HINTLESHAM HALL, SUFFOLK

Set in nineteen acres of its own parkland just 70 miles
from London, Robert Carrier's latest
restaurant adventure, HINTLESHAM HALL,
is the home of the ROBERT CARRIER DINING CLUB
and the HINTLESHAM FESTIVAL
OF MUSIC AND THE ARTS.

Oct 24/14

To Gloria

A great evening the with the McConnell's and London the and fun was us.

in Massey's

It with Warm regards

you John

THE ROBERT CARRIER COOKERY COURSE

By the same author

The Robert Carrier Cookbook
Great Dishes of the World
Cooking for you

THE ROBERT CARRIER COOKERY COURSE

Drawings by Val Biro

W. H. ALLEN · London & New York

A division of Howard & Wyndham Ltd

1974

Printed in Great Britain by Fletcher & Son Ltd, Norwich

for the Publishers W. H. Allen & Co. Ltd,
44 Hill Street, London W1X 8LB

Bound by Richard Clay (The Chaucer Press) Ltd, Bungay, Suffolk

ISBN 0 491 01192 X

To Helena Raderka – 'Queen Bee' of my London Test Kitchen where all these recipes were dreamed up, tried out, retested and then perfected; to Caroline Liddell, Hilary Colbourn and Norma and Christopher Hillier – the expert choppers, stirrers, mixers, saucemakers and bakers; to Gunther Schlender and Terry Boyce, head chefs of my two restaurants, CARRIER'S in London and HINTLESHAM HALL in Suffolk, who lent their professional support; and to Jacqueline Cottee – my Personal Assistant for thirteen years – and Chief Taster – all my grateful thanks for their many years of effort on my behalf. It's been a lot of fun. And, more important, it's a great book.

Contents

Introduction

Cooking is easy; wonderfully easy. And cooking is fun. I firmly believe that every meal we have should be a pleasure, an adventure. And by that I do not mean that we all have to eat complicated dishes and rich sauces every day of our lives; nor do we have to spend all day in the kitchen to prepare the family dinner. But I do believe that we must take advantage of our meal times to produce well-planned, well-presented meals that are delicious to eat.

I personally would much rather have a lightly boiled egg and a perfectly dressed green salad than all the slap-dash meals in the world. And I want variety in my everyday eating. Of course, you'll say 'with two restaurants – one in London and the other in the country – his life is easy'. But you have no idea how, after a lot of entertaining and being entertained, I long for a simple grilled steak and a baked potato. Or, without a thought for the spreading waistline, a plate of steaming hot spaghetti or noodles tossed with fresh butter and grated Parmesan cheese.

My favourite foods are basically simple foods: lightly grilled chicken with mustard and ginger; a Provençal vegetable salad bathed in olive oil and lemon juice flavoured with finely chopped anchovies, sweet onion and fresh herbs; baby lamb chops, marinated with olive oil and dry white wine and then grilled over the open fire; tiny 'pillows' of cheese, crisp fried on the outside and deliciously creamy within. Or, for supper, a slice of home-made *pâté*, and a crisp green salad redolent of fruity olive oil. Add then, the simple luxuries: *gratin dauphinois* (thinly sliced potatoes layered with double cream and freshly grated Parmesan and Gruyère and baked in the oven until creamy and golden); a freshly baked *quiche* filled with a cargo of creamed button onions; a fresh cucumber salad, sprinkled with snippets of fresh tarragon and parsley; and a golden saffron-flavoured *risotto*. All these favourites – easy to make, exciting to serve – you will find in this book. And many more!

You will find, too, that each of the five Sections of this Cookery Course is complete in itself with First Courses, Main Courses,

9

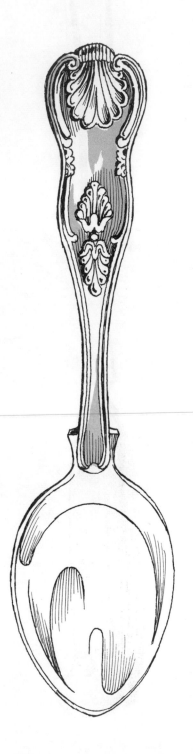

Vegetable Dishes, Salads and Salad Dressings and Sweets and Puddings. And the selection of recipes in each course is more than ample for planning well-balanced and varied menus for every occasion.

Beginner cooks should start at the very beginning of the Cookery Course – First Course (Lessons 1 through 5) – to experiment with simple Company Dinners staged around a superb roast. Study how easy it is to cook a roast of beef, lamb, pork or poultry superbly well. Then try the recipe for 'No-Roast' Roast Beef as an excitingly moist variation on the Rare Roast Beef theme.

This Course also offers an intriguing collection of 'no cook' and 'hardly cook' appetisers and *hors d'œuvres* guaranteed to make entertaining easy, as well as a selection of salad dressings; a recipe for perfect mayonnaise with all the variations; suitable vegetable accompaniments for roasts and grills; and a lesson on delightfully easy fruit desserts and sweets and puddings.

On Grilling

How many of your cookbooks tell you simply to 'grill until done' or 'cook until tender' or 'bake until golden'?

Most of them, I am sure. But not this one. In Section Two, Lesson 8, you will find exact instructions for choosing beef for grilling, followed by notes on how to store beef until ready to use, how much to serve for each portion, how to prepare it for grilling, how to know when it is done (using the 'finger test' or the 'cut edge' test) and finally, what flavoured butters and sauces to serve with it.

But best of all, on pages 204 and 205 you will find a Super Grilling Chart which tells you how to grill beef to perfection according to its cut, thickness and weight; how far it should be from the heat; and just how many minutes cooking time it should have on each side of the steak for the desired degree of doneness: 'blue' or very rare, rare, medium-rare and well-done. It took many months of painstaking testing and retesting in the kitchen to perfect the Grilling and Roasting Charts you will find in the book. Use them to bring exactitude to your cooking.

In the Third Course, Lesson 14 (see pages 367 to 397), you will learn how to create individual masterpieces with long slow-cooking casseroles of meat, fish, poultry and game. In this lesson we go into all the 'whys' and 'wherefores' of casserole cooking. If your cookbook tells you to cook your beef and veal casseroles at a temperature of 375° (Mark 5), throw it away. You'll end up with scraggy, stringy pieces of meat floating about in a delectable sauce. Fine if it's just the sauce you're after; not quite so satisfactory if it is the whole dish!

If you want your stew to be succulently tender, with the meat melting to the bite, and with a deliciously rich sauce, look at our instructions pages 367 to 397. Here you will learn how to cook your casseroles in an oven set to just 225°F. (Mark $\frac{1}{4}$) or 250°F. (Mark $\frac{1}{2}$). At such low heats, the liquids in the casserole keep to a faint, barely perceptible bubble, leaving the meat wonderfully tender and moist without disintegrating into a bundle of dry, tasteless fibres. Your sauce will be richer in texture and flavour, too.

More than a Cook Book

The whole Cookery Course – Lesson by Lesson – is full of helpful hints and professional know-how. More than a Cook Book, it is a step-by-step Course in Cookery which takes you progressively through all the culinary techniques that you need to become a really superb cook, and as you master Section after Section of the Course, learning progressively all the techniques of gourmet cookery, you will be able to choose your favourite dishes from the whole book to make many memorable meals that will astound your friends and delight yourself.

It was André Simon, I think, who first compared good cooks with great actors. 'They both need,' he confided, 'to be fit and strong, for acting and cooking are two of the most exacting professions in the world. And they should also be blessed with artistic temperament for they need recognition from their audience to make sure they are giving of their best.'

I know that I, for one, really enjoy cooking for guests that appreciate good food and say so. In the old days it used to be considered impolite to even mention the food that had been so painstakingly prepared. Those days are gone forever, thank God, and now we can all sit about the table commenting on the dish that is being served to us, talking about its flavour, its texture, remembering other dishes, other savours; and just plain exuberating in the very fact that we are all together, with old friends and new friends, having the time of our lives.

A Way of Life

That is what cooking is all about. Giving a dinner party for two, for four, or for more, can be a wonderfully rewarding experience. Yet, so many cooks I know limit themselves to too small a repertoire of favourite recipes. And too many mothers allow themselves to be ruled by their children's lack of interest in trying out new dishes. How many times on my visits around the world have I met women who profess to be 'real gourmets', but

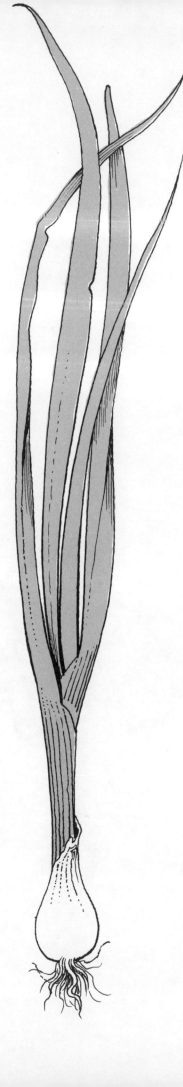

who restrict their daily cooking to chops, steaks, or even hamburgers, because 'that's what the children like'.

Every member of the household – from father to the youngest child – should be made to devote a little time to gastronomic exploration and innovation. It's a dull diet indeed if every day, week in and week out, we sit down to the same things, varying this regular monotony perhaps with a few seasonal delicacies – strawberries, asparagus, summer fruits, game – as they first appear . . . and then falling back into the same old weary routine of daily eating.

We can get so much pleasure and excitement from ringing the changes in our daily menu. The shops are full of possibilities well within our reach, both gastronomically and economically. So, don't get into a food rut. Whether you are feeding the family or special guests, just one or two new dishes a week will make a dramatic difference to your culinary vocabulary and will give them at the same time the pleasure of voting on your latest creations.

It is the small daily variations in our meals that instil new life and interest: a new sauce or garnish for a favourite vegetable; different dressings for various salad combinations; or finding new ways of preparing potatoes, carrots, or Brussels sprouts. So follow the Cookery Course – Lesson by Lesson – and you will soon be a superb cook ready to delight your friends and loved ones with your culinary expertise.

A Short Guide to Culinary Terms

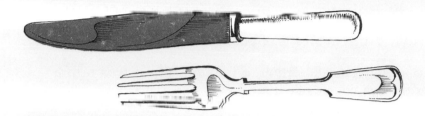

Abaisse French pastry making term to describe a sheet (or layer) of pastry rolled out to a certain thickness.

Abatis Heart, liver, gizzard, neck and wing tips of fowl.

A la In the manner of. **A l'allemande** German style. Often means garnished with sauerkraut, sausages or noodles. **A l'Alsacienne** Alsatian style. Usually garnished with sauerkraut and sausages; sometimes with *foie gras*. **A l'Americaine** Usually dressed with a sauce containing tomatoes, dry white wine and brandy. Sometimes means dishes cooked in American style. **A l'Andalouse** Usually dresses fish, poultry and meat dishes with *aubergines*, peppers and tomatoes. **A l'Aurore** Usually garnished with a rose-coloured sauce. **A la Barigoule** Usually contains artichokes, mushrooms and a brown sauce. **A la Bordelaise** Bordeaux style. A rich wine sauce. **A la Bourguignonne** Burgundy style. With button mushrooms, button onions and a rich wine sauce. **A la Crème** Served with cream or cooked in a cream sauce. **A l'Espagnole** Spanish style. With tomatoes and peppers. **A la Financière** With truffles and Madeira sauce. **A la Flamande** Flemish style. Usually with chicory. **A l'Indienne** Indian style. With curry. **A l'Italienne** Italian style. With pasta or with a rich brown sauce garnished with tomatoes, mushrooms and garlic. **A la Jardinière** Gardener's style. With mixed cooked vegetables. **A la Normande** Norman style. With a fish-flavoured *velouté* sauce garnished with mussels, shrimps, etc. Or with apples. **A la Paysanne** Country style. **A la Polonaise** Polish style. With buttered breadcrumbs, finely chopped parsley and hardboiled eggs. **A la Portugaise** Portuguese style. With tomatoes, onions or garlic. **A la Provençale** Provençal style. With tomatoes, garlic and olive oil.

A la broche Roasted slowly on a revolving spit.

13

Acidify To add lemon juice or vinegar to a sauce or cooked dish.

Acidulated water (1) Water mixed with an acidifying agent – lemon juice or vinegar – used to blanch sweetbreads, veal or chicken. (2) Lemon juice and water in equal quantities added to sliced apples, pears or bananas to stop them turning brown.

Aiguillette Thin, vertically cut strips of prime cuts of meat. Usually cut from breasts of poultry or game.

Appetiser A small portion of food or drink served before – or for the first course of – a meal.

Aspic The culinary name for calf's foot jelly, or jelly made with bones of meat, fish or poultry. Any meat, fish, poultry, game or vegetable may be served 'in aspic'.

Bain-marie A French kitchen utensil designed to keep liquids at simmering point without coming to the boil. It consists of a saucepan standing in a large pan which is filled with boiling water. A *bain-marie* is a great help in keeping sauces, stews and soups hot without over-cooking. In domestic kitchens, a double saucepan can do double duty as a *bain-marie*.

Bake To cook in dry heat in the oven. This term is usually used only for breads, cakes, cookies, biscuits, pies, tarts and pastries. When meats are cooked in the oven, the term used is 'to roast'.

To bake blind To bake a pastry shell without a filling. To keep the sides of pastry shells from collapsing and the bottom from puffing up during baking, place a piece of aluminium foil or wax paper in the bottom of the pastry case and weight this with dried beans or rice (or a combination of the two). When pastry shells have been baked according to recipe directions, the foil or paper is removed and the beans and rice are returned to a storage jar to be used again and again.

Barbecue To cook meat, poultry, game or fish in the open on a grill or spit over charcoal. Originally this term meant cooking a whole animal over an open fire, or in a pit. Barbecued foods are usually basted with a highly-seasoned sauce during cooking time.

Bard To cover meat, poultry, game (and sometimes fish) with thin strips of pork fat or green bacon before roasting or braising.

Baste To pour or spoon liquid over food as it cooks to moisten and flavour it.

Batter Something that is beaten. Usually means the mixture from which pancakes, pudding and cakes are made. The batter used for pancakes and for coating purposes is made of eggs, flour and milk (or sometimes water) and is fairly liquid in consistency.

Beat To mix with a spoon, spatula, whisk, rotary beater or electric blender; to make a mixture smooth and light by enclosing air.

Beurre manié Equal quantities of butter and flour kneaded together and added bit by bit to a stew, casserole or sauce to thicken it. See page 370.

Bind To thicken soups or sauces with eggs, cream, etc.

Bisque A rich cream soup made of puréed fish or shellfish.

Blanch To pre heat in boiling water or steam. This can be done for several reasons; (1) to loosen outer skins of fruits, nuts or vegetables; (2) to whiten sweetbreads, veal or chicken; (3) to remove excess salt or bitter flavour from bacon, gammon, ham, brussels sprouts, turnips, endive, etc.; (4) to prepare fruits and vegetables for canning, freezing or preserving.

Blend To mix two or more ingredients thoroughly.

Boil To cook in any liquid – usually water, wine or stock or a combination of the three – brought to boiling point and kept there.

Boiling point The temperature at which bubbles rise continually and break over the entire surface of a liquid.

Bone To remove the bones from fish, chicken, poultry or game.

Bouillon A clear soup, broth or stock made with beef, veal or poultry and vegetables. Strained before using.

Bouquet garni A bunch or 'faggot' of culinary herbs. Used to flavour stews, casseroles, sauces. A *bouquet garni* can be small, medium or large, according to the flavour required for the dish and, of course, according to what the cook has at hand.

Bread To roll in, or coat with breadcrumbs before cooking.

Brochette See skewer.

Broil See grill.

Brunoise Finely diced vegetables – carrots, celery, onions, leeks (and sometimes, turnips) – simmered in butter and stock until soft. Used to flavour soups, stuffings, sauces and certain dishes of fish and shellfish.

Caramelise To melt sugar in a thick-bottomed saucepan, stirring continuously, until it is a golden-brown syrup.

Chaud-froid A jellied white sauce made of butter, flour, chicken stock, egg yolks, cream and gelatine. Used to give a handsome shiny white glaze to chicken, ham, etc. Brown *chaud-froid* sauce is used to glaze meat and game.

Chill To place in refrigerator or other cold place until cold.

Chop To cut into very small pieces with a sharp knife or a chopper.

Chowder A fish, clam or oyster stew.

Clarify 1. To clear a stock or broth by adding slightly beaten egg whites and crushed egg shells and bringing liquid to the boil. The stock is then cooled and strained before using. 2. To clarify butter: melt butter and pour off clear liquid, leaving sediment behind.

Coat To dust or roll in flour until surface is covered before cooking.

Cocotte 1. A round or oval casserole with a cover. Usually made of iron or enamelled iron. 2. Individual heatproof dishes used for baking eggs. Usually of earthenware or heatproof china.

Cool To allow to stand at room temperature until no longer warm to the touch. (Not to put in the refrigerator.)

Court-bouillon The liquid in which fish, poultry or meat is cooked to give added flavour. A simple *court-bouillon* consists of water to which you have added 1 bay leaf, 2 stalks celery, 1 Spanish onion, 2 carrots and salt and freshly ground black pepper, to taste. Other additives: wine, vinegar, stock, olive oil, garlic, shallots, cloves etc.

Cream To work one or more foods with a heavy spoon or a firm spatula until the mixture is soft and creamy. To cream butter and sugar; beat softened butter with electric mixer (or rub against sides of bowl with a wooden spoon) until smooth and fluffy. Gradually beat or rub in sugar until thoroughly blended.

Croûte The pastry case for *pâtés*, e.g. *pâté en croûte*. Usually a brioche, a rich brioche dough or a hot water crust.

Croûton Bread trimmed of crusts, cut to shape (triangles, hearts, dice), rubbed with garlic (optional) and sautéed in oil or butter.

Cut in To combine fat and dry ingredients with two knives, scissor-fashion, or with a pastry blender. When making pastry.

Deep-fry To cook in deep hot fat until crisp and golden. Also known as French-fry.

Devil 1. To grill food with a mixture of butter, mustard, chutney or Worcestershire sauce and fresh breadcrumbs. 2. To cook or serve with a hot 'devil' sauce.

Dice To cut into small even cubes.

Disjoint To cut poultry, game or small animals into serving pieces by dividing at the joint.

Dissolve To mix a dry ingredient with liquid until it is absorbed.

Dredge To coat with flour (or other fine-particled substance) by dusting, sprinkling, or rolling the food in flour, cornflour, cornmeal, sugar etc.

Dust To sift or sprinkle lightly with a fine-particled substance such as flour, sugar or seasonings.

Duxelles Finely-chopped mushrooms and onion (or shallots), sautéed in butter until soft. Mixture should be quite dry. Used to flavour poached fish and shellfish; dress a fillet of beef or leg of baby lamb before it is wrapped in pastry; or garnish a *papillote*.

Fillet 1. Special cut of beef, lamb, pork or veal; breast of poultry and game; fish cut off the bone lengthwise. 2. To cut any of the above to use in cooking.

Fish fumet A highly concentrated fish stock, made by reducing well-flavoured fish stock. Used to poach fish, fish fillets or fish steaks. Corresponds to essence for meats.

Flake To break into small pieces with a fork.

Flame To pour or spoon alcohol over a dish and ignite it.

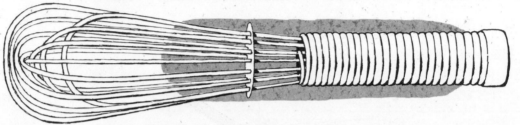

Fold in When a mixture has been beaten until light and fluffy, other ingredients must be 'folded' in very gently with a spatula so that the air will not be lost. Blend in new ingredients little by little, turning mixture very gently. Continue only until the ingredients are evenly blended.

Fricassée To cook chicken or veal in fat until golden, and then in a sauce. *Fricassée* is in fact a form of braising.

Fry To cook in a little fat or oil in a frying-pan.

Garniture The garnish or trimming added to a cooked dish (or served at the same time on a separate dish); vegetables, rice, pasta, pastry shapes, *croûtons*, etc.

Glaze A thin coating of syrup or aspic – sometimes coloured with caramel – which is brushed over sweets, puddings, fruits (syrup) or cooked ham, tongue, chicken, beef, pork, veal etc. (aspic). Food must be cold and quite dry before aspic will set.

Grate To reduce to small particles with a grater.

Gratin To cook '*au gratin*' is to brown food in the oven – usually covered in a sauce and dotted with breadcrumbs, cheese and butter – until a crisp, golden coating forms. A '*gratin*' dish is the heatproof dish used for cooking *au gratin*. Usually oval-shaped, in earthenware or enamelled iron.

Grease To rub lightly with butter, margarine, oil or fat.

Grill To cook by direct heat such as an open fire. In our day, by charcoal, gas or electricity.

Julienne To cut into fine strips the length of a matchstick.

Knead To work dough with hands until it is of the desired elasticity or consistency.

Lard 1. Common cooking fat obtained by melting down of pork fat. 2. Culinary process by which lardons of pork fat or green bacon are threaded through meat, poultry, game (and sometimes fish) to lend flavour and moisture to food.

Lardons 1. Strips of fat or green bacon used as above. 2. Diced pork fat or green bacon, blanched and sautéed to add flavour and texture contrast to certain stews, *daubes*, *ragoûts*, and casseroles.

Liaison To thicken a sauce, gravy or stew: 1. by the addition of flour, cornflour, arrowroot, rice flour, potato flour, or a *beurre manié* (flour and butter); 2. by stirring in egg yolk, double cream, or in the case of certain dishes of poultry or game, blood.

Macédoine 1. A mixture of raw or cooked fruit for a fruit salad. 2. A mixture of cooked diced vegetables garnished with a cream sauce, mayonnaise or aspic, usually served as an *hors-d'œuvre* salad, or as a garnish.

Marinade A highly flavoured liquid – usually red or white wine or olive oil or a combination of the two – seasoned with carrots, onion, bay leaf, herbs and spices. Marinades can be cooked or uncooked. The purpose of a marinade is to impart flavour to the food and to soften fibres of tougher foods.

Marinate To let food stand, or steep, in a marinade. See above.

Mask To cover cooked food with sauce.

Mince To reduce to very small particles with a mincer, chopper or knife.

Mirepoix Finely-diced carrots, onion, celery (and sometimes ham), simmered in butter until soft. Used to add flavour to dishes of meat, poultry, fish and shellfish.

Oven-fry To cook meat, fish or poultry in fat in the oven, uncovered, basting food with fat from time to time.

Panade A mixture of soft breadcrumbs, egg yolk (and sometimes cream).

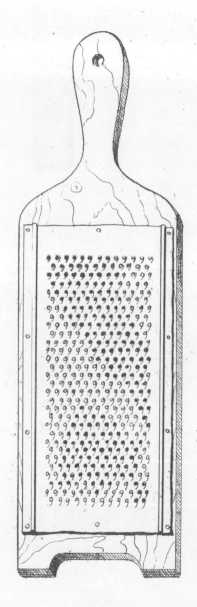

Pommade A thick, smooth paste.

Parboil To pre-cook, or boil until partially cooked.

Pare or Peel 1. To cut off outside skin or covering of a fruit or vegetable with a knife or parer. 2. To peel fruits such as oranges or bananas without using a knife.

Papillote To cook '*en papillote*' is the culinary term for cooking food enclosed in an oiled paper or foil case (*papillote*).

Poach To cook gently in simmering (not boiling) liquid so that the surface of the liquid barely trembles.

Pit To remove pit, stone or seed, as from cherries.

Pound To reduce to very small particles, or a paste, with a mortar and pestle.

Purée To press through a fine sieve or food mill to produce a smooth, soft food.

Quenelle The finely-pounded flesh of fish, shellfish, veal, poultry or game; mixed with egg whites and cream and pounded over ice to a velvety smooth paste. These feather-light dumplings are then poached in a light stock or salted water.

Ragoût A stew made from regular-sized pieces of meat, poultry or fish sautéed in fat until brown and then simmered with stock, meat juices or water, or a combination of these, until tender. *Navarin de mouton* is an example of a 'brown' *ragoût* (Irish stew is a typical 'white' *ragoût*, in which meat is not browned before stewing).

Ramekin A small, earthenware dish for cooking individual portions: eggs, vegetables and seafood *gratin*, etc.

Reduce To cook a sauce over a high heat, uncovered, until it is reduced by evaporation to the desired consistency. This culinary process improves both flavour and appearance.

Render To free fat from tissue by melting at low heat.

Roast To cook meat by direct heat on a spit or in the oven; although 'baking' would be a better term in the latter case, for when meat is cooked in a closed area (oven) vapour accumulates and changes texture and flavour of true roast.

Roux The gentle amalgamation of butter and flour over a low heat; capable of absorbing at least six times its own weight when cooked. 1. To make a white *roux*: melt 2 tablespoons butter in the top of a double saucepan; add 2 tablespoons of sieved flour and stir with a wire whisk for 2 to 3 minutes over water until the mixture amalgamates but does not change colour. 2. A pale *roux*: Cook as above stirring continuously, just a little longer (4 to 5 minutes) or until the colour of *roux* begins to change to pale gold. 3. A brown *roux*: cook as above until mixture acquires a fine, light-brown colour and nutty aroma.

Salmis To cook jointed poultry or game in a rich wine sauce after it has been roasted until almost done. Often done in a chafing dish at the table.

Salpicon Finely diced meat, poultry, game, fish, shellfish or vegetables, bound with a savoury sauce and used to fill *canapés* and individual *hors-d'œuvre* pastry cases. Also used to make *rissoles*, *croquettes* and stuffings for eggs, vegetables and small cuts of poultry or meat.

Sauté To fry lightly in a small amount of hot fat or oil, shaking the pan or turning food frequently during cooking.

Scald To heat to temperature just below boiling point. I use a double saucepan to scald cream or milk. This prevents scorching.

Score To make evenly spaced, shallow slits or cuts with a knife.

Sear To brown and seal the surface of meat quickly over high heat. This prevents juices from escaping.

Sift To put through a sifter or a fine sieve.

Simmer To cook in liquid just below boiling point, with small bubbles of steam rising gently to the surface.

Skewer 1. To keep in shape with skewers. 2. The actual 'skewer' – made of metal or wood – which is used to keep meats, poultry, game etc. in shape while cooking. 3. The 'skewer' – piece of metal or wood – sometimes called 'brochette' used to hold pieces of chicken, fish, poultry etc., to be grilled over charcoal, or under gas or electricity.

Sliver To cut or shred into long, thin pieces.

Steam To cook food in vapour over boiling water. This process is often used in Oriental cooking.

Steep To let food stand in hot liquid to extract flavour or colour.

Stir To mix with a spoon or fork with a circular motion until ingredients are well blended.

Whisk To beat rapidly with a whisk, rotary beater or electric mixer in order to incorporate air and increase volume.

Zest The finely grated rind of lemon or orange.

How to follow a recipe successfully

Read the recipe carefully through to the end. Calculate *total* preparation time, including hold-ups while marinating, chilling, etc. Make sure that you have all the necessary ingredients and utensils before you begin the recipe; and that all utensils are of the correct size.

Assemble ingredients and utensils *before* you start. Remove eggs, butter, meat, etc., from refrigerator in advance so that they will be at room temperature by the time you start to cook.

Do any advance preparation indicated in list of ingredients. The preparation of cake tins, etc., should also be attended to before you start.

Measure or weigh ingredients carefully.

Do not be tempted to alter a recipe in mid-stream until you have prepared it faithfully at least once, and do not telescope or ignore directions and procedures for combining ingredients unless you are a very experienced cook.

Follow cooking and/or baking times and temperature given, but test for doneness about two-thirds of the way through or, conversely, be prepared to increase cooking time if it appears insufficient. Oven heats can vary considerably.

How to measure correctly

All spoon measurements in this book are level.

Accurate measurement is essential to any kind of cooking. A standard set of individual measuring spoons in plastic or metal – 1 tablespoon, 1 teaspoon, $\frac{1}{2}$ teaspoon and $\frac{1}{4}$ teaspoon – is ideal for small quantities and can be bought in many kitchen departments throughout the country. When a recipe calls for a fraction not catered for in the standard set, a dry ingredient can be measured by taking a whole spoonful, then carefully halving or quartering the amount with the tip of a knife and discarding the excess.

Larger quantities

For measuring larger quantities of ingredients you will also need:
A Measuring Jug marked off in fluid ounces and heatproof to withstand boiling liquids. You will also find this useful to use with American recipes, but remember the American pint measures only 16 fluid ounces, and the American cup (or $\frac{1}{2}$ pint) measures 8 fluid ounces.
Kitchen Scales. Select a pair with a large enough pan to hold the quantities you are likely to be measuring. You should be able to measure a pound of flour without spilling.

FIRST COURSE

Lesson 1
Appetisers

Some Appetisers and Hors-d'œuvres You Don't Even Have to Cook

The simplest – and often the best – appetisers of all are those you buy – whole, sliced, smoked or canned – and just open (or unwrap) and serve.

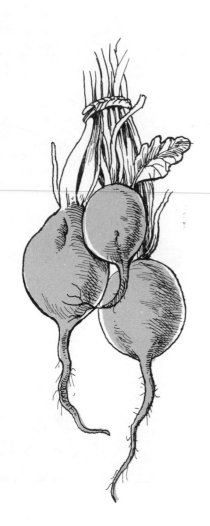

Olives Plump green or black olives – they must be juicy. To make black olives more interesting, place them in a bowl with several tablespoons of olive oil to which you have added a crumbled bay leaf or two and a sprinkling of rosemary spikes, and leave them for several days, turning olives in marinade mixture from time to time. You will find the olives will have plumped up and the herbs will have given them an extra flavour. Use the remains of the oil to add a touch of fruity, herby flavour to your salad dressings.

Radishes Wash radishes in cold water and then trim tops and tails. Serve in individual raviers or *hors-d'œuvre* dishes with coarse salt; or dress them with a little salted olive oil and lemon juice.

Canned anchovies Serve in a small ravier or *hors-d'œuvre* dish, topped with thin strips of canned pimentos or bottled capers. I usually drain off the oil from the can and add fresh olive oil and a squeeze of lemon to bring out their flavour.

Use canned anchovies, too, to decorate and give their unique salty flavour to other *hors-d'œuvre* salads. Thin strips on a fresh tomato salad; coarsely chopped anchovies on a lentil or haricot blanc salad, a potato salad, a hard-boiled egg mayonnaise, or an egg salad; use finely chopped or pounded anchovies to give flavour to a vinaigrette dressing for *hors-d'œuvre* salads.

Canned sardines Above all, choose the best quality you can find. Serve on buttered fingers of toast, garnished with sieved hard-boiled egg yolk, or a little finely chopped parsley and a squeeze of lemon. Or, more simply as they are, in a small ravier or *hors-d'œuvre* dish as part of a mixed *hors-d'œuvre* selection. I like to mash sardines, too, with a little lemon juice, curry powder, finely chopped onion and mayonnaise (page 186) or butter, to serve as a delicious sardine *pâté* or spread.

Canned tuna fish Tuna is one of the most versatile of our canned fishes. Serve it, as it is, in its own oil; combine it with cooked white haricot beans and thinly sliced rings of onion; mix it with canned pimentos or haricots verts in a salad; mash it with lemon juice, finely chopped onion and mayonnaise (page 186) and use it as a delicious tuna *pâté* or spread; use this same mixture to stuff hard-boiled eggs; thin the mixture down with a little more mayonnaise and lemon juice, and use it as a delicious sauce for hard-boiled eggs, a tomato salad or for cold slices of cooked veal.

Canned crab Toss pieces gently with diced tomato, diced avocado and diced hard-boiled egg in a well-flavoured vinaigrette dressing (page 41). Mix gently with a little chopped onion and green pepper in a home-made mayonnaise (page 186); or mash it with a little finely chopped onion, lemon juice and mayonnaise to make a crab *pâté* or spread.

25

Italian sausages One of the best known Italian sausages, now so popular throughout the world that it is also produced in Germany, Hungary and the United States, is *salami*, generally made of lean pork, fat pork and beef, finely ground and highly seasoned, coloured with red wine and pickled in brine before it is air dried. Of the varieties of *salame* to be found in Italy today, there is seemingly no end. Some are highly garlic flavoured, others are mild; some are eaten fresh and others are considered to be at their best when they are more mature. Perhaps the most familiar to us in this country are the *crespone* or *salame de milano*, about 2½ inches in diameter, red-hued and granite-grained, with a very spicy flavour, and the *salame de cremona*, a larger slightly coarser-grained version of the Milano sausage. Try, too, the *salame casalinga*, a rough-marbled sausage with a more distinctive flavour; look for the deep cherry red of the meat and the white waxiness of the fat when it is fresh.

Good, too, for the *hors-d'œuvre* platter are the silver-wrapped *cacciatora* and *turisto* sausages on sale here. They are both good keepers.

One of my favourite Italian sausages is the large, round, rosey-fleshed *mortadella*, a smooth-tasting sausage studded with square white chunks of fat. *Mortadella* is made in Florence and Bologna from the flesh of pigs which feed on the chestnuts and acorns in the surrounding forests. Seasoned with wine, garlic and spices it is a useful sausage, served as it is in thin slices, or made into cornucopiae to hold flavoured cream cheese fillings.

All of the above sausages make eminently suitable appetisers. If you are slicing them yourself – they should be thinly sliced – remove outer skin *first*. It comes off much more neatly this way than from individual slices, when it is apt to tear out lumps of sausage.

Canned vegetables Canned vegetables make wonderful additions to a mixed appetiser selection. Drain them; rinse lightly and then marinate them for at least one hour in a well-flavoured vinaigrette dressing before serving them. A little finely chopped onion, fresh herbs or finely chopped garlic or capers may be added to improve flavour contrast to these impromptu appetiser salads. Try two, or more, of the following:

Artichoke hearts, cut into thin strips, and tossed with a vinaigrette or mayonnaise dressing (page 186).

Tiny pickled beets, sliced, cut into strips or served whole, with a sour cream or vinaigrette dressing (page 41).

Tiny carrots, sliced or served whole, with a vinaigrette dressing (page 41) flavoured with fincly chopped onion and fresh herbs.

Tiny new potatoes, sliced, or served whole with a sour cream or mayonnaise dressing (page 186) to which you have added (1) crumbled cooked bacon, (2) chopped onion and green pepper.

Red pimentos, cut into thin strips, and tossed in a vinaigrette dressing (page 41) flavoured with finely chopped parsley, anchovies and garlic.

Button mushrooms, sliced or served whole in a vinaigrette dressing (page 41) flavoured with finely chopped onion, garlic and fresh herbs.

Haricots verts, sliced or served whole, in a vinaigrette dressing (page 41) flavoured with finely chopped onion.

Haricots blancs, tossed in a vinaigrette dressing (page 41) flavoured with finely chopped onion and anchovies.

Lentils, tossed in a vinaigrette dressing (page 41) flavoured with finely chopped onion and anchovies.

Chick peas, tossed in a vinaigrette dressing (page 41) flavoured with finely chopped onion and fresh herbs.

Red kidney beans, tossed in a vinaigrette dressing (page 41) flavoured with finely chopped onion, garlic and fresh herbs.

Lima beans, tossed in a lemon-flavoured mayonnaise (page 43).

Button onions, sliced or served whole, in a vinaigrette dressing (page 41), flavoured with finely chopped onion and fresh herbs.

Macédoine of legumes, tossed with mayonnaise (page 186) or a vinaigrette dressing (page 41).

Ratatouille, dressed with a little lemon-flavoured vinaigrette dressing (page 42) and sprinkled with finely chopped parsley.

For Special Occasions

Smoked salmon Now that it has almost doubled in price over the past few years, smoked salmon heads the list of 'special occasion' appetisers. Coral-coloured, fine grained and aromatically fragrant, it is at its best when served slightly chilled in paper-thin slices on a lightly oiled platter. I always accompany it with thin slices of buttered brown bread, fresh lemon wedges and pepper from a pepper mill to bring out its naturally smokey flavour.

I like smoked salmon, too, served *à la Russe*. For each serving, place two thin slices of smoked salmon on a mound of lemon-dressed shredded lettuce; and garnish each portion with a table-spoonful each of chopped hard-boiled egg, chopped raw onion, and capers. You'll find the smoked salmon seems to go much further. Another way of making a little smoked salmon seem like a feast is to use a very little of it to flavour a quiche.

Smoked sturgeon Rarer than smoked salmon in our shops, but half the price, smoked sturgeon is usually cut thicker than salmon and served with wedges of lemon. Delicious appetiser which needs coarsely ground black pepper and lemon to bring out its full flavour.

Smoked trout One of my favourite ready-to-serve appetisers is smoked trout. Just skin the trout and serve one for each person with a wedge or two of lemon or a little horseradish chantilly (recipe on page 510) and some buttered brown bread. Or, fillet the trout and serve each person half a smoked fish on a

28

piece of buttered brown bread which you have spread with a little horseradish chantilly. Delicious.

I like, too, to make a *brandade* (a smooth mousse) of smoked trout and serve it in a small individual ramekin or soufflé dish with crisp fingers of toast. To make the *brandade*: pound skinned and boned smoked trout in a mortar with 2 tablespoons each of olive oil, lemon juice and double cream, continuing this process – adding equal quantities of olive oil, lemon juice and cream – until the mousse is smooth and of a spreading consistency.

Smoked eel Fillets of smoked eel make a delicious appetiser, either served on an oiled plate with lemon wedges and thin brown bread and butter, or with horseradish chantilly (page 510).

Smoked oysters Another smoked delicacy to add to your smoked *hors-d'œuvres* platter. Very rich in texture and flavour, so you will find that one or two smoked oysters on toothpicks served with the *hors-d'œuvres* of your choice will be sufficient.

Smoked fish platter Combine servings of smoked salmon, smoked sturgeon and filleted smoked trout and smoked eel on a large serving platter. Decorate dish with lettuce leaves and wedges of tomato and lemon. Serve with thin brown bread and butter. And make sure that you have a coarse grinding mill of black pepper ready, as well as bowls of horseradish chantilly (page 510).

Canned lobster More expensive than the preceding canned fish additions to your *hors-d'œuvres* selection, canned lobster, when tossed gently in a well-flavoured mayonnaise (page 186) or vinaigrette dressing (page 41), can add much to a mixed seafood *hors-d'œuvre* salad. Serve it on its own, with a mayonnaise or a tomato and pimento-flavoured mayonnaise dressing in tall glasses which you have lined with lettuce leaves. Use this same mixture to top a salad made of thinly peeled slices of avocado pear brushed with a vinaigrette dressing.

Fresh vegetables à la vinaigrette The following list of fresh vegetables – raw and cooked, cut into slices, strips, pieces, and in some cases, served whole – are prepared as below and then tossed gently in a well-flavoured vinaigrette sauce (page 41). A choice of finely chopped fresh herbs, onion, garlic, anchovies, capers, etc., may be added to these fresh-tasting appetiser salads according to taste.

Cucumbers, peeled and cut into $1\frac{1}{2}$-inch strips, thin slices, or diced.

Tomatoes, thinly sliced.

Baby carrots, boiled until tender, and cut into strips, thin slices, or diced.

Baby turnips, boiled until tender, and cut into strips, thin slices, or diced.

New potatoes, boiled until tender, and cut into strips, thin slices, or diced.

Leeks, boiled until tender and cut into 2-inch lengths.

Peas, boiled until tender.

Courgettes, boiled until tender, and cut into thin slices.

Broccoli buds, boiled until tender.

Brussels sprouts, boiled until tender.

Cauliflowerets, boiled until tender.

Button mushrooms, cut into thin slices, or diced.

Green and red peppers, with skins and seeds removed and cut into thin slices.

Radishes, thinly sliced.

Fresh vegetables mayonnaise The following fresh vegetables – raw and cooked, cut into slices, strips, pieces, and in some cases, served whole – are prepared as below and then tossed gently in a well-flavoured home-made mayonnaise (page 43).

Cucumbers, peeled and cut into $1\frac{1}{2}$-inch strips, thin slices, or diced.

Baby carrots, boiled until tender, and cut into strips, thin slices, or diced.

Button mushrooms, cut into thin slices or diced.

Baby turnips, boiled until tender, and cut into strips, thin slices, or diced.

New potatoes, boiled until tender, and cut into strips, thin slices, or diced.

Cauliflowerets, boiled until tender.

Red cabbage, coarsely shredded.

Green cabbage, coarsely shredded.

When You Feel Rich

Caviar True caviar, which is always soft grey to grey-black, is the roe of the sturgeon and is the most expensive food in the world. Nowadays the finest caviar comes from inside the USSR or from the Caspian waters under the sovereignty of the Iranian government. Its quality is judged by the size of the eggs. Another test of quality is the amount of salt used in preserving it. The less salt, the better the caviar.

Serve the caviar in the jar or tin it came in, imbedded in cracked ice, or in a glass bowl nestling in ice. Some prefer it with accompanying dishes of finely chopped onion and hard-boiled egg and capers, but I like it on its own, served with crisp biscuits or hot toast, chilled butter and a wedge or two of lemon. Russian cooks make a little caviar go a long way by dabbing a tiny spoonful on top of a small hot Russian pancake called a *blini* (page 493) and accompany it with sour cream. An easier way to make a little caviar seem a lot is to mound crisp rounds of toasted bread with a chilled mixture of cream cheese and sour cream and top each canapé with a tiny spoonful of caviar.

Red caviar, much cheaper than black caviar, is delicious served in the same way.

Oysters Once so plentiful in Britain that they were considered the food of the poor, oysters are now in the luxury class. And every season seems to bring a higher price. Oysters are usually served 'on the half shell' embedded in a plate of cracked ice. I like to flavour mine with a squeeze of lemon juice and a little freshly milled black pepper. In France, however, I have enjoyed them icy cold served with piping hot sausages. A taste, texture and temperature contrast which is quite pleasing.

To open an oyster Take a short, strong bladed oyster or clam knife and work the point into the hinged side of the oyster, until you cut through the 'hinge' and break the tension. Then draw the blade all around the shell to open it. You'll find it is best to work over a bowl to catch any of the precious oyster juices. Make sure there are no flecks of shell left in the open oyster as you serve it.

Simple Fruit-based Appetisers

Grapefruit

Grapefruit, which can be served at any informal meal of the day, makes a particularly quick-and-easy appetiser. However, I find grapefruit left in the half-shell an awkward thing to deal with, even when the segments have been loosened. Your guests will undoubtedly be grateful to you if you go to the trouble of peeling off all the skin and pith, and serve the segments in a glass.

Grapefruit segments can be served on their own, lightly sweetened with icing sugar and decorated with a mint leaf or two, or combined with other sliced citrus fruits, dressed with lemon juice, honey and a little olive oil.

To peel a grapefruit Peeling a grapefruit (or any other citrus fruit, for that matter) is simple when you know the professional way. With a little practice, and providing your knife is razor-sharp, you will find this method takes far less time than the more conventional one.

1 Slice off the two ends of the fruit, taking all the pith and outer membrane away with the peel.

2 Stand fruit on one (cut) end and with sharp, straight, downward strokes, whittle off slices of peel and membrane all around sides, taking the knife down to the bare flesh. Turn fruit on its other end and repeat process.

3 Slice off the ring of peel left around the middle of the fruit, and cut away any scraps of white pith which escaped your knife the first time around. You should be left with a rather angular-shaped fruit.

4 Holding the peeled fruit over a bowl to catch juices, slip the knife blade between each segment and the membrane holding it on either side. Cut the segment out, keeping it whole if possible; remove any pips, and drop the segment into the bowl below. Proceed in this way until all you have left is the central core, with the empty membranes fanned out around it like the leaves of a book.

5 Finally, squeeze the core and membranes firmly in your hand to extract remaining juice, and discard them.

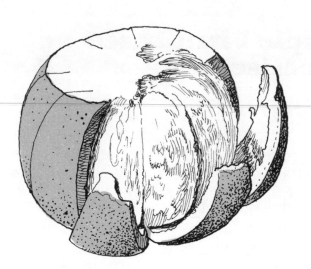

Chilled Melon Appetiser

Serves 4–6

1 Cut melons in half horizontally and scrape out seeds with a spoon.

2 Working over a bowl to catch juices, scoop out melon balls with a special cutter. (If you don't possess one of those, a round ½-teaspoon measure makes a good substitute tool.)

3 Squeeze melon shell to extract remaining juice.

4 Cover bowl with foil and chill melon for at least 2 hours.

5 Just before serving, drain melon balls. Divide juice between 3 serving bowls, preferably Chinese ones.

6 Flavour one bowl with ground ginger; another with ground cloves, and the third with lemon juice and a pinch of monosodium glutamate. If the melon is not a particularly sweet one, you can also add a sprinkling of castor sugar to each bowl.

7 Divide melon balls equally between bowls and toss well. Chill. Guests serve themselves from the 3 bowls.

2 ripe Honeydew melons
1/2 level teaspoon ground ginger
Generous pinch of ground cloves
2 teaspoons lemon juice
Generous pinch of monosodium glutamate
Castor sugar (optional)

Melon with Port

Serves 4

1 Using a very sharp knife with a thin point, cut a plug about $2\frac{1}{2}$ inches in diameter from the melon at the stem end. Slant the knife slightly towards the centre as you cut to taper the plug. Then take a large spoon with a long handle and scoop out all the seeds.

2 Taste a small piece of melon. If it is not sweet enough for you, sprinkle inside with a little castor sugar.

3 Pour port into the melon and replace plug.

4 Put a layer of cracked ice at the bottom of a large bowl. Set the melon on top; cover with foil and chill for several hours.

5 To serve: scoop out flesh with a large serving spoon and make sure everyone has some of the port.

1 ripe melon, about 2 1/2 lb
Sugar (optional)
1/2 pint white port

An Appetiser Spectacular

Italian Antipasto

An antipasto can be hot or cold, a simple platter of paper-thin slices of raw Parma ham (*prosciutto crudo*) and fresh ripe figs or a slice of melon, or a selection of thinly sliced Italian sausages and smoked meats. Vegetables of all kinds are served raw in a salad, or simmered in olive oil and served cold, or stuffed and served either hot or cold, according to the filling.

Then there are the magnificent fish and shellfish of the Mediterranean, and an intriguing variety of deep-fried little appetisers – usually some combination of bread and cheese – of which the best known are probably *mozzarella in carrozza* (slices of Mozzarella cheese sandwiched between two slices of bread, dusted lightly with flour, then dipped in egg beaten with milk, and deep-fried until crisp and golden), and the Roman favourite, *suppli* (little croquettes of rice stuffed with Mozzarella or Provatura cheese which melts when the croquettes are deep-fried and stretches into long threads resembling the *suppli* or 'telephone wires' after which they are named.)

Italy's magnificent white truffles also play their part in the antipasto. Sliced paper-thin and layered in a buttered dish with freshly grated Parmesan, each layer brushed with a little olive oil and sprinkled with salt and white pepper, then the whole baked in a hot oven for a few minutes and served garnished with lemon wedges. Or pounded to a paste with fresh butter and spread on *grissini* (crisp bread sticks), which are then wrapped in a thin slice of prosciutto. Luxury of the highest order!

The version of antipasto which concerns us here, however, is the simplest – and perhaps one of the most effective of all.

You make for your nearest delicatessen, an Italian one if you're lucky, and buy up all the delicacies that take your fancy, a few slices of this, a handful of that, a can of something else. You then complement these with a judicious selection of crisp raw vegetables, sweet peppers, tomatoes, bulbs of Florence fennel, celery, possibly a lettuce, and assemble the lot as impressively and attractively as you know how in large individual portions or in small serving dishes for each person to help himself.

Have a bowl of oil and vinegar dressing to spoon over as you think fit, and serve with crusty Italian or French bread, or *grissini*, and butter.

Some vegetables to choose from (1) *Raw*: tomatoes, fennel, sweet peppers (green, yellow and red), white chicory (Belgian endive), celery, sweet Spanish onion, lettuce; (2) *Preserved or cooked*: artichoke hearts, asparagus tips, pickled mushrooms, red peppers in vinegar, black and green olives in oil, stuffed olives, capers, Italian pickles (*mostardo di Cremona*).

Fish Tunny fish in oil, sardines and anchovy fillets, either flat or rolled round a caper.

Sausages Salami and Mortadella are the obvious choices, but try a slice or two of any other variety you are offered. These are too numerous to list – fat and thin, juicy or dry, highly spiced and peppered, or mild.

Meats *Prosciutto*, of course, although raw smoked Westphalian ham makes an excellent substitute; *bresaola*, a magnificent dried beef which you serve in near-transparent slices, sprinkled with olive oil and lemon juice; and *capocollo*, which is smoked pork.

Italian Antipasto Salad

Serves 4–6

1 Wash lettuce leaves and pat them dry individually. Roll up in a damp tea-cloth and leave in the vegetable compartment of your refrigerator until needed.

2 Wash or wipe remaining vegetables. Slice chicory bulbs lengthwise. Cut fennel into sections. Core, seed and slice peppers into rings. Chill vegetables until needed.

3 Peel and dice Spanish onion coarsely. If you are wary of raw onion, soak it in iced water for 30 minutes to mellow flavour. Then drain thoroughly.

4 Prepare dressing: beat olive oil and lemon juice together until they form an emulsion. Stir in finely chopped garlic and parsley, and season to taste with salt and freshly ground black pepper.

5 To assemble salad: arrange lettuce leaves at the bottom of a large, shallow salad bowl. Arrange prepared vegetables on it in groups.

6 Chop anchovy fillets coarsely. Mix with capers and place in the centre of the salad.

7 Sprinkle with dressing and garnish with sprigs of parsley. Serve immediately.

1 head lettuce
4 bulbs white chicory (Belgian endive)
2 bulbs Florence fennel
1 sweet green pepper
1 sweet red pepper
1 large Spanish onion
4 anchovy fillets
2 level tablespoons capers
Parsley sprigs, to garnish

Dressing

6 tablespoons olive oil
2 tablespoons lemon juice
1/2 clove garlic, very finely chopped
2 level tablespoons finely chopped parsley
Salt and freshly ground black pepper

French Hors-d'œuvres Made Easy

In Paris or any other French city, one of the first things you notice when you enter a small restaurant or bistro is a selection of little rectangular dishes filled with a variety of simple vegetable salads – thin slices of ripe red tomatoes brushed with a little olive oil and wine vinegar and sprinkled with a little finely chopped parsley, green onion tops or chives; some finely shredded carrot dressed with a pinch of sugar and a little lemon juice or a delicate balance of vinegar and oil; a salad made of cooked green beans in a tarragon flavoured vinaigrette dressing; and some halved hard-boiled eggs bathed in a golden home-made mayonnaise. These simple basics are usually accompanied by a dish of crisp white radishes and one of sardines in oil.

Add to this a little saffron rice, tossed while still warm with diced green and red pepper and a well-flavoured vinaigrette; a salad of cooked lentils or haricots blancs, dressed with olive oil and vinegar with a hint of onion and anchovy to give it a lift, and you have a wonderful array of appetite-whets for a super luncheon party or for a supper in the country. With the addition of a few slices of cold cuts or pink boiled ham and fresh bread and butter, you can turn these cool, crisp salads into a whole meal.

French *hors-d'œuvres* are really very easy to produce and we will go through each one of them step by step. Serve them all together in French bistro style, or pick one or two to provide a light appetiser for a family or company meal.

Tomato Salad

Serves 6

6 large ripe tomatoes
Salt and freshly ground
　black pepper
Castor sugar
1 level tablespoon finely
　chopped chives or spring
　onion tops
2 teaspoons wine vinegar
2 tablespoons olive oil

A simple tomato salad can be one of the most refreshing appetisers in the world. Unfortunately, those great, ugly, flavoursome tomatoes that are such a feature of continental vegetable markets are difficult to come by here. The most you can do is beware of tomatoes that look too perfect and too evenly red – these usually taste of nothing at all – or buy from a small-time market gardener who has not sacrificed quality and flavour in the interests of high yield.

1 Wipe tomatoes clean. Stand them on their stem ends and slice them thinly with a very sharp knife.

2 Discard end slices, which are nearly all skin anyway, and fan tomatoes out in rows on a wide, shallow serving dish.

3 Season to taste with salt, freshly ground black pepper and a pinch or two of castor sugar.

4 Sprinkle evenly with finely chopped chives or spring onion tops, wine vinegar and olive oil, adding more of any of these ingredients if you think the tomatoes will take it.

Tomato Onion Salad

Alternate tomato slices and paper-thin slices of Spanish onion in overlapping rows. Dress as above, substituting finely chopped parsley for the chives.

If it is sliced thinly enough, 1 medium-sized onion will be sufficient for a salad made with 6 medium-sized tomatoes and the above dressing.

Grated Carrots

Serves 4–8

depending on the selection
of salads served with it
1 lb young carrots
4 tablespoons olive oil
4 teaspoons lemon juice
Salt and freshly ground
  black pepper
Castor sugar
Lettuce leaves, to garnish

1 Scrape carrots and grate them on the coarsest side of your grater.

2 In a bowl, toss grated carrots with olive oil and lemon juice. Season to taste with salt, freshly ground black pepper and a pinch of sugar, and toss again.

3 Pile up on a dish lined with lettuce leaves and chill lightly until ready to serve.

Carrot Orange Appetiser Salad

Serves 4–8

depending on the selection
of salads served with it

1 lb young carrots
4–6 level tablespoons
  mayonnaise (not too thick
  – see page 43)
Lemon juice
Generous pinch of finely
  grated orange rind
Salt and freshly ground black
  pepper
Lettuce leaves, to garnish

1 Scrape carrots and grate them on the coarsest side of your grater.

2 If mayonnaise is very thick, thin it down with a little lemon juice. Beat in a generous pinch of finely grated orange rind and correct seasoning with more salt and freshly ground black pepper if necessary.

3 Toss grated carrots thoroughly with orange-flavoured mayonnaise. Then taste and add a little more salt, pepper, lemon juice or grated orange rind to 'balance' flavours.

4 Serve as above.

Carrot and Redcurrant Salad

Serves 2–4

depending on the selection
of salads served with it

4 oz redcurrants
4 large, crisp carrots,
  coarsely grated
2–3 level teaspoons castor
  sugar
Juice of **1** lemon
Lettuce leaves, to garnish

To be really successful, this salad should always be prepared with garden-fresh carrots and really plump, ripe redcurrants. Serve it as part of a selection of appetiser salads, or as an accompaniment to a dish of sliced cold meat, pork or lamb especially.

1 Strip redcurrants from stalks. Wash and drain them thoroughly, and toss in a serving bowl with coarsely grated carrots.

2 Flavour to taste with sugar and lemon juice, and chill thoroughly before serving on a bed of lettuce leaves.

37

Green Bean Salad Vinaigrette

Serves 4–6

as part of a selection of
hors-d'œuvre salads

1 1/2 lb fresh young green
  beans
Salt
6–8 tablespoons olive oil
2–3 tablespoons tarragon
  vinegar
Freshly ground black pepper
1–2 level tablespoons very
  finely chopped onion
3–4 level tablespoons very
  finely chopped parsley
1 level teaspoon finely
  chopped fresh tarragon
Pinch of finely chopped
  garlic

There is one simple secret to this salad, but it is a vital one which
will stand you in good stead throughout the entire field of
vegetable cooking: for maximum flavour, cook the beans until
they are just tender but still distinctly crisp to the bite.

1 Top and tail young green beans.

2 Bring a pan of salted water to a brisk boil. Drop in beans (this
immersion in boiling water helps to 'set' the brilliant colour of all
green vegetables); bring to the boil again and simmer until just
tender.

3 Meanwhile, combine olive oil with tarragon vinegar, salt and
freshly ground black pepper, to taste, in a small bowl, and beat
with a fork until they form an emulsion. Stir in very finely
chopped onion, herbs and a pinch of finely chopped garlic, to
taste.

4 As soon as beans are cooked, drain them thoroughly in a
colander and put them in a serving bowl.

5 Pour dressing over steaming beans. Toss thoroughly and taste
for seasoning, adding more salt or freshly ground black pepper
if necessary. Serve cold.

Beetroot Salad Vinaigrette

Serves 4–6

1 lb cold cooked beetroot
3–4 level tablespoons very
  finely chopped onion
2 level tablespoons finely
  chopped parsley
2 tablespoons olive oil
2 teaspoons lemon juice or
  wine vinegar
Salt and freshly ground
  black pepper
Pinch of castor sugar
  (optional)

1 Peel beetroot if necessary and cut into $\frac{1}{3}$-inch dice, or into
small, thin slices, as you prefer. Place them in a bowl.

2 Add remaining ingredients and toss thoroughly but carefully
to prevent crushing beetroot. The slices or cubes should glisten
with dressing. If necessary, add more oil and lemon or vinegar.

3 Chill salad for 1 hour.

4 Just before serving: toss ingredients again, correct seasoning
and turn into a shallow serving dish.

Cucumber Salad

Serves 4–6

1 Peel and slice cucumber thinly – a mandolin cutter is best to slice the cucumber with. In a glass bowl, toss cucumber slices with 1 level tablespoon salt; place a weighted plate on top and leave for at least 1 hour to draw out juices.

2 Wash and drain cucumber slices thoroughly, pressing them lightly against the sides of the sieve to extract as much moisture as possible. Place them in a serving bowl.

3 Prepare a dressing by beating olive oil with wine vinegar, add salt and freshly ground black pepper, to taste, until they form an emulsion. Pour over cucumber slices; toss again and chill for at least 30 minutes before serving.

4 Just before serving, sprinkle salad with finely chopped parsley and tarragon.

1 large cucumber
Salt
3 tablespoons olive oil
1 tablespoon wine vinegar
Freshly ground black pepper
2 level tablespoons finely chopped parsley
1 level tablespoon finely chopped fresh tarragon

Celeriac Salad

Serves 4

1 Peel and wash celeriac. Cut into matchstick strips about $1\frac{1}{2}$ inches long and $\frac{1}{8}$ inch thick.

2 Put celeriac strips in a pan. Cover with cold water; add a good pinch of salt and bring to the boil over a moderate heat. Drain well and put in a bowl.

3 While celeriac is still faintly warm, fold in mayonnaise and season with more salt if necessary, freshly ground black pepper, and either mustard, curry powder (or paste) or paprika.

1 root celeriac
Salt
1/2 pint well-flavoured mayonnaise (page 43)
Freshly ground black pepper
Mustard, curry powder (or paste) or paprika

Carrier's Celeriac Salad

Serves 6

1 Scrub celeriac roots with a stiff brush under running water to remove dirt.

2 Bring a large pan of salted water to the boil. Add lemon juice. Submerge roots in the water and boil gently until tender but still on the crisp side, i.e. *al dente*. This will take about 30 minutes.

3 Peel celeriac roots. Slice them and cut them into strips about 2 inches long and $\frac{1}{4}$ inch thick. Place in a bowl and cover.

4 Make up 1 recipe Sauce Rémoulade on page 188. In Step 2 of the method, fold in prepared celeriac after listed ingredients.

5 Correct seasoning and serve.

Note: You may also like to add a little extra lemon juice or white wine vinegar.

2 celeriac roots, each about 1/2 lb
Salt
2 tablespoons lemon juice
1 recipe Sauce Rémoulade (page 188)

2 cans sardines in oil
1 egg, hard-boiled
1 level tablespoon finely
  chopped parsley
Lemon wedges, to garnish

Sardine and Hard-boiled Egg Appetiser

1 Use a good brand of sardines canned in oil. Drain them thoroughly and arrange head to tail on a rectangular serving dish.

2 Shell hard-boiled egg. Separate yolk from white and sieve them separately.

3 Garnish each sardine lengthwise with a band of sieved egg yolk, or egg white, or finely chopped parsley, alternating the bands of white, yellow and green along the dish.

4 Serve immediately with lemon wedges to squeeze over the top.

Serve as part of a selection of appetisers.

Serves 6–8

1 lb chicken livers
1/2 Spanish onion, finely
  chopped
1 fat clove garlic, finely
  chopped or crushed
1 small bay leaf, crumbled
Generous pinch each of
  dried marjoram and
  thyme
Salt and freshly ground
  black pepper
2 level tablespoons butter
2 tablespoons brandy
About 3 oz thinly sliced fat
  salt pork or fat bacon
6 oz pie veal
1/4 pint double cream

To garnish
Lettuce leaves
Quartered tomatoes
Black olives, pitted

Simple Chicken Liver Terrine

Later on in this course, the whole world of classic *terrines* and *ballotines* will be explored in depth. As a foretaste of things to come, this simple, delicious terrine can be tackled with confidence by any novice.

Just make sure you don't overcook the livers when you sauté them, and watch out for your eyebrows when you flame the brandy.

The terrine improves in flavour if made the day before you wish to serve it.

1 Put livers in a sieve or colander and rinse them quickly under the cold tap. Trim off any membranes or green parts. Dry livers on kitchen paper or a clean cloth.

2 Toss livers in a bowl with finely chopped Spanish onion, garlic, crumbled bay leaf, herbs, and salt and freshly ground black pepper, to taste.

3 Melt butter in a heavy frying-pan. When it is foaming, add chicken liver mixture and toss over a high heat for 4 or 5 minutes until livers are browned on the surface but still a little pink in the middle.

4 Remove pan from heat. Quickly pour on brandy; stand well back and set it alight with a match. Allow flames to die out of their own accord, shaking pan gently; then turn mixture into a bowl and leave to cool.

5 Preheat oven to moderate (375°F. Mark 5).

6 Line base and sides of a 1-lb loaf tin with thin slices of fat salt pork or fat bacon, leaving enough overlapping the sides to fold over the top when tin is full. (If bacon slices have not been cut thinly enough, arrange them, well spaced apart, between two sheets of greaseproof paper and pound them with a mallet or the bottom of a milk bottle until almost paper-thin. Fat salt pork cuts best if thoroughly chilled beforehand, but slices tend to disintegrate if pounded.)

7 Combine cooled liver mixture with pie veal. Put through a mincer fitted with a coarse blade.

8 Beat in double cream. Season to taste with salt and freshly ground black pepper, and beat again until mixture is thoroughly blended.

9 Spoon mixture into lined tin. Tap tin lightly against the table to eliminate air bubbles.

10 Fold overlapping ends of fat salt pork or bacon over the top of the terrine to cover it completely; then seal top of tin with a piece of foil.

11 Place tin in a deep baking dish and pour in hot water to come a third of the way up sides. Bake for 45 to 50 minutes. To test the terrine, plunge a thin skewer into the centre; leave it there for about 10 seconds, then quickly put it to your lips: it should feel hot.

12 Allow terrine to cool. Chill overnight.

13 To serve: loosen terrine by dipping base of tin in hot water for 1 or 2 seconds. Turn it out on to a serving dish lined with lettuce leaves and garnish with quartered tomatoes and a few pitted black olives. Serve 2 thin slices per person.

Note: For a more elegant effect, remove two of the nicest livers when you have sautéed them and slice them thinly. Half-fill tin with minced liver mixture; arrange sliced livers in a row down centre and cover with remaining mixture. Finish as above.

French Vinaigrette Dressing Explained

In many of the foregoing recipes for appetisers and *hors-d'œuvres* we have been using a vinaigrette dressing. So now it is time to experiment with the flavours of a perfect vinaigrette.

Most cooks will agree that a beautifully proportioned and well-seasoned vinaigrette dressing is at least half of any salad. And the best salad dressing allows the cook a wide variety of choice. First of all your vinegar: red wine vinegar, white wine vinegar, cider vinegar, malt or tarragon vinegar. There are several

Basic Vinaigrette Dressing

2 tablespoons wine vinegar
6 tablespoons olive or salad oil
1/4 level teaspoon dry mustard (optional)
Salt and freshly ground black pepper

41

Lemon Vinaigrette

2 tablespoons lemon juice
6 tablespoons olive or salad
    oil
1/4 level teaspoon dry
    mustard (optional)
Salt and freshly ground
    black pepper
1 level tablespoon finely
    chopped parsley
1 hard-boiled egg, finely
    chopped

Vinaigrette Dressing with Fresh Herbs

2 tablespoons wine vinegar
    or lemon juice
6 tablespoons olive or salad
    oil
1/4 level teaspoon dry mustard
    (optional)
Salt and freshly ground
    black pepper
1 level tablespoon freshly
    chopped tarragon, chives or
    fennel, or a combination
    of all three

vinegar strengths on the market – fragile to mellow to sharp. Taste your vinegar as you go, or perhaps use just half of the vinegar called for in the recipe first, then add more to achieve the desired sharpness as you go along, or add a little lemon juice to your vinegar to 'soften' the flavour. ·

The same goes for the oil you choose. There are many available: rich, full flavoured olive oil with the fruity taste of the olive in it, a more refined lighter-flavoured olive oil, other vegetable oils, nut oil. It's up to you to choose any of these or a blend of two or more to get the flavour and body balance that you like best, beautifully proportioned and seasoned.

Then when you have perfected the right blend of oils and vinegars, it is time to make your vinaigrette:

To Make a Perfect Vinaigrette Dressing

1 Mix together wine vinegar, lemon juice, or a combination of the two; add dry mustard if desired and season to taste with salt and freshly ground black pepper.

2 Add olive oil, and beat well with a fork until the mixture emulsifies.

3 Stir in 1 level tablespoon finely chopped herbs. For a 'greener', more fragrant dressing, add 2 to 3 level tablespoons finely chopped herbs.

Note: If dressing is too 'thick', add a little more olive oil and lemon juice, to taste.

Note: The flavour of these dressings can be varied according to your taste. Add a little crumbled Roquefort cheese, a finely chopped clove of garlic, a dash of onion juice or several pinches of curry to ring the flavour changes.

A 'Tour de Main' Makes Perfect Mayonnaise

There seem to be as many theories on the origin of the word mayonnaise as there are ways to serve this delicious sauce. The first has it that the word was created to celebrate a sauce brought back from the wars by the chef of the Duc de Richelieu when his master took Port Mahon in 1756. Islanders used to dress cold meats and fish with a sauce made of raw egg yolk, garlic, salt and olive oil. Richelieu's cook copied the sauce, leaving out the garlic, and *mahonnaise*, or *mayonnaise*, as we know it today, was born.

Another school of thought, led by the great French chef Carême, claimed that this golden sauce should really be called *magnonaise* as it comes from the verb *manier* (to stir). Others are of the opinion that it was originally called *bayonnaise*, as it was first known in France in the region of Bayonne; yet others that the word was really *moyeunaise*, as in old French *moyeu* meant the yolk of an egg.

But whatever the origin of this word we would indeed be poor without the rich golden sauce that springs as if by magic from the marriage of olive oil and egg yolk. It is a powerful and useful accompaniment to cold beef, veal, chicken, cod, lobster, crab and pike. It can be served already mixed with pieces of lobster, chicken, ham, turkey or assorted vegetables. It takes kindly to the addition of fresh herbs, mustard, freshly grated horse-radish, tomato purée, saffron, capers, and finely chopped gherkins and cucumber. It is the perfect accompaniment to hard-boiled eggs, a 'must' with chilled prawns. With a little dry white wine, milk or water added mayonnaise is perfect for potato salad, with liquid gelatine added it becomes a coating for cold chicken and duck.

I use a rotary whisk to mix my mayonnaise – heresy to the wooden spoon and soup-plate teachers of my youth, but I find it makes almost fool-proof mayonnaise and almost no loss to flavour and texture.

Mayonnaise should always be thick enough to cut with a knife (none of these wishy-washy emulsions for me). And for this a substantial quantity of top-quality olive oil must be used.

How to Make Perfect Mayonnaise in the Classic Manner

Makes ½ pint

2 egg yolks
1/2 level teaspoon English or French mustard
Salt and freshly ground black pepper
Lemon juice
1/2 pint olive oil

1 Have all ingredients at room temperature before you start. This is important: eggs straight from the refrigerator and cloudy olive oil are both liable to make a mayonnaise curdle.
2 Make sure that there are no gelatinous threads left on the egg yolks. Put yolks in a medium-sized bowl and set it in a pan or on a damp cloth on the table to hold it steady. Add mustard and a pinch each of salt and freshly ground black pepper, and work to a smooth paste with a spoon or a whisk.
3 Add a teaspoon of lemon juice and work until smooth again.
4 Pour olive oil into a measuring jug. With a teaspoon, start adding oil to egg yolk mixture a drop at a time, beating well between each addition.
5 Having incorporated about a quarter of the oil, step up the

rate at which you add the remainder of the oil, a teaspoon or two at a time, or a steady, fine trickle, beating strongly as you do so. If the mayonnaise becomes very thick before all the oil has been absorbed, thin it down again with more lemon juice or a few drops of cold water. Forcing olive oil into a very thick mayonnaise is another factor which may cause it to curdle. The finished mayonnaise should be thick and shiny, and drop from the spoon or whisk in heavy globs.

6 Correct seasoning, adding more salt, freshly ground black pepper or lemon juice if necessary.

7 If mayonnaise is not to be used immediately, beat in a tablespoon of boiling water to keep it from separating. Cover bowl tightly and leave at the bottom of the refrigerator until ready to use.

Curdled mayonnaise If in spite of all precautions mayonnaise should curdle, you can bring it back by breaking another egg yolk into a clean bowl, beating it lightly with a few drops of lemon juice or water, then adding curdled mayonnaise a teaspoon at a time, beating well between each addition. Mayonnaise will begin to 'take' immediately – in fact, the new emulsion will probably become very thick before the whole of the curdled portion has been added. If so, be sure to keep thinning it down occasionally with a few drops of lemon juice (or water) as you proceed.

Thin mayonnaise Occasionally, mayonnaise which has not exactly curdled nevertheless refuses to become thick. You may also find that mayonnaise left too long in the refrigerator before being used tends to lose 'body'. When this happens, no amount of beating will bring it back to the right consistency and you will have to resort to the measures described for curdled mayonnaise.

Makes about ½ pint

2 egg yolks
1 tablespoon wine vinegar or lemon juice
1/2 level teaspoon each dry mustard and salt
Pinch of freshly ground black pepper
1/2 pint olive oil

Quick Blender Mayonnaise

A simple mayonnaise which can be made in a matter of minutes.

1 Combine egg yolks with wine vinegar or lemon juice, mustard, salt, a pinch of freshly ground black pepper and 2 tablespoons cold water in the container of an electric blender. Cover and blend at moderate speed for 5 seconds, or until well mixed.

2 Remove inner cover of blender and, with the motor turned to maximum speed, add oil in a thin, steady trickle. Correct seasoning and use as required.

Variations on the Mayonnaise Theme

Blender mayonnaise Combine 2 whole eggs, $\frac{1}{4}$ pint olive oil, 4 tablespoons lemon juice or vinegar, $\frac{1}{2}$ level teaspoon each dry mustard and salt, and freshly ground black pepper to taste in electric blender. Cover the container and turn the motor to high. When blended, remove cover and add $\frac{1}{2}$ pint olive oil in a thin steady trickle, blending continuously. Correct seasoning and use as desired.

Horseradish mayonnaise Add juice of $\frac{1}{2}$ lemon and salt to taste to $\frac{3}{4}$ pint mayonnaise. Just before serving, stir in 2 to 3 tablespoons freshly grated horseradish. (For eggs, hard-boiled egg salads or seafood.)

Russian mayonnaise dressing Add 3 tablespoons tomato ketchup, a dash of Tabasco or Worcestershire sauce and 1 level teaspoon each chopped tinned pimentos and chives. (For eggs, cooked vegetable salads and seafood.)

Cucumber mayonnaise Add $\frac{1}{4}$ finely chopped cucumber and 2 tablespoons finely chopped parsley to $\frac{3}{4}$ pint mayonnaise.

Saffron mayonnaise Add powdered saffron to taste.

Mustard mayonnaise Add Dijon or powdered mustard to taste.

Sauce tartare Add 1–2 teaspoons each chopped parsley, tarragon, chervil, capers and gherkins to $\frac{1}{2}$ pint mayonnaise.

Aristocratic Appetiser Trio

This aristocratic trio make three of the finest and easiest *hors-d'œuvres* you could wish for. The other great advantage they have is their simplicity of preparation.

The Artichoke

To choose and store artichokes When buying artichokes, look out for ones that are fresh and heavy for their size, with supple, tightly closed leaves. Stiff, dry leaves and an 'overblown' appearance generally indicate that the artichoke will be tough and woody.

The size of an artichoke is no indication of its quality, but small ones are better for pickling, medium-sized and large ones for serving whole as an appetiser, or in dishes where only the heart is called for.

(**Note**: Never waste the leaves when preparing a dish with artichoke hearts: they can be boiled and served with a vinaigrette or melted butter just like a whole artichoke.)

● Artichokes can be stored in the refrigerator, tightly covered to preserve their moisture.

To prepare whole artichokes

1 With a strong, sharp knife, slice all the leaves off level with the tips of the shortest ones. Strip away any tough outer leaves. Trim base and stem.

2 With a sharp-edged teaspoon, scoop and scrape out the fuzzy chokes, taking care not to leave a single fibre. Remember that an artichoke is the flowerbud of a thistle and that these fibres are not called 'chokes' for nothing.

3 While you are working on the artichoke, keep dipping it into a bowl of water heavily acidulated with lemon juice each time you cut open a fresh surface to prevent it turning brown. The artichoke contains peroxides and oxidising enzymes which cause it – and any steel utensil used with it – to discolour very quickly when exposed to the air. This is not dangerous, but it makes the artichoke look unattractive and spoils its flavour.

To prepare artichoke hearts As above, but strip off all the outer leaves, one by one; then slice round with a sharp knife to remove those closest to the heart and scrape out the choke. Keep the bowl of acidulated water handy and use it frequently to prevent discolouration.

● If you wish to use canned or bottled artichokes – a good standby when fresh ones are out of season – be sure to rinse off all the preserving liquid, as the taste of this might interfere with the flavour of the finished dish.

To boil artichokes

1 To a large pan of water add a handful of salt and some lemon juice (or a squeezed-out lemon half). Bring to the boil.

2 Immerse artichokes and simmer for 30 to 40 minutes, or until you can pull a leaf out easily.

3 Lift out artichokes and leave them to drain standing on their heads in a colander.

To serve whole artichokes (Artichoke hearts present no problem – you simply use a knife and fork.)

The toughest leaves should already have been stripped off and the artichoke will be standing on a large plate, ready to be attacked. Start stripping the remaining leaves off first. Holding a leaf by its point, dip the base in the sauce selected. Then just draw it lightly through your teeth to remove the tender part. Put the inedible part of the leaf on the side of your plate. You will find that the edible pulp on each leaf becomes less substantial as you work your way through to the heart.

If you find the choke is still intact when you get down to the heart, scrape it out with a knife and fork, and eat the heart with a fork.

Fingerbowls of warm water with a slice of lemon floating on top are essential.

Sauces for artichokes
Melted butter
Vinaigrette (page 41)
Mayonnaise (page 43)
Hollandaise (page 190)

Asparagus

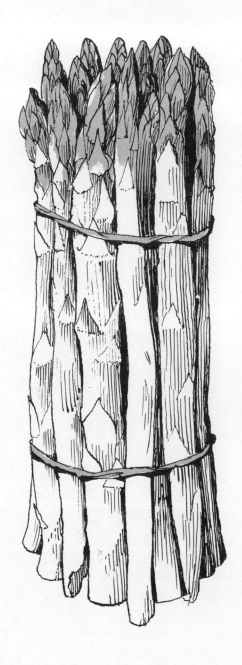

Did you know that asparagus belongs to the same family as the lily-of-the-valley? And that the Greeks and Romans were eating asparagus, both fresh and dried, long before the birth of Christ? And that even before then, it enjoyed a great reputation as a medicine for almost any ailment from toothache to heart disease? However, the most interesting discovery, for me at least, was that in over two thousand years gourmets have failed to improve on the classic method of cooking asparagus. The Roman saying: 'You can do it in less time than it takes to cook asparagus,' shows just how close their method of dealing with it was to ours.

To choose and store asparagus There are several varieties of asparagus available, varying in colour and thickness: *English asparagus* is usually green, either thick or thin. The great *French asparagus*, probably the finest, and certainly the best known, comes from Argenteuil, and is white. Then there is *Italian* or purple Genoa asparagus, and *Belgian* and *German* asparagus both of which are white. (The asparagus tips we buy bottled or canned come from the green variety, as is the variety used for freezing.)

When buying fresh asparagus, avoid any with hard, woody stems or overblown, spreading tips. The stalk should snap easily. Remember that thin stalks are not necessarily the most tender ones.

Bunches should be graded according to thickness, otherwise you will have to grade them yourself, then cook each portion separately to ensure that the stalks are all ready at the same time.

Fresh asparagus can be stored, wrapped, in the bottom of the refrigerator for several days.

To prepare asparagus Wash stalks thoroughly under the cold tap, scrubbing them with a small brush if they are sandy. Remove stray leaf points from stem below the head. Trim stalks; scrape the lower ends with the back of a knife. If stalks are 'woody', break the woody part off – you will find that the stalk snaps off right at the point where the tender part begins. Trim broken edge of stalk with a knife. Put stalks into cold water as you prepare them.

To cook asparagus You can boil or steam asparagus. Both methods are equally good, though steaming is probably safer.

To boil asparagus Grade stalks into bundles of even thickness. Stand bundles upright in a tall saucepan and pour in boiling water to come just under the tips. Salt the water. Bring to the boil; cover tips loosely with a cap of crumpled foil and simmer gently until tender, 10 to 15 minutes from the time water comes to the boil again. In this way, the stalks cook in water, while the more tender tips are steamed. Drain as soon as stems feel tender when pierced with the tip of a sharp knife.

Another method of boiling asparagus, suitable for very tender stalks, is to use a pan wide enough to take the stems sideways. Fill with salted water; bring to the boil and immerse the bundle of asparagus, supporting tips clear of the water on a pillow of crumpled foil so that they cook in steam as before. Bring to the boil and simmer until cooked. Drain immediately.

To steam asparagus You will find a special asparagus steamer invaluable for this, especially as it can also be used for fish, corn on the cob, artichokes and other vegetables. One variety of steamer is oblong and has an adjustable liner with handles which allow you to lift out the cooked stalks (or fish) without breaking them. Another type is a tall tube of stainless steel or aluminium, with a lift-out steamer basket, which allows you to cook stems of asparagus in boiling water, while the heads ride free in the steam.

Sauces for asparagus Serve boiled or steamed asparagus *hot*:

● Sprinkled with flaked toasted almonds and melted butter.

● Masked with a well-flavoured cream sauce into which you have stirred some diced, hard-boiled egg.

● Accompanied by $\frac{1}{4}$ lb melted butter flavoured with 2 tablespoons each lemon juice and finely chopped parsley.

- With Hollandaise or Mousseline Sauce (see pages 190 and 191).

Or *cold*:

- With a plain vinaigrette flavoured with herbs and French mustard, or one into which you have stirred 2 to 3 hard-boiled eggs, a bunch of chives, 6 sprigs fresh tarragon, 3 to 4 sprigs fresh parsley and 1 or 2 cloves garlic, all finely chopped.

- With mayonnaise (see page 43).

- *A la fontenelle.* For this, you serve the cold asparagus with a bowl of melted butter and a soft-boiled egg per person. Each stalk is dipped first in melted butter, then in the soft yolk of the egg.

The Avocado

Surprisingly enough, avocados have something of a reputation of being an acquired taste, so don't waste an avocado on someone unless you're sure that he'll like it.

To choose an avocado Avocados vary considerably in size, from huge, pear-shaped fruit to little ones weighing no more than a few ounces. The skin can be smooth or slightly rough, and the colour a bright green or deep violet.

Pick fruit which are heavy for their size and fairly firm, with just a hint of softness when pressed lightly with a finger. If they are too hard, leave for a day or two at normal room temperature. *Never* try to 'ripen' an avocado in the refrigerator.

To serve an avocado The traditional way of serving an avocado is to slice it in half, remove the stone, which comes out easily enough if the fruit is ripe, and replace it with a vinaigrette dressing.

- Another favourite way is to scoop out some of the flesh, dice it, and combine it with fish or shellfish and a little well-flavoured mayonnaise. Serve piled up in the half-shell. Whichever way you choose, make a point of protecting the flesh from discolouration by brushing it with lemon juice (or spooning over some of the vinaigrette you are going to serve) as soon as you cut it.

Simple Fish-type Appetisers

Herring Fillets in Oil

Serves 4

4 salted herrings
2 medium-sized Spanish
  onions
6 black peppercorns
1–2 bay leaves
1 lemon, thinly sliced
About 1/4 pint olive oil

For this dish you will need raw, salted herrings from a barrel. These are gradually becoming more easily available, and can now be found in many delicatessens, especially those specialising in Eastern European food.

This is a delicious appetiser, well worth the 2 days you will have to wait for it. The long marinating in olive oil with lemon and onion slices mellows the flavour of the herrings, and gives them a soft, almost buttery texture.

1 Wash salted herring fillets thoroughly and remove skins carefully if these have been left on. Leave fillets to soak in water for 24 hours, changing it occasionally.

2 Drain herring fillets thoroughly; pat them dry with paper towels and lay them in a shallow serving dish.

3 Slice onions thinly and separate them into rings. Scatter over herring fillets, together with black peppercorns and pieces of bay leaf, and lay thin lemon slices on top.

4 Pour in just enough olive oil to cover. Then cover dish with foil and leave to marinate in the bottom of the refrigerator for 48 hours before serving.

Pickled Smoked Salmon à la Russe

Serves 4

4 thick slices smoked salmon
1 Spanish onion, thinly
  sliced
3 tablespoons corn oil
2 tablespoons olive oil
2 tablespoons wine vinegar
1 small clove garlic, crushed
1/2 bay leaf
Salt and freshly ground
  black pepper

The advantage of this simple little appetiser is that you do not need to use top-quality smoked salmon. The marinade itself adds a great deal of flavour and changes the texture of the fish to a buttery softness.

1 Select a deep china dish just large enough to take a slice of smoked salmon flat. It should preferably have a tight-fitting lid, but you can use foil instead.

2 Separate onion slices into rings.

3 Arrange alternate layers of smoked salmon and onion rings.

4 Combine next five ingredients in a bowl and beat with a fork to make a dressing. Season generously with salt and freshly ground black pepper.

5 Pour dressing over the salmon and onions. Cover dish tightly and leave to marinate at the bottom of the refrigerator for a week to 10 days.

6 Serve a slice of salmon per person, garnished with a few of the onion rings and accompanied by thinly sliced rye bread.

Taramasalata

Serves 4–6

1 Trim bread slices of crusts and soak bread in cold water for a few minutes.

2 Meanwhile, put smoked cod's roe into the bowl of an electric mixer and beat to a paste.

3 Squeeze bread dry and, with the mixer at full speed, shred it into the bowl, a few pieces at a time. Continue to beat until well blended.

4 Blend in 2 tablespoons lemon juice, the grated onion and mashed garlic, if used.

5 Pour about $\frac{1}{2}$ pint olive oil into a jug with a good pouring lip with which you can control the flow. With mixer still at full speed, pour in olive oil in a fine trickle, rather as you would in the later stages of making mayonnaise.

6 If tarama becomes stiff and waxy before all the oil has been incorporated, thin it down with a little more lemon juice, to taste. Then continue beating in olive oil, a little faster now, until tarama is a beautiful, pale pink, with a firm, spreading consistency.

7 Taste and add more grated onion or lemon juice if desired.

8 Tarama may be served in several ways:
(*a*) mounded up on a serving dish lined with lettuce; garnished with black olives and lemon wedges, and served with hot toast or fresh French bread;
(*b*) piped attractively into individual porcelain dishes; garnished and served in the same way;
(*c*) piped into perfect white mushrooms caps, and sprinkled with a little very finely chopped parsley.

2–3 slices white bread
One 3-oz jar smoked cod's roe
2–3 tablespoons lemon juice
1 level teaspoon grated onion
1/4 clove garlic, mashed (optional)
About 1/2 pint olive oil

Serves 6

1 Head lettuce
8 oz peeled shrimps or
   prawns, or flaked canned
   crab or lobster
1 lemon
Paprika or cayenne

Dressing
1/2 pint thick mayonnaise
   (page 43)
1 teaspoon French mustard
2 teaspoons lemon juice
3–4 level tablespoons tomato
   ketchup
Worcestershire sauce
Tabasco
Salt and freshly ground
   black pepper

Seafood Cocktail

1 To make dressing: prepare $\frac{1}{2}$ pint thick mayonnaise, flavouring it with a teaspoon of French mustard, and about two of lemon juice. Blend in tomato ketchup and flavour to taste with a few drops of Worcestershire sauce and a dash of Tabasco. Correct seasoning.

2 Wash lettuce leaves; dry carefully and shred finely.

3 To assemble cocktails: half-fill 6 round, tall-stemmed glasses (round champagne glasses are the best) with shredded lettuce and divide seafood between them. Spoon dressing over the top allowing about 3 level tablespoons per portion.

4 Cut lemon lengthwise into 6 wedges. With a sharp knife, make an incision between skin and flesh from one tip of each wedge to about half-way up. Clip a wedge on to each glass.

5 Garnish each cocktail with a tiny pinch of paprika or cayenne, and serve.

Fresh Vegetables à la Grecque

Fresh Vegetables à la Grecque: The vegetables of your choice make a wonderfully sophisticated cold vegetable appetiser when cooked in a mixture of olive oil, dry white wine and water, flavoured with aromatics in the manner of cooking that professional chefs call *à la Grecque*.

Mixed Vegetables à la Grecque

Parboil vegetables for 5 minutes, and then poach them gently in an *à la Grecque* sauce for 10 to 15 minutes, or (as in the case of button onions) until tender:

1 Prepare à la Grecque Sauce: Combine first seven ingredients in a saucepan; add salt, freshly ground black pepper and cayenne, to taste; bring to boil, reduce heat and simmer gently over lowest of heats for 30 minutes.

2 Add vegetables of your choice, and simmer until tender (10 minutes for tender vegetables to 40 minutes for onions).

3 Just before serving: correct seasoning; add a little olive oil and sprinkle with finely chopped parsley.

A choice of:

Fingers of aubergine
Celery hearts, cut into thin strips
Celery root, cut into thin strips
Green and red peppers, cut into thin strips
Fennel, sliced or cut into quarters
Carrots, sliced or cut into strips
Courgettes, sliced or cut into strips
Leeks, cut into 2-inch strips
Button onions
Button mushrooms
Cauliflowerets

A la Grecque Sauce:

1 pint water
5 level tablespoons tomato concentrate
5 tablespoons olive oil
5 tablespoons dry white wine
1/2 Spanish onion, finely chopped
1/2 clove garlic, finely chopped
12 coriander seeds
Salt and freshly ground black pepper
Cayenne pepper
Olive oil
Finely chopped parsley

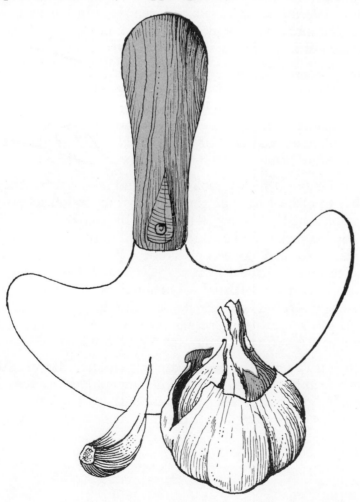

Lesson 2
Simple Egg Dishes

It is rare in cookery to find one single food that can be all things to all dishes. Such a food is the egg.

Served plain boiled in its shell – after a three-minute immersion in gently boiling water – it is the perfect breakfast dish for poet or ploughman. Battles have been fought in my presence on whether it is better to break the egg deftly around the top and then eat the creamy yolk and barely coagulated white with a spoon; or by dipping thin strips of buttered toast into the orifice so created.

As a child in America I used to solve this weighty problem – my mother was a 'spooner', my father was a 'toaster' – by demanding *two* soft-boiled eggs which I could then break into a heated cup, season with salt and pepper, moisten with a few butter bits and eat to my intense satisfaction with both teaspoon and strips of toast. The best of all worlds!

From plain soft-boiled eggs I soon graduated to two eggs, lightly poached and served on well-buttered toast, and then to my favourite Sunday morning breakfast – a 'soft scramble' of egg, flavoured with a spoonful or two of crumbled cooked bacon, diced cooked ham, or thinly sliced mushrooms sautéed in butter before being stirred into the eggs.

Poached Eggs Benedict took these childhood fancies one step further to make a light luncheon dish of my favourite poached eggs on toast. In this case, a thin strip of ham and a fat slice of raw tomato were placed on buttered toast, or on a toasted English muffin. A poached egg was placed on top and the whole bathed in a delicious Hollandaise sauce (page 190). Fried eggs – 'sunny side up' – with the yolks unbroken and unblemished – and hard-boiled eggs – sliced and served hot with butter, simmered sliced onions and a creamy cheese sauce, or cold with a home-made mayonnaise (page 43) – completed my personal egg picture.

But it wasn't until I lived in France, just after the war, that I encountered for the first time the delights of *œufs en cocotte* (eggs baked in butter and cream in individual little baking dishes); *œufs sur le plat* (eggs cooked under the grill in buttered heatproof

54

dishes); and the myriad wonders of French egg cookery: sweet and savoury soufflés of hitherto unimaginable lightness; hot and cold mousses; feathery *quenelles* of poultry or seafood; and filled French omelettes which seemed manna to my eager but unsophisticated palate.

Egg dishes are wonderfully easy to cook. The only three variants to worry about are (1) the freshness of the egg; (2) the correct amount of heat to use; and (3) the amount of time the eggs are to be subjected to it. *Eggs should never be overcooked.* With the exception of the omelette, a gentle heat is best for all egg cookery. And even when making omelettes, it is best not to have the heat too high, or you will end up with a tough, leathery omelette fit only for the waste-disposal unit.

The egg itself is so delicate; its composition changes so quickly when cooking, that just a short time with a gentle heat is enough to cook them. More eggs – boiled, poached, baked, fried – have been ruined, more soufflés and mousses dried out, more egg sauces curdled by too high a heat, than by any other means.

Treat eggs gently for the best results. You'll find that the following simple egg dishes will benefit enormously from a light touch.

Eggs

To break an egg Crack the egg through the middle by hitting it smartly against the side of a bowl; then prise the two halves of the shell apart and allow the yolk and white to drop into the bowl. Clean out any egg white remaining in the shell with your forefinger. Never tempt fortune by breaking several eggs into the same bowl one after the other – it is impossible to guarantee that one of them will not be bad and taint your whole bowl, so far better to break eggs into a cup one at a time and check that each one is fresh before slipping it into the bowl with the rest.

To separate eggs Crack the eggs as above; then, holding a half-shell in each hand, gently slide the yolk back and forth between them, taking care to keep it whole while allowing the white to fall down into a dish below. Drop egg yolk into another bowl and clean out remaining white with your finger as above.

To store eggs Eggs should be stored in the special compartment of the refrigerator (usually in the door) designed for them. Since this is rarely big enough, store the excess in cartons at the bottom of the refrigerator, well away from strong-smelling foods, as they can actually absorb flavours and aromas *through* the shell.

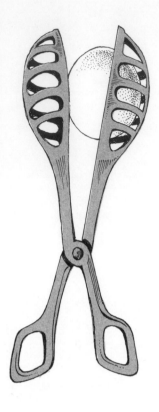

Most recipes call for eggs brought to room temperature, so make a point of taking eggs out of the refrigerator well before you embark on a dish, especially when baking.

Soft-boiled Eggs

You may already have noticed in the past that a new-laid egg takes appreciably longer to boil than a slightly stale one (not to mention a very stale one, which has no business to be boiled anyway).

To soft-boil eggs:

1 Bring a pan of water to the boil. Slip eggs in gently on a spoon, one at a time – make sure eggs are wholly immersed in water, otherwise they will not cook evenly. Lower heat until water is barely bubbling and allow 3 minutes for a classic soft-boiled egg, the white coagulated but still on the soft side and the golden yolk runny, $\frac{1}{2}$ to 1 minute longer if (*a*) the egg is very fresh or (*b*) you prefer it to be set pretty firm.

2 Or slip eggs into boiling water as above. When water reboils, remove pan from heat, cover it and allow eggs to stand for 10 minutes. You will find that the yolk is creamy and the whites have set without being tough.

3 A slightly quicker yet very similar method to Step **2** lowers the eggs into boiling water; draws the pan to the side of the stove (or lowers heat) so that water remains just below boiling-point at a steady 175°F. for about 6 minutes.

4 Or place the eggs in cold water; bring to the boil over a low heat and remove them as soon as water boils. This takes about 10 minutes.

● Once cooked and removed from the heat, no amount of subsequent heating will harden a soft-boiled egg that has been insufficiently cooked.

● Soft-boiled eggs can be reheated, however, by standing them for 3 or 4 minutes in hot but not boiling water.

● If you find a crack in an egg intended for boiling, rub it over with a cut lemon just before you put it in the water, or cover the crack with a piece of gummed paper – the paper will come off, of course, but not before the white has coagulated sufficiently to prevent it escaping into the water.

● To *prevent* an egg cracking when you lower it into boiling water, pierce a tiny hole in the broader end with a needle before cooking it. This releases the pressure caused by the sharp increase in temperature.

Viennese Eggs

Serves 4

8 fresh eggs
3–4 level tablespoons soft
   fresh butter
Salt

1 Soft-boil eggs for 4 minutes.

2 Have ready 4 small, tall glasses set in 4 small, deep bowls containing hot (not boiling) water.

3 As soon as eggs are ready, lift them out with a slotted spoon; slice off tops and scoop 2 eggs out into each glass with a spoon, trying to keep yolks whole if possible.

4 Garnish each glass with a knob of butter and season with a pinch of salt. Serve immediately. The eggs are eaten with a spoon. Or with fingers of hot toast.

Poached Eggs

Only very fresh eggs with a smooth, rounded yolk and a firm white can be poached successfully.

Drop a stale egg into boiling water and the white will wisp away in all directions, to end up finally as an unappetising scum on the surface, leaving a tired, solitary egg yolk bobbing away somewhere in the foamy liquid. The aim is to cook the egg in such a way that the white will set neatly around the yolk, leaving the latter soft and slightly runny inside.

1 Pour 4 pints water into a large, wide saucepan, about 7 pints capacity. Water should be about 3 inches deep. Add 4 tablespoons wine vinegar; bring to the boil; then lower heat to a vigorous simmer.

2 Crack a fresh egg on the side of the pan and, holding the shell as close to the surface of the water as possible, drop the egg in.

3 Then raise heat so that water bubbles up, drawing white up neatly around yolk.

(**Note**: It is preferable to poach just 2 or 3 eggs at a time until you get the knack.)

4 After 2 or 3 minutes, carefully lift out one egg with a slotted spoon – try to remember the location of the one that went in the pan first – and test it by pressing lightly with your finger. If it is not cooked to your liking, lower egg back into pan for a little longer.

5 Lift eggs out with a slotted spoon. Drain them on a cloth or on absorbent paper, and trim ragged edges with a pair of scissors.

● To ensure that eggs are not left with a vinegary flavour, gently rinse with hot water before trimming them.

57

● Poached eggs can be kept for several hours if they are immersed in a bowl of cold water. Drain and dry thoroughly in a clean cloth or absorbent paper before use.

● To reheat poached eggs which have been cooked in advance: slip them into a bowl of hot salted water for 30 to 40 seconds; then drain thoroughly.

Poached Eggs Florentine

Serves 6

6 individual shortcrust pastry cases 4 inches in diameter, prebaked
6 eggs, poached and trimmed
6 level tablespoons Mornay sauce (page 179)
2 level tablespoons freshly grated Parmesan

Spinach mixture

12 oz frozen spinach
2 oz butter
4 level tablespoons freshly grated Parmesan
3–4 tablespoons single cream
Lemon juice
Salt and freshly ground black pepper
Freshly grated nutmeg

1 Prepare spinach mixture: combine frozen spinach with butter in a heavy pan and allow to defrost over a gentle heat, stirring and mashing occasionally with a wooden spoon. Then simmer spinach for 5 to 7 minutes longer, stirring to rid it of excess moisture. Beat in grated Parmesan and cream, and season to taste with a few drops of lemon juice, salt, freshly ground black pepper and a pinch of freshly grated nutmeg.

2 Fill pastry cases with hot spinach mixture and top each one with a poached egg. Spoon hot Mornay sauce over the top and sprinkle with grated Parmesan.

3 Slip pastry cases under a hot grill for a few minutes until tops are bubbling and golden, and serve immediately.

Note: If you have no Mornay or other rich cheese sauce available, simply sprinkle pastry cases more generously with grated Parmesan and grill as above until cheese has melted.

Oeufs en Cocotte

Serves 4

Butter
8 fresh eggs
Salt and freshly ground black pepper
1–2 level tablespoons single cream

1 Butter 4 individual heatproof ramekins (5 fluid oz capacity). Break 2 eggs into each ramekin; sprinkle with a pinch of salt and a few turns of the peppermill.

2 Arrange ramekins side by side in a heavy pan with a lid. (Failing a large enough pan, use a roasting tin and cover it with a sheet of foil.)

3 Pour in boiling water to come a third of the way up sides of ramekins; cover pan or tin tightly and simmer very gently on top of the stove for about 8 minutes for soft eggs, a minute or two longer if you prefer them on the firm side. (Don't let the surface of the eggs persuade you to carry on simmering them too long: a 'watery', unset surface may be concealing rock-hard egg whites underneath, so test by pressing the yolks firmly with a finger – you will soon be able to tell whether the dish is ready or not.)

4 As soon as eggs are cooked to your liking, remove ramekins from water. Swirl about 1 teaspoon cream round the top of each dish and serve immediately.

Hard-boiled Eggs

1 For very fresh eggs: place the required number of eggs in a pan. Pour in cold water to cover; bring to the boil and boil for 10 minutes.

2 For shop-bought eggs: lower eggs into a pan of boiling water. Wait until water comes back to the boil and boil for 10 minutes.

● As soon as eggs are cooked, plunge them into cold water – this makes it easier to shell them without damaging whites. Allow to become quite cold before shelling.

● To shell a hard-boiled egg: tap the egg all round with the back of a knife; then peel off shell, taking great care not to damage surface of egg white.

● Hard-boiled eggs should not be overcooked, or yolks will acquire a greeny-black outer surface where they meet the white.

Hard-boiled Egg Variations – Cold

Stuffed Eggs with Green Mayonnaise

Serves 6

Green mayonnaise
2 egg yolks
Salt and freshly ground black pepper
1/2 level teaspoon French mustard
2 teaspoons lemon juice or wine vinegar
1/2 pint olive oil
Fresh parsley sprigs
Fresh watercress
1 level tablespoon each finely chopped fresh parsley, watercress and tarragon

Stuffed eggs
2 oz buttered shrimps
6 eggs, hard-boiled
4 level tablespoons mayonnaise (above)
Lemon juice
Cayenne pepper
2 level tablespoons finely chopped mixed fresh herbs, to garnish

1 Prepare green mayonnaise a few hours before serving to allow flavours of herbs to develop: in a medium-sized bowl, combine egg yolks with a pinch each of salt and freshly ground black pepper, the mustard and 2 teaspoons lemon juice or wine vinegar. Using a spoon or a small wire whisk, beat yolks to a smooth paste.

2 Incorporate olive oil into egg yolks drop by drop at first, a fine, thin stream as emulsion begins to form, beating steadily between each addition and adding more lemon juice, vinegar (or cold water) if mayonnaise becomes over-thick before all the oil has been beaten in. Put aside.

3 Take 1 ounce each fresh parsley sprigs and watercress, and wash them carefully. Bring a pint of salted water to the boil; plunge in washed herbs and simmer for 6 minutes. Drain and press out as much moisture as possible between the folds of a cloth. Then put herbs in a mortar; crush them finely and purée through a sieve.

4 Reserve 4 level tablespoons mayonnaise for stuffed eggs and blend remainder with puréed herbs; stir in finely chopped parsley, watercress and tarragon, and correct seasoning, adding more salt, freshly ground black pepper and lemon juice or vinegar if necessary. Chill until ready to use.

5 Prepare stuffed eggs shortly before serving as they tend to discolour if prepared too far in advance: pound buttered shrimps to a smooth paste in a mortar. Shell hard-boiled eggs; cut them in half lengthwise and carefully scoop out yolks. Rub yolks over pounded shrimps through a fine sieve and mix well. Reserve whites.

6 Bind pounded shrimp and egg yolk mixture with reserved mayonnaise, and season to taste with lemon juice and a pinch of cayenne.

7 Stuff egg whites with shrimp mixture, piling it up smoothly to resemble whole eggs again.

8 To serve: spread a layer of green mayonnaise in a shallow rectangular ravier or shallow serving dish large enough to take stuffed eggs comfortably side by side. Arrange eggs on top and sprinkle with finely chopped mixed green herbs.

Note: If fresh tarragon is not available, use half the amount of dried tarragon which you have first reconstituted by leaving it to 'infuse' in a little boiling water for 5 minutes. Dry thoroughly before use.

Eggs Stuffed with Cheese and Ham

1 Shell hard-boiled eggs carefully and half them lengthwise. Scoop out yolks and, if necessary, cut a thin slice from the base of each halved egg white to make it stand securely. (Be careful as the white can sometimes be very thin on the base.) Put aside.

2 Mince egg yolks together with ham (or ham sausage) and Gruyère cheese. Stir in cream and finely chopped parsley, and pound to a smooth paste, adding mustard, salt, freshly ground black pepper and a few drops of lemon juice, to taste.

3 Stuff each halved egg white with pounded yolk mixture, rounding it up and smoothing it over to resemble a whole egg again.

4 Arrange stuffed eggs on a bed of lettuce leaves and mask each egg completely with thick, well-flavoured mayonnaise. Sprinkle with a pinch of paprika and decorate with tiny parsley sprigs.

Serves 4 as an appetiser

4 eggs, hard-boiled
4 oz ham or ham sausage
1 oz Gruyère cheese
2 level tablespoons double cream
1 level tablespoon finely chopped parsley
1/4–1/2 level teaspoon prepared French mustard
Salt and freshly ground black pepper
Lemon juice
1/4 pint thick well-flavoured mayonnaise (page 43)
Lettuce leaves
Paprika
Parsley sprigs

Gourmet Eggs Mayonnaise

1 Plunge hard-boiled eggs into cold water as soon as they are cooked. Leave to cool in water; then carefully peel off shells.

2 Cut each egg in half lengthwise and arrange, cut side down, on a porcelain serving dish.

3 Mask each half-egg completely with a tablespoon of mayonnaise, tapping the bottom of the dish if the mayonnaise does not flow smoothly over the egg of its own accord.

4 Dot top of each egg with a few grains of lumpfish roe or red caviar and chill lightly until ready to serve.

Note: To prevent hard-boiled eggs discolouring (*a*) don't shell and halve them until they are quite cold, and (*b*) don't use a metal dish.

Serves 4

4 eggs, hard-boiled
8 level tablespoons thick well-flavoured mayonnaise (page 43)
1–2 level teaspoons lumpfish roe or red salmon caviar

Hard-boiled Egg Variations – Hot

Serves 6

6 eggs, hard-boiled
1 sprig fresh tarragon or
  1/2-level teaspoon dried
  tarragon
3 1/2 oz butter
1 oz flour
1/2 pint milk
Salt and freshly ground black
  pepper
2 level tablespoons Dijon
  mustard
3–4 level tablespoons finely
  chopped chives
1/4 pint double cream

Oeufs à la Dijonnaise

An elegant appetiser, delicately flavoured with tarragon and Dijon mustard. Choose your dried tarragon carefully – fresh tarragon is rarely available – as it varies considerably in flavour from brand to brand.

1 Plunge hot hard-boiled eggs into cold water for a few minutes before shelling them; then remove shells carefully.

2 If you are using fresh tarragon, dip the sprig into boiling water; drain well and chop finely. Dried tarragon should be 'infused' in boiling water for 5 minutes to swell and revive it, then pressed dry between the folds of a clean cloth or absorbent paper.

3 Prepare a sauce: melt 1 oz butter in a heavy pan; add flour and stir over a low heat for 1 minute to make a pale *roux*. Add milk gradually, stirring constantly; bring to the boil and simmer until smooth and thick. Season to taste with salt and freshly ground black pepper. Keep hot.

4 Cut shelled, hard-boiled eggs in half lengthwise and carefully scoop out yolks. Put them in a bowl together with the remaining butter, 1 level tablespoon Dijon mustard, the finely chopped tarragon and chives, and beat with a wooden spoon until smooth and well blended.

5 Stuff egg whites with this mixture, reserving 1 level tablespoon for flavouring the sauce. Arrange stuffed eggs side by side in an ovenproof dish and leave in a warm oven with the door ajar while you finish sauce.

6 Beat double cream, the remaining mustard and the reserved tablespoon of hard-boiled yolk mixture into the sauce, and cook over a very low heat, stirring constantly, for 4 or 5 minutes, until it is very hot and smooth.

7 Mask eggs with hot sauce and serve immediately.

Oeufs à la Tripe

Serves 4

1 Cool hard-boiled eggs under running water; then carefully shell and slice them.

2 Melt half the butter in a heavy saucepan and sauté onion slices slowly until soft and golden but not brown.

3 In another saucepan, melt remaining butter; blend in flour with a wooden spoon and cook for 2 to 3 minutes over a low heat, stirring constantly, to make a smooth, pale *roux*. Gradually stir in hot milk and bring to the boil, stirring. Add *bouquet garni* and peppercorns, and simmer very slowly until sauce has thickened and reduced by about a third, 8 to 10 minutes.

4 Preheat oven to slow (325°F. Mark 3).

5 Strain sauce through a fine sieve; season to taste with salt, freshly ground black pepper and a pinch of freshly grated nutmeg, and stir in cream.

6 Add sautéed onions to sauce; mix well, then carefully fold in sliced eggs.

7 Pour mixture into a 2-pint ovenproof dish; cover with foil and heat through in the oven for 10 to 15 minutes. Serve immediately.

6 eggs, hard-boiled
4 level tablespoons butter
2 large Spanish onions, thinly sliced
2 level tablespoons flour
3/4 pint hot milk
Bouquet garni (parsley, bay leaf, thyme, small stalk celery)
3–4 black peppercorns
Salt and freshly ground black pepper
Freshly grated nutmeg
2 level tablespoons double cream

Hot Curried Eggs

Serves 4–6

1 Cool hard-boiled eggs under cold running water; then carefully peel off shells and cut eggs in half lengthwise.

2 In a heavy pan, melt butter and sauté finely chopped onion for 4 or 5 minutes, until soft and golden.

3 Stir in flour and curry paste or powder, and cook for a further 2 to 3 minutes, stirring constantly.

4 Add hot chicken stock, a little at a time, stirring vigorously to prevent lumps forming. Then bring to the boil, stirring, and simmer for 30 minutes until sauce is thick and smooth, and no longer tastes raw.

5 Remove from heat; beat in cream and chutney, and season to taste with salt, freshly ground black pepper and a few drops of lemon juice to bring out flavours.

6 Fold in halved, hard-boiled eggs and return pan to a low heat for 3 to 4 minutes to heat them through. Serve immediately over plain boiled rice.

6 eggs, hard-boiled
1 oz butter
6 level tablespoons finely chopped onion
1 1/2 level tablespoons flour
1 level teaspoon curry paste (or powder)
1/2 pint hot chicken stock
4 level tablespoons double cream
1 level teaspoon mango chutney
Salt and freshly ground black pepper
Lemon juice

63

Fried Eggs

Do not attempt to fry more than 4 eggs at a time in the average frying-pan, and always make sure they are fresh – a stale egg has a 'watery' white which will run all over the frying-pan instead of remaining firm and rounded. To test an egg for freshness: hold it by the two pointed ends between your thumb and forefinger, and shake it gently up and down. If you can feel the yolk thudding lightly against the shell, the egg is stale.

For 4 eggs, heat 2 level tablespoons butter in a frying-pan until sizzling but not coloured. Break 1 egg at a time into a cup; season with salt and freshly ground black pepper, and slide gently into the pan. Fry eggs very slowly until done to your liking; then lift out carefully with a spatula, drain well and serve on hot plates.

Fried Eggs with Sausages, Bacon and Tomatoes

Grill or fry sausages according to directions below. Then slip lightly-seasoned halved tomatoes into the grill-pan while you fry 2 eggs per person (see above).

Grilled sausages Prick sausages lightly all over with a fork and lay them side by side in the bottom of the grill-pan. Brush with melted lard, dripping or butter, and grill under a moderate heat for 6 to 8 minutes, turning sausages to colour them evenly.

Fried sausages Unless you are hooked on charred and burst sausages, try this method for keeping them whole and crisp, with a juicy centre. Melt about 1 tablespoon lard or dripping in a heavy frying-pan; prick large sausages all over and arrange them in the pan in one layer. Turn them over a moderate heat until they just change colour. When sausages begin to sizzle, pour in 1 tablespoon water, clamp on a lid and continue to cook over a moderate heat until water has been absorbed and sausages are crisp on the underside. Continue adding water and cooking sausages in this manner until they are brown and crisp all over. Drain thoroughly and serve.

Bacon Grill or fry rashers of bacon until done to your liking.

Tomatoes Halved tomatoes, lightly seasoned, may be slipped into the grill-pan a few minutes before bacon is ready, but do not let them reduce to a mush.

Oven-fried Eggs

(Oeufs sur le Plat)

Serves 4

1 Preheat oven to moderately hot (400°F. Mark 6).

2 Lightly butter 4 shallow fireproof dishes that can be served at table.

3 Break 2 eggs into each dish, taking care not to puncture yolks; season with salt and freshly ground black pepper, and dot with remaining butter.

4 Bake eggs for 7 to 8 minutes, or until they are just set but by no means hard. Serve immediately.

2 level tablespoons butter
8 eggs
Salt and freshly ground black pepper

Baked Eggs with Bacon and Cream

Serves 6

1 Preheat oven to moderate (375°F. Mark 5). Butter 6 individual ramekins.

2 In a small pan, sauté chopped bacon in oil until crisp. Drain well and mix with finely chopped parsley. Season with salt and freshly ground black pepper.

3 Sprinkle base of each ramekin with a little of the chopped bacon mixture, and break 1 or 2 eggs carefully on top.

4 Arrange ramekins in a wide pan. Pour in hot water to come half-way up sides and cover loosely with foil. Bake for 16 to 18 minutes, or until eggs are just set.

5 Swirl a tablespoon of cream over top of each ramekin and serve immediately.

Butter
6 level tablespoons finely chopped bacon
1–2 tablespoons olive oil
6 level tablespoons finely chopped parsley
Salt and freshly ground black pepper
6–12 eggs
6 level tablespoons double cream

65

Serves 6

Butter
6 oz ham, finely chopped
6 level tablespoons finely
  chopped parsley
6 level tablespoons fresh
  breadcrumbs
Salt and freshly ground black
  pepper
6–12 eggs

Baked Ham and Eggs

1 Preheat oven to moderate (375°F. Mark 5).

2 Butter 6 individual heatproof ramekins (about $\frac{1}{4}$-pint capacity).

3 Combine finely chopped ham with parsley and fresh bread-crumbs, and season carefully with salt and freshly ground black pepper – ham may already be salty enough.

4 Coat base and sides of each ramekin with chopped ham mixture, using about three-quarters of total amount.

5 Break 1 or 2 eggs into each ramekin and sprinkle with remaining chopped ham mixture.

6 Arrange ramekins in a wide pan with hot water to come halfway up sides and cover loosely with foil.

7 Bake for 16 to 18 minutes, until eggs are just set. Serve immediately.

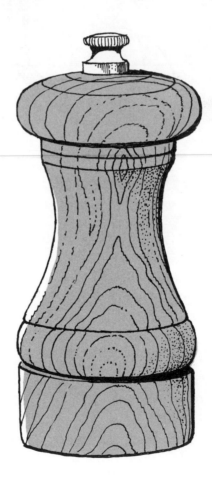

66

Lesson 3
Roasting

It would be impossible to give one ideal roasting temperature to cover every kind of meat. Beef and pork start off at a fast rate and then continue rather more slowly; lamb can be roasted at a high or low temperature throughout – see pages 85 and 86; poultry and veal must be taken more carefully. It all comes down to the robustness and/or quality of the meat, and the degree of doneness you wish to achieve: for a prime cut of beef (or lamb) to be served rare, you could easily keep the temperature high to the end. But if the meat is a delicate one like veal or poultry and needs to be taken right through to well done, then keep the temperature low, or you may dry it out too much.

As you will see, however, I advise reducing the temperature even when the meat can 'take it', mainly because a joint (especially a large one) exposed to high heat throughout its cooking time is liable to cook patchily, i.e. the heat penetrates the surface of the joint too deeply, causing it to be well done, or even overcooked, on the outside, while the interior is still raw.

To Roast Meat

Never cover a roast with a lid, foil or any other device that will cause steam to accumulate around it.

Apart from adding fat to lean meats (veal and poultry – see pages 79 to 121) you should introduce as little moisture as possible for the same reason. By all means, add a tablespoon or two of water to a roasting tin to prevent the natural juices charring, but leave it at that – see page 68.

Remember, if you cover your roast, add too much liquid, or overbaste, you will not be *oven*-roasting but *pot*-roasting – an excellent method in itself, but not the subject of the present lesson.

Basting a roast If a roast is adequately protected by a thick layer of natural fat, it will need little or no basting: the fat itself will do this job for you as it melts and rolls down the sides of the meat.

You will, however, find that in some cases I advise adding a little water to the roasting tin to prevent the natural juices burning. Never exceed the stated amount, or too much steam will be created as it evaporates (you want *dry* heat, remember). More can always be added when it evaporates, but always in the same small quantity. And when you baste, try to scoop up fat only, leaving the juices behind.

Delicate and/or naturally lean cuts of meat are a different matter. It is up to you to provide them with the protection they lack naturally either by continuous basting with pan juices, or with a generous spreading of soft fat. Once this protective covering has melted and flowed off, it is no longer of any use unless you continue to baste it back over the meat from time to time.

Racks and roasting tins When a joint is boned and rolled, or where its own bones are unable to hold it upright, a roasting rack should be used so that the meat won't end up literally stewing in its own juice.

Some consideration should also be given to the size of roasting tin in relation to the joint (or bird) to be cooked. If the tin is too large, the fat and juices that drip from the meat will be distributed so thinly that they will char, and any gravy you make using them will be bitter.

If your choice is restricted to one all-purpose roasting tin, you can make it smaller by inserting a lining of the required size, shaped out of double-thickness foil.

To test a roast Professional chefs can tell the state of a roast by pressing it with a finger – the same test, in fact, as they use for grills (see page 200). The home cook would be better advised to stick to the following method.

Take a sharp, *thin* metal skewer or a long fork with no more than *two* sharp prongs to it. Push the skewer or fork into the thickest part of the meat – right through to the bone, if there is one – and pull it out again. You will be able to tell the state of the meat by the colour of the juices that spurt out (see individual sections). The test spot in poultry is right through the thickest part of the inside leg (i.e. where the leg lies close to the body).

One or two tests should be enough. Resist the temptation (understandable in nervous novices) to jab your roast full of holes like a pincushion. Remember each jab costs you some of the precious juices.

There are times when you may not be able to examine the juices as, for example, when the joint is wrapped in pastry, or in a larding strip. In this case, push in the skewer; leave it there while you slowly count up to 60, then remove it and immediately put it to your lips. If the skewer feels just hot and no more, the meat is very rare – hot but bearable means that it is rare – very hot to unbearably hot means it is medium to well done.

Meat thermometers A meat thermometer can be extremely useful, not least as a confidence booster; but it can also lull you into a false sense of security. (Sugar and deep fat thermometers are different: you can predict exactly what will happen when a syrup reaches a certain temperature, or how hot fat should be to cook and colour a particular ingredient in a given time.)

For one thing, I find meat thermometers too arbitrary. How *can* gadget manufacturers know what *you* mean by rare roast beef? Does your idea of perfectly cooked lamb tally with theirs? Mine certainly doesn't. Secondly, it is difficult to check whether the thermometer is working properly. And thirdly, you only have to insert the thing carelessly for the reading to go haywire.

A meat thermometer should be pushed into the thickest part of the joint, if possible at an angle which will allow you to read the temperature without removing the joint from the oven. Take the greatest possible care to ensure that the tip of the thermometer is not resting in fat or touching bone. And *always* be prepared to overrule the thermometer in favour of the evidence of your own eyes.

To serve a roast To be at its best, roast meat should be served either really hot or really cold. Nothing is less appetising than lukewarm meat or congealing gravy. (The exception is delicate meat like veal or poultry, which loses flavour if served too cold.)

● Choose a large, flat serving platter that will give you plenty of room to carve without having to retrieve morsels from the table.

● Make sure your platter, sauceboat and dinner plates are as hot as safety allows.

● Sharpen your carving knife.

● When the roast is ready, transfer it to the serving dish; *then leave it for 15 to 20 minutes in the turned-off oven with the door ajar* to allow the cooking to subside and the juices, which were still flowing freely when you last pierced the joint, to be reabsorbed by the meat. You will find this 'rest' makes the meat far easier to carve into neat slices, and it also gives you time to make the gravy and do any other last-minute preparation.

● Finally, to avoid that awkward pause during carving, which usually results in a polite guest of honour being forced to watch his meat grow cold before him as he waits for the others to be served, it is a good idea to carve enough for the first round before serving any of it out. Second helpings can then be sliced to order as needed.

1 Chuck, shoulder and arm
2 Ribs
3 Loin
4 Rump
5 Round
6 Shank
7 Plate, Brisket, short ribs
8 Flank
9 Tail

Roasting Beef

The inescapable truth is that only prime cuts of beef will give you a top-quality roast. Indeed, I would go so far as to say that what you can't grill you can't roast. There is one exception to this, topside, which will roast tolerably well, especially if you keep it rare.

How to Choose Beef for Roasting

Beware of pale or unnaturally red beef, beef that looks too perfectly lean and 'compact' in texture, and so-called 'tenderised' beef. Look for a well-hung joint: it will be a rich, succulent dark red, firm and moist to the touch, the meat shot through with flecks of fat and rather coarse-grained. If it comes from a young animal, there will be only a hint of gristle, if any, between the fat and the lean. The fat should be creamy white, not yellow.

Small chunks of beef do not make good roasts: they shrink away to nothing and it is practically impossible to control the degree of rareness. Two ribs or at least a lb rolled meat are the minimum you should go for. Otherwise, pot-roasting is again the answer.

Joints which do not come naturally equipped with an outer coating of fat to keep them moist as they roast must either be *barded* (a thick strip of beef suet is rolled around the entire length of the joint and tied on firmly in several places with string); *larded* (long thin strips of fat salt pork are pulled through the meat with the help of a special needle); or simply rubbed all over with fat (butter, oil, etc.) and then basted more frequently than you would do otherwise with the juices that collect at the bottom of the roasting tin.

Otherwise, it is a mistake to baste too frequently. And if the joint has a good layer of fat on top, you should not have to baste at all: the fat will do it for you as it melts and flows down the sides of the meat.

The following cuts, taken from a good-quality, well-hung young carcass, will all provide reliable roasts. They are listed in order of expense but bear in mind that, as with grilled steaks, many people actually find the firmer, coarser texture of sirloin more satisfying than the delicately expensive fillet.

Fillet (whole) What could be more elegant for a formal dinner party than a whole fillet, roasted plainly, or first spread with a delectable duxelles of finely chopped mushrooms, onions and ham, then carefully wrapped up in a sheet of buttery puff pastry before going into the oven? And really, if you consider that 4 to 5 oz (uncooked weight) makes an ample portion for one, compared with 12 to 16 oz of rib roast or 5 to 8 oz rolled roast, it is not prohibitively expensive for the extra-special occasion, even at today's prices.

A fillet has very little fat of its own. Larding or barding is essential; or you can give it a quick preliminary turn in hot dripping or butter to seal in the juices before transferring the roasting tin to the oven. Three or 4 tablespoons of warm water are also added to the pan, just enough to keep the meat moist without actually steaming it.

You will see in the chart on page 74 that the fillet is the only cut of beef for which I recommend a high oven temperature throughout. This is to ensure that the whole cooking process is carried out as quickly as possible, for the longer this tender joint remains in the oven, the greater the danger of it drying out.

Finally, the natural shape of a whole fillet – nicely rounded at one end, tapering away to nothing at the other – presents a slight problem in that unless certain steps are taken, the thinner end will have cooked to an inedible frazzle by the time the thick end is ready. The answer is to fold about 6 inches of the thin end back on itself and tie the two layers together tightly with string in several places so that the meat has the same diameter throughout.

Rib roast A majestic joint. It should first be seared in a fairly hot oven for about 15 minutes, or until its surface is richly browned and sealed with a crust; then cooking proceeds more gently until the meat has reached the required degree of doneness.

Allow at least 12 oz meat and bone (uncooked weight) per person, 3 to 4 oz more to be on the safe side.

Note that the cooking time per pound for a larger joint is slightly less than that of a small one (see chart on page 74).

Rolled sirloin Another fine cut, ideal for roasting.

Allow 5 to 8 oz uncooked weight per person.

Rolled joints take proportionately longer to cook than those with a larger amount of bone as there is a thicker area of meat for the heat to penetrate.

Topside This requires barding as it has no natural fat to protect it.
Allow 5 to 8 oz per person, and keep it rare if possible.

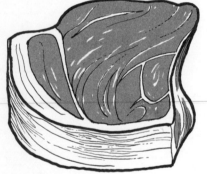

Topside

To Store Beef for Roasting

Remove wrappings; lay the joint on a plate and cover it loosely with greaseproof paper or foil. It can then be stored near the bottom of the refrigerator for a maximum of about 1 week.
Don't forget to allow the meat to come to room temperature again before roasting. (If it has come straight out of the butcher's cold room and you intend to cook it the same day, it need not go into the refrigerator at all.) It's a good idea to rub seasonings into the meat as soon as it comes out of the refrigerator, then leave it at room temperature for 2 to 3 hours so that it can lose its chill and absorb flavours all at the same time.

To Roast Beef

Remove beef from the refrigerator; wipe it dry with a damp cloth and season all over with black pepper, ground as coarsely as your peppermill will make it. Allow joint to come to room temperature.

Fillet Just before roasting the fillet, sear it well on all sides in 4 level tablespoons hot dripping or butter. Transfer fillet to a roasting tin. Insert meat thermometer if used (see page 69). Add 4 tablespoons warm water and roast in a preheated oven, calculating the cooking time according to the chart on page 74.

Rib roast Spread joint all over with 4 level tablespoons dripping or butter. Insert meat thermometer, if used, and lay joint in a roasting tin, fat side up. Roast in a preheated oven, calculating the cooking time according to the chart on page 74, and adding 4 tablespoons warm water to the tin when you lower the temperature after the first 15 minutes.

Rolled sirloin, topside Sear joint on all sides in 4 level tablespoons hot melted dripping or butter. Transfer to a roasting tin, fat side up, and insert meat thermometer, if used. Roast in a preheated oven, calculating the cooking time according to the chart on page 74, and adding 4 tablespoons warm water to the tin when you lower the temperature after the first 15 minutes.

If possible, you should stand rolled joints on a rack *over* the roasting tin so that they do not end up swimming in their own fat and juices instead of cooking in dry heat. If the joint has its own bones to support it, these will keep it upright, well clear of the juices.

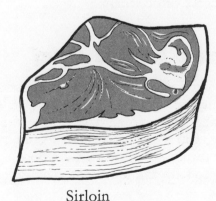

Sirloin

Beef rib

73

Timetable for Roasting Beef (Average only)

Cut	(425°F. Mark 7)	(325°F. Mark 3) per lb	Degree of doneness
Fillet (whole)	8–10 minutes per lb 14 minutes per lb 21–22 minutes per lb		very rare–rare medium-rare–medium well-done juicy–very well-done
Rib roast (2 ribs, about 5 lb)	15 minutes initially then→	16 minutes 25 minutes 31–32 minutes	rare medium well-done
Rib roast (4 ribs, about 11 lb)	15 minutes initially then→	15 minutes 20 minutes 25 minutes	rare medium well-done
Rolled sirloin	15 minutes initially then→	15 minutes 25 minutes 35–37 minutes	rare medium well-done
Top side	15 minutes initially then→	15 minutes 27 minutes 37 minutes	rare medium well-done

The times, given above apply to standard joints of beef of good, average quality and size, such as you would be able to buy from any self-respecting butcher. Highest quality beef and joints of less than average thickness will take slightly less time to reach the same degree of doneness.

To Serve Roast Beef

When the joint is done to your liking, season it to taste with salt and additional freshly ground black pepper. Transfer it to a well-heated platter, large enough to allow the carver to operate comfortably, and leave it to stand for 15 to 20 minutes at the front of the turned-off oven with the door open. This will allow the cooking to stop and the juices to subside, making it easier to carve neatly.

Meanwhile, pour off most of the fat in the roasting tin and use the juices and sediment that remain, reinforced with some red wine, stock or water, and the juices that poured from the roast as it 'set', to make your gravy. Make sure your sauceboat and plates are very hot, too. Congealed gravy is unpleasant.

74

The No-Roast Beef Roast (5 lb or more)

Lovers of perfectly rare beef, pink and juicy from end to end, with just the outer surface richly crusted, should try the following method when next cooking a large joint. I have attempted to adapt it to smaller pieces of beef, too, but have had to admit defeat, which is sad, as the method is otherwise foolproof.

1 Turn the thermostat up to 500°F. (Mark 9) and give the oven at least 20 minutes to heat up before proceeding.

2 Rub joint all over with salt and freshly ground black pepper, and spread it with 4 level tablespoons dripping or butter. Lay it on a rack over a roasting tin.

3 Place meat in the oven. Roast for 5 minutes per lb; then, without opening the oven door, switch off the heat and leave for a further 2 hours. *Do not, under any circumstances, open the oven door during this time.*

4 When the 2 hours are up, open the door and, without removing the tin from the oven, touch the beef with your finger. If it feels hot, go ahead and serve it. However, as some ovens do not retain their heat as well as others (electricity is often rather better than gas in this instance), you may find the beef on the lukewarm side. If so, close the door, relight the oven, still at 500°F. (Mark 9), and give it a further 10 minutes or so. This will raise the temperature of the beef without affecting its rareness.

5 Serve as usual, on a hot platter, accompanied by gravy made with the pan juices.

Serves 6–8

1 sirloin or rib roast of
   beef, about 5 lb
4 level tablespoons dripping
   or butter
1 level tablespoon dry
   mustard
Coarsely ground black
   pepper
2 level tablespoons lightly
   browned flour
Salt

Yorkshire pudding

4 oz plain flour
Pinch of salt
2 eggs
1/4 pint milk

Serves 6

4 oz plain flour
Pinch of salt
2 eggs
1/4 pint milk
2 level tablespoons beef
   dripping or butter

English Roast Beef with Yorkshire Pudding

1 Preheat oven to fairly hot (425°F. Mark 7).

2 Spread roast generously with dripping or butter, and sprinkle with a mixture of dry mustard, coarsely ground black pepper and flour which you have lightly browned in a frying-pan or in the oven.

3 Prepare Yorkshire pudding batter: sift flour and salt into a bowl, and make a well in the centre. Break in eggs; add 2 tablespoons milk and work to a smooth paste with a wooden spoon. Then slowly add remaining milk, beating vigorously. Allow batter to rest for at least 1 hour before using it.

4 Place beef on a rack over a roasting-pan and brown beef for 15 minutes. Then lower heat to 325°F. (Mark 3) and continue to roast, basting occasionally, until beef is done to your liking (see chart on page 74).

5 Thirty to 40 minutes before the end of cooking time, lift the rack with the joint and pour Yorkshire pudding batter into the pan underneath. In this way, both will be ready at the same time.

6 Don't forget to salt beef just before serving it.

Individual Yorkshire Puddings

Yorkshire puddings look most attractive – and taste better, too – if they are baked in individual moulds instead of the usual large roasting tin. If possible, use fluted round tins measuring 3 to 3½ inches across the top. The puddings should be timed to go into the oven when you remove the roast beef – allowing the latter 15 to 20 minutes to 'settle' before carving.

1 Sift flour and salt into a bowl, and make a well in the centre. Break in eggs; add 2 tablespoons milk and work to a smooth paste with a wooden spoon. Then slowly add remaining milk, beating vigorously. Allow batter to rest for at least 1 hour before using it.

2 Put a level teaspoon of dripping or butter in the bottom of each fluted tin; lay tins on a baking sheet and put them in the oven for 2 to 3 minutes to heat up.

3 When fat has melted, remove tins from oven. Quickly pour 3 tablespoons batter into each tin; return tray to top shelf of the oven and bake for 15 minutes, or until puddings are puffed and crisp, and golden brown on top. Serve immediately.

Note: If you prefer to make one large pudding instead of individual ones, use an 11- by 9-inch tin for this quantity of batter.

Roast Fillet of Beef

Fillet of beef cooks in a relatively short time. It is at its best when it is roasted in a fairly hot oven 425°F. (Mark 7) until it is crusty on the outside and rare inside.

1 Turn thermostat up to 425°F. (Mark 7) and give the oven at least 20 minutes to heat up before proceeding.

2 Place fillet on a rack in a shallow roasting-pan, tucking narrow end of fillet under to make the roast evenly thick. Brush generously with softened butter or dripping and season with freshly ground black pepper and a little rosemary and crumbled bay leaf.

3 Roast for 8–10 minutes per pound for very rare to rare; 14 minutes per pound for medium rare to medium well done; 21–22 minutes per pound if you like your meat very well done.

4 Serve with mushrooms, sautéed in butter and lemon juice.

Serves 8–10

1 fillet of beef, 4–6 lb stripped of fat
Melted butter or dripping
Freshly ground black pepper
Rosemary
Bay leaf, crumbled
Salt
Mushrooms, sautéed in butter and lemon juice

Fillet Steak

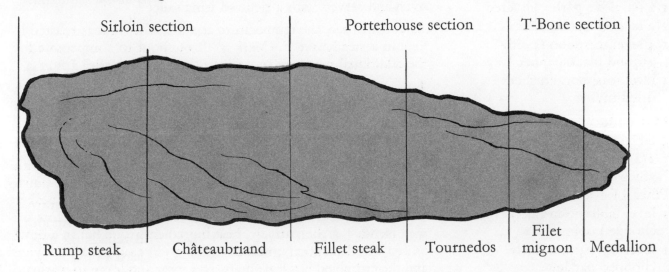

Sirloin section   Porterhouse section   T-Bone section

Rump steak   Châteaubriand   Fillet steak   Tournedos   Filet mignon   Medallion

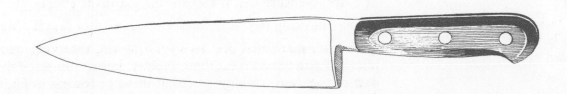

2 lb boned rolled sirloin
2-3 tablespoons olive oil
Salt and freshly ground black
  pepper
1 pint minus 2 tablespoons
  liquid aspic (page 575)
2 tablespoons Madeira

A 2-lb rolled joint of
  roasting beef
1/2 fat clove garlic, slivered
1/2 level teaspoon salt
1/4 level teaspoon freshly
  ground black pepper
1 level teaspoon crushed
  dried thyme

Marinade

4 tablespoons olive oil
1 1/2 tablespoons wine
  vinegar
Pinch of dried oregano
1 level tablespoon finely
  chopped onion
1 level tablespoon finely
  chopped parsley
Salt and freshly ground black
  pepper
1/4 pint red wine
1/2 large bay leaf,
  crumbled

Sauce

1 level tablespoon flour
1/4 pint red wine
Salt and freshly ground black
  pepper

Cold Roast Beef

1 Preheat oven to hot (450°F. Mark 8).

2 Rub beef with oil and season with salt and freshly ground black pepper.

3 Roast for about 25 minutes for rare beef, longer if you prefer it more thoroughly cooked, turning it occasionally. Remove from oven and allow to cool; then chill overnight in the refrigerator, loosely covered.

4 The following day, prepare aspic and flavour with 2 tablespoons Madeira. Allow to cool; pour into a wide, shallow dish and leave to set in the refrigerator.

5 Slice beef thinly and arrange slices, folded over, on a serving dish. Dice or chop aspic and use it to garnish dish.

Roast Beef Provençal

A succulent alternative to plain roast beef – a joint marinated overnight with olive oil, red wine and herbs, then roasted in the oven and served with a rich red wine sauce.

As you will see, the temperature at which the meat is roasted is kept at a steady 425°F. (Mark 7) throughout to compensate for the additional moisture contributed by the marinade.

1 Wipe joint clean with a damp cloth. Make slits about 1 inch deep all over it with the point of a sharp knife and push in slivers of garlic. Rub joint all over with salt, freshly ground black pepper and dried thyme, and place in a shallow, rectangular dish.

2 Prepare marinade: combine olive oil and wine vinegar with oregano, finely chopped onion and parsley, and a generous pinch each of salt and freshly ground black pepper in a plastic beaker with a tight-fitting lid, and shake vigorously until ingredients are well blended. (Alternatively, beat ingredients together in a bowl with a wooden spoon, gradually adding olive oil.) Add red wine and the crumbled bay leaf; pour over meat and leave to marinate overnight at the bottom of the refrigerator, turning meat once or twice to ensure that it absorbs the marinade evenly.

3 The following day, preheat oven to fairly hot (425°F. Mark 7).

4 Transfer marinated beef to a roasting tin, reserving marinade juices. If you have a meat thermometer, insert it into the thickest part of the meat, making sure that it is not resting in fat. Roast for 25 minutes.

5 Pour over marinade juices and continue to roast until beef is done to your liking, basting frequently and calculating total cooking time according to the chart on page 74, but *not* lowering the temperature.

6 When meat is ready, transfer to a heated serving dish and leave at the door of the turned-off oven for 15 minutes to allow the juices to subside and make carving easier.

7 Meanwhile, finish sauce: pour off all but 2 tablespoons fat from the roasting tin. Blend in flour smoothly together with wine and 4 tablespoons water, and bring to the boil on top of the stove, stirring and scraping bottom and sides of tin vigorously with a wooden spoon. Season to taste with salt and freshly ground black pepper, and simmer for 3 minutes, stirring, until sauce has thickened slightly and no longer tastes of raw flour. Serve in a heated sauceboat, together with meat. Tomatoes Provençal (see below) make an excellent garnish.

Tomatoes Provençal

1 Grease a wide, shallow baking dish lightly with butter.

2 Cut tomatoes in half horizontally and arrange them side by side in the dish, cut sides up. Spread lightly with mustard and season with salt and freshly ground black pepper.

3 Toss breadcrumbs with parsley and sprinkle over tomatoes. Trickle ½-level teaspoon olive oil over each tomato.

4 Bake on shelf below meat for 20 minutes, or until breadcrumbs are golden.

Roasting Veal

Veal is a delicate young meat that requires careful cooking. It is best cooked in a little liquid flavoured with aromatics to give it much-needed moistness and flavour. Do not sear veal at a high temperature as you do beef. Cook it in a slow oven (325°F. Mark 3) for 20–40 minutes per pound (see chart on page 81). Veal is at its best when cooked to just the right point of moist tenderness – well cooked, but with a delicate hint of pinkness still in evidence.

What to Look for in Veal for Roasting

Veal is a delicate, young meat. At its best, the flesh should be pale, almost white, faintly tinged with pink. Young veal is fine grained, firm and smooth; the fat is white and satiny. The one drawback this 'immature' meat has is that it has little or no fat so the meat is inclined to be dry. Veal must always be basted with a little oil or butter to keep it moist.

Serves 4–6

Butter
4–6 firm tomatoes
1/4–1/2 level teaspoon
  prepared French mustard
Salt and freshly ground black
  pepper
1–1 1/2 oz soft white
  breadcrumbs
1–1 1/2 level tablespoons
  finely chopped parsley
2–3 teaspoons olive oil

1 Rump
2 Leg
3 Loin
4 Ribs
5 Shoulder
6 Head
7 Breast
8 Shank

What to Avoid

1. Dark meat, it comes from an older animal, fed on grass, and is almost certain to be tough and stringy.

2. Veal that looks 'blown up'. This is usually the result of crude and excessive bleeding to lighten the colour of old veal by force. In the oven, the joint will swell up like a balloon, and then collapse, as tough as the punctured tyre it so closely resembles.

As with beef, only prime cuts of veal make good roasts:

Leg of veal is a good joint for a party. Use a thick slice cut from the centre if possible.

Allow 10 to 12 oz uncooked weight per person, depending on how thick the bone is.

Loin Sold as one joint with bone, or boned and stuffed. Either have it chined and roast it on the bone; or bone it and roll with stuffing. A double loin is called a *saddle* – expensive, but quite spectacular for a party. I often roast the loin until half done; then cut it into thick chump chops with the kidney; season chops to taste with salt, pepper, rosemary and bay leaf; baste with olive oil and bake in the oven in small earthenware dishes.

Allow 12 to 14 oz uncooked meat on the bone per person.

Best end of neck If roasted on the bone, it should be chined. Otherwise, bone and roll it.

Allow 12 to 14 oz uncooked weight on the bone per person.

Shoulder Can be roasted whole, or boned and stuffed. When knuckle is removed, remaining 'oyster' makes a good roasting joint.

Allow 12 to 16 oz uncooked weight on the bone per person.

Breast An economical cut. It is advisable to bone and roll it otherwise carving may be tricky.

Allow 12 to 16 oz uncooked weight on the bone per person.

To Store Veal for Roasting

Unlike other large meat roasts, veal does not keep well and should be used soon after slaughtering. A veal roast can be stored near the bottom of the refrigerator for 3 to 4 days, covered loosely with fresh greaseproof paper or foil.

Remember to bring it back to room temperature before you start cooking it (see page 72).

To Roast Veal

Because of its extremely short life – as a rule no more than twelve weeks – veal never gets the chance to develop much fat, so that its meat is largely made up of connective tissue. For the cook, this means two things:

(1) The scanty fat must be supplemented with butter, or by larding or barding the joint with pork fat or unsmoked bacon, followed by frequent basting with the juices that collect in the tin as a result of this.

(2) The cooking temperature must be kept low to allow the compact tissue to tenderise gradually.

Veal must never be overcooked: for maximum flavour and succulence, there should still be a hint of pink in the beige meat, even though the juices run clear. If using a meat thermometer, take the temperature to 165°F., i.e. 5 degrees under the temperature usually recommended.

Timetable for Roasting Veal (Average only)		
Cut	(325°F. Mark 3) per lb	Degree of doneness
Loin (about 6 lb)	20 minutes	well done but juicy
Best end of neck (about 4 lb)	25 minutes	well done but juicy
Leg (3½–4 lb)	30 minutes	well done but juicy
Brisket (about 2½ lb)	40 minutes	well done but juicy

The times given above apply to joints of average good quality. Rolled joints take longer, as there is a thicker expanse of meat for the heat to penetrate.

Serves 4–6

1 joint of veal to serve 4–6 (a thick centre cut from a leg of veal, or from the shoulder)

2–3 tablespoons softened butter

Salt and freshly ground black pepper

Dried thyme

1/2 lb bacon, thinly sliced

2 cloves garlic

4 carrots, thinly sliced

1 Spanish onion, thinly sliced

2 bay leaves

4 tablespoons olive oil

1/2 pint chicken stock

1/4 pint dry white wine

1 level tablespoon butter

1 level tablespoon flour

Savoury Roast Veal

1 Preheat oven to slow (325°F. Mark 3).

2 Spread joint generously with 2 to 3 level tablespoons softened butter. Season with salt, freshly ground black pepper and dried thyme.

3 Cover veal with thin bacon slices and place meat in a roasting-pan. Surround veal with garlic cloves, sliced carrots and onion and bay leaves.

4 Add olive oil and chicken stock, and roast veal as directed in the chart above, basting frequently to keep it moist. Add a little hot water to the pan if fat tends to scorch during cooking.

5 Transfer joint to a heated serving dish and allow to 'settle' at the door of the turned-off oven.

6 To make gravy: pour off excess fat from roasting tin. Add chicken stock and dry white wine and bring to the boil on top of the stove, stirring and scraping bottom and sides of tin clean with a wooden spoon.

7 Blend 1 level tablespoon each butter and flour together smoothly to make a *beurre manié*. Add to simmering sauce in small pieces; stir and simmer until sauce has thickened slightly. Correct seasoning. Pour into a heated sauceboat and serve with veal.

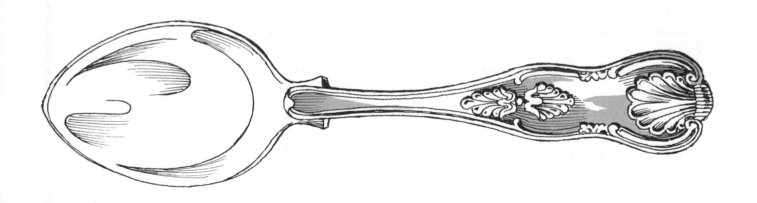

Roast Loin of Veal

1 Have butcher bone and trim a loin of veal for 4 to 6 persons.

2 Preheat oven to slow (325°F. Mark 3).

3 Spread roast generously with softened butter and season with salt, freshly ground pepper and crushed rosemary.

4 Place meat in a roasting-pan and roast it in the preheated oven (325°F. Mark 3) for 20 minutes per pound or until the meat is well done but juicy, basting frequently.

Note: Add a little hot water to the pan if fat tends to scorch during cooking.

5 Transfer joint to a heated serving dish and allow to 'settle' at the door of the turned-off oven.

6 Spoon off excess fat; add chicken stock and dry white wine to roasting tin and cook over a high heat on top of the stove, stirring and scraping bottom and sides of tin clean with a wooden spoon.

7 Correct seasoning and pour into a heated sauce boat and serve with veal.

Serves 4–6

1 roasting joint cut from the the loin of veal (see Step 1)
Softened butter
Salt and freshly ground black pepper
Crushed rosemary
1/4 pint chicken stock
1/4 pint dry white wine

Roasting Lamb

Lamb makes a wonderful roast for beginner cooks. Tender, easy to cook, less expensive than beef, more flavourful than veal, this delicious meat absorbs delicate flavours marvellously. Try dried thyme, crushed rosemary, garlic and onion, a hint of tomato and a little dry white wine and olive oil to moisten it. You'll find it easy to make a reputation with lamb.

How to Choose Lamb for Roasting

Look for a fine-textured meat, lean and lightly pink. The fat should be firm and white, with a pink blush. There should always be a higher proportion of meat to bone and fat.

Not everyone realises that lamb (and mutton even more so) should be well hung. Irrespective of its quality, insufficiently aged lamb is liable to remain tough and chewy even when over-cooked.

1 Leg
2 Loin
3 Ribs
4 Breast
5 Shank
6 Shoulder
7 Neck

Leg of lamb Expensive, but economical, too, thanks to its leanness and the high proportion of meat to bone.

If it annoys you to waste the thin end of the leg where the meat tapers away to bone, pare the meat away from the tip of the bone with a sharp knife, saw off the bare protruding bone (about 6 inches should be enough), then tuck the ends of the meat in neatly and secure with skewers or a few stitches of strong thread. A butcher will do the boning for you in minutes if you don't feel like coping with it yourself.

A leg may also be partially boned to take a stuffing, or completely boned and either stuffed or simply rolled and tied – a good idea when spit-roasting or barbecuing.

As the year advances and the joints grow larger, you can take only half a leg when cooking for a small number of people.

Allow 8 to 12 oz uncooked, unboned meat per person.

Loin One of the finest and most delicate roasts of all, the loin divides into two parts, middle loin and chump end. A 'saddle' or double loin, i.e. the loins from both sides of the animal attached by the backbone, makes a spectacular presentation for a large party.

It is essential to have a loin roast chined by the butcher to avoid carving problems. This usually entails sawing through the bone that runs along the length of the joint, so that when the meat has been cooked, the bone can be removed, leaving the server with the easy job of running his knife down between the chops to separate them.

Allow 8 to 12 oz per person.

Best end of neck Cheaper than loins, best ends provide delicate little cutlets, sweet and succulent. They make excellent roasts, too, either cooked singly; or two at a time, shaped into 'crowns', with the cavity in the centre filled with stuffing; or with the tips of the bones intertwined to make 'guards of honour'.

A best end should be chined like a loin and the tips of the cutlet bones scraped clean of any remaining meat, which would char if left on. Then the protruding tips of the cutlet bones are chopped short, leaving just a couple of inches or so which can be protected from the heat by a wrapping of foil.

It is also very easy to bone a best end completely for stuffing or simply rolling and roasting; just take a sharp knife down the cutlet bones and across the bottom and lift out the meat.

Allow at least 2 cutlets per person.

Shoulder Many people prefer the delicate flavour of shoulder to that of leg. It can be plain-roasted, but is easier to deal with at the table if boned and stuffed. A large shoulder can be divided in two: blade half and knuckle half.

Allow 8 to 12 oz uncooked unboned meat per person.

Breast A very cheap cut, supremely tender and full of flavour, if inclined to be fatty. You can have it boned for stuffing and rolling, but it is infinitely more simple to sandwich two small unboned breasts, fat side outwards, with stuffing, and tie them together tightly with a string.

To Roast Lamb

There are two schools of thought on the subject of roasting lamb. One favours a high heat method; the other prefers a considerably lower temperature. Both ways have their advantages. The high heat method seals more flavour into the meat and gives it a richer crust, but it also makes it shrink more. Low heat results in a slightly more tender joint, and certainly the meat shrinks less, but it also acquires a somewhat boiled appearance. You can make the most of both methods by roasting young lamb at the higher temperature and reserving the low heat method for older meat of more dubious quality.

Use a roasting rack for all boned joints and those joints such as a leg of lamb that cannot rely on their own bones to keep them clear of the juices in the tin.

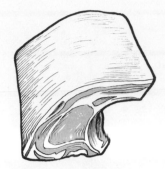

Best end of neck

Shoulder

Breast

Leg of Lamb

Loin

Timetable for Roasting Lamb (Average only)			
Cut	High heat method (400°F. Mark 6) per lb	Low heat method (300°F. Mark 2) per lb	Degree of doneness
Leg (3½–4 lb)	22–23 minutes 26–27 minutes 30–31 minutes	37–38 minutes 41–42 minutes 47–48 minutes	very pink rosé well done
Loin (about 3 lb)	16–17 minutes 20 minutes 25–26 minutes	23 minutes 28 minutes 37 minutes	very pink rosé well done
Best end of neck (whole)	23–24 minutes 30 minutes 40 minutes	45 minutes 60 minutes 80 minutes	very pink rosé well done
Shoulder (4–5 lb)	17–18 minutes 20 minutes 22–23 minutes	21 minutes 26 minutes 30–31 minutes	very pink rosé well done

The times given above apply to joints of average good quality, unstuffed and on the bone. I recognise three degrees of doneness: *very pink*, which in my opinion at least gives unbeatable flavour and succulence, *rosé* or the classic French way of serving roast lamb, and *well done*, which means what it says and not a kitchen cremation.

To Serve Roast Lamb

Transfer roast to a very hot serving platter and let it stand at the open door of the turned-off oven for 15 to 20 minutes before carving, just as you would a beef roast (see page 74).

Make gravy with skimmed pan juices. Any bits and pieces, bones, etc. trimmed off before roasting the joint can be boiled up while the meat is in the oven to make a stock with which to reinforce the gravy. Failing this, use a light beef stock, or white wine diluted with stock or water, and thicken with a little *beurre manié* (equal quantities butter and flour mashed to a smooth paste and stirred into the gravy in tiny pieces). Bring to the boil; simmer for 2 or 3 minutes to cook the flour, and serve in a well-heated sauce boat.

Remember to have thoroughly hot dinner plates ready. Lamb should be eaten either very hot or very cold, never lukewarm.

Savoury Roast Lamb

Serves 6

1 Preheat oven to moderately hot (400°F. Mark 6) or very slow (300°F. Mark 2), depending on whether you are following the high or low heat method (see chart opposite).

2 Beat softened butter, crushed rosemary, and dried thyme with a wooden spoon, gradually adding lemon juice, until smooth. Season generously with salt and freshly ground black pepper.

3 Spread seasoned butter evenly over entire surface of joint. Place lamb on a rack over a roasting tin (or directly in the tin if the joint will support itself), fat side up.

4 Roast lamb as indicated in the chart above, basting occasionally, not frequently.

5 When roast is cooked to your liking, transfer it to a hot serving platter and leave to 'set' for 15 to 20 minutes at the door of the oven before carving.

6 Skim excess fat from the roasting tin. Place tin over direct heat; add beef stock, tomato concentrate and bring to the boil, stirring and scraping bottom and sides of tin vigorously with a wooden spoon to dislodge the crusty bits stuck there.

7 Mash butter and flour to a smooth paste. Add to the tin in tiny pieces, stirring until they have 'dissolved' in the gravy; then bring to the boil and simmer for 2 to 3 minutes until gravy has thickened.

8 Strain gravy; pour into a heated sauce boat and serve with the lamb.

1 medium-sized joint of lamb for roasting
Softened butter
1/2 level teaspoon crushed rosemary
1/2 level teaspoon dried thyme
Juice of 1 lemon
Salt and freshly ground black pepper

To finish gravy
1/2 pint beef stock
1–2 tablespoons tomato concentrate
1 level tablespoon butter
1 level tablespoon flour

Serves 6

1 boned shoulder of lamb
(3 1/2–4 lb boned weight,
see Step 1)
2 level tablespoons flour
Salt and freshly ground black
pepper
2 tablespoons melted butter
2 tablespoons olive oil
A little dry white wine

Stuffing

1/2 Spanish onion, finely
chopped
4 level tablespoons butter
Two 6-oz packets frozen
spinach
1/2 lb pork sausage meat
1 egg, beaten
1 level tablespoon finely
chopped parsley
Generous pinch each of
rosemary and thyme
Salt and freshly ground black
pepper
Pinch of freshly grated
nutmeg

Roast Stuffed Shoulder of Lamb

1 Have butcher bone shoulder of lamb but leave it unrolled. Lay meat out flat on a board, skin side down. If there is excess fat in the meat, cut it out with a very sharp knife, taking care not to pierce the outer skin.

2 Prepare stuffing: sauté finely chopped onion in half the butter until transparent but not browned.

3 Heat spinach gently, uncovered, until completely defrosted; drain thoroughly in a sieve, pressing it with the back of a spoon; then simmer gently in the remaining butter until cooked.

4 In a large bowl, combine onion and spinach with sausage meat, beaten egg, finely chopped parsley and a generous pinch each of rosemary and thyme. Season to taste with salt, freshly ground black pepper and freshly grated nutmeg. Mix well.

5 Preheat oven to slow (325°F. Mark 3).

6 With a long needle and strong thread, 'darn' any holes in the outer skin of the lamb. Spread stuffing between every layer, filling all the crevices so that when the joint is rolled and sliced, the spinach stuffing will produce a marbled effect.

7 If there are any loose flaps at the end of the meat, bring them up over the stuffing and sew them firmly to the sides. Then bring sides of meat together and sew securely along every seam, pushing stuffing back into the meat if it tends to seep out, and making a neat, smooth roll.

8 Dust meat with flour and season generously with salt and freshly ground black pepper. Place a sheet of foil in a roasting tin and lay meat on top; bring up sides of foil slightly, but do not seal meat. Pour over melted butter and olive oil.

9 Roast for 2 hours, basting occasionally with pan juices. Then raise heat to 400°F. (Mark 6), open foil out and roast lamb for about 30 minutes longer, or until golden brown and cooked to your liking.

10 To serve: remove threads from meat and transfer it to a heated serving dish. Pour juices from foil into tin; add a little dry white wine to the juices in the tin and heat through. Spoon over roast.

Roast Shoulder of Lamb with Apricot Stuffing

Middle Eastern cooks have long appreciated the affinity that dried fruits, especially apricots, have for lamb. Discover for yourself how the sharpness of the apricots perfumed with herbs and grated lemon rind imparts a delicious flavour to the meat.

1 Ask your butcher to bone shoulder of lamb but not to roll it. It should weigh about 2¾ lb when boned.

2 Preheat oven to moderate (375°F. Mark 5).

3 To make stuffing: chop 5 oz soaked apricots and 3 oz soaked and stoned prunes coarsely. In a large bowl, combine chopped fruit with breadcrumbs, butter, egg yolks, finely chopped onion, parsley, herbs and grated lemon rind. Mix well and season generously with salt, freshly ground black pepper and a generous pinch of cayenne.

4 Lay boned shoulder of lamb out on a board, skin side down. Spread with stuffing, pushing it into every crevice. Fold in scrappy ends of meat and roll shoulder neatly. Sew along 'seams' with a strong needle and thread.

5 Dissolve sugar in ¼ pint water. Add remaining apricots and prunes, and simmer together for about 5 minutes.

6 Season joint all over with salt and freshly ground black pepper. Place it in a roasting tin lined with foil and surrounded with poached apricots and prunes. Spoon poaching syrup over fruit.

7 Roast meat for 30 minutes; then raise temperature to moderately hot (400°F. Mark 6) and continue to roast for about 45 minutes if you like lamb pink, 15 minutes longer for well done. Baste joint occasionally with pan juices and bring up sides of foil to cover it loosely if it browns too quickly.

8 To serve: remove threads from meat and transfer it to a heated serving dish. Surround with fruit. Skim pan juices if necessary; pour into a heated sauce boat and serve with lamb.

Serves 6

1 shoulder of young lamb, about 3 1/2 lb (see Step 1)

1/2 lb dried apricots, soaked

1/2 lb dried prunes, soaked and stoned

3 oz fresh white breadcrumbs

1 oz softened butter

2 egg yolks

1 Spanish onion, finely chopped

4 level tablespoons finely chopped parsley

1/4 level teaspoon dried rosemary

1/4 level teaspoon dried thyme

Grated rind of 1 lemon

Salt and freshly ground black pepper

Cayenne pepper

3–4 oz castor sugar

Serves 4–6

2 best ends neck of lamb, weighing 3/4–1 lb when boned (see Step 1)

4 oz pie veal

2 egg whites

5 level tablespoons double cream

1 oz finely chopped carrot

1 oz finely chopped celery

1 oz finely chopped onion

4 oz finely chopped white button mushrooms

2 oz butter

Salt and freshly ground black pepper

4 level tablespoons finely chopped parsley

2 tablespoons dry sherry

1 tablespoon brandy

Freshly grated nutmeg

8 oz puff pastry, home-made or bought

1 egg yolk

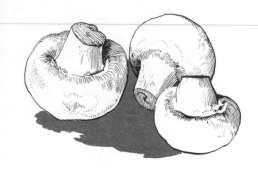

Carré en Croute

1 Ask your butcher to bone the best ends of lamb.

2 Put the pie veal through the fine blade of your mincer. Then put the minced veal, egg whites and double cream in separate bowls and chill until needed.

3 Prepare a stuffing: sauté finely chopped carrot, celery, onion and button mushrooms in half the butter over a low heat, stirring occasionally, for about 20 minutes, or until vegetables have softened and excess moisture evaporated. Season to taste with salt and freshly ground black pepper. Cool and chill – about 1 hour in the refrigerator should be enough.

4 When all the ingredients are thoroughly cold, turn minced veal into a large bowl. Season generously with salt; then add the egg whites one at a time, beating vigorously with a large wooden spoon or spatula until well blended.

5 Still beating vigorously, add the cream gradually and continue to beat mixture to a smooth mousse.

6 Finally, beat in finely chopped parsley, sherry, brandy and the chilled vegetable mixture, and season to taste with salt, freshly ground black pepper and freshly grated nutmeg.

7 Preheat oven to fairly hot (425°F. Mark 7).

8 Lay best ends out flat with the fat side to the board. Sprinkle with salt and freshly ground black pepper.

9 Divide the vegetable–veal mousse between them, spreading it evenly over the entire surface.

10 Roll best ends up tightly and secure with thin string.

11 Spread best ends with remaining butter. Put them on a baking sheet and roast for 15 minutes. Remove from the oven and allow to cool.

12 Reduce oven temperature to moderate (350°F. Mark 4).

13 Cut puff pastry in half and roll each piece out into a 12- by 7-inch rectangle.

14 Beat egg yolk lightly with a teaspoon of cold water.

15 When best ends are cold, discard strings and lay each roll in the centre of one of the rectangles of pastry. Bring sides of pastry up to enclose meat completely. Brush seams with beaten egg yolk and seal them carefully, trimming away excess pastry.

16 Lay parcels on a baking sheet, seam side down. Decorate tops with leaves and flowers made from the scraps of pastry and put in the refrigerator to rest for 30 minutes.

17 Brush all over with beaten egg yolk and bake as follows: 35 minutes if you like your meat very pink, 45 minutes for medium and 55 minutes for well done.

18 Serve in thick slices, accompanied by a simple fresh Tomato Sauce (see below).

Tomato Sauce

Serves 4–6

1 Chop peeled and seeded tomatoes into ¼- to ½-inch dice.

2 In a heavy pan, sauté finely chopped onion gently in olive oil for 4 to 5 minutes until transparent and very soft but not coloured.

3 Add three-quarters of the diced tomato, the sugar and oregano, and season lightly with salt and freshly ground black pepper. Simmer for 10 to 15 minutes, or until tomatoes are reduced to a rich, thick sauce.

4 Stir in remaining tomato dice and heat through for just a minute or two longer.

5 Remove pan from heat. Correct seasoning, adding more sugar, salt or freshly ground black pepper if necessary; stir in finely chopped parsley and serve.

2 lb fresh ripe tomatoes, peeled and seeded
4 level tablespoons finely chopped onion
2 tablespoons olive oil
1/4 level teaspoon castor sugar
1/4 level teaspoon oregano
Salt and freshly ground black pepper
2 level tablespoons finely chopped parsley

Leg of Lamb in Pastry

Serves 6–8

1 Have your butcher bone the leg of lamb and remove most of the fat.

2 Clean kidneys. Remove cores and skins if this has not been done by the butcher, and cut kidneys into ¼-inch dice.

3 In a heavy frying-pan, sauté kidneys in half the butter for 1 minute. Add thinly sliced mushrooms, diced truffles if used, and herbs; season to taste with salt and freshly ground black pepper, and sauté for a further 3 or 4 minutes until golden.

4 Remove pan from heat. Pour over brandy and, standing well back, quickly set it alight with a match. Let flames burn themselves out and leave until lukewarm.

5 Blend in *pâté de foie gras*. Chill

6 Preheat oven to moderate (375°F. Mark 5).

7 Lay boned leg out flat, skin side down. Spread with mushroom–kidney stuffing and roll back into shape. Tie up securely or sew along seams with a needle and strong thread.

1 small leg of lamb, about 3 lb (see Step 1)
4 lamb's kidneys
4 level tablespoons butter
5 oz white button mushrooms, thinly sliced
1–2 truffles, diced (optional)
Generous pinch of thyme
Generous pinch of rosemary
Salt and freshly ground black pepper
2 tablespoons brandy
4 level tablespoons *pâté de foie gras*
8 oz puff pastry, frozen or home-made
1 egg yolk, lightly beaten

8 Place stuffed leg in a roasting tin. Roast for 1 hour, turning carefully once or twice. Remove from oven and allow to cool.

9 Increase oven temperature to hot (450°F. Mark 8).

10 Roll pastry out into a rectangle about 14 by 12 inches.

11 When lamb is cool, spread it with remaining butter and lay it on the pastry. Wrap lamb in pastry; seal edges of 'parcel' very carefully and trim off excess pastry. Make leaves out of pastry scraps and use them to decorate top of parcel.

12 Transfer parcel to a heavy baking sheet. Brush lightly with cold water and bake for 10 minutes. Then brush with beaten egg and return to the oven for a further 10 minutes, until parcel is puffed and golden. Serve hot.

Stop press! For super-succulent meat, give the lamb a 'fix' as follows: take an ordinary hypodermic syringe – a chemist will sell you one if you can get him to believe what it's for – and pump about 1 tablespoon dry red wine into the lamb on all sides before wrapping it in pastry. It really does work!

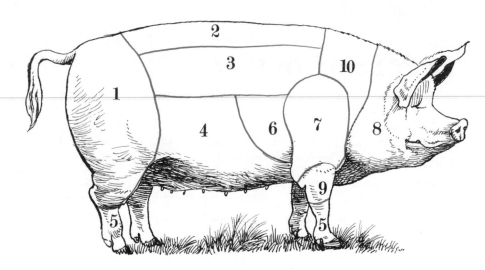

1 Leg
2 Backbone
3 Loin
4 Belly
5 Feet
6 Ribs
7 Shoulder
8 Head
9 Hock
10 Spare rib and
Bladebone

Roasting Pork

It is high time we stopped paying attention to the alarmists who, not without a little relish, I suspect, put around dire warnings about what will happen to us if we eat 'rare' pork. True, raw pork meat may harbour tiny parasites called trichinae which can be transmitted to humans if the temperature of the meat is not raised high enough to kill them first. However, the temperature at which trichinae organisms no longer survive is officially stated to be 137°F. If you then take the meat a further 45 degrees, you will have a tender roast of pork – beige, not pink, right to the bone, deprived of neither juices nor flavour – which you can enjoy with complete peace of mind.

What to Look for in Pork for Roasting

Good pork should be pale pink, smooth in texture, with a fine grain and a fair proportion of very white fat. The skin should not be too thick. And above all, there should be no unpleasant smell. In fact, smell and colour are the two best indications of pork of top quality. I find that if the pork is too dark, the meat tends to be dry and tough; and if the pork fat is soft, flabby and badly coloured, the pork is not fresh.

Leg or half leg of pork One of the most economical and best cuts for large families. In America, when I was a child, we often had a roast leg of pork for Sunday lunch, served hot with whipped sweet potatoes, whipped turnips or parsnips, crisp red Harvard beets cooked in orange juice, and home-made apple sauce. A leg of pork does not seem to be standard fare in Britain, and often must be ordered in advance from the butcher.

Loin of pork A loin of pork – one thick chop for each guest – makes a very acceptable roast, with its 'crackling' expertly scored to facilitate carving. Unfortunately, the crackling is often removed before selling in order to cut away some of the valuable fat for use for larding or barding meats and pâtés. For notes on perfect crackling, see page 95. Always make sure your butcher chines the loin to make carving easier.

A boned loin of pork (ask your butcher for the bones to roast with the boned joint to add extra flavour to the roast) is easier to handle and makes a more elegant roast. I like to cut slits through boned loin so that a flavoursome stuffing of forcemeat, or dried apricots, prunes and onions, or for special occasions, thinly sliced white truffles can be pressed down between the slices before cooking.

Fillet This is the leanest and choicest cut of pork, having no fat whatsoever. It is naturally the most expensive. Treat it as you would fillet of beef: cut it into medallions and sauté it as you would a tournedos; or season generously with salt and freshly ground black pepper and roast it for 15 minutes in a hot oven; allow it to get cold; brush fillet with Dijon mustard; wrap it in flaky pastry and bake it until pastry is puffed and golden.

Spare ribs and joints cut from the shoulder Fairly lean and moderately priced, these make excellent small roasting joints. They can be pot roasted or casseroled as well as roasted.

The shoulder may be purchased either with the bone, or boned and rolled. This cut makes an excellent roast when stuffed with a herb stuffing.

Blade bone Cut from behind the head, or top of foreleg. I like it for stuffing with bone removed. An inexpensive joint, delicious when roasted.

Hand and spring Well-flavoured joint cut from the foreleg. Can be boned (knuckle removed) and rolled. Inexpensive.

Belly Often rather fat, usually salted and boiled, this cut is sometimes rolled for an inexpensive roast.

Hand and spring

What to Avoid

1. Dark meat.
2. Soft, flabby, badly coloured fat.
3. Coarse-textured meat.

How Much Pork to Serve

Allow 1 good-sized chop, 6 to 8 oz boned and rolled meat, 8 to 12 oz meat on the bone per person.

To Store Pork for Roasting

A pork roast, transferred to fresh wrappings or simply covered loosely with greaseproof paper or foil, can be stored for about 4 days in the coldest part of the refrigerator, up to 6 days if the joint is a large one.

Remember to let the meat come back to room temperature before roasting it.

To Roast Pork

The English have a lesson to teach their neighbours – the French included – in the way they prepare crackling. However, as there is nothing like keeping an open mind, in cooking especially, you should not fail to try the alternative method we suggest, minus crackling, on page 95. Your family may find it hard to forgive you when they see what you've done, but the flavour of the dish should soon win them over. And there is nothing to stop you roasting the rind you have removed in the pan together with the joint if you wish.

To make crackling It is far better to undertake the scoring of the rind yourself unless your butcher can be relied on not to hack it about with a few random strokes which are usually far too deep and spaced too far apart to help the server carve reasonable slices. Pork rind is very tough, so for safety's sake, equip yourself with a strong, short, sharp knife. A linoleum cutter fitted with a new blade makes an ideal tool with which you can exert sufficient pressure to control the direction and depth of the cuts without slipping.

Score the rind at close intervals, following the direction you will take when carving the joint. Alternatively, you can criss-cross the rind with diagonal scores ½ inch apart to make diamonds; then, when it comes to serving, remove the crackling before carving the joint and divide it up separately.

To ensure crackling that is crisp enough to bite on and not chewy, rub the scored rind thoroughly with olive oil, plenty of salt, and freshly ground black pepper to taste. The joint is then set fat side up in a roasting tin (on a rack if necessary) and subjected to an initial 15 minutes in a hot oven (450°F. Mark 8) before lowering the temperature to very slow (300°F. Mark 2) to ensure the thorough, steady cooking it needs.

Pork roast without crackling Almost every other nation – French and Americans included – prefers to remove the rind and some of the fat before roasting pork. (The French save the precious fat they have cut off for larding or barding other meats less well-endowed by nature.)

Seasonings are rubbed into the meat and exposed fat, or the joint is bathed in a marinade – more for flavour than texture – before roasting in exactly the same way as one would an English roast.

Glazed pork roast To glaze a pork roast you reverse the cooking procedure: first you roast the meat for the specified length of time per lb at 300°F. (Mark 2); then you sprinkle the fat with brown sugar (or pour over a sweet glazing sauce – see under basting sauces for ham) and return the roast to a fairly hot oven (425°F. Mark 7) to glaze.

Pork joints, especially those that are awkward to carve on the bone, may be boned and rolled with stuffing like any other meat. Loins should be chined by a butcher.

Pork is practically self-basting provided the fat stays on top so that it can run down the sides of the joint as it melts, but take a look at it and spoon over some of the pan juices occasionally. If the crackling appears to be browning too fast, protect it with a *loose* covering of foil.

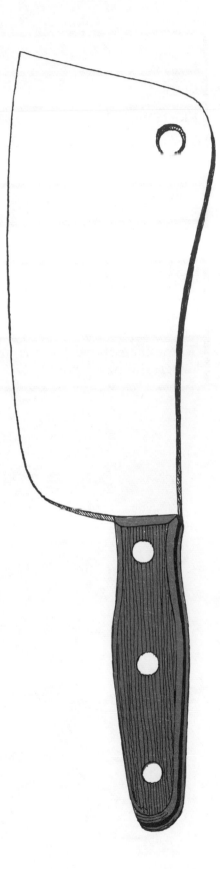

Timetable for Roasting Pork (Average only)			
Cut	(450°F. Mark 8)	(300°F. Mark 2) per lb	Degree of doneness
½ leg (about 4 lb)	15 minutes initially then→	40 minutes	well done
Loin	15 minutes initially then→	37–38 minutes	well done
Spare rib joint	15 minutes initially then→	50 minutes	well done
Blade bone	15 minutes initially then→	50 minutes	well done
Hand and spring	15 minutes initially then→	28 minutes	well done
Belly	15 minutes initially then→	36–37 minutes	well done

The timing above result from tests with pork of average quality, on the bone. If using a thermometer, the meat should reach a temperature of between 180° and 185°F.

To Serve Roast Pork

Transfer joint to a large, thoroughly hot serving platter and leave it to rest for 15 to 20 minutes in the turned-off oven with the door ajar. (Because of the comparatively high temperature the meat achieves, there is less danger than with other meats of pork being cold by the time you are ready to serve it.)

Pour off excess fat from pan juices. Set roasting tin over direct heat and add ½ pint light chicken or beef stock. Bring to the boil, scraping bottom and sides of tin thoroughly with a wooden spoon to dislodge the crusty bits stuck there.

Have ready a *beurre manié* (1 level tablespoon each butter and flour mashed to a smooth paste). Add it to the gravy in tiny pieces, stirring until they have 'dissolved' into the gravy; bring to the boil and simmer for 3 to 4 minutes, stirring occasionally, until sauce has thickened.

Stir in any juices that have collected under the joint; correct seasoning; strain and serve in a well-heated sauce boat together with the meat.

French Pork Roast

1 Preheat oven to hot (450°F. Mark 8).

2 With a sharp knife, cut the rind off the loin as neatly as possible. If the joint is very fat, take some of this off as well so that the meat is left with an even layer no more than $\frac{1}{3}$ inch thick. With the point of your knife, make incisions all over the joint about 1 inch deep.

3 Blend butter with French mustard, crumbled bay leaf and thyme.

4 Season pork with salt and freshly ground black pepper, and spread with mustard butter, making sure it goes deep into the incisions.

5 Roast in the usual way (see above), lowering heat to 300°F. (Mark 2) after the first 15 minutes.

1 loin of pork, about 2 lb, chined
4 level tablespoons softened butter
1 1/2 level tablespoons French mustard
1 bay leaf, crumbled
1/2 level teaspoon dried thyme
Salt and freshly ground black pepper

Roast Pork à la Provençale

Serves 4

1 Ask your butcher to skin pork loin and chine it to make carving easier.

2 Soak dried mushrooms in a little warm water for at least 30 minutes; then pour mushrooms and their soaking water into a small pan and simmer gently until they are soft and swollen, and water has almost completely evaporated.

3 Put aside 3 pieces of mushroom and cut remainder into 12 strips. Peel 1 garlic clove and cut into 12 slivers.

4 Make 12 deep slits in the fat of the pork with the point of a sharp knife, and push a strip of mushroom and garlic well down into each slit. Season meat with salt and freshly ground black pepper. Place it on a dish; cover with foil and leave at room temperature for 1 hour to absorb flavours.

5 Preheat oven to hot (450°F. Mark 8).

6 Transfer pork to a roasting tin and roast for 15 minutes; then reduce heat to 300°F. (Mark 2) and continue to roast until pork is cooked through but still moist (i.e. 37 to 38 minutes per lb), basting occasionally with pan juices plus a tablespoon or two of boiling water if these are scarce.

7 Meanwhile, finely chop remaining garlic clove. In a small pan, sauté chopped onion and garlic in butter for 3 to 4 minutes until softened. Cool.

8 Chop reserved soaked mushrooms finely and combine in a

2 lb (4 good chops) loin of pork, skinned and chined (see Step 1)
6 dried mushroom pieces (see Note)
2 large cloves garlic
Salt and freshly ground black pepper
3 level tablespoons finely chopped onion
1 level tablespoon butter
8 oz pork sausage meat
6 level tablespoons freshly grated Parmesan
1 level tablespoon finely chopped parsley
1/2 level teaspoon each finely chopped fresh tarragon and chives
4 large ripe tomatoes
6 oz large tight white mushrooms
5 tablespoons olive oil

bowl with sautéed onion mixture, sausage meat, grated Parmesan and chopped herbs. Mix well and season to taste with salt and freshly ground black pepper.

9 Slice off tops of tomatoes and scoop out pulp and seeds, taking care not to break shells. Sprinkle lightly with salt and leave up-side down on a rack to drain for a few minutes.

10 Wipe or wash mushrooms clean and carefully remove stems.

11 Stuff tomatoes and mushroom caps with sausage meat mixture, smoothing tops over neatly.

12 Twenty minutes before pork is to be served, sauté stuffed tomatoes and mushrooms gently in olive oil for 3 to 4 minutes until golden all over. Then cover the pan and cook over a low heat for about 15 minutes until tender but not disintegrating.

13 To serve: transfer pork to an oval, heated serving dish and surround with stuffed tomatoes and mushroom caps. Moisten with pan juices and serve hot.

Note: Dried mushrooms can be bought in large pieces (top-quality ones are frequently dried whole), often threaded on to a string, or in small packets of broken pieces. For this recipe you need the equivalent of 6 medium-sized pieces at least an inch long and about ½ inch wide. If there is any liquid left in the pan when you have finished simmering them, pour it over the meat or add it to the stuffing as it is full of flavour.

Roast Pork with Grapes

Serves 6

1 Ask your butcher to skin, bone and roll a lean loin of pork. The rolled joint should weigh just under 3 lb after being prepared.

2 Combine marinade ingredients. Pour over joint in a deep dish and leave to marinate, covered, at the bottom of the refrigerator for 24 hours. Turn pork several times during this time to keep it thoroughly coated with marinade.

3 When ready to cook pork, preheat oven to moderate (375°F. Mark 5).

4 Drain pork, reserving marinade, and put it in a roasting tin. Sprinkle pork with salt and freshly ground black pepper. Pour about $\frac{1}{4}$ pint cold water around it and roast, basting occasionally with its own juices, until cooked through but still moist. It will take about $1\frac{3}{4}$ hours, or 35 minutes per lb.

5 Ten minutes before taking pork out of the oven, prepare garnish: melt butter in a large, deep frying-pan and sauté grapes for 4 to 5 minutes until golden brown. Reserve.

6 When pork is cooked, transfer to a deep, hot, flameproof serving dish. Pour 3 tablespoons gin over it, stand well back and set alight with a match. (Or if you find it easier, pour gin into a heated metal ladle, set it alight and quickly pour all over the meat.)

7 Skim fat from juices left in the roasting tin. Pour back into the tin any juices that have collected around the pork on the serving dish and return pork on its dish to the turned-off oven to keep hot while you finish sauce.

8 To finish sauce: add grape juice, white wine and reserved marinade to the roasting tin, and bring to the boil on top of the stove, scraping bottom and sides of tin with a wooden spoon to dislodge any crusty morsels stuck there. Allow to simmer for 2 to 3 minutes longer.

9 Meanwhile, work butter and flour to a smooth paste in a small cup (to make a *beurre manié*).

10 Strain sauce into the frying-pan over sautéed grapes and, with the pan set on a low heat, stir in *beurre manié* in small pieces. Continue to stir until sauce comes to the boil and simmer for 3 or 4 minutes longer to cook the flour. Season to taste with salt and freshly ground black pepper.

11 To serve: spoon sauce and grapes over and around pork. Any excess sauce and grapes should be served with the meat in a heated sauce boat or bowl. Serve pork very hot, cut into thick slices.

4 lb lean loin of pork
Salt and freshly ground black pepper
3 tablespoons gin
1/4 pint unsweetened grape juice
1/4 pint dry white wine
2 level tablespoons butter
2 level tablespoons flour

Marinade
8 juniper berries, crushed
2 cloves, crushed
1 clove garlic, crushed
3 tablespoons olive oil
6 tablespoons dry white wine

Garnish
2 level tablespoons butter
1 lb seedless white grapes

Serves 4

2 lb lean loin of pork (4
  thick chops) (see Step 1)
1 tablespoon olive oil
Salt and freshly ground black
  pepper
4 oz plump prunes, soaked
  overnight
4 oz dried apricots, soaked
  overnight
2 Spanish onions, very
  coarsely chopped
Generous pinch of thyme
1 level tablespoon butter
2 tart crisp eating apples

Roast Pork with Dried Fruits

You will have to start this dish the day before you plan to serve
it by leaving the dried fruit to soak overnight.

1 Ask your butcher to chine the loin of pork to make carving
easy; but tell him to leave the skin on.

2 Preheat oven to hot (450°F. Mark 8).

3 Wipe the pork with a damp cloth. If there are any bristles on
the skin, singe them off over an open flame.

4 With a strong, sharp knife, cut into the skin in parallel lines
½ inch apart going at a slant in one direction, then in the other,
to make diamonds.

5 Lay pork in a roasting tin. Rub oil into the skin and season the
whole joint generously with salt and freshly ground black pepper.

6 Roast pork for 15 minutes.

7 While pork is in the oven, drain soaked fruits, reserving liquids.
Pit prunes. Mix fruit with coarsely chopped onion and add a generous seasoning of thyme, salt and freshly ground black pepper.

8 Remove pork from the oven. Surround with fruit and onion
mixture, and dot it with butter.

9 Return roasting tin to the oven and immediately turn temperature down to very slow (300°F. Mark 2).

10 Quarter, peel and core apples.

11 When pork has been back in the oven for 15 minutes, mix
apples gently with fruit in the roasting tin.

12 Continue to roast until pork is tender, about 45 minutes
longer, basting occasionally with soaking liquid from fruit.
(Total cooking time for pork, about 1 hour 15 minutes at both
temperatures.)

13 To serve: transfer pork to a heated serving dish and surround
with fruits; skim pan juices if necessary; spoon over fruit and
serve immediately.

Old English Gammon Baked in Pastry

Serves 10–12

A 4 1/2- to 5-lb middle cut of
  gammon
1 1/2 lb plain flour
Butter
About 3 oz browned
  breadcrumbs

1 Soak the gammon for a minimum of 12 hours in a large bowl
of cold water, changing water twice during this time.

2 Sift flour into a bowl. Work in enough cold water to make a
soft but not sticky dough. (It will take between 16 and 17 fluid
oz.) Turn dough out on to a floured board and knead lightly
until smooth.

3 Cut off a piece of dough weighing between 4 and 6 oz; wrap in a piece of greaseproof paper and reserve for later use. Divide remaining dough in half. Roll one piece out to roughly the shape of the gammon joint, but nearly twice the size. Repeat with the other piece of dough.

4 Preheat oven to slow (325°F. Mark 3).

5 Choose a large roasting tin and a rack (a cake rack or one out of the grill-pan). Line rack with a double thickness of foil and brush liberally with melted butter.

6 Drain gammon joint and dry thoroughly. Tie joint with string so that it will stay in shape while cooking.

7 Lay joint, flat side down, on one of the sheets of dough. Cover with a second sheet. Bring edges of dough together and seal them tightly, folding and pinching them together. Joint should now be completely encased, with no holes anywhere in the dough for steam or juices to escape.

8 Lay wrapped joint on foil-lined rack. Stand rack in a roasting tin.

9 Bake joint on shelf below centre of oven for 1 hour.

10 Remove joint from oven and carefully turn it over. If pastry casing has cracked and some of the juices have escaped into the roasting tin, pour them back in through the crack; then use some of the reserved raw dough to plug up the crack.

11 If you wish to use a meat thermometer at this stage, take some more of the raw dough; roll it into a ball and press on top of pastry crust, roughly in the centre. Then push thermometer through this so that tip is resting in centre of joint.

12 Replace in the oven and bake for a further hour, or until thermometer registers 160°F.

13 Allow joint to cool for 30 minutes before cracking open the crust. Discard pastry crust. It has now done its moisturising job. Then remove skin, which should pull off quite easily while joint is warm.

14 *If ham is to be served hot:* Cut off string. Press browned breadcrumbs into fat where skin has been removed and serve immediately on a heated serving dish.

15 *If ham is to be served cold:* Leave string around it. Coat fat surfaces with browned breadcrumbs as before. Place joint, flat side down, on a board. Place another board on top and weight down heavily with bags of flour, sugar, cans, etc. Leave to become quite cold. Remove string. Press on more crumbs if necessary. Slice as required.

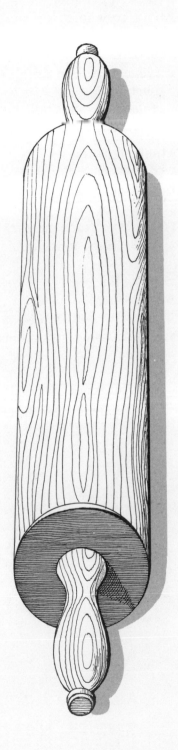

A 4-lb joint of lightly
smoked gammon

About 20 whole cloves

2 tablespoons oil

2 oz dark soft brown sugar

1/2 level teaspoon dry
mustard

1 tablespoon pineapple juice

1 tablespoon cider vinegar

Mustard sauce

1 oz butter

1 oz flour

3/4 pint hot milk

1/2 chicken stock cube

4 level tablespoons double
cream

2 egg yolks

2–3 level teaspoons dry
mustard

Salt and freshly ground black
pepper

Baked Gammon with Mustard Sauce

1 Soak gammon in a large bowl of cold water for 24 hours, changing water several times.

2 The following day, drain gammon and place it in a large saucepan with plenty of fresh cold water to cover. Slowly bring to the boil and simmer for 30 minutes, or until the skin can be taken off easily. Leave the pan containing the gammon under cold running water until gammon is cool enough to handle.

3 Preheat oven to moderately hot (400°F. Mark 6).

4 Pare skin off gammon with a sharp knife and discard it. Score fat of gammon in a diamond pattern and spike each diamond with a whole clove.

5 Lay gammon in a roasting tin; brush with oil and roast for 1 hour, basting occasionally with pan juices.

6 Meanwhile, prepare glaze: work brown sugar to a paste with mustard, pineapple juice and cider vinegar, and set aside until ready to glaze gammon.

7 Prepare Mustard sauce: melt butter in a heavy pan; stir in flour and cook, stirring, for 3 minutes to make a smooth golden *roux*. Gradually add hot milk, stirring constantly to avoid lumps. Dissolve stock cube in a little of the hot sauce; add to sauce and simmer gently, stirring occasionally, for about 20 minutes. Keep hot.

8 After an hour's baking, remove gammon from the oven. Pour over the glaze and return to the oven for a further half-hour, or until cooked through, basting frequently.

9 When gammon is ready to serve, finish sauce. Stir in cream; bring to the boil; remove from heat and beat in egg yolks. Work mustard to a smooth paste with a tablespoon of hot sauce, and beat into sauce. Season to taste with a little salt and freshly ground black pepper. Reheat if necessary, but do not let sauce come to the boil again, or egg yolks may curdle. Serve hot with slices of gammon.

Sweet Glazes for Gammon, Ham and Bacon

Pineapple and Brown Sugar Glaze

1 Mix ingredients together smoothly.

2 Pour glaze over parboiled and skinned joint and bake in a slow oven (325°F. Mark 3) for 1 hour, basting frequently, until glaze becomes syrupy and meat a rich red-brown.

Enough for a 2-lb joint

4 oz Demerara sugar
1 level teaspoon dry mustard
6 tablespoons pineapple juice

Spiced Apple Glaze

1 Combine sugar, apple juice and spice in a small pan, and stir over a moderate heat until sugar has dissolved.

2 Pour glaze over parboiled and skinned joint, and bake as above, basting frequently.

Enough for a 2-lb joint

4 oz Demerara sugar
4–6 tablespoons apple juice
1/8 level teaspoon mixed spice

Roasting Chicken

It wasn't until the 16th Century that Henri IV of France declared that a 'chicken in the pot every Sunday' should be the right of every Frenchman. And it was not until centuries later that politicians both in America and Britain were fighting for the same right: a chicken every Sunday.

Today, thanks to new methods of production and promotion, better refrigeration and transportation, we can have chicken every day of the week if we want it.

In fact, chicken is now our national dish. Inexpensive, readily available, sold fresh or frozen, in whole or in pre-packaged parts, chicken makes an easily prepared, inexpensive meal for one or for a family of five.

But the ready availability of poultry today brings with it some obvious disadvantages. Chickens, especially, don't taste the same as they used to. New commercial methods of feeding and battery systems of rearing have made the chicken cheaper and more available, but they have made it a different product.

And a plain roast chicken is no longer the delicacy it used to be. Today's cooks have to rub it with butter, stuff it with French cream cheese and fresh herbs, or dust it with powdered paprika or saffron to give it an exciting flavour (see following recipes).

A Dictionary of Chicken Terms

Poussins Baby chickens, weighing about 2 pounds. Usually best spit-roasted, halved and grilled or cooked whole in a casserole. One bird per portion.

Broilers or broiler-fryers Chickens about 9 weeks old, weighing $1\frac{1}{2}$ to 3 pounds. Tender, with creamy smooth-textured skin and flexible breast-bone cartilage. Half a broiler is usually considered a portion, except for the very large ones. Disjoint broilers before sautéeing.

Frying chickens Larger broilers. Usually about $2\frac{1}{2}$ pounds. Can be split or cut into individual serving pieces for frying and sautéeing.

Roasting chickens Tender chickens of $3\frac{1}{2}$ to $4\frac{1}{2}$ pounds. The best ones have well-rounded bodies and full breasts. Roasting chickens are used for roasting, for casserole dishes and for most fricassées.

Boiling fowls Mature birds weighing 4 to 8 pounds with a richer fuller flavour. Not as tender however as a roasting chicken. They need long, slow poaching or simmering to achieve tenderness. Excellent for soups and broths.

Capons are unsexed male birds. Large and delicately flavoured, they are excellent roasted, casseroled or poached in chicken stock.

Poulardes Unsexed female birds. Fine flesh and fine flavour.

In judging a chicken, notice the bony lower legs and feet, which in a young bird are thick and heavy looking. As a bird ages, these become thin and dry. The breastbone of a young chicken is flexible and soft enough to break easily when pressed with the fingers.

Remove wrappings; remove giblets from carcass, if there are any. Then lay bird on a plate and cover it loosely with grease-proof paper or foil. It can then be stored near the bottom of the refrigerator for 2 or 3 days.

If the bird is frozen, keep frozen until 24 hours before cooking. Then unwrap and leave in your refrigerator overnight. Or, if quicker defrosting is necessary, place chicken, still wrapped, in cold water for 2 to 4 hours. When completely thawed; pat dry and sprinkle cavity with salt before roasting in the usual way.

To Truss Poultry for Roasting

Pluck bird and singe if necessary. Cut off feet at the first joint. Lay the bird on its back and turn the wings under; bring the legs close to the body and pass a metal or wooden skewer first through the flesh of the wing, the middle of the leg and the body; then out the other side through the other leg and the wing.

Pass a piece of string over each end of the skewer; bring it round the vent; fasten the legs tightly and tie securely.

To Roast a Chicken

Chicken, when roasted without a stuffing to add flavour and substance, needs an extra fillip of butter and dried herbs – rosemary, marjoram, sage or thyme – to lend it excitement, or as in the two recipes below – a touch of paprika, or a hint of saffron and lemon.

Basic Roast Chicken with Paprika

Serves 4

1 Preheat oven to fairly hot (425°F. Mark 7).

2 Wipe bird clean both inside and out with a damp cloth, or absorbent paper. Season cavity with salt and freshly ground black pepper.

3 Put 3 oz butter in a bowl. With a wooden spoon, work in paprika and a generous seasoning of salt and freshly ground black pepper.

4 Take half of the seasoned butter; place it in the cavity of the bird.

1 tender chicken, about 3 1/2 lb dressed weight
Salt and freshly ground black pepper
Butter
1/2 level teaspoon paprika
Flour
Sprigs of watercress, to garnish
Dry white wine

5 Lay chicken on its breast. Bring its wings round and lay them flat across the back. Draw neck skin over the back. Pass a skewer through one wing, through the neck skin and then through the other wing.

6 Now turn chicken on to its back. Tie legs together with string; then draw string under the 'parson's nose' and tie tightly.

7 Spread remainder of seasoned butter over breast of chicken. Sprinkle chicken with more salt and freshly ground black pepper.

8 Lay chicken on its side in a roasting tin. Roast for 20 minutes until slightly browned.

9 Turn bird on to its other side and roast for a further 15 to 20 minutes.

10 Reduce oven temperature to 350°F. (Mark 4). Turn bird on to its back. Sift a dusting of flour over the breast; baste with 3 or 4 tablespoons boiling water and continue to roast for another 20–25 minutes, or longer, until chicken is tender, basting frequently. If you push a skewer through the thickest part of the inside leg, the juices should run quite clear and golden. Similarly, when you tip the chicken up, juices from the cavity should be clear.

11 When chicken is tender, remove trussing skewer, string, etc.; drain bird and transfer to a heated serving dish. Garnish with sprigs of watercress.

12 Pour off most of fat remaining in roasting tin. Add a little dry white wine; place tin over a high heat and boil for 5 minutes, stirring and scraping bottom and sides of pan clean with a wooden spoon.

13 When this gravy is reduced to about $\frac{1}{2}$ its original quantity, season to taste with salt and freshly ground black pepper, and stir in 1 level teaspoon butter. Pour into a heated sauceboat and serve with chicken.

I particularly like the roast chicken with saffron and lemon that I was served recently in Central France: an unusual combination of tender chicken served with mushrooms in a creamy velouté sauce flavoured with the sharp clear bite of lemon—both juice and peel—and the rich savour of saffron. Typically French in feeling (witness its subtle sauce), but with more than a hint of its African heritage—the Arabs have used lemon and saffron with chicken for centuries—this dish makes a wonderful addition to your store of favourite chicken dishes.

Roast Chicken
with Lemon and Saffron

1 Preheat oven to fairly hot (425°F. Mark 7).

2 Wipe bird clean both inside and out with a damp cloth, or absorbent paper. Season cavity with salt and freshly ground black pepper.

3 Put 3 oz butter in a bowl. With a wooden spoon, work in powdered saffron, finely chopped garlic and lemon juice. Season generously with salt and freshly ground black pepper.

4 Take half of the seasoned butter and place it in the cavity of the bird.

5 Lay chicken on its breast. Bring its wings round and lay them flat across the back. Draw neck skin over the back. Pass a skewer through one wing, through the neck skin and then through the other wing.

6 Now turn chicken on to its back. Tie legs together with string; then draw string under the 'parson's nose' and tie tightly.

7 Take remainder of the seasoned butter; flatten it out with your fingertips and spread over the breast of the chicken.

8 Sprinkle chicken with more salt and freshly ground black pepper.

9 Lay chicken on its side in a roasting tin. Roast for 20 minutes until slightly browned.

10 Turn bird on to its other side and roast for a further 15 to 20 minutes.

11 Reduce oven temperature to 350°F. (Mark 4). Turn bird on to its back. Sift a dusting of flour over the breast; baste with 3 or 4 tablespoons boiling water and continue to roast for another 20–25 minutes, or longer, until chicken is tender, basting frequently. If you push a skewer through the thickest part of the inside leg, the juices should run quite clear and golden. Similarly, when you tip the chicken up, juices from the cavity should be clear.

12 While chicken is roasting, combine egg yolks, cream, sliced mushrooms, lemon juice and strips of lemon peel in a bowl.

13 Melt butter in the top of a double saucepan. Stir in flour and cook over water, stirring constantly, until well blended.

14 Caramelise sugar by browning 2 level teaspoons sugar with enough water to obtain a very smooth syrup. Stir into sauce. Remove pan from heat until chicken is done.

Serves 4

1 tender chicken, about 3 1/2 lb dressed weight
Salt and freshly ground black pepper
Butter
1/4 level teaspoon powdered saffron
1 small clove garlic, finely chopped
Juice of 1/2 lemon
Flour
Watercress

Sauce
2 egg yolks
1/4 pint double cream
1/4 lb button mushrooms, sliced
Juice of 1/2 lemon
Peel of 1/2 lemon, cut in thin matchsticks
2 level tablespoons butter
2 level tablespoons flour
2 level teaspoons sugar
6 tablespoons dry white wine

15 When chicken is tender, remove trussing skewer, string, etc.; drain bird and transfer to a heated serving dish. Garnish vent with sprigs of watercress.

16 Pour off most of the fat remaining in roasting tin. Add 6 tablespoons dry white wine; place tin over a high heat and boil for 5 minutes, stirring and scraping sides of pan clean with a wooden spoon.

17 To finish sauce: Return double saucepan to heat; add juices and egg, cream and mushroom mixture and whisk over boiling water until thick. Do not let sauce boil or it will curdle.

18 Correct seasoning. Pour sauce into a heated sauce boat and serve with the chicken.

Basic Roast Chicken with Stuffing

The simplest stuffing of all – which doesn't make it any the less good.

1 Preheat oven to moderate (350°F. Mark 4).

2 To make stuffing: cut bread into ⅓-inch cubes.

3 In large frying-pan, fry bacon slices in half the butter until crisp. Remove bacon; add finely chopped onion to the pan and sauté over a moderate heat until soft and golden. Remove from pan with a slotted spoon.

4 Add remaining butter to the frying-pan. When it has melted, add bread cubes and toss over a moderate heat until they have taken up all the fat and turned a light golden colour.

5 Crumble fried bacon rashers into a mixing bowl. Add sautéed onion, bread cubes and herbs, and toss lightly with a fork until well mixed.

6 In another, smaller bowl, beat egg with milk or stock. Pour over bread mixture, tossing with the fork to distribute liquid evenly. Season stuffing with salt and freshly ground black pepper.

7 Wipe chicken clean both inside and out.

8 Fill cavity of chicken with bread stuffing. Skewer or sew vent up with a few stitches of strong thread.

9 Lay chicken in a roasting tin. Rub with salt and freshly ground black pepper, and spread with softened butter.

10 Roast chicken for about 1 hour 15 minutes, basting frequently with its own juices (supplemented if necessary with a tablespoon or two of boiling water).

Serves 4

A 3- to 3 1/2-lb roasting chicken

Salt and freshly ground black pepper

2 level tablespoons softened butter

Bread stuffing

3–3 1/2 oz trimmed stale white bread

2–3 slices lightly smoked bacon

2 level tablespoons butter

1 Spanish onion, finely chopped

3 level tablespoons finely chopped parsley

Generous pinch of crumbled thyme

Generous pinch of rosemary leaves, crumbled

1 egg

4 tablespoons milk or chicken stock

Salt and freshly ground black pepper

11 To serve: transfer chicken to a heated serving dish. Discard skewers or thread, and keep hot.

12 Pour 2 or 3 tablespoons water into the roasting tin and bring to the boil over a moderate heat, stirring and scraping base and sides with a wooden spoon to dislodge crusty bits stuck there. Simmer for a minute, stirring. Taste for seasoning; pour into a heated sauce boat and serve with the chicken.

Roast Chicken with sausages This is prepared in exactly the same way as Basic Roast Chicken with stuffing (page 108), with the addition of 1 lb best-quality pork sausages.

Twist sausages in half if they are large, to give about 16 fat little chipolata shapes.

Add them to the roasting tin when you have basted with boiling water (Step 10, above) and continue to roast as directed in the master recipe.

Roast Chicken with Herbs

Serves 4

1 Preheat oven to fairly hot (425°F. Mark 7).

2 Wipe bird clean both inside and out with a damp cloth, or absorbent paper. Season cavity with salt and freshly ground black pepper.

3 Put 2 oz butter in a bowl. With a wooden spoon, work in dried rosemary and marjoram and a generous sprinkling of lemon juice. Season with salt and freshly ground black pepper, to taste.

4 Put half of the seasoned butter in the cavity of the bird.

5 Lay chicken on its front. Bring its wings round and lay them flat across the back. Draw neck skin over the back. Pass a skewer through one wing, through the neck skin and then through the other wing.

6 Now turn chicken on to its back. Tie legs together with string; then draw string under the 'parson's nose' and tie tightly.

7 Spread remainder of seasoned butter over breast of chicken. Sprinkle chicken with more salt and freshly ground black pepper.

8 Lay chicken on its side in a roasting tin. Roast for 20 minutes until slightly browned.

9 Turn bird on to its other side and roast for a further 15 to 20 minutes.

A tender roasting chicken (about 3 1/2-lb dressed weight)
Salt and freshly ground black pepper
Butter
1/4 level teaspoon dried rosemary
1/4 level teaspoon dried marjoram
Lemon juice
Flour
Paprika
Sprigs of watercress, to garnish
6 tablespoons dry white wine

10 Reduce oven temperature to 350°F. (Mark 4). Turn bird on to its back. Sift a dusting of flour over the breast; sprinkle bird lightly with paprika; baste with 3 or 4 tablespoons boiling water and continue to roast for another 20 to 25 minutes, or longer, until chicken is tender, basting frequently. If you push a skewer through the thickest part of the inside leg, the juices should run quite clear and golden. Similarly, when you tip the chicken up, juices from the cavity should be clear, without a trace of pink.

11 When chicken is tender, remove trussing skewer, string, etc.; drain bird and transfer to a heated serving dish. Garnish dish with sprigs of watercress.

12 Pour off most of fat remaining in roasting tin. Add dry white wine; place over a high heat and boil for 5 minutes, stirring and scraping bottom and sides of pan clean with a wooden spoon.

13 When juices are reduced to about $\frac{1}{4}$ of their original quantity, check seasoning and stir in 1 level teaspoon butter. Pour over chicken.

Serves 4

Two 1 1/2-lb chickens, with giblets
4 level tablespoons softened butter
Parsley sprigs, to garnish

Dill stuffing
4 oz fine stale white breadcrumbs
8 tablespoons milk
2 level tablespoons softened butter
2 eggs, separated
The chicken livers
3–4 level tablespoons finely chopped fresh dill
Salt and freshly ground black pepper

Roast Spring Chickens
à la Polonaise

Half a roast spring chicken perfumed with a light, dill-flavoured breadcrumb stuffing makes a handsome portion for one. The best accompaniments are Polish-style, too: a green salad dressed with sour cream (page 111) and boiled new potatoes tossed with butter and finely chopped parsley or dill.

1 Wipe chickens clean both inside and out. Clean livers. Put aside until required.

2 Preheat oven to moderate (350°F. Mark 4).

3 Put breadcrumbs in a bowl. (Use crumbed soft rolls in preference to plain bread if possible, as they give a better flavour and texture.) Sprinkle with milk, tossing lightly with a fork, and leave to soak for 15 minutes.

4 In a mixing bowl, beat softened butter and egg yolks until well blended.

5 Chop up chicken livers coarsely. Squeeze breadcrumbs lightly to extract any milk that has not been absorbed – in fact, there should be none if crumbs were stale and fine enough. Combine the two and put them through the fine blade of a mincer.

6 Blend breadcrumb mixture thoroughly with butter and egg yolks. Mix in finely chopped fresh dill and season to taste with salt and freshly ground black pepper.

7 Whisk egg whites until stiff but not dry. Fold into stuffing lightly but thoroughly.

8 Loosen skin all over breast of each chicken by carefully easing your hand – or a blunt wooden spoon – down between skin and breast meat. Take great care not to tear skin. If it refuses to come away from breast easily at any point, don't force it: instead use the tip of a sharp knife or a pair of small scissors to cut them apart.

9 Push enough stuffing between skin and breast to cover the entire breast with a thin, even layer. Fill cavity of each chicken with remaining stuffing.

10 Skewer or sew cavities up, making sure at the same time that stuffing cannot slip out from under the breast skin. Truss chickens.

11 Melt butter in a roasting tin large enough to take chickens comfortably side by side. When butter is very hot, turn them over in it to coat them thoroughly; then lay them on their backs in the tin.

12 Roast chickens, basting frequently with their own juices, for 1 hour, or until juices run clear when a skewer is pushed through the thickest part of the leg, close to the body.

13 To serve: remove chickens from roasting tin and, with a very sharp knife, slice each one in half right down the middle. Put two halves together again and arrange on a heated serving dish. Decorate with parsley sprigs and serve with pan juices, new potatoes and lettuce with sour cream dressing.

Lettuce with Sour Cream Dressing Turn a carton of sour cream into a porcelain or earthenware salad bowl. Beat lightly with a spoon, adding salt, freshly ground black pepper, a pinch of sugar and a few drops of lemon juice, to taste.

Break carefully washed and dried leaves of 1 large lettuce over the dressing, and toss until each leaf has a thin, creamy coating. Correct seasoning and serve.

To Roast Ducks and Geese

For best results, duckling and geese should always be roasted. Boiled goose, preserved goose, duckling *en daube* and charcoal grilled duck and goose are among the few exceptions that I know.

To prepare a duck for roasting

A duck is a very fat bird. It is best to cut all visible fat from openings before cooking, and then to pour off excess fat occasionally as it accumulates in the pan during cooking.

Singe the duck, and then, using a pair of kitchen tweezers (or the point of a small knife and your thumb) remove any remaining pin feathers. Then wash the bird quickly in warm water and dry it in a cloth. Cut off feet and wings at the first joint; brush bird lightly with melted butter or a little oil and season generously with salt and fresh ground black pepper, inside and out.

To roast duckling

Put bird, prepared as above, in a shallow roasting pan breast side down. Roast duck (4 to 5 lb) for 2 to 2½ hours in a preheated slow oven (325°F. Mark 3).

After about 1½ hours cooking time, turn breast side up and continue roasting until the thigh joint moves easily up and down.

To prepare a goose for roasting

Singe the goose and remove any pin feathers, as above. Remove excess fat from the bird in the following manner: Prick fatty parts of goose with a fork; place bird in preheated moderately hot oven (400°F. Mark 6) for 15 minutes, or until fat begins to run; then remove goose from oven. Tip goose to let fat in body cavity run out and pour off fat from pan. Return to oven, and repeat this process 2 or 3 times.

Roast Goose with Calvados

1 goose (6 to 8 lb)
Melted butter
Salt and freshly ground black pepper
4-6 tablespoons calvados or cognac
Dry breadcrumbs

Brush goose, prepared as above, lightly with melted butter and season generously with salt and freshly ground black pepper, inside and out. Place the bird in a shallow roasting pan, breast side down. Roast the bird for 3½-4 hours in a preheated slow oven (325°F. Mark 3).

After 2½ hours of cooking time, turn the bird breast side up and continue roasting until the skin is well browned. When the thigh joint moves easily, the goose is done.

Flame goose with heated Calvados, or cognac, and sprinkle lightly with dry breadcrumbs; raise oven heat to 450°F. (Mark 8) and cook, 10 to 15 minutes more, or until breadcrumbs are golden brown.

Roast Duck

Serves 4

1 Preheat oven to moderate (350°F. Mark 4).

2 Wipe duck clean both inside and out with a damp cloth.

3 Chop orange coarsely, rind and all, and put it in a bowl.

4 Peel and chop onion coarsely; mix with orange. Season generously with thyme, salt and freshly ground black pepper, and moisten with olive oil.

5 Pack duck cavity tightly with orange and onion mixture, including any juices which may have drained to the bottom of the bowl.

6 'Seal' duck completely: with a needle and strong thread, sew neck skin to the back; then push 'parson's nose' into the vent and sew up the opening. Truss duck.

7 Rub duck all over with salt and freshly ground black pepper. Lay it on a rack over a roasting tin and prick all over with a sharp fork.

8 Roast duck, basting frequently with its own fat, until skin is crisp and brown, and juices run clear when leg is pierced with a skewer through the thickest part, close to the body. It will take between $1\frac{3}{4}$ and 2 hours.

9 When duck is ready, lift it out of the roasting tin and pour off all but 1 tablespoon fat.

10 Remove trussing strings from duck. Unravel threads; open up cavity and drain off all the juices into the roasting tin. The orange-onion mixture inside can now be discarded as it has done its flavouring and moisturising job, and is not meant to be eaten. Place duck on a serving dish and keep hot while you finish sauce.

11 Place roasting tin over a moderate heat. Blend in flour smoothly with a wooden spoon; then add chicken stock gradually, stirring and scraping bottom and sides of tin vigorously to incorporate all the sediment into the sauce. Season to taste with salt and freshly ground black pepper; bring to the boil, stirring, and simmer for 2 minutes.

12 Strain sauce into a heated sauce boat and serve with the duck.

1 oven-ready duck, about 4 lb
1 large orange
1 Spanish onion
Generous pinch of thyme
Salt and freshly ground black pepper
1 tablespoon olive oil
1 level tablespoon flour
1/2 pint chicken stock

Serves 4

1 oven-ready duck, about
  4 lb
4 level tablespoons butter
Salt and freshly ground black
  pepper
2 oranges
2 lemons
6 peaches
1 level tablespoon sugar
1 tablespoon wine vinegar
10 tablespoons dry white
  vermouth
1 1/2 level teaspoons
  cornflour
2 tablespoons peach liqueur
  or orange curaçao
2 level tablespoons
  redcurrant jelly
Sprigs of fresh watercress

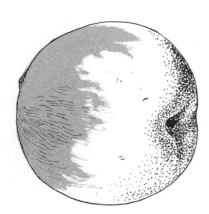

Roast Duck with Peaches

1 Preheat oven to moderate (350°F. Mark 4).

2 Melt butter in a deep roasting tin on top of the stove and sauté duck until crisp and golden on all sides. Season with salt and freshly ground black pepper.

3 Transfer roasting tin to the oven and roast duck for 50 to 60 minutes or until tender, basting occasionally with the fat which collects in the pan. Test duck by pushing a fork or skewer through the thickest part of the leg nearest the breast; it is ready when juices run clear.

4 While duck is roasting, remove zest from oranges (with a potato peeler). Cut zest into thin strips. Squeeze lemons and oranges.

5 Drop peaches in boiling water, one by one, to loosen skin. Remove each peach from water with a slotted spoon after a minute or two. Holding peach in a clean kitchen towel, gently remove loosened skin. Cut peaches in half, removing stones.

6 Melt sugar in wine vinegar over a low heat and simmer, stirring, until it turns a deep golden caramel. Stir in the lemon juice, orange juice and vermouth; mix well and season to taste with salt and freshly ground black pepper. Sieve 4 peeled peach halves into sauce and simmer very gently for 5 minutes. Keep warm.

7 When duck is cooked, transfer to a heated serving dish. Surround with remaining 8 peeled peach halves and return to the oven, leaving the door ajar, to keep hot while you finish sauce.

8 Mix cornflour to a smooth paste with peach liqueur or curaçao. Drain almost all the fat from the roasting tin. Stir in syrup and cornflour paste, and cook over a moderate heat until sauce is smooth and thickened, scraping bottom and sides of pan to dislodge any crusty bits stuck there. Finally, add redcurrant jelly, and strips of orange zest; stir until jelly has melted and taste for seasoning, adding more salt or freshly ground black pepper if necessary.

9 Remove duck from the oven and spoon some of the sauce over the duck and peaches. Garnish duck with sprigs of fresh watercress. Serve remainder of sauce separately in a heated sauce boat.

Roast Duck with Sauerkraut

Serves 4

1 In a large, deep frying-pan, sauté diced fat salt pork until pieces are transparent and fat runs.

2 Add coarsely chopped onion and fry until soft and transparent.

3 Peel and core apples, and cut into $\frac{1}{2}$-inch cubes. Add to the pan and toss quickly over a high heat until golden. Watch apples carefully: the pieces should remain very firm indeed so that they still retain their shape when the stuffing is served.

4 Remove pan from heat. Stir in brown sugar, thyme and caraway seed, and put aside.

5 Drain sauerkraut but do not squeeze it dry. Put it in a large bowl, loosening shreds out with your fingers or two forks. Then add apple-onion mixture and salt and freshly ground black pepper, to taste, and toss lightly until well mixed.

6 Preheat oven to slow (325°F. Mark 3).

7 Wipe duck inside and out with a damp cloth and dry thoroughly. Season cavity with salt and freshly ground black pepper.

8 Stuff duck with sauerkraut mixture and truss securely. (If you have some stuffing left over, put it in a buttered ovenproof dish; cover with foil and place in the oven with the duck $\frac{1}{2}$ hour before the end of cooking time.)

9 Lay duck in a roasting tin and roast for about $2\frac{1}{2}$ hours: 1 hour on each side and a final half-hour on its back. It is ready when the leg moves freely and there is no trace of blood deep down in the joint.

10 Serve duck on a heated dish, surrounded with any remaining stuffing that had to be cooked separately.

1 oven-ready duck, 4 1/2–5 lb
4 oz fat salt pork, finely diced
1 Spanish onion, coarsely chopped
2 cooking apples
2 level tablespoons soft brown sugar
Pinch of thyme
1/2 level teaspoon caraway seed
One 1-lb jar sauerkraut in brine
Salt and freshly ground black pepper

Serves 4

1 oven-ready duck, 4 1/2–
   5 lb
Salt and freshly ground black
   pepper
6 oz fresh white
   breadcrumbs
10 oz pork sausage meat
1 medium-sized onion,
   grated
1/4 level teaspoon each dried
   thyme and rosemary
1 small apple, cored and
   coarsely chopped

Basting sauce
1 pint lager
3 oz brown sugar
Pinch of ground cloves
2 tablespoons wine vinegar
1 level teaspoon dry mustard

Roast Duck with Beer

A magnificent dish. It may be served either hot or cold. The beer basting sauce gives the duck a rich brown glaze which retains its sheen even when the duck is cold, and looks incredibly pretty and inviting.

1 Wipe duck clean and season inside generously with salt and freshly ground black pepper.

2 In a large bowl, combine breadcrumbs with sausage meat, grated onion, herbs and chopped apple. Season generously with salt and freshly ground black pepper.

3 Stuff duck with this mixture, and truss or skewer it firmly to make sure that the stuffing does not spill out during cooking.

4 Preheat oven to slow (325°F. Mark 3).

5 Prepare basting sauce: combine lager with brown sugar, cloves, wine vinegar and mustard, and stir until sugar has melted.

6 Place duck on a rack in a roasting tin and pour basting sauce over it. Roast for about 2 hours, or until duck is tender and cooked through, basting every 30 minutes with pan juices.

7 To serve hot: transfer duck to a heated serving dish; skim fat from pan juices and serve separately in a heated sauce boat. If you are planning to serve duck cold, continue to baste it frequently with skimmed pan juices as it cools in order to build up a rich glaze.

To Roast Turkey

Until recently, fairly large turkeys were much sought after. I can remember my mother worrying whether a twenty-pound bird would go into her oven. And, of course, then would come the resultant problems: how to make the family eat turkey day after day until the huge bird was reduced to its carcass for a final 'turkey soup'. Today a turkey of any size may be roasted.

How to prepare a turkey for roasting As you would chicken. If bird is to be stuffed, allow about ½ cup stuffing per pound of turkey.

How to roast a turkey Roast turkey in a slow oven (325°F. Mark 3) according to this guide or as in recipes:

Ready-to-cook Turkey	Approximate Roasting Times
(weight before stuffing)	
6 pounds	3 to 3½ hours
6 to 8 pounds	3½ to 4 hours
8 to 12 pounds	4 to 5½ hours
12 to 16 pounds	5½ to 6 hours
16 to 20 pounds	6½ to 8 hours

Basic Roast Turkey with Orange Gravy

1 Preheat oven to fairly hot (425°F. Mark 7).

2 Wipe turkey both inside and out with a damp cloth or absorbent paper. Pick off any stray feathers or quills.

3 To make flavouring (this is intended *only* as a flavouring for the meat and will be discarded before serving): dice orange, peel and all; peel and dice onion. Toss together in a bowl with olive oil, herbs and a generous seasoning of salt and freshly ground black pepper.

4 Stuff body cavity of turkey loosely with this mixture.

5 To truss bird: sew or skewer vent tightly to prevent juices escaping. Draw neck skin over back, not too tightly, and fasten in place with metal skewers or wooden toothpicks. Cut off ends of wings to use for the giblet stock. Tie legs together with string and fasten string around tail.

6 Season turkey generously all over with salt and freshly ground black pepper, and lay it in a roomy roasting tin, breast side up.

7 Over a low heat, melt butter for basting sauce in a heavy pan. Remove from heat before it starts to sizzle.

8 Cut a piece of double-thick muslin large enough to drape over turkey and cover it, legs and all. Rinse under the cold tap and wring out as dry as possible. Soak cloth in melted butter and gently squeeze out excess. Drape muslin over turkey.

9 Roast turkey on lowest shelf of oven for 15 minutes. Then reduce temperature to moderate (350°F. Mark 4) for the rest of the cooking time.

10 To make basting sauce: combine remainder of melted butter with dry white wine, orange juice and finely chopped garlic. Crumble in a stock cube for seasoning and stir until dissolved.

Serves 8

1 medium-sized turkey, about 10 lb dressed weight
Salt and freshly ground black pepper

Flavouring mixture
1 orange
1 Spanish onion
2 tablespoons olive oil
1/4 level teaspoon dried rosemary
1/4 level teaspoon dried oregano
Salt and freshly ground black pepper

Basting sauce
8 oz butter
1/4 pint dry white wine
Juice of 2 small oranges
1 clove garlic, finely chopped
1 chicken stock cube

Orange gravy
Giblet stock (see Step 13)
2 level tablespoons butter
2 level tablespoons flour
Juices from roasting tin
Salt and freshly ground black pepper

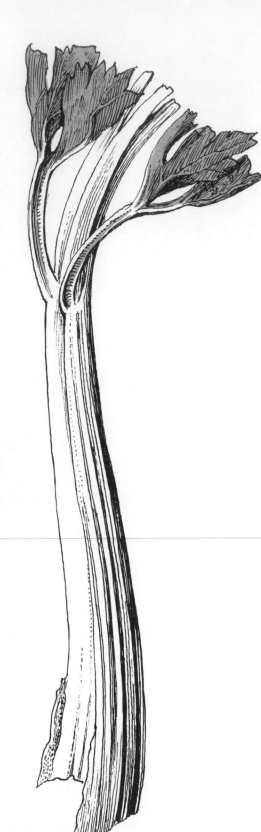

11 Baste turkey with some of this buttery liquid at the end of the first 15 minutes, and every 15 minutes thereafter, making sure that the muslin is completely remoistened with this liquid or the pan juices each time.

12 The total roasting time, including the first 15 minutes at the higher temperature, is calculated at between 12 and 15 minutes per lb, but this can only be a guide. The important thing to remember is that with a turkey you are dealing with two different kinds of meat, the delicate white meat of the breast, and the dark leg meat, which needs longer cooking. A balance must therefore be struck by roasting the bird just long enough to cook the legs through without drying out the breast. Test the leg by pushing a skewer into the thickest part close to the body – the juices should *just* run clear. If you then cut the string, the leg joint should wiggle loosely in its socket.

13 While turkey is roasting, prepare a stock with its giblets: Wash the neck, heart, gizzard and wing tips, and place them in a pan with 1 Spanish onion, coarsely chopped, 1 bay leaf, 4 sprigs each celery tops and parsley, and a little salt and freshly ground black pepper. Add $\frac{1}{4}$ pint dry white wine and enough water to cover. Bring to the boil; skim; lower heat and simmer gently for $1\frac{1}{2}$ hours, topping up with more water as necessary. Add liver and simmer for 30 minutes longer.

14 When turkey is tender, discard the muslin, flavouring ingredients from the body cavity, as well as strings, skewers, etc., used to truss the bird. Transfer bird to a hot serving dish and keep hot in the turned-off oven while you prepare orange gravy. Like roast meat, turkey is easier to carve if it is left for 15 minutes to allow juices to 'settle'.

15 Strain giblet stock. Chop giblet meats finely.

16 Pour juices and crusty bits from roasting tin into a bowl. Leave for a minute to allow all the fat to come to the surface so that you can skim it off. (The bulb baster method – see page 160 – is neat and quite safe provided you hold the baster dead vertical.)

17 Melt butter in a heavy pan, blend in flour and stir over a low heat for 2 minutes to make a pale *roux*.

18 Gradually add strained giblet stock and skimmed pan juices stirring vigorously to prevent lumps forming. Bring to the boil and simmer, stirring, until gravy has thickened and flour is cooked, 6 to 8 minutes.

19 Add chopped giblets; heat through and correct seasoning. Pour into a hot sauce boat and serve with turkey.

English Roast Turkey with Sausage Meat Stuffing and Chestnuts

Serves 8–10

1 To make Sausage Meat Stuffing: in a large frying-pan, cook bacon slices until fat runs and bacon turns crisp. Remove from pan with a slotted spoon and crumble into a large bowl.

2 Add butter to fat remaining in pan. Heat until frothy. Then add bread cubes and toss over a moderate heat until they are crisp on the outside but still feel soft and spongy inside when pressed. Add to crumbled bacon.

3 Add remaining ingredients. Mix by hand until thoroughly blended.

4 Having peeled and skinned chestnuts, cook them in boiling stock, or simply in salted water, until they are quite tender, about 20 minutes.

5 Drain chestnuts thoroughly, reserving stock; return them to the hot, dry pan. Add butter; moisten with 1 or 2 tablespoons of the stock, and swirl around until chestnuts are coated with buttery liquid. Season with salt and freshly ground black pepper.

6 Preheat oven to fairly hot (425°F. Mark 7).

7 Wipe turkey both inside and out with a damp cloth or absorbent paper. Pluck out any stray feathers or quills.

8 Free the skin from the breast by working your hand down under the skin from the neck end. If skin refuses to come away at any point, do not force it or you may cause it to tear. Instead, separate the meat from the underside of skin with the tip of a small knife, or snip it free with a pair of scissors. Proceed carefully until you have loosened skin almost to the end of the breast and down each side to the legs.

9 Stuff breast with sausage meat mixture, pushing it right down and over sides of breast to keep the meat moist. Try not to pack it too tightly, however, as it does tend to swell. Draw the neck skin over the back, not too tightly, and either sew or fasten it in position with metal skewers or toothpicks.

10 Chestnuts should be stuffed *loosely* into the body cavity. (Any left over can be added to the pan juices to reheat about half-hour before bird is ready to come out of the oven; then strained out of the sauce with a slotted spoon just before serving.) Skewer vent shut.

11 Finishing trussing bird as directed in Step 5 of preceding recipe.

1 medium-sized turkey, about 10 lb dressed weight
Salt and freshly ground black pepper

Sausage meat stuffing
3 oz fat bacon slices
2 level tablespoons butter
4 oz stale trimmed white bread, cut into 1/3-inch cubes
1 lb pork sausage meat
1/2 lb boned pork spare-rib, minced
1 small onion, finely chopped
2 level tablespoons finely chopped parsley
1/4 level teaspoon dried thyme
1/4 level teaspoon dried marjoram
Pinch of dried sage
4 tablespoons turkey giblet (page 118) or chicken stock (page 162)
1 egg, beaten
Salt and freshly ground black pepper

Chestnut stuffing
2 lb chestnuts, peeled and skinned (see page 120)
Turkey giblet or chicken stock (optional)
1–2 tablespoons butter
Salt and freshly ground black pepper

Basting sauce
8 oz butter
1/4 pint turkey giblet or chicken stock

12 Lay bird, breast side up, in a roomy roasting tin. Season generously with salt and freshly ground black pepper, and with a sharp toothpick or skewer, prick the breast skin all over – this too, helps to prevent it bursting should the stuffing swell.

13 Cover bird with butter-soaked muslin and roast as directed in Steps 8–12 of preceding recipe, using remainder of butter mixed with stock as your basting sauce.

14 When turkey is cooked, discard muslin, trussing threads and skewers, and transfer to a hot serving dish. Keep hot in the turned-off oven while you finish gravy.

15 Skim pan juices. You may find this easier to do if you pour them off into a bowl first – see Step 16 of preceding recipe. Return to the roasting tin and bring to the boil, scraping off all the crusty bits from bottom and sides of pan with a wooden spoon.

16 Correct seasoning if necessary. Gravy may also be thickened with a teaspoon of cornflour, worked to a smooth paste with cold water before it is stirred in and brought to the boil.

17 Pour gravy into a hot sauce boat and serve with turkey.

To Peel Chestnuts

There are several ways of tackling this – blanching in boiling water, deep-frying, grilling, roasting in a hot oven – but the following is, to my mind, the most efficient and least messy of them all.

1 With the tip of a small knife, cut a slit in the shell on the rounded side of each chestnut.

2 Heat 3 tablespoons cooking oil in a wide, heavy saucepan.

3 Add enough chestnuts to make more or less a single layer, and sauté over a high heat for about 5 minutes, shaking pan to keep chestnuts on the move and prevent them charring.

4 Transfer chestnuts to a colander with a slotted spoon. Rinse briefly so that they are cool enough to handle.

5 Shell chestnuts and peel away their thin inner skins. They are now ready for cooking.

If you are preparing anything over a pound of chestnuts, you will probably have to fry them off in batches. The oil in the pan will do for several batches.

Allowing for shells, skins and the odd bad or wormy nut, you can on average count on getting $\frac{1}{2}$ lb meat from 1 lb chestnuts.

Sausage and Prune Stuffing for Turkey

(to be started the night before)

1 The night before you intend to make stuffing, put prunes to soak in a bowl of water, and sultanas or raisins in port.

2 The following day, drain and pit prunes.

3 Fry bacon slices in their own fat until crisp. Remove bacon from pan and crumble (or snip with kitchen scissors) into a large bowl.

4 Add olive oil and 1 level tablespoon butter to fat remaining in the pan, and sauté finely chopped onion over a moderate heat, stirring frequently, for 6 to 8 minutes until soft and golden. Drain onion thoroughly with a slotted spoon, pressing with the back of the spoon so that as much fat as possible remains in the pan, and add to bowl.

5 Add a further 2 level tablespoons butter to fat remaining in frying-pan, and heat until frothy. Add bread cubes and toss over a moderate heat until they have absorbed all the fat and are lightly crisp. Add to bowl.

6 Add sausage meat to frying-pan. Sauté gently for 10 to 12 minutes, stirring and crumbling it with a fork so that it turns a uniform beige throughout. Remove to bowl containing prepared ingredients.

7 Pour sultanas (or raisins) together with port into the frying-pan. Bring slowly to boiling point, stirring and scraping pan clean of crusty bits with a wooden spoon. Pour contents of pan into bowl.

8 Add chopped turkey liver, if used, beaten egg, parsley and thyme to bowl, and mix until ingredients are thoroughly blended. Season to taste with salt and freshly ground black pepper. Use as required.

Sufficient stuffing for the breast of a medium-sized turkey (about 10 lb)

6 oz plump prunes

4 oz sultanas or seedless raisins

1/4 pint tawny port

3 slices back bacon, rinds removed

1 tablespoon olive oil

3 level tablespoons butter

1 Spanish onion, finely chopped

4 oz stale white bread, cut into 1/3-inch cubes

12 oz sausage meat

1 turkey liver, chopped (optional)

1 egg, beaten

1 level tablespoon finely chopped parsley

1/2 level teaspoon dried thyme

Salt and freshly ground black pepper

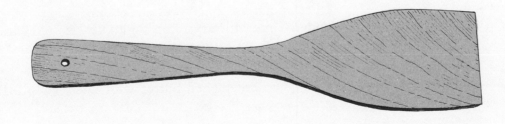

Lesson 4

Vegetable Accompaniments for Roasts and Grills

Boiled New Potatoes

Serves 3–4

1 lb small new potatoes
(20–24)
Coarse salt
Butter

1 Wash potatoes and either scrape them or, if they peel easily, simply rub off a neat band of skin round the middle of each potato with your finger.

2 Put potatoes in a pan. Cover with cold water; add a small handful of salt and bring to the boil.

3 Simmer potatoes until they feel soft when pierced with a fork. The small ones specified in this recipe will take about 18 minutes.

4 Drain well and serve with plenty of butter and coarse salt, to taste.

Boiled New Potatoes and Peas

Serves 4

1 lb small new potatoes
(20–24)
Coarse Salt
1 sprig of mint
1 small pk frozen peas
Butter
Finely chopped parsley

Scrape new potatoes and boil them as above, adding a small sprig of mint to the cooking water. Drain well; add 1 small packet frozen peas, cooked and drained, and 2 to 3 tablespoons melted butter. Turn into a heated serving dish. Garnish with finely chopped parsley and serve immediately.

Boiled Potatoes with Parsley Butter

Serves 4–6

1 1/2 lb potatoes
Salt
2 oz butter, melted
2 level teaspoons finely
chopped parsley
1/2 teaspoon lemon juice

1 Peel potatoes and cook in boiling salted water until just tender. Time will vary according to the size and variety of potato used. Drain, return to pan and toss over gentle heat to evaporate any remaining moisture.

2 Combine hot melted butter with finely chopped parsley and lemon juice.

3 Dress potatoes with hot parsley butter. Turn into a heated dish and serve immediately.

Foil-baked New Potatoes

Serves 4

New potatoes cooked in this way are permeated with a marvellous concentration of flavour and aroma. Try them, too, baked with a sprig of fresh dill instead of the mint.

1 Preheat oven to moderately hot (400°F. Mark 6).

2 Scrape potatoes; wash and dry them thoroughly, and lay them in the centre of a large square of aluminium foil.

3 Bury mint leaves among potatoes. Season to taste with coarse salt and freshly ground black pepper, and dot with butter.

4 Seal potatoes tightly in foil. Lay the packet on a baking sheet.

5 Bake for 1 hour.

6 Undo the parcel – the fragrance will be irresistible. Transfer potatoes to a heated serving dish and serve immediately.

1 lb small new potatoes
4–6 leaves fresh mint
Coarse salt and freshly ground black pepper
2 level tablespoons butter

Whipped (Puréed) Potatoes

Serves 4–6

1 Peel potatoes and, if they are very large, cut them up roughly into even-sized pieces.

2 Boil potatoes in salted water until they feel soft when pierced with a fork, but are not disintegrating. (Overcooked potatoes will produce a water-sodden purée, not a fluffy one as you might expect.)

3 As soon as potatoes are cooked, drain them thoroughly and toss in the dry pan over a moderate heat until remaining moisture has completely evaporated.

4 Mash potatoes to a smooth purée; or rub them through a fine wire sieve and return them to the pan.

5 Gradually beat in hot milk with a wooden spoon. (If potatoes are particularly dry, you may need to use more milk.) Then add melted butter and cream, and continue to beat vigorously until purée is light and fluffy.

6 Season purée to taste with salt, freshly ground black pepper and a grating of fresh nutmeg, and beat over a moderate heat until purée is thoroughly hot again. Take great care not to let purée boil, or it may discolour. Serve immediately.

Note: Although ideally a potato purée should be served as soon as it is prepared, you can keep it hot for up to ½ hour by putting it in a buttered mixing bowl over hot water, covered with well-buttered greaseproof paper. Just before serving, beat purée up again to restore its texture.

2 lb floury potatoes
Salt
1/4 pint hot milk
2 oz butter, melted
3 level tablespoons double cream
Freshly ground black pepper
Freshly grated nutmeg

Serves 4

1 lb potatoes
1 level tablespoon dripping
   or oil
1 level tablespoon butter
Salt and freshly ground black
   pepper

Roast Potatoes

1 Preheat oven to moderately hot (400°F. Mark 6).

2 Peel potatoes and if they are very large, cut them into even-sized chunks each weighing about 2 oz. Wash and dry potatoes thoroughly.

3 Melt dripping or oil and butter in a roasting tin. When fat is almost smoking hot, add potatoes. Turn them over to coat them thoroughly with fat and sprinkle with salt and freshly ground black pepper.

4 Roast potatoes, turning them occasionally, for 35 to 40 minutes, or until they are crisp and golden, and feel soft when pierced with a fork. (Cooking time will vary slightly, depending on the variety and age of potatoes.)

Note: Some people prefer to parboil potatoes for 5 to 7 minutes before roasting them. In this case, use larger pieces; dry them carefully and score them lightly before putting them into the fat.

You will find that parboiling softens the surface of the potatoes slightly, allowing them to absorb the fat better, with the result that they have more of a crust.

Serves 6

6 medium-sized cold,
   previously baked potatoes
4 tablespoons single cream
2 oz softened butter
4–6 level tablespoons
   freshly grated Parmesan
Salt and freshly ground black
   pepper

Cheese-baked Potatoes

1 Preheat oven to moderate (375°F. Mark 5).

2 Cut a thin slice from each potato, and with a spoon, scoop out the pulp into a bowl, leaving a firm shell.

3 Mash potato pulp smoothly with cream, butter and Parmesan, and season with salt and freshly ground black pepper, to taste.

4 Pile potato purée back into shells and place potatoes on a wire rack.

5 Bake for 25 to 30 minutes or until potatoes are thoroughly hot.

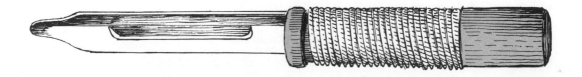

Baked Potato Loaves

Serves 4–6

1 Preheat oven to fairly hot (425°F. Mark 7).

2 Empty packet of instant mashed potato into a bowl. Beat in ¾ pint boiling water and 4 level tablespoons butter.

3 When purée is smooth, beat in egg and 2 level tablespoons Parmesan. Season to taste with salt, freshly ground black pepper and a pinch of garlic salt, if liked.

4 Shape mixture into 8 little loaves of equal size. Cut 2 diagonal slashes on top of each one.

5 Butter a large baking sheet. Arrange loaves on it and brush with melted butter.

6 Sprinkle loaves with a mixture of breadcrumbs and remaining Parmesan.

7 Bake near top of oven for 15 to 20 minutes, or until golden. Serve immediately.

One 5-oz packet (or 5–6 servings) instant mashed potato
Butter
1 egg, beaten
3 level tablespoons grated Parmesan
Salt and freshly ground black pepper
Pinch of garlic salt (optional)
1 level tablespoon white breadcrumbs

Boiled Green Beans

Serves 3–4

Follow this method and you will never again run the risk of overcooking green beans – the most common mistake people make with this delicate vegetable.

1 Top and tail green beans. They should be young enough not to require stringing.

2 Bring a pan of salted water to the boil. Throw in beans; bring to simmering point again and cook gently for 5 minutes, or until beans are just tender, but still slightly crisp to the tooth.

3 Drain; plunge into cold water for 5 minutes and drain again.

4 When ready to serve, season beans generously with salt and freshly ground black pepper, and toss in melted butter until heated through. Serve immediately.

1 lb baby green beans
Salt and freshly ground black pepper
3–4 level tablespoons butter

Green Beans Amandine

Serves 3–4

1 Prepare beans as in master recipe for Boiled Green Beans above.

2 Add toasted slivered almonds and finely chopped parsley to hot buttered beans; toss well and serve immediately.

1 recipe Boiled Green Beans (see above)
1 oz slivered almonds, toasted
2 level tablespoons finely chopped parsley

Herbed Green Beans

Serves 3–4

1 lb baby green beans
Salt
3–4 level tablespoons butter
2 level tablespoons finely chopped chervil
2 level tablespoons finely chopped parsley
1 level tablespoon finely chopped chives
Freshly ground black pepper

1 Top and tail green beans. They should be young enough not to require stringing.

2 Bring a pan of salted water to the boil. Throw in the beans; bring to simmering point again and cook gently for 5 minutes, or until beans are just tender, but still slightly crisp to the tooth.

3 Drain; plunge into cold water for 5 minutes, then drain again.

4 Pound butter with finely chopped herbs and season with a little salt and freshly ground black pepper.

5 When ready to serve, season beans generously with salt and freshly ground black pepper, and simmer in the herb butter until heated through. Serve immediately with the buttery juices poured over.

Boiled Carrots

Preparation Trim tops and tails of carrots. If they are young, you need only scrub or scrape them. Old carrots should be peeled.

Average-size carrots (about 8 to the lb) can be left whole or thinly sliced. Small carrots (the finger-thick ones that come about 28 to the lb) should be left whole.

To Cook Carrots

1 Cover with salted water; bring to the boil and lower heat to a moderate simmer. Cover tightly with a lid and boil gently.

Average-size carrots will be cooked but still slightly crisp after 15 minutes. If you prefer them to be very soft, cook for 3 to 4 minutes longer. *Finger-thick carrots* take 15 minutes, and *thinly sliced ones* only 5 to 8 minutes.

2 To serve: drain thoroughly; toss with melted butter and season to taste with salt, freshly ground black pepper and a pinch of sugar to bring out their natural sweetness. Garnish with chopped parsley and serve immediately.

Glazed Carrots

Serves 4

1 pound small carrots
4 level tablespoons butter
4 tablespoons chicken stock
1 level tablespoon sugar
Salt

1 Scrape carrots; slice thickly and place in a small saucepan; cover with cold water and blanch. Drain.

2 Simmer blanched carrots with butter, chicken stock, sugar and salt to taste, until carrots have absorbed the liquid without burning and have taken on a little colour.

Boiled Spinach

1 Spinach requires meticulous washing, leaf by leaf, to remove every possible speck of sand or grit. Discard any yellowed, pale or blemished leaves as you go, and pull away stems. If they are tender, they will snap off at the base of the leaf; but, if tough, the stem will probably rip away the whole length of the leaf.

2 Shake leaves to get rid of excess moisture – not too energetically – and pack them into a saucepan. Turn heat up fairly high; cover tightly and allow to cook in the water left clinging to the leaves (no salt at this stage).

3 From the moment you hear sizzling noises emanating from the pan, cook for 1 to 2 minutes longer, uncovering pan to turn leaves over with a fork so that the uncooked layer on top takes the place of the cooked leaves underneath. Remove from heat.

4 Drain cooked spinach in a colander, pressing firmly to extract remaining moisture. If desired, chop it up, using two sharp knives scissor-fashion.

5 Return spinach to the dry pan; dress with a little butter and season to taste with salt, freshly ground black pepper and a little freshly grated nutmeg.

6 Stir over a low heat until butter has melted and spinach is thoroughly hot. Serve immediately.

Spinach with Rosemary

1 Melt butter in a heavy pan; add frozen spinach and allow to thaw over a very low heat, stirring occasionally.

2 When spinach has thawed completely, sprinkle with crushed dried rosemary and season to taste with salt and freshly ground black pepper. Cover pan and simmer gently, stirring or shaking pan occasionally, for 10 to 15 minutes longer, or until spinach is tender and fragrant with rosemary.

3 Transfer to a heated serving dish and serve hot.

Note: If using *powdered* rosemary, cut the amount by about half as it is much more concentrated in flavour.

Serves 6

4 level tablespoons butter
4 6-oz packets frozen leaf
  spinach
1–2 level teaspoons crushed
  dried rosemary (see Note)
Salt and freshly ground black
  pepper

2 lb fresh spinach
3 tablespoons salad oil
1 level teaspoon salt
Freshly ground black pepper
A pinch of monosodium
  glutamate
1 tablespoon soy sauce (or
  sake or dry sherry)

Chinese Sautéed Spinach

1 Wash the spinach leaves thoroughly in several changes of water. Discard any yellowed, pale or blemished leaves as you go, and pull away stems. (If they are tender, they will snap off at the base of the leaf; but if tough, the stem will probably rip away the whole length of the leaf.)

2 Drain spinach.

3 Heat oil in a large frying-pan; add spinach, salt, freshly ground black pepper and a pinch of monosodium glutamate and cook over a medium heat for about 3 minutes, stirring constantly.

4 Add the soy sauce (or sake, or dry sherry), to taste.

5 Serve immediately.

Serves 4

1 1/2 lb small brussels sprouts
Salt and freshly ground black
  pepper
2 tablespoons melted butter
Lemon juice

Boiled Brussels Sprouts

1 Cut off stem ends and remove any wilted or damaged outer leaves from small brussels sprouts. (If brussels sprouts are older, remove tough outer leaves entirely.) Nick a small cross in their stems to help them cook evenly.

2 Soak sprouts in cold water with a little salt for 15 minutes. Drain well.

3 Drop sprouts into a large pan of boiling salted water and simmer, uncovered, for 5 minutes. Cover pan and continue to cook for 7 (if very young) to 15 minutes longer, or until sprouts are just tender.

4 Drain well and season generously with salt and freshly ground black pepper. Toss in melted butter and lemon juice to taste, to give added flavour. Serve immediately, topped with a pat of butter.

Boiled Cabbage

For plain boiled cabbage, the simplest method is the best.

Preparation

Loose-leaf green cabbage Strip away outer leaves until you reach the tighter, paler leaves of the inner 'heart'. Trim off exposed stalk, plus a little more. Leave the heart intact.

Wash all the leaves thoroughly in cold water. (A soft brush is good for dislodging remnants of soil.)

Stack half a dozen leaves one on top of the other and roll tightly into a sausage. With a sharp knife (and keeping your fingertips safely tucked under), slice the bundle into strips $\frac{1}{4}$ inch wide. Slice remaining leaves and heart into strips as well.

Crinkle-leaf (Savoy) cabbage This is prepared as loose-leaf cabbage, except that it has more heart. Deal with the outer leaves as above. When you come to the heart, where the leaves do not strip away so readily, trim the stem and slice heart into quarters. Wash cabbage. Cut out the central core from each wedge of heart.

Slice cabbage leaves and heart into strips as above.

White cabbage Trim stem; peel off any bruised or discoloured outer leaves and discard them. Rinse cabbage.

Slice the cabbage in four and cut out the central core from each quarter. Slice cabbage into $\frac{1}{4}$-inch strips.

To Cook Cabbage

1 Bring $\frac{1}{2}$-inch salted water to the boil in a saucepan – medium or large depending on the amount of cabbage to be cooked.

2 Add cabbage strips and bring to the boil again. Cover pan with a tight-fitting lid.

3 Continue to cook until cabbage is tender but still on the crisp side, with plenty of 'bite'. *Loose-leaf and white cabbage* will take no more than 5 minutes; *crinkle-leaf cabbage* even less, between 3 and 4 minutes.

4 Drain cabbage.

5 Melt a lump of butter in the hot, dry pan. Return cabbage to pan and toss with a fork, adding more salt and plenty of freshly ground black pepper, to taste. Serve immediately, topped with more butter if desired.

Courgettes au Beurre

1 Wipe courgettes clean and peel thin strips off them lengthwise with a potato peeler so that you have alternating bands of white and green.

2 Drop courgettes into a pan of cold salted water; bring to the boil, cover and simmer for just 5 minutes. Drain thoroughly.

3 In a large sauté pan or a deep, heavy frying-pan with a lid, heat butter until it just begins to bubble. Lay courgettes in it side by side in one layer; cover and simmer for 5 to 10 minutes, shaking pan occasionally, until courgettes are tender but not disintegrating and a deep golden colour all over.

Serves 4–6

2 lb (12 small) courgettes
Salt
4 level tablespoons butter
Coarse salt and freshly
  ground black pepper
Finely chopped parsley

4 Season courgettes with coarse salt and freshly ground black pepper. Transfer to a heated serving dish; pour over some of the butter in which they were simmered, and sprinkle with finely chopped parsley. Serve immediately.

French Peas

Serves 4

1–1 1/4 lb frozen peas
4 level tablespoons butter
4 tablespoons chicken stock
   made with a cube
1 level tablespoon sugar
Salt
Lettuce leaves, to garnish

1 Put peas in a small pan; cover with cold water and bring to the boil over a high heat. As soon as water boils, drain peas thoroughly and return them to the pan.

2 Add butter and chicken stock; season to taste with sugar and salt, and simmer gently, shaking pan occasionally, until liquid has been absorbed and peas are tender.

3 Serve on a bed of lettuce leaves.

Peas au Beurre

Serves 4

1 lb frozen peas
4 level tablespoons butter
4 tablespoons chicken stock
Salt and freshly ground black
   pepper
Lemon juice

1 Place peas in a small saucepan. Add just enough cold water to cover and bring to the boil. Remove from the heat and drain.

2 Replace peas in the saucepan with butter and chicken stock. Season with a little salt and freshly ground black pepper. Simmer, half-covered with a saucepan lid, until the liquid is almost all absorbed and the peas are tender.

3 Serve with pan juices and a little lemon juice sprinkled over.

Note: You can add 2 or 3 spring onions, finely chopped, in Step 2, for extra flavour.

Boiled Cauliflower

Preparation Trim off the base of a cauliflower, taking the remains of the outer leaves with it. Leave the fine, light green leaves intact. Using a potato peeler, hollow out the stem about 2 inches deep.

Immerse cauliflower, head down, in a bowl of cold salted water.

To Cook Cauliflower

1 Select a saucepan one size larger than the cauliflower. Pour in ½-inch salted water and bring to the boil.

2 Lower cauliflower stem end down into boiling water. Bring back to the boil again before covering pan with a tight-fitting lid.

An average-sized cauliflower (about $1\frac{1}{2}$ lb) will be cooked to perfection – tender but with a slight crispness still in evidence – in 15 minutes, but you may prefer it a little softer.

3 Carefully remove cauliflower to a colander to drain while you melt some butter in the hot dry pan.

4 To serve: arrange cauliflower in a heated serving dish. Pour over melted butter and serve immediately.

Cauliflower Cheese

1 and **2** Prepare and cook cauliflower as directed in the master recipe.

3 While cauliflower is cooking, prepare cheese sauce: melt butter in a heavy pan; blend in flour smoothly with a wooden spoon and stir over a low heat for 2 minutes to make a pale *roux*.

4 Gradually add milk, stirring vigorously to prevent lumps forming; bring to the boil, stirring, and simmer for 4 or 5 minutes until sauce no longer tastes of raw flour.

5 Beat in cheese over a low heat until melted; add mustard and season to taste with salt and freshly ground black pepper. Keep hot.

6 Drain cauliflower thoroughly and lay it in a deep, heated serving dish. Mask with hot cheese sauce and sprinkle with toasted almonds or buttered breadcrumbs. Serve immediately.

Serves 4–6

1 recipe Boiled Cauliflower (see opposite)
2–3 level tablespoons chopped toasted almonds or buttered breadcrumbs

Cheese sauce
1 oz butter
1 oz flour
1/2 pint milk
4 oz mature Cheddar, grated
1/2 level teaspoon French mustard
Salt and freshly ground black pepper

Grilled Aubergines

Good with lamb especially.

Serves 6 as a vegetable, or 3 as an appetiser

3 medium-sized fat ripe
  aubergines
Salt
3 cloves garlic, slivered
Freshly ground black pepper
2 tablespoons olive oil
2 level tablespoons freshly
  grated Gruyère

1 Wash aubergines and wipe them dry. Trim off stem ends and cut each aubergine in half lengthwise. Score cut surfaces deeply with a sharp knife and rub them with salt. Leave aubergines, cut sides down, for at least 30 minutes to allow salt to draw out bitter juices.

2 Drain aubergines thoroughly, squeezing them lightly to get rid of as much excess moisture as possible. Wipe them dry with kitchen paper.

3 Push garlic slivers into scores made in the cut surface. Sprinkle with freshly ground black pepper.

4 Place aubergine halves, cut sides up, in a grill-pan, and sprinkle each half with a teaspoon of olive oil and one of freshly grated Gruyère.

5 Grill slowly for 15 to 20 minutes, or until aubergines are soft through and golden brown on top. Serve immediately.

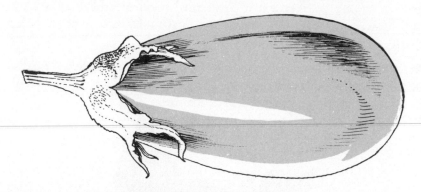

Harvard Beets

Serves 4–6

2 level teaspoons cornflour
2 1/2 oz sugar
1/2 level teaspoon salt
1/8 level teaspoon freshly
  ground black pepper
4 tablespoons orange juice
3 tablespoons wine vinegar
4–6 tablespoons cold water
  or beetroot liquid
1 lb small cooked or canned
  beetroot, thinly sliced
1 level tablespoon butter

1 In a heavy saucepan, mix cornflour with sugar, salt and freshly ground black pepper. Add orange juice, vinegar and water or beetroot liquid, and stir until smooth.

2 Cook cornflour mixture over a low heat, stirring constantly, for 3 to 4 minutes until sauce is smooth and thick, and no longer tastes of cornflour.

3 Add sliced beetroot and heat through gently. Stir in butter just before serving. Serve hot.

Basic Green Salad

When making a basic green salad the quality of one's oil and vinegar are of the utmost importance. I like a fruity olive taste in my olive oil and prefer the oils from Provence or Tunisia for salads. If, for some reason, the oil which I am using is not fruity enough, I soak ripe olives in it for a day or two to give it body. If you prefer a lighter oil, use corn oil or arachide.

Second most important fact in salad making is the choice of the right wine vinegar. There are many commercial varieties available in the better food departments of our major stores. It is merely a matter of experiment until you find the right one for you. I prefer a red wine vinegar, with not too sharp a bite and, having found it, I stuff two or three sprigs of fresh tarragon into it to give it a wonderful tarragon flavour.

There are several schools of thought on the care and handling of salad greens. Purists like to wash the leaves in cold water and then to dry the salad with a clean tea towel, leaf by leaf, thereby assuring that no excess liquids will dilute the precious salad dressing.

Other salad buffs prefer to wash their greens in cold water and then drain them dry in a wire salad basket, in which they are shaken lightly to remove excess moisture. In either case, the leaves are best refrigerated until crisp before serving.

I usually break or tear large salad leaves such as Cos as I feel that torn or broken leaves never take on an unattractive brown edge.

When making salads at the table don't overlook the drama of handsome accessories – a giant bowl, spoon and fork for tossing the salad, small individual bowls for the different salad ingredients to be used, attractive olive oil and wine vinegar cruets, a tall pepper mill and salt mill . . . and, of course, chilled plates for the salad itself to be served on.

Toss is really just a turn of phrase. One should really 'roll' the salad when mixing it. With salad spoon in your right hand, fork in your left, go down to the bottom of your salad bowl with one tool while going up and over with the other. Roll the salad in this way until every leaf shines with dressing.

Cos lettuce, endive, chicory, young tender spinach leaves, watercress, fennel, celery, green pepper and avocado pear make wonderful additives to a green salad.

Chef's flavour tricks Sprinkle a little salt in a wooden salad bowl; mash a garlic clove into salt with the back of a wooden spoon.

Be adventurous Keep a salad tray of wine and herb vinegars, oils and seasonings handy for your salads. Then all you have to do is add your finely chopped fresh herbs and garnishes and you are ready to be a salad *chef par excellence*!

Tossed Green Salad

Serves 4–6

1–2 heads lettuce
French Dressing (below)

1 Wash lettuce leaves well in a large quantity of water.

2 Drain well and dry thoroughly in a cloth or a salad basket so that there is no water on them to dilute the dressing.

3 To serve; pour French Dressing into salad bowl and arrange prepared lettuce leaves on top. At the table, give a final toss to the ingredients to ensure that every leaf is glistening with dressing. Check seasoning and serve.

Green Salad Variations

1 Add other salad greens in season – Cos lettuce, endive, chicory, batavia, young spinach leaves, watercress and French mâche (corn salad).

2 Add finely chopped garlic or shallots, or a combination of the two, to salad dressing.

3 Add fresh green herbs – finely chopped chervil, basil, tarragon or chives – to the dressing.

4 For crunch appeal, add diced celery, green pepper or fennel.

5 Add sliced or diced peeled avocado pear which you have tossed in lemon juice to preserve colour.

Basic French Dressing - Vinaigrette Sauce

1 tablespoon lemon juice
1–2 tablespoons wine vinegar
1/4 teaspoon dry mustard
Coarse salt and freshly
    ground black pepper
6–8 tablespoons olive oil

1 Combine lemon juice, wine vinegar and dry mustard in a bowl.

2 Season to taste with coarse salt and freshly ground black pepper.

3 Add olive oil, and beat with a fork until mixture emulsifies.

Bohemian Dressing

1 Blend mustard, salt and castor sugar to a smooth paste with tarragon vinegar.

2 Stir in next four ingredients and put aside for 1 hour.

3 Remove garlic clove.

4 Add olive oil, a tablespoon at a time, beating with a fork until dressing emulsifies.

Makes just under ½ pint

1/2 level teaspoon dry mustard

1/2 level teaspoon salt

1/4 level teaspoon castor sugar

3 tablespoons tarragon vinegar

1 level teaspoon finely chopped shallot

1 level teaspoon finely chopped parsley

1/2 level teaspoon finely chopped tarragon

1 clove garlic, lightly crushed

9 tablespoons olive oil

Champagne Dressing

A nonchalant dressing to whisk up before your guests on a champagne occasion.

1 Combine olive oil and lemon juice in a small bowl or jug, and beat with a fork until they form an emulsion. Season to taste with salt and freshly ground black pepper.

2 Beat in iced champagne a little at a time so as not to destroy the emulsion, and use immediately. Dressing loses its 'kick' and emulsion tends to separate after 10 to 15 minutes.

Enough for 2 large lettuces

8 tablespoons olive oil

1 tablespoon lemon juice

Salt and freshly ground black pepper

8 tablespoons iced champagne

Honey Dressing

1 Combine olive oil with white wine vinegar, and beat with a fork until they form an emulsion.

2 Add honey and beat again until thoroughly blended.

3 Season to taste with salt, freshly ground black pepper and a generous pinch of dry mustard.

Makes about ¼ pint

6–8 tablespoons olive oil

2 tablespoons white wine vinegar

1 level tablespoon clear honey

Salt and freshly ground black pepper

Generous pinch of dry mustard

Lesson 5

Super Sweets that are Simple to Make

I find it amusing that some of the most popular sweets served in my restaurant – provoking a minor riot among our regular customers if they are taken even temporarily off the menu – are the ones that any novice cook could make without turning a hair. This surely proves my point, if proof were needed, that a simple little sweet can, in the right circumstances, give more pleasure than the richest, most ambitious creation of a talented pastry-cook. Indeed, there are times when a bowl of fresh fruit, perfectly ripe and unblemished, is all you need to round off a meal.

Later on in this course we shall explore the vast world of tarts and pies, ice creams and moulded sweets, elegant crêpes and traditional family puddings. But for the moment, let us concentrate on fruit, how to whip up a cream or mousse, and how to handle a classic egg custard. With just these simple techniques mastered, you will have an impressive repertoire of sweets at your finger-tips.

How to Serve Fresh Fruit

A bowl of apples, pears, oranges, grapes – the most common everyday fruits – become a dish fit for a king when a little trouble is taken over their choice and presentation. I would far rather be served a perfectly ripe apple, fragrant, crisp and unblemished, than some expensive, out-of-season curiosity that had been forced to maturity before its time and flown in from some distant corner of the globe.

There is nothing to stop you serving fresh fruit as the finale to a formal meal either. Fruits that would normally be washed – apples and plums, for example, but not peaches, apricots or bananas – look stunning if presented half-submerged in a bowl of cold water set over cracked ice.

Small (sharp) knives and forks should be provided, a sifter of castor sugar, a dish of lemon wedges for those who want them, and a small pair of scissors to cut off individual bunches of grapes. If you possess a set of finger-bowls, here is your chance to use them. The water should be lukewarm with a thin slice of lemon or a single red rose petal floating on the surface.

Fruit Salads

Let the season dictate your choice of fruits for a mixed salad. With the selection available to us all year round, it should rarely be necessary to fall back on canned or frozen varieties. Keep those as an emergency standby for adding a touch of colour or glamour when the choice of fresh fruit is limited, never as a major component. A fresh fruit salad should rely on *fresh* fruit – canned and frozen fruit come into their own in the Baked Fruit Compote on page 143.

Making a fruit salad is no excuse for using unripe fruit, and fruit past its prime. A few blemishes won't matter, but select for flavour as carefully as if you were serving the fruit whole. If you use oversoft fruit, it is likely to turn spongy as it absorbs the syrup and juices from its companions.

Give some thought, too, to the colours in your salad and liven it up with touches of strong colour – bright red cherries, sharp green or purple grapes. If all else fails, you can slice in an unpeeled red apple.

To prepare fruit for a salad Before you start any peeling or slicing, squeeze plenty of lemon juice into a medium-sized bowl (2 lemons for a large portion should be enough). It is usually most convenient to use the serving bowl for assembling the salad, so get that out as well. A pastry brush for painting the cut surfaces of fruit too fragile to be tossed in lemon juice will come in useful. And remember to use a knife that will not be affected by the acids in the fruit: either silver, silver-plated or stainless steel.

Citrus fruit Start your preparation by peeling and segmenting your oranges, grapefruit, etc., into the serving bowl (see pages 31 and 32). Their acid juices will help the lemon in preserving the colour of fruits prone to discolouration.

Apples and pears should be quartered, peeled, cored and thinly sliced straight into the bowl of lemon juice. Toss thoroughly to ensure surfaces are all coated with the juice and leave for 10 to 15 minutes. Then transfer to the serving bowl with a slotted spoon, leaving behind the lemon juice to use with the next fruit.

Grapes If they are small, leave them whole. Large grapes with tough skins – white ones are tougher than black – and pips

should be peeled, halved and seeded. Drop them straight into the serving bowl.

Peaches must be peeled. The method is similar to that used for peeling tomatoes. Put a couple of peaches in a sieve and pour enough boiling water over them to loosen their skins. Then peel peaches, holding them in a soft cloth to protect your fingers and avoid bruising the fruit. Cut them in half; remove stones and slice peaches lengthwise into lemon juice. They must be coated with lemon juice as quickly as possible as they soon start to turn brown. Use the pastry brush if you are afraid of crushing the slices.

Apricots are treated like peaches.

Plums have tough, unpleasant skins and should be peeled. Loosen the skins first by dipping the fruit for, say, 60 seconds in boiling water, not much longer or the plum will become mushy. Peel, cut in half and remove stones. If the plums are large, they should be quartered. Some varieties may discolour slightly. To be on the safe side, brush them with lemon juice before adding them to the serving bowl.

Melon Cut thick segments; scrape out seeds and cut the fruit out of its rind with a sharp knife. Slice segments horizontally into the serving bowl. Alternatively, you can take a large chunk of melon, scrape out all the seeds and scoop the flesh out with a melon baller.

Pineapple A fresh pineapple is cut up into small pieces (otherwise known by the coy name of 'tidbits') in the same way as a melon, only instead of scraping out the seeds, you must cut out the woody core that runs down the centre.

Cherries Rinse and dry them. Remove stems and use a gadget specially designed for cherries (and olives) to punch out stones.

Currants – red, black or white – should be picked over carefully for stems, and if necessary, rinsed in a colander and shaken dry.

Bananas Use firm, unbruised fruit. Peel off skins and slice fruit into rounds. Bananas discolour easily, so brush surfaces thoroughly with lemon juice as soon as they are cut. Add bananas to fruit salad just before serving.

Strawberries, raspberries, etc. Strawberries must be hulled, but neither they, nor similar soft fruit like raspberries or blackberries, should be washed unless absolutely necessary.

If you are doubtful about some strawberries, try the following method of cleaning them, which is less drastic than washing:

lay the fruit on a damp kitchen towel; roll the towel up loosely, twist the ends to prevent the fruit falling out and, holding the cloth straight but not taut by its two ends, shake it up, down and sideways several times. Any particles of sand or soil will transfer themselves to the cloth, yet the fruit will remain dry. Add ripe strawberries and raspberries to fruit just before serving.

To dress a fruit salad Fruit for a salad should always be dressed well ahead of time and allowed to macerate for several hours before serving. The only exceptions are bananas, which turn slimy and unpleasant if left soaking too long, and delicate soft fruits like strawberries and raspberries, which sometimes acquire a pulpy 'defrosted' look. For this reason, they should be tossed into the bowl just before serving.

There are several ways of dressing a fruit salad. You can use a simple sugar and water syrup combined with fruit juice and/or wine and/or liqueur.

Pour it over prepared fruits, turning them gently until they are thoroughly mixed. Cover the bowl with foil and leave to macerate in the bottom of the refrigerator for 2 or 3 hours, longer if possible.

On the other hand, it seems a shame to add water to fruits which, given time, will release plenty of pure, natural juice of their own. If you layer the fruit in the bowl with siftings of icing sugar, some fresh orange juice and/or wine to start the ball rolling, and a sprinkling of liqueur – just enough to enhance the flavour of the fruit without overwhelming it – between each layer, then leave the bowl, covered with foil, in the bottom of the refrigerator for at least 6 hours, the fruits themselves will provide an abundant syrup, fragrant and fresh-tasting as only natural juices can be.

To serve fruit salad Just before serving, you can decorate the salad with a few chopped nuts – almonds, walnuts or pistachio nuts – or shredded coconut, to give some texture contrast.

Serve fruit salads very cold, but not chilled, or a lot of their fragrance will be lost. They look best in glass bowls or coupes, very pretty in large goblets.

Many people like cream with a fruit salad – I prefer it on its own, with perhaps just a dish of delicate biscuits to accompany it.

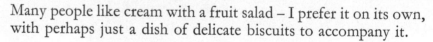

Minted Apples

1 Sprinkle raisins with 1 tablespoon crème de menthe in a cup and leave to soak until needed.

2 Peel and core apples, leaving them whole.

3 Combine sugar and lemon juice with ¾ pint water in a wide, heavy pan. Stir over a moderate heat until sugar has dissolved; then flavour syrup with remaining crème de menthe and deepen colour slightly if necessary with a drop or two of green food colouring.

4 Poach apples in the syrup for 5 to 7 minutes, or until just tender, turning them once or twice.

5 Transfer apples to a serving dish with a slotted spoon.

6 Combine soaked raisins with chopped almonds. Fill centre of each apple with this mixture. Allow to cool.

7 Boil poaching liquid until reduced to a light syrup (225°F. on a sugar thermometer). Cool slightly.

8 Spoon syrup over each apple to cover it with a delicate green glaze. Chill until ready to serve.

Serve 1 or 2 apples per person

4 level tablespoons raisins or sultanas

3–4 tablespoons crème de menthe

8 tart dessert apples

1/2 lb sugar

Juice of **2** lemons

Green food colouring (optional)

6 level tablespoons chopped blanched almonds

Banana Flambé

Simple but very spectacular and rich in flavour. Take care not to let the bananas become mushy.

1 Peel bananas. Brush each one with lemon juice as soon as you peel it to avoid discolouration; then leave to absorb lemon flavour for a few minutes.

2 Melt butter in a large, heavy frying-pan into which bananas will fit side by side; add orange juice, grated orange rind and sugar. Stir over a low heat until sugar has dissolved.

3 Arrange bananas side by side in the pan and brown them gently all over, taking care not to burn sauce or overcook bananas.

4 Remove pan from heat; pour over rum and immediately set a match to it.

5 Serve as soon as the flames have died down.

Serves 4

4 large bananas or 8 small ones

Juice of 1/2–1 lemon

1 oz butter

Juice and finely grated rind of 1 orange

1 oz castor sugar

1–2 tablespoons rum

1 large ripe pineapple
6 level tablespoons icing
 sugar
3 tablespoons Cointreau
3 tablespoons rum
1/2 pint double cream
3 tablespoons Kirsch
Coarsely grated rind of 1
 orange

Pineapple Romanoff

1 Slice top off pineapple.

2 With a long, thin, sharp kitchen knife, cut all around the inside of the pineapple from the cut end about a third of an inch in, taking great care not to damage shell. Then cut flesh into four segments to make it easier to handle, and scoop out carefully, leaving shell intact. Put the shell aside.

3 Dice pineapple flesh and toss segments in a bowl with 4 level tablespoons icing sugar. Pour over them a mixture of Cointreau and rum. Cover bowl and put in the refrigerator to chill.

4 One hour before serving: whip cream until soft peaks form. Sweeten with remaining icing sugar and flavour with Kirsch.

5 Spoon whipped cream into macerated pineapple, tossing until every chunk is coated with creamy liqueur mixture.

6 Pile into pineapple shell – or into individual dishes – and dust with coarsely grated orange rind. Keep cold until time to serve.

Serves 8

8 firm ripe dessert pears
8 oz sugar
Thinly pared strip of lemon
 peel
Vanilla essence
3/4–1 pint vanilla ice cream

Chocolate sauce
6 oz bitter chocolate
2 oz butter
6 level tablespoons double
 cream
6 tablespoons single cream
Vanilla essence (optional)

Pears 'Belle Hélène'

1 Preheat oven to moderate (350°F. Mark 4).

2 Peel, halve and core pears, and arrange them in one layer in a large baking dish, flat side down.

3 Combine sugar and lemon peel with $\frac{3}{4}$ pint water in a heavy pan. Bring to the boil, stirring until sugar has melted, and flavour to taste with vanilla essence.

4 Pour syrup over pears; cover dish tightly with foil and bake for 15 to 20 minutes, or until pears are tender but not disintegrating.

5 With a slotted spoon or fish slice, transfer pears carefully to a large, shallow dish.

6 Pour syrup into a pan; boil until reduced to a quarter of the original volume; then strain over pears. Cool and chill until ready to serve.

7 Meanwhile, prepare chocolate sauce: stir chocolate with butter over hot water until smoothly melted. Gradually beat in double and single cream; then bring to the boil and simmer over direct heat for 2 to 3 minutes, stirring constantly. Flavour to taste with a few drops of vanilla essence if liked.

(**Note**: This simple sauce may be cooled and reheated just before serving. If it should curdle, you can restore the emulsion by beating in a tablespoon of cold water.)

8 To serve: place a scoop of ice cream in each of 8 individual coupes. Press a pear half gently to either side of each scoop of ice cream and glaze with a little of the remaining syrup. Serve hot chocolate sauce separately.

Boiled Fruit Compote

Serves 6

1 Preheat oven to moderate (350°F. Mark 4).

2 Rinse fruit and place in a baking dish with 2 pints boiling water. Cover dish tightly with foil and bake for 1 to 1¼ hours, or until fruit is plump and soft.

3 Pour off cooking juices into a pan. Add sugar, grated orange rind and lemon juice, to taste, and stir over a low heat until sugar has dissolved; then simmer for 5 minutes.

4 Pour syrup over fruit in a serving dish. Add orange slices and chill until ready to serve.

5 Just before serving, sprinkle with slivered almonds.

12 oz mixed dried fruit: apricots, peaches, apples, figs, prunes, raisins or sultanas
3 level tablespoons sugar
2 level teaspoons finely grated orange rind
Juice of 1 lemon
1 orange, peeled and thinly sliced
1 oz blanched almonds, slivered

Baked Fruit Compote

Serves 6

1 Cover prunes with strong hot tea and leave to soak for 4 hours before assembling compote. Defrost raspberries, following directions on packet.

2 Drain peach halves, greengages and lychees, reserving their syrup. Slice lychees and put them aside until just before serving compote. Drain loganberries and soaked prunes.

3 In a large glass serving bowl, combine peach halves with greengages, prunes, raspberries and loganberries, mixing very gently to avoid crushing fruit.

4 Combine peach, greengage and lychee syrup; measure out ¼ pint and flavour to taste with brandy. Pour over fruits in the bowl and chill until ready to serve.

5 Just before serving, sprinkle compote with slices of lychee and the toasted, slivered almonds.

18 large dried prunes
1/2 pint strong hot tea
One 8 oz packet frozen raspberries
One 13 oz can peach halves
One 13 oz can greengages
One 7 3/4 oz can lychees
One 7 1/2 oz can loganberries
1–2 tablespoons brandy
2 oz blanched slivered almonds, toasted

Serves 6

1 1/2 lb ripe red cherries
2 punnets ripe strawberries
1 punnet red currants
2 punnets ripe raspberries
Cognac
Lemon juice
Icing sugar
Raspberry purée (see below)

Serves 6

2 punnets fresh raspberries
2–3 tablespoons lemon juice
2–3 level tablespoons icing
   sugar

Serves 4–6

3 slices fresh pineapple
4 tablespoons Kirsch
3 large, juicy oranges
3/4 pint double cream
4–6 oz Barbados sugar

Red Fruit Bowl with Raspberry Purée

1 Pit cherries; hull strawberries; strip red currants from their stalks.

2 In a glass bowl, combine prepared fruit with raspberries. Flavour to taste with cognac, lemon juice and sifted icing sugar, tossing fruit gently to avoid crushing them, and chill for at least 30 minutes before serving.

3 Serve accompanied by a bowl of chilled raspberry purée.

Raspberry Purée

Wash fresh raspberries and rub through a fine sieve (or purée in an electric blender, then rub through a sieve). Flavour to taste with lemon juice and icing sugar. Chill.

Fruit in a Blanket

A deliciously simple sweet which you can vary to your heart's delight by using other combinations of fresh fruits in season, flavouring them with a suitable liqueur in place of the Kirsch. Soft summer fruit tossed in Grand Marnier or sliced fresh peaches in brandy are magnificent served 'in a blanket'.

1 Cut pineapple slices into eighths. Sprinkle with Kirsch and leave to macerate while you prepare oranges.

2 Using a razor-sharp knife, and working over a dish to catch juices, peel oranges right down to the flesh, taking all the white pith and membrane away with the peel. Slice oranges horizontally, discarding any pips as you come across them; then cut slices into quarters.

3 In a glass serving bowl, toss pineapple and orange pieces together with their juices.

4 Whip cream until just stiff enough to hold its shape. Spread thickly over fruit, smoothing out top with back of spoon. Chill until ready to serve.

5 Just before serving, cover cream with a thick, even layer of Barbados sugar and chill until ready to serve.

Creams and Custards

There seem to be whole generations of cooks to whom the word 'custard' still signifies a packet of cornflour dyed a virulent shade of yellow that I defy any chicken to match. How sad and how unnecessary. It can't be explained by economy either, for in these days of spiralling costs, the price of eggs is one of the few items on the grocery bill that has held down tolerably well.

Learning how to make a real egg custard is a basic cooking technique that you will employ time and again, not only in the recipes that follow in this lesson, but also for making fillings for cakes and tarts, Bavarian cream (a custard and whipped cream concoction set with gelatine to make it firm enough to unmould – see page 553), ice creams of all kinds, and indeed every time you use eggs to thicken a dish, be it savoury or sweet.

Custards can be divided into two main categories:

1 Egg custard (Crème Anglaise) A custard mixture thickened exclusively with egg yolks is bound to curdle if allowed to get too hot or subjected to a rapid change in temperature. The yolks simply scramble. On the other hand, a custard will not thicken unless allowed to reach a certain temperature. The answer is to filter the heat so that the temperature rises very gradually, giving you time to make up your mind when the mixture has had enough and remove it from the heat. When a custard is cooked on top of the stove, a double saucepan will protect it (page 146).

For baked custards such as the classic Crème Caramel (page 149), use a *bain-marie*: stand the baking dish in a roasting tin or some other fairly deep oven pan and pour in hot water to come about half-way up the sides of the dish containing the custard. Provided the oven heat is kept low enough so that the water surrounding the dish does not boil, your custard will set perfectly smooth.

2 Egg and starch custard A custard mixture that contains an appreciable amount of starch (flour, cornflour or potato flour, for example) can safely be boiled. Indeed, people often make the mistake of not boiling it long enough to cook away the raw taste of the starch.

The classic example of an egg and starch custard is *crème pâtissière* or confectioner's custard, used when a rather firm mixture is required to layer in a cake, or to act as a filling for a French fruit tart (see page 443).

Note: In the recipe for *Crème Anglaise* on page 148, a teaspoon of cornflour is suggested as an additional safeguard which will allow you to take the custard a few degrees higher without fear of curdling. Although the custard is not boiled, there is no danger of the cornflour leaving a raw taste provided you do not exceed the amount specified in the recipe.

How to use a double saucepan If you are at all serious about cooking, I would thoroughly recommend you to get a double saucepan. True, every cook should be prepared to improvise, but your life will be made considerably easier if you are not forced to perform a complicated balancing act with two badly fitting pans at the same time as you are trying to concentrate on cooking a delicate sauce.

It is sometimes said that a heavy single saucepan is just as effective, provided you keep the heat under it low enough but, unless you can recognise all the warning signs, you may not be fast enough to whisk it off the heat in time.

A double saucepan has rounded sides, allowing your spoon to get into the corners easily, whereas your ordinary heavy pan may not, with the result that, unless you take great care, part of the mixture coagulates before the rest has thickened.

● Always make sure that the top half of the pan is clear of the water below. This is simply done: make sure the base of the top half is dry; fit the two together, then take them apart again and check that the base of the top part is still dry.

● Before fitting the pans together again, bring the water in the bottom part to the boil and lower heat to a mere simmer.

● Pour the mixture to be cooked into the top part; fit the two together again and cook as directed in your recipe, keeping the mixture constantly on the move with a wooden spoon, especially on the base and around the edges.

To make an egg custard Scalding, whisking, coating and curdling are the operative words here. Once you understand their meaning, you should have no trouble in making a simple egg custard.

Scalding Start by scalding the milk. If you are using a double saucepan, pour the milk into the top half and place it over gentle, *direct* heat. Leave it until surface just begins to tremble, and as it were, 'gathers up its strength' to rise. As soon as you see this happening, lift the pan off the heat to prevent it coming to the boil.

● Be careful, especially if your pan is thin, not to scorch the milk. Nothing can camouflage the taste of scorched milk and you will have to throw it out and start again.

● If you are flavouring your custard with a vanilla pod, split it open and scald it together with the milk. Then, for maximum flavour, draw the pan aside, cover it and let the milk infuse with the pod for a further 15 minutes. The pod can then be fished out, wiped dry and stored in a tightly stoppered jar until you need it again.

Whisking While the milk is heating gently, combine the egg yolks and sugar in a bowl large enough to hold them *and* the milk comfortably. If you are adding a little cornflour, this must be blended thoroughly with the dry sugar *before* you add the egg yolks; otherwise, when it comes into contact with the wet egg, the cornflour tends to form little pockets that no amount of whisking will disperse.

Beat the yolks and sugar together with a whisk until light and thick enough to leave a trail on the surface when the beaters are lifted. Make sure that there are no tell-tale specks of undissolved sugar left in the mixture either.

Now start adding the hot milk to the beaten egg mixture in a thin stream, whisking vigorously to lower the overall temperature and prevent the yolks curdling from the shock of sudden contact with heat. Stop whisking as soon as the two are smoothly blended. If you beat in too much froth, you will make it difficult to judge when the custard starts coating the back of your spoon.

Pour mixture into the top of a double saucepan and fit it over the bottom part.

Coating Now comes the most critical part of the operation. Stir the mixture steadily and patiently over lightly simmering water. The first sign that something is happening is a tendency for the liquid to splash less and turn rather sluggish. Start lifting out the spoon occasionally and holding it rounded side up. The custard is cooked when a distinct coating adheres to the wood. Test it by drawing your finger quickly down the coated spoon. The sides of the trail should remain quite distinct. If they flow together again, carry on cooking and stirring for a little while longer.

As soon as the custard has thickened sufficiently, remove the top part of the pan from the heat and plunge its base into cold water to arrest the cooking process. Carry on stirring for a minute or two longer until the temperature has come down to a safe level.

Curdling The most expert cook will occasionally curdle a custard, but if it is caught soon enough, it can just about be saved. The first warning signs are a vague, soft lumpiness, practically imperceptible, and a faint watery texture appearing around the outside rim of the pan. If you see this happen, don't hesitate: plunge the base of the pan in cold water and whisk the custard as hard as you can. If you are lucky, this will restore its smoothness, or you may at least succeed in preventing the curds getting larger. If not, then I am afraid you have no alternative but to start again.

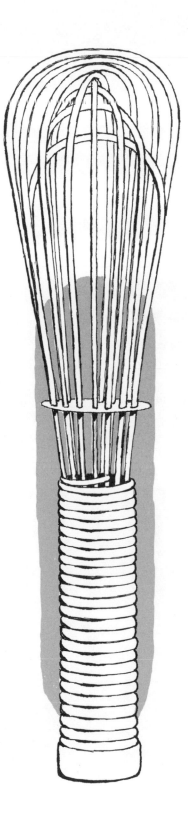

To finish custard *If the custard is to be served hot,* beat in flavourings, strain through a fine sieve into a bowl; cover and keep hot over warm (*not* boiling, *nor* simmering) water until ready to serve.

If custard is to be served cold, strain it through a fine sieve. Pour into a jug or bowl and allow to cool, stirring frequently to prevent a skin forming on top. Then chill until ready to serve. By cooling the custard in a narrow-necked jug you minimise the area on which a skin could form.

● Chocolate or instant coffee should be added before straining, while the custard is still hot enough to melt them.

● Liqueurs or essences should not be added until the custard is more or less at the temperature at which it is to be served, as their strength (of flavour) varies quite considerably according to whether the custard is hot or cold.

Crème Anglaise

Makes ½ pint

3/4 pint milk
4 egg yolks
1–2 oz castor sugar
1 level teaspoon cornflour (optional)
Flavouring (see method)

This light custard sauce makes a delicious alternative to whipped cream for serving with ice cream, fruit-based desserts and other creams or moulds. If you are worried about curdling the custard, add the cornflour as a safeguard.

1 Pour milk into the top of double saucepan and bring to the boil over direct heat.

2 Whisk egg yolks with sugar and cornflour, if used, until thick and creamy. Add boiling milk gradually, beating vigorously.

3 Return mixture to top of double saucepan and cook over simmering water, stirring constantly, until custard coats back of spoon. Take great care not to let it reach boiling point or the egg yolks will curdle. As soon as custard has thickened, plunge base of pan into cold water to prevent further cooking.

4 Strain custard and stir in flavouring.

5 If custard is to be served hot, serve immediately, or keep hot by placing pan in *warm* water. Otherwise, pour custard into a jug and allow to cool, stirring occasionally to prevent a skin forming on the surface; then cover jug and chill until ready to serve.

Flavourings A classic *Crème Anglaise* is flavoured with vanilla, but liqueur or strong coffee may also be used. For a chocolate *crème*, melt about 2 oz bitter chocolate in the milk before adding it to the egg yolks, and use only 1 oz sugar in the basic recipe.

Crème Caramel

A caramel cream should be smooth and limpid in texture with not a bubble in evidence when you cut through it.

1 Preheat oven to moderate (350°F. Mark 4).

2 Combine milk and cream in a pan with vanilla pod and castor sugar, and bring to the boil. Remove pan from heat; cover and leave to infuse for 5 to 10 minutes.

3 Meanwhile, beat whole eggs with the egg yolk lightly in a large bowl.

4 Remove vanilla pod from milk (it can be wiped dry and stored in a stoppered jar for future use). Stir milk mixture into beaten eggs – do *not* beat them in; this, together with a too-hot oven, is what usually causes the air bubbles. Flavour to taste with vanilla essence.

5 Prepare caramel: select a straight-sided, 1½ pint metal mould. Add sugar and water, and swirl pan over a low heat until dissolved. Raise heat and boil rapidly, without stirring, until syrup turns into a rich, dark caramel. Watch it like a hawk, drawing the caramel away from the heat before it is quite ready, as it carries on cooking from the heat of the mould and will burn at the slightest provocation.

6 Holding handle of mould in a thick cloth, swirl caramel around with the greatest possible care so that bottom and sides of mould are well coated. Cool slightly.

7 Pour in egg mixture; cover mould with a piece of foil and stand it in a baking tin. Pour in hot water to come half-way up sides of mould.

8 Transfer to the oven and immediately reduce temperature to 325°F. (Mark 3). Bake custard for 35 to 40 minutes, or until set.

9 Cool mould; then turn out carefully on to a deepish serving dish to catch the caramel syrup.

Individual Caramel Creams

To make individual creams, prepare the same amount of custard and caramel, cooking the latter in a small, heavy saucepan.

Divide hot caramel between 6 individual heatproof dariole or turret moulds, swirling it around base and sides quickly before it starts setting. Add egg mixture and cover moulds as above.

Stand moulds in a baking tin with hot water to come half-way up sides, and bake as above for 35 to 40 minutes.

Serves 4–6

1/2 pint milk
1/4 pint single cream
A piece of vanilla pod, split
2 oz castor sugar
3 eggs
1 egg yolk
1/2 teaspoon vanilla essence

Caramel
4 oz granulated sugar
1 tablespoon water

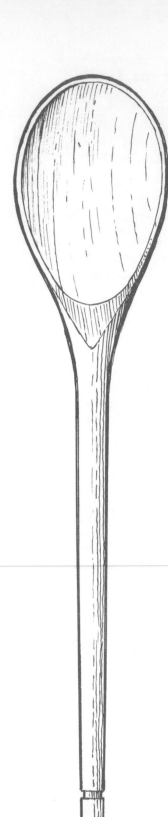

Orange Caramel Cream

Prepare the basic custard mixture as described for Crème Caramel (page 149), but add 2 level teaspoons very finely grated orange rind and a strip of orange peel as well as the vanilla pod and sugar to the creamy milk before scalding it. Then leave to infuse for at least 10 minutes – the longer you leave the mixture, the more pronounced will be the orange flavour of the cream.

Remove vanilla pod and orange peel. Strain milk mixture into beaten eggs.

Finish custard as directed for Crème Caramel, omitting vanilla essence.

Prepare a caramel for the mould with 4 oz sugar, dissolving it in 2 tablespoons orange juice rather than water, but this time do not let it cook to such a deep colour. You don't want too much bitterness to interfere with the delicate orange flavour.

Bake as above.

Chocolate Caramel Cream

Break 3 oz bitter chocolate into small pieces and combine with milk, cream, vanilla pod and 1 oz castor sugar, following basic method for Crème Caramel (page 149). Bring to the boil, stirring. Add 1 level teaspoon instant coffee; cover and leave to infuse.

Remove vanilla pod and finish custard as directed for Crème Caramel, omitting vanilla essence.

Prepare a light golden caramel for the mould with 4 oz sugar, dissolving it in 1 tablespoon cold water.

Coat mould with caramel. Pour in chocolate custard mixture and bake as above.

Coffee Caramel Cream

In this version, the milk, cream, vanilla pod and sugar are brought to the boil, and flavoured with 3 level tablespoons instant coffee before being left to infuse.

Remove vanilla pod and finish custard as directed for Crème Caramel, omitting vanilla essence. Bake in a mould coated with a light golden caramel as for Chocolate Caramel Cream.

Floating Islands
(Oeufs à la Neige)

Serves 4

A marvellously delicate sweet, equally at home in the nursery and as a finale to the most sophisticated dinner party.

1 In a heavy saucepan, combine ½ pint milk with the cream, 2 level tablespoons sugar and a vanilla pod which you have split lengthwise. Bring to the boil slowly; remove from heat and leave, covered, to infuse for half-hour. Remove vanilla pod; rinse and dry it thoroughly, and store in a stoppered jar for future use.

2 Blend cornflour smoothly with a little of the cream mixture. Stir back into the pan and bring to the boil slowly, stirring constantly. Simmer for 2 or 3 minutes until cornflour no longer tastes raw.

3 Beat egg yolks lightly in a bowl. Add cornflour cream in a very thin stream, beating vigorously. Return to the pan and cook over a low heat, stirring constantly, until sauce coats back of spoon. Take great care not to let it boil, or egg yolks will curdle. Put sauce aside to cool while you prepare 'islands', giving it an occasional stir to prevent a skin forming on top.

4 To prepare 'islands': combine remaining milk with 1 pint water in a wide, deep frying-pan.

5 Add a pinch of salt to the egg whites in a spotlessly clean and dry bowl, and whisk until soft peaks form. Gradually whisk in castor sugar and continue to whisk to a stiff, glossy meringue.

6 Bring milky water to the boil and reduce heat to a bare simmer.

7 Take up an eighth of the meringue mixture on a large spoon, shape it into a mound and drop on to the surface of the simmering milk.

8 Cook 3 or 4 'islands' at a time for just 4 minutes, flipping them over carefully with a fork half-way through. Do not overcook them, or they will start disintegrating.

9 As soon as it is ready, lift each island out with a slotted spoon and lay it on a wire rack to drain thoroughly. This is very important; otherwise, islands will continue draining on to the custard sauce.

10 To serve: pour sauce into a glass serving dish and pile 'islands' gently on top. Sauce should be about ¾ inch deep. Chill until ready to serve.

3/4 pint milk
1/2 pint single cream
2 level tablespoons sugar
1 vanilla pod, split
2 level teaspoons cornflour
4 egg yolks
Salt
3 egg whites
3–4 oz castor sugar

Oeufs à la Neige au Caramel

1 Prepare and assemble *œufs à la neige* (page 151).

2 Combine 3 oz sugar with 2 tablespoons water in a heavy pan and stir over a low heat until sugar has melted. Then boil rapidly to a golden brown caramel.

3 Spoon a little hot, liquid caramel over each meringue and allow to harden before serving.

Oeufs à la Neige aux Oranges – my favourite

1 Prepare sauce as above, but substitute 2 thinly pared strips of orange zest for the vanilla pod and when still warm, flavour the sauce with 4 teaspoons Grand Marnier.

2 Assemble the dish and let it stand for the full hour before serving. For some magic reason, the sauce impregnates the meringues with a most delicate orange flavour as it waits.

Oeufs à la Neige au Café

1 Prepare according to the master recipe, adding 1 level tablespoon instant coffee dissolved in a teaspoon of boiling water to the sauce before removing it from the heat.

Serves 4–6

3 eggs
1 oz castor sugar
3 oz bitter chocolate
Salt

Quick Chocolate Mousse

Nothing could be simpler for a quick, rich little sweet.

1 Separate eggs.

2 Beat yolks with castor sugar until creamy and lemon-coloured.

3 Break chocolate into the top of a double saucepan and melt over simmering water.

4 Add melted chocolate to beaten egg yolk mixture, beating vigorously until smoothly blended.

5 Add a pinch of salt to egg whites and whisk until stiff but not dry.

6 Fold egg whites into chocolate mixture lightly but thoroughly, using a metal spoon or spatula – don't overfold, or you will end up with less mousse.

7 Spoon mixture into a 1-pint dish (or 4 or 6 individual dishes) and chill until set, about 2 hours.

Petits Pots au Chocolate à l'Orange

Serves 4

4 oz dark bitter chocolate
2 oranges (1 large, 1 medium-sized)
1 oz butter
Grand Marnier or cognac
2 eggs, separated

One of the most popular sweets I have ever served in my restaurant. The quantities given below will serve four, with maybe a little left over. For six, simply use another egg – the pots will be slightly paler in colour, but still very rich.

1 Break chocolate into the top of a double saucepan.

2 Finely grate the rind of 1 large orange; squeeze its juice and add both to the chocolate, together with butter.

3 Heat over simmering water, stirring occasionally, until chocolate has melted. Then remove pan from heat; add 1 tablespoon Grand Marnier or cognac, and beat until smooth.

4 In a bowl, beat egg yolks thoroughly. Strain in chocolate mixture through a fine sieve, beating constantly. Allow to cool.

5 In another bowl, beat egg whites until stiff but not dry. Fold into chocolate mixture gently but thoroughly with a spatula.

6 Pour mixture into individual (¼ pint) pots or soufflé dishes. (Do not use metal pots, as chocolate may discolour.) Chill until set.

7 Just before serving, cut 2 thin slices from the centre of the remaining orange. Quarter each slice and lay 2 quarters, point to point, on top of each pot. Pour over a teaspoonful of Grand Marnier or cognac; swirl around very gently so that entire surface is moistened, and serve immediately.

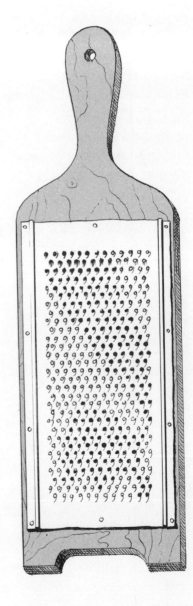

Serves 6

4–6 large firm dessert pears
Lemon juice
4 oz sugar
Vanilla pod
1/4–1/2 teaspoon vanilla
essence

Crème pâtissière

3 level tablespoons castor
sugar
2 level tablespoons cornflour
3/4 pint milk
4 egg yolks
4 level tablespoons butter
1 tablespoon Grand Marnier
1/4–1/2 teaspoon vanilla
essence

To finish dish

12 almond macaroons
4 teaspoons Grand Marnier
1/4 pint double cream
1 level teaspoon castor
sugar
Crystallised violets (optional)

Poire Vefour

An exquisite sweet from the Grand Vefour in Paris, one of France's most famous three-star restaurants. There is nothing difficult about making it, though, providing you take it carefully stage by stage.

1 Peel pears; cut them in half lengthwise and remove cores. Brush each pear liberally with lemon juice as soon as you have prepared it to prevent discolouration.

2 In a wide pan, combine sugar and vanilla pod with 1 pint water. Stir over a low heat until sugar has dissolved; then bring to the boil.

3 Lower in pear halves; bring to the boil again and cover surface with a piece of greaseproof paper. Poach very gently, for 15 to 20 minutes until pears are tender but without a trace of mushiness.

4 Remove pan from heat. Taste syrup and intensify vanilla flavour with a little essence. (The restaurant describes it as '*un sirop très vanillé*'.) Allow pears to cool in their syrup.

5 Meanwhile, prepare *crème pâtissière*: combine castor sugar with cornflour in the top of a double saucepan. Add cold milk gradually, stirring with a wooden spoon to blend ingredients smoothly, and bring to the boil over a moderate, direct heat, stirring constantly. Simmer for 3 to 4 minutes until sauce has thickened and no longer tastes floury. Remove from heat.

6 Beat egg yolks lightly with a whisk. Pour in hot cornflour sauce in a thin stream, beating vigorously. Then pour back into top of double saucepan and cook over lightly simmering water, stirring, until sauce is thick, about 5 minutes. Take care not to let it come to the boil, or egg yolks may curdle.

7 Remove pan from heat. Pass sauce through a fine sieve into a bowl and allow to cool slightly. Then add the butter; beat until completely melted, and flavour with Grand Marnier and vanilla essence.

8 To assemble dish: select a shallow serving dish large enough to take the pear halves in one layer. Cover bottom of dish with half the *crème pâtissière*, smoothing it out evenly with a spatula.

9 Cut macaroons in half. Sprinkle them with 2 teaspoons Grand Marnier and scatter evenly over the *crème pâtissière* – use the crumbs as well.

10 Spread remaining *crème pâtissière* evenly over the macaroons.

11 Drain poached pears thoroughly and arrange them on top, rounded sides up.

12 Whisk double cream lightly with remaining Grand Marnier and a teaspoon of castor sugar, and use it to decorate top of dish. Dot with a few crystallised violets if you have them, and chill lightly until ready to serve.

Note: You can fish out the vanilla pod when you have finished, dry it carefully and store it in a screw-top jar for future use.

SECOND COURSE

Lesson 6
Soups and Stocks

Basic Stocks

No one who is interested in cooking and good food can consider him- (or her-) self to have mastered his art until he has learnt to simmer all the goodness from a piece of meat, a few vegetables and a bunch of herbs into a sparkling, clear stock of beef or chicken, and furthermore learnt how to combine this home-made stock with vegetables and milk or cream into a rich, velvety fresh-tasting purée.

Why stock? The French word for stock is *fond: fond brun* or brown stock, *fond blanc* or white stock. (Fish stock, by the way, goes under the name of *fumet*.) But the really interesting point about this is the fact that the word *fond* also means 'basis' or 'foundation', for without a good stock there could be few soups, practically no savoury sauces – with the obvious exception of emulsions like mayonnaise and other cold sauces – and certainly no aspics worth tasting. You would also be hard put to it to find a worthy substitute for moistening casseroles and pot roasts, or for reinforcing their flavours.

Stock cubes I am the last person to decry the value of stock cubes. They are indispensable in the modern kitchen, providing they are used with discrimination.

Stock made with cubes is excellent for quick sauces and as a base for soups, especially creams and purées, which derive a rich flavour from their other ingredients.

However, they are not suitable for sauces which are to be subjected to prolonged reduction, as the monosodium glutamate with which they are invariably seasoned and the salt with which their 'shelf life' is preserved, tend to overpower all other flavours.

For clear broths, chicken cubes are better than beef cubes, and they become quite good if you add a few chopped vegetables – celery, carrot, etc. – to them before simmering them in water. Be careful not to over-reduce the stock, though, during this 'flavouring' operation. In fact, it is a good idea to allow for reduction by using an extra ¼ pint of water per cube.

Finally, you should experiment with all the different brands of stock cubes available in your local shops. I have found an appreciable difference between those which I liked least, and the best ones which, for the record, were Swiss.

Making Stocks

Serious stock-making calls for only one slightly out-of-the-way piece of equipment – a large pot of, say, 8-pint capacity.
This is important.
The essence of a good home-made stock lies in gentle simmering for a period of several hours, during which time the liquid reduces by about half. It stands to reason, therefore, that if there is not much of it to start with, you will have precious little to show for your efforts at the end of 3 or 4 hours' evaporation.

The pot must also be large enough (1) not to boil over or splash; and (2) so that you have enough room to manoeuvre when you skim fat and scum from the surface.

The basic ingredients What goes into your stock-pot is your own affair, but remember as you read through the following recipes that you only get out what you put in. If the stock is to end up as a consommé, for example, then a good proportion of meat to bone is advisable. Otherwise, meaty bones (with plenty of marrow if possible) will do the trick.

You can even make a very passable stock with just vegetables: finely chop carrots, leek, onion, celery, and any other vegetables you may have at hand, and – here's the secret – sauté gently in a little butter and oil until lightly coloured. Cover the pan tightly and 'sweat' vegetables for 10 to 15 minutes over a low heat. A little diced fat salt pork or mild, unsmoked bacon sautéed in the fat before adding vegetables will strengthen flavour even further. Add water – 2 pints per lb of vegetables - a stock cube (see page 158), a *bouquet garni*, and a squashy tomato or two if you have them, and simmer gently for an hour before straining – not the most subtle of stocks but a perfectly acceptable launching pad for a vegetable soup.

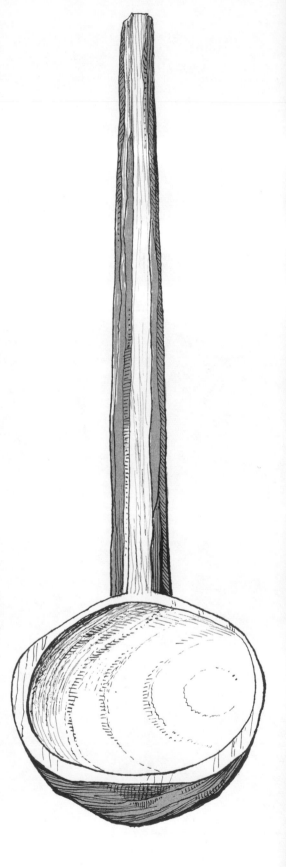

159

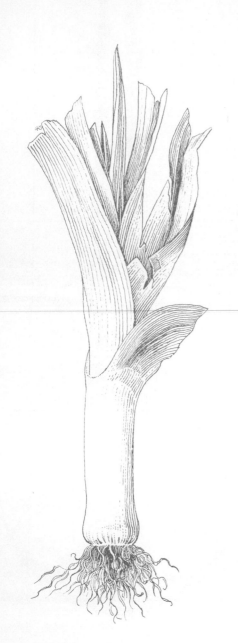

Skimming stock Stock is skimmed at two stages – first to rid it of the scum that the heat (and salt) draws out of the meat and bones, and which, if not removed, will be driven back into the liquor, and secondly to remove excess fat.

Scum Use a slotted spoon. Don't start skimming until the white foam has collected into a definite scum – otherwise it will just filter back through the slits in the spoon. Then skim at regular intervals until surface is quite clear. Peppercorns, dried herbs etc. should not be added until the end of this operation as you are liable to skim them out with the scum.

Fat If stock is not to be used immediately, the fat presents no problem. You simply wait until it congeals on the surface and lift it off in slabs. It is best not to remove fat from the surface until you need the stock, as it provides an effective seal which helps the stock to keep fresh longer.

For a very greasy stock, a bulb-baster is the answer. Strain stock into a glass or pyrex jug, a portion at a time. Wait for a few minutes until fat has settled on the surface; then plunge bulb-baster down to the bottom; draw out clear stock and transfer to another container. In this way, you can be sure of leaving all the fat behind. Remember, however, to hold the bulb-baster *vertical* at all times. If you tilt it at an angle, there is a danger that it may spurt hot stock while you are transferring it from one container to another.

To clarify stock – see recipe for Beef Consommé (page 164).

To keep stock Never store stock without first straining out the bones and vegetables. Left in, the latter will quickly cause it to sour, even in the refrigerator.

Strained stock should be poured into a non-metal container – a tall one is best as it takes up less room than a bowl – and stored in the refrigerator, where it will keep for about a week before it needs to be reboiled.

Unrefrigerated stock should be boiled up every day in warm weather, or every second day in winter.

Surplus stock gives you a marvellous opportunity to try your hand at making a meat glaze (see page 182).

Classic Beef Stock I

Makes 3 pints

1 Ask your butcher to remove the meat from the shin (or neck) of beef and shin of veal, and to chop the bones up into large chunks.

2 Preheat oven to very hot (475°F. Mark 9).

3 Trim any excess fat from the meat.

4 Put beef and veal bones, and the ham in a roasting tin. Add roughly chopped onions and carrots and sliced leeks and celery, and dot with dripping.

5 Roast bones and vegetables in the oven for 40 to 45 minutes, turning occasionally, until richly browned.

6 Scrape contents of roasting tin into a large saucepan, casserole or stock-pot. Add boned meat, ham, mushroom stalks or trimmings and soft tomatoes.

7 Add ½ pint cold water to roasting tin; bring it to the boil and scraping bottom and sides of tin with a wooden spoon to dislodge all the crusty bits and sediment stuck there. Pour over vegetables, and then add 5½ pints cold water.

8 Place pan over a low heat and bring to the boil. Allow foam to settle into a scum on the surface; skim it off with a slotted spoon, then add a little salt (not too much – remember stock will reduce), which will draw out more scum. Skim again.

9 When all the scum has been drawn out of the meat and bones, throw in herbs, bay leaf, clove and black peppercorns, and leave stock to simmer gently for 3 hours.

10 Strain stock through a fine sieve into a large bowl and allow to cool before skimming off fat. Store until ready to be used.

Note: Meat can be eaten with coarse salt and freshly ground black pepper, or combined with fresh vegetables to make another portion of stock.

3 lb shin or neck of beef on the bone (see Step 1)

1 lb shin of veal on the bone (see Step 1)

1 small ham bone (about 1/2 lb) or 1/4 lb lean ham

2 Spanish onions, roughly chopped

3 large carrots, roughly chopped

2 leeks, thickly sliced

3–4 stalks celery, thickly sliced

2 oz beef dripping

A few mushroom stalks or trimmings

2–3 soft over-ripe tomatoes

Salt

3 sprigs parsley

1 sprig thyme or a pinch of dried thyme

1 bay leaf

1 clove

9 black peppercorns

1 lb veal knuckle (chopped
  by your butcher)
1 lb beef knuckle (chopped
  by your butcher)
2 Spanish onions, roughly
  chopped
2 large carrots, roughly
  chopped
2 stalks celery, roughly
  chopped
2 leeks, thickly sliced
2 oz beef dripping
2 chicken feet, well scrubbed
  (optional)
2 lb boned shin of beef
A few mushroom stalks or
  trimmings
2–3 soft over-ripe tomatoes
Salt
3 sprigs parsley
1 sprig thyme or a pinch of
  dried thyme
1 bay leaf
1 clove
9 black peppercorns

Classic Beef Stock II (Quick Method)

The method for this stock is very similar to that of the preceding recipe, but quicker.

1 Dot bones with dripping and roast them together with the vegetables as directed in the preceding recipe.

2 Combine roasted bones with 5½ pints water in a large pan.

3 Rinse out roasting tin with ½ pint water. Add to the pot, together with chicken feet, shin of beef, mushrooms stalks or trimmings, and soft tomatoes.

4 Bring to the boil. Skim; add remaining ingredients and cook as above, but for 2 hours only, or until stock has reduced to between 3½ and 4 pints.

5 Strain through a fine sieve. Cool and store.

1 boiling fowl, 3–3 1/2 lb,
  with feet if possible for
  their gelatine content
1 veal knuckle, about
  1 1/2 lb
3 large carrots
3 Spanish onions
1 leek
2 stalks celery
2–3 over-ripe tomatoes
Salt

Chicken Stock

1 Put boiling fowl in a large stock-pot or saucepan, together with its feet, well scrubbed, and the veal knuckle. Cover with 6 pints cold water and very slowly bring to the boil.

2 Meanwhile, chop up carrots, onions, leek, celery and tomatoes roughly.

3 When water starts to bubble, add a tablespoon of salt. This will help to draw all the scum from the meat and bones to the surface, where it can easily be skimmed off with a slotted spoon. Skim several times until water ceases to throw up scum.

4 Add chopped vegetables, herbs, bay leaf, cloves and whole peppercorns; bring to the boil and skim again if necessary.

5 Lower heat and leave stock to simmer for 2 to 2½ hours, or until meat falls away from the chicken carcass and stock is richly flavoured and reduced by about half.

6 Correct seasoning. Ladle stock through a fine sieve or a colander lined with muslin. Allow to cool; then store in the refrigerator. Stock should set into a firm clear jelly.

White Stock

1 Ask your butcher to bone the meat and to chop the bones roughly.

2 Put the meat and all the bones in a large pan or stock-pot and cover with 6 pints cold water. Bring to the boil over a very low heat.

3 Meanwhile, clean the vegetables and chop them roughly.

4 When pot comes to the boil, raise the heat and wait until a thick layer of scum has formed on the surface. Skim this off with a slotted spoon; then add a good pinch of salt, which will help to draw out yet more scum, and continue to skim until surface of liquid is clear. (Veal bones throw up more scum than beef or chicken.)

5 Add prepared vegetables to the pot, together with herbs, cloves and peppercorns. Bring back to the boil and skim again if necessary.

6 Simmer stock for 2 to 2½ hours, or until meat and vegetables are disintegrating, and the stock is well flavoured and reduced by about half. Skim off remaining scum and any fat as they come to the surface.

7 Strain stock through a fine sieve or a colander lined with muslin, and season to taste.

8 Allow stock to cool. Then store in the refrigerator in an earthenware or enamelled (not metal) container.

3 sprigs parsley
1 sprig thyme
1 bay leaf
2 cloves
8 whole peppercorns

Makes 3 pints

3 lb knuckle of veal, or 2 lb knuckle of veal and 1 lb knuckle of mutton (see Step 1)
1 small ham bone (see Step 1)
3 large carrots
3 Spanish onions
2 stalks celery
1 leek
2–3 over-ripe tomatoes
Salt
3 sprigs parsley
1 sprig thyme
1 bay leaf
2 cloves
8 white peppercorns

Makes 3 pints

2–3 lb beef bones (see Step 1)

1 small ham bone, about 8 oz (see Step 1)

2 Spanish onions, roughly chopped

2 stalks celery, roughly chopped

2 leeks, thickly sliced

2 carrots, roughly chopped

2 oz beef dripping or butter

A few mushroom stalks or trimmings, if available

2–3 over-ripe tomatoes, if available

Salt

2–3 sprigs parsley

1 sprig thyme or a pinch of dried thyme

1 bay leaf

1 clove

9 black peppercorns

Simple Bone Stock

This simple stock is cheaper than the others because no meat is used, apart from scraps which may have been left on the bones. It is obviously not as rich and you will probably find it too thin to serve as a consommé on its own, but it is still eminently suitable as a base for soups and sauces, or for flavouring casseroles.

1 Charm your butcher into giving you nice, meaty bones, including one or two marrow bones if possible, and ask him to chop them up roughly.

2 Preheat oven to very hot (475°F. Mark 9).

3 Rinse bones and put them in a roasting tin together with roughly chopped and sliced vegetables. Dot with dripping or butter.

4 Proceed as directed for Classic Beef Stock I (page 161), leaving the pot to simmer for about 3 hours, or until liquid has reduced by about half.

5 Strain stock through a fine sieve.

Soups

Makes 2 pints (serves 6)

12 oz lean beef, minced

2 leeks, fairly finely chopped

2 stalks celery, fairly finely chopped

2 carrots, fairly finely chopped

1/2 Spanish onion, fairly finely chopped

2 soft over-ripe tomatoes (optional)

Whites and shells of 2 eggs

3 pints beef stock

Beef Consommé

1 Combine ingredients in a large saucepan and bring to the boil over a low heat, stirring frequently to prevent anything sticking to the bottom of the pan.

2 Stop stirring when a thick pad of foam starts forming on the surface. Leave to simmer very gently for 1 hour.

3 Line a large sieve or colander with muslin. Strain consommé through it into a bowl; cool and chill.

4 Carefully lift off fat which has coagulated into a layer on top of the consommé. Transfer consommé to storage jars and store in the refrigerator until needed. It will keep for several weeks if brought to the boil and rebottled in rinsed and dried jars every 7 days.

Note: If you wish to use consommé as soon as you make it, skim grease off the top by soaking it up with absorbent paper or by siphoning off stock with a bulb-baster (see page 160).

Chicken Consommé

This is the one of the few exceptions to the rule of not using stock cubes to make a consommé, but if you use cubes you must use good ones which are not overseasoned with monosodium glutamate. The consommé may not be quite as fine as one made with fresh stock, but with the flavouring of the veal and vegetables, it makes a very acceptable substitute.

Follow the method for Beef Consommé (page 164).

Garnished Consommés

Few things can rival a carefully simmered consommé as an elegant beginning to a formal dinner party. And having gone to all this trouble, you can, with just a little more effort, enhance your consommé with an elegant garnish.

Consommé à l'Orange

Garnish each bowl of piping hot beef consommé (page 164) with $\frac{1}{2}$ to 1 level teaspoon finely shredded watercress leaves and a half-slice of unpeeled orange (taken from the centre of the orange), cut into 3 wedges.

Tarragon Consommé

Add 3 sprigs fresh tarragon to 2 pints cold beef consommé (page 164). Bring to the boil over a low heat; cover pan and leave in a warm place, e.g. on the pilot light of a gas stove, for 20 minutes.

Strain consommé through a fine sieve (or a coarser sieve lined with muslin). Serve each portion garnished with 2 or 3 tarragon leaves blanched in a little consommé, or a sprinkling of coarsely chopped fresh tarragon.

Madeira or Sherry Consommé

Flavour 2 pints beef consommé (page 164) with a tablespoon of Madeira or dry sherry just before serving.

Makes 2 pints (serves 6)

- 12 oz pie veal, minced
- 1 medium-sized leek, fairly finely chopped
- 1 stalk celery, fairly finely chopped
- 1 large carrot, fairly finely chopped
- 1 Spanish onion, fairly finely chopped
- Whites and shells of 2 eggs
- 3 pints chicken stock (or the same amount of stock made with 2 1/2 chicken stock cubes)

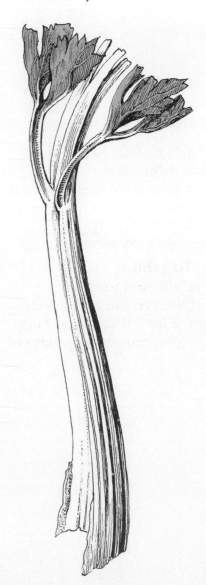

Consommé with Pasta

Larger noodles, of which the Italians make an infinite variety, all slightly different in shape and size, can also be used to garnish a consommé.

Use 2 oz for 2 pints beef (page 164) or chicken consommé (page 165) and simmer for 15 to 18 minutes. If you are using a stock cube, cook as directed on the packet. Serve immediately.

Serves 6

2 oz lettuce leaves
2 oz spinach leaves
2 oz sorrel leaves
2 pints beef (page 164) or chicken consommé (page 165)

Green Consommé

1 Wash leaves carefully. Pat them dry in a cloth and shred finely.

2 Put shredded leaves in a pan. Pour over boiling water to cover; bring back to the boil and simmer for 1 minute.

3 Drain leaves thoroughly and stir into hot consommé. Serve immediately.

Note: If sorrel is not available, flavour consommé with a few drops of lemon juice.

Serves 6

1 lb ripe red tomatoes
2 stalks celery
2 pints clear, well-flavoured chicken stock (page 162)
Salt and freshly ground black pepper

To garnish

1/2 lb firm tomatoes
One 7 oz can red pimentos
1–2 level tablespoons finely chopped parsley or chervil

Consommé Rose

1 Chop ripe tomatoes and celery roughly. Place them in a large pan with chicken stock; bring to the boil and simmer for 30 minutes.

2 To make garnish: peel and seed tomatoes, and cut them into small dice, about $\frac{1}{8}$ inch square. Drain pimentos and dice them also.

3 Strain stock through a muslin-lined sieve. Add diced tomato and pimento garnish; season to taste with salt and freshly ground black pepper, and bring just to boiling point again.

4 Remove from heat and ladle into individual bowls. Sprinkle with finely chopped parsley or chervil, and serve immediately.

Consommé Niçoise

Prepare 1 portion of Consommé Rose (above). Stir in 2 oz cooked diced green beans and 2 oz finely diced cooked potatoes together with the original garnish, and serve in individual bowls, sprinkled with finely chopped parsley or chervil.

Consommé Italienne

Prepare 1 portion of Consommé Rose (page 166). Before garnishing with tomato and pimento, add 1½ oz vermicelli and simmer for 3 to 4 minutes until tender. Serve immediately as above.

Creole Chicken Consommé

Rinse 3 oz long-grain rice in a sieve under the cold tap until water runs clear. Shake out as much moisture as possible and dab dry with a cloth.

Bring 2 pints chicken consommé (page 165) to a brisk boil. Dribble in rice; stir once or twice to dislodge any grains stuck to the bottom of the pan. Cover and simmer very gently for 15 to 18 minutes, until rice is just tender.

Serve immediately, otherwise rice will carry on cooking from the heat of the consommé even after the pan is removed from the heat, and may become mushy.

Chicken Consommé with Vermicelli

Vermicelli also makes a pretty garnish for a plain chicken consommé (page 165).

Use 1½ oz dry noodles for every 2 pints consommé and cook as page 166. Serve immediately.

Zuppa alla Pavese

Serves 6

6 rounds French bread
3 level tablespoons butter
3 level tablespoons freshly grated Parmesan
6 very fresh eggs (see note)
2 pints well-flavoured hot beef consommé (page 164)

This famous Italian soup is supremely elegant and very simple to make, but you must use very fresh eggs, otherwise the white will run all over the bottom of the bowl and turn into a nasty froth when it comes in contact with the boiling consommé.

1 Fry rounds of French bread in butter until golden on both sides.

2 Lay a round of bread at the bottom of each of 6 soup bowls. Sprinkle each round with ½ level tablespoon freshly grated Parmesan.

3 Break an egg into each bowl to one side of (not over) the bread, taking great care not to break the yolk.

4 Bring consommé to a bubbling boil and, without removing pan from the heat, carefully ladle consommé into each bowl. Serve immediately.

Serves 6

1 1/2 lb onions
Butter
3 tablespoons olive oil
1/2 level teaspoon castor
  sugar
2 1/2 pints beef stock (page
  161)
6 rounds French bread
4 tablespoons brandy
1/2 level teaspoon French
  mustard
Salt and freshly ground
  black pepper
12 level tablespoons freshly
  grated Gruyère

Soupe à l'Oignon Gratinée

1 Peel and slice onions thinly.

2 In the pan in which you intend to make the soup, heat 3 level tablespoons butter with oil and sugar. Add onion rings and cook over a moderately low heat for 15 to 20 minutes, stirring to brown them evenly.

3 When onions have turned soft and golden brown, stir in beef stock gradually. Bring to the boil; lower heat and simmer gently, covered, for 1 hour. Soup should have reduced to about 2 pints.

4 Fifteen minutes before soup is ready, preheat oven to hot (450°F. Mark 8).

5 Toast rounds of French bread and spread them with butter.

6 When soup is cooked, stir in brandy and French mustard, and taste for seasoning, adding salt or freshly ground black pepper if necessary.

7 Put a round of toasted French bread in each of 6 ovenproof soup bowls. Ladle soup and onion rings over the top; wait a second until toast floats up to the surface, then heap 2 level tablespoons grated Gruyère on each round.

8 Bake bowls of soup in the oven for 10 to 15 minutes until cheese is golden brown and bubbling. Serve immediately.

Note: The soup can also be baked in a wide ovenproof casserole or soup tureen.

Avgolemono

(Greek Egg and Lemon Soup)

1 Bring chicken stock to the boil in a pan and poach chicken joint for 15 to 20 minutes until flesh comes away from the bone easily.

2 Remove chicken joint from stock and leave until cool enough to handle. Strain stock through a fine sieve into a clean pan.

3 Skin and bone chicken joint, and cut flesh into very thin slivers.

4 In a bowl, beat eggs lightly with lemon juice. Add a ladleful of hot stock to the egg mixture, beating vigorously with a whisk.

5 Bring remaining stock to the boil. Remove from heat; add cooked rice and slivered chicken, and stir in egg mixture. Season to taste with salt and freshly ground black pepper, and return to a very low heat for 3 or 4 minutes, stirring constantly, until soup is hot and creamy. Do not allow soup to boil again, or eggs may curdle.

6 Stir in finely chopped parsley and serve immediately.

Serves 6

2 1/2 pints chicken stock (page 162)

1 chicken joint (leg or breast)

3 eggs

2 tablespoons lemon juice

6–8 level tablespoons cooked long-grain rice

Salt and freshly ground black pepper

2–3 level tablespoons finely chopped parsley

Chicken Soup with Matzo Balls

1 In a large saucepan, combine stock with coarsely chopped celery and the whole onion. Bring to the boil; cover and simmer very gently for about 45 minutes.

2 Meanwhile, sift matzo meal, salt and baking soda into a bowl. Stir in finely chopped parsley and grated lemon rind.

3 Make a well in the centre. Add egg yolks, olive oil and 3 tablespoons iced water, and mix to a stiff, smooth paste.

4 Whisk egg white until stiff but not dry. Fold into the matzo paste, making sure that the entire mixture is thoroughly blended. If any lumps of matzo remain, they will be unpleasantly hard.

5 Strain celery-flavoured stock into a clean pan and taste for seasoning, adding salt or freshly ground black pepper if necessary, and perhaps a few drops of lemon juice.

6 Bring stock to a brisk boil and drop in the matzo mixture in teaspoonfuls. There should be 18 to 20 balls. Simmer for 15 minutes. (If the pan you are using is not very wide, you may have to poach the matzo balls in two batches, since if they are too close together they will not rise properly.)

7 Serve 3 or 4 matzo balls in each portion of soup.

Serves 4–6

2 1/2 pints well-flavoured chicken stock (page 162)

2 stalks celery, coarsely chopped

1 Spanish onion

Salt and freshly ground black pepper

Lemon juice (optional)

Matzo balls

1 1/2-oz fine matzo meal

Generous pinch of salt

Generous pinch of baking soda

1 level tablespoon finely chopped parsley

1/2 level teaspoon finely grated lemon rind

2 egg yolks

2 tablespoons olive oil

3 tablespoons iced water

1 egg white

Serves 6

2 long carrots, peeled and
thinly sliced
2–3 stalks celery, thinly
sliced
3–4 leaves of leek, thinly
sliced
2 pints hot consommé (page
164)
3–4 tablespoons Madeira
Finely chopped parsley, to
garnish

Lemon dumplings

2 oz coarse stale
breadcrumbs
1/4 level teaspoon grated
lemon rind
Generous pinch of dried
thyme
1 level teaspoon finely
chopped parsley
2 level tablespoons softened
butter
1 egg yolk
Salt, freshly ground black
pepper and freshly grated
nutmeg

Consommé with Lemon Dumplings

1 To make lemon dumplings: knead ingredients to a smooth paste, adding salt, freshly ground black pepper and a pinch of freshly grated nutmeg. Roll into 36 neat balls.

2 Bring a pan of salted water to the boil and poach dumplings for 30 to 40 minutes until tender. Drain thoroughly.

3 Simmer thinly sliced vegetables in a little consommé until cooked through, 8 to 10 minutes.

4 Combine with remaining consommé and stir in Madeira, to taste.

5 Serve hot, each portion garnished with 6 lemon dumplings and a sprinkling of finely chopped parsley.

Note: If carrots and celery stalks are thick, halve or quarter them lengthwise before slicing them.

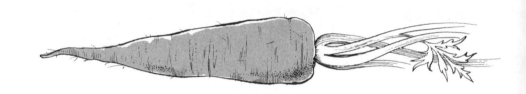

Serves 4

2 lb very ripe, fresh tomatoes
1 pint beef stock (page 161)
Salt and freshly ground
black pepper
Generous pinch of sugar
Lemon juice (optional)
1–2 level teaspoons tomato
concentrate (optional)
1 oz rice, cooked
1 level tablespoon finely
chopped dill or parsley

Fresh Tomato Soup

To make when tomatoes are at their cheapest and most flavoursome.

1 Wash tomatoes; chop them roughly and put them in the top of a double saucepan. Add 2 tablespoons water. Set pan over simmering water and cook for 15 to 20 minutes, until tomatoes are very soft and pulpy, mashing occasionally with a wooden spoon.

2 Rub tomatoes and their juices through a fine sieve into a saucepan.

3 Stir in beef stock. Bring to the boil and season to taste with salt, freshly ground black pepper, a good pinch of sugar and a few drops of lemon juice, if necessary. If you feel the tomato flavour does not come through strongly enough, add a little tomato concentrate diluted in a tablespoon of the soup.

4 Just before serving, stir in cooked rice and sprinkle with finely chopped dill or parsley.

Country Potato Soup

1 Peel or scrape vegetables as necessary and slice them thickly.

2 Put vegetables in a large pan; cover with stock and bring to the boil. Put the lid half-on to prevent stock reducing too much, and simmer gently for 40 to 45 minutes, or until vegetables are practically disintegrating.

3 Prepare garnish: if using bread, remove crusts, cut bread into small dice and sauté in butter until crisp and golden; drain on paper towels. If using bacon, cut into tiny dice and fry in butter for 3 or 4 minutes until crisp; drain in the same way.

4 When soup is cooked, purée vegetables and stock through a fine sieve.

5 Rinse and dry the pan. Melt butter in it and fry finely chopped onion slowly for 6 to 8 minutes until richly coloured but not burnt, otherwise it will taste bitter.

6 Sprinkle with flour and continue to stir over a low heat for a further 2 or 3 minutes to make a nutty *roux*.

7 Add sieved soup gradually, stirring to prevent flour lumping; bring to the boil and dilute with more stock (or a little milk) if necessary.

8 Season soup with a pinch of dried marjoram, salt and freshly ground black pepper, to taste, and simmer for 5 to 10 minutes longer before serving.

9 Serve soup with *croûtons* or bacon garnish in a separate dish for each person to sprinkle over his bowl as he likes.

Serves 6

1 lb floury potatoes
1–2 large carrots
1–2 stalks celery
2–2 1/2 pints beef stock
 (page 161)
1 level tablespoon butter
1/2 Spanish onion, very
 finely chopped
1 level tablespoon flour
Generous pinch of dried
 marjoram
Salt and freshly ground black
 pepper

To garnish

4 oz bread slices and 4
 level tablespoons butter,
 or 4 oz bacon and 2 level
 tablespoons butter

Polish Barley and Mushroom Soup

Serves 6

1 Spanish onion, halved and thinly sliced

4 oz button mushrooms, chopped

1 level tablespoon butter

4 oz pearl barley, soaked (see note)

2 1/2 pints well-flavoured beef stock (page 161)

1 large or 2 small carrots, diced

Salt and freshly ground black pepper

8 oz potatoes, peeled and diced

1/2 pint creamy milk

Serve this hearty peasant soup at a family meal in winter. Although in the traditional version stock flavoured with dried mushrooms is used, these are expensive as well as hard to come by in England and fresh mushrooms make a good alternative.

If it is not convenient to leave the barley soaking overnight, you can soften it quickly as follows: cover with cold salted water, bring to the boil and boil for 3 minutes; then remove from heat and leave to soak for ½ hour before draining and using.

1 In a large pan, sauté thinly sliced onion and chopped button mushrooms in butter until soft and golden.

2 Drain barley thoroughly and add to pan together with beef stock, diced carrots and salt and freshly ground black pepper, to taste. Bring to the boil; cover pan and simmer gently for 30 minutes.

3 Add diced potatoes and simmer for 10 minutes longer, or until potatoes are cooked but not disintegrating, and other vegetables are soft.

4 Stir in creamy milk; bring to boiling point again and serve very hot.

Creamed Mushroom Soup

Serves 6–8

1 1/2–2 pints chicken stock (page 162)

1 piece dried mushroom (optional)

4 level tablespoons butter

1 Spanish onion, finely chopped

1 lb button mushrooms

4 level tablespoons flour

1 small bay leaf

1/2 pint single cream

Salt and freshly ground black pepper

1 If using a piece of dried mushroom to perfume the stock, rinse it in cold water. Bring stock to the boil; add the mushroom; cover the pan; remove from heat and leave to soak until required.

2 In the pan in which you intend to prepare soup, melt all but 1 level tablespoon of the butter and sauté finely chopped onion until transparent but not coloured.

3 Wipe or wash mushrooms clean and trim stems. Pat mushrooms dry and put aside 4 oz of the whitest ones to serve as a garnish. Chop remainder finely.

4 Stir chopped mushrooms into sautéed onions; cover pan and stew over a very low heat for 10 minutes.

5 Blend in flour over a low heat. Then gradually incorporate hot stock, taking care not to allow lumps to form.

6 Add the bay leaf; bring to the boil, stirring frequently; lower heat and leave soup to simmer gently for 15 minutes.

7 Fish out the bay leaf, and the dried mushroom if you can locate it, and rub soup through a sieve, or purée in an electric blender, a portion at a time.

8 Return soup to the rinsed and dried pan. Stir in cream and season to taste with salt and freshly ground black pepper.

9 Slice reserved button mushrooms thinly and sauté quickly in remaining tablespoon of butter. Drain and add to soup.

10 Reheat soup gently, adding a little more stock or cream (or milk) if it is too thick for your taste, and serve immediately.

Chilled Chicken Avocado Soup

Serves 8

A sensationally pretty summer soup. Serve it in small bowls as it is very rich indeed.

1 Chill stock thoroughly.

2 Peel and halve avocados, and remove stones. Cut one avocado half into small, neat dice. Brush avocados generously with lemon juice as soon as you cut them to prevent discolouration.

3 Purée avocado halves with chilled chicken stock until smooth, either in an electric blender, or by rubbing them together through a very fine sieve. Season to taste with salt and white pepper.

4 Add Tabasco and cream; blend thoroughly and taste again for seasoning.

5 Stir in diced avocado and chill until ready to serve.

3 pints well-flavoured chicken stock (page 162)
4 large avocado pears
Juice of 1 large lemon
Salt and white pepper
6 drops Tabasco
1/4 pint double cream

Broccoli Cream Soup

Serves 6

Equally good served hot, each bowl garnished with a paper-thin slice of lemon, or cold, sprinkled with chopped chives or young spring onion tops.

1 Put broccoli in a large pan with thinly sliced celery and onion. Pour in boiling chicken stock; bring to the boil again and simmer for 15 to 20 minutes, or until vegetables are very soft.

2 Blend soup to a purée in an electric blender, or rub through a fine sieve.

3 Season to taste with ground cloves, salt and freshly ground black pepper, and thin down to the desired consistency with cream. If serving hot (see note above), reheat very gently, stirring, without letting soup come to the boil again.

2 10-oz packets frozen broccoli
1 stalk celery, thinly sliced
1 small onion, thinly sliced
1 1/2 pints boiling chicken stock (page 162)
Generous pinch of ground cloves
Salt and freshly ground black pepper
About 1/2 pint double cream

Lesson 7
Sauces and Butters

Some Basic Sauces

You can tell the importance that a nation attaches to sauce-making from the position of the sauce chapter in its cookbooks. In a French book, sauces will be right at the top of the list, together with stock-making and soups. The Americans are more likely to relegate the sauce section somewhere towards the end, if they include one at all. Cakes and pastries and pies are what come first on that side of the Atlantic.

To my mind, neither attitude is reasonable. The American one just doesn't fit into my philosophy of cooking, but that may be argued as a matter of taste. On the other hand, to support the French is to council a path of perfection, knowing full well that even the dedicated home cook will flatly refuse to follow it. Only in a restaurant can one demand that stocks and glazes be on hand at all times; and that highly trained chefs make it their sole task to produce sauces taking many hours of careful attention.

Inevitably, the next question will be, 'In that case, why bother about sauces at all?' There are two answers to this. Firstly, certain processes that one employs in sauce-making must be mastered before one can go on to other important areas. What is a soufflé, after all, but a *thick white sauce* into which you have folded whisked egg whites? Secondly, not all sauces are as time-consuming and tedious to prepare as one might imagine. There is a whole range of emulsion sauces – mayonnaise, Hollandaise, even the sweet Sabayon – that take minutes to prepare once you've got the knack; yet what a difference they can make to your culinary repertoire.

A sauce should be like the frame around a painting, bringing out but not getting in the way of the image it surrounds, drawing your attention to its good points, sometimes camouflaging a weakness and, very occasionally, even more costly and rare than the painting itself. In other words, a sauce can make or break the dish that it 'frames'.

Techniques of sauce-making Sauces fall neatly into two categories, those that rely on a blending of fat and flour (the *roux*) for their thickening, and the emulsions, formed by beating fat (oil or butter) into egg yolks. The latter can be done cold (in which case oil is used) or over gentle heat (in which case you would use butter, or simply rely on the yolks themselves to provide the necessary body).

Flour-based Sauces

In the simplest terms, you start with a fried mixture of fat and flour (the *roux*); incorporate liquid into it and, when the two are smoothly blended into a sauce, you let it simmer until (*a*) the raw taste of the flour has been cooked out, and (*b*) the sauce has been reduced to the desired degree of concentration.

A *white sauce* is made with a pale *roux* and a light stock (chicken or veal). For a *brown sauce* the *roux* is cooked to a darker shade and blended with a rich beef stock.

To make roux In a heavy saucepan, melt the required amount of butter over a low heat. When it is frothy but not coloured, add flour and stir until the two are smoothly combined. The usual proportion of butter to flour is 1:1, so you should have no difficulty in blending the two together.

Continue to simmer the mixture, stirring constantly and reaching into the corners around the base of the pan with a wooden spoon. This is important because the mixture colours unevenly if left undisturbed.

Classic French cookery recognises three 'shades' of *roux*:

Roux blanc (white or uncooked *roux*) for delicate white and cream sauces – 2 to 3 minutes' stirring over a low heat.

Roux blond (a lightly coloured, i.e. 'blonde' *roux*) for rather richer white sauces – 4 to 5 minutes' stirring over a low heat.

Roux brun (brown *roux*) is intended for rich brown sauces. The *roux* should be stirred until it turns a rich, golden brown colour and gives off a deliciously nutty aroma. If you are using a heavy pan which retains a lot of heat, lift it away from the stove a few seconds before the *roux* reaches the desired stage, or you may find it going too far.

To combine roux with liquid This is the only stage where you have to exercise care. Remove the saucepan from the heat while you get your stock, milk or whatever. Then return pan to a low heat and gradually start adding the liquid, beating and stirring vigorously with your spoon between each addition. Initially, the *roux* will absorb the liquid and even seem to stiffen

up as it swells. However, as you continue blending in the liquid, somewhat faster now, it will thin down into a sauce.

Continue stirring over a low to moderate heat until the sauce thickens and comes to the boil. Then lower heat even further and simmer gently, stirring frequently, for a further 8 to 10 minutes to cook out the raw, floury taste.

● Many beginner cooks prefer to use a double saucepan to make their sauces. In this case, melt your butter in the top of the double saucepan directly over the heat; stir in your flour and cook, stirring constantly to the desired 'shade' of *roux*. Then, place top of double saucepan over gently simmering water before adding your liquid and finishing your sauce. You never have to worry about your sauce burning if you follow this double saucepan method.

● A sauce is less likely to turn lumpy if the *roux* and liquid are both roughly at the same temperature when brought together. If you'd feel happier with this additional safeguard, then *either* plunge the base of the pan into cold water for a second before adding the liquid, *or* heat the liquid, whichever is the more convenient.

Flavouring a sauce The quality of your sauce will largely depend on the quality of the stock that went into it in the first place, but the secret of a classic sauce can be summed up in one word: *reduction*.

Taste a sauce when it has first been made; then let it cook for an hour or two either over a low direct heat, or preferably over simmering water, and you'll hardly recognise it. For some reason, you won't achieve the same result if you use a concentrated stock and cook the sauce just long enough to remove the floury taste. The magic succeeds only when all the ingredients are allowed to simmer together slowly, blending into each other in their own good time.

To enrich a sauce A few tablespoons of cream, an egg yolk or a little butter whisked in at the last moment will transform the most mundane of sauces.

Cream may either be added before simmering the sauce, or towards the end of cooking. If the sauce contains a lot of acid (lemon or vinegar), it is safer to add cream at the end and not allow the sauce to boil again, otherwise it may curdle. A sauce should never be boiled once *sour* cream has been added.

Egg yolk(s) should be beaten lightly in a bowl before being added to the sauce.

● If the sauce contains a high proportion of flour (i.e. the egg yolk is not necessary to thicken the sauce), simply remove the pan from the heat, whisk in the egg yolk and stir for a minute or two longer until the heat of the sauce itself has 'cooked' the yolk slightly.

● If egg yolks are intended to help the flour thicken the sauce as well as flavour it, first whisk a little of the hot sauce into the bowl of beaten egg yolks; then whisk this mixture into the main body of the sauce off the heat. When mixture is well blended, return pan to a low heat and stir sauce until it has thickened. I make it a rule *never* to boil a sauce again once egg yolks have been added, even when I am reasonably confident that the flour content would be high enough to protect them and prevent them scrambling.

Butter enriches flavour, improves texture and gives a sauce a beautiful gloss. Remove the pan from the heat; wait a second or two, then incorporate butter, a small piece at a time, beating with a wire whisk between each addition. This should be done at the last moment before serving for, if the sauce has to be reheated, the butter will separate and make it oily.

Meat glaze Just a teaspoonful of meat glaze will do for a brown sauce what butter does for a delicate white one. (page 182)

To keep sauces hot A pan of sauce can be kept hot for several hours by standing it, covered, in a larger container of hot (*not* boiling) water.

In order to prevent a skin forming on top, cover the surface with a piece of buttered greaseproof paper; or dot it with small flakes of butter to keep the surface moist as they melt, then whisk the melted butter into the sauce just before serving.

If a skin *does* form, don't try to disperse it with a whisk because nine times out of ten you won't be successful. Simply strain the sauce through a fine sieve and reheat gently.

Perfect Gravy: Step by Step

Your favourite Sunday roast – beef, pork, turkey or chicken – can give you wonderful gravy to glorify mashed potatoes and yet making perfect gravy can be the making or breaking of a new cook's reputation. Try my easy directions below:

1 First lift the roast to a heated platter and keep warm. (The meat will carve better with this little 'rest' while you fix the gravy.) Leaving crusty bits in roasting tin, pour fat and meat juices into a measuring jug. When the fat comes to the top of juices, spoon off 4 tablespoons of the fat into the roasting pan.

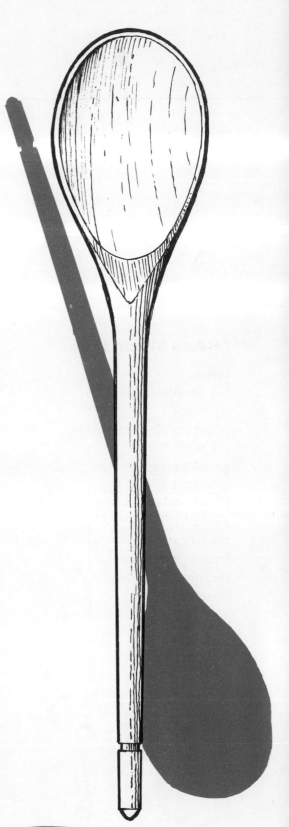

2 Stir 4 tablespoons flour into pan and blend flour and fat with a wire whisk. Keeping heat very low, cook and stir till frothy. For richer colour and flavour, brown flour in the fat to a light tan.

3 Remove roasting tin from heat and pour in the liquid all at once – ¾ pint. Stir to blend and to loosen the crusty bits. Then return to pan to heat.

For the liquid, use meat juices plus stock, water or milk.

4 Season gravy to taste with salt and freshly ground black pepper and perhaps a dash of a favourite herb like rosemary, and a tablespoon or two of red or white wine, Port or Madeira.

Allow the gravy to simmer for about 5 minutes. Strain into a hot gravy boat and serve immediately.

Makes about 1 pint

Butter
1/2 Spanish onion, finely chopped
3 level tablespoons flour
1 1/2 pints milk
2 oz lean veal or ham, finely chopped
1 stalk celery, finely chopped
1 small sprig thyme
1/2 bay leaf
White peppercorns
Freshly grated nutmeg
Salt

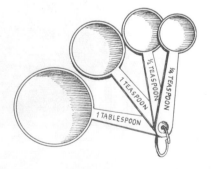

Classic Béchamel Sauce

Do not be tempted to shortcut the process of making this sauce – the slow reduction of fine sauces as exemplified in this recipe is one of the cardinal rules of great cooking.

1 In a thick-bottomed saucepan or in the top of a double saucepan, melt 3 level tablespoons butter over direct heat and sauté onion very gently until transparent but not coloured.

2 Add flour and continue to cook, stirring constantly, for a few minutes, taking great care not to let *roux* colour.

3 Scald milk and add to *roux* gradually, stirring constantly to prevent lumps forming. Continue to cook, stirring, until sauce becomes thick and smooth.

4 In another pan, simmer chopped lean veal (or ham) and celery in 1 level tablespoon butter over a very low heat. Add thyme, bay leaf, a few white peppercorns and a pinch of freshly grated nutmeg. Cook for 5 minutes, stirring to prevent veal from browning.

5 Combine contents of pan with sauce; mix well and bring to the boil over direct heat. Then cook over hot water for about $1\frac{1}{4}$ hours, or until sauce is reduced to just over 1 pint. Season to taste with salt.

6 Strain sauce through a fine sieve into a bowl, pressing meat and onion with a wooden spoon to extract all their juices. If not using sauce immediately, cover surface with tiny pieces of butter to stop a skin from forming.

Quick Béchamel-Cream Sauce

Makes about 1 pint

1 Combine milk, stock cube, peppercorns and bay leaf in a pan; bring to the boil, stirring to make sure cube has dissolved; remove from heat, cover and leave by the side of the stove to 'infuse' for 15 minutes.

2 Meanwhile, in another pan, melt butter and simmer finely chopped onion over a low heat for 5 to 7 minutes until soft and transparent, making sure butter does not colour.

3 Blend in flour with a wooden spoon and continue to stir over a low heat for 2 to 3 minutes longer to make a pale *roux*.

4 Gradually add infused milk, beating vigorously with the spoon to prevent flour lumping.

5 When sauce is smooth, add cream and bring to the boil, stirring. Simmer gently, uncovered, for 10 minutes, stirring frequently.

6 When sauce is thick, with no trace of flour in its flavour, season to taste, adding salt if necessary and a pinch of freshly grated nutmeg. Strain through a fine sieve and use as required.

Note: Sauce may be enriched by beating in an egg yolk at the last moment, and you can flavour it with a little grated Parmesan or a drop of lemon juice just enough to bring out the other flavours without making its own identity obvious.

Ingredients:
- 1 pint milk
- 1 chicken stock cube
- 6–8 black peppercorns
- 1 small bay leaf
- 3 level tablespoons butter
- 1 small onion, very finely chopped
- 4 level tablespoons flour
- 1/4 pint single cream
- Salt
- Freshly grated nutmeg

Mornay Sauce

Makes 1 pint

1 Beat egg yolks in a bowl with cream until well mixed.

2 Heat Béchamel Sauce in a heavy pan, stirring with a whisk and when hot but not boiling, add beaten egg mixture in a thin stream, beating vigorously with the whisk. Continue to stir over a moderate heat until sauce just reaches boiling point. Remove from heat.

3 Beat in butter, and freshly grated Parmesan and Gruyère, and when sauce is smooth again, season to taste with salt, white pepper, a pinch of freshly grated nutmeg and a few drops of lemon juice to intensify cheese flavour. Serve hot.

Ingredients:
- 2 egg yolks
- 4 tablespoons double cream
- 1 pint Béchamel sauce, quick or classic method (see above and page 178)
- 2 level tablespoons butter
- 4 level tablespoons freshly grated Parmesan
- 4 level tablespoons freshly grated Gruyère
- Salt and white pepper
- Freshly grated nutmeg
- Lemon juice

Makes about ¾ pint

2 level tablespoons butter
2 level tablespoons flour
3/4 pint milk
3 oz sharp Cheddar cheese, grated
1 egg yolk, lightly beaten
Salt and freshly ground black pepper
Freshly grated nutmeg
A few drops of lemon juice

English Cheese Sauce

1 Melt butter in the top of a double saucepan over direct heat. Blend in flour smoothly and cook over a low heat, stirring constantly, for about 3 minutes to make a pale *roux*.

2 Gradually add milk, stirring vigorously with a wire whisk to prevent lumps forming. Bring to the boil and simmer for 3 minutes, stirring.

3 When sauce is smooth and well blended, remove from heat. Beat in grated Cheddar and the lightly beaten egg yolk, and season to taste with salt, freshly ground black pepper and a pinch of freshly grated nutmeg.

4 Cook sauce over lightly simmering water for 20 minutes, or until thick and creamy, stirring occasionally.

5 Strain sauce if desired; correct seasoning and add a few drops of lemon juice to enhance cheese flavour.

Makes about 1 pint

2 oz butter
2 oz plain flour
1 1/2 pints well-flavoured chicken stock
6 white peppercorns
2 oz mushroom trimmings (stems and peelings), washed

Chicken Velouté Sauce

1 In the top of a double saucepan, melt butter over a low heat. Add flour and cook gently, stirring, until *roux* turns a pale golden colour.

2 Bring stock to the boil in a separate pan. Add it to the *roux* gradually, stirring vigorously with a whisk to prevent lumps forming.

3 When sauce is smooth and well blended, stir in peppercorns and mushroom trimmings. Bring to the boil and cook over simmering water, stirring occasionally and skimming surface from time to time, until sauce has reduced to two-thirds of the original quantity and is very thick but light and creamy. About 1¼ hours.

4 Strain sauce through a fine sieve and if it is not to be used at once, dot the surface with tiny flakes of butter to prevent a skin forming on top.

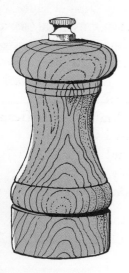

White Chaudfroid Sauce

A coating sauce for cold eggs, chicken and game.

1 Sprinkle gelatine over 3 to 4 tablespoons cold water in a cup and leave to soak for a few minutes.

2 Bring *Velouté* sauce to the boil in a heavy saucepan, stirring frequently. Remove from heat; add softened gelatine and beat until dissolved.

3 Whisk double cream with egg yolk until thick; add to sauce and whisk until smoothly blended. Season to taste with salt and white pepper.

4 Strain sauce through a fine sieve and allow to cool.

5 Use sauce before it starts to set.

Note: I sometimes add a little highly flavoured, thick home-made mayonnaise to add savour to this sauce.

Makes about 1 pint

2 level teaspoons powdered gelatine
1/2 pint *Velouté* sauce
1/4 pint double cream
1 egg yolk
Salt and white pepper
Home-made mayonnaise (optional—see note opposite)

Mushroom Sauce

The perfume of dried wild mushrooms imparts a far richer, meatier flavour to a sauce than cultivated mushrooms could ever do. Use it to sauce meat dishes such as beef olives, or serve it over rice, cracked wheat or buckwheat.

1 Cover mushrooms with ¾ pint hot water and leave to soak for several hours, or overnight if possible.

2 Transfer soaked mushrooms to a small pan, together with their soaking liquid. Bring to the boil and simmer for 10 minutes, or until mushrooms are soft and plump. Drain off mushroom liquor and reserve it. Chop mushrooms finely.

3 Melt butter in a heavy saucepan and sauté finely chopped onion until soft and golden. Sprinkle with browned flour and continue to stir over a low heat for a few minutes longer.

4 Pour in reserved mushroom liquor, a little at a time, stirring constantly to prevent lumps forming. Then add finely chopped mushrooms; bring to the boil over a moderate heat, stirring, and simmer for 6 or 7 minutes until sauce no longer tastes of raw flour.

5 Finally, stir in cream; season sauce to taste with salt and freshly ground black pepper, and reheat gently.

Note: To brown flour, either shake it in a heavy pan over a moderate heat until it turns a deep golden brown, taking great care not to let it burn; or spread it on a baking sheet and bake in a hot oven for a few minutes, again watching it carefully to avoid colouring too much.

Makes about ½ pint

1 oz dried mushrooms
1 1/2 oz butter
2 level tablespoons finely chopped onion
1 oz browned flour (see note below)
1/4 pint double cream
Salt and freshly ground black pepper

Makes about ¾ pint

1 level tablespoon butter
1 level tablespoon flour
1/2 pint hot fish stock
  (page 327)
1/4 pint (4 oz) buttered
  shrimps, or 4 oz cooked
  shrimps plus 1 level
  tablespoon butter
4 level tablespoons double
  cream
Salt and white pepper
Cayenne
Lemon juice
1–2 tablespoons brandy
  (optional)

Makes ¾ pint

2 level tablespoons finely
  diced fat salt pork
2 level tablespoons butter
1 1/2 Spanish onions,
  coarsely chopped
2 medium-sized carrots,
  coarsely chopped
1 stalk celery, coarsely
  chopped
1 bay leaf
1/4 level teaspoon dried
  thyme
3 level tablespoons flour
1 level tablespoon tomato
  concentrate
3/4 pint beef stock (canned
  or from a cube)
5–6 tablespoons dry white
  wine
3 tablespoons quick meat
  glaze (see note)
Freshly ground black pepper

Shrimp Sauce

1 Melt butter in a heavy, medium-sized pan. Add flour and stir over a low heat for 2 to 3 minutes to make a pale *roux*.

2 Add hot fish stock a little at a time, beating vigorously with a wooden spoon or a wire whisk to prevent lumps forming. Bring to the boil, stirring, and simmer gently for 15 minutes.

3 Meanwhile, mash half of the buttered shrimps lightly with a fork. (If plain cooked shrimps are used, pound half of them with 1 level tablespoon butter.)

4 Add all the shrimps – both mashed and unmashed – to the sauce, together with double cream, and simmer for a further 5 minutes.

5 Remove pan from heat and season sauce to taste with salt, white pepper, a pinch of cayenne, and a few drops of lemon juice to intensify flavours. The sauce may also be enriched with 1 or 2 tablespoons brandy just before serving.

Quick Espagnole Sauce

The 'quickness' of a quick Espagnole sauce to a large extent depends on finding a substitute for meat glaze, which, although not difficult to make, takes more time to prepare than most home cooks, however enthusiastic, are prepared to give.

Quick Meat Glaze

I *can* give you a very simple substitute for meat glaze, but only on condition that you use the best-quality canned consommé you can find: take a 15-oz can of consommé; add 1 large onion and 2 tomatoes, finely chopped and boil it fast until reduced to half its original quantity. Strain sauce, return to pan and reduce to just 3 tablespoons of dark glaze. If the consommé you used was reasonably good, the glaze will have a more than tolerable flavour (although you'll probably not need to add any salt at all to the sauce).

1 In a heavy pan, sauté finely diced fat salt pork in butter until transparent.

2 Add coarsely chopped vegetables, bay leaf and thyme, and continue to sauté briskly until well browned all over.

3 Sprinkle vegetables with flour; lower heat and continue to sauté, stirring, for 2 to 3 minutes longer until flour is a rich golden colour.

4 Dilute tomato concentrate with a little of the stock and stir it into the pan. Then gradually add remaining stock and the wine, stirring constantly to prevent lumps forming.

5 When sauce thickens, add meat glaze; bring to the boil, stirring, and simmer for about 20 minutes with the lid half-on, stirring occasionally.

6 Press sauce through a fine sieve. Season to taste with freshly ground black pepper.

Note: The sauce may be used immediately or stored for 2 days in an air-tight container in the refrigerator.

Quick Brown Sauce

Makes about ½ pint

1 Melt butter in a heavy pan. Add roughly chopped onion and carrot, parsley, thyme and bay leaf. Brown vegetables thoroughly, stirring occasionally with a wooden spoon and scraping bottom of pan.

2 Dust with flour and continue to cook until this has browned as well.

3 Stir in tomato concentrate and stock cube dissolved in ¾ pint hot water, scraping bottom of pan vigorously to dislodge the brown sediment. Season lightly with freshly ground black pepper. Simmer for 45 minutes, stirring occasionally.

Note: The sauce may be used immediately, or stored for 2 days in an air-tight container in the refrigerator.

Makes about ½ pint

2 level tablespoons butter
1 Spanish onion, roughly chopped
1 medium-sized carrot, roughly chopped
3 sprigs parsley
1 sprig fresh thyme or 1/4 level teaspoon dried thyme
1/2 bay leaf
2 level tablespoons flour
1 level teaspoon tomato concentrate
1 beef stock cube
Freshly ground black pepper

White Onion Sauce

Makes about ¾ pint

1 Melt butter in a heavy saucepan; add roughly chopped onions and sauté gently until soft and transparent. Blend in flour and continue to cook, stirring, for 2 to 3 minutes longer.

2 Combine milk with ¼ pint chicken stock (or water). Add to onion and flour mixture gradually, stirring constantly; bring to the boil and simmer gently, covered, for 15 minutes longer.

3 Pour sauce into the goblet of an electric blender and blend at high speed for 1 minute. Then strain through a fine sieve and return to rinsed-out pan.

4 Carefully fold in whipped cream and egg yolk (if used). Season to taste with salt and freshly ground black pepper, and a pinch each of sugar and freshly grated nutmeg. Stir over a very low heat for 1 to 2 minutes longer, taking care not to let sauce come to the boil again, and serve immediately.

2 oz butter
1 1/2 lb onions, roughly chopped
2 level tablespoons plain flour
1/2 pint milk
3/4 pint chicken stock (page 162) (or water)
4 level tablespoons whipped cream
1 egg yolk, lightly beaten (optional)
Salt and freshly ground black pepper
Pinch of sugar
Freshly grated nutmeg

Side Sauces made from Espagnole or Brown Sauce

There are many side sauces made from Espagnole or Brown Sauce: sauce demi-glace, Madeira, bordelaise, bourguignonne, chasseur, bigarade and lyonnaise, to mention just a few. I give you here a selection of recipes for some of the most useful in everyday cooking. The others can be found in any good French cookbook.

Sauce Demi-Glace

Makes about ½ pint

1 pint Brown Sauce (page 183)
Chopped stems and peelings of 6 large mushrooms
6 tablespoons dry sherry or or Madeira
1–2 tablespoons meat glaze (page 182)

Simmer chopped mushroom stems and peelings in dry sherry or Madeira until liquid is reduced by half.

Reduce Brown Sauce to half the original quantity. Then add meat glaze, mushrooms and juices to this mixture, and simmer over a low heat for 15 minutes. Strain before serving.

Sauce Madeira

Makes about ½ pint

1 pint Espagnole (page 182) or Brown Sauce (page 183)
6 tablespoons Madeira

Reduce Espagnole or Brown Sauce to half the original quantity. Add Madeira. Heat the sauce well, but do not let it boil, or the flavour of the wine will be lost.

Sauce Bordelaise

Makes about ½ pint

3/4 pint Brown Sauce (page 183)
2 shallots, finely chopped
1 clove garlic, finely chopped
1 glass red Bordeaux
1 bay leaf
2 tablespoons finely sliced beef marrow
Salt
1 teaspoon finely chopped parsley
A squeeze of lemon juice
Freshly ground black pepper

Simmer finely chopped shallots and garlic in a small saucepan with wine and bay leaf until wine is reduced to half the original quantity. Add Brown Sauce and simmer for 20 minutes, carefully removing any scum that rises. Strain the sauce and return it to the saucepan.

Poach finely sliced marrow in boiling salted water for 5 minutes; drain and add to the sauce with finely chopped parsley, lemon juice, and salt and freshly ground black pepper, to taste.

Sauce 'Fines Herbes'

Remove leaves from sprigs of parsley, tarragon and chervil. Reserve them to garnish sauce. Chop stems and simmer gently in dry white wine for 5 minutes. In another saucepan, melt 2 level tablespoons butter, and add 1 finely chopped shallot and the strained liquid in which herb stems were cooked. Cook this mixture until it is reduced to half the original quantity. Add Espagnole or Brown Sauce and cook for 10 to 15 minutes. Take off heat, add lemon juice and 'finish' by swirling in 1 tablespoon butter. When butter has been completely incorporated into the sauce, add herb leaves. Serve with meat, eggs or poultry.

Makes about ½ pint

3 sprigs parsley
3 sprigs tarragon
3 sprigs chervil
6 tablespoons dry white wine
3 level tablespoons butter
1 shallot, finely chopped
3/4 pint Espagnole (page 182) or Brown Sauce (page 183)
Juice of 1 lemon

Sauce Lyonnaise

Finely chop onions and sauté in 2 level tablespoons butter until golden brown. Add dry white wine and simmer until reduced to half the original quantity. Add Espagnole or Brown Sauce and cook gently for 15 minutes; add 1 teaspoon chopped parsley, and 'finish' by swirling in 1 level tablespoon butter.

Makes about ¼ pint

2 medium-sized onions
3 level tablespoons butter
6 tablespoons dry white wine
3/4 pint Espagnole (page 182) or Brown Sauce (page 183)
Chopped parsley

Quick Blender Mayonnaise

A simple mayonnaise which can be made in a matter of minutes.

1 Combine egg yolks with wine vinegar or lemon juice, mustard, salt, a pinch of freshly ground black pepper and 2 tablespoons cold water in the container of an electric blender. Cover and blend at moderate speed for 5 seconds, or until well mixed.

2 Remove inner cover of blender and, with the motor turned to maximum speed, add oil in a thin, steady trickle. Correct seasoning and use as required.

Makes about ½ pint

2 egg yolks
1 tablespoon wine vinegar or lemon juice
1/2 level teaspoon each dry mustard and salt
Pinch of freshly ground black pepper
2 tablespoons cold water
1/2 pint olive oil

Makes ½ pint

2 egg yolks
1/2 level teaspoon English or
   French mustard
Salt and freshly ground black
   pepper
Lemon juice
1/2 pint olive oil

Classic Mayonnaise

1 Make sure all ingredients are at room temperature before you start.

2 Remove any gelatinous threads left on the egg yolks. Put yolks in a medium-sized bowl and set it on a damp cloth on the table to hold it steady. Add mustard and a pinch each of salt and freshly ground black pepper, and work to a smooth paste with a spoon or a wire whisk.

3 Add a teaspoon of lemon juice and work until smooth again.

4 Pour olive oil into a measuring jug. With a teaspoon, start adding oil to egg yolk mixture a drop at a time, beating well between each addition.

5 Having incorporated about a quarter of the oil, step up the rate at which you add the remainder of the oil, to a steady, fine trickle, beating strongly as you do so. If the mayonnaise should become very thick before all the oil has been absorbed, thin it down again with more lemon juice or a few drops of cold water. Forcing olive oil into a very thick mayonnaise is another factor which may cause it to curdle. The finished mayonnaise should be thick and shiny, and drop from the spoon or whisk in heavy globs.

6 Correct seasoning, adding more salt, freshly ground black pepper or lemon juice if necessary.

Makes about ½ pint

1/2 pint thick, home-made
   mayonnaise (see above)
1 oz fresh parsley sprigs
1 oz fresh watercress leaves
Salt
2 level tablespoons finely
   chopped parsley
1 level tablespoon finely
   chopped watercress
1 level tablespoon finely
   chopped fresh tarragon
   (see note page 187)
Freshly ground black pepper
Lemon juice

Green Mayonnaise

(Sauce Verte)

1 Prepare mayonnaise with a flavouring of French mustard and lemon juice or wine vinegar.

2 Wash parsley sprigs and watercress thoroughly.

3 Bring a pint of salted water to the boil. Plunge in parsley and watercress, and boil for 6 minutes. Drain thoroughly and press as dry as possible between the folds of a cloth.

4 Pound blanched greens to a paste in a mortar. Rub through a fine sieve to make a smooth purée.

5 Beat purée into mayonnaise, together with finely chopped herbs, and if necessary correct seasoning with more salt, freshly ground black pepper and lemon juice.

6 Chill for a few hours before serving to allow flavour of herbs to develop.

Note: When fresh tarragon is not in season, you can substitute half the amount of dried tarragon, but first 'reconstitute' it by leaving it to infuse in a cup of boiling water for 5 minutes; drain well, pat dry and use as above.

Sauce Niçoise

1 Place all the ingredients in the goblet of an electric blender. Blend at top speed for 1 minute.

2 Chill for at least 2 hours. Serve in a sauce boat.

Excellent with cold boiled potatoes, hard-boiled eggs or cold fish.

Makes about 1 pint

1/2 pint well-flavoured mayonnaise (page 186)
one 7 1/2-oz can red pimentos, drained
2 level tablespoons tomato concentrate
1 tablespoon lemon juice
1/4 level teaspoon finely chopped fresh tarragon or 1/8 level teaspoon dried tarragon

Aïoli

A Provençal mayonnaise flavoured with crushed garlic. It is served with salt cod, hard-boiled eggs, plainly cooked vegetables and snails, or stirred into the famous Provençal fish soup known as *bourride*. In the earliest versions, no egg yolks were used: instead, the sauce was a simple emulsion of crushed garlic, breadcrumbs or mashed potato, and olive oil. Some recipes still use breadcrumbs or mashed potato for thickening.

Adopt the same precautions as when making mayonnaise (see opposite).

1 Peel the garlic cloves and crush them to a smooth paste in a mortar with a little salt. Add a tablespoon of olive oil and blend well.

2 Beat the egg yolks and mix them thoroughly with the garlic paste. Add the remaining olive oil very gradually, beating all the time, until the sauce has the consistency of mayonnaise. The *aïoli* will thicken gradually until it reaches a stiff, firm consistency.

3 Season to taste with additional salt, a little freshly ground black pepper and lemon juice.

4 Cover bowl tightly and chill lightly until ready to use.

Makes about ½ pint

4 large cloves garlic
Salt
8–10 fluid oz olive oil
2 egg yolks
Freshly ground black pepper
Lemon juice

Makes about ½ pint

1/2 pint thick, well-flavoured
  mayonnaise (page 186)
1 level tablespoon finely
  chopped fresh tarragon,
  and basil or chervil
1 level tablespoon finely
  chopped parsley
1 clove garlic, crushed
1/2–1 level teaspoon dry
  mustard
1 level teaspoon capers
2 small pickled gherkins,
  finely chopped
1 level teaspoon pounded
  anchovy fillets
  or anchovy paste
2 hard-boiled eggs, finely
  chopped

Sauce Rémoulade

A robust sauce to be enjoyed with cold meat, especially roast beef
and cooked ham. Excellent, too, with cold seafood: shrimps,
prawns, lobster.

Fold ingredients into thick well-flavoured mayonnaise and mix
well. Serve chilled.

Makes about ¾ pint

4 hard-boiled egg yolks
1 raw egg yolk
2 level teaspoons French
  mustard
2 teaspoons lemon juice or
  wine vinegar
1 teaspoon water
1/2 pint olive oil
2 level teaspoons chopped
  capers
2 level teaspoons chopped
  gherkins
1 level tablespoon finely
  chopped parsley
1/4 level teaspoon finely
  chopped tarragon
Salt and freshly ground black
  pepper

Sauce Tartare I

1 Rub hard-boiled egg yolks through a fine sieve into a bowl;
add the raw egg yolk and mix with a spoon until smoothly
blended.

2 Beat in mustard, 1 teaspoon lemon juice or wine vinegar and
1 teaspoon water.

3 Add olive oil, a few drops at a time at first, then in a thin
trickle as for mayonnaise, beating constantly.

4 Mix chopped capers and gherkins, finely chopped parsley and
tarragon with the emulsion.

5 Season to taste with remaining lemon juice or wine vinegar,
salt and freshly ground black pepper.

Sauce Tartare II

1 Place egg yolks in a bowl together with mustard and a pinch each of salt and freshly ground black pepper. Set it on a damp cloth on the table to prevent bowl slipping, and beat vigorously until smoothly blended.

2 Add 1 teaspoon lemon juice or wine vinegar and continue beating until smooth.

3 Pour in olive oil a few drops at a time, then in a thin stream, beating continuously as for a mayonnaise. If emulsion thickens too quickly, thin down with more lemon juice, vinegar or cold water.

4 When emulsion is thick and glossy, add chopped capers, gherkins and herbs, and mix well.

5 Season to taste with salt and freshly ground black pepper, a pinch of sugar and remaining lemon juice or wine vinegar.

Sauce Ravigote (Cold)

1 Rub hard-boiled egg yolks through a fine sieve; blend thoroughly with raw egg yolks.

2 Beat in mustard and add olive oil in a thin trickle, beating constantly as you would for mayonnaise.

3 Fold in finely chopped parsley, shallot, chives or spring onion tops, capers and tarragon, and season to taste with lemon juice or wine vinegar, salt and freshly ground black pepper. Serve chilled.

Makes about ¾ pint

2 egg yolks
1/2 level teaspoon French mustard
Salt and freshly ground black pepper
1–3 teaspoons lemon juice or wine vinegar or water
1/2 pint olive oil
1 level tablespoon chopped capers
1 level tablespoon chopped gherkins
1 level teaspoon each finely chopped parsley, tarragon and chervil
Pinch of sugar

Makes just under ½ pint

3 hard-boiled egg yolks
2 raw egg yolks
1 level teaspoon French mustard
1/4 pint olive oil
1 level tablespoon finely chopped parsley
1 level teaspoon finely chopped shallot
1/2 level teaspoon finely chopped chives or spring onion tops
1/2 level teaspoon finely chopped capers
1/4 level teaspoon finely chopped tarragon
1–2 teaspoons lemon juice or wine vinegar
Salt and freshly ground black pepper

Hollandaise

To the French, a sauce is the basic secret of all good cooking. To them, a grilled or baked fish is just a fish. But when you top it with a smoothly golden Sauce Hollandaise – a flavoursome emulsion of egg yolks, lemon juice and butter – you've created a masterpiece.

And Hollandaise Sauce is surprisingly easy to make if you use a double boiler to protect the delicate emulsion from excessive heat. Your sauce must never come to the boil or you'll end up with a separated 'curdle' that even the cat wouldn't eat.

Serve this elegant sauce with fish, with broccoli or asparagus, with delicate veal; add a little whipped cream to it and you have Sauce Mousseline; add the finely grated rind and juice of a blood orange and you have Sauce Maltaise.

Classic Hollandaise Sauce

Makes about ½ pint

Lemon juice
1 tablespoon water
Salt and white pepper
8 oz softened butter
4 egg yolks

1 In the top of a double saucepan, combine a teaspoon of lemon juice with a tablespoon of cold water and a pinch each of salt and white pepper.

2 Put softened butter on a plate and divide into 4 pieces of equal size.

3 Add egg yolks and 1 piece butter to the liquid in the pan and place over hot water. Stir rapidly with a wire whisk for about 5 minutes, or until butter has melted completely and mixture begins to thicken, making sure water underneath never comes to the boil.

4 Incorporate remaining pieces of butter one at a time, whisking vigorously and stirring from the bottom of the pan.

5 When sauce is thick and emulsified, beat for 2 to 3 minutes longer; then correct seasoning, adding more salt, white pepper or lemon juice to taste. Strain if necessary and serve.

Quick Hollandaise Sauce

Makes about ½ pint

8 oz butter
4 egg yolks
Lemon juice
Salt and white pepper

1 Melt butter in a small, heavy pan, taking care that it does not bubble or sizzle.

2 Heat the goblet of an electric blender by leaving it full of hot water for a few minutes.

3 In the goblet, combine egg yolks with 1 teaspoon lemon juice, 1 tablespoon cold water, and a pinch each of salt and white pepper.

4 Switch blender to moderate speed and, when yolks are well mixed, remove inner cover and pour in hot butter in a thin stream. If butter is poured in slowly enough, sauce will thicken before your eyes. However, if it remains too liquid, pour it into the top of a double saucepan and stir over hot, but not boiling, water for a few seconds to thicken it; conversely, an over-stiff sauce may be thinned by beating in a tablespoon or two of very hot water.

5 Taste for seasoning, adding more salt, pepper or lemon juice, if necessary, and keep sauce warm over *warm* water.

Mustard Hollandaise

Makes about ½ pint

1/2 pint Hollandaise sauce (page 190 or 191)
1–2 level tablespoons English mustard
Lemon juice (optional)

This sauce is particularly good with fried or poached fish.

1 Prepare Hollandaise according to classic or quick method.

2 Beat in mustard to taste and a drop or two of lemon juice if necessary, and serve immediately.

Sauce Mousseline

Makes just over ½ pint

1/2 pint Hollandaise sauce (page 190 or 191)
4 tablespoons double cream, whipped

A delicate sauce that goes beautifully with fish or poached vegetables.

1 Prepare Hollandaise sauce according to classic or quick method.

2 Remove Hollandaise from heat and fold in whipped cream, a tablespoon at a time. Take care not to incorporate cream too rapidly, or sauce will curdle. Serve immediately.

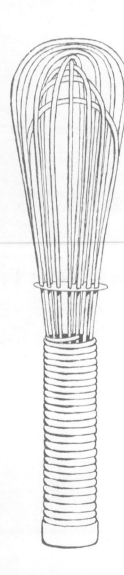

Makes about ½ pint

Rind of 1 blood orange
4 tablespoons water
4 egg yolks
8 oz softened butter, divided
    into four pieces
Juice of 1–2 blood oranges
Salt and white pepper

Sauce Maltaise

A lovely pink sauce traditionally served with asparagus but also excellent with other green vegetables and poached or steamed fish.

1 Finely grate orange rind and place in a small pan with 4 tablespoons water; bring to the boil and blanch gently for 2 minutes. Drain blanched rind thoroughly and pat dry between the folds of a cloth or absorbent paper.

2 In the top of a double saucepan, combine grated rind with egg yolks, 2 oz butter (1 piece) and 1 tablespoon orange juice.

3 Place pan over hot but not boiling water, and beat mixture vigorously with a wire whisk until butter has melted and sauce begin to thicken.

4 Add second piece of butter, beating vigorously and constantly with the whisk. As butter melts and sauce thickens again, beat in third piece of butter, making sure you reach all corners of the pan with your whisk.

5 Add last piece of butter and whisk until completely incorporated into sauce.

6 Remove top of saucepan from heat. Flavour to taste with about 2 or 3 tablespoons more orange juice, and season with salt and freshly ground white pepper. Strain and serve immediately.

Note: If sauce should curdle when *hot*, pour 1 to 2 teaspoons cold water into a bowl and *very slowly* beat in curdled sauce with your whisk. If curdled sauce is *cold*, use hot water in the same manner as above.

This sauce can be kept overnight, but there is a strong possibility that it will curdle when reheated. Bring it back by resorting to one of the methods described above.

The sauce should be reheated slowly over hot water in the top of a double saucepan, whisking constantly.

Classic Sauce Béarnaise

Makes about ¾ pint

Like its near cousin, Hollandaise sauce, the secret of a successful Béarnaise is never to let the water in the bottom of the double saucepan boil, or the sauce will not 'take'. Béarnaise sauce is the perfect accompaniment to grilled steak; try it, too with grilled, poached or fried fish.

1 Combine coarsely chopped herbs, chopped shallot, crushed black peppercorns, tarragon vinegar and white wine in the top of a double saucepan. Bring to the boil and cook over a high heat until liquid is reduced to about 2 tablespoons in the bottom of the pan. Remove from heat.

2 Beat egg yolks with a tablespoon of water and combine with reduced liquid in the top of the double saucepan. Stir briskly with a wire whisk over hot but not boiling water until light and fluffy.

3 To egg mixture add a piece of butter at a time, whisking briskly until completely incorporated. As sauce begins to thicken, increase the butter to several pieces at a time, whisking it in thoroughly as before until sauce is thick.

4 Season to taste with salt, lemon juice and cayenne.

5 Strain sauce through a fine sieve and serve.

3 sprigs tarragon, coarsely chopped
3 sprigs chervil, coarsely chopped
1 level tablespoon chopped shallot
2 black peppercorns, crushed
2 tablespoons tarragon vinegar
1/4 pint dry white wine
3 egg yolks
1 tablespoon water
1/2 lb softened butter, diced
Salt
Lemon juice
Cayenne pepper

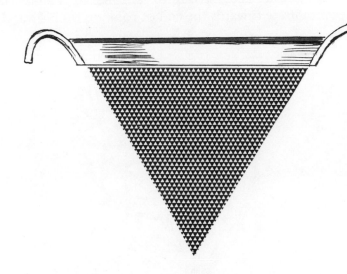

193

French Tomato Sauce for Vegetables, Fish or Eggs

Makes ½ pint

2 level tablespoons butter
2 level tablespoons finely
  chopped ham
1 small carrot, finely chopped
1 small turnip, finely
  chopped
1 medium-sized onion, finely
  chopped
1 stalk celery, finely chopped
2 level tablespoons flour
1/2 pint boiling beef stock
  (page 161)
1 14-oz can Italian tomatoes
  or 1 lb summer-ripe fresh
  tomatoes, peeled and
  chopped
1 level teaspoon tomato
  concentrate
1/2 level teaspoon sugar
Bouquet garni 1 sprig each
  thyme, marjoram and
  parsley, and 1/2 bay leaf)
Salt and freshly ground black
  pepper
1 teaspoon lemon juice

1 Melt butter in a thick-bottomed saucepan; add finely chopped ham and vegetables. Sauté gently until onion is soft and transparent.

2 Sprinkle ham and vegetables with flour, and stir over a low heat for 1 to 2 minutes longer, or until flour is golden.

3 Remove pan from heat and add boiling stock, tomatoes and tomato concentrate, sugar, *bouquet garni*, and a pinch each of salt and freshly ground black pepper.

4 Bring to the boil, stirring constantly, and simmer for about 30 minutes, or until sauce is thick and smooth. If sauce reduces too quickly, thin it down again with a few more tablespoons of stock or water.

5 Strain sauce through a fine sieve into a bowl, pressing vegetables firmly against sides of sieve to extract juices. Add more salt and freshly ground black pepper if necessary, and sharpen flavour with lemon juice.

Note: Sometimes colour of sauce is rather pale, especially if fresh tomatoes have been used. If this happens, you can improve both colour and flavour by stirring in a little more tomato concentrate towards the end of cooking time – but don't overdo it.

Super Italian Tomato Sauce for Pasta

Makes 1 pint

1 In a large, heavy saucepan, sauté finely chopped onions and garlic in olive oil until onion is soft and transparent but not coloured.

2 Stir in tomato concentrate and continue to cook, stirring constantly, for 2 to 3 minutes longer.

3 Add canned tomatoes, bay leaves, herbs and lemon peel. If using saffron, dissolve it in hot wine before adding it to the pan; otherwise add wine on its own.

4 Season lightly with salt and freshly ground black pepper (remember that salt will gain strength as sauce reduces). Blend thoroughly and simmer gently, stirring occasionally, for 45 minutes, or until sauce is very thick.

5 Rub tomato sauce through a fine sieve and return to pan. Reheat gently; then season to taste with 2 to 3 teaspoons Worcestershire sauce, more salt or freshly ground black pepper if necessary, and a pinch of sugar.

2 Spanish onions, finely chopped
2 cloves garlic, finely chopped
4 tablespoons olive oil
4 level tablespoons tomato concentrate
One 1 lb 12 oz can Italian peeled tomatoes
2 bay leaves
4 level tablespoons finely chopped parsley
1/4 level teaspoon dried oregano
Generous pinch of basil
1 small strip lemon peel
Pinch of saffron strands (optional)
6 tablespoons dry white wine, heated
Salt and freshly ground black pepper
2–3 teaspoons Worcestershire sauce
Pinch of sugar

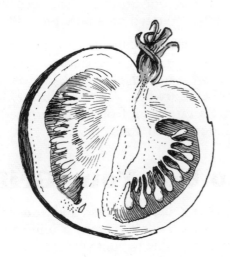

Lesson 8
Grilling

The first cookery lesson man ever taught himself was when he discovered that his game tasted a great deal more palatable if he first speared it on a stick and turned it over the glowing embers of an open fire.

Of course, this original, unknown genius was, strictly speaking, discovering the barbecue, and nothing has been evolved since to replace the magnificent aroma and flavour of meat, fish or vegetables cooked over smouldering wood or charcoal.

Few of us nowadays would care to rely exclusively on an open fire for cooking our meat. Winter weather, tower-flat living and the very restricted number of cuts to which this method can be applied would render it both uncomfortable and expensive. But practically every aspiring cook can lay his hands on the equipment necessary for indoor grilling – even bedsitter cooks often find their gas-rings mounted on a portable grill.

So let us revise this ancient culinary lesson together. There is no magical secret about it, only one cardinal rule: *grilling demands your undivided attention from start to finish*. Never attempt to combine it with other activities. As you will see, sometimes only seconds separate a rare steak from medium, medium from well-done, and well-done from disaster.

How to Use Your Grill

● Successful grilling depends first and foremost on HEAT. Insufficient heat causes meat to turn a uniform, rubbery grey, makes it utterly impossible to control the degree of rareness, and inevitably dries out the precious juices of delicate foods such as poultry and fish instead of cooking them in.

● Get into the habit of lighting your grill, turned up to maximum, about 20 minutes before you intend to start cooking – possibly a little less if you have a super-modern efficient grill. Then test the temperature: a slice of fresh bread 3 inches from the source of heat should brown to toast on one side within 35 to 40 seconds.

● The next thing you must watch is the distance at which you grill. Generally speaking, the more delicate the food (or thinner the slice), the closer to the heat it should be – 3 inches is a good average distance – so that the precious juices are safely sealed in by fierce heat before they have a chance to escape. Thick chunks must also be sealed, but set them about 5 inches from the source of heat.

● Finally, the grill-pan itself: most foods do best on the grid. You will find that the instructions that come with cookers usually recommend leaving the pan in position while the grill is pre-heating. Unless you then use the grid, (*a*) you cannot adjust the distance at which the food is exposed to the source of heat, and (*b*) the bottom of the grill-pan gets so hot that food sizzles on contact and cooks simultaneously on *both* sides – making a nonsense of the carefully calculated number of minutes required for each side.

● If you prefer the cooking juices to accumulate around the food instead of draining through the bars of the grid, you can line the grid with foil. This has the advantage of making it easier to baste, but if the juices are very copious, there is the danger that, towards the end, the steak, or whatever, will be simmering gently in a puddle of juice instead of cooking under dry heat as it is meant to.

What Can You Grill?

To most people, the very word 'grill' is almost synonymous with 'steaks', and to some extent they would be right: glorious, charred beef steaks that reveal a juicy pink centre as you cut through rich brown crust and crisp fat; thick fish steaks, from the humble cod to salmon and turbot, cooked to the point where the flesh can just be eased away cleanly from the bone.

But that's not the end of the story by any means. There are also lamb chops and cutlets, baby chickens, majestic Dover soles, lobsters and langoustes that have been sliced down the middle and saturated with herb-flavoured butter, even the odd thick rasher of bacon, a few kidneys, tomatoes and mushrooms.

Veal and pork – rather dry in themselves – are easier to handle in a frying-pan, but with careful basting (often helped by a pre-liminary 'bath' in a moisturising marinade) and scrupulously accurate timing, they can also be grilled very successfully. My favourite way of dealing with veal and pork chops is to mark them on the grill on each side and then finish them in a table-spoon or two of butter and oil in a heat-proof frying-pan or gratin dish in the oven. And, if you prefer not to take any risks

at all, turn them into kebabs, which will give you the opportunity
to thread little squares of fat salt pork or bacon on to the skewers
between each piece of meat.

What Beef Can You Grill?

Big beautiful beef steaks of all shapes and sizes: Americans revel in
them; the British, who first thought of them and bred them, and
even organized 'eating clubs' in their honour in the eighteenth
century, now spend most of their time yearning for them; while in
France *filet mignons*, *entrecôtes* and *aloyaux* are standard items on
the menu, with *pommes frites*, of course, and a tossed green salad.

How to Choose Beef for Grilling

Providing your choice isn't limited to precut, prepackaged
supermarket steaks, there are two ways of going about this. You
either buy individual steaks – rump, sirloin, fillet or porterhouse –
or one supersize slab, say 2 lb to serve four.

Apart from relying on your butcher, you can usually tell the
quality of a good steak by its appearance. The raw meat should
be shot through with tiny, thin flecks of fat, and the fat around it
should be white and firm.

You will soon discover that, although the texture of a steak cut
is closely related to its price, the same does not by any means
apply to its flavour. Most people agree that rump or sirloin are
far more robust in flavour than the delicate fillet, which is the
most expensive of all, and many claim to prefer their firmer
texture to the buttery softness of the latter.

Here, then, in order of price and tenderness, are the cuts of beef
suitable for grilling.

The fillet is a long, narrow muscle running along the backbone, thicker at one end and tapering away to nothing at the
other. As it is very lean, steaks cut from the fillet are frequently
larded or barded (see pages 14 and 19). The fillet is divided into
several classic cuts, though nowadays you may be hard put to
find a butcher who knows how to differentiate between them!

(1) The Châteaubriand is a large, thick steak cut from the
thickest end of the fillet, weighing from 12 oz to 2 lb and serving
2 to 5 people. After grilling, it is usually finished off in the oven
and served with a *Béarnaise sauce* (see page 202).

(2) The fillet steak is cut from the middle of the fillet. A
4-oz steak over 1 inch thick makes a neat portion.

(3) The tournedos, cut towards the thin end or 'tail' of the fillet, makes up with thickness what it lacks in diameter. It should be at least 1½ inches tall and weigh about 4 oz. A tournedos often has a thin strip of fat tied around it with a piece of string, which adds moisture and also helps to keep the meat in shape while it is cooking.

(4) The medallion, similar to the tournedos but smaller still, is cut from the 'tail' of the fillet or *filet mignon*. It weighs about 3 oz.

(5) Sirloin or entrecôte steak Cut from the top part of the sirloin, 1 to 1½ inches thick. Entrecôte steaks are correctly cut from between two wing ribs.

(6) Porterhouse steak Cut from the wing ribs of the sirloin. Usually 1½ to 2 inches thick.

(7) T-bone steak Very popular in America. The T-bone steak is cut directly through the T-shaped bone across the sirloin.

(8) French rib steak Thick cut of the sirloin, complete with bone.

(9) Rump steak This is an excellent piece of fleshy meat. Some of the most flavoursome steaks are cut from this part. Usually cut about 1½ inches thick.

(10) Minute steak Thin slice of entrecôte. Must be cooked very quickly.

To Store Steak

A steak can be stored in the refrigerator for 3 to 5 days on a plate loosely covered with a fresh sheet of greaseproof paper or foil, but you must remember to bring it out at least an hour, and more like 3 hours if it's a thick super-steak, before you intend to grill it, to allow the meat to come to room temperature. In fact, a supersteak bought straight from the butcher's cold room is best not stored in the refrigerator at all if you intend to cook it the same day.

To Prepare Steak for Grilling

If your steak has a border of fat, trim this down but don't cut it all away – in moderate quantities it tastes delicious when crisply cooked. Then slash the fat neatly at regular intervals; otherwise it will contract at a different rate from the meat and cause the steak to buckle and curl up when exposed to the heat. Finally, if it is an individual steak, give it a good whack with a meat bat.

(With a super-size sirloin or porterhouse you will need several whacks to flatten it out to the required thickness – see tables on pages 204 and 205.)

To Season Steak

To salt or not to salt? Some people maintain that salting meat before grilling it tends to draw out the moisture and prevents it from browning properly. In practice, we can find little evidence to support this theory – I suspect it is a hangover from the days when only very coarse-grained salt was available. To be on the safe side, however, season meat with freshly ground black pepper as soon as you take it out of the refrigerator to allow its fragrance to penetrate the meat, but leave salting until the last moment. And while you're about it, try a light sprinkling of herbs together with the pepper: the Provençal blend of thyme, savory, basil, parsley, bay leaf and fennel gives an exciting flavour, but you can do your own experimenting with whatever you have available on your spice rack. Just remember to tread carefully: dried herbs are about twice as powerful as fresh ones.

To Moisturise Steak

Just before grilling, brush the steak generously with a mixture of half melted butter-half olive oil to keep it moist and help it brown. Beef steaks do not normally require basting once they are under the grill.

To Grill Steak

Grill your steaks according to the timetables on pages 204 and 205. A *blue* steak (*au bleu* in French restaurant parlance) means one which is charred brown on the outside but just hot in the centre; *rare* implies that the red juices inside are still flowing freely; in a *medium* steak, the juices have set, but the centre is still very pink; and in a *well-done* steak, the last traces of pinkness have just turned to beige, leaving the meat moist and juicy, *not* dry.

● The importance of accurate timing to successful grilling cannot be over-emphasised. You should literally stand over it with your watch in your hand.

Is It Ready?

Professional chefs can tell the state of a steak simply by pressing it with a finger: as the cooking progresses, the fibres of the meat contract, so that the degree of doneness can be assessed remarkably accurately from the resilience of the meat.

However, you would have to practise on an awful lot of steaks to develop a 'feel' for this little trick, so it is probably more practical to stick to the following method: make a small slit down the centre with the point of a sharp knife and take a look. If the steak is not ready, quickly put it back under the grill. The heat soon seals the cut up and the amount of juice that escapes is too small to make any difference to it.

Three Butters for Steaks

Maître d'Hôtel Butter

For grilled fish, steak, lamb chops and hamburgers, and plain boiled vegetables.

1 Cream butter in a bowl with a wooden spoon.

2 Add finely chopped parsley and lemon juice, and beat until thoroughly blended.

3 Season to taste with salt and freshly ground black pepper.

4 Pat into a neat roll and chill until firm.

Note: Maître d'hôtel butter can also be served hot: melt the butter over a low heat and combine with remaining ingredients.

Makes about 4 oz.

4 oz butter
1–2 level tablespoons finely chopped parsley
1–2 tablespoons lemon juice
Salt and freshly ground black pepper

Green (Parsley or Watercress) Butter

Watercress butter makes a good garnish for chops and steaks, while a pat of parsley butter can transform a dish of plain boiled vegetables.

1 In a bowl, combine finely chopped watercress or parsley with softened butter.

2 Flavour with lemon juice and season to taste with salt and freshly ground black pepper. Pat into a neat roll and chill until firm.

Makes about 4 oz

3 level tablespoons finely chopped watercress (or parsley)
4 oz softened butter
1–2 teaspoons lemon juice
Salt and freshly ground black pepper

Makes about 6 oz

2 oz Roquefort cheese
4 oz butter
3–4 level tablespoons finely
  chopped parsley, chervil or
  chives
Juice of 1 small lemon

Makes about ¾ pint

3 sprigs tarragon, coarsely
  chopped
3 sprigs chervil, coarsely
  chopped
1 level tablespoon chopped
  shallot
2 black peppercorns, crushed
2 tablespoons tarragon
  vinegar
1/4 pint dry white wine
3 egg yolks
1 tablespoon water
1/2 lb softened butter, diced
Salt
Lemon juice
Cayenne pepper

Makes about ½ pint

1 pint Espagnole (page 182)
  or Brown sauce (page 183)
6 tablespoons Madeira

Roquefort Butter

Magnificent with grilled meat dishes, or fish.

1 Pound Roquefort with butter until smooth and well blended. Beat in finely chopped herbs and lemon juice to taste.

2 Shape into a neat roll and chill until firm.

Four Super Sauces for Steaks

Béarnaise sauce

Like its near cousin, Hollandaise sauce, the secret of a successful Béarnaise is never to let the water in the bottom of the double saucepan boil, or the sauce will not 'take'. Béarnaise sauce is the perfect accompaniment to grilled steak; try it, too, with grilled, poached or fried fish.

1 Combine coarsely chopped herbs, chopped shallot, crushed black peppercorns, tarragon vinegar and white wine in the top of a double saucepan. Bring to the boil and cook over a high heat until liquid is reduced to about 2 tablespoons in the bottom of the pan. Remove from heat.

2 Beat egg yolks with a tablespoon of water and combine with reduced liquid in the top of the double saucepan. Stir briskly with a wire whisk over hot but not boiling water until light and fluffy.

3 To egg mixture add a piece of butter at a time, whisking briskly until completely incorporated. As sauce begins to thicken, increase the butter to several pieces at a time, whisking it in thoroughly as before until sauce is thick.

4 Season to taste with salt, lemon juice and cayenne.

5 Strain sauce through a fine sieve and serve.

Madeira sauce

Reduce Espagnole or Brown sauce to half the original quantity. Add Madeira. Heat the sauce well, but do not let it boil, or the flavour of the wine will be lost.

Perigourdine Sauce

1 Add tomato concentrate to 1 pint Espagnole or Brown sauce and reduce sauce to half the original quantity.

2 Combine finely chopped truffles and Madeira in a small saucepan and simmer gently until the wine is reduced to half the original quantity.

3 Strain reduced Espagnole (or Brown) sauce into Madeira and truffles and simmer sauce for a few minutes longer, skimming if necessary. Season with freshly ground black pepper to taste.

Makes about ½ pint

1 pint Espagnole or Brown sauce (page 182 or 183)

1–2 level tablespoons tomato concentrate

2–3 truffles, finely chopped

6 tablespoons Madeira

Freshly ground black pepper

Sauce Bordelaise

1 In a small pan, combine first four ingredients and simmer until wine is reduced to half the original quantity.

2 Stir in Brown sauce and continue to simmer gently for a further 20 minutes, carefully skimming off any scum as it appears on the surface.

3 Strain sauce through a fine sieve and return to the (washed and dried) pan.

4 Bring a small pan of salted water to the boil. Lower heat. Drop in thinly sliced beef marrow and poach gently for 2 to 3 minutes.

5 Add to sauce, together with finely chopped parsley and lemon juice. Correct seasoning with salt and freshly ground black pepper if necessary, and keep hot over hot water until required.

Makes about ½ pint

2 shallots, finely chopped

1 clove garlic, finely chopped

1/4 pint red Bordeaux

1 bay leaf

1/2 pint Brown sauce (page 183)

Salt

2 level tablespoons thinly sliced beef marrow

1 level teaspoon finely chopped parsley

A squeeze of lemon juice

Freshly ground black pepper

To Grill an Individual Steak

Individual steaks should be between $\frac{3}{4}$ and 1 inch thick. With anything under $\frac{3}{4}$ inch you are faced with an almost impossible task of getting the surface brown and crusty while at the same time keeping the centre moist and pink. So unless you *like* steak done to leather, keep thin steaks for quick dry-pan-frying (see page 607).

Note: If, for some reason, you're desperate to grill a thin piece of steak, try chilling it thoroughly first; brush it with softened butter and pop it straight under a preheated grill without allowing it to come to room temperature. If you're lucky, this will give the surface time to brown before the cold steak cooks right through to the centre.

Timetable for Individual Beef Steaks

Cut	Weight	Thickness	Distance from heat	Cooking time each side	Degree of doneness
Fillet	4–6 oz	$1\frac{1}{4}$ inches	3 inches	2 minutes 3 minutes $3\frac{1}{2}$ minutes 4–$4\frac{1}{2}$ minutes	blue rare medium well done
Tournedos	4 oz	$1\frac{1}{2}$ inches	3 inches	3 minutes $4\frac{1}{2}$ minutes 6 minutes 7–8 minutes	blue rare medium well done
Châteaubriand (serves 2–3)	16 oz	$1\frac{1}{4}$ inches	5 inches	7 minutes 9 minutes 10–11 minutes 12–13 minutes	blue rare medium well done
Sirloin, porterhouse or rump	8 oz	$\frac{3}{4}$ inch	3 inches	2 minutes 3 minutes 4 minutes 5–6 minutes	blue rare medium well done
Thick sirloin, porterhouse or rump	11–12 oz	$1\frac{1}{4}$ inches	3 inches	$2\frac{1}{2}$–3 minutes 3–$3\frac{1}{2}$ minutes 5 minutes 6–7 minutes	blue rare medium well done
T-bone	15–16 oz (Weight including bone)	$\frac{3}{4}$ inch	3 inches	3 minutes 4 minutes 6 minutes 8–9 minutes	blue rare medium well done

To Grill a Super-size Sirloin for Four

A super-size steak, which serves four easily, is no more extravagant than individual steaks for the same number of people, but as a presentation it's a knock-out. Add to this the fact that one large steak is far easier to cope with under a normal-sized household grill than, say, four individual pieces, plus the fact that, armed with an adequately heated grill and meticulous timing you can pinpoint the degree of rareness you wish to achieve with deadly accuracy – something you can never be sure of when roasting meat in the oven – and you have an ideal dish to serve at a small dinner party for good friends.

Just choose your companions carefully so that as far as possible they all like their meat grilled to the *same* degree. One 'well-done' against three 'blues' could present problems! But even then, all is not necessarily lost. You will find that a large piece of meat like this carries on cooking on the serving platter for several minutes after leaving the grill, and for this reason you should normally carve and serve it as quickly as possible. However, should one of your guests prefer less underdone meat than the rest, leave his portion right to the end. By then, the meat remaining on the platter will have advanced by about one stage, i.e. from blue to rare, rare to medium, and so on.

Super-size steaks should be carved diagonally across the grain into very thin slices.

Timetable for Super-size Beef Steaks

Cut	Weight	Thickness	Distance from heat	Cooking time each side	Degree of doneness
Super sirloin or porterhouse	2 lb	Flattened to 2 inches*	5 inches	11 minutes 15 minutes 20 minutes 25 minutes	blue rare medium well done
Super rump	2 lb	2 inches	5 inches	7–8 minutes 10 minutes 12 minutes 15–16 minutes	blue rare medium well done

* Flatten super sirloin or porterhouse to 2 inches before grilling for added tenderness. Meat will gradually resume shape as it cooks.

The Gourmet Hamburger Steak

Finally, when you're sighing for a steak but money is short, try this delectable piece of make-believe.

The chopped sirloin steak is an ingenious trick adopted by top-class American restaurant kitchens for using up scraps cut from the sirloin and rump, or even fillet ends. They simply put the lot through the coarse blade of a mincer, together with some suet if the meat is very lean; season generously with garlic powder and salt (or garlic salt) and freshly ground black pepper; shape the meat into a thick steak and grill it as usual.

Per super portion

8 oz lean roasting beef, e.g. topside
2 level tablespoons finely minced beef suet
Garlic powder or garlic salt
Salt and freshly ground black pepper
Melted butter and olive oil

Before you start sneering at the notion of scraps of rump and fillet crowding out your refrigerator, try applying the trick to a chunk of meat one category removed from a grilling cut – i.e. a piece for roasting, like topside. Although for want of a better name, we've called it a gourmet hamburger, I think you'll agree that it bears little resemblance to the mean little patties that usually go under this designation, and as for your older friends and relations who haven't kept on good terms with their dentist, you'll probably be doing them a favour, as well as your budget.

1 Preheat grill for 20 minutes at maximum temperature before cooking hamburger.

2 Meanwhile, put beef and suet through the coarse blade of your mincer.

3 Season mixture generously with a good dash of garlic powder or garlic salt, some salt if you're using garlic powder, and freshly ground black pepper. Shape lightly into a steak $1\frac{1}{2}$ inches thick.

4 Lay steak on a rack in the grill-pan set 3 inches from the heat; brush generously with a mixture of melted butter and olive oil, and grill for 6 minutes on each side for a medium steak, 8 minutes if you prefer it well done. (A rare one would be difficult to achieve, since the loose texture of minced meat allows the heat to penetrate far too quickly.)

Tournedos à la Henri IV
(Tournedos with Béarnaise Sauce)

Serves 4

4 tournedos steaks
Freshly ground black pepper
Olive oil
Béarnaise sauce (page 202)
4 thick slices white bread
Butter
Salt

1 Sprinkle steaks on both sides with freshly ground black pepper and brush them lightly with olive oil.

2 Preheat grill for 20 minutes at maximum temperature before cooking steaks.

3 Prepare Béarnaise sauce according to directions on page 202, and keep hot in a double saucepan over hot water.

4 Trim bread slices into neat rounds slightly larger than steaks.

5 Heat a little olive oil and butter in a frying-pan, and when hot, sauté bread slices gently until crisp and golden on both sides. Drain on absorbent paper and keep hot.

6 Grill steaks to your liking, following the chart on page 204. Season to taste with salt.

7 Arrange sautéed bread rounds on a heated serving dish. Lay a tournedos on each round and serve immediately, accompanied by the Béarnaise sauce in a separate, heated sauce boat.

Planked Steak

The 'plank' is a thick wooden board approximately 12 by 16 inches on which you present the steak together with its garnish. Before using a board for the first time, you will have to 'season' it – rather like an iron frying-pan – by brushing it with olive oil, putting it into a cold oven and setting the thermostat to slow (325°F. Mark 3). Leave the board in the oven for a total of 25 minutes; then remove it, brush with more oil and allow to cool.

1 Trim the steak, slit the fat around it and season both sides with freshly ground black pepper and salt as directed in the introduction to grilling on page 196. Put it aside while you prepare garnish.

2 Preheat oven to moderately hot (400°F. Mark 6).

3 Peel potatoes; cut them up into even-sized chunks and simmer in salted water until soft but neither waterlogged, nor disintegrating.

4 Drain potatoes thoroughly; return them to the pan and toss over a moderate heat for 2 to 3 minutes to evaporate remaining moisture.

5 Mash potatoes smoothly or rub them through a fine sieve into a bowl.

6 Beat egg yolk lightly with double cream. Add to hot potato purée, together with 2 level tablespoons butter, and beat vigorously with a wooden spoon until smoothly blended. Season to taste with salt, freshly ground black pepper and a pinch of freshly grated nutmeg.

7 Light the grill, set to maximum, in preparation for grilling the steak.

8 Butter a baking sheet.

9 Scrape potato purée into a piping bag fitted with a ¼-inch star nozzle and pipe 4 potato 'nests' on the baking sheet.

10 Bake potato nests for 15 to 20 minutes on the top shelf of the oven until puffed and golden.

11 Meanwhile, cut tomatoes in half; sprinkle with salt and freshly ground black pepper; brush with olive oil and grill for about 10 minutes, cut side up, or until soft but not squashy.

12 When potato nests are done, arrange them, together with grilled tomato halves, around the edge of the plank. Fill each nest with 2 level tablespoons buttered peas and 2 glazed button onions.

Serves 4

1 super sirloin, porterhouse or rump steak weighing 2 lb

Freshly ground black pepper and salt

Melted butter and olive oil, for grilling

Garnish

1 lb floury potatoes

Salt

1 egg yolk

2 level tablespoons double cream

Softened butter

Freshly ground black pepper

Freshly grated nutmeg

4 firm tomatoes

Olive oil

8 level tablespoons cooked buttered peas

8 small glazed button onions (see page 376)

Sprigs of watercress, to decorate

13 Transfer plank to the oven. Shut the door and switch the oven off.

14 Grill steak to your liking following the chart on page 205.

15 Lay steak in centre of plank. Sprinkle with salt; decorate with watercress sprigs and serve immediately.

Serves 4

4 sirloin steaks, about 8 oz each
Salt and freshly ground black pepper
Butter and oil, for grilling
Fresh watercress, to garnish

Bercy sauce

1/4 lb beef marrow, diced
4 shallots, finely chopped
1/2 pint dry white wine
1/2 lb softened butter, diced
2 level tablespoons finely chopped parsley
Lemon juice
Salt and freshly ground black pepper

Entrecôtes Bercy

Bercy is the name of a big wine depot in Paris, so naturally recipes named after it include wine. Entrecôtes Bercy are probably the most famous of them all.

1 Prepare Bercy sauce before grilling steaks, but first light the grill so that it will be hot enough when you need it.

2 Poach diced beef marrow in boiling water; drain and cool.

3 In the top of a double saucepan, simmer finely chopped shallots in white wine over direct heat until liquid is reduced to about 2 tablespoons.

4 Remove from heat and whisk until slightly cooled; then fit pan over base containing hot water and gradually whisk in diced softened butter until sauce thickens.

5 Stir in diced beef marrow and finely chopped parsley, and season to taste with lemon juice, salt and freshly ground black pepper. Keep hot.

6 Grill steaks until done to your liking (see page 204). Transfer to a heated serving dish. Garnish with sprigs of watercress and serve immediately with Bercy sauce.

Grilling Lamb

Second only to beef in the grilling stakes, lamb benefits enormously if first marinated in olive oil and lemon juice with plenty of herbs, garlic, of course, and perhaps a little chopped onion. This has the twofold aim of (1) keeping the meat moist – lamb can be dry, and certainly will be if you overcook it – and (2) adding zest to the flavour.

What Lamb Can You Grill?

Chops are the best: loin chops, juicy big *chump chops* and *best end chops*. In the United States, *leg chops* or *steaks* are popular cuts for the charcoal grill, but they must be taken from a very young animal, otherwise you may find them rather chewy.

To Grill Lamb

Proceed exactly as for beef, heating the grill well in advance and making sure your meat is at room temperature (see page 199).

● If you have not used a marinade, brush the meat generously with a mixture of half melted butter and half olive oil.

● Marinated lamb chops or steaks should be drained thoroughly before grilling; then, if the marinade is made with olive oil, use that for basting the meat while it is cooking.

● Grill your lamb chop or steak according to the table below. Unlike the four degrees of cooking for beef steaks, we recognise only two stages where lamb is concerned: *rosé* or a succulent pink, which is how I like it, and *well done*.

Note: If the thought of serving lamb rare has never occurred to you, or even put you off in the past, I do urge you to try it at least once. I think it will be a revelation, with a richness of flavour and a moist tenderness which you never before imagined that grilled lamb could possess.

Timetable for Grilling Lamb

Cut	Weight	Thickness	Distance from heat	Cooking time each side	Degree of doneness
Loin chop	4 oz	1 inch	3 inches	4 minutes 6 minutes	rosé well done
Best end chop	3 oz	1 inch	3 inches	4 minutes 6 minutes	rosé well done
Chump end	6 oz	¾ inch	3 inches	4 minutes 6 minutes	rosé well done
Leg steak	9 oz	¾ inch	3 inches	4 minutes 6 minutes	rosé well done

Marinades for Grilled Lamb Chops and Steaks

Enough for 6 large chops or 12 baby ones

1/4 pint lemon juice
1/4 pint oil: olive or corn
4 level teaspoons finely chopped fresh mint
1 level teaspoon grated lemon rind
1 clove garlic, finely chopped
Salt and freshly ground black pepper

Lemon Mint Marinade

1 Blend first five ingredients together thoroughly in a bowl.

2 Season chops with salt and freshly ground black pepper, and arrange them side by side in a shallow dish just large enough to take them in one layer.

3 Pour over marinade and leave for at least 2 hours, longer if possible, turning chops occasionally to ensure they remain thoroughly coated.

Enough for 6 large chops or 12 baby ones

6–8 tablespoons dry white wine
6–8 tablespoons olive oil
2–3 cloves garlic, finely chopped
2–3 small bay leaves, finely crumbled
Salt and freshly ground black pepper.

Garlic Wine Marinade

1 Combine first four ingredients in a small bowl.

2 Season chops with salt and freshly ground black pepper, and arrange them side by side in a shallow dish just large enough to take them in one layer.

3 Pour over marinade and leave for at least 2 hours, longer if possible, turning chops occasionally to ensure they remain thoroughly coated.

Enough for 4 lamb leg steaks weighing 8 to 10 oz each

1 large Spanish onion
2 level tablespoons finely chopped parsley
1 tablespoon lemon juice
1 level teaspoon salt
1/4 level teaspoon each powdered cumin, cayenne pepper and finely crushed black peppercorns

Moroccan Spice Marinade

This is a dressing rather than a marinade, excellent for flavouring and tenderising lamb steaks. Use it, too, for Moroccan brochettes of lamb.

1 Peel Spanish onion and grate it to a purée on the finest surface of your grater.

2 Combine grated onion with remaining ingredients.

3 Coat lamb steaks evenly with this mixture, pressing it in well.

4 Leave to absorb flavours for at least 2 hours.

Lamb and Courgette Brochettes

1 Cut lamb into 1-inch cubes and put them in a large bowl. Add all the marinade ingredients and toss thoroughly to coat lamb evenly. Leave to marinate in a cool place for at least 3 hours, preferably longer, tossing meat occasionally to keep it well coated.

2 Half an hour before you are ready to cook brochettes, wash or wipe courgettes clean and trim stem ends. Slice thinly. Cut tomatoes in half.

3 Light grill, set at maximum, to allow it about 20 minutes' preheating.

4 Drain lamb. Thread cubes on to 4 large skewers alternately with sliced courgettes, spearing a tomato half on to the beginning and end of each skewer.

5 Arrange brochettes on the grill-pan. Brush all over with olive oil, and season to taste with salt and freshly ground black pepper.

6 Grill for 10 to 12 minutes, or until brochettes are done, turning skewers from time to time so that they cook evenly.

7 Arrange brochettes on a heated flameproof serving dish. Sprinkle with dried thyme.

8 Just before serving, flame with brandy. Serve as soon as the flames have died down.

Serves 4

1 1/2 lb shoulder of lamb
2–4 small courgettes
4 small firm round tomatoes
Olive oil
Salt and freshly ground black pepper

Marinade

1 clove garlic, finely chopped
1/4 Spanish onion, finely chopped
2 level tablespoons finely chopped parsley
6 tablespoons olive oil
4 tablespoons dry white wine
2 tablespoons lemon juice
Salt and freshly ground black pepper
2 bay leaves, crumbled

To flame

1 level teaspoon dried thyme
3 tablespoons brandy

Grilling Veal

Veal is such a delicate, dry meat that grilling is not usually recommended. Far better to sauté it in a frying-pan, where plenty of butter and oil will keep it moist.

However, if you are confident that you have bought a really prime chop (8 oz in weight and about $\frac{3}{4}$ inch thick), brush it generously with melted butter and oil; lay it on a rack lined with foil and grill 3 inches from the heat for 5 minutes on each side, basting frequently with the juices that collect around it, plus more butter and oil if these are rather scarce. Then place veal in a preheated oven for a few minutes more to finish cooking without drying out.

Veal should be taken through to the point where it is well done but *not* dry. If anything, the clear juices should err on the pink side so that the meat loses nothing of its delicate succulence.

● Test for doneness by nicking the meat close to the bone. Season with salt, freshly ground black pepper and a squeeze of lemon, and serve immediately, topped with a pat of butter.

● For added flavour, soak chop for a couple of hours in the wine and lemon marinade (page 211) before grilling it.

Serves 6

1 lb veal (or lamb) sweetbreads
Salt
24 button onions
1 1/2 lb boned leg of veal
Freshly ground black pepper
3 level tablespoons finely chopped parsley
1/4 pint white wine
1 tablespoon lemon juice
2 tablespoons olive oil
2 tablespoons melted butter

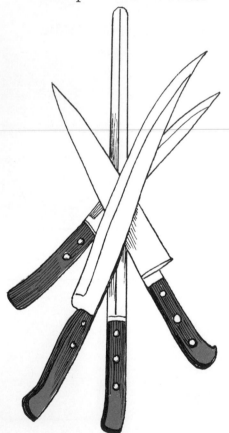

Sweetbread and Veal Brochette

1 Wash sweetbreads carefully. Put them in a pan with cold salted water to cover; bring to the boil over a moderate heat and blanch for 2 minutes. Cool the sweetbreads by leaving the pan under cold running water.

2 Peel button onions and blanch as above for 5 minutes; cool under running water.

3 Cut veal into 24 one-inch cubes, discarding any pieces of skin or gristle. Divide sweetbreads into 24 pieces as well, making them all as near to the same size as possible. (If you have small pieces left over, you can thread several of them on to the skewer at a time.)

4 Take 6 long metal skewers and assemble each one in the following order: a piece of veal, followed by a piece of sweetbread and 1 button onion, allowing 4 sets of ingredients per skewer.

5 Lay brochettes side by side in a large shallow dish or baking tray. Season generously with salt and freshly ground black pepper, and sprinkle with finely chopped parsley. Combine wine with lemon juice, pour over brochettes and leave to marinate for 1 hour, turning skewers occasionally so that they remain evenly coated with dressing.

6 About 20 minutes before cooking brochettes, light the grill turned to its maximum setting.

7 When ready to cook brochettes, combine olive oil with melted butter in a small dish. Drain brochettes thoroughly, reserving marinade, and brush them all over with the butter and oil mixture. Place them on a grill-pan under the grill; reduce heat to moderate and grill brochettes for about 20 minutes, or until cooked through and golden, turning skewers occasionally.

8 Transfer skewers to a heated serving dish.

9 Add reserved marinade to drippings in the grill-pan and bring to the boil, scraping up any crusty bits adhering to bottom and sides of pan with a wooden spoon. Strain into a heated sauce boat and serve immediately with brochettes. A dish of saffron rice tossed with green peas makes a first-class accompaniment.

Grilling Pork

Much of what has been said above with the reference to grilling veal can also, to a lesser extent, be applied to pork. Remember, too, that of all meats pork is the one that *must* be cooked to a uniform beige right through. Make sure the meat is done by making a small cut down by the bone, where the meat always cooks more slowly. It should be juicy, but without a trace of pink.

● **A loin chop** 1 inch thick, or a *rib chop* $\frac{3}{4}$ inch thick (both about 6 oz in weight) will take $5\frac{1}{2}$ to 6 minutes on each side, set 3 inches under a thoroughly preheated grill. Brush with butter as it cooks to prevent meat drying out. Pork, too, can be finished in the oven after it has been marked and browned on both sides under the grill.

Flavourings Instead of ordinary butter, you can brush the pork with a pounded lemon and parsley butter, or one flavoured with juniper, shallot, sage, rosemary, or mixed herbs.

Grilled Pork Chops

Serves 4

4 tender pork chops, 3/4–1-inch thick
Salt and freshly ground black pepper
4 tablespoons olive oil
2 tablespoons dry white wine
2 level tablespoons finely chopped onion
2 bay leaves, crumbled

1 Two hours before you are ready to grill pork chops, lay chops in a flat porcelain or earthenware rectangular baking dish just large enough to hold them in one layer. Season chops generously with salt and freshly ground black pepper and spoon over olive oil, dry white wine, finely chopped onion and crumbled bay leaves. Allow chops to marinate in this mixture, turning them once in the two hours.

2 Twenty minutes before you are ready to grill chops, preheat grill at maximum temperature and turn on the oven set at moderately hot (400°F. Mark 6).

3 Place chops on the rack of the grill pan; slide pan under the grill so that chops are 3 inches away from the heat and grill them for 5–6 minutes on each side, basting them with marinade juices from time to time.

4 Transfer pork chops to rectangular baking dish; pour over pan juices and give them about 10 minutes more in the oven, or until chops are cooked through.

1 1/2 lb pork loin, shoulder
  or fillet
4 bay leaves
Thinly sliced onion
Thinly sliced tomato
Olive oil
Finely chopped onion
Salt and freshly ground black
  pepper

Grilled Pork Brochettes

1 Choose tender and fairly lean pork from the loin, shoulder or fillet. Cut it into even-sized pieces about 1 inch square.

2 Thread pork cubes on 4–8 metal skewers (according to their size) alternately with small pieces of bay leaf and thin onion and tomato slices. Brush pork and vegetables with olive oil; roll in finely chopped onion and season generously with salt and freshly ground black pepper.

3 Twenty minutes before you are ready to grill brochettes, pre-heat grill at maximum temperature.

4 When ready to grill: place brochettes on the grid of your grill pan; slide pan under the grill so that brochettes are 3 inches away from the heat and grill them for 7 to 8 minutes, turning brochettes once during cooking time.

Grilling Chicken

Half a tender young spring chicken grilled until its skin crackles crisply, and served with a tossed green salad, is a dish fit for a king.

Grilling a whole chicken is not to be recommended. If it is small – say, no more than 2 lb drawn weight – split it down the middle and serve half a chicken per person. If larger, divide it into quarters or joints.

To halve a chicken Place the chicken on a chopping board, breast side up, with its neck towards you. With a large sharp knife, cut right through the centre of the breast, starting at the vent and cutting towards you. Slip the knife down the side of the breast bone, through the rib cage, and finally through the wish-bone.

Open the carcass out with your hands; then lay knife blade against the carcass and press down to cut chicken in two. I like to use a cleaver at this point as it is quicker. Chop off centre of backbone with knife or cleaver to give you two even-sided portions. Remove wing tips and ends of the leg joints. Keep backbone and wing tips and other trimmings to make a stock.

To Grill Chicken Halves

1 Two hours before you are ready to grill chicken, marinate chicken halves in a mixture of 6 tablespoons each dry white wine and olive oil, flavoured with 1 small clove of garlic finely chopped, 2 level tablespoons finely chopped onion, 2 crumbled bay leaves, a generous pinch each of paprika and cayenne pepper and salt and freshly ground black pepper, to taste.

2 Twenty minutes before you are ready to grill chicken, preheat grill at maximum temperature and turn on the oven set at moderately hot (400°F. Mark 6).

3 Line rack of grill-pan with a double-thickness of aluminium foil and lay chicken halves, cut side up, on the rack of the pan.

4 Slide pan under the grill so that chicken halves are about 3 inches from the heat and grill for 10 minutes, basting occasionally with its own juices plus a teaspoon or two of the marinade juices, if necessary. Then, turn the chicken pieces over; brush with pan juices and marinade and grill them on the other side for another 10 minutes.

5 Transfer foil lining and chicken halves to a large flat baking dish or roasting pan; pour over remaining marinade juices and give it about 10 more minutes in the oven to finish cooking.

6 To test chicken for doneness; cut it with the tip of a sharp knife at the drumstick. The meat should come away from the bone without any trouble, and the juices that pour out should be a clear golden colour.

To Grill Chicken Joints

Breast and wing joints, leg and thigh joints make wonderfully practical grills. Especially now that we can purchase the chicken pieces of our choice, chilled or frozen.

I like to marinate the chicken joints in the marinade above; or rub them with a 'devill'd mixture' of 1 level teaspoon each of salt, coarsely ground black pepper, ground ginger and dry mustard, softened with a little sugar, to taste, and then, brushed with olive oil and melted butter just before grilling.

Preheat grill as above and then grill breast and wing joints for 8 minutes on each side, brushing from time to time with marinade juices or melted butter and olive oil. Leg and thigh joints need a little more time. You'll find the three special marinades for lamb (see page 210) will also do wonders for grilled chicken.

Serves 4

A 3 1/2-lb roasting chicken
1 leek, white part only, split
3 stalks parsley
1 clove garlic, halved
1 bay leaf
1/4 teaspoon dried thyme
4–5 black peppercorns
1/4 pint dry white wine
Salt
Milk
7 level tablespoons butter
4 level tablespoons flour
1 level tablespoon finely
  chopped parsley
Freshly ground black pepper
5–6 oz fresh white
  breadcrumbs
4 eggs

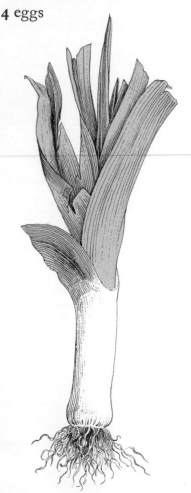

Chicken St Menehould

1 Divide chicken into eight joints, two from each breast and two from each leg.

2 Arrange them in a wide, heavy pan. Add next 6 ingredients. Pour over wine, together with $\frac{3}{4}$ pint water, and sprinkle with salt. Bring to simmering point over a low heat; cover pan and simmer gently until chicken is tender, about 20 minutes.

3 Remove pan from heat and leave chicken to cool in its stock.

4 Strain chicken stock; measure it and if necessary reduce to $\frac{1}{2}$ pint by fast boiling. Then make up to $\frac{3}{4}$ pint with milk.

5 In a medium-sized pan, melt 3 level tablespoons butter. Blend in flour with a wooden spoon and stir over a low heat for a minute or two longer to make a pale *roux*.

6 Gradually add stock and milk mixture, stirring vigorously to avoid lumps. Bring to the boil and simmer for 5 to 6 minutes longer, stirring, until very thick and smooth. Beat in chopped parsley; season with more salt if necessary and freshly ground black pepper, and leave until cold and solid enough to spread thickly.

7 Skin chicken joints carefully and pat them dry with absorbent paper. Spread thickly with cold sauce mixture and quickly roll in breadcrumbs. Chill joints until firm.

8 In a wide, shallow dish, beat eggs lightly with a fork until well mixed. Coat chicken joints all over with beaten egg; drain and cover with a second coating of breadcrumbs. Chill until quite firm again.

9 Prepare a moderate grill. Melt remaining butter in a small pan.

10 Arrange chicken joints on a rack in a grill-pan. Brush all over with melted butter and grill until crisp and golden brown. Continue turning and brushing joints with butter until evenly browned all over and hot through. Serve immediately.

Butters to go with Grilled Meats, Poultry and Fish

Garlic Butter I

1 Soften butter slightly in a mortar or bowl.

2 Add finely chopped garlic and parsley, and pound to a smooth paste.

3 Season to taste with lemon juice, salt and freshly ground black pepper to taste, and mix well.

4 Shape into a neat roll and chill until firm, tightly wrapped in foil to prevent garlic flavour contaminating other foods in the refrigerator.

Makes about 4 oz

4 oz butter
1–2 plump cloves garlic, finely chopped
1–2 level tablespoons finely chopped parsley
Lemon juice
Salt and freshly ground black pepper

Garlic Butter II

1 Peel garlic cloves; drop them into a pan of boiling water and simmer for 8 to 10 minutes. Drain well and pat dry.

2 Crush cloves to a paste in a mortar. Add butter and pound until smooth.

3 Season to taste with salt. Shape into a neat roll and chill as above.

Makes about 6 oz

2 oz garlic cloves
4 oz butter
Salt

Beurre Blanc

Beurre Blanc or 'white butter' is usually served hot with poached or steamed fish. Take care not to let sauce separate when whisking in butter, or all you will have is – melted butter. This is definitely '*a tour de main*' recipe. You'll have to get the 'knack' before it will work every time.

1 Combine finely chopped shallots with dry white wine in an enamelled or stainless steel pan or bowl (aluminium might discolour), and simmer until liquid is reduced to about 1 tablespoon, which will take about 30 minutes. If it evaporates too quickly, add a little more wine.

2 Transfer reduced mixture to a bowl and place over a saucepan of hot water. (Use a saucepan which will hold the rim of the bowl firmly and make quite sure that bottom of bowl is not touching water.)

Makes 6–8 oz

3 shallots, finely chopped
1/4 pint dry white wine
6–8 oz softened butter, diced
White wine vinegar
Salt and freshly ground black pepper

3 Gradually whisk in diced butter a few pieces at a time, until sauce becomes thick.

4 Flavour sauce with a few drops white wine vinegar, and season to taste with salt and freshly ground black pepper. Strain and serve immediately.

Anchovy Butter

Makes about 6 oz

2 oz anchovy fillets
4 oz unsalted butter

Use to garnish fish, grilled beef or veal, and some egg dishes. You can substitute anchovy paste for the fillets, but the flavour will be less subtle.

1 Rinse anchovy fillets thoroughly and pat them dry.

2 Pound anchovies to a paste in a mortar; add butter and pound again until smooth and well blended.

3 Shape into a neat roll and chill until firm.

Green Butter

Makes just over ½ lb

1/2 lb softened butter
2 hard-boiled eggs, sieved
2 tablespoons olive oil
1–2 cloves garlic, crushed
12 spinach leaves
6 lettuce leaves
6 sprigs watercress
6 sprigs parsley
2 shallots, finely chopped
2 level tablespoons capers, chopped
1/2 level teaspoon French mustard
Lemon juice
Salt and freshly ground black pepper

Delicious with poached or grilled fish – halibut, turbot and salmon in particular.

1 Place softened butter, sieved hard-boiled eggs, olive oil and crushed garlic cloves in an electric blender, and blend until creamy. (If you do not have an electric blender, pound ingredients to a creamy paste in a mortar.) Add more oil if mixture seems too dry.

2 Remove stems from spinach leaves. Blanch spinach, lettuce, watercress, parsley sprigs and shallots. Drain thoroughly; chop together finely and add to the butter mixture, together with capers and French mustard.

3 Beat until well blended; then beat in lemon juice, salt and freshly ground black pepper, to taste. Chill until ready to serve.

Roquefort Chive Butter

Makes about 6 oz

2 oz Roquefort cheese
4 oz butter
3–4 level tablespoons finely chopped chives
Juice of 1 small lemon

Magnificent with grilled steak or lamb chops

1 Pound Roquefort with butter until smooth and well blended. Beat in finely chopped herbs and lemon juice to taste.

2 Shape into a neat roll and chill until firm.

Shallot Butter

Serve with grilled meat dishes, or fish.

1 Peel shallots and drop them whole into a pan of boiling water. Boil for 1 minute; drain well and pat dry. Chop shallots very finely.

2 Beat butter until creamy. Add finely chopped shallots and beat vigorously until well blended. Season to taste with salt.

3 Shape into a neat roll and chill until firm.

Makes about 6 oz

2 oz shallots
4 oz butter
Salt

Tarragon Butter

Made with fresh tarragon, this butter has a very light, subtle flavour. Use it to garnish delicate dishes of fish, eggs and poached chicken.

1 Strip leaves from tarragon sprigs and drop them into a small pan of boiling salted water. Boil for 2 minutes; then drain in a sieve and rinse thoroughly under the cold tap.

2 Pat leaves dry. Put them in a mortar and pound to a paste (or chop them finely and put them in a bowl).

3 Add butter and pound until smooth and well blended. Season to taste with salt and freshly ground black pepper.

4 Shape butter into a neat roll and chill until firm.

Makes 8 oz

4 sprigs fresh tarragon
Salt
8 oz butter
Freshly ground black pepper

White Wine Butter (Chilled)

Serve with steamed or poached fish.

1 Beat butter until very light and fluffy.

2 Add wine a few drops at a time, beating vigorously between each addition.

3 Beat in finely chopped parsley and season to taste with salt and freshly ground black pepper. Chill until ready to serve.

Makes about 4 oz

4 oz softened butter
5–6 tablespoons dry white wine
2–3 level tablespoons finely chopped parsley
Salt and freshly ground black pepper

Makes about 4 oz

3 level tablespoons finely
chopped watercress (or
parsley)
4 oz softened butter
1–2 teaspoons lemon juice
Salt and freshly ground black
pepper

Watercress or Parsley Butter

Watercress butter makes a good garnish for chops and steaks,
while a pat of parsley butter can transform a dish of plain boiled
vegetables.

1 In a bowl, combine finely chopped watercress or parsley with
softened butter.

2 Flavour with lemon juice and season to taste with salt and
freshly ground black pepper. Pat into a neat roll and chill until
firm.

Makes about 4 oz

4 oz butter
1 level teaspoon curry paste
1/2 level teaspoon tomato
concentrate
Salt

Curry Butter

Curry butter should always be made with curry paste and not
powder, which gives a much coarser, drier flavour. Serve it with
a rich, oily fish – mackerel is ideal – or as a garnish for a bowl of
plain steamed rice.

1 Pound butter with curry paste and tomato concentrate until
smooth and well blended. Season to taste with a pinch of salt.

2 Shape into a neat roll. Wrap tightly in foil (or pack into a
tightly covered container) to prevent curry aroma transferring
to other foods in the refrigerator, and chill until firm.

Makes about 4 oz

4 oz butter
1–2 level tablespoons finely
chopped parsley
1–2 tablespoons lemon juice
Salt and freshly ground black
pepper

Maître d'Hôtel Butter

For grilled fish, steak, lamb chops and hamburgers, and plain
boiled vegetables.

1 Cream butter in a bowl with a wooden spoon.

2 Add finely chopped parsley and lemon juice, and beat until
thoroughly blended.

3 Season to taste with salt and freshly ground black pepper.

4 Pat into a neat roll and chill until firm.

Note : *Maître d'hôtel* butter can also be served hot: melt the
butter over a low heat and combine with remaining ingredients.

Lesson 9
More Exciting Vegetable Dishes

To big-city dwellers, the so-called 'exotic' vegetables – aubergines, sweet potatoes and the like – have long been a familiar sight on the stalls of street markets, often only a little more expensive than they would be in their native land. In the provinces, however, it was a different story until much more recently. But in the last few years I have been surprised and delighted to find a growing selection appearing in the windows of greengrocers even in remote country towns. The trouble is that while few people know what to *do* with an aubergine or a pepper, and consequently the demand stays small, the provincial shop is likely to be discouraged from widening the selection even further.

The *raison d'être* for this chapter is part-exotic, but even more a way of showing you how you can get right away from the 'boiled greens' or 'two tired veg'-type of dish by applying just a little more effort and imagination.

Vegetable purées Take this small section on vegetable purées, for example. They are, if anything, less tricky to do well than boiling (or steaming) a fresh vegetable to perfection. And if you have an electric blender or a sturdy *mouli-legumes*, the actual work is minimal compared to the result.

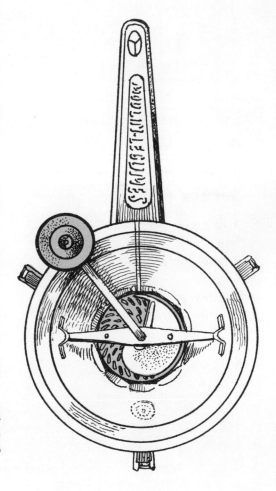

● The vegetables should be cooked to complete softness, but if you get them *mushy*, you will have to evaporate excess moisture by beating the purée vigorously over a low heat.

● If the purée still seems too slack and watery, beat in some hot mashed potato, or even simpler, a tablespoon or two of instant potato purée. I frequently sieve the purée instead of blending it, and then mix it with the contents of the sieve – skins, husks or whatever – to add texture, as well as body.

● A dash of cream, a lump of butter and some seasoning (and don't forget a pinch of sugar to bring out the natural sweetness that many vegetables possess), and you have a side dish to accompany a gourmet-class main course.

Vegetable Purées

Pea, Sweetcorn or Carrot Purée

Serves 4–6

1 1/2 lb frozen peas or 1 lb frozen sweetcorn or 1½ lb fresh carrots, thinly sliced

4 tablespoons chicken stock (page 162)

4 level tablespoons butter

1–2 level tablespoons instant potato powder

1–2 level tablespoons double cream

Salt and freshly ground black pepper

Lemon juice and sugar (optional)

1 Place frozen peas or sweetcorn, or thinly sliced raw carrots, in a pan. Add chicken stock and butter.

2 Bring to the boil; push a sheet of greaseproof paper down into pan on top of vegetables; reduce heat to moderate and simmer until very tender: about 5 minutes for frozen vegetables, 10 to 12 minutes for fresh carrots.

3 Pour contents of pan into a blender. Add instant potato powder. Turn to maximum speed and blend for 2 minutes, stopping occasionally to scrape down sides of goblet with a spatula. (If a blender is not available, put vegetables through a *mouli* or rub through a sieve. In the case of sweetcorn, return contents of sieve to purée to give it bulk and texture.)

4 Return purée to pan. Beat vigorously with a wooden spoon over a moderate heat until purée is thoroughly hot again, adding just enough cream so that it still holds its shape.

5 Season purée to taste with salt and freshly ground black pepper. In addition, pea purée will be improved by a squeeze of lemon juice, sweetcorn by ½ level teaspoon sugar. Serve immediately.

Note: If you wish, you can serve a tablespoon or two of the cooked peas or sweetcorn kernels for garnish. Carrot purée looks well with a garnish of finely chopped parsley.

Purée of Green Beans

Serves 4–6

1 lb green beans

Salt

4 level tablespoons double cream

Freshly ground black pepper

Freshly grated nutmeg

Use an electric blender for a particularly smooth purée. You can bind the purée with a little butter instead of cream; or it is excellent cold, mixed with a little well-flavoured mayonnaise (page 43).

1 Trim beans; wash them and drain well.

2 Bring a pan of water to the boil. When it begins to bubble, add a generous pinch of salt and the beans. Boil briskly for 30 minutes, or until very tender. Drain thoroughly.

3 Purée beans through a fine sieve and return to the pan. Reheat over a moderate heat, beating vigorously with a wooden spoon to evaporate excess moisture.

4 Add cream; mix well and season to taste with salt, freshly ground black pepper and a pinch of freshly grated nutmeg.

5 Spoon into a heated serving dish and serve immediately.

Purée of Brussels Sprouts

Serves 4

1 Place brussels sprouts and chicken stock in a pan. Bring to the boil over high heat; cover pan tightly and continue to cook over a moderately high heat for 5 minutes, or until sprouts are tender.

2 Pour contents of pan into the goblet of an electric blender and blend to a purée. (You will have to stop machine several times to scrape down sides.) Add cream and egg yolk, and carry on blending to a smooth purée.

3 Scrape purée into the top of a double saucepan and cook over simmering water, beating in lemon juice, salt, freshly ground black pepper and a pinch each of freshly grated nutmeg and sugar, to taste. Last of all, beat in butter.

4 Continue to cook purée until thoroughly hot again, with the consistency of thick whipped cream. Serve immediately.

1 lb frozen brussels sprouts
4 tablespoon chicken stock (page 162)
2 level tablespoons double cream
1 egg yolk
1/2 teaspoon lemon juice
Salt and freshly ground black pepper
Freshly grated nutmeg
Pinch of sugar
1 level tablespoon butter

Artichoke Purée

Serves 6

1 Scrub artichokes clean and drop them into a pan of boiling salted water. Bring to the boil and simmer for 15 to 20 minutes, or until tender. Drain artichokes thoroughly and peel them as soon as they are cool enough to handle.

2 Press artichokes through a sieve or purée in a vegetable mill. Return purée to the rinsed-out pan and stir over a moderate heat to evaporate excess moisture. Purée will thicken quite considerably, and the rather delicate artichoke flavour will be intensified.

3 Beat in cream and gradually add butter in small pieces, still beating.

4 When butter has melted, remove pan from heat. Beat in egg yolks if used – these greatly improve the rather dull colour of the purée – season to taste with salt and freshly ground black pepper, and serve very hot, garnished with finely chopped parsley.

3 lb Jerusalem artichokes
Salt
3 level tablespoons lightly whipped cream
3 level tablespoons butter
3 egg yolks (optional)
Freshly ground black pepper
Finely chopped parsley

Serves 4

2 lb fresh peas
1 lettuce heart, shredded
12 tiny spring onions or **1/2** Spanish onion, sliced
3 sprigs parsley
4 tablespoons chicken stock (page 162) (or water)
4 oz butter
Sugar
Salt
1–2 boiled potatoes (optional – see above)

Purée Saint-Germain

A light, delicate purée which can also be made with frozen peas. If you find it too thin – the texture depends on the quality and age of the peas – blend in one or two hot boiled potatoes.

1 Put peas in a pan with the shredded lettuce heart, spring onions or onion slices, parsley, chicken stock (or water), half the butter, and sugar and salt, to taste. Bring to the boil and simmer until peas are tender.

2 Discard parsley sprigs. Drain peas, reserving liquor. Strain liquor.

3 Blend peas to a smooth purée in an electric blender.

4 Turn pea purée into the top of a double saucepan; beat in a little of the strained liquor and the remaining butter, and reheat thoroughly. Serve immediately.

Serves 4

1 lb frozen peas
4 level tablespoons butter
4 tablespoons strong chicken (cube) stock
1/2 Spanish onion, very finely chopped
Salt and freshly ground black pepper
About **1/2** lb floury potatoes

Purée Clamart

A light, fluffy purée of fresh or frozen peas with an enticing colour and a rich, delicious flavour. Puréed potato is blended into the peas in just sufficient quantity to make it hold its shape, the amount varying slightly according to the variety and age of the peas, and the dryness of the potato purée.

1 Cover peas with cold water in a pan; bring to the boil. Drain.

2 Return peas to pan with butter, chicken stock, very finely chopped onion, and a pinch each of salt and freshly ground black pepper; cover and simmer until peas are tender and have absorbed most of the liquid.

3 Meanwhile, peel and boil potatoes in salted water. Drain; toss over a moderate heat to evaporate remaining moisture; then press through a sieve. Put about half of potato purée in a large bowl.

4 Purée cooked peas, together with any remaining liquor, in an electric blender. (Do *not* use a sieve, which would trap the pea skins and leave a soup-like mixture requiring too much potato to thicken it.)

5 Gradually add blended peas to potato purée in bowl, beating vigorously. If purée does not hold its shape when lifted with a spoon, beat in a little more potato.

6 Add more salt or freshly ground black pepper if necessary, and keep hot over a pan of simmering water until ready to serve.

Super Potato Dishes

Sweet Potatoes

These exotic vegetables deserve to be better known in this country. You will often find them in West Indian shops and street markets: gnarled, red, tubular roots that can grow to an amazing size. Avoid the very big ones, though, for they tend to be fibrous. Although sweet potatoes haven't the slightest connection with potatoes, they certainly are sweet, with a mealy, crumbly texture which I find goes well with meat and poultry. Sometimes the flavour is reminiscent of chestnuts, sometimes more like baked or roast parsnips.

Boiled Sweet Potatoes

Scrub sweet potatoes and cut them into suitable chunks that will fit readily into your saucepan. Bring a pan of salted water to the boil. Add potatoes and cook for 15 to 20 minutes, or until soft. (Test with the point of a knife as you would ordinary potatoes.)

Drain, peel and serve hot with butter and salt.

Baked Sweet Potatoes

Scrub sweet potatoes. Dry them and bake in a moderate oven (375°F. Mark 5) for 40 to 50 minutes, or until they feel quite soft when squeezed gently. Remove potatoes from oven, peel and then mash them with butter and double cream, as you would ordinary potatoes. Season generously with salt and freshly ground black pepper.

Roast Sweet Potatoes

Peel sweet potatoes and cut them into chunks. Boil in salted water for 10 minutes and drain. Then either put them in the roasting tin with the meat (add an extra tablespoon or two of butter if meat juices are scarce) or roast them in a separate baking dish, adding 4 level tablespoons butter per lb of sweet potato. They will take 45 to 50 minutes, depending on the size of the chunks.

Sautéed Sweet Potatoes with Orange

Delicious with pork or poultry. Peel sweet potatoes; cut them into chunks and boil as above. When they are tender, drain them thoroughly and cut into ¼-inch dice.

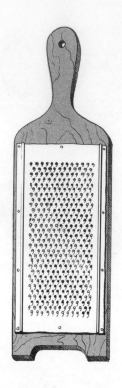

For 1 lb diced sweet potato, melt 4 level tablespoons butter in a frying-pan. Sauté diced potatoes gently for 5 minutes, turning them to colour them evenly.

Add ½ level teaspoon finely grated orange rind and continue to sauté until potatoes are crisp and golden.

Remove pan from heat. Sprinkle potatoes with 2 tablespoons orange juice; toss lightly and serve immediately in a heated serving dish.

Sweet Potato Chips

Scrub sweet potatoes and cook in boiling salted water for 10 minutes. Drain, peel and cut into chips.

Deep-fry in oil heated to 375°F. for 5 minutes, or until crisp and golden, with a soft, floury centre.

Drain on absorbent paper and serve immediately, sprinkled with salt.

Swedish Potato Pancakes

Old potatoes
Salt and freshly ground
    black pepper
Oil or lard, for frying

Though not, strictly speaking, deep-fried, these are a cross between a potato crisp and a pancake. They make an attractive garnish for meat or game, or even just a snack of bacon and egg.

1 Peel potatoes and grate them coarsely on a plate, making the shreds as long as possible. Season to taste with salt and freshly ground black pepper.

2 In a large, heavy frying-pan, heat just enough oil or lard to cover the base with a thin film.

3 Drop level tablespoonfuls of potato into the hot pan, well spaced apart, and quickly spread them out with the back of the spoon, making each one a thin, round, lacy network of potato strips. (The starch in the potato will make the shreds stick together.)

4 Fry until the underside of each pancake is crisp and golden brown. Then flip it over and continue to fry until the other side is brown and potato shreds are cooked through. Add more oil or lard to the pan as necessary.

5 Drain pancakes on absorbent paper and keep hot in a very slow oven (300°F. Mark 2) while you prepare more in the same way. They will remain crisp provided you don't stack them on top of each other.

Rösti

(Swiss Potato Cake)

1 With a stiff brush, scrub potatoes clean under running water.

2 Put potatoes in a large pan. Cover with water; add salt and bring to the boil. Simmer for 15 minutes, or until potatoes are three-quarters cooked. Remove pan from heat. Cover and leave for 15 minutes. Then cool under cold running water.

3 When potatoes are cool enough to handle, peel off skins. Grate potatoes as coarsely as possible into a large bowl.

4 Add the very finely chopped onion and 1 level tablespoon butter in small flakes, and toss lightly with a large fork to mix them in without crushing potatoes. Season generously with salt and freshly ground black pepper.

5 In a heavy, 9-inch frying-pan (base measurement), heat remaining butter and bacon fat or olive oil together. When fat is quite hot, add potato mixture. Pat it lightly into a cake with straight sides – the mixture must not be too compact, to allow steam to escape – and fry over a gentle heat for 15 minutes, or until underside is crusty and well browned. Shake pan gently from time to time to make sure bottom of cake has not stuck.

6 Heat a flat plate slightly larger in diameter than the top of your frying-pan.

7 When *rösti* is cooked underneath, turn it out on to the plate and quickly slip it straight back into the frying-pan. Continue to fry gently for a further 10 to 15 minutes, or until the other side is crisp and well browned.

8 Turn out on to a hot, flat serving dish and serve immediately, cut in wedges like a cake.

Note: I sometimes sprinkle the raw potato cake with a little freshly grated Gruyère cheese while it is cooking to add a little more flavour.

Serves 4

About 1 1/2 lb large old potatoes

Salt

1 Spanish onion, very finely chopped

2 level tablespoons butter

Freshly ground black pepper

2 tablespoons bacon fat or olive oil

Freshly grated Gruyère (optional)

Serves 6

2–2 1/2 lb potatoes
1 large green pepper
1 large Spanish onion
1 level tablespoon flour
4 level tablespoons finely
  chopped parsley
4 oz freshly grated cheese
Pinch of cayenne
Salt and freshly ground black
  pepper
1/4 pint hot milk
1/4 pint double cream
2 level tablespoons butter

Potatoes O'Brien

Particularly good with lamb or pork.

1 Preheat oven to moderately hot (400°F. Mark 6).

2 Peel potatoes and cut them into ¼-inch dice. Place them in a bowl. Slice pepper in half; remove core and seeds, and chop flesh finely. Add to potatoes. Peel and chop onion finely; toss lightly with diced potatoes and pepper.

3 Sprinkle with flour, chopped parsley and grated cheese, and toss again. Then season to taste with a pinch of cayenne, salt and a little freshly ground black pepper, bearing in mind that the mixture may already be quite peppery because of the green pepper.

4 Spread potato mixture evenly in a 3-pint, ovenproof dish; pour over milk and cream; dot with butter and bake for 1 hour, or until potatoes are soft, with a crisp, golden brown topping.

Serves 4

1 lb new potatoes
2 level tablespoons butter
1/4 pint double cream
8 level tablespoons freshly
  grated Gruyère
4 level tablespoons freshly
  grated Parmesan
Salt and freshly ground black
  pepper

Gratin Dauphinois I

1 Peel or scrape potatoes and slice them very thinly (about $\frac{1}{16}$ inch thick). Rinse thoroughly and leave to soak in a bowl of cold water for 15 minutes.

2 Select a shallow ovenproof dish about 9 by 5 inches. Grease with 2 level teaspoons of the butter.

3 Preheat oven to very slow (300°F. Mark 2).

4 Drain potato slices and dry them thoroughly with a cloth or absorbent paper.

5 Arrange a quarter of the potato slices in the dish in overlapping rows; pour over 2 level tablespoons cream; sprinkle with 2 level tablespoons Gruyère and 1 level tablespoon Parmesan; dot with 1 level teaspoon butter; and finally, season to taste with salt and freshly ground black pepper.

6 Repeat layers exactly as above, making four in all, and ending with grated cheese and butter.

7 Bake *gratin* for 1 hour 20 minutes, or until potatoes feel tender when pierced with a sharp skewer and are golden and bubbling on top. Allow to 'settle' for a few minutes before serving.

● If top browns too quickly, cover with a sheet of foil.

● If and when you use old potatoes, the cooking time will be slightly shorter.

Gratin Dauphinois II

Serves 4

1 Peel or scrape potatoes and slice them very thinly (about 1/16 inch thick). Rinse thoroughly and leave to soak in a bowl of cold water for 15 minutes.

2 Select a shallow ovenproof dish about 9 by 5 inches. Grease with butter.

3 Preheat oven to moderate (350°F. Mark 4).

4 Drain potato slices and dry them thoroughly with a cloth or absorbent paper.

5 Arrange a quarter of the potato slices in the dish in over-lapping rows; sprinkle evenly with 3 level tablespoons grated Gruyère, and salt and freshly ground black pepper, to taste.

6 Continue in this manner until potatoes and cheese are used up, finishing with a layer of cheese.

7 Pour over milk and cream.

8 Bake for 1 hour, or until potatoes feel tender when pierced with a sharp skewer and are golden and bubbling on top.

1 lb new potatoes
2 level teaspoons butter
12 level tablespoons (4 oz) freshly grated Gruyère
Salt and freshly ground black pepper
1/4 pint milk
1/4 pint double cream

Pommes Sautées à la Lyonnaise

Serves 3–4

1 Scrub potatoes clean and boil them in their jackets in salted water until *just* cooked – it won't hurt if they remain slightly undercooked. Plunge into cold water and leave to cool.

2 When potatoes are cold, peel and slice them $\frac{1}{8}$ inch thick. Combine with shredded onion, mixing carefully to avoid breaking potato slices.

3 Melt butter in a heavy frying-pan. When hot, add potato-onion mixture and sauté over a moderate heat, turning frequently with a spatula, until mixture is crisp and golden. Season to taste with salt and freshly ground black pepper towards the end of cooking time.

4 Turn potato mixture on to a heated serving dish and serve immediately, sprinkled with finely chopped parsley.

1 lb even-sized potatoes
Salt
1 medium-sized Spanish onion, finely shredded
4 level tablespoons butter
Freshly ground black pepper
2 level tablespoons finely chopped parsley

Serves 4

2 lb large potatoes
3 level tablespoons butter
1 tablespoon olive oil
Salt and freshly ground black
  pepper
Finely chopped parsley, to
  garnish

Pommes Parisiennes

1 Peel, wash and dry potatoes.

2 Holding a potato firmly in one hand, press the bowl of a 1-inch Parisienne cutter (the same gadget you use to make melon balls) into the flesh, open side down. Twist gently from side to side until you can scoop out a neat ball of potato. Scoop as many balls as you can out of each potato – the trimmings can be used in a *vichyssoise* (leek and potato soup), or boiled and mashed.

3 Dry potato balls thoroughly.

4 Select a large, heavy frying-pan which will hold all the potato balls in one layer. Melt butter and oil in it and, when foaming subsides, add potato balls. Sauté over a moderate heat, shaking pan frequently, so that potato balls brown evenly, for 15 minutes, or until they are crisp and golden on the outside, and feel soft when pierced with the point of a knife. Season to taste with salt and freshly ground black pepper.

5 Drain potato balls thoroughly and serve immediately, sprinkled with finely chopped parsley.

Serves 4–6

2 lb old potatoes
Salt
Butter
3 level tablespoons freshly
  grated Parmesan
Freshly ground black pepper
2 eggs
1 level tablespoon stale white
  breadcrumbs

Pommes Viennoises

1 Peel potatoes and boil them in salted water until they feel soft when pierced with a fork.

2 Preheat oven to fairly hot (425°F. Mark 7).

3 When potatoes are cooked, drain them thoroughly, tossing them in a dry pan over a moderate heat to evaporate remaining moisture.

4 Mash hot potatoes to a smooth purée, or rub them through a wire sieve, adding 4 level tablespoons butter, 2 level tablespoons freshly grated Parmesan, and salt and freshly ground black pepper, to taste.

5 Whisk 1 egg vigorously. Add to potato purée and beat until thoroughly blended.

6 Divide purée into 12 equal portions. Roll each portion into a fat oval, and pat into the shape of a small loaf. Cut diagonal slashes on top of each 'loaf'.

7 Butter a large baking sheet. Transfer potato loaves to it and brush tops with remaining egg, beaten. Sprinkle each loaf with remaining grated Parmesan and breadcrumbs, mixed.

8 Bake loaves for about 20 minutes, or until puffed and golden brown. Serve immediately.

Pommes Dauphine

1 Peel potatoes; cut them up if they are very large and boil in salted water until cooked but not mushy. Drain well and toss in a dry pan over a low heat to evaporate all excess moisture.

2 Press potatoes through a sieve into a bowl. Beat in 2 level tablespoons butter and the lightly beaten egg yolks, and season to taste with salt, freshly ground black pepper and freshly grated nutmeg. Cool.

3 Meanwhile, combine remaining butter with $\frac{1}{4}$ pint water in a heavy pan. Bring to the boil over a moderate heat.

4 Sift flour on to a sheet of greaseproof paper.

5 When water boils, remove pan from heat and quickly pour in flour all at once. Beat vigorously with a wooden spoon until well mixed; then return pan to a low heat and continue to beat for 2 to 3 minutes longer until paste forms itself into a ball around the spoon, leaving bottom and sides clean. This mixture is called a *panada*. It should not be overcooked or it will become oily.

6 Remove the saucepan from the heat and add the eggs one at a time, beating each one in very thoroughly until the dough is of a good consistency.

7 Put a pan of oil on to heat.

8 Blend potato purée smoothly with (*choux*) paste. Correct seasoning.

9 Spoon potato mixture into a piping bag fitted with a plain, $\frac{1}{2}$-inch nozzle. Pipe out 1-inch lengths on to a sheet of lightly oiled greaseproof paper, snipping them off with a pair of kitchen scissors. (Dip scissors in hot water occasionally to prevent mixture sticking to them.)

10 When temperature of oil reaches 350°F. – a bread cube should brown in 90 seconds – carefully drop in 15 to 20 little rolls at a time and deep-fry for 5 minutes, or until puffed and golden.

11 Drain thoroughly on absorbent paper and serve immediately.

Pommes Lorette

Prepare as above, but coat the little potato rolls in finely chopped blanched almonds before deep-frying them. You will need about 6 oz almonds for this recipe.

2 lb floury potatoes
Salt
4 level tablespoons butter
2 egg yolks, lightly beaten
Freshly ground black pepper
Freshly grated nutmeg
4 oz plain flour
3 eggs
Oil for deep-frying

Serves 4

1 1/2 lb shelled broad beans,
  fresh or frozen
12 button onions
1 small or 1/2 large head
  lettuce
4 level tablespoons butter
1/2 level teaspoon crumbled
  savory or thyme
1/4 level teaspoon castor sugar
Salt and freshly ground black
  pepper
4 tablespoons beef stock
  (page 161)
Dash each of Worcestershire
  and soy sauces
4 level tablespoon finely
  chopped parsley

Broad Beans and Lettuce

1 Remove skins of any beans which are large and tough. Peel button onions carefully. Wash and drain lettuce thoroughly.

2 Melt butter in a saucepan and sauté onions until golden brown.

3 Add broad beans; cover and simmer for 5 minutes if frozen, 10 to 12 minutes if fresh.

4 When beans are tender but still very firm, add lettuce, savory (or thyme), sugar, and salt and freshly ground black pepper, to taste. Moisten with stock; add Worcestershire and soy sauces, and simmer gently for a further 5 minutes.

5 Turn beans into a deep, heated serving dish. Sprinkle with finely chopped parsley and serve immediately.

Serves 4

1 1/2 lb broad beans, fresh
  or frozen
Salt
Butter
1 oz plain flour
3/4 pint milk
1 egg yolk, lightly beaten
Freshly ground black pepper
Freshly grated nutmeg
1–2 level tablespoons freshly
  grated Parmesan
1–2 level tablespoons freshly
  grated Gruyère

Gratin of Broad Beans

1 Simmer fresh beans in a large pan of boiling salted water for 10 to 15 minutes, or until tender. (For frozen beans, follow directions on packet.)

2 To make sauce: melt 1 oz butter in a heavy saucepan and stir in flour; stir over a low heat for 2 minutes to make a pale *roux*. Then gradually add milk and bring to the boil, stirring vigorously until sauce is smooth and thick. Simmer gently for 7 to 10 minutes, stirring frequently.

3 Remove pan from heat. Mix in the lightly beaten egg yolk.

4 Season sauce lightly with salt, taking into account the saltiness of the cheese which you will sprinkle on top, and more generously with freshly ground black pepper and a pinch of grated nutmeg, to taste.

5 Butter a gratin dish.

6 When beans are tender, drain them. Remove outer skins if they are very tough.

7 Fold beans into sauce and pour into gratin dish. Sprinkle with a mixture of grated Parmesan and Gruyère, and dot with 2 level tablespoons butter.

8 Brown dish under a hot grill until top is crisp and bubbling, and serve immediately.

Jerusalem Artichokes au Gratin

Serves 4

Excellent with roast or grilled meat, or, more simply, with a few rashers of crisp bacon.

1 Scrub artichokes clean and drop them into a pan of boiling salted water. Bring to the boil and simmer for 15 to 20 minutes, or until tender. Then drain thoroughly and peel as soon as artichokes are cool enough to handle.

2 Butter a 3-pint ovenproof dish and slice artichokes into it. Preheat oven to fairly hot (425°F. Mark 7).

3 In a heavy pan, melt 1 oz butter; add flour and stir over a low heat for a minute or two to make a pale *roux*.

4 Gradually add milk, stirring constantly until sauce is smooth, and bring to the boil; simmer, stirring occasionally, for 7 to 10 minutes.

5 Remove sauce from heat. Beat in 2 oz butter and the egg yolks, followed by 2 oz each grated Parmesan and Gruyère. Season to taste with salt and freshly ground black pepper.

6 Spoon sauce over artichokes, making sure they are completely covered, and sprinkle remaining cheese over the top.

7 Bake for 15 minutes, or until bubbling and golden brown, and serve immediately.

2 lb Jerusalem artichokes
Salt
Butter
1 oz flour
1 pint milk
3 egg yolks
3 oz freshly grated Parmesan
3 oz freshly grated Gruyère
Freshly ground black pepper

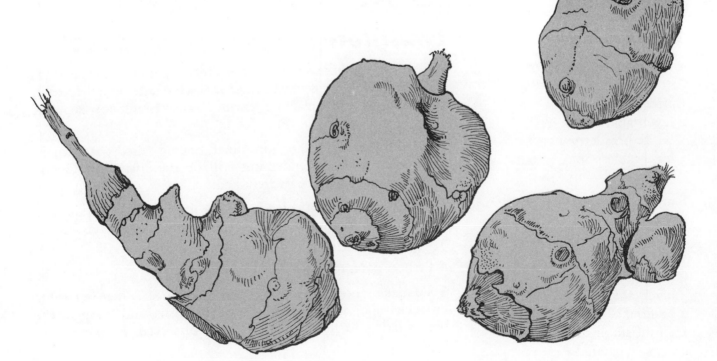

Serves 3–4

1 medium-sized vegetable
marrow, about 2 lb
1 tablespoon olive oil
2 level tablespoons butter
1 Spanish onion, finely
chopped
1 fat clove garlic, finely
chopped
4 ripe tomatoes, peeled and
seeded
1 level tablespoon tomato
concentrate
2 level tablespoons finely
chopped parsley
Generous pinch of oregano
Salt and freshly ground black
pepper
2 oz grated Cheddar
1 oz stale white breadcrumbs

Vegetable Marrow au Gratin

If using part of a very large marrow for this dish, be sure to
scrape out all the woody membranes, as no amount of cooking
will make them soft.

1 Preheat oven to moderately hot (400°F. Mark 6).

2 Peel marrow, divide it in half and scoop out seeds and membranes with a spoon. Cut flesh into 1-inch dice.

3 In a sauté pan or deep frying-pan, heat oil with 1 level tablespoon butter and sauté finely chopped onion and garlic over a
low heat until soft and transparent, 4 to 5 minutes.

4 Add peeled and seeded tomatoes and tomato concentrate and
continue to cook, stirring constantly, for 2 more minutes.

5 Add cubed marrow and herbs, and season to taste with salt
and freshly ground black pepper. Sauté over a moderate heat
until marrow is golden, turning contents of pan with a spatula to
mix them thoroughly.

6 Transfer marrow and onions to a baking dish. Mix grated
cheese and breadcrumbs together, and sprinkle them over the
top. Dot surface with remaining butter.

7 Bake for 30 minutes, or until marrow feels soft when pierced
with a fork and topping is crisp, golden and bubbling. Serve hot.

Serves 4

1 medium-sized cauliflower
Salt
Butter
2 level tablespoons fresh
white breadcrumbs
3 level tablespoons grated
Cheddar

Sauce
1 pint milk
1 chicken stock cube
1/2 bay leaf
6 black peppercorns
3 level tablespoons butter
2 oz flour
1/4 pint single cream
2 eggs, separated
Squeeze of lemon juice
Salt and freshly ground black
pepper

Cauliflower Soufléed au Gratin

1 Separate cauliflower into flowerets as follows. Cut into
quarters; slice away central core from each quarter and discard it,
together with any remaining leaves. Flowerets will now separate
easily and naturally.

2 Cook flowerets, covered, in $\frac{1}{2}$-inch boiling salted water for 10
to 15 minutes until tender but still on the crisp side. On no
account should they be overcooked.

3 Drain flowerets in a colander. Put colander over the saucepan
in which they were cooked; cover with the lid and leave (off the
heat) until needed.

4 Preheat oven to moderate (375°F. Mark 5).

5 To make sauce: pour milk into a medium-sized pan; crumble
in stock cube; add bay leaf and peppercorns, and bring to the
boil, stirring to make sure cube has dissolved. Remove from
heat.

6 In another pan, melt butter. Blend in flour with a wooden spoon and cook over a low heat, stirring, for 2 to 3 minutes to make a pale *roux*.

7 Gradually add flavoured milk, beating vigorously with the spoon to prevent lumps forming. Bring to the boil, stirring until sauce is thick and smooth, and simmer gently, uncovered, for 10 minutes, stirring frequently.

8 Butter a 2- to 2½-pint gratin dish.

9 Remove sauce from heat; beat in cream and egg yolks. Taste and add a squeeze of lemon juice and salt and freshly ground black pepper.

10 Strain sauce through a fine sieve into a bowl. Cool to luke-warm if cream and egg yolks have not already lowered the temperature sufficiently.

11 Whisk egg whites until stiff but not dry. Fold into tepid sauce with a metal spoon or spatula.

12 Spoon half of sauce evenly over base of gratin dish. Arrange cauliflowerets on top and cover with remaining sauce.

13 Mix breadcrumbs and cheese together; sprinkle evenly over surface and dot with 1 level tablespoon butter.

14 Bake cauliflower until sauce is puffed, with a crisp golden topping, about 30 minutes. Serve immediately.

Italian Cauliflower Mousse

Serves 4–6

1 Clean cauliflower, cut into quarters and cook in boiling salted water until very soft.

2 Preheat oven to moderate (350°F. Mark 4).

3 Drain cauliflower and rub through a fine sieve.

4 Beat in the eggs, egg yolk and double cream. Season generously with freshly ground black pepper and grated nutmeg.

5 Transfer to a well-buttered soufflé dish with a band of aluminium foil tied around it, or a deep charlotte tin, and place in a pan of hot water on top of the stove.

6 Bring water to the boil; then transfer to the oven and bake for 45 to 50 minutes, or until set.

7 Unmould on to a serving dish and mask with Hollandaise sauce. Garnish with sprigs of parsley and poached cauliflower flowerets.

1 large cauliflower
Salt
3 eggs
1 egg yolk
1/4 pint double cream
Freshly ground black pepper
Freshly grated nutmeg
Butter
Hollandaise sauce (page 190)
Sprigs of parsley
Flowerets of cauliflower, poached

Courgettes Soufflées

Serves 3–4 as an appetiser, 6 as an accompaniment

6 courgettes
Butter
Salt and freshly ground black pepper
1/4 pint Béchamel sauce (page 178)
2 egg yolks
Freshly grated Parmesan cheese
2 egg whites

1 Wash courgettes and cut them in half lengthwise. Scoop out flesh with a spoon, taking care not to pierce shells.

2 Cook courgette pulp in 2 level tablespoons butter until reduced to a thick purée. Season generously with salt and freshly ground black pepper.

3 Butter a baking dish that will hold courgette shells comfortably side by side.

4 Make a Béchamel sauce.

5 Remove sauce from heat and beat in egg yolks, one by one. Add cooked courgette pulp and freshly grated Parmesan, to taste. Check seasoning.

6 Preheat oven to slow (325°F. Mark 3).

7 Whisk egg whites until stiff but not dry and fold gently into lukewarm mixture.

8 Arrange courgettes shells in the buttered baking dish. Fill with soufflé mixture and bake for 25 minutes. Serve immediately.

Souffléed Aubergines

Serves 4 as an appetiser, 8 as an accompaniment

2 large aubergines or 4 medium-sized ones
Salt
1/2 pint milk
1 small onion, stuck with 2–3 cloves
1 bay leaf
4–5 black peppercorns
1 1/2 oz butter
1 oz flour
1 small onion, finely chopped
1/2 lb ripe tomatoes, skinned, seeded and chopped
1 clove garlic, finely chopped
2 level tablespoons finely chopped parsley
2 level teaspoons tomato concentrate
1–2 tablespoons lemon juice
2 eggs, separated
1 oz freshly grated Parmesan

An unusual and delicious way to deal with aubergines. Serve the 'soufflés' hot.

1 Halve aubergines lengthwise. With a sharp knife, make deep slashes in the cut surface, taking care not to break through skins. Rub generously with salt and leave upside down in a colander for at least 1 hour to allow bitter juices to drain away.

2 Preheat oven to slow (325°F. Mark 3).

3 Rinse aubergine halves in cold water, pressing them firmly but gently to rid them of as much moisture as possible, and dry thoroughly with a cloth or kitchen paper.

4 Arrange aubergine halves in a baking dish, cut sides up, and bake for 20 to 30 minutes, or until flesh is very soft. Remove from oven; cool slightly and scoop out flesh with a spoon, taking care not to damage shells.

5 Pour milk into a saucepan; add the onion stuck with cloves, bay leaf and peppercorns. Bring to the boil; remove pan from heat, cover and leave milk to infuse for at least ½ hour.

6 Melt 1 oz butter in a small saucepan; stir in flour to make a *roux* and cook over a low heat for 1 minute, taking care not to let it colour.

7 Strain milk and add to *roux* gradually, stirring constantly to prevent lumps forming. Bring to the boil and continue to cook, stirring, for 2 or 3 minutes until sauce thickens.

8 Melt remaining butter in another heavy pan and sauté finely chopped onion until transparent. Add peeled, seeded and chopped tomatoes, finely chopped garlic and parsley, tomato concentrate and lemon juice. Simmer for 2 minutes, stirring.

9 Combine tomato mixture with white sauce. Beat in 2 egg yolks and stir over a very low heat until mixture thickens. Remove from heat and allow to cool.

10 Chop aubergine flesh finely and add to sauce; mix well.

11 Whisk egg whites until stiff but not dry, and fold gently but thoroughly into sauce.

12 Pile mixture into aubergine shells. Sprinkle with finely grated Parmesan and bake for 10 to 15 minutes, or until filling is well risen and golden on top. Serve immediately.

Aubergines au Gratin

1 Peel and dice aubergines; salt them liberally and leave to drain in a colander for 1 hour. Then rinse off salt with cold water and shake diced aubergines dry in a cloth.

2 Combine olive oil and 2 level tablespoons butter in a frying pan, and sauté aubergines until golden. Remove from pan and reserve.

3 Preheat oven to moderate (375°F. Mark 5).

4 Add 2 level tablespoons butter to fats in the pan; add finely chopped onion and sauté until the onion just begins to turn colour.

5 Add tomato concentrate, peeled, seeded and coarsely chopped tomatoes and finely chopped garlic and parsley and mix well.

6 Add allspice, cinnamon, sugar and salt and freshly ground black pepper, to taste, and simmer mixture, stirring occasionally, for 5 minutes.

7 Add diced, sautéed aubergines and pour into a well-buttered gratin dish (or, if you prefer, individual soufflé dishes); sprinkle with breadcrumbs; dot with butter and bake in a preheated moderate oven 375°F. (Mark 5) for 30 minutes.

Serves 4 as an appetiser, 8 as an accompaniment

4 aubergines
Salt
4 tablespoons olive oil
Butter
1 Spanish onion, finely chopped
2 level tablespoons tomato concentrate
6 ripe tomatoes, peeled, seeded and coarsely chopped
2 cloves garlic, finely chopped
4 level tablespoons finely chopped parsley
1/4 level teaspoon each of allspice, cinnamon and sugar
Freshly ground black pepper
Breadcrumbs

Serves 3–4

12 oz runner beans
Salt
1 Spanish onion, finely
chopped
8 oz ripe tomatoes, peeled
and chopped
4 level tablespoons finely
chopped parsley
Olive oil
Freshly ground black pepper
1–2 level teaspoons sugar

Runner Beans à la Turque

A wonderful appetiser – or light luncheon dish – to serve in summer with plenty of fresh bread to mop up the sauce.

1 String runner beans and slice them thinly lengthwise (or use a special gadget for slicing beans). Sprinkle beans generously with salt, rubbing it into them lightly with your hands, and put them aside for 1 hour to soften and 'wilt' slightly.

2 Rinse beans in a colander. Shake off excess moisture and put them in a heavy pan.

3 Add chopped onion, tomatoes and parsley; mix well and pour in 2 tablespoons olive oil and ½ pint boiling water. Season to taste with freshly ground black pepper – you are unlikely to need salt, as it will not all have been rinsed off the beans – and add sugar.

4 Bring to the boil; lower heat and simmer gently, uncovered, until beans are tender, 20 to 30 minutes, depending on their age. If sauce becomes too thick, dilute with a little more boiling water.

5 Turn beans into a shallow serving dish. Cool; correct seasoning and dribble another tablespoon of olive oil over the surface. Serve lukewarm or chilled.

Serves 4

1–1 1/2 lb carrots, sliced
6 oz thickly sliced bacon,
diced
2 level tablespoons butter
2 small onions, finely
chopped
4 level teaspoons sugar
Salt and freshly ground black
pepper
4 tablespoons chicken (cube)
stock
2 level tablespoons finely
chopped parsley

Glazed Carrots with Bacon

Serve with poultry or a delicate meat such as veal.

1 In a heavy pan, cover carrot slices with cold water; bring to the boil, remove from heat and drain thoroughly.

2 Rinse and dry the pan, and simmer diced bacon in butter until lightly browned.

3 Add blanched carrots and finely chopped onions, toss lightly and sprinkle with sugar. Season to taste with salt and freshly ground black pepper, and moisten with chicken stock.

4 Simmer gently until carrots are soft and all the liquid has been absorbed, about 15 minutes.

5 When carrots are tender, transfer them to a heated serving dish. Garnish with finely chopped parsley and serve immediately.

Dried Pulse Vegetables

Dried vegetables (pulses) are a marvellous standby in the kitchen. They can be stored almost indefinitely, are inexpensive, easy to cook, and can be turned into rich, satisfying and extremely economical one-dish meals or sophisticated salads.

Soaking Once upon a time, no one would have contemplated cooking dried vegetables without first leaving them to soak overnight in cold water. The beans or peas were, as likely as not, several years old and practically fossil-hard. Nowadays, although soaking overnight certainly does no harm and still remains the safest method of dealing with dried vegetables, it is rarely necessary except for chick peas and occasionally, brown lentils. If you have forgotten to put them in to soak the previous evening, it will be enough to place them in a pan, cover with plenty of cold water and bring to the boil. Remove pan from heat, cover with a lid and leave undisturbed for an hour or two to soften.

It is important to use plenty of water, especially if leaving pulses to soak overnight; otherwise you may find in the morning that they have absorbed it all and could have had more.

Cooking pulses Each season, dried vegetables seem to cook more quickly. I suspect, though I have no evidence to support my theory, that this is largely due to improved drying methods as well as a fast turnover in the shops. Not so long ago, chick peas required prolonged soaking, followed by several hours' simmering to soften them. Nowadays they rarely take more than an hour to cook, and I have even, to my amazement, found pre-soaked chick peas that were tender within 20 minutes.

● Start cooking pulses in unsalted water unless the recipe states otherwise. Salt slows down the softening process.

Dried peas These come in two forms, whole and split, the latter minus its wrinkled green outer skin. Puréed dried peas make an excellent accompaniment to serve with hearty dishes of fat salt or smoked meat, especially if the purée is blended with some fresh green peas, which gives it a light, silky texture. Thinned down with ham stock, milk or water, pea purée can be turned into a warming winter soup.

Split peas are used mainly for soup, but also for that English classic, pease pudding, a favourite accompaniment to boiled pork. In addition, you can cook them according to any of the recipes for brown lentils.

Dried peas, especially whole ones, should always be soaked. Allow at least 1½ hours' cooking for whole peas, 30 to 45 minutes for split peas.

Lentils There are two types of lentils available, the red or Egyptian lentil, the most common in our shops, and the German lentil, which is greenish brown in colour and much larger than the red lentil. The two react quite differently to cooking – the red lentil needs little or no soaking and disintegrates to a purée within 10 minutes when cooked. The brown lentil, while it cooks quickly (15 minutes is my record), will keep its shape even after prolonged cooking, making it ideal for long-simmered casseroles and simple salads dressed with olive oil and vinegar. The two types should never be interchanged in recipes, for obvious reasons.

Beans

Haricot beans There's a lot more to the haricot bean than a tin and tomato sauce. Unfortunately, we can rarely enjoy fresh haricot beans as the French do, straight from the pod of the green (French) bean. Ours are usually left to mature and then dried.

That the Americans should have evolved so many bean dishes – Boston baked beans being only one of many – is not surprising, for the bean is a native of America, and the very word 'haricot' is the French version of the Aztec word for bean *ayacotl*.

Inevitably, too, the French have come up with a rival delicacy, the magnificent *cassoulet*. And there are few things to rival their way of serving a dish of roast baby lamb with haricot beans, fresh this time.

As winter fare, beans are hard to beat: a big pot of them simmered long and slow with rich seasonings will satisfy the keenest appetites.

Although I often find that soaking makes little difference to the cooking time of haricot beans, it is a wise precaution. Allow about $1\frac{1}{2}$ hours of gentle simmering.

Flageolets A choice variety of haricot – the pods are picked and shelled while the seeds are still a pale green colour. The French use them both fresh and dried. In this country they are rarely found, even in their dried form, and when they are, they tend to be rather expensive.

Red kidney beans Red kidney beans are the seeds of the runner bean left to mature, shelled and dried. They cook within 30 to 45 minutes, but must be soaked first.

Butter beans Large, flat beans, creamy white in colour. They are prepared and cooked in the same way as haricot beans, but for a slightly shorter time – say 1¼ hours rather than 1½ hours.

Chick peas or *pois chiches* (*garbanzos* in American cookbooks) should always be soaked before cooking. They will take anything from 15 minutes upwards of steady simmering to soften, and much, much longer if they are old. However, since it is practically impossible to overcook them, they are ideal for simmering in casseroles.

Lentils in Red Wine

Serves 4

A good, strong dish to serve with pork or sausages, or game. Do not attempt to make it with small red lentils – they will disintegrate into an unsightly mush, and in any case, their flavour is too delicate. Like so many dishes made with wine, this one improves with reheating.

1 Put lentils in a bowl and pour over 2 pints boiling water. Leave to soak for a minimum of 2 hours. Then drain, rinse under the cold tap and drain again thoroughly.

2 In a heavy pan, combine lentils with remaining ingredients, adding salt and freshly ground black pepper to taste. Bring to the boil; cover and simmer for 35 to 40 minutes, or until lentils are soft but still hold their shape, and liquid is almost completely absorbed. Stir occasionally to prevent lentils sticking to bottom of pan, taking care not to crush them as they become softer.

3 When ready to serve, remove *bouquet garni* and garlic clove. Turn lentils into a heated serving dish and serve very hot.

8 oz large brown lentils
1/2 pint red wine
1 small carrot, sliced
1 small onion, sliced
1 whole clove garlic
Bouquet garni (2 sprigs parsley, 1 sprig thyme, 1/2–1 small bay leaf)
4 oz smoked streaky bacon, cut in strips
Salt and freshly ground black pepper

Lentils Provençal

Serves 6–8

1 Cover lentils with 3 to 4 pints boiling water and leave to soak for at least ½ hour. Then drain; rinse thoroughly under the tap and drain again.

2 Place lentils in a heavy saucepan. Cover with lightly salted water. Add the whole onion, peeled, and bring to the boil. Simmer lentils until tender but not disintegrating. Their cooking time will depend on their age and quality, but start checking on them occasionally after the first half-hour.

3 While lentils are cooking, drain the anchovy fillets thoroughly and pound to a paste with butter, using a mortar and pestle if available.

4 When lentils are tender, drain thoroughly. Discard onion.

1 lb large brown lentils
Salt
1 Spanish onion
1 small can anchovy fillets
4 oz butter
4 tablespoons olive oil
1 clove garlic, finely chopped
Freshly ground black pepper

241

5 Heat olive oil in a heavy pan. Add lentils and finely chopped garlic, and heat through gently, shaking pan to prevent lentils sticking to the bottom.

6 Add anchovy butter; mix gently until butter has melted. Then season to taste with freshly ground black pepper – anchovies will probably have made the dish salty enough.

7 Spoon lentils into a heated serving dish and serve very hot.

Pease Pudding

A pease pudding is simmered in a pot with boiled meats – usually ham, bacon or beef – and then served with the meat in the traditional old English style. If no ready-made stock is available, flavour the cooking water lightly with chicken or beef stock cubes (say 1 cube per quart of water) and a piece of bacon.

1 Drain soaked peas thoroughly. Tie them up loosely in a cloth (an old tea-cloth or a double-thickness of butter muslin).

2 Submerge the bundle of peas in a large pan of boiling stock and boil for 3 hours.

3 When peas are very tender, lift out the bundle. Reserve cooking stock. Rub peas through a sieve into a bowl.

4 Beat eggs lightly with cream. Blend into puréed peas, together with softened butter, and season to taste with salt, freshly ground black pepper and sugar.

5 Rinse the boiling cloth and wring out thoroughly. Pile pea purée in the centre and tie up again, quite tightly this time.

6 Bring cooking stock back to the boil. Lower bundle into it and add a little boiling water if necessary so that it is completely submerged. Boil pudding for a further 30 minutes.

7 Untie pudding and serve steaming hot.

Note : You can make the texture of the pudding more interesting by crushing a few tablespoons of the cooked peas lightly and blending them into the purée, so that it is not completely smooth.

Serves 4

1 lb split peas, soaked overnight
Stock (page 161 or 162), or water and stock cubes and bacon (see Note)
2 eggs
2 level tablespoons double cream
2 level tablespoons softened butter
Salt and freshly ground black pepper
1/4–1/2 level teaspoon castor sugar

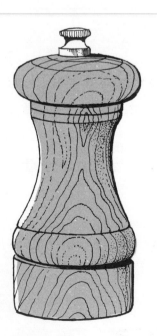

Hummus
(Puréed Chick Pea Appetiser)

Serve as a dip with hot Greek bread, or as an accompaniment for charcoal-grilled skewers. *Tahina* may be found in Greek and Oriental food shops.

1 Drain soaked chick peas. Cover with fresh (unsalted) water; bring to the boil and simmer until quite soft, 45 minutes to 1 hour, depending on age and quality. Drain thoroughly and reserve one-third for garnish.

2 Peel garlic cloves. Crush them to a pulp with $\frac{1}{4}$ level teaspoon salt, using the side of a strong-bladed knife.

3 Put remaining two-thirds of chick peas in the container of an electric blender. Add crushed garlic, the juice of $1\frac{1}{2}$ lemons, tahina paste and $\frac{1}{4}$ pint cold water. Blend to a smooth purée, gradually adding up to $\frac{1}{4}$ pint more cold water until purée has the consistency of a thick mayonnaise. Flavour to taste with freshly ground black pepper and more lemon juice and salt if necessary.

4 Pour hummus into a shallow serving dish. Dribble a little olive oil over the top if liked and decorate with a large star made up of alternating thin bands of brown cumin and red paprika or cayenne. Dot with whole chick peas.

6 oz chick peas, soaked overnight
2 cloves garlic
Salt
Juice of 1 1/2–2 lemons
1/4 pint *tahina* (sesame seed paste)
Freshly ground black pepper
Olive oil (optional)
Ground cumin
Paprika or cayenne

Easy Cassoulet

1 Cover haricot beans generously with cold water and leave them to soak overnight.

2 The following day, drain beans and put them in a large saucepan. Cover with a fresh portion of cold water and add the bacon, onions, thyme, bay leaf, 1 clove garlic, 4 level tablespoons lard or dripping and salt and freshly ground black pepper, to taste. Bring to the boil and simmer until beans are soft, about $\frac{1}{2}$ hour, or longer, depending on quality of beans. Drain beans, reserving liquor and bacon.

3 In the meantime, cut breast of lamb into serving pieces. Melt 4 level tablespoons of remaining lard or dripping in a large frying-pan and sauté pieces of lamb until golden.

4 To assemble *cassoulet*: place sautéed lamb in the bottom of a large, earthenware casserole; divide bacon into chunks and place together in centre. Cover with half of the cooked beans; add remaining garlic clove and peeled and seeded tomatoes. Top with remaining beans.

1 3/4 lb dried white haricot beans
1 pound bacon, in one piece
2 spanish onions, thinly sliced
Thyme
1 bay leaf
2 cloves garlic
10 level tablespoons lard or dripping
Salt and freshly ground black pepper
2 pounds breast of lamb
8 large, ripe tomatoes, peeled and seeded
4 level tablespoons tomato concentrate
Freshly grated breadcrumbs

5 Dilute tomato concentrate with $\frac{1}{2}$ pint of the reserved bean liquor and add to casserole, together with remaining lard or dripping.

6 Sprinkle entire surface generously with freshly grated breadcrumbs and cook *cassoulet* in a very slow oven (300°F. Mark 2) for $2\frac{1}{2}$ hours. Cover casserole with a lid or a piece of aluminium foil after first hour of cooking to prevent too thick a crust forming on top. Serve hot from casserole.

Boston Baked Beans

Serves 8

1 1/2 lb dried haricot beans

1 lb salt pork or bacon, in one piece

2 Spanish onions, finely chopped

4 level tablespoons butter

2 level teaspoons dry mustard

4 level tablespoons molasses or treacle

4 level tablespoons brown sugar

Salt and freshly ground black pepper

4–6 level tablespoons tomato ketchup

2–4 tablespoons melted bacon fat

A magnificent dish for a cold winter's night. The traditional earthenware bean pot used for this famous dish had a wide, rounded base tapering to a narrow neck.

1 Soak beans overnight in cold water. If this is not convenient, use the following method instead to soften them and make them swell: put beans in a large saucepan and cover generously with cold water; bring to the boil and boil for 2 minutes; then remove pan from heat, cover and leave to soak for at least 1 hour.

2 Drain soaked beans; cover with fresh water and bring to the boil again. Simmer for 30 to 40 minutes, or until bean skins burst when blown upon.

3 Drain beans, this time saving about 1 pint of their soaking liquid.

4 Scald pork or bacon; drain and divide in half. Slash rind in several places with a sharp knife. Place one piece of pork in the bottom of a deep, ovenproof casserole.

5 Preheat oven to very slow (275°F. Mark 1).

6 Sauté finely chopped onions in butter until soft and golden. Stir in dry mustard, molasses or treacle, sugar, 1 level teaspoon each salt and freshly ground black pepper, and the reserved bean water. Bring to the boil, stirring. Pour into beans and mix well. Then spoon beans over pork in casserole.

7 Push remaining piece of pork into beans so that rind remains above the surface. Cover casserole with a lid.

8 Bake in centre of oven for about 5 hours, stirring every hour, and adding a little boiling water if beans dry out too quickly.

9 Uncover casserole and gently stir in tomato ketchup, taking care not to break beans. Check seasoning. Drip melted bacon fat over beans and return casserole to the oven to colour them and brown the pork. Serve hot.

French Duck and Bean Casserole

Serves 4–6

1 Put beans in a saucepan and cover with about 3 pints water. Bring to the boil and simmer for 2 minutes. Remove pan from the heat; cover and allow to stand for 1 hour.

2 Replace pan on heat; bring to the boil and simmer beans in the same water until tender, 1 to $1\frac{1}{2}$ hours, depending on quality. Add more water during cooking if liquid is absorbed too quickly.

3 Cut duckling into serving portions; season generously with salt and freshly ground black pepper and sauté in olive oil until golden on all sides.

4 Preheat oven to moderate (350°F. Mark 4).

5 Drain beans and place them in a 4-pint, heatproof casserole. Add duck pieces and stir in remaining ingredients. Cover tightly.

6 Bake casserole for 1 to $1\frac{1}{2}$ hours, then uncover and continue to bake for a further 30 minutes.

7 Skim off excess fat; correct seasoning and serve very hot straight from casserole.

10 oz dried haricot beans
1 tender duckling
Salt and freshly ground black pepper
4 tablespoons olive oil
1/2 pint chicken stock
1/2 pint strained canned tomatoes
2 Spanish onions, finely chopped
2 cloves garlic, crushed
2 tablespoons melted butter
4 canned pimentos, very finely chopped

Chili con Carne

Serves 4–6

In spite of repeated warnings, recipes using Mexican chili powder seem to have caused more trouble than all the others put together in a writing career spanning over fifteen years. So please do not, repeat *not*, confuse Mexican chili powder with powdered chillies. The former is a strong but palatable Mexican blend of spices and peppers (Spice Islands, McCormick's and Wagners are well-known names to look for) and the traditional seasoning for chili con carne; the latter is so hot that more than a pinch of it renders a dish inedibly fiery.

1 Cut beef and pork into bite-sized cubes, trimming fat as you go. In a thick-bottomed, flameproof casserole, sauté meats, finely chopped onion and garlic in bacon fat until golden brown.

2 Cover with boiling beef stock or red wine. If red wine is used, add it straight from the bottle, then bring to the boil over a gentle heat. Cover casserole and simmer gently for 1 hour.

3 Blend chili powder and flour with a little of the hot pan juices, and add to casserole, together with bay leaves, cumin, oregano, and salt and freshly ground black pepper, to taste.

4 Simmer over a low heat until meat is tender.

5 Taste for seasoning. Serve hot with boiled red beans and rice.

2 lb lean beef
1 lb fresh pork
1 Spanish onion, finely chopped
4 cloves garlic, finely chopped
2 level tablespoons bacon fat
1 pint well-flavoured beef stock or red wine
4 level tablespoons Mexican chili powder (see note)
1 level tablespoon flour
2 bay leaves
1/2 level teaspoon powdered cumin
1/2 level teaspoon dried oregano
Salt and freshly ground black pepper
Boiled red beans and rice, to serve

Lesson 10

Simple Baked Cakes, Sweets and Sweet Sauces

Making Cakes

There are four main varieties of cake making which we will study in this lesson.

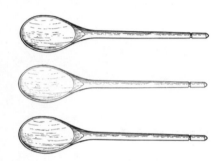

Creamed Batter Cakes

The simplest example is a Victoria Sandwich Sponge.

Butter and sugar are beaten together until light and fluffy. Eggs are beaten separately until frothy. Then the eggs are beaten into the creamed mixture, a few tablespoons at a time. (If all the ingredients have been brought to room temperature, there will be a less likelihood of curdling at this stage, which, though unimportant, is unnecessary.) Finally, flour sifted with baking powder (or self-raising flour) is folded in with a metal spoon.

People tend to be over-enthusiastic when it comes to creaming, believing, wrongly, that the harder they beat, the better the cake will be. But, in fact, it is all too easy to overcream. Tell-tale signs are air-bubbles just under the top crust, and crumbly edges. The texture should be fairly fine, the crust thin and smooth, and the cake generally of a uniform colour and thickness.

Once you know how to make a simple Victoria Sponge, you can go on to any fruit cake based on the same principle, including Christmas cake.

A creamed cake relies on baking powder and/or eggs to give it lightness.

Whisked Sponge Cakes

Basically, a whisked mixture of eggs and sugar, with flour, or flour and cornflour, folded in. This is the lightest type of sponge possible. It should be eaten fresh, as it tends to dry out quickly.

Genoese-type Cakes

If melted butter is folded into the batter, it becomes a Genoese cake. The butter makes it richer and also helps it to keep better. Whisked sponges rise because of the air that has been whisked into them. Therefore you must take every care not to deflate the whisked mixture by overfolding, not to mention mixing or beating.

Cakes where the Fat and Sugar are Melted Together

Here, the fat and sugar (pure, or in the form of a syrup) are melted together and mixed to a batter with eggs and dry ingredients.

These cakes are baked slowly because of the cream of tartar or bicarbonate of soda used to leaven them, both of which have a slow chemical reaction.

Baking Tins

Good baking tins that don't warp or buckle are a sound investment, for they will last you a lifetime. I have never been particularly taken with the non-stick type, possibly because I don't really trust them wholeheartedly and usually end up either greasing or lining them 'just in case'. However, I am a great believer in loose-bottomed tins which make it that little bit easier to cope with a cake that has stuck in spite of your precautions.

If you enjoy making cakes, you will want to collect a set of various-sized tins. Obviously, if a recipe calls for a tin or tins of a certain diameter, either the baking time – even the temperature, if possible – or the total amount of mixture will have to be adjusted if you change the size.

You will need:

Sandwich (layer cake) tins: two or, ideally, three in *each diameter* from the standard 7 inches upwards.

Deep round cake tins: from 6 inches upwards.

A Swiss roll tin: either 12 by 9 inches or 14 by 9 inches.

Baking sheets: heavy and strong. Inferior-quality ones are prone to buckling as they heat up. Make sure they fit your oven properly, with a 2 inch gap around the sides.

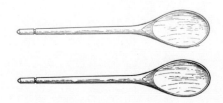

Square cake tins, a *tubular plain or fluted tin* for angel cakes, babas and gugelhupfs, and individual *bun* and *patty* tins can be added to your collection as you need them.

Cooling racks (at least two).

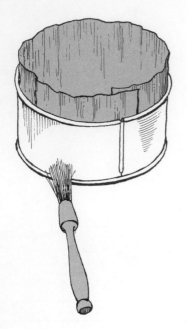

Preparation of Cake Tins

A session of cake-making should always start with the preparation of the tin or tins:

● For light sponges and layer cakes that cook comparatively rapidly you can either:

1. Brush base and sides of tin with melted butter; line base with a neat circle of greaseproof paper and brush that with melted butter as well; or . . .

2. Brush with melted butter as above; then coat with a mixture of equal parts flour and castor sugar, knocking tin against side of table to shake off the surplus. This gives a sponge cake a light, dry coating which is particularly pleasant.

● Heavy fruit cakes that are to spend quite a long time in the oven need more robust protection with a double thickness of buttered greaseproof paper on the base and around the sides. If the cake is to be left to 'mature' over a period of time, leave the lining paper attached.

When baking a very large cake, cover the top of the cake with greaseproof, brown paper or foil if it looks as if it's going to darken too much before it has cooked through to the centre.

The Basic Ingredients

A cake on the table is bound to be the focal point of attention for man, woman and child alike. Don't risk disappointment by using ingredients of doubtful quality.

Flour If you read American cookbooks, you will surely have come across 'cake' or 'pastry' flour. This is a soft, weak, low-gluten flour – the opposite of the strong flour used for baking with yeast. The point here is that, whereas breads should have a good framework and a firm, open texture, with cakes you are trying to make the crumb as light and delicate as possible.

All our recipes have been tested with a good-quality plain flour similar to types available throughout the country. We have then 'softened' this as necessary with cornflour, potato flour or some other starch, to make our own version of 'cake flour'.

248

Serious cake-makers will already have their pet brands of flour. If you have not done so already, it will be worth your while to experiment with the brands available in your area until you find the flour that suits you best.

Keep your flour dry in a tightly stoppered jar, and *always* sift it before use for lightness' sake, even if it doesn't look lumpy.

Fat As usual, there is nothing to beat butter for flavour, if not lightness. For family cakes, however, you may prefer to substitute margarine or one of the whipped fats, or even better, a combination of 2 parts butter to 1 part other fat.

You will save yourself a lot of effort if the fat is softened to kitchen temperature before you start creaming it, but don't heat it until it becomes oily: this destroys its ability to trap air, so that no amount of creaming will make it light and fluffy, and the resulting cake is heavy.

Eggs The best eggs for baking are neither too fresh – not less than, say, three days old – nor stale. A very fresh egg, whole or separated, will not beat up to the same volume as one that has been left for a few days. A stale egg will not improve the flavour of the cake, even if it is not stale enough actually to spoil it.

As you are very unlikely, unless you keep chickens, to have the problem of overfresh eggs, it is more useful to know how to recognise a stale or bad egg (see page 64).

● Eggs should be used at room temperature.

● Our recipes have been tested with so-called 'standard' eggs, weighing about 2 oz.

Raising agents Apart from the air that can be incorporated into the egg yolks and whites and/or simply the batter by vigorous beating, chemical raising agents also play an important part in cake-making.

Baking powder is the most familiar example. To ensure that it remains in possession of all its powers, keep the tin tightly closed and replace any that may have become stale.

● Finally, don't use more baking powder than the recipe specifies in the mistaken belief that the cake will benefit from this. It won't. The texture will be short instead of tender, and the cake will have a nasty aftertaste.

Self-raising flour Many people prefer to use self-raising flour instead of plain flour and baking powder. This is all right, provided the proportion of flour to powder matches that required by the recipe: 1 level teaspoon per 4 oz flour.

Otherwise, stick to plain flour and baking powder, sifted together to ensure that they are perfectly blended.

Baking soda (bicarbonate of soda) Used in sticky heavy cakes like gingerbread, for example, has a slower action than baking powder. It should always be dissolved in a little cold water before use.

Flavourings Vanilla and grated lemon or orange rinds are the two most common flavourings for cakes.

A word here about essences. There is a vast difference between cheap, synthetic essence, say vanilla or almond, and the real thing. Once you have used the latter, you will never want to change back. Pure essences have a delicate flavour which does not become crude and unpleasant, even if you've used a little too much by mistake.

However, the best way of introducing vanilla flavour into a cake is to use vanilla sugar – sugar (icing or castor) that has been packed around a couple of vanilla pods in a tall jar, tightly stoppered and left to absorb their flavour. Replenish the jar as the sugar is used up, and the vanilla pods will last indefinitely, or at least for several years.

Baking a Cake

● Have the oven preheated to the required temperature.

● Place the baking tin(s) in the centre (unless the recipe states otherwise) of the oven. If you have to use 2 rungs, you may need to switch the tins over two-thirds of the way through, or once the cakes have 'set', to allow them to brown evenly.

● Don't open the oven door unless absolutely necessary, and then close it carefully, without slamming.

To test for doneness ● A light, sponge-type cake is ready when it shrinks away slightly from the sides of the tin and springs back into shape when you press it lightly with a finger.

● A heavier (fruit) cake is best tested with a long skewer, preferably one with a twist. Push it gently right through the thickest part of the cake and draw it out again. The skewer should feel quite dry to the touch, with no sticky bits of batter adhering to it.

● Another favourite way of testing a cake, quite reliable with heavy cakes, is to listen to it. If you can hear a slight buzzing noise (this is known as the cake 'singing') it is not done and should go back into the oven.

Turning out a cake

All cakes should be left to 'settle' before being turned out of their tins, sponge-type cakes for a minute or two, heavy cakes for 10 to 15 minutes.

● If you are a perfectionist and don't want the marks of the cake rack on top of your sponge, turn it out on to a clean towel and then invert it on to the cake rack so that it cools resting right side up.

● Fruit cakes, too, should be left to cool right side up.

Victoria Sandwich Sponge

Makes 2 7-inch layers

Slightly softened butter
4 oz castor sugar
1/4 teaspoon vanilla essence
1/4 level teaspoon finely
   grated lemon rind
2 eggs
4 oz plain flour
1 level teaspoon baking
   powder
Redcurrant jam or a
   flavoured butter cream
   (page 166)
Icing sugar

1 Preheat oven to moderate (350°F. Mark 4).

2 Lightly butter two 7-inch sandwich tins and line bases with circles of *very* lightly buttered greaseproof paper.

3 Combine 4 oz butter with the castor sugar, vanilla essence and finely grated lemon rind in a large bowl. Cream together with a wooden spoon until light and fluffy.

4 In another bowl whisk eggs until light and frothy. Beat whisked eggs, a few tablespoons at a time into creamed butter and sugar mixture.

5 Sift flour and baking powder over creamed mixture. Fold in lightly but thoroughly with a metal spoon or spatula.

6 Divide batter evenly between prepared sandwich tins and level off tops with your spatula.

7 Place tins in preheated oven and bake for 25 minutes or until they are a good golden brown. Test for doneness: your cake is ready when it shrinks away slightly from the sides of the tin and springs back when pressed lightly with a finger.

Note: Always place baking tins in the centre of the oven. And if you are using 2 rungs, it is a good idea to switch the two tins over two-thirds of the way through cooking time to allow them to brown evenly.

8 When cakes are done, turn out on to a folded cloth and carefully peel off base papers. Then turn right side up again and allow to cool on a wire rack.

9 When layers are cold, sandwich with warm redcurrant jam or a rich chocolate- or butterscotch-flavoured butter cream and top with a sprinkling of icing sugar.

Makes 2 8½-inch layers

Butter for baking tins
6 eggs, separated
8 oz castor sugar
2 tablespoons lemon juice
  (or water)
Finely grated rind of 1/2
  lemon
Generous pinch of salt
3 oz plain flour
1 oz cornflour

Basic Whisked Sponge I

1 Preheat oven to moderate (350°F. Mark 4).

2 Lightly butter two 8½-inch sandwich tins and line bases with circles of *very* lightly buttered greaseproof paper.

3 Combine egg yolks, castor sugar, lemon juice (or water), finely grated lemon rind and salt in the bowl of an electric mixer. Place egg whites in another bowl, spotlessly clean and dry.

4 Sift flour and cornflour together four times.

5 Whisk egg yolk mixture at maximum speed for 5 minutes. Alternatively, if whisking by hand, whisk steadily until mixture is light and fluffy.

6 Wash and dry your whisk carefully. Whisk egg whites until soft peaks form.

7 Gradually resift flour and cornflour over surface of egg yolk mixture, folding it in lightly with a large metal spoon or spatula.

8 Fold in whisked egg whites.

9 Divide mixture evenly between prepared cake tins. If necessary, level off tops with the back of your spoon or spatula.

10 Bake for 20 to 25 minutes, or until sponges are well risen and a rich golden colour on top. They are ready when a light dent made with the finger springs back into shape.

11 Remove sponges from the oven. Leave to 'settle' for a minute or two; then slip a knife blade around the sides to loosen them, and turn out on to wire cooling racks. Peel off lining papers and allow to cool completely before sandwiching with jam, cream, etc.

Makes 2 8½-inch layers

Melted butter
3 oz plain flour
3 oz cornflour
3/4 level teaspoon baking
  powder
6 eggs
6 oz castor sugar
1 teaspoon vanilla essence
  or other flavouring

Basic Whisked Sponge II

1 Preheat oven to moderately hot (400°F. Mark 6).

2 Brush two 8½-inch sandwich tins with melted butter. Line bases with greaseproof paper and brush these with melted butter as well.

3 Sift flour with cornflour and baking powder three times.

4 Separate eggs, placing whites in one large, spotlessly clean and dry bowl, yolks in another.

5 Add sugar and vanilla essence (or other flavouring) to egg yolks, and whisk until mixture is pale and creamy, and leaves a trail on the surface when beaters are lifted.

6 Wash and dry your whisk carefully. Whisk egg whites until stiff but not dry.

7 Whisk egg whites into beaten yolk mixture. Fit bowl over a pan of hot water and continue to whisk mixture until thick and light again.

8 Remove bowl from heat. Gradually sift flour mixture over the surface, at the same time folding it in lightly but thoroughly with a large metal spoon or spatula. Do not overfold.

9 Divide batter evenly between cake tins.

10 Bake for 20 minutes, or until cakes are well risen and golden brown on top, and spring back when pressed lightly with a finger. They should also have shrunk slightly from the sides of the tin.

11 Remove cakes from the oven and leave for 2 to 3 minutes before turning out on to wire racks. Peel off lining paper and leave cakes to become quite cold before using.

Basic Genoese Sponge Cake

Makes 2 7½–8-inch layers

Excellent for layer cakes, iced cakes and *petits fours*.

1 Preheat oven to moderate (350°F. Mark 4).

2 Sift flour with cornflour three times.

3 Take the bowl in which you intend to whisk up the cake and select a large saucepan over which it will fit firmly. Pour 2 inches water into the pan and bring to the boil.

4 Place about 5 oz unsalted butter in another, smaller pan; lower it into the heating water so that the butter melts without sizzling or bubbling. Remove pan from water.

5 Brush two 7½- or 8-inch sandwich tins with a little melted butter. Line bases with greaseproof paper and brush with butter as well.

6 Combine eggs, castor sugar and vanilla essence or grated lemon rind in the bowl. Set it over barely simmering water and whisk vigorously until very thick, light and lukewarm.

7 Remove bowl from heat. Stand bowl on a cool surface and continue to whisk until mixture leaves a distinct trail on the surface when beaters are lifted (3 to 5 minutes if beating with an electric mixer at high speed).

8 Gradually resift flour mixture over surface, at the same time folding it in lightly but thoroughly with a large metal spoon or spatula.

3 oz plain flour
1 oz cornflour
About 5 oz unsalted butter
4 eggs
4 oz castor sugar
1 teaspoon vanilla essence or finely grated rind of 1/2 lemon

9 Add 8 tablespoons melted butter and continue with the folding motion until it has been completely absorbed. This may take slightly longer than you expect, so work as lightly as you can to avoid deflating the mixture.

10 Divide batter evenly between prepared tins.

11 Bake for 15 to 20 minutes, or until cakes are well risen, golden brown on top and springy to the touch.

12 Turn out on to wire racks. Peel off lining paper and allow cakes to cool completely before using.

Genoese au Moka

Makes 2 7½–8-inch layers

Melted butter
1 level teaspoon instant coffee
2 1/2 oz plain chocolate
2 oz plain flour
1 oz cornflour
4 eggs
3 oz castor sugar
1 teaspoon vanilla essence

1 Preheat oven to moderate (350°F. Mark 4).

2 Brush two 7½- to 8-inch sandwich tins with melted butter. Line bases with greaseproof paper and brush them with butter as well.

3 In a small basin, dissolve instant coffee in 4 teaspoons boiling water. Add chocolate, broken into small pieces. Set basin over a pan of simmering water and allow chocolate to melt, stirring occasionally to blend it smoothly with coffee. Remove from heat and allow to cool.

4 Sift flour and cornflour together three times.

5 Combine eggs, castor sugar and vanilla essence in a large bowl. Set bowl over a pan of barely simmering water and whisk until mixture is thick, light and lukewarm.

6 Remove bowl from heat and continue whisking until mixture has cooled and is thick enough to leave a distinct trail on the surface when beaters are lifted (3 to 5 minutes if beating with an electric mixer at high speed).

7 Gradually resift flour mixture over surface, at the same time folding it in lightly but thoroughly with a large metal spoon or spatula.

8 Fold in melted chocolate mixture as quickly and as lightly as possible.

9 Divide batter evenly between prepared tins.

10 Bake for 15 to 20 minutes, or until cakes are well risen, golden brown on top and springy to the touch.

11 Turn out on to wire racks. Peel off lining paper and allow cakes to cool completely before using.

Angel Food Cake

This feathery, light cake should not be cut with a knife but gently torn apart into portions with a knife and fork.

Serve with a light, pouring Chocolate Sauce.

1 Preheat oven to moderate (350°F. Mark 4). Have ready a 9-inch tube cake tin, making sure that it is spotlessly clean and free of grease; otherwise the cake will not rise properly.

2 Sift flour with cornflour and salt. Sift castor sugar separately. Then resift flour mixture three times with 3 oz of the sugar.

3 Mix egg whites with lemon juice and 1 tablespoon cold water. Whisk until foamy; then add cream of tartar and continue to whisk until stiff but not dry.

4 Whisk in remaining 5 oz castor sugar, a tablespoon at a time. (If you are using an electric mixer, start adding sugar a little earlier to avoid overbeating.)

5 Add vanilla and almond essence.

6 Sift about 2 tablespoons of the flour and sugar mixture over egg whites and fold in quickly but thoroughly with a large metal spoon. Continue folding flour mixture in gradually until it has all been incorporated into egg whites.

7 Pour mixture carefully into prepared tin.

8 Bake cake for about 45 minutes, or until it is firm and springs back when pressed lightly with a finger.

9 Remove cake from oven and immediately invert tin at an angle, upside down, so that the cake hangs free – a milk-bottle is good for this.

10 Leave cake like this for about 1½ hours, or until quite set and cold. Then gently shake it out of the tin on to a serving dish.

Chocolate Sauce

1 In a heavy pan, melt chocolate with butter over a low heat, stirring with a wooden spoon.

2 Gradually beat in double and single cream; bring to the boil and simmer for 2 to 3 minutes, stirring frequently.

3 Strain sauce through a fine sieve into a bowl and serve hot or lukewarm. This sauce can also be reheated successfully by placing the bowl in a pan of hot (not boiling) water and stirring until liquid and smooth again.

Makes 10–12 portions

3 oz plain flour
1 oz cornflour
1/2 level teaspoon salt
8 oz castor sugar
10 egg whites
1 tablespoon lemon juice
1 level teaspoon cream of tartar
1/2 teaspoon vanilla essence
1/4 teaspoon almond essence

Makes about 1 pint

9 oz bitter chocolate
3 oz butter
6 fluid oz double cream
6 fluid oz single cream

Makes 10–12 portions

2 oz plain flour
1 oz cocoa powder
1 oz cornflour
1/2 level teaspoon salt
8 oz castor sugar
10 egg whites
1 tablespoon lemon juice
1/2 level teaspoon cream of
    tartar
2 teaspoons coffee essence

Chocolate Angel Food Cake

Serve as above, with a chocolate or light orange sauce (page 255 or 277).

1 Preheat oven to moderate (350°F. Mark 4). Have ready a 9 inch tube cake tin, making sure that it is spotlessly clean and free of grease, as otherwise the cake will not rise properly.

2 Sift flour with cocoa powder, cornflour and salt. Sift castor sugar separately. Then add 3 oz of the sugar to the flour mixture and resift three times.

3 Mix egg whites with lemon juice and 1 tablespoon water. Whisk until foamy; then add cream of tartar and continue to whisk until stiff but not dry.

4 Whisk in remaining 5 oz castor sugar, a tablespoon at a time. (If you are using an electric mixer, start adding the sugar a little earlier to avoid overbeating.)

5 Finally, beat in coffee essence.

6 Sift about 2 tablespoons of the flour and sugar mixture over egg whites and fold in quickly but thoroughly with a large metal spoon. Continue adding flour mixture gradually until it has all been incorporated.

7 Pour mixture carefully into prepared tin.

8 Bake cake for about 45 minutes, or until it is firm and springs back when pressed lightly with a finger.

9 Remove cake from oven and immediately invert tin at an angle, upside down, so that the cake hangs free – a milk-bottle is good for this.

10 Leave cake like this for about 1½ hours, or until quite set and cold. Then gently shake it out of the tin on to a serving dish.

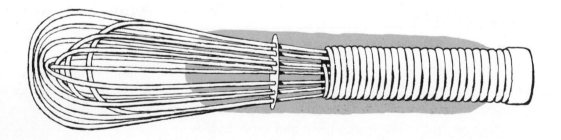

Dobostorte

Layer upon layer of feathery sponge cake sandwiched with chocolate cream and topped with a crackling sheet of caramel.

1 Preheat oven to moderate (350°F. Mark 4).

2 Trim 6 sheets of greaseproof paper so that they will lie flat on your baking sheets. With a pencil, mark a circle 8½ inches in diameter on each sheet of paper. Brush all over with melted butter.

3 Prepare batter for Basic Genoese Sponge Cake (Steps 6–9).

4 Divide sponge mixture evenly between prepared sheets of greaseproof paper, smoothing it out with a spatula or knife so that it covers marked circles neatly with an even layer.

5 Depending on how many baking sheets you have (and the size of the oven), the layers of sponge will have to be baked in two or three batches. Transfer 2 or 3 layers carefully on to baking sheets and bake for about 10 minutes, or until springy to the touch and golden but not brown. (The remaining layers will come to no harm provided the waiting time is kept to a minimum.)

6 As soon as the first batch of layers is ready, slip them off on to a flat surface, still attached to their sheets of greaseproof paper. Cover with a damp, clean cloth and leave for 2 to 3 minutes. Meanwhile, place the next 2 (or 3) layers of sponge on baking sheets and continue baking as before.

7 Now ease baked layers of sponge off lining paper with the aid of a spatula or a broad-bladed knife. The edges will probably have turned rather crisp. Using a plate or baking tin as a guide, trim layers down to 8-inch rounds. Leave to cool.

8 Having baked all 6 rounds, spread hazelnuts out on a baking sheet and toast them in the oven at the same temperature for 15 minutes, or until their papery skins become crisp and brittle, and can easily be rubbed off between the palms of your hands.

9 To make Chocolate filling: whisk eggs and sugar over hot water until thick and pale, and beaters leave a trail on the surface when lifted. Remove from heat.

10 Add grated chocolate and continue to whisk until completely dissolved. Cool.

11 Blend in vanilla essence and instant coffee dissolved in 1 tablespoon boiling water. Leave until quite cold.

12 In another bowl, beat butter with a wooden spoon until soft and fluffy. Gradually add chocolate mixture, beating vigorously. Chill until stiff enough to spread.

Makes 12 portions

Sponge layers
1 recipe Basic Genoese Sponge Cake (page 253)
Melted butter, for baking sheets
4 oz shelled hazelnuts, toasted (see Step 8)
4 oz sugar, for caramel
Flavourless oil

Chocolate filling
4 eggs
4 oz castor sugar
4 oz dark chocolate, grated
1 teaspoon vanilla essence
2 level tablespoons instant coffee
7 oz unsalted butter

257

13 To prepare caramel: first select the best-looking of the sponge layers and place it on a flat surface. In a small, heavy pan, dissolve sugar over a low heat; then cook to a rich golden caramel, swirling pan around to colour caramel evenly, and watching it like a hawk to prevent it burning. (It is a good idea to remove pan from heat a few seconds before caramel has reached the desired shade, as it continues to deepen in colour from the heat of the pan itself.)

14 Have ready a lightly oiled knife. Quickly pour hot caramel evenly over entire surface of sponge layer. Leave it for about 45 seconds; then mark it into 12 portions with the oiled knife, pressing quite deeply so that caramel will divide easily when cake is cut. Allow to become quite cold.

15 Skin toasted hazelnuts and chop coarsely.

16 To assemble cake: sandwich 5 layers with chocolate filling, using about two-thirds of the total amount. Having spread top with more filling, carefully lay caramel-coated layer in position. Spread sides with remaining filling and coat with chopped, toasted hazelnuts.

17 Leave cake for several hours in a cool place such as the bottom of the refrigerator to allow it to become quite firm before serving.

Family Chocolate Cake

A rich, moist chocolate cake which can easily be whipped up on a Sunday afternoon in time for tea.

Makes 8–10 portions

Butter
7 oz plain flour
4 level tablespoons cocoa powder
2 level teaspoons instant coffee powder
2 level teaspoons baking powder
1 level teaspoon baking soda
2–3 teaspoons lemon juice
6–7 fluid oz milk
6 oz castor sugar
2 eggs
1/2 teaspoon vanilla essence
Glaze
4 level tablespoons sharp-flavoured jam or orange marmalade
4 tablespoons orange juice
Liqueur or rum (optional)

1 Preheat oven to moderate (375°F. Mark 5).

2 Butter two 8-inch layer cake tins.

3 Sift flour three times with cocoa, instant coffee and baking powder.

4 In a small cup, dissolve baking soda in 3 to 4 teaspoons water.

5 Stir sufficient lemon juice into the milk, a little at a time, to curdle it.

6 Cream 4 oz softened butter with sugar until light and fluffy; then beat in a tablespoon of the sifted flour mixture.

7 Beat eggs very thoroughly and start adding to the butter mixture alternately with flour mixture and curdled milk, beating vigorously between each addition. The cake batter should remain comparatively stiff, so stop adding curdled milk if it should seem to be turning too liquid.

8 Finally, beat in baking soda and vanilla essence.

9 Divide batter evenly between prepared cake tins and smooth out with a spatula.

10 Bake for 20 to 25 minutes, or until cakes are springy to the touch and have shrunk slightly from sides of tins.

11 Leave cakes to cool in tins for a minute or two; then turn out on to wire racks and allow to become quite cold.

12 When cakes are cold, lay them 'top crust' down and prick surfaces lightly all over with a fork.

13 Combine jam or marmalade and orange juice in a small pan, and simmer over a low heat until melted and slightly syrupy. Cool slightly and if you wish, flavour with liqueur or rum.

14 Pour glaze over pricked surfaces and allow to soak in.

15 To make filling: cream butter with icing sugar until light and fluffy; then beat in the egg yolk, followed by melted chocolate. If filling is too soft, chill for a few minutes in the refrigerator before spreading on soaked surfaces of cake layers.

16 Put layers together.

17 To make chocolate icing: melt chocolate in a double saucepan and beat in butter. Add rum, and continue to beat until icing is glossy.

18 Pour icing over top of cake and allow to set before serving.

Filling
2 oz unsalted butter
4 oz icing sugar, sifted
1 egg yolk
4 oz bitter chocolate, melted

Icing
2 oz bitter chocolate
1 oz butter
1 tablespoon rum

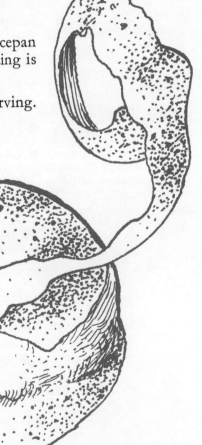

Makes 6–8 portions

Softened butter
4 oz castor sugar
4 egg yolks
10 oz best-quality bitter
  dessert chocolate
1/4 teaspoon almond essence
4 oz plain flour
1/2 level teaspoon baking
  powder
5 egg whites
2 level tablespoons sieved
  apricot jam
Lemon juice (optional)
4 oz granulated sugar

Sachertorte

The original recipe for *Sachertorte*, an exquisite chocolate cake which has defied all imitators for many years, is a jealously guarded secret, known only to the finest pastry shops in Vienna. Here is my version. Serve it as they do at Sacher's, topped with a generous dollop of feathery whipped cream.

1 Preheat oven to slow (300°F. Mark 2).

2 Grease a 7½-inch cake tin lightly with butter.

3 In a large bowl, cream 4 oz butter with sugar until light and pale-coloured. Add egg yolks and beat until very light and fluffy. (If an electric mixer is used, all three ingredients can be beaten together at top speed from the start.)

4 Melt 6 oz chocolate over hot water; beat it gradually into the creamed butter mixture, together with almond essence.

5 Sift flour with baking powder. Resift over bowl of chocolate-butter mixture, folding it in lightly with a large metal spoon until completely incorporated.

6 Beat egg whites until stiff but not dry. Fold them carefully into the cake mixture with the same spoon.

7 Pour mixture into prepared cake tin; level off top and immediately put into the oven.

8 Bake cake for 1 hour, or until firm and well risen.

9 When cake is ready, remove from the oven and allow to cool for 10 minutes; then turn out on to a cake rack and carefully turn over again so that cake is resting right side up. Leave to become quite cold.

10 Brush top and sides of cake with sieved apricot jam. (It will spread more easily if you warm it slightly first.)

Note: I often add a little lemon juice to sharpen flavour of jam.

11 Make an icing: melt remaining chocolate over hot water.

12 In a heavy pan, dissolve sugar in 4 fluid oz water. Bring to just below boiling point, then quickly whisk in melted chocolate and continue to beat until smooth. Bring to the boil, stirring constantly, and cook syrup until it reaches 240°F. on a sugar thermometer.

13 Remove pan from heat and immediately pour icing over the whole cake, using a palette knife to make sure that sides are completely covered. Icing will set very quickly, so work fast. Do not touch until quite set, as this will spoil the gloss.

Scotch Shortbread

The accepted formula for Scotch shortbread is 2-4-6: 2 oz sugar, 4 oz butter, 6 oz flour, but I find I get a much finer texture by substituting 1 oz cornflour for 1 oz of the flour. Alternatively, an ounce of fine semolina in place of the cornflour gives a coarser, more crumbly texture which many people like.

1 Preheat oven to slow (325°F. Mark 3).

2 In a bowl, cream castor sugar with softened butter until light and fluffy.

3 Sift flour once with cornflour; then sift them together into the bowl and work with creamed mixture to make a dough which holds together. Knead lightly until smooth.

4 Roll dough into a circle about ⅓ inch thick. Transfer to a baking sheet. Prick all over and mark edges with the tines of a fork. Mark into 8 wedges with the back of a knife.

5 Bake shortbread for 25 to 30 minutes, or until lightly coloured but not brown.

6 Dust hot shortbread liberally with castor sugar. Cut through marks into individual portions and transfer to a wire rack to cool. Store in an airtight container.

Makes 8 wedges

2 oz castor sugar
4 oz butter, softened
5 oz plain flour
1 oz cornflour (see note)
Castor sugar, to dust

Walnut Roll

1 Select a Swiss roll tin 9 by 14 inches in size and brush it lightly with oil; line tin with greaseproof paper, and oil the paper lightly as well.

2 Preheat oven to moderate (350°F. Mark 4).

3 Sift flour, salt and baking powder into a small bowl.

4 Grind walnuts coarsely in a small *mouli* – nuts must not be ground too finely, or they will release too much oil and make the cake heavy.

5 Whisk egg yolks with 4 oz castor sugar over hot water until mixture leaves a trail on the surface when beaters are lifted.

6 Remove bowl from heat and continue whisking until cool. Fold in ground walnuts with a metal spoon.

7 Wash and dry your whisk carefully so that no trace of the egg yolk mixture remains. Then whisk egg whites stiff but not dry. Fold into walnut mixture gently but thoroughly.

8 Finally, fold in sifted flour mixture.

9 Pour batter into prepared tin and level it off with a spatula.

Makes 8 portions

Oil for baking tin
2 level tablespoons plain
   flour
Pinch of salt
1/2 level teaspoon baking
   powder
4 oz walnuts
6 eggs, separated
Castor sugar
Sifted icing sugar, to
   decorate

Filling
3/4 pint double cream
3–4 oz castor sugar

10 Bake for 20 to 25 minutes, or until well risen and springy to the touch.

11 While cake is in the oven, prepare a surface for rolling it: lay a damp cloth on the table; cover with a sheet of greaseproof paper and sprinkle with 1 level teaspoon castor sugar.

12 Turn cake out on to sugared paper and carefully peel off lining paper. Lay a fresh sheet of greaseproof paper in its place and carefully roll cake up together with papers and cloth, starting at one of the longer sides. Leave to cool.

13 When roll is cool, whip cream until it forms soft peaks and sweeten to taste with castor sugar.

14 Carefully unroll cake and remove top paper. Spread cake evenly with whipped cream and roll it up again, this time without the aid of the cloth and paper underneath.

15 Lay on a long, flat serving dish, seam side down, and dust liberally with sifted icing sugar.

Note: Do not fill roll too far in advance. If icing sugar begins to dissolve, dust again just before serving.

Biscuits à la Cuillère

(Sponge Fingers)

1 Preheat oven to moderate (375°F. Mark 5).

2 Line 2 baking sheets with lightly buttered greaseproof paper.

3 Sift flour and cornflour into a bowl.

4 In another bowl, whisk egg yolks and castor sugar together until thick and pale. Add vanilla essence.

5 Wash and dry your whisk carefully. In a third bowl, whisk egg whites until stiff but not dry.

6 Using a large metal spoon or spatula, fold beaten egg whites lightly but thoroughly into egg yolk mixture alternately with sifted flour mixture, a third or a half at a time.

7 Spoon mixture into a piping bag fitted with a plain ½-inch nozzle.

8 Pipe on to buttered paper in 3½-inch lengths, making about 20 in all.

9 Dust sponge fingers generously with sifted icing sugar.

10 Bake for 12 minutes, or until firm to the touch and a pale golden colour.

Makes about 20 portions

Butter
3 1/2 oz plain flour
1/2 oz cornflour
3 eggs, separated
3 oz castor sugar
2–3 drops vanilla essence
Sifted icing sugar

11 Allow sponge fingers to cool for a minute or two; then ease them off papers with a spatula and leave on a wire rack until completely cold.

Rich Coffee Cake

1 Preheat oven to moderate (375°F. Mark 5).

2 Butter two 8-inch sandwich tins and line the bases with circles of lightly buttered greaseproof paper.

3 Sift flour, then resift twice more with baking powder.

4 Cream 8 oz butter with castor sugar until very light and fluffy.

5 Add egg yolks, one at a time, beating vigorously between each addition.

6 Dissolve instant coffee in 3 tablespoons boiling water and beat into the creamed mixture, followed by sifted flour and baking powder.

7 Whisk egg whites until stiff but not dry and fold into cake batter gently but thoroughly.

8 Divide batter evenly between prepared tins, smoothing tops evenly with a spatula.

9 Bake for 20 to 25 minutes, or until layers are well risen, springy to the touch and golden brown.

10 Turn layers out on to wire racks; peel off lining papers and leave to become quite cold.

11 To make filling: beat butter in a bowl until soft and fluffy; add sugar, egg yolk and coffee essence, and continue to beat vigorously for 5 to 6 minutes longer.

12 Whisk cream with milk until firm and fluffy; then beat into butter cream until filling is smooth and fairly stiff again. (Should cream separate, beat vigorously – with an electric hand beater, if available – until it emulsifies again.)

13 Sandwich cake layers with two-thirds of the cream filling and spread remainder evenly around sides. Roll coated sides in toasted-flaked almonds and place cake on a serving plate.

14 To make icing: dissolve instant coffee in 1 tablespoon boiling water; add vanilla essence and gradually stir into the sifted icing sugar. When icing is smooth, beat in softened butter.

15 Spread icing evenly over top of cake and allow to set.

Makes 10–12 portions

Butter
8 oz plain flour
3 level teaspoons baking powder
8 oz castor sugar
4 eggs, separated
2 level tablespoons instant coffee
2 oz flaked almonds, toasted

Filling
4 oz unsalted butter
3 oz castor sugar
1 egg yolk
1 tablespoon coffee essence
1/4 pint double cream
2 tablespoons cold milk

Icing
1 level tablespoon instant coffee
1/4 teaspoon vanilla essence
4 oz icing sugar, sifted
1 level tablespoon softened butter

Christmas Cake

Butter and greaseproof paper
for cake tin

8 oz softened butter

6 oz soft dark brown sugar

8 oz plain flour

4 eggs

2 level tablespoons liquid
honey

8 oz sultanas

8 oz currants

8 oz seedless raisins

4 oz chopped mixed peel

4 oz glacé cherries, finely
chopped

2–3 oz hazelnuts, chopped

1–2 oz blanched almonds,
chopped

2 oz walnuts, chopped

Finely grated rind of 1/2
orange

Finely grated rind of 1/2
lemon

1/2 teaspoon vanilla essence

1/2 level teaspoon mixed
spice

1/2 level teaspoon ground
cinnamon

1/4 level teaspoon freshly
grated nutmeg

Pinch of salt

2–4 tablespoons brandy

1 Butter a deep round cake tin 9 inches in diameter. Line base and sides with double-thick greaseproof paper, buttered on the inside.

2 Before starting to mix the cake, assemble ingredients and do all the advance preparation (chopping, etc.) indicated in the list above. If the fruit has to be washed, dry it carefully between the folds of a clean cloth.

3 Get out your two largest mixing bowls, and one smaller one.

4 In the largest bowl, combine butter and brown sugar. Sift flour into the second bowl. In the third, smallest bowl, whisk eggs until light and airy.

5 Cream butter and sugar with a wooden spoon until light and fluffy. Add honey and beat well.

6 Add flour and beaten eggs alternately to creamed mixture, a little at a time, beating vigorously between each addition.

7 In the now empty flour bowl, combine all the remaining ingredients except brandy. Mix well.

8 Add to the creamed mixture and stir vigorously until thoroughly mixed.

9 Preheat oven to cool (250°F. Mark $\frac{1}{2}$).

10 Spoon cake mixture into prepared tin; level off top with the back of your spoon; then make a slight but distinct indentation in the centre to counteract any tendency the cake may have to rise in a dome as it bakes.

11 Bake cake for about $3\frac{1}{2}$ hours, or until a thin wooden spill or metal skewer pushed down the centre comes out clean. If top of cake browns too quickly, cover loosely with a sheet of brown paper or foil.

12 When cake is ready, remove it from its tin (leave the lining paper attached to the base and sides) and lay it on a rack, right side up.

13 Prick surface of cake deeply with a thin skewer. Sprinkle with brandy and leave to cool.

14 When cake is quite cold, wrap it up in fresh greaseproof paper or foil and store in an airtight tin until needed.

Note: The above mixture can be divided between smaller tins. You should allow roughly 1 hour's baking per lb of uncooked mixture, but always test to make sure.

To decorate a Christmas cake

1 Three weeks before the cake is required, unwrap it and brush top and sides with warmed, sieved apricot jam.

2 Cover top and sides of cake with marzipan (see below) (you will need about $1\frac{1}{2}$ lb for a 9-inch cake), and leave in a closed cupboard to dry out for about 1 week. If you attempt to ice over the marzipan before it is dry, it will show through the icing.

3 Ice cake, applying two coats for a really smooth finish, and leave to set hard before decorating.

Almond Marzipan or Paste

Makes 2–2¼ lb

This is a basic recipe for almond paste. Use it to decorate cakes or to make into *petits fours* and sweets.

1 Combine ground almonds with sugars in a large bowl. Mix well.

2 Add vanilla and almond essence, rum or brandy if used, and lemon juice, together with eggs. Knead thoroughly by hand until paste is smooth and pliable.

1 lb ground almonds
1/2 lb castor sugar
1/2 lb icing sugar, sifted
1 teaspoon vanilla essence
1/4 teaspoon almond essence
4 tablespoons rum or brandy
  (optional)
Juice of 1 lemon
2 eggs, lightly beaten

Simple American Frosting

1 Place egg whites and salt in the bowl of an electric mixer. Start beating at slow speed; then, as whites foam up, increase speed and continue to whisk until stiff but not dry.

2 Meanwhile, combine sugar and $\frac{1}{4}$ pint cold water in a medium-sized pan. Place over a moderate heat, swirling pan gently until sugar has melted; then boil rapidly until syrup reaches a temperature of 240°F.

3 With mixer at high speed, pour hot syrup over stiffly beaten egg whites. Add chosen flavouring or colouring and continue to whisk until syrup is cool and very thick.

4 Use immediately to layer or cover cake. Leave for at least 3 hours to allow outer surface to harden.

Makes enough to sandwich and cover top and sides of a 3-layer cake 7–8 inches in diameter (or a 2-layer cake 9 inches in diameter)

2 egg whites
Pinch of salt
12 oz sugar
1/4 pint cold water
Flavourings
Colourings

Basic Butter Cream

Makes enough to sandwich an 8- to 9-inch layer cake

2 oz softened butter
4 oz icing sugar, sifted
1 egg yolk (optional)
Flavourings and colourings, as desired

1 Beat butter with a wooden spoon, or whisk in an electric mixer, until light and fluffy.

2 Gradually beat in sifted icing sugar.

3 For a richer, smoother-textured cream, beat in egg yolk.

4 Flavour and/or colour as desired.

Butter Cream Mousseline

Makes enough for the middle, top and sides of a 2-layer cake 7–8½-inches in diameter

2 egg yolks
5 level tablespoons sugar
5 oz unsalted butter, softened

A marvellous, velvety cream for filling and decorating cakes, rich, yet practically light enough to eat by the spoonful, and so versatile: in addition to the variations given below, you could flavour the basic cream with finely chopped toasted nuts, pounded praline, grated orange or lemon rind, and/or any liqueur you fancy, beating them in at the end, after the butter.

1 In the bowl of an electric mixer, if you have one, whisk egg yolks until thick and pale.

2 Combine sugar and 5 tablespoons cold water in a pan. Swirl pan gently over moderate heat until sugar has melted; then bring to the boil and boil vigorously until syrup reaches 215°F.

3 Immediately pour boiling hot syrup over beaten egg yolks in a thin stream, whisking vigorously. Continue to whisk until mixture is thick and tepid.

4 Incorporate softened butter in small pieces or flakes, whisking them in one at a time. Continue to whisk steadily until cream is thick and fluffy again. If necessary, chill slightly until thick enough to spread.

Vanilla mousseline Flavour basic cream with a few drops of vanilla essence.

Coffee mousseline Whisk 1 level tablespoon instant coffee dissolved in 2 teaspoons boiling water into basic cream.

Chocolate mousseline Melt a 3½ or 4 oz bar dark chocolate over hot water, working it smooth with a spoon or spatula. Cool to lukewarm and whisk into basic cream a tablespoon at a time.

A teaspoon of strong coffee or a few drops of vanilla essence complement the flavour of the cream beautifully.

Simple Baked Sweets

Baked sweets need never imply heavy sweets, but the very fact that most of them are *served* hot makes them seem more substantial and filling.

This makes it particularly important to plan your menu carefully – for a satiated appetite will not look kindly on a bread pudding, however light and tender it may be, or even a baked apple stuffed with fruits.

Menu-planning also comes in on a purely practical level. If the oven is to be used for the meat course, for example, make sure that the temperature it requires does not clash with that of the sweet. On the other hand, you can usually rely on the oven being hotter towards the top and cooler towards the bottom, so it may be feasible to accommodate the sweet either above or below the other dish. Remember, though, when roasting meat, that it does not take kindly to the presence of another dish in the oven, particularly if it gives off a lot of steam.

Finally, don't make the mistake of relegating baked puddings solely to the winter months. A Baked Alaska, filled with sliced fresh strawberries and ice cream before being baked in meringue, and bathed in *Grand Marnier*, or *clafoutis*, a creamy batter pudding stuffed with sliced apples and pears, or ripe black cherries – these are the essence of high summer.

Cinnamon Baked Apples

Serves 4

1 Preheat oven to moderate (350°F. Mark 4).

2 Peel and core apples, and stuff each cavity with 2 soaked and pitted prunes.

3 Combine brown sugar and cinnamon in a dish. Roll apples in cinnamon sugar and arrange them side by side in a baking dish.

4 Top each apple with about 2 level teaspoons golden syrup and 1 level teaspoon butter. Dot dish with remaining butter.

5 Bake apples for 25 minutes, or until tender but not disintegrating.

6 With a wide spatula, transfer apples to a heated serving dish.

7 Blend cream into syrupy juices; spoon over apples and serve immediately.

4 large cooking apples
8 large prunes, soaked and pitted
4 level tablespoons light brown sugar
1/8 level teaspoon ground cinnamon
3 level tablespoons golden syrup
3 oz butter
4–6 level tablespoons double cream

Serves 4

4 large cooking apples
Softened butter
4 oz light brown sugar
Finely grated rind of 1 large
  lemon
4 level tablespoons finely
  chopped almonds
Chilled whipped cream, to
  serve

Florentine Baked Apples

1 Preheat oven to moderate (350°F. Mark 4).

2 Wash and dry apples, and core them.

3 Lightly butter a baking dish large enough to take apples side by side.

4 In a bowl, combine 6 level tablespoons softened butter with brown sugar; stir in grated lemon rind and finely chopped almonds.

5 Stuff apple cavities loosely with this mixture. Arrange them in a baking dish and pile remaining sugar mixture over the top.

6 Bake apples for 35 to 40 minutes, or until they are soft but not disintegrating, and sugar mixture piled on top has melted down the sides and caramelised.

7 Serve apples lukewarm with chilled whipped cream.

Serves 6

6 eating apples
1 lb puff pastry
1 1/2 oz castor sugar
Ground cloves
1 1/2–2 oz butter
1 egg, beaten, to glaze

Normandy Baked Apples

1 Preheat oven to hot (450°F. Mark 8).

2 Peel apples; core them carefully from the stem and without going to the bottom.

3 Roll pastry out $\frac{1}{8}$ inch thick; cut out six 6-inch squares.

4 Moisten apples slightly and place each one in the centre of a pastry square. Sprinkle each apple with a little sugar and a generous pinch of ground cloves. Push a knob of butter into each cored cavity.

5 Bring pastry up sides of apples to enclose them completely, and seal tightly, moistening seams with a drop of water if necessary, and trimming off any excess pastry.

6 Roll out remaining pastry and cut out 'leaves' to decorate tops of apples. Alternatively, you can make a slightly more elaborate and very pretty decoration as follows: roll out remaining pastry thinly and cut out circles to fit tops of apples like little caps; press down lightly but firmly, then make 'leaves' from remaining scraps of pastry and arrange these on top so that tips of 'leaves' overlap sides of cap.

7 Brush apples with beaten egg. Place them on a baking sheet and bake for 10 minutes; then lower oven temperature to 425°F. (Mark 7) and continue to bake for a further 20 minutes, or until pastry is puffed and a rich golden colour. Serve hot or warm, dusted with more castor sugar if liked.

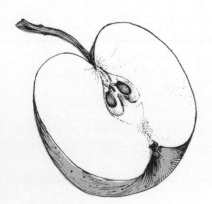

268

Baked Apples Alaska

Serves 4

1 Preheat oven to moderate (350°F. Mark 4).

2 Peel and core apples. Arrange them side by side in a baking dish and moisten with wine. Cover dish tightly with foil and bake for 35 to 40 minutes, or until apples are tender but not disintegrating. Turn apples once or twice while they are baking so that they absorb the wine in the bottom of the dish evenly.

3 When apples are tender, drain them, reserving 4 tablespoons of their cooking liquor. Allow apples to become quite cold.

4 Stuff central cavity of each apple with raspberries. Lay them in a wide, shallow baking dish, well spaced apart, and chill for at least 30 minutes.

5 Increase oven temperature to very hot (475°F. Mark 9).

6 Combine egg whites with reserved apple liquor in a large bowl and whisk until stiff peaks form.

7 Gradually whisk in castor sugar and continue to whisk vigorously to a stiff meringue. Flavour with a few drops of vanilla essence.

8 Spoon meringue into a piping bag fitted with a large fluted nozzle.

9 Remove apples from the refrigerator and, working quickly, spread them with ice cream. Pipe meringue in a spiral around each apple to cover it completely. Dust tops with sifted sugar.

10 Bake apples for 2 or 3 minutes, just long enough to set the surface of the meringue and tinge it with brown, and serve at once.

4 large cooking apples
1/4 pint dry white wine
4 oz fresh or frozen
    raspberries, defrosted
4 egg whites
4 oz castor sugar
Vanilla essence
1 family block vanilla ice
    cream
Sifted icing sugar

Baked Bananas

Serves 2–4

Simple baked bananas make an excellent winter sweet, enjoyed by children and adults alike. Serve them with cream if liked.

1 Preheat oven to moderate (375°F. Mark 5).

2 Butter an ovenproof baking dish, using all of the butter.

3 Peel bananas and cut them in half lengthwise.

4 Arrange banana halves side by side in the dish, and sprinkle with sugar, grated orange rind and orange juice.

5 Bake for about 15 minutes, or until bananas are soft and sugar has completely melted. Serve hot or lukewarm.

1 oz butter
4 bananas
4 level tablespoons castor
    sugar
Freshly grated rind and
    juice of 1 orange

Serves 4–6

2 lb cooking apples
Juice of 1 lemon
7–8 oz butter
4 level tablespoons castor
   sugar
Piece of vanilla pod
1/2 jar apricot jam, sieved
1 egg yolk
1 small loaf of white bread

Hot Apple Charlotte

Crisp, buttery slices of bread enclosing a smooth apple filling.

1 Preheat oven to moderately hot (400°F. Mark 6).

2 Peel, core and slice apples into a bowl of water acidulated with lemon juice to prevent discolouration.

3 Drain apples and put them in a heavy saucepan with 2 level tablespoons of the butter, the castor sugar and vanilla pod. Cover tightly and cook over a low heat until apples are reduced to a purée.

4 In the meantime, butter a 1-pint charlotte mould generously, using some of the remaining butter.

5 Remove vanilla pod from apples and rub them through a sieve. Add 2 level tablespoons of the sieved apricot jam and mix well. Then beat in egg yolk and allow purée to cool.

6 Cut bread into $\frac{1}{4}$-inch-thick slices and trim off crusts. Trim half the slices into squares of the same depth as the charlotte mould; then cut them in half to make rectangles. Cut the remaining slices into quarters to make small squares.

7 Melt remaining butter over a low heat without letting it sizzle or colour.

8 Dip bread squares in melted butter and arrange them in an overlapping pattern all over the base of the mould. Dip rectangles in butter and use them to line sides of mould. These, too, should overlap to make a firm case when charlotte is turned out.

9 Spoon cold apple purée into bread-lined mould; there should be enough to fill the mould generously.

10 Bake charlotte for 35 to 40 minutes.

11 When charlotte is ready, put a serving dish on top and invert mould on to it. Leave for a few minutes to settle, then carefully remove mould.

12 Melt remaining apricot jam over a low heat, stirring. Use it to glaze top and sides of charlotte. Serve hot.

Clafoutis with Apples and Pears

Serves 6–8

Serve this French farmhouse sweet right out of the dish you cook it in. At its best lukewarm.

1 Preheat oven to moderate (350°F. Mark 4).

2 Butter a shallow ovenproof dish about 15 by 9 inches. Don't use a tin because it conducts the heat too fiercely and tends to make the bottom and sides of the pudding too tough instead of soft and creamy.

3 Beat whole eggs and egg yolks together with a pinch of salt until well mixed. Add castor sugar and beat until light; then gradually sift in flour, beating vigorously until mixture is quite smooth and free of lumps.

4 Melt 2 level tablespoons butter over a low heat, taking care not to let it bubble, and incorporate smoothly into egg batter, followed by milk and vanilla essence, beating vigorously until batter is smooth and well blended again.

5 Peel, core and slice apples and pears thinly. Toss slices with lemon juice to preserve colour and sprinkle with sugar mixed with cinnamon.

6 Scatter sliced fruits evenly over prepared baking dish and cover with batter.

7 Dot with 2 level tablespoons butter and bake for about 45 minutes, or until *clafoutis* is golden and set, but still creamy inside.

8 Serve hot or lukewarm, with a light dusting of sifted icing sugar flavoured with a little cinnamon.

Note: To make a cherry *clafoutis*, substitute 1 lb ripe black cherries, stemmed and pitted, for sliced fruits and proceed as in recipe above.

Butter
4 eggs plus 2 egg yolks
Pinch of salt
4 1/2 oz castor sugar
3 1/2 oz plain flour
1 pint milk
1/2 teaspoon vanilla essence
3/4 lb tart eating apples
3/4 lb ripe pears
Juice of 1 lemon
1 level tablespoon sugar
1/4 level teaspoon cinnamon
Sifted icing sugar and
  cinnamon, to serve

Souffléed Rice Pudding with Orange Sauce

Serves 4

A deliciously fragrant, light rice pudding. Make the orange sauce which goes with it first, so that it has time to cool. (See page 272.)

1 Grease a 1½-pint soufflé dish generously with butter and coat with granulated sugar, shaking out excess. Stand dish in a deep roasting tin and put aside.

2 Bring a pint of water to the boil and dribble in rice through your fingers. Boil for 5 minutes; drain well and return to the pan.

3 Add milk; bring to the boil and simmer for 10 to 12 minutes until milk has been absorbed.

4 oz short-grain rice
1/2 pint milk
Thinly pared zest of 2 large
  oranges
2 oz butter
2 oz light brown sugar
Salt
3 eggs, separated
Orange sauce (page 272)

For baking dish
Butter
Granulated sugar

4 Preheat oven to moderate (350°F. Mark 4).

5 Thinly pare zest (coloured part of rind) from oranges with a potato peeler and cut into fine strips. Cover with cold water; bring to the boil; simmer for 5 minutes and drain thoroughly.

(**Note**: Squeeze the oranges and use their juice in the sauce.)

6 When rice has absorbed milk, remove pan from heat. Stir in blanched zest, butter, brown sugar and a pinch of salt. Cool slightly.

7 Beat egg yolks lightly and stir them into the lukewarm rice mixture.

8 Add a pinch of salt to egg whites in a bowl and beat until stiff but not dry. Stir a quarter of them into the rice mixture to loosen it; then carefully fold in the rest.

9 Spoon rice mixture into prepared soufflé dish. Pour hot water into roasting tin to come a third of the way up sides of dish and bake for 40 to 45 minutes, or until pudding is well risen and set.

10 Serve immediately, accompanied by a jug of orange sauce.

Makes about ½ pint

1/2 pint fresh orange juice (oranges left over from pudding plus 1–2 more)

2–3 level teaspoons finely grated orange rind

4 tablespoons lemon juice

4 level tablespoons castor sugar

1 level tablespoon cornflour

1 level tablespoon butter

1 tablespoon orange liqueur (Curaçao, Grand Marnier, Cointreau)

Orange Sauce

1 Simmer fresh orange juice with finely grated rind for 2 minutes. Remove from heat.

2 Blend lemon juice smoothly with castor sugar and cornflour.

3 Stir cornflour mixture into orange juice in a thin stream. Bring to the boil again, stirring constantly, and simmer for 5 minutes, stirring, until sauce is thick and translucent.

4 Remove pan from heat. Stir in butter until melted and allow to cool, stirring occasionally to prevent a skin forming on top.

5 Flavour sauce with orange liqueur and serve lukewarm or cold. Do *not* chill it, through, or it will set.

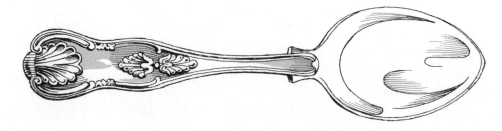

Chocolate Breadcrumb Pudding

Serves 4–6

1 Preheat oven to moderate (350°F. Mark 4).

2 Butter a 3-pint ovenproof baking dish.

3 Break chocolate into the top of a double saucepan. Stir in single cream and instant coffee, and heat gently over simmering water until chocolate has melted, stirring occasionally to blend ingredients smoothly.

4 Add sugar, salt and 1 level tablespoon butter, and stir until melted.

5 In a large bowl, beat egg yolks until well mixed. Pour in hot chocolate cream in a thin stream, beating vigorously to prevent egg yolks curdling.

6 Fold in breadcrumbs thoroughly and allow to cool. Then flavour to taste with vanilla. If using Maraschino cherries, drain them thoroughly, cut them in half and fold them in.

7 Beat egg whites until stiff but not dry. Fold lightly and quickly into bread mixture with a spatula or a large metal spoon.

8 Pour mixture into prepared baking dish and bake for 45 to 50 minutes, or until pudding is well risen and springy to the touch in the centre.

9 Serve hot, with chilled whipped cream.

Butter
4 oz dark chocolate
1/2 pint single cream
1 level tablespoon instant coffee
2 oz castor sugar
1/4 level teaspoon salt
4 eggs, separated
3 oz fresh white breadcrumbs
Vanilla essence
One 4-oz jar Maraschino cherries (optional)
Whipped cream, to serve

Adam and Eve Pudding

Serves 4–6

A comforting family pudding for a cold day. Try it, too, made with fresh sliced pears, or even canned or bottled fruit. Serve with thin cream.

1 Preheat oven to moderate (375°F. Mark 5).

2 Peel, core and slice apples thickly into an 8- to 10-inch baking dish. Add lemon and orange juice, grated orange rind, a pinch of cinnamon and 2 tablespoons water, and toss well.

3 Sprinkle apples with chopped walnuts and sugar. Cover baking dish tightly with foil and bake in the oven for about 15 minutes while you prepare topping.

4 To make topping: cream butter and sugar together until light and fluffy. Add beaten eggs gradually, beating well between each addition.

5 Sift flour with baking powder and salt. Stir into creamed mixture alternately with milk, and mix lightly until batter is smoothly blended.

2 lb apples
Juice of 1 small lemon
Juice and finely grated rind of 1/2 orange
Pinch of cinnamon
2 level tablespoons chopped walnuts
2 level tablespoons castor sugar

Topping
4 oz butter
4 oz castor sugar
2 eggs, well beaten
4 oz plain flour
1 level teaspoon baking powder
Pinch of salt
1–2 tablespoons milk

273

6 Spread batter evenly over apples and return dish to the oven for a further 30 minutes, or until topping is well risen and springy to the touch, with a rich golden top. Serve hot.

Brown Betty

A 'betty' is an American pudding made up of layers of buttered bread cubes (or breadcrumbs) and fruit, lightly spiced and baked in the oven. Brown betty is traditionally made with apples and brown sugar.

Serves 4–6

4–6 slices (about 6 oz) stale bread, cubed

4 tablespoons melted butter

1 1/2–2 lb tart, crisp eating apples, peeled, cored and thinly sliced

8 oz dark brown sugar

1 level teaspoon ground cinnamon

1/4 level teaspoon freshly grated nutmeg

1/4 level teaspoon ground cloves

Generous pinch of salt

1 level teaspoon finely grated lemon rind

1 oz seedless raisins

2 tablespoons lemon juice

1 Preheat oven to moderate (375°F. Mark 5).

2 Toss bread cubes with melted butter. Scatter a third of them over the base of a rectangular, 2-pint baking dish and arrange half of the apple slices on top.

3 Mix together brown sugar, spices, salt and grated lemon rind. Sprinkle half of this mixture evenly over apples, together with a few of the raisins and 1 tablespoon lemon juice.

4 Cover with half of the remaining bread cubes, followed by remaining apples, sugar mixture, raisins and lemon juice.

5 Top with remaining bread cubes and sprinkle with 4 tablespoons water.

6 Bake pudding for 40 minutes, or until top is crisp and golden brown. Serve warm with a jug of cream

Baked Alaska

This famous sweet is easy to prepare if you work quickly and follow the preliminary instructions carefully – the board, cake and ice cream are all poor conductors of heat, while foil deflects it – which all helps to achieve the seemingly impossible combination of a hot shell and an ice-cold filling.

Choose your fruit according to what is available – soft fruit, peaches, pineapple or mixed fruit salad are all good, fresh, tinned or frozen.

Serves 6

1 8-inch sponge flan case or layer of sponge cake

1/2 lb sliced strawberries, or other fruit

3–4 tablespoons orange juice

Grand Marnier, brandy or some other suitable liqueur (optional)

1 family block vanilla ice cream

1/4 level teaspoon cream of tartar

4 egg whites

3 oz castor sugar

Icing sugar, sifted

1 Preheat oven to hot (450°F. Mark 8).

2 Take a wooden board at least 2 inches larger in diameter than sponge flan case. Cover board smoothly with aluminium foil. Place flan in centre.

3 Prepare fruit, cutting it into slices if necessary, and saving any juices which escape.

4 Prick base and sides of flan case or sponge with a fork. Sprinkle with 4 tablespoons orange juice (or 3 tablespoons orange juice and a tablespoon of Grand Marnier), plus the juices which have escaped from the fruit.

5 Fill flan with fruit. If a plain sponge layer is used, leave a ½-inch gap of cake showing around sides.

6 Slice ice cream and cover fruit with it. Place in freezing compartment of refrigerator while you make meringue. (It is not advisable to leave it there too long, though, or the fruit will freeze hard and still be unpleasantly icy when you take the Alaska out of the oven.)

7 Add cream of tartar to egg whites and whisk until stiff. Add sugar gradually and continue beating to a stiff, glossy meringue.

8 Spread meringue over ice cream and sides of cake, covering it completely, and peak it all over with the flat side of a knife. Dust generously with sifted icing sugar.

9 Bake at once for about 5 minutes, or until tips of meringue are lightly browned, but take care not to let the meringue burn.

10 Serve immediately. You can make the sweet even more spectacular by flaming it with a tablespoon of Grand Marnier, or some other liqueur, depending on your choice of fruit. Serve quickly before the flames go out.

Sweet Sauces

Chocolate Rum Sauce

1 Melt chocolate in a bowl over a pan of hot water. Remove from heat and beat in rum and grated orange rind.

2 Warm milk in a saucepan. Work cornflour smoothly with a little of the milk; then pour back into remaining milk and bring to the boil, stirring. Simmer until mixture thickens and loses its raw taste, about 4 minutes.

3 Add cooked cornflour mixture to the melted chocolate gradually, beating vigorously, and continue to beat until sauce is smooth and shiny. Serve hot or cold.

Serves 4–6

4 oz bitter chocolate
1 tablespoon rum
1/4 level tablespoon finely grated orange rind
1/2 pint milk
1 level tablespoon cornflour

Rich Apricot Sauce

Makes just under ½ pint

1 15 1/2-oz can apricot halves in syrup
1 level tablespoon castor sugar
1 level teaspoon arrowroot
2 tablespoons lemon juice
2 teaspoons apricot brandy

Serve hot with cake-type puddings; lukewarm with creams and ices.

1 Drain apricot halves, reserving syrup, and purée through a fine sieve. Add castor sugar and blend thoroughly.

2 Blend arrowroot smoothly with 3 tablespoons apricot syrup and stir into apricot purée, together with 2 tablespoons lemon juice.

3 Stir over a moderate heat until sauce reaches boiling point. Then reduce heat and simmer, stirring, for 5 to 6 minutes, or until sauce has thickened and become translucent.

4 Allow to cool slightly; then flavour to taste with apricot brandy, and a few drops more lemon juice if desired.

Cold Apple Sauce

Makes about 1 pint

2 lb cooking apples
2–3 lemon slices
2 level tablespoons sugar
1/2 teaspoon vanilla essence
2 tablespoons cream (optional)
Cinnamon (optional)

1 Wipe, quarter and core apples.

2 Cut quartered apples into thick slices and put them in a large saucepan together with 2 to 4 tablespoons water, the lemon slices and sugar. Bring to the boil; cover pan tightly and simmer gently for 10 minutes, or until apples are fluffy.

3 Remove lemon slices and purée sauce through a fine sieve.

4 Flavour to taste with vanilla essence and add more sugar if necessary. Stir in cream for a richer sauce and add a pinch of cinnamon if liked.

Butterscotch Sauce

Makes 2 pints

4 oz butter
6 oz granulated sugar
5 oz Demerara sugar
11 oz golden syrup
Pinch of salt
8 fluid oz double cream

A delicious, all-purpose butterscotch sauce. It keeps well stored in a screw-top jar in the refrigerator and can also be deep-frozen.

1 Combine all ingredients except double cream in a saucepan. Stir over a low heat until ingredients have melted and mixture comes to the boil; then cook very slowly for 20 minutes, stirring occasionally.

2 Remove from heat and allow to cool.

3 Add cream and beat vigorously until smooth.

Orange Sauce

Equally good served warm or cold with cake and steamed puddings, as well as ices.

1 In a measuring jug, combine grated orange rind with orange and lemon juice. There should be ½ pint liquid. Make it up to 1 pint with water.

2 Mix arrowroot smoothly with some of the diluted juice; then combine with remaining juice and pour into a pan.

3 Bring to the boil, stirring constantly, and simmer for 2 to 3 minutes until sauce is thick and translucent.

4 Beat in sugar and butter over a low heat until dissolved.

5 Beat egg yolks lightly in a bowl until well mixed. Pour hot sauce over them in a thin stream, beating vigorously with the whisk.

6 Pour sauce back into rinsed and dried pan, and stir over a low heat for a minute or two longer until sauce thickens slightly. Take great care not to let sauce boil, or egg yolks may curdle.

7 Strain sauce through a fine sieve; allow to cool slightly, then flavour to taste with a little Grand Marnier.

8 Serve sauce warm or cold.

Makes about 1 pint

Finely grated rind of **2** oranges
Juice of **4** large oranges
Juice of **1/2** lemon
2 level tablespoons arrowroot
3 level tablespoons castor sugar
2 level tablespoons butter
2 egg yolks
1–2 teaspoons Grand Marnier

THIRD COURSE

Lesson 11
Scrambled Eggs and Omelettes

Scrambled Eggs
(*Oeufs Brouillés*)

Although far from requiring the *tour de main* necessary for making a French omelette – more about that later on in this lesson – in their own simple way, perfect scrambled eggs need just as much care and attention.

● **The pan** they are cooked in must be a heavy one. You can choose between a wide saucepan or a deep frying pan, but in either case keep the depth of liquid egg down to about an inch, so that the heat can permeate the whole mass of egg evenly as you stir.

● **The heat** should be kept low, so that the first curds do not start forming too quickly – otherwise they will be solid and tough by the time the rest of the egg has had a chance to thicken. If in spite of these precautions the eggs seem to be cooking too quickly, remove pan from heat and, still stirring, give the mixture a chance to cool down a little before proceeding.

● Still on the subject of heat, it is a good idea to remove the pan from the stove a few seconds before the eggs are scrambled to your liking. Keep on stirring *off* the heat for a few seconds longer, and the mixture will finish cooking from the heat of the pan itself.

● The eggs should be stirred until well mixed. Never beat them, or you will also beat in air bubbles which will make it impossible to achieve a creamy, smooth texture for your scrambled eggs however carefully you cook them.

● Scrambled eggs make a surprisingly rich little dish. Two eggs per person plus one 'for the pan' are ample.

Basic Scrambled Eggs

1 Break eggs into a bowl. Add salt and freshly ground black pepper, to taste, and stir well with a fork (don't beat) until yolks and whites are thoroughly mixed. Stir in double cream or water – water will make extremely fluffy eggs; cream gives a richer, smoother texture.

2 Select a heavy frying pan or saucepan (see note above). Add a good tablespoon butter and heat until sizzling but not coloured. Then swirl butter around so that bottom and sides of pan are coated.

3 Pour in eggs all at once; set pan over a low heat and immediately start stirring with a large wooden spoon. Keep stirring, making sure the spoon reaches the corners of the pan and keeping the whole mass of liquid egg on the move, until eggs are creamy and almost ready.

4 Remove pan from the heat and stir for a few seconds longer until eggs are ready. Then fold in a few flakes of cold butter (almost $\frac{1}{2}$ level teaspoon). Correct seasoning with a little more salt and freshly ground black pepper if necessary, and serve at once on a hot plate, or in one of the little containers described below.

To make 1 portion

3 eggs
Salt and freshly ground black
   pepper
1 level tablespoon double
   cream or water
Butter

Containers for Scrambled Eggs

Add a delightful finishing to your scrambled eggs by serving them in a delicate pastry shell, a crisply baked, scooped-out dinner roll or a golden fried bread croustade.

Pastry cases 8 oz shortcrust pastry rolled out very thinly will line 6 individual fluted tart tins 4 inches in diameter. Bake 'blind' in a moderate oven (375°F. Mark 5) for 10 to 12 minutes, or until crisp and golden. (See page 431.)

If not used immediately, reheat pastry cases before filling them with scrambled eggs.

Bread rolls With the point of a sharp knife, cut a circle about $1\frac{1}{2}$ inches in diameter in the top of a crisp, round dinner roll. Then carefully scoop out soft pith inside, leaving a shell about $\frac{1}{4}$ inch thick.

Brush inside of roll generously with melted butter; lay on a baking sheet and slip into a moderate oven (375°F. Mark 5) for 10 minutes until hot and crisp.

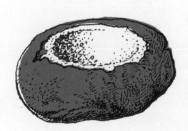

Croustades Cut a slice of bread $\frac{3}{4}$ inch thick and stamp out a circle $2\frac{1}{2}$ inches in diameter with a plain round biscuit cutter. Take another cutter $1\frac{1}{2}$ inches in diameter and cut down into the circle of bread to within $\frac{1}{4}$ inch of the bottom (i.e. $\frac{1}{2}$ inch deep). Carefully scoop out centre to make a firm case.

In a shallow dish, beat an egg with 2 tablespoons milk and a pinch each of salt and freshly ground black pepper.

Heat a $\frac{1}{4}$-inch layer of mixed butter and oil in a frying pan until a small cube of bread dropped into it browns within 60 seconds.

Dip the prepared bread case quickly on both sides in beaten egg. Shake off excess and immediately drop into hot fat. Fry until crisp and a rich golden colour all over. Drain on absorbent paper and use immediately.

Scrambled Eggs with Smoked Salmon and Chives

Serves 1

3 eggs
Salt and freshly ground black pepper
1 level tablespoon double cream or water
1 1/2 level tablespoons butter
1 1/2 oz smoked salmon, cut into thin strips
A few drops of lemon juice
1–2 level teaspoons finely chopped chives or spring onion tops

1 Break eggs into a bowl. Add salt and freshly ground black pepper, to taste, and stir well with a fork (don't beat) until yolks and whites are thoroughly mixed. Stir in double cream or water – water will make extremely fluffy eggs; cream gives a richer, smoother texture.

2 Melt butter in the pan in which you intend to scramble eggs. Add strips of smoked salmon and toss gently over a low heat for a few seconds only until they change colour.

3 Pour in eggs and finish cooking as in Basic Scrambled Eggs.

4 Just before serving, stir in a few drops of lemon juice and the finely chopped chives or spring onion tops. Serve immediately.

Scrambled Eggs with Mushrooms

Serves 1

1 1/2 oz white button mushrooms
Butter
3 eggs
1 level tablespoon double cream
Salt and freshly ground black pepper

1 Wipe mushrooms clean and trim their stems. Slice mushrooms thinly and sauté in 1 level tablespoon butter for about 5 minutes. Keep warm.

2 Prepare and scramble eggs as directed in Basic Scrambled Eggs (page 281).

3 When eggs are on the point of setting, stir in sautéed mushrooms and their butter. Finish cooking and serve immediately.

Scrambled Eggs with Cheese

Serves 1

Steps **1–3** as in Basic Scrambled Eggs (page 281).

4 When eggs are on the point of setting, remove pan from heat; add grated cheese and continue to stir until melted. Correct seasoning and intensify cheese flavour with a few drops of lemon juice, if liked. Serve immediately.

3 eggs
Salt and freshly ground black pepper
1 level tablespoon double cream
Butter
1 oz freshly grated Parmesan plus 1/2 oz freshly grated Gruyère, or 1 oz grated mature Cheddar
A few drops of lemon juice (optional)

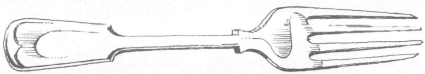

Scrambled Eggs with Buttered Shrimps

Serves 1

1 Heat the shrimps through gently in their butter in a small saucepan.

2 Proceed as for Basic Scrambled Eggs (page 281), folding in the shrimps and their butter when eggs are on the point of setting. Serve immediately.

1–2 oz buttered (potted) shrimps
3 eggs
Salt and freshly ground black pepper
1 level tablespoon double cream
Butter

Scrambled Eggs with Asparagus Tips and Ham

Serves 1

1 As in Basic Scrambled Eggs (page 281).

2 Melt 1 level tablespoon butter in the pan in which you intend to scramble eggs. Add chopped asparagus tips and ham, and toss over a gentle heat for 1 or 2 minutes until thoroughly hot.

Steps **3** and **4** as in Basic Scrambled Eggs (page 281).

3 eggs
Salt and freshly ground black pepper
1 level tablespoon double cream
Butter
3 canned asparagus tips, chopped
2 level tablespoons finely chopped ham

Serves 4

8 anchovy fillets
4 slices white bread
5 level teaspoons butter
2 teaspoons olive oil
8 eggs
2 tablespoons cream, milk or
    water
Salt and freshly ground black
    pepper
Cayenne pepper
4 plump black olives, pitted
    and quartered
1 level tablespoon finely
    chopped parsley

Scrambled Eggs Provençale

1 Preheat oven to very slow (300°F. Mark 2).

2 Slice anchovy fillets in half lengthwise.

3 Cut bread into rounds about 3 inches in diameter. Sauté lightly in 2 teaspoons each butter and olive oil until just golden on both sides. Transfer to a baking sheet and put into the oven to keep warm.

4 Break eggs into a bowl; add cream, milk or water, and salt, freshly ground black pepper and cayenne to taste, and mix lightly.

5 Scramble eggs in remaining butter until cooked but creamy.

6 Spoon scrambled eggs on to fried bread rounds. Garnish with a lattice-work of anchovy strips; dot each portion with 4 pieces of olive and sprinkle with a pinch of finely chopped parsley. Serve immediately.

Serves 2–3

2 tablespoons olive oil
1 green pepper, seeded,
    cored and thinly sliced
1 Spanish onion, thinly
    sliced
1/2 clove garlic, crushed
2–4 level tablespoons diced
    cooked ham
Salt and freshly ground black
    pepper
1 level tablespoon butter
6 eggs
1 level tablespoon freshly
    grated Parmesan (optional)
4 firm ripe tomatoes, peeled,
    seeded and roughly chopped

Basque Pipérade

Although usually classed as an omelette, this Basque dish of eggs and vegetables is more like a glorified version of scrambled eggs. You can either stir the eggs into the softened vegetables and cook them as described below; or, for a more elegant occasion, scramble the eggs separately – see recipe for Basic Scrambled Eggs – then spoon them neatly on top of the vegetables just before serving.

1 Heat olive oil in a large, deep frying pan and sauté thinly sliced green pepper until softened.

2 Add thinly sliced onion, crushed garlic and diced cooked ham; season to taste with salt and freshly ground black pepper, and stir in butter. Simmer vegetables for about 25 minutes, or until practically reduced to a purée, stirring occasionally.

3 Meanwhile, break eggs into a bowl and stir vigorously with a fork until well mixed, adding salt and freshly ground black pepper to taste, and grated Parmesan if used.

4 Add peeled, seeded and chopped tomatoes to simmering vegetables, and cook gently for 4 or 5 minutes longer. Tomatoes should not be allowed to disintegrate.

5 Pour eggs over hot vegetable mixture and stir over a low heat until just set but still soft and slightly wet. Serve immediately.

The Omelette

It may seem incongruous when you think that one of the shortest culinary operations of all – cooking an omelette takes no more than a minute from start to finish, even less once you acquire the knack – has evoked so many pages of advice and admonition from cookery writers over the years.

Yet this is not quite as absurd as it appears. Several quite dextrous operations have to be fitted into those few seconds and will probably require a few trial runs before you master the procedure.

So don't despair if your first attempt is a flop – soon you will be turning out perfect French omelettes, oval-shaped and plump, golden and buttery on the outside, moist and creamy and just set in the middle, as easily and automatically as the most experienced chef.

The Omelette Pan

Ideally, you should have a special pan reserved for omelettes just as the books say – a heavy French black iron pan with rounded sides and a characteristic flat handle is the one usually recommended. Before embarking on the first omelette, the pan must be 'seasoned': it is washed and dried, heated, coated all over with oil and left to stand overnight. Then, the following day, the excess oil is wiped off and the pan is rubbed clean with salt.

Henceforth the pan is never washed again, only wiped clean with kitchen paper between sessions. Anything that sticks to the surface can be rubbed off with a little dry salt.

This is the ideal. However, I wonder how many cooks are prepared to sacrifice money and/or kitchen space to a special omelette pan.

My own opinion is that, provided your pan is a heavy one – copper, cast-iron or aluminium as the case may be – and has a good smooth, spotlessly clean surface, there are other factors involved which are far more important.

● The size of the pan is important: if it is too small, the omelette will be unmanageably thick and either crack when you fold it, or refuse to fold at all; too large, and the omelette will be thin and leathery. Keep the depth of egg mixture at about $\frac{1}{4}$ inch, no more. A 3-egg omelette for one will take a 6-inch pan. For a 5-egg omelette, which serves two, use a 7- or 8-inch pan.

● For more than two servings, it is better to make several small omelettes which are far easier to handle than one gigantic one.

● The weight of the pan is important: the omelette cooks so quickly that it is impossible to disperse the heat evenly if the pan is a thin one.

● Having found in the past that omelettes seemed to cook more successfully on gas than on electricity, I now make a point of switching on the electric ring if I intend to use electricity a few minutes in advance to make sure it is thoroughly hot before I start cooking an omelette on it.

● The eggs and butter you use for an omelette should be of the very best. And as with scrambled eggs, you should never beat, only stir the eggs vigorously in a bowl with a fork or a wire whisk just enough to mix the yolks and whites before pouring them into the pan.

● If you plan to fill your omelette, the filling should be prepared in advance and be ready to spoon down the centre of the omelette just before it is folded.

● Finally, an omelette must be served as soon as it is ready. If it is kept waiting, it soon becomes tough and leathery.

Basic French Omelette

(Omelette Nature)

Serves 1

3 fresh eggs
1 teaspoon cold water
Salt and freshly ground black
   pepper
Generous pinch of freshly
   grated Parmesan
Butter

1 Break eggs into a bowl. Add a teaspoon of cold water; season to taste with salt and freshly ground black pepper, and a generous pinch of grated Parmesan, just enough to intensify the egg flavour without making its own taste felt. Stir vigorously with a fork or a wire whisk until yolks and whites are well mixed.

2 Melt $\frac{1}{2}$ to 1 level tablespoon butter in the omelette pan over a high heat, swirling it around so that bottom and sides of pan are entirely coated.

3 As soon as foaming subsides and butter is on the point of changing colour, pour in eggs all at once.

4 Now is the time to start working. As soon as the eggs are in, take the handle of the pan in your left hand and start shaking it back and forth over the heat. At the same time, scrape the bottom of the pan with a large fork held as flat as possible in your right hand, back and forth several times in one direction, then back and forth at right angles, and bringing in the sides so that the eggs cook evenly. Continue working like this for a few seconds, with both hands on the move. Then discard the fork and allow the bottom to set for a few seconds longer. You should feel the omelette slipping freely over the surface of the pan, but the surface should still be soft and moist.

5 Remove pan from the heat. Take the fork again and use it to fold the nearside edge of the omelette over to the centre. Then tilt the pan down *away* from you and give the handle a few sharp knocks so that the omelette slips down the pan and the unfolded part slides up the side farthest away from you. Fold this side over the centre. Your omelette is now neatly folded in three.

6 Take a heated serving dish in your left hand and carefully tip the pan up at right angles to that the omelette flops out with the folded edge underneath.

7 Quickly brush surface with a knob of butter speared on the end of a knife. Serve immediately.

Note: For a supremely light omelette, fold a tablespoon of stiffly beaten egg white into the eggs before they have completely set.

Asparagus Omelette

Prepare a Basic French Omelette (page 286). Just before folding it, scatter 2 or 3 hot cooked asparagus stalks, cut into 1-inch lengths, down the centre.

Fold omelette. Turn out; brush with butter and serve garnished with a sprinkling of finely chopped parsley.

Serves 1

3 eggs
1 teaspoon cold water
Salt and freshly ground black
   pepper
Generous pinch of freshly
   grated Parmesan
Butter
2–3 cooked asparagus stalks
Finely chopped parsley

Cheese Omelette

1 Mix the eggs together in a bowl as directed in Basic French Omelette (page 286), adding freshly grated Parmesan and Gruyère. A tablespoon of double cream may also be added if you want a particularly creamy omelette.

Steps **2–7** as in Basic French Omelette (page 286).

Serves 1

3 eggs
Salt and freshly ground black
   pepper
2 level tablespoons freshly
   grated Parmesan
2 level tablespoons freshly
   grated Gruyère
1 level tablespoon double
   cream (optional)
Butter

Serves 1

3 eggs
Salt and freshly ground black
  pepper
Generous pinch of freshly
  grated Parmesan
Butter

Mushroom filling
2 oz button mushrooms,
  thinly sliced
1 oz shredded Spanish onion
2–3 tablespoons cold water
1 level tablespoon flour
2 tablespoons cold chicken
  stock
Salt and freshly ground black
  pepper
1/2 level tablespoon finely
  chopped parsley and dill
2 level tablespoons double
  cream

Serves 1

3 eggs
Salt and freshly ground black
  pepper
Generous pinch of freshly
  grated Parmesan
Butter

Tomato filling
4 oz firm ripe tomatoes
1 level teaspoon butter
1/2 level teaspoon
  concentrated tomato purée
1 level teaspoon finely
  chopped parsley
Pinch of dried oregano
  (optional)
Salt and freshly ground black
  pepper
Pinch of sugar

Mushroom Omelette

1 Prepare Mushroom filling before making the omelette: combine thinly sliced mushrooms and shredded onion in a small pan with 2 or 3 tablespoons cold water. Simmer, covered, for 4 or 5 minutes until softened.

2 Blend flour smoothly with cold chicken stock and stir into mushroom mixture. Bring to the boil again, stirring, and simmer for 2 or 3 minutes longer until thickened.

3 Season to taste with salt and freshly ground black pepper; stir in finely chopped herbs and cream, and heat through. Remove from heat and keep warm while you prepare omelette.

4 Prepare and cook the omelette as directed in Steps **1–4** of Basic French Omelette (page 286).

5 Just before folding the omelette, spoon mushroom filling down centre. Fold the omelette in three; turn out on to a heated plate; brush with butter and serve immediately.

Tomato Omelette

1 Prepare Tomato filling before making the omelette: peel, seed and chop tomatoes coarsely. Melt butter in a small pan; add all but 1 level tablespoon of the chopped tomatoes, the tomato purée, finely chopped parsley, oregano if used, and salt, freshly ground black pepper and a pinch of sugar, to taste. Simmer for 4 to 5 minutes until tomatoes have dissolved to a thick purée. Then stir in reserved chopped tomato and keep warm while you prepare omelette.

2 Prepare and cook the omelette as directed in Steps **1–4** of Basic French Omelette (page 286).

3 Just before folding the omelette, spoon tomato filling down the centre. Fold the omelette in three; turn out on to a heated plate; brush with butter and serve immediately.

Italian Anchovy Omelettes

Serves 4

Moist little omelettes flavoured with anchovy and grated Parmesan. Make a large omelette instead if you prefer.

1 Break eggs into a bowl and stir with a fork just enough to combine yolks and whites. Add grated Parmesan and freshly ground black pepper, to taste.

2 Make 4 flat little omelettes, using 1 level tablespoon butter to fry each omelette on one side only. Spoon a little softened anchovy butter over each omelette; fold in two and serve immediately.

8 eggs
2 level tablespoons freshly grated Parmesan
Freshly ground black pepper
4 level tablespoons butter
2–3 level teaspoons anchovy butter (page 218), softened

Aubergine and Tomato Omelette

Serves 4–6

A rich, thick omelette to serve as a substantial summer luncheon dish, followed by a fresh green salad.

1 Peel aubergines and cut flesh into dice. Leave them to soak in a bowl of salted water for at least $\frac{1}{2}$ hour.

2 Heat half the olive oil in a deep, heavy frying pan. Add finely chopped onion and diced tomatoes, and sauté gently for a few minutes.

3 Drain aubergines thoroughly, squeezing out as much as possible of their bitter juices between the palms of your hands.

4 Add them to the simmering tomato mixture and mix well. Season to taste with salt and freshly ground black pepper, and cook gently for about 25 minutes, stirring occasionally with a wooden spoon.

5 Add finely chopped garlic and parsley; mix well and cook for a minute longer. Remove from heat and keep warm.

6 Beat eggs lightly with a fork. Season to taste with salt and freshly ground black pepper.

7 Heat remaining oil in a large, heavy omelette pan; pour in eggs and stir over a moderate heat until they begin to thicken. Then spoon aubergine mixture down centre, reserving two or three tablespoons for a garnish.

8 Continue to cook until omelette is golden brown on the underside but still creamy on top; then slide it up one side of the pan and fold it over on itself. Slip folded omelette out carefully on to a heated serving dish. Brush with melted butter; garnish with remaining aubergine mixture and serve immediately.

3 ripe aubergines
Salt
8 tablespoons olive oil
1 Spanish onion, finely chopped
2 lb ripe red tomatoes, peeled, seeded and diced
Freshly ground black pepper
1 clove garlic, finely chopped
4 level tablespoons finely chopped parsley
8 eggs
1–2 tablespoons melted butter

Potato Omelette

(Omelette Parmentier)

Serves 2

3 eggs
1/2 tablespoon water
Salt and freshly ground black
  pepper
1 1/2 level tablespoons butter
4 level tablespoons finely
  diced fat salt pork or fat
  bacon
3 oz cold cooked potato, cut
  into 1/2-inch cubes
1 level teaspoon each finely
  chopped parsley and chives
  or spring onion tops

This omelette is not folded in three, but browned on both sides and served flat like its Italian counterpart, the *frittata*. (See pages 291 and 292.)

1 In a bowl, combine eggs with $\frac{1}{2}$ tablespoon water and a pinch of salt and freshly ground black pepper, and stir with a fork or a wire whisk until well mixed.

2 Melt 1 level tablespoon butter in a 6-inch omelette pan and sauté diced fat salt pork until fat runs and pork bits are golden brown. Remove them from the pan with a slotted spoon and reserve them.

3 Sauté potato cubes in remaining fat until golden. Then return pork bits to the pan, together with finely chopped herbs, and salt and freshly ground black pepper, to taste.

4 Pour eggs over the hot potato mixture and cook like an omelette until set and golden underneath. Then turn it upside down on to a hot plate of the same diameter as the top of the pan, and quickly melt remaining butter in the pan before carefully slipping the flat omelette back in to brown the other side.

5 Serve in wedges from a flat, heated serving dish.

Spinach Omelette

Serves 1

3 eggs
Salt and freshly ground black
  pepper
Generous pinch of freshly
  grated Parmesan
1/2 clove garlic (optional)
Butter

Spinach filling
1–2 level tablespoons butter
3 oz frozen chopped spinach
Salt and freshly ground black
  pepper
Freshly grated nutmeg
1–2 level teaspoons double
  cream

1 Prepare Spinach filling before making the omelette: melt butter in a small pan; add frozen spinach and heat gently until it has completely defrosted and excess moisture has evaporated. Season to taste with salt, freshly ground black pepper and a pinch of freshly grated nutmeg, and stir in a little cream. Keep warm while you prepare omelette.

2 Prepare and cook the omelette as directed in Steps **1–4** of Basic French Omelette (page 286). When making a spinach omelette, I sometimes rub the pan with a cut clove of garlic before starting.

3 Just before folding the omelette, spoon spinach filling down the centre. Fold the omelette in three; turn out on to a heated plate; brush with butter and serve immediately.

Bacon Soufflé Omelettes with Cheese Sauce

1 Start with the Cheese sauce: melt butter in a small, heavy pan; add flour and cook over a very low heat for 2 minutes to make a pale *roux*, stirring constantly with a wooden spoon. Add milk gradually, beating vigorously to avoid lumps. Bring to the boil, stirring, and simmer for 10 to 12 minutes, or until sauce loses its raw, floury taste.

2 Remove from heat; stir in grated cheese and beat until smooth. Season with Worcestershire sauce, and salt and freshly ground black pepper, to taste. Cover top of sauce with a circle of dampened greaseproof paper to prevent a skin forming, and keep hot.

3 Grill or fry bacon until cooked through, and cut into ½-inch strips.

4 Beat egg yolks with 2 tablespoons cold water until light and frothy. Season lightly with salt and freshly ground black pepper.

5 Light grill, setting it at the highest temperature.

6 Whisk egg whites until stiff but not dry, and gently fold into egg yolk mixture.

7 Cook the mixture in two batches, or using two 8- or 9-inch omelette pans simultaneously: melt 1 level tablespoon butter in each pan. Pour in half the omelette mixture and, swirling lightly with a fork, allow base to set and colour over a steady heat. Then slip omelettes under a hot grill for a few minutes, just long enough to puff and set the top, and colour it slightly.

8 Scatter half of the bacon strips over half of each omelette and carefully fold in two. Slip omelettes out on to heated serving dishes. Mask with hot cheese sauce and serve immediately.

Serves 4

8 oz bacon

6 eggs, separated

2 tablespoons cold water

Salt and freshly ground black pepper

2 level tablespoons butter

Cheese sauce

1 oz butter

1 oz flour

1 pint hot milk

4 oz hard Cheshire or Cheddar cheese, grated

2 teaspoons Worcestershire sauce

Salt and freshly ground black pepper

Italian Frittata

1 Heat 2 tablespoons olive oil in a small frying pan and sauté finely chopped onion for 3 or 4 minutes until soft and lightly coloured. Allow to cool.

2 Break eggs into a bowl. Add cooled sautéed onion, finely chopped herbs and salt and freshly ground black pepper, to taste, and stir vigorously with a fork or a wire whisk until well mixed.

3 Combine remaining olive oil with 1 level teaspoon butter in a heavy, 8-inch frying pan, and heat until sizzling.

Serves 2-3

3 tablespoons olive oil

1/2 Spanish onion, finely chopped

8 eggs

1 level tablespoon each finely chopped fresh parsley, mint or basil

Salt and freshly ground black pepper

2 level teaspoons butter

4 Pour in egg mixture all at once and cook as you would an omelette for 40 to 45 seconds, until golden brown and set underneath, but still very creamy on top.

5 Invert a hot flat plate on top of the pan, slightly larger in diameter than the latter; then carefully turn plate and pan upside down so that frittata is transferred to the plate.

6 Melt remaining teaspoon of butter in the pan; then slide frittata back in to cook and set the other side for just 20 to 30 seconds longer. It should remain soft and creamy in the middle. Serve immediately, cut in wedges like a cake.

Note: When fresh chives are available, you can substitute 2 level tablespoons, finely chopped, for the sautéed onion, adding them with the other chopped herbs.

Remember, too, that only half the amount of dried herbs should be used when substituting them for fresh ones, as they are much stronger in flavour. And a dried herb is greatly improved if you first 'reconstitute' it by infusing it for a few minutes in boiling water, then draining it thoroughly on absorbent paper.

Frittata con la Ricotta

(Italian folded Omelette with Cottage Cheese)

Ricotta, which is a very delicate curd cheese used extensively in Italian cooking, can be bought in many Italian delicatessens. If you can't get it, substitute well-drained cottage cheese.

1 Prepare tomato sauce in advance: heat oil in a small pan and sauté finely chopped onion for 3 or 4 minutes until soft and golden.

2 Add canned tomatoes, together with their juice, a good pinch of basil, and sugar, salt and freshly ground black pepper, to taste. (Season lightly at this stage, bearing in mind that the sauce will reduce as it simmers.)

3 Simmer sauce for 20 minutes until thickened, stirring and mashing occasionally with a wooden spoon.

4 Rub sauce through a fine sieve and taste for seasoning. Keep hot.

5 To make omelette: in a bowl, beat cheese with 1 level tablespoon grated Parmesan, the finely chopped parsley, and salt and freshly ground black pepper, to taste.

6 In another bowl, stir eggs vigorously with a fork or a wire whisk until thoroughly blended, adding remaining tablespoon of grated Parmesan, and salt and freshly ground black pepper, to taste.

Serves 2 substantially

Tomato sauce

1 teaspoon olive oil

1 level tablespoon finely chopped onion

One 14-oz can peeled tomatoes

Generous pinch of dried basil

Pinch of sugar

Salt and freshly ground black pepper

Omelette mixture

4 oz ricotta or cottage cheese (see note)

2 level tablespoons grated Parmesan

1 level tablespoon finely chopped parsley

Salt and freshly ground black pepper

4 eggs

1/2–1 level tablespoon butter

7 Melt butter in a 6- or 7-inch omelette pan. When it is hot but not coloured, pour in egg mixture and cook as you would a French omelette.

8 When omelette is set and golden underneath but still very moist on top, spread centre with cheese mixture and continue to cook for a few seconds longer to allow it to heat through.

9 Fold omelette in three. Turn out on to a hot serving dish and mask with hot tomato sauce. Serve immediately.

Basic Sweet Omelette

Fewer eggs are needed for an individual sweet omelette than a savoury one as the sweetness makes it more filling. Use cognac, Kirsch or rum, or any sweet liqueur such as Grand Marnier or Cointreau, to flame the omelette.

1 Break eggs into a small bowl. Add salt, sugar and a teaspoon of cold water, and stir vigorously with a fork or a wire whisk until mixed.

Steps **2–6** as in Basic French Omelette (page 286).

7 Sprinkle the folded omelette with castor sugar. Heat liqueur gently in a large metal spoon; set it alight and pour over the omelette. Serve immediately.

Serves 1

2 fresh eggs
Pinch of salt
1 level tablespoon castor sugar, vanilla-flavoured if possible
1 level teaspoon butter

To flame
1/2 level teaspoon castor sugar
1 teaspoon liqueur (see note)

Sweet Omelette Fillings

The fillings below can be used to garnish both plain sweet omelettes and soufflé ones. One portion is ample to fill a Basic Sweet Omelette. Allow a double portion of filling for each recipe of Basic Sweet Soufflé Omelette, replacing the Grand Marnier in the basic egg mixture with a tablespoon of the liqueur used to flavour the filling.

Remember that an omelette filling should always be prepared before the omelette itself.

Jam Omelette

Choose a well-flavoured jam – apricot, raspberry or damson are particularly good, and so is marmalade. Warm it gently; then mix 2 level tablespoons of it with a few drops of lemon juice.

Spoon down middle of omelette; fold and serve immediately, sprinkled with a little castor sugar.

Banana Omelette

Peel a small banana (3–4 oz unpeeled weight) and cut it into ½-inch chunks. Toss in a teaspoon of butter over a high heat for 1 or 2 minutes until golden but not mushy. Flame with ½ teaspoon rum which you have first heated in a metal spoon and set alight. Sharpen flavour with a few drops of lemon juice and keep warm.

Just before folding the omelette, spoon banana chunks and juices down the centre. Fold omelette and turn out on to a hot plate.

Sprinkle with ½ level teaspoon castor sugar; flame with a teaspoon of rum and serve immediately.

Cherry Omelette

Take 6 ripe black cherries, fresh or canned. Cut them in half and remove stones. Toss cherries in a teaspoon of butter over a high heat for 1 or 2 minutes. Flame with ½ teaspoon Kirsch which you have first heated in a metal spoon and set alight. Keep warm.

Just before folding the omelette, spoon cherries and juices down the centre. Fold omelette and turn out on to a heated plate.

Sprinkle with ½ level teaspoon castor sugar; flame with a teaspoon of Kirsch and serve immediately.

Pear Omelette

Peel, core and thinly slice half a ripe, fragrant dessert pear. Toss slices in a teaspoon of butter over a high heat for 2 to 3 minutes until golden and tender but not mushy. Flame with ½ teaspoon Kirsch which you have first heated in a metal spoon and set alight. Keep warm.

Just before folding the omelette, spoon pear slices and juices down the centre. Fold omelette and turn out on to a hot plate.

Sprinkle with ½ level teaspoon castor sugar; flame with a teaspoon of Kirsch and serve immediately.

Soft Berry Omelette

Sprinkle 12 ripe raspberries or blackberries with ½ level teaspoon castor sugar and ½ teaspoon Kirsch. Toss lightly and leave to macerate for 30 minutes. (If using frozen berries, allow them to defrost completely in the Kirsch and sugar mixture.)

Spoon berries and juices down middle of omelette just before folding it. Then fold the omelette; sprinkle with $\frac{1}{2}$ level teaspoon castor sugar, and flame with $\frac{1}{2}$ to 1 teaspoon Kirsch.

For a strawberry omelette, macerate 8 to 12 berries, depending on size, in $\frac{1}{2}$ teaspoon each castor sugar and Grand Marnier or Cointreau.

Spoon down the omelette; fold it; sprinkle with $\frac{1}{3}$ level teaspoon castor sugar and flame with $\frac{1}{2}$ to 1 teaspoon Grand Marnier.

Sweet Soufflé Omelette

Serves 2–3

Our basic sweet soufflé omelette is flavoured with orange, but you can use vanilla instead (vanilla-flavoured castor sugar plus a few drops of essence if necessary to intensify the flavour).

It is important to use unsalted butter for frying the omelette – salted butter tends to burn, and there is no way of preventing this as the omelette mixture is not stirred once it goes into the pan. Too much salt may also spoil the flavour.

Finally, the secret of a feathery soufflé omelette is to cook it as quickly as possible – it will become tough and rubbery if it is overcooked – and serve it as soon as it's ready.

1 Separate eggs.

2 Beat egg yolks with castor sugar and grated orange rind until light and creamy. Add Grand Marnier gradually, beating constantly.

3 Add a pinch of salt to the egg whites and beat until stiff but not dry. (Make sure your whisk is spotlessly clean and dry after the egg yolk mixture, otherwise your egg whites will not 'mount up' properly.)

4 Fold beaten egg whites into yolk and sugar mixture.

5 Melt butter in an 8-inch omelette pan over a moderate heat, swirling it around so that entire surface is coated.

6 When butter is hot and foaming, pour in egg mixture and allow it to find its own level. Cook over a steady, moderately low heat for *60 to 90 seconds only* until underside is set and golden – egg mixture will still be quite cool on top.

7 Slip pan under a hot, preheated grill and hold it close to the heat for *20 to 30 seconds*. Remove as soon as top of omelette has puffed up and set and coloured delicately.

8 Fold omelette in two with a spatula. Slip out on to a hot plate and dust with sifted icing sugar. Serve immediately.

3 eggs
2 level tablespoons castor sugar
1/2 level teaspoon finely grated orange rind
1 tablespoon Grand Marnier
Pinch of salt
1–2 level teaspoons unsalted butter
Sifted icing sugar

Serves 2–3

4 level tablespoons apricot
  jam
1 tablespoon lemon juice
4 eggs
2 level tablespoons vanilla-
  flavoured castor sugar
Pinch of salt
1–2 level tablespoons
  unsalted butter
1 tablespoon rum

Apricot Rum Soufflé Omelette

1 Heat apricot jam in a small pan, adding a tablespoon of lemon juice to thin it down to heavy pouring consistency. Keep warm.

2 Separate eggs.

3 Beat yolks with half the castor sugar until fluffy and lemon-coloured.

4 Beat egg whites with a pinch of salt until stiff but not dry. (Be sure to wash and dry the beaters carefully after beating the egg yolks, or your whites will not come up stiffly.)

5 Heat an 8-inch omelette pan until a drop of water sizzles and rolls on contact. Add the butter and allow it to melt without colouring.

6 Fold stiffly beaten egg whites into yolk mixture and immediately pour into the hot pan.

7 Lower heat to moderate and cook steadily until omelette is set and golden brown underneath.

8 Slip pan under a hot, preheated grill, as close to the heat as possible, and keep it there just long enough to puff and colour the surface of the omelette. It should remain creamy in the middle. If it is overcooked, it will turn rubbery.

9 As soon as omelette is puffed and golden, remove from heat. Spread warm jam over half of it and fold in two with a spatula.

10 Slip omelette out on to a heated serving dish. Sprinkle with remaining castor sugar and flame with rum which you have first heated gently in a metal ladle and set alight. Serve immediately.

Italian Apple Frittata

A fragrant, quick omelette to make at a moment's notice – ideal as a snack for jaded appetites. If you are nervous about inverting the omelette, you can cheat a little and brown the top under a hot grill instead.

1 Make a smooth batter with the flour, salt and milk. Stir in well-beaten eggs, sugar, grated lemon rind and vanilla, and beat until thoroughly blended.

2 Peel, core and slice apples into rings; fold them into the egg batter.

3 Melt half the butter in a large, thick-bottomed frying pan. When it is sizzling, pour in apple mixture, distributing apple slices evenly over the entire surface. Cook steadily over a moderate heat until underside of omelette is set and golden, and omelette is no longer runny.

4 Turn omelette out on to a plate of the same diameter as the frying pan. Melt remaining butter in the frying pan; then slip omelette back into pan to brown the other side.

5 Serve very hot with a dusting of sifted icing sugar.

Serves 2

2 level tablespoons plain flour
Pinch of salt
6 tablespoons milk
2 eggs, well beaten
1 level tablespoon castor sugar
Grated rind of 1 lemon
1/2 teaspoon vanilla essence
2 medium-sized eating apples
About 2 level tablespoons butter
Icing sugar

297

Lesson 12
Soufflés

The soufflé, a half-forgotten and much neglected culinary classic, is ready to come to your rescue. The marvellous versatility of this airy dish will make you wonder how you managed so long without it.

For the appetising use of left-overs there is nothing to equal it. For economy in extending small bits of luxury – lobster, fresh crab, finely chopped fresh herbs, caviar, pheasant – it cannot be bettered.

Try my basic cheese soufflé, a careful combination of grated Gruyère and Parmesan – and add chopped cooked spinach or slivers of golden fried courgettes. Or go Spanish with slices of mushroom, green peppers, tomatoes and Bayonne ham. Or take a page from a French country cook: sauté diced cooked potatoes in oil with finely chopped onion, and toss lightly into your soufflé mixture before folding in the stiffly beaten egg whites.

I have never made a Chinese soufflé – with bean sprouts, water chestnuts, prawns and mushrooms – but I don't see why it shouldn't be equally delicious in its own distinctive Oriental way!

It is probably true to say that the procedure of making a soufflé involves as many skills and techniques as any other branch of cooking. Yet all it is is a thick, highly flavoured, sauce-like base rich in egg yolks, combined with stiffly beaten egg whites which cause it to rise to a spectacular height when subjected to the heat of the oven.

The Soufflé Dish

Soufflés are baked in specially designed, round porcelain or earthenware dishes with straight, fairly low sides. Since the soufflé mixture is intended to mushroom up into a crust well clear of the top of the dish, the latter must be carefully greased with butter, especially around the rim, to prevent the soufflé getting stuck on its way up. As a further aid to the soufflé on its journey, the inside of the dish is coated with breadcrumbs or grated cheese (in the case of a savoury soufflé), or granulated sugar (in the case of a dessert soufflé) to provide a rough surface with some 'grip' for it to cling to as it rises.

The Soufflé Mixture

The preparation of a soufflé can be broken down into four separate stages:

Stage 1 – The sauce or foundation The sauce base for a *savoury soufflé* may be a simple Béchamel, a thick reduced purée of fish, meat or vegetables, or a combination of the two.

A *sweet soufflé* usually has as its foundation a *crème pâtissière* (custard), or simply a sweetened and heavily reduced fruit purée.

This base is enriched with egg yolks and allowed to cool until it is just lukewarm before proceeding.

● Alternatively, you can break off at this point and allow the base to become quite cold, provided you reheat it again slightly before carrying on to Stage 2.

Stage 2 – Whisking the egg whites Once you embark on Stage 2, there is no turning back. The soufflé must be completed, baked and served without delay. So calculate 2 to 3 minutes for beating the egg whites, and a further 2 minutes or so to fold them into the sauce base. Add to this the baking time specified in the recipe – then make sure that everyone is assembled at the table as zero hour approaches. No one minds waiting for a few minutes when a soufflé is on its way, but a soufflé will wait for no one. Those few crucial minutes make all the difference between a gloriously tall, feathery creation trembling from the oven, and an exhausted, rubbery pillow.

The next step is to beat as much air as possible into the egg whites. Make sure that (*a*) the egg whites are free from the slightest trace of yolk, and at room temperature; and (*b*) that your bowl and whisk are spotlessly clean and dry. Grease is the greatest enemy of whisked egg whites.

Add a pinch of salt to them; then whisk steadily until peaks hold their shape with soft firmness when the beaters are lifted out. As soon as this stage is reached, stop beating – overbeaten egg whites are as useless as underbeaten ones.

If you are using a hand-held electric mixer to beat the egg whites, start off at low speed; then, as whites foam up and their texture changes, increase speed to moderate and continue to beat until stiff peaks form, turning the bowl this way and that, and moving the beaters over the entire surface so that every part of the mass of egg whites comes under them.

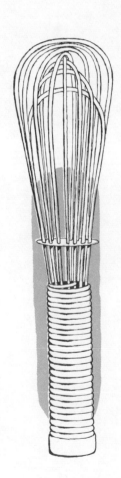

With a fixed electric mixer, you will have to keep scraping the whites down to the beaters with a spatula to ensure even beating.

Stage 3 – **Folding in egg whites** The beaten egg whites must now be folded into the tepid sauce without delay.

If the sauce base is very thick and heavy, loosen it by stirring in a dollop or two of the beaten egg white. Then scoop the remainder out on to the surface of the sauce and, using a spatula or a large metal spoon, combine the two as quickly and as lightly as possible, cutting through at right angles, and drawing the sauce up and over the mountain of egg white with a gentle over-and-under motion, while at the same time turning the bowl round and round with your other hand. The aim is to combine the mixture with the least number of air-deflating strokes, and the whole operation should take no more than a minute to complete. Do not be tempted under any circumstances to use a stirring, far less a beating motion. Far better to stop while a few flecks of unblended egg white are still in evidence.

Spoon the mixture into the prepared soufflé dish and level off top lightly with a spatula or the back of a spoon.

If you want your soufflé to have a head, draw a 'ring' about 1 inch deep all around the outer perimeter of the soufflé with the flat side of a knife or spatula.

Stage 4 – **Baking the soufflé** There are two ways of baking a soufflé (with the inevitable one or two exceptions such as a chocolate soufflé – see page 320). Either it goes straight into the oven on a shelf slightly below centre; or the dish is first set in a deep baking tin, and an inch of boiling water is poured in around it and brought back to a gentle boil on top of the stove before being transferred to the oven. The latter method is best for the less robust (usually sweet) soufflés: it protects the eggs in the mixture from curdling and ensures that the soufflé does not rise unevenly.

The temperature remains the same in both cases: the oven is preheated to 400°F. (Mark 6) and reduced to 325°F. (Mark 3) as soon as the soufflé goes in. This gives it just long enough at the higher temperature to allow the heat to penetrate the cold dish without affecting the soufflé, which itself proceeds to bake at the lower temperature. If the higher temperature were maintained, the soufflé would probably curdle, and a heavy, unyielding crust would form over the exterior before it had had a chance to rise to its full potential.

To test if a soufflé is ready To a certain extent, the degree of cooking is a matter of taste: some people prefer the creamier texture of a slightly undercooked soufflé, but if you want it to retain its handsome appearance as long as possible, you would be advised to stick to the full baking time.

A baked soufflé should tremble slightly when you shake the dish, but not wobble, and a thin skewer pushed down to the bottom should come out clean – if foamy traces of the mixture have stuck to it, leave the soufflé in the oven for a few minutes longer.

Old wive's tales If your thermostat is accurate, and the oven has been fully preheated, there is no reason why you should tiptoe around the kitchen while a soufflé is in the oven.

I have even dug a spoon into a soufflé, discovered that it was still raw, and returned it to the oven – whereupon, having recovered from the initial shock, it has proceeded to puff up to even more majestic heights than before.

I certainly don't recommend this drastic treatment, but it does go to prove that soufflés are far more robust and less temperamental creatures than we have been led to believe.

Basic Cheese Soufflé

The simplest and best soufflé of them all. However, the choice of cheese merits a special note. Contrary to most dishes, which call for *freshly* grated Gruyère and Parmesan, a soufflé requires the cheese to be on the dry side. So, just this once, grate your cheese in advance; spread it out quite thinly on a baking sheet and leave it for a few hours at the bottom of the refrigerator before using it.

Another point to watch is that the sauce base must be cooled *before* you beat in the cheese. The aim is to prevent the cheese from melting until it has been thoroughly dispersed throughout the mixture, beaten egg whites and all.

1 Grease a 2½-pint soufflé dish generously with butter, paying particular attention to the inside rim, and dust all over with a mixture of stale breadcrumbs and dry grated Parmesan. Stand dish in a deep baking tin and put aside.

2 Preheat oven to moderately hot (400°F. Mark 6).

3 Melt butter in a heavy saucepan; blend in flour and stir over a low heat for 2 to 3 minutes to make a pale *roux*.

4 Heat milk in a separate pan. Add to *roux* gradually, stirring vigorously to prevent lumps forming; bring to the boil and

Serves 4–6

3 level tablespoons butter
3 level tablespoons flour
1/2 pint milk
5 egg yolks
3 oz dry grated Gruyère
2 oz plus 1 level tablespoon dry grated Parmesan
Salt and freshly ground black pepper
Freshly grated nutmeg
Cayenne pepper
Scant 1/4 level teaspoon dry mustard
6 egg whites

Soufflé dish
Butter
1 level tablespoon stale fine breadcrumbs
1 level tablespoon dry grated Parmesan

simmer over a moderate heat for 2 to 3 minutes longer, stirring, until sauce is thick and smooth.

5 Remove pan from heat. Cool sauce slightly; then beat in egg yolks, one at a time. Pour sauce into a large bowl and allow to cool to lukewarm.

6 Add grated Gruyère and 2 oz grated Parmesan to tepid sauce; blend thoroughly and season generously with salt, freshly ground black pepper, a pinch each of freshly grated nutmeg and cayenne, and a little dry mustard.

7 Select another large bowl and make sure it is spotlessly clean and dry. Put egg whites in it; add a pinch of salt and whisk until stiff but not dry.

8 Stir a large dollop (about 2 heaped tablespoons) beaten egg white into the tepid sauce; then fold in remainder with a spatula or a metal spoon, working as quickly and lightly as possible.

9 Spoon soufflé mixture into prepared dish and lightly level off top with the back of the spoon or spatula. Pour an inch of boiling water into the baking tin and bring back to the boil over a gentle heat.

10 As soon as water bubbles, transfer tin to the oven and immediately lower temperature to 325°F. (Mark 3). Bake for about 40 minutes, or until soufflé is well puffed and almost done, but still very wobbly. Then increase heat to 400°F. (Mark 6) again and give it another 10 minutes to finish cooking and brown the top. Halfway through cooking time, sprinkle top of soufflé with remaining tablespoon of grated Parmesan to give a crisp, flavoursome crust. Soufflé is ready when a thin skewer pushed into the centre comes out clean. Serve immediately.

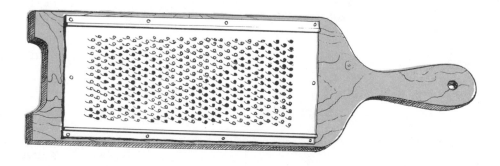

Basic proportions The basic recipe given above can be cut down or extended as follows:

	1½-*pint dish (serves 3–4)*	3½-*pint dish (serves 6–8)**
Butter	2 level tablespoons	4 level tablespoons
Flour	2 level tablespoons	4 level tablespoons
Milk	7 fluid oz	¾ pint
Egg yolks	3	6
Dry grated Gruyère	2 oz	4 oz
Dry grated Parmesan	1½ oz	3 oz
Salt and freshly ground black pepper	to taste	to taste
Freshly grated nutmeg	to taste	to taste
Cayenne pepper	to taste	to taste
Dry mustard	generous pinch	¼ level teaspoon

Butter plus 1 level tablespoon each fine stale breadcrumbs and dry grated Parmesan for soufflé dish.

1 level tablespoon dry grated Parmesan sprinkled over top of soufflé halfway through baking time.

Cooking time: 400°F. (Mark 6) turned down to 325°F. (Mark 3) plus 400°F. (Mark 6) to brown top	30 minutes plus 10 minutes	40 minutes plus 10 minutes

* For a larger number of people make soufflés in two dishes.

Soufflé Variations

The following soufflés are all variations on the theme of the Basic Cheese Soufflé, with the amount of cheese decreased to make way for the new flavour.

Serves 4–6

1 recipe Basic Cheese Soufflé
(page 301) made with 2 oz
grated Gruyère and 1 oz
grated Parmesan

1/4 pint sour cream

2–3 level tablespoons red
caviar, lightly crushed

Serves 4–6

1 recipe Basic Cheese Soufflé
(page 301) made with 2 oz
grated Gruyère and 1 oz
grated parmesan

3–4 oz thinly sliced smoked
salmon, diced

Béarnaise sauce made with
4 oz butter (page 193)

Serves 4–6

1 recipe Basic Cheese
Soufflé (page 301) made
with 1 oz grated Gruyère
and 1 oz grated Parmesan

8 oz smoked haddock
fillets

1 level tablespoon butter

1 level tablespoon flour

4 level tablespoons double
cream

Soufflé au Caviar

Steps **1–8** as for Basic Cheese Soufflé (page 301).

9 Beat sour cream lightly with a fork to even out its texture.
Fold in red caviar.

10 Spoon half of soufflé mixture into prepared dish; spread
evenly with sour cream and red caviar, and cover with remaining
soufflé mixture, levelling it out neatly with the back of your
spoon.

11 Finish soufflé according to directions in basic recipe.

Smoked Salmon Soufflé

Steps **1–8** as for Basic Cheese Soufflé (page 301).

9 Fold diced smoked salmon into Béarnaise sauce.

10 Spoon half of soufflé mixture into prepared dish; spread
evenly with smoked salmon and Béarnaise sauce, and cover with
remaining soufflé mixture, levelling it out neatly with the back
of your spoon.

11 Finish soufflé according to directions in basic recipe.

Creamed Haddock Soufflé

Steps **1** and **2** as for Basic Cheese Soufflé (page 301).

3 Prepare haddock mixture: cover fillets with cold water and
bring slowly to the boil. Cover pan; remove from heat and leave
to stand for 15 minutes. Drain and separate with a fork into large
flakes.

4 In a heavy pan, sauté haddock flakes lightly in butter for 1 or
2 minutes to colour them slightly, taking care not to crush them.
Dust with flour; cook for 1 minute longer and stir in double
cream. Remove from heat and allow to cool.

5 Prepare Cheese Soufflé as directed in Steps 3–8 of basic recipe,
cutting down Gruyère and Parmesan by 1 oz each.

6 Spoon half of soufflé mixture into prepared dish. Cover evenly
with haddock mixture and top with remaining soufflé mixture,
levelling it off neatly with the back of your spoon.

7 Finish soufflé according to directions in basic recipe.

Sweetbread Soufflé

1 Wash sweetbreads thoroughly and leave them to soak in cold water for 1 hour, changing water 2 or 3 times.

2 Drain sweetbreads thoroughly. Place them in a small pan; cover with cold water; bring to the boil and simmer for 5 minutes. Cool under cold running water.

3 When sweetbreads are cold, drain well and carefully remove any membranes and tubes. Slice sweetbreads and cut into ½-inch squares.

4 In a heavy pan, melt butter. Blend in flour with a wooden spoon and stir over a low heat for 2 or 3 minutes to make a pale *roux*.

5 Gradually add milk, double cream and Madeira, stirring briskly to prevent lumps forming. Bring to the boil and simmer for 2 minutes, stirring, to make a thick sauce.

6 Remove pan from heat. Fold in sliced sweetbreads and season to taste with salt, freshly ground black pepper and a few drops of lemon juice.

7 Prepare cheese soufflé as directed in Steps **1–8** of basic recipe (page 301).

8 Spoon half of soufflé mixture into prepared dish; cover with sweetbreads and Madeira sauce, and top with remaining soufflé mixture, levelling it out evenly with the back of your spoon.

9 Finish soufflé according to directions in basic recipe.

Serves 4–6

1 recipe Basic Cheese Soufflé made with 2 oz grated Gruyère and 1 oz grated Parmesan

Sweetbread garnish
8 oz sweetbreads
1 level tablespoon butter
1 level tablespoon flour
3 tablespoons milk
2 level tablespoons double cream
2 tablespoons Madeira
Salt and freshly ground black pepper
Lemon juice

Soufflé aux Courgettes

1 Prepare courgettes before soufflé: wipe them clean, slice them into thin rounds, and sauté in butter for 2 to 3 minutes until soft and golden on both sides. Season to taste with salt and freshly ground black pepper, and put aside to cool.

2 Combine finely chopped herbs on a plate and use them to coat courgette slices on both sides.

3 Prepare cheese soufflé as directed in Steps **1–8** of basic recipe (page 301).

4 Spoon half of soufflé mixture into prepared dish; cover with a layer of herbed courgette slices and top with remaining soufflé mixture, levelling it out evenly with the back of your spoon.

5 Finish soufflé according to directions in basic recipe.

Serves 4–6

1 recipe Basic Cheese Soufflé (page 301) made with 2 oz grated Gruyère and 1 oz grated Parmesan

Courgette garnish
4 oz courgettes
2 level teaspoons butter
Salt and freshly ground black pepper
2 level tablespoons finely chopped parsley
1/2 level teaspoon dried chopped chives or spring onion tops
1/4 level teaspoon dried oregano

Serves 3–4

Butter

1/2 lb plus 1 oz very white
   button mushrooms

1 medium-sized onion

1 1/2 level tablespoons flour

1/8 pint single cream

1/8 pint well-flavoured
   chicken stock (page 162)

2 egg yolks

2 oz cooked white chicken
   meat, slivered

Salt and freshly ground black
   pepper

Freshly grated nutmeg

3 egg whites

Mushroom Chicken Soufflé

1 Butter a $1\frac{1}{2}$-pint soufflé dish generously, paying particular attention to the top rim. Place it in a deep baking tin and put aside.

2 Preheat oven to moderately hot (400°F. Mark 6).

3 Chop $\frac{1}{2}$ lb mushrooms very finely and the onion rather coarsely. Sauté together in $\frac{1}{2}$ level tablespoon butter until softened, stirring with a wooden spoon to evaporate as much moisture as possible. Then blend to a purée in a liquidiser and rub through a fine sieve into a large bowl.

4 Slice remaining ounce of button mushrooms thinly and toss in a little butter for a few minutes until softened. Put aside.

5 In a heavy saucepan, melt 1 level tablespoon butter. Add flour and stir over a low heat for 2 to 3 minutes to make a pale *roux*.

6 Add cream and chicken stock gradually, stirring vigorously to prevent lumps forming, and cook for 2 to 3 minutes longer, stirring, until sauce is thick and smooth.

7 Blend hot sauce thoroughly with mushroom purée. Then beat in egg yolks, one at a time; fold in sautéed mushrooms and the chicken slivers, and season generously with salt, freshly ground black pepper and a pinch of freshly grated nutmeg. Allow mixture to cool to lukewarm.

8 In a large, spotlessly clean bowl, whisk egg whites with a pinch of salt until stiff but not dry. Fold into mushroom sauce as quickly and lightly as possible with a spatula or a large metal spoon.

9 Spoon soufflé mixture into prepared dish; pour an inch of boiling water into the baking tin and bring back to the boil over a gentle heat.

10 Transfer soufflé to the oven and immediately reduce temperature to 325°F. (Mark 3). Bake for 30 minutes; then increase temperature to 400°F. (Mark 6) again for about 10 minutes, or until soufflé is cooked through, with a golden brown crust. Serve immediately.

Salmon Soufflé

Serves 4-6

1 Grease a 2½-pint soufflé dish generously with butter and dust with flour, shaking out excess. Stand dish in a deep baking tin and put aside.

2 Preheat oven to moderately hot (400°F. Mark 6).

3 In a small bowl, combine canned salmon with cream and mash thoroughly with a fork.

4 Melt butter in a double saucepan over lightly simmering water. Add flour and cook for 2 to 3 minutes, stirring, to make a smooth pale *roux*.

5 In a heavy pan, bring milk just to boiling point. Add to *roux* in a thin stream, beating constantly to prevent lumps forming. Beat in mashed salmon and continue to cook over simmering water for 5 minutes longer, stirring occasionally.

6 Put egg yolks in a large bowl and beat lightly until well mixed; then gradually beat in hot salmon mixture. Add lemon juice and season generously with salt, freshly ground black pepper and a good pinch of cayenne. Allow to cool to lukewarm.

7 In another bowl, whisk egg whites with a pinch of salt until stiff but not dry. Fold in salmon mixture as quickly and lightly as possible, using a spatula or a large metal spoon.

8 Spoon mixture into prepared soufflé dish and level off top. Pour an inch of boiling water into tin and bring back to the boil over a gentle heat.

9 Transfer to the oven and immediately lower heat to 325°F. (Mark 3). Bake for 45 minutes until well risen; then increase temperature to 400°F. (Mark 6) for a further 5 to 10 minutes to firm the soufflé and brown the crust. Serve immediately.

One 7 1/2-oz can red salmon
2 tablespoons double cream
4 level tablespoons butter
3 level tablespoons flour
1/2 pint milk
4 egg yolks
2-3 teaspoons lemon juice
Salt and freshly ground black pepper
Cayenne pepper
5 egg whites
Butter and flour for soufflé dish

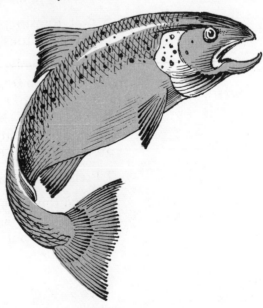

Soufflé garnish

Butter and flour for soufflé
  dish
3 fresh tomatoes, peeled and
  sliced
1 level tablespoon finely
  chopped parsley
1/4 level teaspoon dried basil
1/4 level teaspoon dried
  oregano
2 level tablespoons freshly
  grated Parmesan

Tomato purée

1 oz fat salt pork or bacon,
  very finely chopped
6 level tablespoons finely
  chopped onion
2 lb fresh ripe tomatoes,
  roughly chopped
1/4 level teaspoon dried
  oregano
1/2 bay leaf
1 sprig parsley

Soufflé mixture

2 level tablespoons butter
3 level tablespoons flour
1/2 pint milk
4 egg yolks
2 level tablespoons freshly
  grated Parmesan
Salt and freshly ground black
  pepper
Cayenne pepper
5 egg whites

Tomato Soufflé

A perfectly passable, fluffy tomato soufflé can be made simply by
flavouring your sauce base with concentrated tomato purée. The
soufflé will *look* pretty, but its flavour cannot be compared to the
version we give below. Here, fresh ripe tomatoes are combined
with fat salt pork or bacon, onions and herbs, then simmered
gently until reduced to a richly concentrated purée which has
none of the crude harshness of commercial paste, yet is thick
enough not to affect the texture of the soufflé.

1 First prepare your soufflé dish and garnish it: grease a $2\frac{1}{2}$-pint
dish generously with butter and dust it with flour, paying particular attention to the rim. Cover bottom of dish with tomato slices
and sprinkle them evenly with finely chopped parsley, basil,
oregano and 1 level tablespoon freshly grated Parmesan. Put
aside until required.

2 Prepare tomato purée: in a large, heavy pan, render fat salt
pork or bacon by frying it gently for 3 to 4 minutes until the fat
runs and the tiny pieces become translucent. Add finely chopped
onion and sauté for a further 4 to 5 minutes until soft and
golden. Then stir in roughly chopped tomatoes, oregano, bay
leaf and the sprig of parsley; bring to the boil and allow to simmer
gently for 40 to 50 minutes, stirring occasionally. The mixture
should be reduced to about $\frac{3}{4}$ pint of thick purée.

3 Meanwhile, prepare soufflé base sauce: melt butter in another
heavy pan, blend in flour with a wooden spoon and stir over a
low heat for 2 to 3 minutes to make a smooth, pale *roux*.

4 Heat milk and add it to the *roux* very gradually, beating constantly, to prevent lumps forming. Then simmer gently, stirring
frequently, until sauce is very thick and smooth, and reduced to
about half of its original volume. This will take 20 to 25 minutes.

5 Beat tomato purée into base sauce and bring to the boil,
beating vigorously. Remove from heat.

6 Beat egg yolks lightly and add them to the tomato mixture,
together with freshly grated Parmesan. Mix well; rub through a
fine sieve into a large bowl and season generously with salt,
freshly ground black pepper and a good pinch of cayenne.
Allow mixture to cool to lukewarm, stirring occasionally to
prevent a skin forming on top.

7 Preheat oven to moderately hot (400°F. Mark 6).

8 When tomato mixture is tepid, put the egg whites in a large,
spotlessly clean and dry bowl. Add a pinch of salt and whisk
until stiff but not dry.

9 With a large spatula or metal spoon, fold beaten egg whites into tomato mixture as quickly and lightly as possible.

10 Spoon mixture into prepared soufflé dish. Level top lightly with the back of the spoon or spatula and sprinkle with remaining tablespoon of Parmesan.

11 Place soufflé in the oven and immediately lower temperature to 350°F. (Mark 4). Bake soufflé for 40 minutes until well puffed with a rich golden crust. Then test it by shaking the dish slightly – if the soufflé is still very wobbly, give it 5 to 10 minutes longer.

(**Note**: The skewer test is not quite so reliable for this soufflé, as its texture remains rather creamy even when fully cooked.)

Spinach and Ham Soufflé

1 Prepare soufflé dish: grease base and sides of a 2½ pint dish generously with butter, and coat with a mixture of freshly grated Parmesan and stale white breadcrumbs, shaking out excess.

2 Preheat oven to moderately hot (400°F. Mark 6).

3 Prepare soufflé mixture: melt 5 level tablespoons butter in a heavy pan, blend in flour and stir over a low heat for 2 to 3 minutes to make a pale *roux*. Remove pan from heat.

4 Bring milk just to boiling point in a separate pan. Add to *roux* very gradually, stirring vigorously between each addition to avoid lumps. When sauce is smooth, return pan to a moderate heat; bring to the boil, stirring constantly, and simmer for 3 to 4 minutes longer until sauce is very thick and no longer tastes of raw flour.

5 Remove pan from heat and allow to cool slightly. Beat in egg yolks, one at a time; then turn mixture into a large bowl and allow to cool to lukewarm.

6 Meanwhile, melt remaining tablespoon of butter in a small pan and sauté diced ham until lightly coloured. Remove ham with a slotted spoon and put aside.

7 In the same butter, thaw frozen spinach over a low heat, stirring and mashing occasionally with a wooden spoon; then simmer for 5 to 7 minutes, stirring frequently to evaporate as much moisture as possible. Spinach should be very dry.

8 Add spinach to cooling sauce, together with freshly grated Parmesan, and beat with a wooden spoon until thoroughly blended. Then stir in sautéed ham and season generously with

Serves 4–6

Soufflé dish
Butter
1 level tablespoon freshly grated Parmesan
1 level tablespoon stale white breadcrumbs

Soufflé mixture
6 level tablespoons butter
5 level tablespoons plain flour
3/4 pint hot milk
5 egg yolks
4–6 level tablespoons finely diced ham
8 oz chopped frozen spinach
3–4 level tablespoons freshly grated Parmesan
Salt and freshly ground black pepper
Freshly grated nutmeg
Cayenne pepper
6 egg whites

Topping
1–2 level tablespoons freshly grated Parmesan

salt, freshly ground black pepper, and a pinch each of freshly grated nutmeg and cayenne.

9 Add a pinch of salt to egg whites in a large bowl and whisk until stiff but not dry. Fold into lukewarm sauce as quickly and as thoroughly as possible, using a metal spoon.

10 Pour mixture into prepared soufflé dish and level off with the back of the spoon.

11 Place soufflé in the oven. Reduce temperature to 325°F. (Mark 3) and bake for 35 to 40 minutes, or until soufflé is well puffed and golden brown. Halfway through baking time, open oven door and sprinkle top of soufflé with a tablespoon of freshly grated Parmesan without removing it from the oven. Serve immediately.

Asparagus Soufflé

Serves 6

1 1/2 lb fresh asparagus
Salt
1 lemon
6 narrow wafer-thin slices
   Parma or Westphalian ham
2 level tablespoons butter
3 level tablespoons flour
1/8 pint single cream
5 egg yolks
Freshly ground black pepper
6 egg whites
1–2 level tablespoons grated
   Parmesan
Butter and flour for soufflé
   dish

There is no need to use the very best asparagus for this soufflé – it is going to end up as a purée anyway. Just make sure you have 6 tender stalks for the garnish.

1 Rinse asparagus and scrape woody stems if necessary.

2 Bring a large pan of salted water to the boil with the juice of $\frac{1}{2}$ lemon (a fish kettle is ideal for this). Drop in asparagus stalks and poach gently for 15 to 20 minutes until just tender. Drain, reserving some of the cooking liquor, and allow to cool.

3 Grease a $3\frac{1}{2}$-pint soufflé dish with butter, paying particular attention to the top rim, and dust with flour, shaking out excess. Set in a deep baking tin and put aside until needed.

4 Preheat oven to moderately hot (400°F. Mark 6).

5 Select 6 of the best asparagus stalks and trim their stems so that the tips come level with the top of the soufflé dish when held upright. Wrap each stalk in a paper-thin slice of Parma (or Westphalian) ham. Put aside.

6 Chop remaining asparagus roughly and rub through a fine wire sieve (or purée in an electric blender, then rub through a sieve to eliminate any woody fibres).

7 Melt butter in a heavy pan. Add flour and stir over a low heat for 2 to 3 minutes to make a smooth, pale *roux*.

8 Combine cream with $\frac{1}{8}$ pint reserved asparagus liquor ($\frac{1}{4}$ pint liquid in all) and add to *roux* a little at a time, stirring vigorously to prevent lumps forming. Beat in asparagus purée and bring to the boil, stirring vigorously. Remove pan from heat.

9 In a large bowl, beat egg yolks lightly with a wire whisk. Pour on hot asparagus sauce very gradually, beating vigorously until well blended.

10 Season mixture to taste with salt and freshly ground black pepper, and add a few drops of lemon juice to bring out asparagus flavour if you think it necessary. Allow to cool to lukewarm.

11 Put egg whites in a large, spotlessly clean and dry bowl. Add a pinch of salt and whisk until stiff but not dry. Turn out on to soufflé mixture all at once and with a large metal spoon or spatula fold in as quickly and as lightly as possible.

12 Spoon mixture into prepared soufflé dish and level out top lightly with the back of the spoon or a spatula. Then push in ham-wrapped asparagus stalks upright at equal intervals in a circle about $1\frac{1}{2}$ inches in from outside rim of dish. Sprinkle top of soufflé with grated Parmesan.

13 Pour an inch of boiling water into the baking tin and bring to the boil again over a gentle heat.

14 As soon as water bubbles, transfer to the oven. Reduce temperature to 350°F. (Mark 4) and bake soufflé for 40 to 45 minutes, or until firm and well puffed, with a rich golden crust. There will be attractive little dips to show the position of each whole asparagus stalk. Make sure each person gets one as you spoon out the soufflé.

Baked Egg Soufflé

1 Preheat oven to moderately hot (400°F. Mark 6).

2 Butter a $1\frac{1}{2}$-pint soufflé dish, paying particular attention to the rim, and stand it in a deep baking tin.

3 In a heavy pan, blend potato flour smoothly with double cream. Add 1 level tablespoon butter and stir over a low heat until mixture acquires a coating consistency. (Do not take sauce beyond this stage, as the fat in the cream will cause it to separate.)

4 Separate yolks and whites of 3 eggs. Beat yolks into lukewarm sauce, together with grated Gruyère and Parmesan, and season to taste with salt, freshly ground black pepper and a pinch of freshly grated nutmeg.

5 Whisk egg whites until stiff but not dry. Fold lightly but thoroughly into cheese sauce.

6 Spoon two-thirds of soufflé mixture into prepared dish. Make 4 indentations with the back of the spoon and carefully break in

Serves 4

Butter
2 level teaspoons potato flour
7 level tablespoons double cream
7 eggs
2 oz grated Gruyère
3 level tablespoons grated Parmesan
Salt and freshly ground black pepper
Freshly grated nutmeg

4 remaining eggs. Top with remaining soufflé mixture and level off neatly.

7 Pour hot water into baking tin to come halfway up sides of soufflé dish. Bring water to the boil again over a gentle heat. Transfer to the oven and immediately reduce heat to 325°F. (Mark 3).

8 Bake soufflé for 30 minutes. Then turn thermostat to 400°F. (Mark 6) for a final 5 to 7 minutes. Serve immediately, including an egg in each portion.

Fish Soufflé

1 To poach fish: first preheat oven to moderate (350°F. Mark 4).

2 Grease an ovenproof dish generously with butter and scatter half of the finely chopped onion over the bottom. Season fish fillets with salt and freshly ground black pepper, and arrange in the dish. Sprinkle with remaining onion and the lemon juice; cover with a buttered paper and bake for 10 to 15 minutes, or until fish flakes easily with a fork.

3 Remove fish from baking dish and flake coarsely. Strain cooking liquor through a fine sieve. Allow both to cool.

4 Increase oven temperature to moderately hot (400°F. Mark 6).

5 Grease a 2½-pint soufflé dish generously with butter, paying particular attention to the top rim, and dust with flour, shaking out excess. Cut a double thickness of greaseproof paper or foil about 4 inches deep and long enough to go around the dish with a couple of inches' overlap. Rub with butter and tie securely around dish with string, buttered side inwards. 'Collar' should extend about 2 inches above rim of dish. Stand dish in a deep baking tin and put aside until needed.

6 Melt butter in a heavy pan; stir in flour and cook over a low heat, stirring constantly, for 2 to 3 minutes to make a smooth, pale *roux*.

7 Pour reserved fish liquor into a measuring jug and make up to ½ pint with milk. Then pour into a small pan; add grated onion and bring to the boil.

8 Add scalded milk mixture to *roux* a little at a time, beating vigorously to prevent lumps forming. Bring to the boil, stirring constantly, and simmer for 2 to 3 minutes longer until sauce thickens.

9 Whisk egg yolks lightly in a large bowl. Add hot sauce gradually, beating constantly. Then add grated Parmesan and French mustard; mix well and season to taste with salt, freshly ground

Serves 4–6

To poach fish
Butter
2 level tablespoons finely chopped onion
8 oz boned, skinned fish fillets: halibut, turbot or sole
Salt and freshly ground black pepper
1 teaspoon lemon juice

Soufflé mixture
3 level tablespoons butter
3 level tablespoons flour
Milk
1 level tablespoon grated onion
5 egg yolks
2 level tablespoons grated Parmesan
1/2 level teaspoon French mustard
Salt and freshly ground black pepper
1–2 teaspoons lemon juice
Cayenne pepper
3 level tablespoons finely chopped parsley
6 egg whites
Butter and flour for soufflé dish

black pepper, a little lemon juice and a pinch of cayenne. Stir in finely chopped parsley and allow to cool.

10 When sauce is lukewarm, put egg whites into another large, spotlessly clean and dry bowl; add a pinch of salt and whisk until stiff but not dry.

11 Turn beaten egg whites out on to sauce all at once and, using a metal spoon or spatula, fold in as quickly and lightly as possible. Towards the end of this operation, scatter surface of mixture with fish flakes and fold them in as well.

12 Spoon soufflé mixture into prepared dish and level top with the back of a spoon or spatula. Pour an inch of boiling water into the baking tin and bring to the boil again over a gentle heat.

13 As soon as water bubbles, transfer to oven and immediately lower heat to 350°F. (Mark 4). Bake soufflé for 45 to 50 minutes, or until well risen and golden brown on top. Centre of soufflé will remain slightly creamy.

14 Carefully peel paper 'collar' and serve soufflé immediately.

Vegetable Soufflé

Serves 3–4

Butter
1/4 pint milk
1/2 chicken stock cube
1 level teaspoon grated onion
4 level tablespoons plain flour
1/4 pint single cream (see Note)
3 oz cooked carrots, chopped to size of peas
3 oz cooked peas
3 eggs
Salt and freshly ground black pepper
1/2 pint light tomato sauce (page 194), to serve

An ideal dish to make on Sunday evening with the vegetables left over from lunch. We have used carrots and peas, but you could easily use 6 oz of just one vegetable. Celery and sweetcorn are particularly good alternatives.

1 Preheat oven to moderate (350°F. Mark 4). Butter a 2-pint metal ring mould, paying particular attention to the rim.

2 Combine milk and ½ stock cube in a pan. Bring to boiling point, making sure cube has dissolved, and remove from heat.

3 In a heavy, medium-sized pan, melt 3 level tablespoons butter. Add grated onion and cook over a very low heat for 5 minutes. Blend in flour with a wooden spoon and cook gently for 2 minutes longer, stirring constantly, to make a pale *roux*.

4 Gradually add hot flavoured milk, beating vigorously to prevent lumps forming. When sauce is smooth, stir in cream. Bring to the boil and simmer for 2 minutes, stirring. Add cooked vegetables and simmer for 1 minute longer. Remove from heat.

5 Separate eggs, dropping whites into one bowl, spotlessly clean and dry, and yolks into another.

6 Beat egg yolks lightly. Pour them into the hot sauce, stirring vigorously. Return pan to a low heat and cook gently for 1

minute longer, or until sauce has thickened, taking great care not to let it boil, or egg yolks may curdle.

7 Remove pan from heat and allow to cool to lukewarm, stirring occasionally to prevent a skin forming on top. Season generously with salt and freshly ground black pepper.

8 Whisk egg whites until stiff but not dry. Using a large metal spoon or spatula, fold them gently but thoroughly into lukewarm sauce.

9 Spoon mixture carefully into prepared ring mould, and immediately transfer to the oven.

10 Bake for 25 to 30 minutes, or until soufflé has risen well above the top of the mould and is golden and firm to the touch.

11 To serve: cover ring mould with a heated serving dish and invert the two quickly so that soufflé is not squashed. Carefully remove mould. Serve soufflé immediately, accompanied by a light tomato sauce.

Note: You can use $\frac{1}{2}$ pint creamy milk instead of the combination of milk and single cream, in which case, scald the whole amount with the stock cube.

Serves 4–6

5 egg yolks
3 oz vanilla-flavoured icing sugar
3 level tablespoons plain flour
3/4 pint milk
A 3-inch piece of vanilla pod
1 level tablespoon butter
Few drops of vanilla essence (see Note)
6 egg whites
Pinch of salt
Butter and granulated sugar for soufflé dish

Basic Vanilla Soufflé

1 Grease a $2\frac{1}{2}$-pint soufflé dish generously with butter, paying particular attention to the inside top rim. Dust all over with granulated sugar and shake out excess. Stand dish in a deep roasting tin.

2 Preheat oven to moderately hot (400°F. Mark 6).

3 In the top of a double saucepan, stir egg yolks lightly with a wooden spoon to break them up. Sift in vanilla-flavoured icing sugar and beat until smooth; then sift in flour and continue to blend lightly with the spoon until mixture is quite smooth and free of lumps.

4 In another pan, slowly heat milk with vanilla pod until it just reaches boiling point. Remove vanilla pod and pour milk into egg yolk mixture in a thin stream, beating constantly and vigorously.

5 Set pan over simmering water and cook, stirring constantly, until mixture becomes a thick, smooth custard. This will take 7 to 10 minutes. Take great care not to let custard boil, or egg yolks may curdle.

6 Remove pan from heat and beat in butter. Then pour custard into a large bowl and leave to cool, stirring occasionally to prevent a skin forming on top.

7 When custard is lukewarm, taste it and, if necessary, strengthen flavour with a few drops of vanilla essence.

8 Select another large bowl and make sure it is spotlessly clean and dry. Put egg whites in it; add a pinch of salt and whisk until stiff but not dry. Then fold egg whites into cooling custard, using a large metal spoon and working as quickly and as lightly as possible to avoid knocking any more air than necessary out of them. Mixture should remain light and feathery to the end.

9 Spoon soufflé mixture into prepared dish and level off top. Pour boiling water into roasting tin to come about 1 inch up sides of soufflé dish and heat gently on top of the stove until water bubbles again.

10 Transfer tin and soufflé dish to the oven and immediately lower heat to 325°F. (Mark 3). Soufflé will take 40 to 45 minutes to bake, but take a look at it after 35 minutes. When ready, it will have puffed up well clear of the rim of the dish and have a rich, golden crust. It should still tremble very slightly when you shake the dish gently, but a thin skewer pushed into the centre will come out clean. Serve immediately.

Note: If you do not keep a supply of vanilla-flavoured icing sugar at hand, you will have to rely on more vanilla essence for your flavouring, but add it with care – too much results in an unpleasantly synthetic aftertaste.

Basic proportions The basic recipe given above can be cut down or extended as follows:

	1½-pint dish (serves 3–4)	3½-pint dish (serves 6–8)*
Egg yolks	3	6
Vanilla-flavoured icing sugar	2 oz	4 oz
Plain flour	2 level tablespoons	4 level tablespoons
Milk	½ pint	1 pint
Vanilla pod	piece	piece
Butter	2 level teaspoons	4 level teaspoons
Vanilla essence	to taste	to taste
Egg whites	4	8
Salt	pinch	generous pinch

Cooking time: Preheat oven to 400°F. (Mark 6) oven turned down to 325°F. (Mark 3). 35–40 minutes 40–45 minutes. * For a larger number of people make soufflés in two dishes.

Serves 4–6

1 recipe Basic Vanilla Soufflé (page 314) minus 4 tablespoons milk and vanilla flavouring
1 oz castor sugar
4 tablespoons lemon juice
1 level teaspoon finely grated lemon rind

Lemon Soufflé

Steps **1–5**. Follow directions for Basic Vanilla Soufflé, leaving out vanilla flavouring and 4 tablespoons of the milk, and adding an extra ounce of castor sugar to the sauce.

6 Remove pan from heat. Beat in lemon juice and finely grated lemon rind, and allow custard to cool to lukewarm before completing soufflé as directed in the master recipe. Serve immediately.

Orange Soufflé

Steps **1–5**. Follow directions for Basic Vanilla Soufflé, leaving out vanilla flavouring and making milk up to ¾ pint again with orange juice. Rub sugar lumps all over the skin of the orange until they are thoroughly impregnated with orange oil and add them to the custard with the sugar specified in the master recipe. (You will probably find that the milk and orange juice mixture curdles when it is heated, but don't worry: it will come back again as the custard thickens.)

6 Remove pan from heat. Beat in lemon juice and marmalade, if used, and allow custard to cool to lukewarm before completing soufflé as directed in the master recipe. Serve immediately.

Coffee Praline Soufflé

Steps **1–5**. Follow directions for Basic Vanilla Soufflé, leaving out vanilla flavouring.

6 Remove pan from the heat and beat in instant coffee. Allow custard to cool; then beat in 3 oz coarsely crushed praline.

7 Finish soufflé and bake it as directed in the master recipe, sprinkling top with remaining coarsely crushed praline 10 minutes before taking it out of the oven. Serve immediately.

Praline

1 In a heavy pan, melt sugar with lemon juice and 4 tablespoons water over a low heat. Then raise heat and boil syrup to a golden brown caramel (340°F. on a sugar thermometer).

2 Meanwhile, prepare a cold surface (marble, metal, or a large flat dish) by brushing it lightly with flavourless oil.

3 As soon as caramel is ready, remove pan from heat and quickly mix in well-toasted almonds. Pour out on to prepared surface and leave to cool and harden.

4 When praline is cold, ease it off the surface with a spatula. Use as required.

Soufflé aux Marrons Glacés

Serves 4–6

1 recipe Basic Vanilla
 Soufflé (page 314)
1–2 tablespoons Kirsch
4 oz Marrons glacés
 (glazed chestnuts), chopped

Steps **1–7** Follow directions for Basic Vanilla Soufflé, flavouring lukewarm soufflé mixture with Kirsch (step 7). Step **8** As in Basic Vanilla Soufflé.

9 Spoon half of mixture into prepared soufflé dish. Scatter the chopped glazed chestnuts over the top, and cover with remaining soufflé mixture.

10 Bake as Basic Vanilla Soufflé.

Soufflé Harlequin (Soufflé Panaché)

Serves 4–6

1 recipe Basic Vanilla Soufflé
 (page 314) minus butter
1 1/2 oz plain chocolate,
 grated
1 level teaspoon instant
 coffee
2 level teaspoons butter
Few drops of vanilla essence
1 extra egg white
Salt

Although we prefer to give a completely different method for making a soufflé which is wholly flavoured with chocolate, we have found that, in the case of a vanilla–chocolate combination, the plain mixture is light enough to counteract any heaviness caused by the chocolate.

Harlequin soufflés can be made with various combinations – orange and lemon, orange and chocolate, coffee and vanilla, or even coffee and chocolate.

Steps **1–5**. Follow directions for Basic Vanilla Soufflé.

6 Remove pan from heat and divide hot custard equally between two large bowls.

7 Add grated chocolate and instant coffee to one half of custard, and beat until completely dissolved. Beat butter into remaining half. Allow both portions to cool slightly.

8 Flavour vanilla mixture with a little essence if necessary, and add a few drops to the chocolate mixture as well.

9 Put 3 egg whites in one bowl and 4 in another. Add a pinch of salt to each and beat them separately until stiff but not dry. Fold 3 egg whites into the vanilla mixture and 4 into the chocolate mixture.

10 Spoon a third of the vanilla mixture into the prepared soufflé dish, keeping it to one-half of the dish using a piece of cardboard cut to fit soufflé dish; then spoon a third of the chocolate mixture in beside it to make an even layer of half-chocolate and half-vanilla. Turn the dish a third of the way round so that the next portions of vanilla and chocolate will overlap the original ones, and spoon in half of the remaining mixtures side by side using cardboard as before. Give the dish another turn and spoon in the remaining vanilla and chocolate mixtures. Level off top with the back of your spoon, taking care not to combine the two mixtures.

11 Bake soufflé as directed in Basic Vanilla Soufflé. (You may find that it needs 4 or 5 minutes longer in the oven.) Serve immediately.

Soufflé au Grand Marnier

Serves 6

1 Prepare soufflé dish as directed in master recipe for vanilla soufflé above, and stand it in a roasting tin. Put aside.

2 Put egg yolks in the top of a double saucepan. Sift in flour, followed by icing sugar, working mixture with a wooden spoon until smoothly blended.

3 In another pan, bring milk just to boiling point. Pour over egg yolk mixture in a thin stream, beating vigorously.

4 Set pan over simmering water and cook, stirring constantly, until custard becomes thick and smooth, 7 to 10 minutes. Beat in butter.

5 Pour custard into a large bowl. Allow to cool slightly; then flavour with half the Grand Marnier.

6 Preheat oven to moderately hot (400°F. Mark 6).

7 Cut sponge cake into tiny dice and sprinkle with remaining Grand Marnier.

8 In another large bowl, sprinkle egg whites with a pinch of salt and whisk until stiff but not dry. Fold into cooling custard with a large metal spoon or spatula.

9 Spoon half of soufflé mixture into prepared dish; scatter evenly with liqueur-soaked sponge and top with remaining soufflé mixture, levelling it off lightly with the back of the spoon or spatula.

10 Pour 1 inch boiling water around soufflé dish in roasting tin and heat gently on top of the stove until water bubbles again. Quickly transfer to oven and immediately reduce temperature to 325°F. (Mark 3).

11 Bake soufflé for 30 minutes; then carefully, without removing soufflé from oven, sprinkle top with a tablespoon of granulated sugar and continue to bake for 10 to 15 minutes longer, or until soufflé is cooked through.

12 Serve immediately accompanied by a bowl of lightly whipped and sweetened cream flavoured to taste with Grand Marnier.

5 egg yolks
3 level tablespoons plain flour
4 level tablespoons icing sugar
3/4 pint milk
1 level tablespoon butter
6 tablespoons Grand Marnier
1 1/2 oz sponge cake
6 egg whites
Pinch of salt
1 level tablespoon granulated sugar
Butter and granulated sugar for soufflé dish
Lightly whipped sweetened cream, flavoured with Grand Marnier, to serve

Serves 4–6

3 level tablespoons cornflour

4 level tablespoons castor sugar

1/2 pint milk

A 3 1/2-oz bar plain chocolate, grated

2 level teaspoons powdered coffee

1 level tablespoon double cream

1/4 level teaspoon finely grated orange rind

3 egg yolks

1/2 teaspoon vanilla essence

5 egg whites

Pinch of salt

Butter and granulated sugar for soufflé dish

Chocolate Soufflé

Cornflour must be used as thickener here instead of flour to counteract the richness of the chocolate, and the soufflé is baked at a higher temperature to help 'lift' the heavier mixture.

1 Grease a 2½-pint soufflé dish quite heavily with butter, paying particular attention to the rim, and coat it with granulated sugar, shaking out excess.

2 In a heavy pan, mix cornflour with 3 level tablespoons castor sugar. Add milk gradually, stirring with a wooden spoon, and when smoothly blended, place pan over moderate heat and stir until mixture just reaches boiling point. Remove from heat; add grated chocolate, powdered coffee, double cream and finely grated orange rind, and beat vigorously until smooth. Pour into a large bowl and allow to cool to lukewarm.

3 Combine egg yolks with vanilla in a bowl and whisk lightly just to mix them. Pour into lukewarm chocolate mixture and beat until smooth again.

4 In another, larger bowl, whisk egg whites with salt until soft peaks form; then add remaining tablespoon of castor sugar and continue to whisk to a stiff, satiny meringue.

5 Using a metal spoon or spatula, stir a large dollop of meringue into chocolate mixture; scoop remaining meringue into the bowl and fold it in as quickly and carefully as you can.

6 Spoon mixture into prepared soufflé dish and immediately transfer to the oven, at the same time turning temperature down to 375°F. (Mark 5). Take a look at the soufflé after 35 minutes: if it still seems very wobbly, give it 5 to 10 minutes longer. It should have puffed up well above the rim of the dish, and a skewer inserted right through the centre should come out clean. Serve immediately. If you wish to gild the lily, accompany your soufflé with a bowl of very cold, lightly whipped cream.

Serves 6–8

6 oz plump dried apricots

2 tablespoons apricot brandy

4 egg whites

Pinch of salt

Pinch of cream of tartar

6–8 level tablespoons castor sugar

Butter and granulated sugar for soufflé dish

Dried Apricot Soufflé

1 Grease a 2½-pint soufflé dish generously with butter, paying particular attention to the inside rim, and dust with granulated sugar, shaking out excess. Set dish in a deep baking tin and put aside.

2 Preheat oven to moderately hot (400°F. Mark 6).

3 Put apricots in a saucepan with water to cover. Bring to the boil and simmer for 20 minutes, or until apricots are soft and swollen. Then drain and reduce to a purée in an electric blender.

Rub purée through a fine sieve into a large bowl, and allow to cool before flavouring with apricot brandy.

4 When apricot purée is just lukewarm, put egg whites in another large bowl and add a pinch each of salt and cream of tartar. Beat with a whisk until soft, moist peaks form; then whisk in castor sugar, a tablespoon at a time, and continue to whisk to a stiff, glossy meringue.

5 With a large metal spoon or spatula, fold meringue into tepid apricot purée as quickly and lightly as possible.

6 Spoon into prepared soufflé dish, levelling top lightly with the back of your spoon or spatula. Pour an inch of boiling water into baking tin and heat gently on top of the stove.

7 As soon as water bubbles, transfer soufflé to the oven and immediately reduce heat to 325°F. (Mark 3). Bake soufflé for 35 minutes, or until well risen and almost ready; then increase temperature to 350°F. (Mark 4) and continue to bake for 10 to 15 minutes longer until soufflé is golden brown on top and no longer wobbles when you shake the dish. Serve immediately.

● The soufflé is very rich in flavour and you will not want to serve huge portions.

Prune Soufflé

This is prepared in exactly the same way as the Dried Apricot Soufflé (page 320), substituting a purée made with 10 oz dried prunes, simmered in water until soft, then stoned and liquidised, and, when lukewarm, flavoured with 3 tablespoons Kirsch and a tablespoon of lemon juice.

It is also advisable to keep the sugar in the beaten egg whites down to 6 level tablespoons – otherwise you may find the soufflé too sweet.

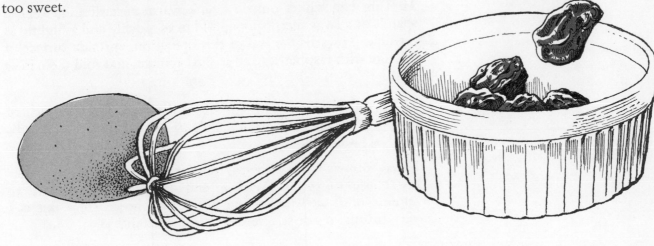

Serves 4–6

12 oz frozen raspberries
4 tablespoons Kirsch
2 oz castor sugar
5 egg yolks
4 oz icing sugar
3 level tablespoons flour
3/4 pint less 4 tablespoons
   milk
1/2 level teaspoon finely
   grated lemon rind
3 tablespoons lemon juice
1 level tablespoon butter
2 oz stale sponge cake
6 egg whites
Salt
Butter and granulated sugar
   for soufflé dish

Raspberry Lemon Soufflé

1 Place frozen raspberries in a wide dish. Sprinkle with Kirsch and castor sugar, and leave to defrost completely, about 2 hours, turning occasionally.

2 Grease a 2½-pint soufflé dish with butter, paying particular attention to the top rim, and dust with granulated sugar, shaking out excess. Set soufflé dish in a deep baking tin and put aside until needed.

3 Preheat oven to moderately hot (400°F. Mark 6).

4 Put egg yolks in the top of a double saucepan. Sift in icing sugar; beat with a wire whisk until light and well blended; then sift in flour, beating constantly until mixture is smooth.

5 In another pan, bring milk to boiling point. Remove from heat and add to egg yolk mixture in a thin stream, beating vigorously.

6 Set pan over simmering water and cook, stirring constantly, for 7 to 10 minutes, until custard is thick and smooth. Then remove from heat and beat in finely grated lemon rind, juice and butter. Pour custard into a large bowl and allow to cool to luke-warm, stirring occasionally to prevent a skin forming on top.

7 Drain raspberries thoroughly in a sieve, reserving juices.

8 Cut sponge cake into neat, ¼-inch dice. Toss lightly with raspberry juices until thoroughly saturated but not crumbly. Any juice which has not been absorbed by the sponge cake may be beaten into the cooling custard.

9 Place egg whites in a large, spotlessly clean and dry bowl. Add a pinch of salt and whisk until stiff but not dry.

10 Turn egg whites out on to lukewarm custard and, using a spatula or a large metal spoon, fold in as quickly and as lightly as possible. Towards the end of this operation, sprinkle surface of mixture with raspberries and soaked sponge, and fold them in as well.

11 Spoon mixture into prepared soufflé dish. Pour an inch of boiling water into the baking tin and gently bring back to the boil over a low heat.

12 As soon as water bubbles, transfer to the oven. Immediately lower heat to 350°F. (Mark 4) and bake soufflé for 45 to 50 minutes until well puffed and just set in the centre – this is a very creamy, moist soufflé. Serve immediately.

Soufflé Vesuvius

Serves 6–8

A rather amusing cross between a soufflé and a cake, baked in a ring mould, turned out on to a baking sheet lined with buttered foil, then filled with a true soufflé mixture and baked again.

In this version, we have flavoured the ring with praline and used our apricot soufflé for the filling, but you can substitute some other fruit, or chocolate, for the latter, provided you keep the uncooked mixture rather stiff so that it rises upwards rather than outwards. Otherwise, the ring tends to crack open under the pressure.

1 Grease a plain 8-inch (2 pint) ring mould with butter. Tie a band of buttered aluminium foil around the outside so that it comes about 2 inches above the rim. Stand another band of the same height inside the inner rim.

2 Preheat oven to moderately hot (400°F. Mark 6).

3 In a large bowl, cream softened butter with an electric mixer (or a wooden spoon) until light and fluffy.

4 Gradually beat in sugar, and when mixture is light again, sift in flour, beating vigorously.

5 Bring milk to the boil in a large, heavy pan. Pour into creamed mixture in a thin stream, beating vigorously.

6 Pour mixture back into saucepan and cook over a moderate heat, stirring constantly, until it thickens and starts coming away from sides of pan.

7 Remove pan from heat and beat in egg yolks one at a time. Allow sauce to cool to lukewarm and flavour with vanilla essence.

8 In a spotlessly clean bowl, and using a clean, dry whisk, beat egg whites until stiff but not dry.

9 Beat crushed praline into tepid sauce, and flavour very lightly with a few drops of almond essence.

10 With a large metal spoon or spatula, fold beaten egg whites into praline sauce as quickly and as lightly as possible.

11 Spoon mixture into prepared ring mould. Set mould in a deep baking tin and pour in boiling water to come halfway up its sides.

12 Bring water back to the boil over a gentle heat. As soon as bubbles begin to break on the surface, transfer to the oven and immediately lower temperature to 350°F. (Mark 4). Bake for 35 minutes, or until mixture is well risen and reasonably firm to the touch.

Soufflé ring

4 oz butter, softened
4 oz castor sugar
4 oz plain flour
3/4 pint milk
4 egg yolks
1/2 teaspoon vanilla essence
5 egg whites
3 oz dark praline, crushed
  (page 317)
A few drops of almond
  essence
Butter for ring mould

Soufflé filling

1 recipe Dried Apricot
  Soufflé (page 320)
Butter
Icing sugar

13 While ring mould is in the oven, make up 1 recipe of the Dried Apricot Soufflé on page 320, folding in the stiffly beaten egg whites at the last moment.

14 Line a large, heavy baking sheet with foil and grease generously with butter.

15 When ring mould is ready, remove it from the oven. Discard the bands of foil and let the mould 'settle' for 1 or 2 minutes; then carefully turn it out in the centre of the foil-lined baking sheet.

16 Pile apricot soufflé mixture in the centre of the mould. Place baking sheet in the oven and again reduce the temperature, this time to 325°F. (Mark 3). Bake for 35 minutes. Then turn temperature up to 350°F. (Mark 4) and bake for a final 10 minutes, or until apricot filling is well puffed and golden, but still slightly creamy in the centre.

17 Dust with icing sugar and serve immediately. You can, if you like, accompany it by a bowl of chilled whipped cream lightly flavoured with apricot brandy, but this is not really necessary.

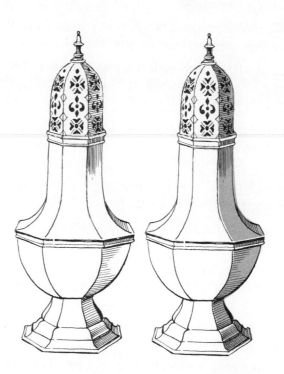

Lesson 13
Fish and Shellfish

Fish can be one of the most delicious dishes on your menu. Treat it gently; flavour it with fresh fish stock, lemon juice, dry white wine or a delicate sauce; and above all don't over cook it. You'll find that you will soon enjoy cooking fish dishes. After all, fish is inexpensive; it is never tough; and it's wonderfully easy to cook, once you know how.

Many cooks think that there is nothing in the world as difficult to cook really well as fish, for its delicate flavour is so easily lost, and its light creamy flakiness so quickly destroyed. Indeed, until fairly recently in this country we did *not* know how to prepare fish properly. It was usually overcooked – boiled to a tasteless rag in water with a little vinegar added – or fried in breadcrumbs, oatmeal or just plain flour until it was crisp and hard, which entirely ruined its delicate texture and flavour.

How to Choose Fish in the Market

The first step towards cooking fish superbly is knowing how to recognise healthy, fresh fish in the market. It is surprisingly easy. Just look for the following indications.

You can tell that a fish is fresh when its eye is rounded and bright, not sunken and dull; when the body is firm, almost stiff, not weak and flabby; when the scales are close fitting, and when the body leaves no imprint when you press it with your fingers.

One of the best indications of a really fresh fish is its mild odour. Learn to distinguish the mild odour of a healthy fish from the strong smell of stale fish.

Do Not Buy Fish

If it has too strong an odour; if the scales come off easily; if the eye is sunken in its socket; if the fish droops weakly over the counter; and if the area over the stomach or around the vent is green or blackish in colour.

Keeping Fish

Fresh Fish Should Be Used as Soon as Possible

If you are going to serve it on the following day, wash it, pat it dry, wrap it loosely in waxed paper and keep it in the refrigerator until ready to use.

Keep frozen fish, unopened, at a 10-degree temperature. I prefer to thaw frozen fish in the refrigerator. Cook as soon as it is thawed. If it is frozen fillets or fingers, I sometimes cook them while still frozen. In either case, do not refreeze frozen fish after it has thawed. It will lose both flavour and texture.

Keep fish away from butter, sweets and puddings to prevent the fish affecting delicately flavoured foods.

To Steam Fish

Oval Steamer Method

There are oval steamers on the market for poultry, meats or vegetables that double wonderfully well as fish steamers. Consisting of oval double saucepans with perforated bottoms to allow the steam to rise, and covers to keep steam in, they make a remarkable fish steamer.

To steam a fish in an oval steamer:
Place fish in a well-buttered oval baking dish that just fits inside the steamer, allowing about an inch round for the steam to rise. Sprinkle with 2 tablespoons each finely chopped onion and mushrooms; moisten with 6 tablespoons dry white wine, canned clam juice or well-flavoured fish stock, and place over boiling water to which you have added a clove or two of garlic for flavour. Cover tightly and steam until fish flakes easily with a fork.

Fish Kettle Method

For a larger fish – or a greater number of small fish, fish steaks or fillets – use a long fish kettle complete with cover and perforated rack. To transform this kettle into a steamer, place rack on heat-proof porcelain ramekins to allow liquid to boil below rack and the steam to rise.

Most fish kettles are big enough to poach or steam a young salmon, or a large centre cut of a larger salmon, a number of lobsters, plenty of oysters or clams, 6 to 12 trout, several chickens, or a large platter of meat and vegetables in the Chinese manner. Try flavouring your steaming liquid with sliced onion, several bay leaves, 10–12 coriander seeds, 10–12 peppercorns, a generous amount of salt, several garlic cloves and a little dry white wine. Season the fish with salt and freshly ground black pepper, and stuff cavity with stalks of fresh or dried fennel, bay leaves, thyme, lemon slices and garlic. You'll find steamed fish is delicious.

To Poach Fish

One of the easiest ways of cooking fish fillets and small fish steaks or cutlets was taught to me in Paris by the great French restaurateur, René Lasserre. His easy method is to the art of poaching what 'oven-frying' is to deep-frying. So I call it 'oven-poaching'.

To 'oven-poach' fillets of sole for four: butter a shallow heatproof gratin dish generously; sprinkle it with a level tablespoon or two of chopped mushrooms (stems will do) and the same amount of chopped shallots; lay in your fish fillets which you have first anointed with a little lemon juice and seasoned with salt and freshly ground black pepper to taste. Sprinkle the fillets with a little more chopped mushrooms and shallots and cover them with the bones and trimmings of the fish to give added flavour and moisture. Place a piece of well-buttered aluminium foil over fish and cook in a hot oven (450°F. Mark 8) until the fish is tender and opaque (about 8 to 12 minutes).

Another variation on this same recipe just adds 2 to 4 tablespoons each reduced fish stock and dry white wine.

To serve: lift fish out carefully, draining it well, and place it on a heated serving dish. Keep warm. Thicken pan liquids slightly with a *beurre manié* or with an egg yolk mixed with a little double cream and lemon juice, to taste. Serve with the fish. This manner of cooking fish is guaranteed to bring out the utmost in flavour of the most delicate fish.

Fish Stock from Trimmings

A well-flavoured fish stock can be made at little expense or effort from fish trimmings. This stock can be used for cooking the fish or for making a sauce to accompany it. There is no comparison between a sauce made with a well-flavoured fish stock and one in which milk or water forms the liquid part. So if you have your fish filleted by your fishmonger, ask for the fish trimmings to be included with the fish.

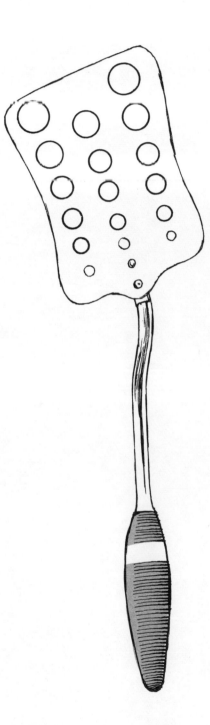

To make the stock, wash the trimmings, discarding any black-looking skin, and break the bones in pieces. Put them in an enamelled saucepan with just enough water to cover them, and add a few parsley stalks, a sliced onion, a few white peppercorns and a little salt. Simmer for at least $\frac{1}{2}$ hour and then strain ready for use. White wine may be added with the water.

Any white fish or the trimmings of white fish – haddock, cod, halibut or flounder – may be used for fish stock. Mackerel, herring and salmon are too oily and too strong in flavour. Uncooked trimmings, however, make a better stock than those which have already been cooked. A cod's head is an economical foundation for a well-flavoured fish stock. And always ask your fishmonger for heads and bones of sole. I also like to add a lobster shell, or the heads and shells of prawns and shrimps, when available.

To Grill Fish

Wash and clean fish; dry them lightly and score the skin across diagonally on both sides to prevent it cracking during cooking. Season with salt and freshly ground black pepper, and brush with olive oil or melted butter. Or marinate fish for 2 hours before cooking in equal quantities of olive oil and dry white wine with a little finely chopped garlic and a crumbled bay leaf or two. Or the fish may be split open, the bones removed, and then lightly coated with flour, egg and breadcrumbs, or fine oatmeal.

Always heat the grid thoroughly and grease it well before you place the fish on it. Keep the fish rather close to the fire while cooking or it will become flabby. Cook fish for 8 to 12 minutes according to its thickness, and turn it at least once during cooking time. I like to serve grilled fish with lemon quarters and *maître d'hôtel* or *fines herbes* butter.

Charcoal-grilled Fish

The odorous smoke from a charcoal or wood fire – with the scent of burning dried fennel stalks, sprigs of thyme or rosemary, or a sprig of bay leaves – makes grilled fish a dish 'fit for a king'. Use a hinged grill when grilling fish over an open fire so that you can turn your fish easily without danger of breaking its tender flesh.

Flour and oil all fish lightly before grilling, and if you are using fish steaks or fish fillets, be sure to baste them frequently with olive oil and lemon juice during cooking time.

328

Whole fish, with skins intact, require less attention. Stuff cavities of fish with herbs before grilling them – a selection of fennel, parsley and thyme – and then baste them with olive oil and lemon juice as they grill.

To Bake Fish

The simplest method of baking fish is to place it in a well-buttered heatproof baking dish with a little finely chopped onion and mushroom, and salt and freshly ground black pepper, to taste; cover it with buttered waxed paper or foil, and cook in a moderate oven (375°F. Mark 5) until fish flakes with a fork. The fish may be served with or without sauce.

Otherwise the fish may be first poached for a few minutes in a little fish stock and then baked *au gratin* with butter, finely chopped parsley, mushrooms and shallots, and sprinkled with freshly grated breadcrumbs and Parmesan cheese; or a little Béchamel or Velouté Sauce may be poured around the fish before it is dotted with butter and sprinkled with chopped parsley, mushrooms, shallots and cheese.

To Fry Fish

When properly fried, fish should be a light golden brown and dry and crisp in texture, as free from fat as if it had never touched it. I like to deep-fry fish in a combination of lard and oil to give added flavour; for pan-frying or oven-frying I use butter or olive oil, or combination of the two.

Small fish are better fried whole, large ones should be filleted or cut into steaks or cutlets.

I like to 'flavour' fish fillets or steaks with a little lemon juice and dry white wine seasoned generously with salt and pepper about an hour before frying.

To fry well, fish should be as dry as possible. So, pat fish dry with a clean cloth or paper towel before coating it with seasoned flour, fine oatmeal or cornmeal, beaten egg and dry breadcrumbs, or a frying batter. This coating serves two purposes: (1) to keep fat from entering the fish while it is immersed in the hot cooking fat or oil; and (2) to add a flavoursome crunchy coating to the fried fish, which adds enormously to the delicately flavoured flesh within.

If seasoned flour, or flour and milk, are used as a coating, apply it just before the fish is to be cooked, or the flour will become moist and the fish will not fry well. Batter, too, should be applied only at the last moment. But the fish may be coated with egg and dry breadcrumbs some time before it is to be fried – even the night before if the fish is to be served for breakfast.

Pan-frying Fish

This method of cooking sautés delicately flavoured fish such as sole, plaice, brill or trout in $\frac{1}{8}$ inch butter in a frying-pan. Finely chopped parsley, lemon juice or slivered almonds are sometimes added to the sauce obtained. It is a good idea to add a little olive oil to the butter first to keep it from browning during the cooking process. Allow it to sizzle; lay in the prepared fish and cook gently, making sure that the entire bottom surface of the fish is in contact with the butter. When the fish begins to take on colour, add more butter. Then turn the fish with a fish slice or a palette knife and continue to cook until it flakes easily with a fork.

Oven-frying Fish

Heat the oven to 400°F. (Mark 6). Cover the bottom of a shallow baking dish with butter and a little olive oil (about $\frac{1}{4}$ inch), and heat the dish in the oven until the butter sizzles. Brush fish with olive oil or melted butter and roll it in dry breadcrumbs mixed with chopped fresh herbs (parsley, chervil, chives, etc.) and a little grated lemon rind. Cook in the oven until tender, turning once during cooking time.

Deep-frying Fish

Deep-fried fish should never be greasy. Thus the temperature of the fat or oil used for frying is of prime importance. It must be hot enough to seal the protective coating of flour, oatmeal, corn-meal, egg and breadcrumbs, batter or pastry at the very moment of immersion. This prevents grease from penetrating the food and keeps in the flavour and juices of the fish. Deep-frying is simple when you know how. Vegetable fats and oils are the most pleasant to use – with a little lard added for extra flavour. Test the heat of your fat with an inch cube of day-old bread. If the temperature is right for deep-frying, the bread will brown on both sides in about 40 seconds.

Do not put too many pieces of fish into the fat or oil at one time, or it will cool down so much that it will soak through the coating or batter. If you use a frying basket, do not let pieces overlap or the fish will not cook through. Cook until fish are golden brown; then lift out and drain on paper towels.

If a frying basket is not used, a perforated spoon or skimmer is best for lifting out fish.

1 Use enough fat or oil to cover fish completely.

2 Do not allow fat to smoke or boil.

3 The temperature of the fat should vary as little as possible during cooking.

4 If fat becomes too hot or begins to smoke, drop a slice of raw potato into it to reduce temperature.

5 Always allow the fat or oil to reheat before adding a fresh lot of fish.

6 If you plunge fish into the fat a second time, the temperature of the second cooking should be higher than that of the first.

Oven-baked Fish

Oven-baked fish – whether you use the basic method below, or add a little dry white wine, fish or chicken stock and one or more exotic aromatics – brings out the best in a whole fish, or a thick steak of cod, halibut, turbot or flounder. Try, too, fillets of your favourite fish, wrapped around a savoury stuffing, and baked in the same manner.

You'll find that Oven-baked Fish becomes one of your most useful party dishes.

First of all, try the Simple Baked Fish recipe below, using $1\frac{1}{2}$-inch-thick steaks of turbot, halibut or cod.

The Simplest Method of Baking Fish You've Ever Tried

1 Butter a baking dish generously with softened butter. Then sprinkle the dish with 2 tablespoons each of chopped celery, chopped mushroom stalks, chopped onion and chopped carrot. Season vegetables with salt and freshly ground black pepper.

2 Lay the fish steaks on the vegetables and season with salt and freshly ground black pepper and lemon juice, to taste.

3 Lay fish bones and trimmings over fish, if available, to give added flavour to the pan juices. (Make a habit of asking your fishmonger for some bones and trimmings of sole when you purchase any fish, for this very reason).

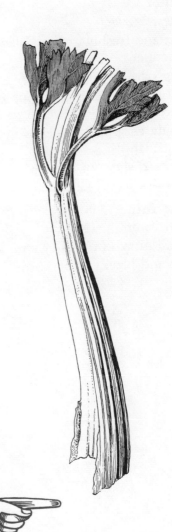

4 Cover tightly with a well-buttered piece of aluminium foil and bake fish in a preheated moderately hot oven (400°F. Mark 6) for 20 minutes.

5 Remove foil and fish bones and trimmings; baste fish well with the liquids formed; and bake for another 10 minutes, or until lightly browned.

6 Serve fish steaks with boiled new potatoes and strained pan juices to which you have added $\frac{1}{4}$ pound butter and 2 tablespoons finely chopped parsley, and lemon juice to taste.

Waterzooï de Poisson
(A Creamy Fish Stew)

For this creamy Belgian casserole, assemble as varied a selection of fish as your fishmonger will provide. The version below is made with salt-water fish – turbot, haddock, plaice and mackerel, but the dish is equally good made with fresh-water varieties.

1 Wash and clean fish, and cut them into even-sized chunks, reserving trimmings for *fumet*. (Ask fishmonger to give you extra trimmings if you do not think you will have enough.)

2 To make *fumet*: put fish trimmings in a large pan; cover with $1\frac{3}{4}$ to 2 pints water, and add parsley sprigs, salt and peppercorns, to taste. Bring to the boil, skimming off scum as it rises to the surface, and simmer, skimming occasionally, for 20 minutes. Strain through a fine sieve.

3 In the pan or casserole in which you intend to cook the *waterzooï*, sauté blanched diced celery in 2 level tablespoons butter until golden brown.

4 Add fish chunks and *bouquet garni*; season to taste with salt and freshly ground black pepper, and pour in prepared *fumet*. Bring to the boil over a low heat and simmer gently for about 10 minutes, or until fish chunks flake easily with a fork but are not disintegrating.

5 Remove fish from pan with a slotted spoon and arrange in a deepish, heated serving dish. Keep hot while you finish sauce.

6 Beat egg yolks with cream.

7 Remove pan from heat and pour egg and cream mixture into simmering sauce, stirring constantly until thickened. If sauce refuses to thicken from the heat of the pan itself, return to a low heat and stir until it does so, but take great care not to let it boil, or egg yolks will curdle. Taste for seasoning.

8 Pour sauce over fish. Sprinkle with finely chopped parsley and serve immediately, with buttered slices of toasted French bread.

Serves 3–4

1 1/2 lb fish (see note)
4 oz celery, diced and
 blanched
Butter
Bouquet garni
Salt and freshly ground black
 pepper
2 egg yolks
4–6 level tablespoons double
 cream
Finely chopped parsley, to
 garnish
Toasted slices of French
 bread, to serve

Fish fumet
Fish trimmings
Small bunch of parsley sprigs
Salt and black peppercorns

Fisherman's Pie

Serves 6

1 Soak smoked haddock fillets in cold water for 2 hours. Drain them and place them in a saucepan with equal quantities of milk and water to cover. Bring to a fast boil. Remove pan from heat; cover and leave for 15 minutes. Then carefully drain haddock, reserving cooking liquor.

2 Melt 2 oz butter in the top of a double saucepan; stir in flour and cook over boiling water for 3 minutes, stirring constantly, to make a smooth, pale *roux*.

3 Gradually add cream and ½ pint of the hot haddock liquor, stirring vigorously to prevent lumps forming, and continue to cook over boiling water, stirring occasionally, for about 30 minutes, or until sauce is thick and smooth. Season to taste with freshly ground black pepper and a pinch of freshly grated nutmeg

4 In a frying pan, sauté peeled shrimps or prawns and sliced scallops in a little butter for just 2 to 3 minutes until golden. Sprinkle with lemon juice. Remove from heat.

5 Butter a deep, 4-pint pie dish.

6 Remove skin and any remaining bones from haddock fillets, and separate fish into large chunks. Arrange them in the pie dish, together with sautéed shrimps and scallops, and their juices.

7 Shell mussels and combine them with seafood in the pie dish.

8 Pour over sauce. Put dish aside to cool.

9 In the meantime, preheat oven to moderate (375°F. Mark 5).

10 Roll two-thirds of pastry out to the same size as top of pie dish; fit it over fish and shellfish in dish, moistening and pinching edges to dish. Roll out remaining pastry; cut into strips about ½ inch wide and arrange over pastry in lattice fashion. Brush top of pie with beaten egg yolk and make vents in pastry to allow steam to escape.

11 Bake pie for 30 minutes, or until pastry crust is golden brown. Serve hot.

1 1/2–2 lb smoked haddock fillets
Milk
Butter
2 level tablespoons flour
1/2 pint double cream
Freshly ground black pepper
Freshly grated nutmeg
4 oz peeled shrimps or prawns
4 scallops, cleaned and sliced
Juice of 1/2 lemon
24 mussels, steamed open (see page 360)
6–8 oz shortcrust pastry (page 432)
1 egg yolk beaten with 1 tablespoon milk, to glaze

Serves 8–10

1 small cooked lobster, at
   least 1 lb
4 oz peeled prawns
1 small lemon sole
1/2 lb turbot
4 oz white button mushrooms
2 tablespoons lemon juice
1 cucumber
Salt
4 oz black olives
2 small green peppers
1 stalk celery
2 level tablespoons finely
   chopped parsley
Freshly ground black pepper

Fish stock (see Step 3)
1 small carrot
1 small piece celery
4 sprigs parsley
Pinch of thyme
1 bay leaf
4 black peppercorns
1/4 pint dry white wine

Dressing
8 fluid oz olive oil
8 tablespoons wine vinegar
2 tablespoons dry white wine
1/2 Spanish onion, very
   finely chopped
1 level tablespoon finely
   chopped chives
Salt and freshly ground black
   pepper

Saffron rice
1 1/4 pints chicken stock,
   made with 2 cubes
1/4 level teaspoon saffron
   strands
6 tablespoons dry white wine
12 oz long-grain rice
Salt and freshly ground black
   pepper

Fish and Rice Salad for a Party

A large-scale and rather complicated salad, excellent for an important buffet.

1 Remove meat from lobster (see page 363). Cut it into chunks where possible and place it all in a bowl together with peeled prawns.

2 Skin and fillet sole (see page 342).

3 In a medium-sized pan, combine sole trimmings and a few pieces of lobster shell with stock ingredients. Add ¾ pint water. Bring slowly to the boil; cover and simmer for 30 minutes.

4 Meanwhile, prepare a dressing in another pan: beat olive oil, wine vinegar and dry white wine with a fork until mixture emulsifies; add finely chopped onion and chives, and season to taste with salt and freshly ground black pepper. Put aside, covered, until required.

5 Strain fish stock through a sieve lined with kitchen paper.

6 Pour 1 inch of strained stock into a deep, wide frying pan. Bring to the boil; remove from heat. Lay sole fillets in stock. After 3 minutes, turn them over and leave them for 2 to 3 minutes longer until just cooked.

7 Carefully remove sole fillets from stock. Cut into chunks and place in a warmed bowl. Cover and keep hot.

8 Cook turbot in the same stock for 10 to 12 minutes over a low heat, turning once.

9 Remove turbot from pan; skin, bone and cut it into chunks. Place in another warmed bowl. Cover and keep hot.

10 Add 4 tablespoons hot fish stock to prepared dressing and mix well. Pour off ¼ pint dressing and reserve for later use. Heat remaining dressing gently until very warm.

11 Dress all the prepared fish and shellfish with warm dressing and leave to cool again, during which time they will absorb flavours.

12 Meanwhile, prepare saffron rice: make up chicken stock with 2 cubes and 1¼ pints boiling water in a large pan. Pour 3 or 4 tablespoons hot chicken stock over saffron strands in a cup and leave to soften and 'infuse' for 10 minutes. Then mash saffron strands against sides of cup with a spoon to extract maximum colour and flavour.

13 Bring chicken stock to the boil with infused saffron and dry white wine. Gradually stir in rice and season to taste with salt and freshly ground black pepper. Reduce heat to a simmer; cover pan and cook gently, undisturbed, for 20 minutes, or until nearly all the liquid has been absorbed and rice is almost, but not quite, cooked. Remove pan from heat. Leave it on one side, still covered, to finish cooking and then gradually cool to lukewarm.

14 Meanwhile, prepare vegetables: wash or wipe mushrooms clean; trim stems and slice mushrooms thinly. Quickly toss them with lemon juice to prevent discolouration.

15 Peel cucumber and halve it lengthwise. Scoop out seeds with a teaspoon. Cut cucumber into $\frac{1}{4}$-inch dice. Place in a colander and toss with a little salt. Leave to drain.

16 Pit olives and slice them into rings. Put them in a bowl.

17 Halve, core and seed peppers. Cut them into strips $\frac{1}{8}$ inch wide and $1\frac{1}{2}$ inches long. Add to olives.

18 Cut celery into $\frac{1}{4}$-inch dice. Add to olives and peppers, and toss lightly.

19 When rice is lukewarm, carefully scoop it into a large mixing bowl. Drain off some of the dressing in which fish and shellfish were marinating and carefully, using a fork to avoid crushing grains, mix it into the rice.

20 Add drained mushrooms and cucumber, the olives, pepper strips, celery and finely chopped parsley, and continue to mix gently until thoroughly blended.

21 Finally, add fish and shellfish, together with remains of the dressing in which they were marinated. Fold them into the rice and vegetables, taking great care not to break the pieces.

22 Use some of the reserved dressing if salad is not moist enough. Correct seasoning and chill lightly until ready to serve.

Note: When coping with large quantities such as these, I find the best mixing tools are usually a pair of (clean) hands!

Cod

Greek Skewered Cod

Serves 6

1 1/2 lb cod (thick end of
  fillet)
4 tablespoons olive oil
2 tablespoons lemon juice
1 bay leaf, crumbled
Salt and freshly ground black
  pepper
4 firm, medium-sized
  tomatoes
3 small onions
Rice or shredded lettuce to
  serve

1 Combine olive oil, lemon juice, crumbled bay leaf and salt and freshly ground black pepper, to taste, in a small bowl to make basting sauce.

2 Cut cod into chunks (1 to $1\frac{1}{2}$ inches square). You should have about 30 in all – any scrappy thin pieces should be rolled up into pieces the same size as chunks.

3 Slice tomatoes $\frac{1}{4}$ inch thick and onions $\frac{1}{8}$ inch thick.

4 Thread six 8- or 9-inch metal skewers with alternate pieces of fish, tomato and onion slices, starting and ending with a chunk of fish, and dividing ingredients equally between skewers.

5 Line rack of grill pan with foil. Arrange skewers on it; brush with half the basting sauce and place under a preheated hot grill. Reduce heat to moderate and grill for 4 to 5 minutes.

6 Turn skewers; baste with remaining sauce and continue to grill for 4 to 5 minutes longer, or until fish flakes easily with a fork.

7 Serve immediately on a bed of rice or shredded lettuce, spooning some of the cooking juices over skewers.

Marinated Cod Steaks

Serves 4

4 slices fresh cod, about
  1 inch thick
Marinade recipe 1 or 2
Butter
Onion
Well-flavoured fish stock
  (page 327), or canned clam
  juice
Salt and freshly ground black
  pepper
8 heart-shaped croûtons
4 slices grilled bacon
2 tablespoons finely chopped
  parsley

1 Marinate cod slices for at least 4 hours in Marinade 1 or 2.

2 Place marinated cod steaks in (A) a well-buttered gratin dish with 1 tablespoon finely chopped onion and 2 to 4 tablespoons fish stock or clam juice; season to taste with salt and freshly ground black pepper; place in double steamer; cover and steam until tender (15 to 20 minutes); or (B) in a saucepan on a bed of sliced onion; add $\frac{1}{4}$ pint fish stock, clam juice and just enough water to cover fish; season to taste with salt and freshly ground black pepper; cover pan, bring to a boil; lower heat and simmer gently for 15 to 20 minutes, or until fish flakes easily with a fork.

3 To serve: Place fish steaks on a heated serving dish; (A) pour over pan juices; garnish with croûtons, grilled bacon and finely chopped parsley, or (B) remove fish steaks to a heated serving dish and keep warm. Reduce fish stock to $\frac{1}{4}$ of its original quantity over a high heat; and strain a few tablespoons over fish. Garnish as above.

Cod Marinade 1

1 Combine olive oil and dry white wine and flavour with finely chopped parsley and onion, crumbled bay leaf and salt and freshly ground black pepper, to taste.

2 Marinate fish in this mixture for at least 2 hours, turning fish from time to time.

4 tablespoons olive oil
4 tablespoons dry white wine
2 level tablespoons finely chopped parsley
2 level tablespoons finely chopped onion
1 bay leaf, crumbled
Salt and freshly ground black pepper

Cod Marinade 2

1 Combine lemon juice and Pernod with olive oil and flavour with fennel seeds (or chopped fennel leaves). Add salt and freshly ground black pepper, to taste.

2 Marinate fish in this mixture for at least 2 hours, turning fish from time to time.

2 tablespoons lemon juice
2 tablespoons Pernod
4 tablespoons olive oil
1 level teaspoon fennel seeds or chopped fennel leaves
Salt and freshly ground black pepper, to taste

Italian Poached Cod with Cold Sauce

1 Place cod steaks in a large frying pan; cover with cold water which you have flavoured with lemon juice and salt and freshly ground black pepper, to taste.

2 Bring to the boil; turn off heat and allow to steep in hot water for 10–12 minutes. Remove steaks from liquid and place on a serving dish and allow to cool.

3 While cod steaks are steeping, combine sauce ingredients and chill.

4 When ready to serve, pour sauce over poached cod and serve.

Serves 4–6

4–6 cod steaks
Juice of 1 lemon
Salt and freshly ground black pepper

Sauce
4 level tablespoons finely chopped Spanish onion
4 level tablespoons finely chopped parsley
2 cloves garlic, finely chopped
8 tablespoons olive oil
Juice of 1/2 large lemon
Salt and freshly ground black pepper

Serves 8

1 1/2 pints lager
1 carrot, sliced
1 Spanish onion, sliced
1 stalk celery, sliced
4 sprigs parsley
8 black peppercorns
5 cloves
1 bay leaf
8 thick cod steaks

Sauce

1 oz butter
1 oz flour
1/2 pint milk
1/2 pint fish liquor (see Step 3)
4 level tablespoons freshly grated Parmesan
4 oz Gruyère, diced
2 egg yolks, lightly beaten
1 level tablespoon butter
4 level tablespoons double cream, whipped
Salt and freshly ground black pepper

Serves 4

4 fillets fresh haddock
Lemon juice
Salt and freshly ground black pepper
Salted water
Sprigs of fresh parsley
Boiled potatoes
1/4 pound butter, melted

Cod Steaks in Beer

This dish is also excellent if prepared in advance, then baked in a preheated moderate oven (375°F. Mark 5) for 20 minutes before serving.

1 Pour lager into a deep frying pan large enough to take 4 cod steaks side by side. Add sliced vegetables, parsley sprigs, peppercorns, cloves and the bay leaf; bring to the boil, cover and simmer for 15 minutes.

2 Lay half the cod steaks in the simmering liquid and cook gently for 15 to 20 minutes, or until they flake easily when tested with a fork, turning them once. Transfer cod steaks to a shallow baking dish or a heatproof serving dish, using a fish slice to avoid breaking them; keep hot. Cook remaining steaks in the same way.

3 Boil remaining cooking liquor briskly until reduced to about ½ pint. Strain through a muslin-lined sieve.

4 To make sauce: melt butter in a heavy pan; blend in flour and cook over a low heat for 2 minutes, stirring constantly, to make a pale *roux*.

5 Gradually add milk and bring to the boil, stirring constantly until sauce is thick and smooth, and no longer tastes of flour.

6 Stir in strained fish liquor; add freshly grated Parmesan, diced Gruyère and lightly beaten egg yolks, and cook over a very low heat, beating vigorously with a wooden spoon until sauce is smooth and hot again, and taking care not to let it boil, or egg yolks may curdle.

7 Stir in butter and whipped cream, and season to taste with salt and freshly ground black pepper.

8 Pour sauce over cod steaks. Slip under a hot grill until top is golden brown and bubbling. Serve immediately.

Haddock

Fresh Haddock with Lemon Butter

1 Cut fillets into manageable portions; season with lemon juice, salt and freshly ground black pepper, and poach them gently in simmering salted water for about 20 minutes, or until fish flakes easily with a fork.

2 Transfer haddock fillets to a heated serving dish and garnish with sprigs of parsley and boiled potatoes.

3 Serve with melted butter seasoned to taste with lemon juice, salt and freshly ground black pepper.

Baked Fresh Haddock

Serves 4–6

1 Preheat oven to moderate (375°F. Mark 5).

2 Sauté finely chopped onion and mushrooms in 2 tablespoons butter until onion is transparent.

3 Wipe cleaned and scaled fish well with a damp cloth and place it in a well-buttered shallow baking dish in which you have sprinkled half the onion and mushroom mixture.

4 Cover fish with remaining onions and mushrooms; season with finely chopped parsley, and salt and freshly ground black pepper, to taste, and add ¼ pint double cream or dry white wine.

5 Bake in a moderate oven (375°F. Mark 5) until fish flakes easily with a fork.

6 Serve immediately in the baking dish.

1 small fresh haddock (about 3 lb)
1/4 Spanish onion, finely chopped
8 button mushrooms, finely chopped
Butter
2 tablespoons finely chopped parsley
Salt and freshly ground black pepper
1/4 pint double cream or dry white wine

Smoked Haddock Mousse

Serves 4

The sad thing about smoked haddock is its cheapness – otherwise it would certainly be treated with greater respect than it is today.

1 Soak fish in cold water for about 1 hour to remove excess salt. Then drain; place in a saucepan and cover with the milk and ½ pint water. Bring to the boil, simmer for 2 to 3 minutes, and put aside.

2 Preheat oven to moderate (350°F. Mark 4).

3 Brush a plain, 1½-pint ring mould generously with oil.

4 In a heavy pan, melt butter; add flour and stir together over a low heat for 2 minutes to make a pale *roux*.

5 Drain fish. Add cooking liquor to *roux* gradually, stirring vigorously to make a smooth sauce. Cook over a moderate heat, stirring, until sauce comes to the boil, and simmer for 4 to 5 minutes longer. Then remove pan from heat; stir in cream and season generously with salt and freshly ground black pepper.

6 Remove all bones and skin from haddock, and blend fish to a purée in an electric blender together with ½ pint of the sauce and the egg yolks. Taste purée for seasoning. It should be rather strongly flavoured.

7 When haddock mixture is quite smooth, spoon it into mould and level off top. Place mould in a deep baking dish with hot water to come three-quarters of the way up sides.

8 Bake mousse until firm, 30 to 35 minutes.

1 lb smoked haddock
1/2 pint milk
Oil for mould
3 oz butter
3 oz flour
1/4 pint single cream
Salt and freshly ground black pepper
3 egg yolks
Juice of 1/2 lemon
2 level tablespoons finely chopped parsley
Pinch of cayenne

9 Stir lemon juice, finely chopped parsley and a pinch of cayenne into remaining sauce, and reheat gently.

10 When ready to serve: carefully unmould mousse on to a flat heated serving dish. Spoon hot sauce over sides and centre of mousse, and serve immediately.

Herrings

Grilled Herrings with Mustard

Serves 4

4 fresh herrings
2 tablespoons flour
Salt and freshly ground black
    pepper
Olive oil
French mustard
Freshly grated breadcrumbs
4 tablespoons melted butter
Boiled new potatoes

1 Clean and scale herrings, taking care not to break the delicate skin underneath; cut off heads; wash and dry carefully.

2 Make 3 shallow incisions on sides of each fish with a sharp knife.

3 Dip herrings in seasoned flour; brush them with olive oil and grill on a well-oiled baking sheet for 3 to 4 minutes on each side.

4 Arrange herrings in a shallow ovenproof gratin dish; brush them liberally with French mustard; sprinkle with freshly grated breadcrumbs and melted butter, and put in a very hot oven (475°F. Mark 9) for 5 minutes. Serve in the gratin dish with boiled new potatoes.

Baked Herrings

Serves 4

4 fresh herrings
Butter
Fresh breadcrumbs
Finely chopped parsley
Salt and freshly ground
    black pepper
Lemon wedges

1 Clean and scale herrings, taking care not to break the delicate skin underneath; cut off heads; wash and dry carefully.

2 Remove roes; detach skin and pound roes with an equal amount of softened butter. Force mixture through a fine sieve; mix in 2 to 4 tablespoons fresh breadcrumbs, flavour with finely chopped parsley, and season to taste with salt and freshly ground black pepper.

3 Slit herrings down backbone with a sharp knife and remove backbone carefully, snipping both ends free with kitchen scissors.

4 Stuff herrings with roe mixture and place fish in a lightly buttered shallow ovenproof dish. Sprinkle lightly with breadcrumbs, finely chopped parsley and melted butter.

5 Cover fish with buttered paper and bake in a moderately hot oven (400°F. Mark 6) for 15 to 20 minutes, or until cooked through. Just before serving, brown under grill. Serve with lemon wedges.

Salmon

Sautéed Salmon Steaks

1 Choose centre cuts of salmon about $\frac{3}{4}$ inch thick.

2 Rub steaks well on both sides with flour.

3 Melt butter in a heavy frying pan or shallow heatproof casserole, and when hot, sauté steaks lightly.

4 When steaks are light brown, add white wine and seasonings.

5 Cover and simmer, with frequent basting, on top of stove until cooked (about 30 minutes). When salmon is cooked, sprinkle with finely chopped parsley and serve.

Serves 4

4 fresh salmon steaks
Flour
4 tablespoons butter
1/4 pint dry white wine
Bay leaf
Salt
White pepper
Pinch of celery seed
2 tablespoons finely chopped parsley

Grilled Salmon Steaks

1 Season both sides of salmon steaks to taste with salt and freshly ground black pepper, and leave to stand at room temperature for 15 minutes.

2 Place steaks on a buttered, preheated baking sheet; brush with 2 tablespoons melted butter and grill for 3 to 5 minutes about 3 inches from heat.

3 Turn steaks, brush with remaining butter and grill until fish flakes easily with a fork (3 to 5 minutes).

4 Serve with lemon and parsley butter and lemon wedges.

5 *To make lemon and parsley butter:* Pound slightly softened butter in a mortar with finely chopped parsley, and lemon juice, salt and freshly ground black pepper to taste.

Serves 4

4 large salmon steaks
Salt and freshly ground black pepper
4 tablespoons melted butter
Lemon wedges

Lemon and parsley butter
1/4 pound slightly softened butter
2 tablespoons finely chopped parsley
Lemon juice
Salt and freshly ground black pepper

Peppered Salmon Steaks

1 Press crushed peppercorns into the flesh of the salmon steaks with the heel of your hand and sprinkle with salt to taste.

2 Brush steaks with melted butter and sprinkle with lemon juice.

3 Grill steaks about 4 inches from the heat for 8 to 10 minutes on each side, brushing with melted butter when you turn them over.

4 When steaks are done, place them on a heated serving dish and garnish with finely chopped parsley.

Serves 4

4 salmon steaks, 3/4 inch thick
2 level tablespoons coarsely crushed black pepper
Salt
4 tablespoons melted butter
Juice of 1/2 lemon
2 level tablespoons finely chopped parsley

Serves 4

2–3 fresh salmon steaks
(about 1 1/2 inches thick)
6 tablespoons olive oil
2 tablespoons lemon juice
1/2 Spanish onion, finely
chopped
4 tablespoons finely chopped
parsley
Salt and freshly ground black
pepper
4 small onions, sliced
4 tomatoes, sliced
Lemon juice

Serves 4

4 soles, about 12 oz each
1 lemon
4 level tablespoons finely
chopped parsley
Salt and freshly ground black
pepper
About 4 oz butter
8 oz button mushrooms,
sliced
1/2 pint dry white wine
1 level tablespoon flour
1/4 pint double cream
1 egg yolk

Salmon Brochettes

1 Cut fresh salmon steaks into 1-inch cubes and marinate for at least 2 hours in olive oil, lemon juice, finely chopped onion and parsley, and salt and freshly ground black pepper, to taste.

2 Place fish cubes on a skewer alternately with a slice of onion, a slice of tomato.

3 Grill over charcoal or under the grill, turning frequently and basting from time to time with marinade sauce.

4 To serve: Remove cooked fish from skewer on to serving plate and sprinkle with lemon juice.

Sole

Sole Bonne Femme

1 Clean soles. Ask the fishmonger to remove the black skin, or do it yourself as follows: make a small incision above the tail and pare away enough skin to give you a good grip; then pull skin sharply towards the head. Lay soles, skinned side up, on a board.

2 Cut the lemon in half; cut one half into thin slices for garnish. Keep remaining half to season fish.

3 Preheat oven to moderate (375°F. Mark 5).

4 Make an incision in each fish down the length of the backbone on the skinned side and slide a thin knife blade under each side. Lift up fillets carefully and sprinkle the pockets with finely chopped parsley (using half of the total amount), a few drops of lemon juice, and salt and freshly ground black pepper, to taste.

5 Butter an ovenproof baking dish large enough to take all the fish in one layer. Sprinkle dish with sliced mushrooms; arrange fish on top and dust with remaining chopped parsley. Add dry white wine and just enough water to cover soles.

6 Cover dish with a buttered paper; bring to simmering point on top of the stove and transfer to the oven. Bake for about 20 minutes, or until fish flakes easily with a fork.

7 When fish are cooked, transfer them to a heated serving dish and keep warm while you finish sauce.

8 Reduce cooking liquor to about half by boiling it briskly over a high heat.

9 Make a *beurre manié* by mashing 1 level tablespoon each butter and flour together to a smooth paste. Thin it down with a little of the reduced stock; then pour back into the pan; bring to the boil, stirring constantly, and simmer for 2 to 3 minutes to cook flour and thicken sauce.

10 Add cream; remove from heat and beat in the egg yolk and the remaining butter in small pieces.

11 When sauce is smooth and shiny, pour over soles. Garnish dish with lemon slices and serve immediately.

Sole with Crevettes

1 Have your fishmonger skin and fillet sole, and ask him to let you have the trimmings from them.

2 To make fish stock: place sole trimmings in a pan with a pint of cold water. Add a little salt; bring slowly to the boil; skim and add remaining ingredients. Simmer gently, covered, for 30 minutes; then remove lid and continue to simmer for a further 30 minutes. Strain stock through a fine sieve into a measuring jug.

3 Season fillets on both sides with salt and freshly ground black pepper. Lay fillets on a board skin side (or with the side that *was* skinned) upwards. Sprinkle with lemon juice.

4 Shell crevettes; remove heads but leave on the two fins right at the end of the tail. Reserve shells and trimmings.

5 Preheat oven to moderate (375°F. Mark 5).

6 Place a crevette at the wider end of each fillet and roll up. The tail of the crevette should stick out at one end.

7 Arrange rolled sole fillets tightly side by side in a deep, heat-proof casserole or baking dish. The tails of the crevettes will stick up in the air. Pour over wine. Cover casserole with a buttered paper.

8 Place casserole over a moderately low heat; bring to simmering point; transfer to the oven and bake for 10 minutes, or until fish flakes easily with a fork, but is not overcooked.

9 Carefully drain off liquor from casserole into the measuring jug. Keep sole hot. Note the quantity of fish stock and wine; pour into a pan; add shells, heads etc. from crevettes and boil rapidly until reduced to ½ pint.

10 To make sauce: in the top of a double saucepan, melt butter over direct heat. Blend in flour with a wooden spoon and stir over a low heat for 2 to 3 minutes to make a pale *roux*.

Serves 4

2 large sole, about 1 3/4 lb each
Salt and freshly ground black pepper
Lemon juice
8 crevettes, with shells, about 8 oz
1/4 pint dry white wine
Butter

Fish stock
Fish trimmings (see Step 1)
Salt
1 carrot, chopped
1 leek, white part only, chopped
Small strip of lemon zest
6 black peppercorns
3–4 sprigs parsley
1 bay leaf

Sauce
2 level tablespoons butter
2 level tablespoons flour
Reduced fish liquor (see Step 9)
1/4 pint double cream
2 egg yolks
2–3 teaspoons Pernod
Lemon juice
1 level tablespoon finely chopped parsley
Salt and freshly ground black pepper

11 Gradually add reduced fish liquor, stirring vigorously to prevent lumps forming; bring to the boil and simmer for 2 or 3 minutes, stirring. Remove from heat.

12 Stir in cream and beat in egg yolks. Fit top of pan over base containing simmering water and cook gently, stirring, until sauce has thickened again. Take care not to let it boil, or egg yolks may curdle.

13 Flavour sauce with Pernod and a few drops of lemon juice; stir in finely chopped parsley and correct seasoning if necessary. Spoon sauce over rolled fillets of sole, avoiding crevette tails, and serve.

Serves 8

1 1/4 lb fillets of sole (weight after filleting)
3 egg whites
Salt, freshly ground black pepper and cayenne
3/4 pint double cream
6 oz fresh white breadcrumbs
3 eggs
4 level tablespoons finely chopped parsley
2 level tablespoons finely chopped tarragon
1 level tablespoon finely chopped chives
Fresh fennel or tarragon sprigs
Thin strips of pork fat
Mousseline-Hollandaise sauce (page 345)

Pain de Sole

1 Prepare a fish mousseline: set aside 4 good-sized fillets of sole and put remainder of fish through a mincer. Stir in 2 unbeaten egg whites; then rub fish mixture through a fine sieve into a bowl.

2 Set bowl in a larger bowl containing ice cubes. Work mixture with a spatula, adding a little salt, which will make fish stiffen and change its consistency, freshly ground black pepper and a pinch of cayenne, to taste. When fish 'stiffens', add ½ pint cream, a little at a time, working paste vigorously with the spatula. Cover bowl and leave mousseline at the bottom of the refrigerator until needed.

3 Prepare herb forcemeat: put fresh breadcrumbs in a bowl. Beat whole eggs lightly and whisk in remaining cream until it forms soft peaks. Add this to breadcrumbs, together with finely chopped herbs, and mix well. Season to taste with salt and freshly ground black pepper.

4 Beat remaining egg white until foamy.

5 Season reserved fillets of sole with salt and freshly ground black pepper.

6 Select a rectangular 4-pint terrine and arrange 2 or 3 sprigs of fresh fennel or tarragon decoratively on the base. Line base and sides of terrine with long, thin strips of pork fat, making sure they overlap at both ends so that they can be folded over the top of the terrine when it is full.

7 To assemble the *pain de sole*: spread base and sides of terrine with an even layer of mousseline, using about two-thirds of the total amount. Brush with lightly beaten egg white and place 2 whole fillets of sole on this bed. Brush fillets with more egg white and cover with half of the forcemeat. Brush with egg white again; lay remaining fillets of sole on top and brush them also. Cover fillets with remaining forcemeat; brush with egg white; then fill dish with remaining mousseline.

8 Fold over overhanging strips of pork fat so that top of mousseline is completely covered. If not to be cooked immediately, cover with a lid and place in refrigerator. Remove terrine from refrigerator 2 hours before you intend to put it into the oven.

9 Preheat oven to very slow (300°F. Mark 2).

10 Place covered terrine in a pan with boiling water to come a third of the way up its sides. Bake for $1\frac{3}{4}$ to 2 hours, or until a sharp skewer pushed through the centre and held there for a few seconds feels hot on the palm of your hand.

11 Turn *pain de sole* out on to a heated serving dish and serve warm, cut in thick slices, accompanied by a Mousseline-Hollandaise sauce (see below).

Mousseline-Hollandaise Sauce

Serves 8

Lemon juice
Salt and white pepper
1/4 lb softened butter
4 egg yolks
4–6 tablespoons whipped cream

1 Combine 1 teaspoon lemon juice with a tablespoon of cold water, and salt and white pepper, to taste, in the top of a double saucepan.

2 Divide softened butter into 4 equal pieces.

3 Add egg yolks and a quarter of the butter to the liquid in the saucepan, and stir mixture rapidly and constantly with a wire whisk over hot but not boiling water until butter has melted and mixture begins to thicken.

4 Add the second piece of butter and continue whisking. As the mixture thickens and the second piece of butter melts, add the third piece of butter, stirring from the bottom of the pan until it has melted. Be careful not to allow water over which sauce is cooking to boil at any time. Add rest of butter, beating until it melts and is incorporated into the sauce.

5 Now remove top part of pan from the heat and continue to beat sauce for 2 to 3 minutes longer.

6 Replace pan over hot but not boiling water for 2 minutes more, beating constantly. By this time the emulsion should have formed and your sauce will be rich and creamy. 'Finish' sauce with a few drops of lemon juice, to taste; strain.

7 Just before serving, fold in whipped cream and season to taste with a little more salt or white pepper if necessary.

Note: If at any stage in the operation the mixture should curdle beat in 1 or 2 tablespoons cold water to rebind the emulsion.

Trout

Trout à la Grecque

Timing is all-important to the success of this attractive dish.

1 Select a heavy, oval, heatproof casserole long enough to hold trout comfortably without bending them. In it dissolve stock cubes in $1\frac{1}{2}$ pints water.

2 Peel carrots, turnips and potatoes. Cut them into $\frac{1}{4}$-inch dice. Place potatoes in a bowl of cold water.

3 Bring chicken stock to the boil. Add diced carrots and turnips; lower heat to simmering point; cover and cook gently for 5 minutes.

4 Drain potatoes thoroughly and add them to the casserole, together with frozen peas. Bring to the boil again; lower heat to simmering point; cover and continue to simmer for a further 4 minutes. Keep testing potatoes towards the end of this time: they should be soft, but on no account overcooked.

5 Submerge trout in stock and vegetables; bring rapidly to the boil; then cover casserole again; remove from heat and allow trout to cook from the heat of the pan itself for 10 minutes. Then plunge casserole into cold water to cool contents quickly and prevent it cooking any further.

6 When casserole is quite cold, chill until ready to serve. It may be left overnight if more convenient.

7 Just before serving, combine dressing ingredients in a bowl and beat with a fork until emulsified. Dressing should be quite highly flavoured and seasoned.

8 To serve: remove trout from casserole, taking care not to break them, and drain on absorbent paper.

9 Drain vegetables; place them in a bowl and toss gently with 4 tablespoons dressing. Taste and correct seasoning if necessary.

Serves 2–4

2 trout, about 1 lb each
1 1/2 chicken stock cubes
1/2 lb carrots
1/2 lb baby turnips
1/2 lb potatoes
1/4 lb frozen peas
Twists of lemon, to garnish

Dressing
6 tablespoons olive oil
1 tablespoon dry white wine
2–3 teaspoons lemon juice
1 level tablespoon fincly
  chopped parsley
1 level tablespoon finely
  chopped chives (optional)
1 level teaspoon grated onion
Salt and freshly ground black
  pepper
6–8 fennel seeds

10 Arrange trout in the centre of a large oval dish. Surround with dressed vegetables. Spoon more of the dressing over the fish and garnish with twists of lemon. Serve very cold, accompanied by remaining dressing.

Serve ½ fish per person as an appetiser; a whole one as the main course of a light summer lunch.

Trout with Almonds

Serves 4–6

1 Season cleaned trout with salt and a little freshly ground black pepper. Dip them in milk and then in flour, shaking off excess.

2 In a large frying pan (or two pans) which will take the trout in one layer, melt half the butter with olive oil. Sauté fish until they are golden brown on both sides and flesh flakes easily with a fork, 4 to 5 minutes on each side. Remove to a heated platter.

3 Drain fat from pan and add remaining butter. When it has melted, add flaked almonds and sauté, shaking pan continuously, until almonds are golden brown. Take care over this, as they burn easily. Sprinkle with lemon juice and finely chopped parsley.

4 Pour buttery sauce and almonds over trout, and serve immediately.

4–6 fresh trout, cleaned
Salt and freshly ground black
   pepper
Milk
Flour
1/4 lb butter
1 tablespoon olive oil
4–6 level tablespoons flaked
   almonds
Juice of 1/2 lemon
2–4 level tablespoons finely
   chopped parsley

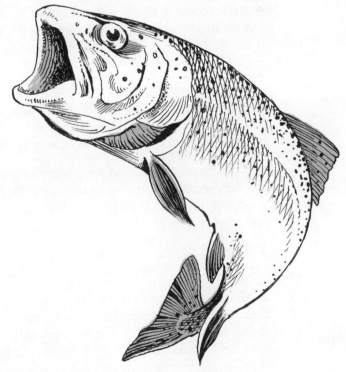

Turbot

Blanquette of Turbot

Serves 8 as an entrée, garnished with crescents of puff pastry, or 4–6 as a main course served with rice

2 lb turbot
5 oz butter
1/2 pint dry white wine
24 button onions
2 level tablespoons castor sugar
Salt and freshly ground black pepper
8 oz tight white button mushrooms
1 oz flour
1 egg yolk
1/3 pint (7 fluid oz) double cream
Lemon juice
3–4 level tablespoons finely chopped parsley
Crescents of puff pastry (page 456) or plain-boiled rice, to serve

Stock

4 leeks, white parts only, thinly sliced
4 carrots, thinly sliced
1 oz butter
Fish heads and trimmings
2 onions, each stuck with 1 clove
Bouquet garni (4 sprigs parsley, 2 sprigs thyme, 1 large bay leaf)
Salt and freshly ground black pepper

Turbot is ideal for a blanquette as it is less likely to disintegrate during cooking than a fish like cod or haddock. However, you should be just as careful not to overcook it, leaving it on the firm side if anything.

1 First prepare stock: in a large pan or casserole, sauté thinly sliced leeks and carrots in butter until lightly coloured. Cover with 3 pints water and add fish heads and trimmings (ask your fishmonger for these when you buy the fish), the onions stuck with cloves, *bouquet garni*, and a light seasoning of salt and freshly ground black pepper. Bring to the boil and simmer until reduced by half, about 20 minutes. Strain stock through a fine sieve and keep hot.

2 Cut turbot in 24 even-sized cubes.

3 Heat 2 oz butter in a heavy pan until lightly coloured and sauté turbot cubes until a pale golden colour on all sides, taking great care not to break them.

4 Add strained stock and dry white wine; bring to the boil over a moderate heat and simmer very, very gently until turbot is cooked through but still firm, 10 to 15 minutes.

5 Meanwhile, put button onions in a small pan and cover with water. Add 1 oz butter, the sugar, and salt and freshly ground black pepper, to taste. Bring to the boil and simmer until liquid has boiled away and onions are lightly caramelised, shaking pan towards the end to colour them evenly. Keep hot.

6 Wipe mushrooms and trim stems; leave them whole if they are very small, halve or quarter them if larger. Put mushrooms in a small pan with 1 oz butter and toss over a gentle heat until softened. Keep hot.

7 When turbot is ready, remove from pan with a slotted spoon and keep hot. Simmer cooking liquor until reduced to 1 pint.

8 Melt remaining 1 oz butter in a large pan or casserole; add flour and stir over a low heat for 2 minutes to make a pale *roux*. Gradually stir in reduced cooking liquor, beating vigorously to prevent lumps forming, and bring to the boil, stirring constantly; then lower heat and simmer for 10 minutes, stirring occasionally. Remove from heat.

9 Beat egg yolk with cream and lemon juice, to taste. Add to sauce; mix well; return pan to a very low heat and continue to stir until sauce thickens, taking care not to let it come to the boil, or egg yolk may curdle.

10 Fold in turbot and mushrooms; correct seasoning, adding more salt, freshly ground black pepper or lemon juice if necessary, and heat through gently.

11 Turn blanquette into a large, heated serving dish. Sprinkle with finely chopped parsley and garnish with glazed button onions. Serve very hot, garnished with crescents of puff pastry or rice.

Poached Halibut Hollandaise

Serves 4

1 Place halibut steaks in a large frying-pan. Add cold water to just cover steaks and season with lemon juice, sliced onion, bay leaf, peppercorns and salt, to taste.

2 Bring to the boil; reduce heat and simmer for 10 minutes or until fish flakes easily with a fork. Do not overcook.

3 Drain steaks thoroughly on a clean kitchen towel.

4 Place steaks on a hot serving dish and spoon a little Hollandaise sauce over each steak. Serve remaining sauce in a sauce boat.

5 Garnish dish with sprigs of fresh watercress or parsley, and lemon wedges.

6 To make Hollandaise sauce: in the top of a double saucepan, combine a teaspoon of lemon juice with a tablespoon of cold water and a pinch each of salt and white pepper.

7 Put softened butter on a plate and divide into 4 pieces of equal size.

8 Add egg yolks and 1 piece butter to the liquid in the pan and place over hot water. Stir rapidly with a wire whisk for about 5 minutes, or until butter has melted completely and mixture begins to thicken, making sure water underneath never comes to the boil.

9 Incorporate remaining pieces of butter one at a time, whisking vigorously and stirring from the bottom of the pan.

10 When sauce is thick and emulsified, beat for 2 to 3 minutes longer; then correct seasoning, adding more salt, white pepper or lemon juice to taste. Strain, if necessary, and serve.

4 halibut steaks, 1 1/2 inches thick
Juice of 1 lemon
1/2 onion, finely sliced
1 bay leaf
6 peppercorns
Salt
Fresh watercress or parsley sprigs
2 lemons, cut into wedges

Hollandaise sauce (Makes about 1/2 pint)
Lemon juice
Salt and white pepper
8 oz softened butter
4 egg yolks

Scallops

One of my favourite kinds of shellfish – and one still within the means of most mortals – scallops taste as good as they look, with their creamy round lobes and bright red corals resting on the half-shell.

If you are ever lucky enough to find the 'miniature' variety (sadly, most of these seem destined to be exported to North America), these are even sweeter in flavour.

When buying scallops in the shell, make sure they are tightly closed. This indicates that they are still alive and safe to eat.

To open a scallop

Slip a short, stubby knife blade between the shells as near to the hinge as you can get. This is to be found at the centre of the straight back edge, where the ribbing on the shells converges to a point. Cut through the hinge level with the shell. This will release the tension and the shell can be prised apart quite easily.

To clean a scallop

1 Remove scallop from half-shell. Discard the black piece sticking to it and the little tube trailing from the end.

2 Wash scallop carefully under cold running water to remove every trace of sand. The 'beard' is either retained, in which case make sure it is free of sand, or discarded, as you prefer.

Serves 4-6

8–12 large scallops, with
   corals
1/2 small onion, chopped
Bouquet garni (2 sprigs
   parsley, 1 sprig thyme,
   1 small bay leaf)
1/2 pint dry white wine
Salt and freshly ground black
   pepper

Basic Poached Scallop

1 Rinse scallops if necessary. Trim off any ragged edges, but leave red 'corals' attached. They are a delicacy.

2 Place scallops in a small pan. Add chopped onion, *bouquet garni*, dry white wine and, if necessary, a little cold water so that scallops are just covered with liquid. Season lightly with salt and freshly ground black pepper.

3 Bring scallops to simmering point over a moderately low heat, and poach gently for 5 minutes. (If scallops are small, they will be ready even sooner.) Take great care not to overcook them or their delicate texture will be ruined and they will turn tough and fibrous.

4 As soon as scallops are ready, lift them out of the pan with a slotted spoon. Use as required. Large scallops are usually sliced thickly in two or three. Small ones may be left whole, or halved.

Some Variations on the Basic Poached Scallops Theme

Poached Scallops Mornay

Steps **1–4** as in basic recipe on opposite page.

5 Make a Mornay Sauce (page 179); add beaten egg yolks and double cream; correct seasoning; add poached sliced scallops and heat gently until warmed through. Do not allow to boil or eggs will curdle. Serve with boiled rice.

Serves 4–6

8–12 large scallops, with corals
1/2 small onion, chopped
Bouquet garni (2 sprigs parsley, 1 sprig thyme, 1 small bay leaf)
1/2 pint dry white wine
Salt and freshly ground black pepper
Mornay Sauce (page 179)
2 egg yolks, beaten
4 tablespoons double cream
Boiled rice, to serve.

Deep-fried Scallops and Bacon

Steps **1–4** as in basic recipe on opposite page.

5 Combine beaten eggs and a little milk in a flat bowl, and season to taste with salt, freshly ground black pepper and cayenne.

6 Dip sliced poached scallops (or whole if they are small) in egg mixture and then in fresh breadcrumbs and allow to set in the refrigerator for at least 1 hour before cooking.

7 When ready to serve, melt butter in a large, thick-bottomed frying pan; add olive oil; bring to frying temperature and cook bacon slices until crisp. Remove and keep warm.

8 Add prepared scallops and cook in hot fat until they are golden brown. Serve immediately accompanied by crisp bacon and wedges of lemon.

Serves 4–6

8–12 large scallops, with corals
1/2 Small onion, chopped
Bouquet garni (2 sprigs parsley, 1 sprig thyme, 1 small bay leaf)
1/2 pint dry white wine
Salt and freshly ground black pepper
2 eggs, beaten
Milk
Cayenne
Fresh breadcrumbs
1/4 lb butter
1/4 pint olive oil
6 slices bacon
Lemon wedges

Serves 4–6

8–12 large scallops with
  corals
1/2 small onion, chopped
Bouquet garni (2 sprigs
  parsley, 1 sprig thyme,
  1 small bay leaf)
1/2 pint dry white wine
Salt and freshly ground black
  pepper
6 ounces finely chopped
  button mushrooms
2 ounces finely chopped
  Spanish onion
Butter
2 level tablespoons finely
  chopped parsley
4 tablespoons reduced Fish
  Velouté Sauce
Freshly grated Parmesan
Fresh breadcrumbs

Makes 2/3 pint

2 level tablespoons butter
2 level tablespoons flour
1 pint boiling fish stock or
  canned clam juice
Salt and white pepper
Lemon juice

Coquilles St Jacques au Gratin

Steps **1–4** as in basic recipe (page 350).

5 Simmer finely chopped button mushrooms and finely chopped Spanish onion in 4 level tablespoons butter until soft. Reserve.

6 Add finely chopped parsley and reduced Fish Velouté Sauce to mushroom and onion mixture. Note: I sometimes just add 4 tablespoons reduced fish stock which I have thickened with ½ level teaspoon each flour and butter mashed to a smooth paste.

7 Toss poached, sliced scallops in this mixture and fill cleaned scallops shells or individual heatproof dishes with this mixture.

8 Sprinkle with a little freshly grated Parmesan and fresh bread-crumbs; sprinkle with a little melted butter and put under the grill until bubbling hot and golden brown.

Fish Velouté Sauce

1 Melt butter in the top of a double saucepan; add flour and cook for a few minutes to form a pale *roux*.

2 Add boiling stock (or canned clam juice) and salt and pepper to taste, and cook, stirring vigorously with a whisk until well blended.

3 Reduce heat and simmer gently, stirring occasionally and skimming from time to time until the sauce is reduced to two-thirds of the original quantity and is thick but light and creamy.

4 Flavour with lemon juice to taste and strain through a fine sieve.

Note: Fish Velouté – makes an excellent sauce on its own when a little double cream and 1 or 2 egg yolks are added.

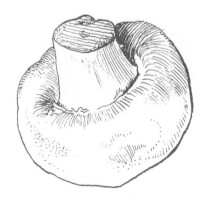
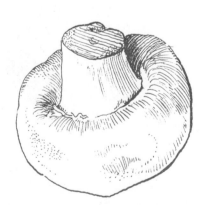

Coquilles Saint-Jacques à la Bretonne

Serves 4

An excellent hot *hors-d'œuvre* which can be prepared in advance and slipped under a hot grill to reheat and brown the top just before serving.

1 If fresh scallops are available, shell and clean them, following directions. The 'beard' should be retained – in Brittany this is served with the rest of the scallops and it is delicious. Wash scallops carefully in running water to remove every trace of sand.

2 If using frozen scallops, allow them to thaw completely.

3 Cut each scallop into large dice, leaving the coral in one piece.

4 Place scallops, corals and 'beards' in a small pan; add wine, and salt and freshly ground black pepper to taste, and poach very gently for about 5 minutes. Drain, reserving poaching liquor, and keep hot.

5 Put stale breadcrumbs in a bowl and sprinkle with milk.

6 In a small pan, sauté finely chopped onion and shallot in 2 oz butter until soft and golden. Add scallops and continue to sauté for 2 to 3 minutes, stirring gently with a wooden spoon. Stir in cognac.

7 Add soaked breadcrumbs, together with crushed garlic and finely chopped parsley, and simmer for 2 to 3 minutes longer, stirring constantly.

8 Sprinkle with flour and moisten with reserved poaching liquor. Season to taste with salt and freshly ground black pepper, and allow to simmer gently for a final 5 or 6 minutes, stirring. The sauce should have the consistency of a Béchamel.

9 Scrub 4 empty scallop shells clean. (If preparing the dish with frozen scallops, use individual heatproof ramekins instead.) Divide scallops and sauce equally between them; sprinkle with fresh breadcrumbs and dot with remaining butter.

10 Just before serving, place shells or dishes under a preheated, very hot grill until tops are golden brown and bubbling.

8 large scallops, fresh or frozen
1/4 pint dry white wine
Salt and freshly ground black pepper
3 oz stale white breadcrumbs
6 tablespoons milk
1 Spanish onion, finely chopped
1 shallot, finely chopped
3 oz butter
1 tablespoon cognac
1 clove garlic, crushed
2 level tablespoons finely chopped parsley
1 level tablespoon flour
4 level tablespoons fine white breadcrumbs

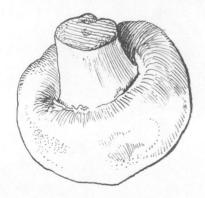

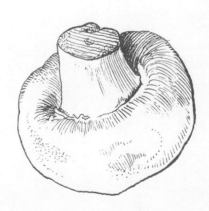

Serves 6

6 large scallops, with corals

1/2 pint dry white wine

3 level tablespoons finely chopped onion

2–3 sprigs parsley

1 sprig thyme or 1/4 level teaspoon dried thyme

1 bay leaf

Salt and freshly ground black pepper

6 oz bacon in one piece

4–5 level tablespoons flour

4–6 level tablespoons fine dry white breadcrumbs

1 egg

Oil for deep-frying

Hollandaise sauce (page 190), to serve

Scallop Brochettes

1 Wipe scallops; put them in a small pan and add white wine, finely chopped onion and herbs. Season to taste with salt and freshly ground black pepper. Bring to a gentle boil; lower heat and simmer for about 5 minutes, or until scallops are just cooked. Remove from heat.

2 Take scallops out of pan with a slotted spoon. Separate corals and cut them in two across the width. Slice white parts in three. Drop scallops and corals back into cooking liquor and leave to cool.

3 Meanwhile, cut bacon into 12 batons, each about 1 inch long and $\frac{1}{2}$ inch thick. Put them in a small pan; bring to the boil; simmer for 2 minutes and drain. Cool.

4 Sift flour on to one flat plate, and scatter breadcrumbs over another one. In a shallow dish, beat egg lightly with a tablespoon of cold water.

5 When scallops and bacon are cool, drain them and dry them thoroughly with absorbent paper.

6 Dust scallop slices, corals and bacon batons with flour; dip each piece in beaten egg, allowing excess to drain off, and coat with breadcrumbs, making sure they cover the entire surface.

7 Thread ingredients on to six 6-inch skewers, assembling each one as follows: 1 slice scallop, 1 baton bacon, 1 piece coral, scallop, bacon, coral and scallop. Chill skewers until ready to fry them.

8 Heat a pan of oil for deep-frying to 400°F., or until a cube of bread browns in 45 seconds.

9 Plunge skewers (about three at a time) into hot oil and deep-fry for 2 minutes, or until nicely browned. Drain on paper towels. Allow fat to reach 400°F. again before frying remaining skewers.

10 Serve immediately with Hollandaise sauce.

354

Crab

Found both in salt and fresh water, crabs are available more or less all the year round, but are at their best from May to August. Crabs contain less meat for their size than lobsters, but the meat is a good deal sweeter and many people prefer its delicate flavour.

To Choose a Crab

Choose heavy crabs of medium size; the light ones tend to be watery. The male crab – recognised by its larger claws – is considered better than the hen, but this is far less important than the weight test.

To Shell a Cooked Crab

You will need a cleaver or a heavy knife with a strong blade, plus a wooden mallet or rolling pin, blunt-ended pincers and a metal skewer or wooden toothpicks, a board on which to work, and two bowls.

1 Lay crab on its back with its tail flap nearest you and the large claws at the side farthest away from you. If the crab is a small one, you will probably be able to separate the chest section from the hard carapace by placing your thumbs under the tail flap and pushing upwards. If it is a mature crab, it will be easier to prise the two sections apart with the tip of your cleaver, pushing it down between carapace and chest section at the tail. Put aside the chest section with claws and legs attached.

2 Take the carapace; turn it around and remove the mouthpiece together with the stomach, which resembles a crumpled greaseproof bag. Lift out transparent membranes and any white gills which may have come loose from the chest section. These go under the dubious name of 'dead men's fingers'.

3 Scoop out the creamy meat into a bowl. If you are careful, you will be able to keep it in reasonably large pieces. Where it joins the shell the meat will have a reddish hue, changing to greenish grey towards the centre. All of this is edible.

4 Take the chest section. Break off claws and legs close to body.

5 *Legs:* In a small crab, the only part of the legs worth shelling is the first joint or thigh. Separate this from the remaining sections by bending it back *against* the joint so that the cartilage is drawn out of it as the two come apart. When all the thigh pieces have been separated, lay them flat on your board, one at a time, and give them a good whack with the side of your cleaver. Pick off cracked shell and place pieces of meat in the second bowl. If the crab is a large one, it will pay you to take the remaining leg joints, separating them as before so that the cartilage is drawn out before you crush the shells and remove meat.

6 *Claws:* Pull the smaller part of each claw back on itself so that it comes away with the cartilage from the larger claw. Then divide claw into joints in the same way. Crack each piece of claw by hitting it smartly with the side of your cleaver or the wooden mallet. Pick off shell, keeping pieces of meat as large as possible, and making sure they are quite free of shell splinters. Put meat in the second bowl.

7 Now clean your board and take the chest section. Peel off all the feathery white gills attached to the underside. If it is a small crab, all you can do is dig as much meat as possible out of the holes left by the legs and claws, and then from the centre, using a skewer or toothpick. If you are dealing with a large crab, chop the chest section in four with your cleaver to get at the quite considerable amount of meat nestling in the crevices inside. Pick this out with your fingers, feeling around carefully to make sure that you do not include any splinters of shell with the meat.

8 Take the empty shell. On the underside you will notice that there is a distinct separation line running around the border. Tap the shell firmly with a wooden mallet or the end of your rolling pin so that it breaks off at this line. Alternatively, use a pair of flat-nosed pliers to snap the shell off level with the line, piece by piece. Scrub interior of shell thoroughly with a brush and make sure there is nothing left in the crevices. Scrub exterior of shell, using a light abrasive if necessary, to remove any dissolved patches. Dry shell thoroughly. Polish the outer surface with a wad of kitchen paper soaked in olive oil.

Dressed Crab

The usual way of serving dressed crab in the shell is as follows:

1 Shell crab as directed above, keeping white and brown meat separate.

2 Trim and polish shell.

3 Mix white meat with a well-flavoured lemon mayonnaise (page 43 using lemon juice instead of Wine Vinegar) in the proportion of 3 level tablespoons mayonnaise to 4 oz meat. Correct seasoning if necessary.

4 Dark meat should be dressed with a piquant sauce, e.g. Ravigote (page 189), in the proportion of 2 tablespoons to 4 oz meat. Add a few drops more of wine vinegar and correct seasoning.

5 The dressed white meat is filled into either side of the crab shell, leaving a central panel clear for the dark meat.

6 Hard-boiled egg white chopped with a stainless steel knife is strewn thickly over the white sections, and sieved egg yolks are used to cover the dark panel in the centre.

7 As a final touch, sprinkle a thin line of finely chopped parsley down the two sides where white meat meets dark.

Délices de Crabe

We have no less than three ways of presenting this dish. In the first and simplest version, the creamy crabmeat filling is rolled into balls, egg-and-breadcrumbed and deep-fried. Or you can roll each portion up in a thin crêpe, coat with egg and bread-crumbs, and deep-fry again. The third variation turns the crab into a delicious, crisp, Middle Eastern *börek*. All three make excellent appetisers or 'fingerfood' to serve with drinks.

1 Drain juices from can of crabmeat into a measuring jug and make up to $\frac{1}{4}$ pint with milk. Pour into a pan. Add the next 5 ingredients; bring to the boil over a low heat. Remove; cover and leave to infuse for 10 minutes.

2 Meanwhile, pick over crabmeat, removing any stray pieces of shell or cartilage.

3 In a medium-sized pan, melt butter. Blend in flour with a wooden spoon and cook over a low heat, stirring, for 2 to 3 minutes to make a pale *roux*.

4 Strain infused milk. Add to *roux* gradually, stirring vigorously to prevent lumps forming. Bring to the boil and cook, stirring constantly, for 2 to 3 minutes. Sauce will be very thick indeed. Remove from heat.

Basic Crabmeat Filling

One $7\frac{3}{4}$-oz can crabmeat
Milk
1 bay leaf
1/2 chicken stock cube
Small strip of lemon zest
1–2 parsley sprigs
1 small onion, quartered
1 oz butter
1 oz flour
1 level teaspoon tomato concentrate
4–6 level tablespoons double cream
2 teaspoons brandy
Salt and freshly ground black pepper
Pinch of cayenne
Squeeze of lemon juice
Oil

5 Beat in tomato concentrate, double cream and brandy, and when smooth, mix in crabmeat. Season to taste with salt if necessary, freshly ground black pepper and a pinch of cayenne, and sharpen flavour with a squeeze of lemon juice.

6 Grease a flat plate lightly with oil. Spread crabmeat mixture out on it evenly into a circle roughly 7 inches in diameter. Cool. Cover tightly with foil or plastic wrap and chill until firm.

Deep-fried Crabmeat Balls

Makes 24 Balls

1 recipe Crabmeat Filling
  (page 357)
Beaten egg
Fine white breadcrumbs
Oil for deep-frying

1 Divide cold crabmeat mixture into 24 equal portions. Roll into balls.

2 Dip each ball in beaten egg; lift out with a slotted spoon and roll in breadcrumbs. Repeat egg-and-breadcrumbing once more.

3 Arrange crabmeat balls on a plate and chill while you heat oil for deep-frying.

4 Heat pan of oil to 375°F.

5 Deep-fry crabmeat balls, a portion at a time, for 2 or 3 minutes, or until crisp and golden. Drain on absorbent paper and serve immediately.

Crisp Crabmeat Rolls

Makes 24 Rolls

Double recipe Basic Crêpe
  Batter (page 489)
1 recipe Crabmeat Filling
  (page 357)
Beaten egg
Fine white breadcrumbs
Oil for deep-frying

1 Prepare and fry 24 crêpes 6 inches in diameter as described in the basic recipe, stacking them on a plate under a folded cloth to keep them moist.

2 Divide cold crabmeat mixture into 24 equal portions. Shape into little rolls.

3 To make pancake rolls: place a roll of crabmeat at one edge of a pancake; roll over once so that filling is enclosed in pancake; fold in left- and right-hand sides, and roll up completely.

4 Coat each roll with beaten egg, allowing excess to drain off, and roll in breadcrumbs.

5 Heat a pan of oil for deep-frying to 375°F.

6 Lay 4 or 5 rolls in the frying basket; lower them into hot fat and deep-fry for 3 to 4 minutes until crisp and golden. Drain on absorbent paper and serve immediately.

Crab Börek

Makes 24 Börek

Greek pastry known as 'phyllo' or 'filo' is an almost transparent, paper-like pastry, very similar to strudel dough in appearance. It can be bought from Cypriot shops in this country in tightly rolled, standard-size sheets sealed in cellophane. Any left over should be resealed carefully in plastic or foil as it becomes brittle and useless if left exposed to the air for any length of time. Always brush Greek pastry with a little melted butter before using it (to make pastry more pliable).

1 Preheat oven to fairly hot (425°F. Mark 7).

2 Divide cold crabmeat mixture into 24 equal portions. Roll into balls.

3 Take one sheet of phyllo pastry at a time, keeping remainder wrapped in a damp cloth to prevent it drying out (see note above). Cut it in half lengthwise.

4 To shape *börek*: brush a half-sheet of phyllo with melted butter. Place a ball of crabmeat mixture in one corner, slightly off centre and 1 inch in from the edge. Fold sheet over it so that it is halved lengthwise again. You now have a long strip of pastry. Brush with more melted butter. Take the short end with filling and fold it over slightly to seal in filling. Then take the (same) end and fold it over itself, making a triangle. Continue folding the strip over and over on to itself, keeping it in the shape of the triangle. Tuck in the end neatly.

5 Arrange triangles on a buttered baking sheet and brush tops all over with more melted butter.

6 Bake *börek* for 10 to 15 minutes until puffed and golden.

Note: If not to be served immediately, the unbaked pastries may be stored in the refrigerator so that they are cooked just before serving.

Makes 24 Börek

1 recipe Crabmeat Filling
(page 357)
12 sheets phyllo pastry
(see Note)
About 6 oz melted butter

Mussels

It's a pity mussels are so cheap. Perhaps if they weren't, people would appreciate them more, for they are very fine indeed, especially in late autumn and during the winter.

People tend to be nervous about mussels, having heard that they can be dangerous if taken from polluted waters, but you have no grounds for worrying about those you buy in shops – by law these have to undergo thorough cleansing in special sea water tanks before they reach the public.

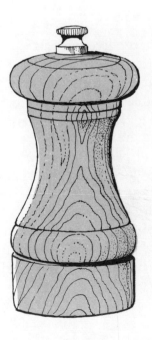

What you do have to be careful about is the odd dead mussel in a batch. This can be dangerous, as they go off quickly, so to be on the safe side, discard any that (*a*) are not tightly closed by the time you've finished scrubbing and 'bearding' them; and (*b*) any that are *still* closed at the end of cooking.

To clean mussels Equip yourself with a hard scrubbing brush. Put the mussels in the kitchen sink and scrub them one by one under running cold water. Be really conscientious about this, for any sand that remains on their shells is likely to find its way into the finished dish.

As you scrub each mussel, pull away the dark, frond-like 'beard' with the help of a short-bladed knife.

Drop each mussel into a large bowl of clear water as you prepare it.

To steam mussels open This is quite easy. Simply take a heavy-based saucepan with a tight-fitting lid. Add the mussels, together with flavouring herbs, wine, a little chopped shallot, or whatever your recipe calls for. Cover pan tightly.

Set pan over a high heat and cook the mussels, shaking the pan gently from time to time, for no more than 5 to 7 minutes. By this time all the mussels that are going to open will have opened.

Discard any that are still tightly closed.

Don't overcook mussels or they will be tough and a lot of flavour will have been lost.

Moules Farcies

Serves 2

24 large live mussels
Butter
1 shallot, finely chopped
4 tablespoons dry white wine
1/4 level teaspoon dried thyme
Small piece of bay leaf
2–4 level tablespoons finely chopped parsley
2 plump cloves garlic
2 teaspoons lemon juice
2 oz stale white breadcrumbs
Salt and freshly ground black pepper

Mussels in bubbling hot garlic butter, with a crisp coating of golden brown breadcrumbs.

1 Scrub mussels clean under cold running water and remove 'beards'. Discard any that are not tightly closed by the end of this operation.

2 Melt $\frac{1}{2}$ oz butter in a wide, heavy pan with a tight-fitting lid, and sauté finely chopped shallot until golden. Stir in dry white wine, thyme and bay leaf, and half the finely chopped parsley, and simmer for 1 minute. Add mussels, cover tightly and cook over a high heat, shaking pan frequently, for 5 to 7 minutes, or until mussels have all opened. Discard any that are still closed.

3 Drain mussels and carefully remove top shell from each one.

4 Peel and crush garlic cloves to a paste and add them to $\frac{1}{4}$ lb butter, together with the remaining parsley, and beat until smooth and well blended.

5 Slip a piece of garlic butter over each mussel in its half-shell and arrange them side by side in a wide, heatproof dish. Sprinkle with lemon juice; scatter breadcrumbs over the top and season with salt and freshly ground black pepper.

6 Cook under a hot grill until butter has melted and breadcrumbs are sizzling and golden brown. Serve immediately.

Moules au Safran

Half the fun of this mussel dish, a cross between a soup and a stew similar to a *mouclade*, is using your fingers, so large napkins and finger bowls are a necessity. Serve with fresh French bread to mop up the delicious sauce.

1 Scrub mussels clean and remove 'beards'. Discard any shells that are cracked or that have not closed tightly by the end of this operation.

2 Put mussels in a heavy pan with a tight-fitting lid. Add half the wine and a *bouquet garni*; cover and cook over a high heat, shaking pan frequently, for 5 to 7 minutes, or until mussels have all opened. Discard any that remain closed – they, too, are suspect.

3 Take mussels from the pan, shaking back any liquor left in their shells. Remove top shell from each mussel and arrange mussels in a wide serving dish. Keep hot. Strain liquor through a sieve lined with fine muslin.

4 To make sauce: in a heavy pan, simmer finely chopped onion and crushed garlic in butter until transparent.

5 Moisten with strained mussel liquor and remaining wine; add cayenne and saffron, and cook over a fairly high heat for 5 minutes until reduced by about one-third.

6 Stir in cream; bring to the boil again and remove from heat.

7 Beat in the egg yolk and season to taste with salt and freshly ground black pepper.

8 Pour sauce over mussels; sprinkle dish generously with finely chopped parsley and serve immediately.

Serves 4

3–4 pints mussels
1/4 pint dry white wine
Bouquet garni (1 sprig parsley, 1 sprig thyme, 1 bay leaf)
2–3 level tablespoons finely chopped parsley, to garnish

Sauce

1 Spanish onion, finely chopped
1 clove garlic, crushed
2 level tablespoons butter
Generous pinch of cayenne pepper
1/4 level teaspoon powdered saffron
1/4 pint double cream
1 egg yolk
Salt and freshly ground black pepper

2 quarts mussels
2 level tablespoons finely
chopped shallots
2 sprigs parsley
1/4 level teaspoon thyme
1 bay leaf
Salt and freshly ground black
pepper
4–6 tablespoons dry white
wine
2 tablespoons wine vinegar
Olive oil
2 level tablespoons coarsely
chopped parsley

Salade de Moules

1 Scrub mussels thoroughly under cold running water and remove 'beards'. Discard any that are cracked or still open by the end of this operation.

2 Place mussels in a large, heavy pan with a tight-fitting lid. Add finely chopped shallots, parsley, thyme and bay leaf; season very lightly with salt and freshly ground black pepper, and moisten with dry white wine.

3 Cover pan tightly. Place over a high heat and cook for 5 to 7 minutes, or until mussels have opened. Discard any that remain closed – they, too, are suspect.

4 Remove pan from heat. As soon as mussels can be handled, scoop them out of their shells with a teaspoon into a bowl. You may, if you wish, pull off their dark little outer frills, but this is not necessary. Cover and keep warm.

5 Taste mussel liquor. If it is not too salty, boil it for a few minutes to reduce it and intensify the flavour. Pour a little mussel liquor through a sieve lined with double-thick muslin or a piece of kitchen paper. If very salty, add a little more dry white wine.

6 Combine 2 tablespoons each mussel liquor and wine vinegar in a small bowl. Beat in enough olive oil to make a good dressing. Stir in half the chopped parsley and season to taste with salt and freshly ground black pepper.

7 Pour dressing over warm mussels; toss lightly to coat them evenly and allow to cool. Then chill until ready to serve.

8 Just before serving, arrange mussels in a shallow serving dish and garnish with remaining parsley. Serve very cold.

Lobster

To Choose a Lobster

Live A live lobster should be vigorous and active. If its movements are weak and sluggish, this is an indication that it has been out of the water for some time and that it may already have been living off its own reserves (for which *you* are now being asked to pay) for weeks. So above all, make sure it's still heavy for its size.

Boiled Weight is again the only sure test of quality. To check for freshness, pull the tail out straight and let go: it should spring back sharply into its original position i.e. pressed tightly against the body.

To Boil a Lobster

Plunge the lobster (live) into a large pan of boiling salted water to which you have added a few peppercorns, a bay leaf and a sprig of thyme. Bring back to the boil again quickly, and poach for 5 minutes per lb. *Don't* overcook.

To Shell a Boiled Lobster

Equip yourself with a cleaver (or, failing this, a heavy knife with a strong blade), a teaspoon, a metal skewer or a wooden toothpick or two, a rolling pin, a wooden board on which to work, a small bowl and a plate.

1 Lay lobster on the board, with its hump facing upwards, and with the cleaver split it in half lengthwise, severing the shell and meat at the same time.

2 Take one lobster-half at a time. With your finger, scoop out the stomach, which is to be found almost immediately behind the head and looks just like a little greaseproof paper bag. Somewhere in the vicinity, you should be able to locate the intestinal vein. Remove this as well.

3 With your teaspoon, scrape out the creamy, grey-green matter in the chest and put it in the bowl. Add to this any bright red coral (this is the roe, so it will only be present in a female lobster).

4 Break off the pliable tail from the chest. Scoop out meat from half-tails, using either the skewer or the teaspoon, and keeping pieces as large as possible. Place meat on the plate and discard any small pieces of shell.

5 Break off the claws together with the hinged double-joints that connect them to the chest. Separate claws from double-joints.

6 Split joints in two. Remove meat with skewer and add to the plate.

7 Now take a claw. Gently prise the smaller part back on itself to separate it from the main claw. As it comes away, it will draw a large, fan-like piece of cartilage out of the main part of the claw. Discard this and skewer flesh out of the smaller claw. Add to plate.

8 Crack the larger claw with a whack or two of your cleaver or rolling pin. Prise off shell, keeping pieces of meat as large as possible. Add to plate.

9 Now take pieces of chest. Pull off the outer shell. If there is any more creamy substance adhering to the outer shell, scrape this off and add to the bowl containing coral.

10 Pull off the four spidery legs attached to each side of the chest.

11 With your skewer or toothpick, scrape meat out of chest, digging into the crevices of the rib-like cartilage with your skewer to extract every morsel. Add meat to plate.

12 Finally, take each leg and divide it into joints. Lay joints, one at a time, on your board and, with the rolling pin, roll over them firmly in one direction so that meat is squeezed out. Add to plate.

A cooked lobster weighing about 12 oz in the shell will provide you with about 6 oz meat.

Serves 4

2 live lobsters (about 2 lbs each)
Boiling salted water, or a well-flavoured *court-bouillon* (opposite)
Melted butter
Lemon juice
Salt, paprika and cayenne pepper
Finely chopped fresh tarragon or chives

Simple Boiled Lobster – Hot

One of the most delicious shellfish dishes in the world. But very expensive. You can procure live lobsters from your fishmonger, but they have to be ordered well in advance.

1 Fill a large saucepan three quarters full of salted water, or a well-flavoured *court-bouillon* and bring to the boil. (Along the Southern coast of France, they sometimes cook live lobsters in a highly flavoured *soupe de poissons* mixture complete with *rouille*. It makes a wonderfully aromatic dish.)

2 Plunge the lobsters, head first, into the boiling liquid; bring to the boil again and boil quickly for 1 minute; then lower heat and simmer gently for 25 minutes, removing any scum that rises during cooking.

3 Remove cooked lobsters; drain well and rub shell with a little melted butter to make it shine.

4 Crack claws and split body in half down the middle, removing intestine, stomach and the spongy looking gills (as directed above).

5 Place the prepared lobster halves on a heated serving dish; brush meat with a little melted butter and serve immediately with a piquant sauce made of additional melted butter, flavoured with lemon juice and salt, paprika and cayenne pepper, to taste. When available, add a little finely chopped fresh tarragon or chives.

Wine Court-Bouillon for Fish

1 Combine ingredients in a large saucepan or fish kettle and bring to the boil. Skim, and boil for 45 minutes.

2 Strain and cool.

Note : For a simpler *court-bouillon* substitute water for dry white wine and add a little wine, wine vinegar or lemon juice, to taste.

1 bottle dry white wine
3/4 pint water
1/4 pound carrots, sliced
1/4 pound onions, sliced
1 handful parsley stalks
1 bay leaf
1 sprig thyme
Coarse salt
12 fennel seeds (optional)
12 peppercorns
Pinch of cayenne pepper

Cold Lobster Mayonnaise

Serves 4

Steps **1–3** in Simple Boiled Lobster recipe (see page 364), rubbing cooked lobster shell with a little olive oil (instead of melted butter) to make it shine.

4 Place the prepared lobster halves on a serving dish; garnish dish with lettuce leaves and tomato and lemon wedges and serve with homemade Mayonnaise or Sauce Verte (Green Mayonnaise).

2 live lobsters (about 2 pounds each), cooked in boiling salted water or a well-flavoured *court-bouillon* as above
Olive oil
Lettuce leaves
Tomato wedges
Lemon wedges
1 recipe Mayonnaise (page 43) or Sauce Verte (page 186)

Lobster – New York Style

Serves 4

1 Cut cooked lobsters in half lengthwise. Crack claws. Remove lobster meat from the shells and cut into dice.

2 Melt butter and lemon juice in a frying-pan; add diced lobster meat and sauté for a few minutes. Flavour with a pinch each of Paprika and cayenne pepper. Flame with cognac. Keep warm.

3 Combine beaten egg yolks and double cream in the top of a double saucepan and cook over water, stirring constantly, until the mixture coats the back of a spoon. Do not let mixture come to the boil, or the sauce will curdle.

4 Add lobster meat and pan juices and heat through. Season to taste with salt, freshly ground black pepper, paprika and cayenne. Serve on a bed of boiled rice. Garnish dish with lemon wedges.

2 cooked lobsters (about 2 pounds each)
4 level tablespoons butter
Juice of 1/2 lemon
Paprika and cayenne pepper
4 tablespoons heated cognac
2 egg yolks, well beaten
1/2 pint double cream
Salt and freshly ground black pepper
Boiled rice
Lemon wedges

Serves 6

4 shallots, finely chopped

4 tablespoons butter

1/4 pint dry white wine

1/2 lb button mushrooms,
  thinly sliced

1 pint thick Béchamel sauce
  (page 178)

1/2 lb cooked lobster, sliced

1/2 lb shelled prawns

1/2 lb cooked sole, sliced

1/2 lb cooked scallops, sliced
  or quartered

24 mussels, cooked and
  shelled

Salt and freshly ground black
  pepper

Seafood Casserole

1 In a saucepan, sauté shallots in half the butter until transparent; add wine and simmer until reduced to 2 or 3 tablespoons.

2 Sauté mushrooms in remaining butter until soft; add to shallot mixture.

3 Strain Béchamel sauce in a pan; carefully fold in prepared seafood, together with mushroom-shallot mixture.

4 Heat through gently, adding salt and freshly ground black pepper, to taste, and thinning sauce down with a little more dry white wine (or stock left over from cooking seafood) if mixture seems too thick.

5 Serve immediately with saffron rice and green peas.

Lesson 14
Casseroles

Casseroling

To be able to coax an inexpensive cut of meat to juicy tenderness in a richly flavoured sauce that owes little to flour and nothing at all to cubes or powders, is a feat to be proud of. And casserole cookery is a wonderfully easy way to make even the least desirable cuts of meat taste delicious. You can marinate the meat in wine, olive oil and herbs to tenderise it before it is cooked. Or just 'seize' it in a little butter or olive oil, flavour it with aromatic herbs and a touch of garlic, and then simmer it for an hour or two in a sauce made rich with stock, wine or cream.

The best cuts of beef to casserole are the top part of the shin, the rump, the topside, the brisket, or the flank.

Veal shoulder, breast, knuckle and shin make wonderful casseroles as they take kindly to long, slow cooking in a well-flavoured sauce. The leg of lamb, shoulder and breast are the best cuts for casseroles, although best end of neck and middle neck can also be used. Any cut of pork is suitable for casseroling if it is not too fat.

Any poultry or game bird – whole or jointed – is perfect for casseroling.

Preparing Meat for Casseroling

1 Meat is usually cut into cubes about $1\frac{1}{2}$ inches square for a casserole, although it can also be cut into thick slices or left whole. Poultry can be jointed, quartered, halved or left whole, according to the recipe. Make sure pieces of meat are thoroughly dry, or they will steam and not brown properly when you fry them. If the recipe tells you to dust them with seasoned flour, do so at the last moment – the flour seems to draw out moisture and makes the meat damp and tacky again if left too long.

2 Larding Top quality beef – rib or fillet – does not have to be larded; but it is usually wise to lard a rump or round of beef, a roast of veal or a leg of mutton with strips of bacon fat as long as the piece of meat to be cooked and about $\frac{1}{2}$ inch wide. Season these first with pepper and spices, sprinkle with chopped parsley and marinate for about 2 hours in a little brandy; then insert the strips into the meat with a special larding needle. Most butchers will lard meat for you.

3 Marinating The flavour of meat intended for braising is greatly improved by marinating it for a few hours in the wine which is to be the moistening agent in cooking. Roll the meat in a mixture of salt, pepper and finely chopped herbs, and place it in an earthenware casserole just large enough to hold it, on a bed of thickly sliced and fried carrots and onions, a generous *bouquet garni*, a clove or two of garlic, and some blanched, fried fat bacon. Cover the meat with wine and marinate it overnight in this mixture, taking care to turn it several times during this period.

4 Sautéeing After having marinated the meat, drain it well and pat it dry with a clean cloth.

Heat the fat in a heavy frying-pan – using olive oil, bacon fat, butter mixed with a little olive oil to keep it from browning, or lard, or a combination of all these, to colour the meat and seal in its juices. Brown meat thoroughly on all sides.

1 Don't overcrowd the pan. If you do, the steam released by the meat will not be able to escape and before you know where you are, the cubes/slices will be simmering in their own juice. Once they do this, nothing will make them brown.

2 Control the heat under the pan carefully so that the meat browns steadily and thoroughly. If the pan gets too hot, the meat will burn and instead of enhancing the flavour of your casserole, you will probably end up with a bitter taste, especially if the meat was floured. Burnt flour is *not* browned flour. The same rule applies when sautéeing finely chopped onions and garlic. Unless the heat is carefully controlled, the sugar in the onions will burn and turn them black long before they have softened, which is not only unattractive but bitter as well.

If the recipe tells you to soften onions without colouring them, do so with the heat right down at simmering point throughout.

Deglazing the frying-pan The sediment and morsels that remain behind in the pan after browning your meat and vegetables hold the very essence of their flavours. Instead of rinsing them down the sink, make it a rule always to *deglaze* your pan – whether the recipe tells you to add liquid to the casserole or not – and add the precious juices to the cooking pot.

You need use no more than 3 or 4 tablespoons water. When you have finished browning the meat, onions, etc., remove pan from heat, add water and scrape the bottom and sides clean with a wooden spoon – this is easy while the pan is hot. So, return pan to heat; stir vigorously until liquid has reduced to just a tablespoon or two, then sprinkle over meat and vegetables.

At other times, for a more distinctive flavour, use a few tablespoons of dry red or white wine, a little cider, wine vinegar or brandy to deglaze your pan. Proceed as above.

Casseroling

Place the vegetables and herbs from the marinade in the bottom of a heavy casserole just large enough to hold the meat; place the meat on this bed of aromatics and pour in enough of the juices from the marinade to cover the vegetables amply. Add well-flavoured stock; place the casserole on the stove and bring it to the boil. Skim froth from the top of the liquid; lower heat so that the casserole barely simmers; cover and cook gently on top of the stove until the meat can be pricked deeply without giving blood. Then remove the meat to another casserole just large enough to hold it; strain the sauce through a piece of muslin over the meat; cover the casserole and place it in a preheated cool oven (225°F. Mark $\frac{1}{4}$–250°F. Mark $\frac{1}{2}$) and cook until tender, stirring or basting from time to time to keep the top of the meat moist. Above all, be sure that the meat cooks very gently so that the meat will be tender and the fat will rise gradually to the surface of the liquid.

Slow oven cooking I find that all casseroles – vegetables as well as meats, poultry, fish and game – respond wonderfully well to low heat cookery. Over the years I have gradually reduced the temperature at which I like to cook stews, daubes, ragoûts and casseroles to 225°F. (Mark $\frac{1}{4}$) or 250°F. (Mark $\frac{1}{2}$). And when cooking on top of the stove I like to use an asbestos or wire mat to help keep the cooking down to a faint, barely perceptible simmer. This low oven temperature is not hot enough to bring the ingredients up to simmering point so before you put the casserole into the oven, make sure you bring it gently to the bubble on top of the stove.

If you do not know your oven very well, it is a good idea, the first few times you use this method, to check up on the state of the casserole rather more frequently than you would do otherwise. Thermostats vary, and you may find you have to adjust the setting slightly to keep the casserole at simmering point.

'Dry' Casserole Cooking

In this version you add no liquid at all. The simplest example (French Casserole of Beef, page 373) sautés plenty of onions, adds the beef, cut into 2-inch cubes, seasoning and a fresh lump of butter for flavour, covers the casserole and leaves it to simmer very gently. When you lift off the lid after about 2 hours, you will find that the onions have dissolved into a delicious, abundant sauce that requires no further thickening or flavouring.

The only stipulation here is that the casserole be tightly covered.

In fact, you could go further and seal it hermetically with a simple flour and water paste to prevent any of the precious juices escaping.

To Finish a Casserole

When your casserole is cooked, your sauce may need thickening. If this is to involve simmering or boiling, lift the meat out first with a slotted spoon and keep it hot in a covered bowl. Next, skim the sauce of fat if necessary, either by drawing a spoon over the surface, or by 'dusting' it with sheets of absorbent kitchen paper until all the fat has been absorbed. To thicken the sauce, use one of the following:

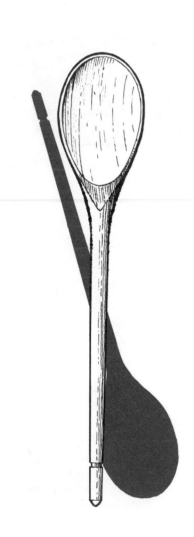

Reduction The simplest way, provided the casserole has not been too highly seasoned and already has some thickening – either 'melted' vegetables or a dusting of flour before the meat was sautéed – is to boil the sauce briskly, stirring constantly to stimulate evaporation, until it has reduced to the desired consistency. It can then be rubbed through a fine sieve or left as it is.

Beurre manié This is made by combining equal volumes (not weights) of butter and flour in a small bowl or cup, and mashing them to a smooth paste. Take up tiny pieces of this paste on the tip of your spoon and stir them into the simmering sauce. Because of its high butter content, the paste will have no difficulty in dissolving without giving the flour a chance to form lumps. Bring to the boil and simmer for 3 or 4 minutes to ensure flour is cooked and no longer tastes raw.

Flour or cornflour worked smoothly with water and stirred briskly into the simmering sauce (to prevent lumps forming) is a quick, if crude way, of thickening and one that I do not particularly like. Flour on its own tends to make a sauce unnecessarily heavy, and cornflour, while lighter and eminently suitable for some sauces, especially sweet ones, gives a characteristic 'slippery' texture quite out of place in a robust meat casserole. All in all, it is better to stick to the classic *beurre manié*.

Egg yolks For creamy blanquettes of veal and lamb and delicate chicken dishes, egg yolks make the ideal thickener, but they must be handled with care if your sauce is not to curdle.

First, the egg yolks are beaten lightly until thoroughly mixed, sometimes with cream, occasionally with a little flour to reinforce them. Then you dilute them with a few tablespoons of the sauce so that there will be enough of this cool mixture to lower the temperature of the hot sauce to a safe level when the two are combined.

Remove the pan of sauce from the heat and make sure it has come quite off the boil. Stir in the beaten egg yolk mixture, and when thoroughly blended, return the pan to a *low* heat.

Stir sauce until it thickens, taking the greatest possible care – particularly if no flour has been added – not to let it boil, or it will curdle.

Take the same precautions when reheating a casserole that has been thickened with egg yolks; stand the pan or casserole in a baking tin of hot water and let it warm up gradually over a low heat without coming to the boil.

Once you have finished your sauce, all that remains to be done is to correct the seasoning, return the meat to the sauce and make sure it is thoroughly hot again.

Basic Beef Stew

Serves 4

You will find all the basic rules of successful stewing and casseroling neatly wrapped up in this one simple dish: first, the steady browning of the meat and vegetables; secondly the reduction of the moistening agent to intensify flavour without swamping ingredients; thirdly, controlling the temperature so that the meat is at no time subjected to more than a faint simmering, whether it be cooked on top of the stove, or in the oven.

1 If you intend to use the oven, preheat it to cool (225°F. Mark ¼).

2 Cut beef into 1-inch cubes, removing gristle and excess fat as you go.

3 Put flour into a strong paper bag and season generously with salt and freshly ground black pepper.

4 Put beef cubes in the bag, a handful at a time, and shake well, holding bag firmly shut. Repeat until cubes are all evenly coated with a good dusting of flour.

2 lb stewing beef
4 level tablespoons flour
Salt and freshly ground black pepper
5–6 level tablespoons butter or beef dripping
3–4 Spanish onions, thinly sliced
6 medium-sized carrots, thickly sliced
1 pint beef stock (page 161)
Generous pinch of mixed herbs

5 In a large, deep frying-pan, melt 3 level tablespoons butter or dripping and sauté thinly sliced onions over a moderate heat until soft and golden brown. Transfer to a heavy, flameproof casserole with a slotted spoon.

6 Add remaining butter or dripping to the pan and sauté thickly sliced carrots until they, too, are richly browned. Remove carrots to casserole.

7 Add a little more fat to the frying-pan if necessary and sauté beef cubes over a steady heat until richly browned all over. (Do not attempt to fry more beef cubes at a time than will fit into the pan in one layer.) Transfer to casserole.

8 Pour stock into the frying-pan and bring to the boil, scraping bottom and sides with a wooden spoon to dislodge all the flavoursome morsels stuck there. Continue boiling and stirring until stock is reduced to about half the original quantity.

9 Stir reduced stock into meat and vegetables, and add a generous pinch of mixed herbs.

10 Cover casserole tightly and *either* simmer very gently indeed on top of the stove, stirring occasionally and using an asbestos mat if the heat cannot be lowered sufficiently; *or* transfer to the oven. In either case, meat should be meltingly tender within 2 hours, but test it after $1\frac{1}{2}$ hours if you are using one of the better cuts.

11 Correct seasoning; skim if necessary and serve.

French Beef Stew

Serves 4–6

2 1/2–3 lb lean beef
Flour
Salt and freshly ground black pepper
1 level tablespoon butter
2 tablespoons olive oil
1/2 lb fat salt pork, diced
2 Spanish onions, coarsely chopped
2 cloves garlic, chopped
Generous pinch of thyme
2 bay leaves, crumbled
1/3 pint red wine
1 beef stock cube
12 button mushrooms
12 button onions

1 Cut beef into 1- to $1\frac{1}{2}$-inch cubes, discarding fat and gristle. Toss in flour seasoned with salt and freshly ground black pepper.

2 Heat butter and olive oil in a heatproof casserole; when fat begins to bubble, add diced salt pork, chopped onions and garlic, and sauté until onions are soft and just begin to turn golden.

3 Add beef and thyme and crumbled bay leaves and cook, stirring frequently, until meat is well browned on all sides.

4 Pour red wine into a small pan and boil until reduced to half the original quantity.

5 Pour reduced wine over beef and add just enough boiling beef stock (made with a cube) to cover meat. Cover casserole and simmer slowly for about 2 hours, or until beef is tender and the sauce is thick.

6 Half an hour before beef is ready, add button mushrooms and onions.

7 Correct seasoning with more salt or freshly ground black pepper, and serve straight from the casserole.

Note: A tablespoon or two of red wine just before serving will add extra bouquet to this dish.

French Casserole of Beef

This fabulously flavoured French casserole uses down-to-earth shin of beef cut into 2-inch cubes to make one of the richest stews you've ever tasted. You start with no liquid at all and yet finish with an abundant sauce.

1 Preheat oven to cool (225°F. Mark ¼).

2 Cut beef into cubes about 2 inches square, discarding excess fat and gristle.

3 Combine olive oil and half the butter in a heavy casserole and sauté thinly sliced onions over a moderate heat until soft and just beginning to turn golden.

4 Dust beef with well-seasoned flour. Add to casserole and sauté, stirring constantly, until beef is well-browned.

5 Add garlic, dried orange peel, cloves, *bouquet garni* and the remaining butter. Cover casserole tightly and bake in the oven for 2 hours, or until meat is meltingly tender and onions have disintegrated into a thick, highly flavoured brown sauce. Alternatively, simmer the casserole on top of the stove over the lowest possible heat for the same length of time, using an asbestos mat to protect it if it starts cooking too fast.

6 Remove orange peel and *bouquet garni*; skim sauce; correct seasoning and serve.

Serves 4–6

2 1/2 lb shin of beef
4 tablespoons olive oil
4 oz butter
4 Spanish onions, thinly sliced
Salt and freshly ground black pepper
Flour
2 cloves garlic
1 strip orange peel which you have dried out in the oven
2 cloves
Bouquet garni (2 sprigs thyme, 4 sprigs parsley, 2 bay leaves)

A 3-lb joint lean top rump
   of beef
3 cloves garlic, quartered
4 oz fat salt pork (with rind)
3 tablespoons olive oil
4 shallots, finely chopped
4 tomatoes, peeled, seeded
   and coarsely chopped
2 cloves garlic, finely
   chopped
12 button onions
4 oz button mushrooms,
   quartered
4 sprigs parsley
1/2 pint well-flavoured beef
   stock (page 161)

Marinade
3 slices lemon
1 bay leaf
Pinch of thyme
1 level tablespoon finely
   chopped mixed herbs
   (parsley, tarragon, chives)
1/4 pint dry white wine
3 tablespoons olive oil
Salt and freshly ground black
   pepper

Daube of Beef à l'Ancienne

To be started the day before serving.

1 Make 12 small incisions all over top rump of beef with the tip of a sharp knife and bury a quarter-clove of garlic in each one.

2 Combine marinade ingredients in a large bowl, adding salt and freshly ground black pepper to taste. Add meat and marinate for 12 hours (or overnight), turning meat occasionally.

3 Drain beef thoroughly, reserving marinade, and pat it dry.

4 Remove rind from the piece of fat salt pork and reserve it. Dice pork and sauté in olive oil until golden.

5 Remove pork bits; over a steady heat brown beef thoroughly on all sides in the resulting amalgamation of pork fat and olive oil.

6 Preheat oven to cool (225°F. Mark $\frac{1}{4}$).

7 Place pork rind in the bottom of a heavy, ovenproof casserole. Lay joint of beef on top and surround with sautéed pork bits, finely chopped shallots, tomatoes, garlic, whole button onions, quartered button mushrooms and parsley sprigs. Strain reserved marinade juices over meat and add beef stock.

8 Bring casserole to the boil over a very low heat; then cover tightly and transfer to the oven.

9 Bake casserole for $1\frac{3}{4}$ to $2\frac{1}{4}$ hours, or until meat is meltingly tender, checking occasionally that liquid in casserole never advances beyond the faintest simmer.

10 To serve: remove beef to a heated platter. Spoon over some of the pan juices and pour remainder into a heated sauce boat. Serve meat in thick slices, accompanied by pan juices and whipped potatoes (page 123).

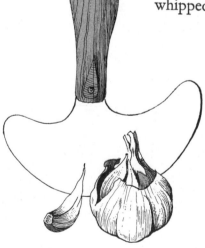

Beef Pot Roast with Madeira Mushroom Sauce

Serves 6–8

A rich pot roast which improves even further if left overnight (the joint kept whole) or prepared in the morning, and reheated again in a slow oven before serving.

1 Cut fat salt pork or bacon into small strips. Make quite deep incisions at regular intervals all over beef with the point of a sharp knife, and push strips of fat in as deeply as possible.

2 Preheat oven to cool (225°F. Mark $\frac{1}{4}$).

3 Melt butter in a heavy, 5- or 6-pint casserole, and brown meat richly and evenly over a steady, moderate heat, together with finely chopped carrots and onions.

4 When meat is thoroughly browned all over, add herbs and quartered, seeded tomatoes. Pour in stock and dry white wine, and season to taste with salt and freshly ground black pepper. Bring to simmering point over a low heat. Cover pan tightly and transfer to the oven. Bake for about $2\frac{1}{2}$ hours, with the pan juices barely at simmering point, turning joint and basting it occasionally with its own pan juices.

5 When meat is tender, remove it from the pan and keep hot.

6 Skim pan juices of excess fat if necessary, and rub juices and vegetables through a fine sieve. Pour back into the casserole and boil vigorously, stirring, until reduced by one-half.

7 Return meat to the casserole together with sliced mushrooms. Bring to simmering point again. Replace cover and return casserole to the oven (or simmer very, very gently on top of the stove) for about 45 minutes longer to finish cooking and allow flavours to develop and fuse.

8 Just before serving, lift out meat, allowing juices to drain back into casserole. Slice meat thickly and arrange on a heated serving platter. Keep hot.

9 To finish sauce: stir in cream and Madeira, and simmer over a low heat until slightly thickened, stirring constantly and scraping bottom and sides of casserole with a wooden spoon. Correct seasoning carefully, adding more salt or freshly ground black pepper if necessary.

10 Spoon some of the sauce over beef slices and serve remainder separately in a heated sauce boat.

8 oz fat salt pork or streaky bacon, in one piece

A 4-lb joint of topside of beef

3–4 oz butter

4 large carrots, very finely chopped

4 Spanish onions, very finely chopped

2 sprigs parsley

2 sprigs thyme or 1/2 level teaspoon dried thyme

2 small bay leaves

8 ripe tomatoes, quartered and seeded

1 pint rich beef stock (page 161)

8–10 tablespoons dry white wine

Salt and freshly ground black pepper

1 lb button mushrooms, thinly sliced

1/3 pint (7 fluid oz) double cream

8 tablespoons Madeira

Serves 6

2 lb lean stewing steak, e.g.
buttock, cut in 2 slices
3/4 to 1 inch thick
4 level tablespoons flour
Salt and freshly ground black
pepper
2 Spanish onions, sliced
Butter
Olive oil
About 1/2 pint beef stock
(page 161)
1/2 pint Madeira
1/2 lb button onions
1/2 lb baby carrots or 1/4 lb
button mushroom caps
Sugar
Lemon juice
4 level tablespoons finely
chopped parsley

Madeira Steak Casserole

1 Preheat oven to cool (250°F. Mark ½).

2 Trim beef slices of fat and gristle if necessary.

3 Season flour with 1 level teaspoon salt and freshly ground black pepper, to taste. Coat beef slices with seasoned flour; lay them on a firm surface and pound them out with a meat mallet or rolling pin to about half their original thickness. Divide slices into 6 neat, even-sized portions. Put aside.

4 In a large, heavy frying-pan, sauté sliced onions steadily in 2 level tablespoons each butter and olive oil until soft and a rich golden brown colour, 10 to 15 minutes. Transfer to a heatproof casserole with a slotted spoon, leaving behind as much of the fat as possible.

5 Add a further 2 tablespoons butter and oil to the frying pan, and when hot, brown steaks thoroughly on both sides, two at a time. Transfer to the casserole and keep hot.

6 When all the steaks have been browned, pour off any fat remaining in the pan. Add ½ pint each beef stock and Madeira, and bring to the boil, scraping bottom and sides of pan clean with a wooden spoon. Boil briskly, stirring, until liquid is reduced by about one-third. Pour over steak and onions.

7 Heat casserole gently on top of the stove until it barely comes to simmering point. Cover tightly and transfer to the oven.

8 Bake casserole for 2 hours, or until meat is tender enough to cut with a fork, adding a little more stock if necessary.

9 While casserole is in the oven, prepare vegetable garnish. You can use button onions and either baby carrots (or thickly sliced large carrots) or button mushroom caps.

Glazed button onions Place button onions in a heavy pan with 2 level tablespoons butter, 2 level teaspoons castor sugar and 8 tablespoons stock. Press a sheet of greaseproof paper down on top of them; bring to the boil and simmer until onions are soft and stock has evaporated. Then caramelise onions in the butter left behind, shaking pan gently so that they turn an even, golden colour.

Glazed carrots Prepare in the same way as button onions, but do not allow them to colour so deeply. If carrots are young, more stock may be needed to soften them.

Sautéed mushroom caps Wipe mushroom caps clean and sauté until softened in a mixture of half butter/half olive oil with a generous squeeze of lemon juice to keep them white.

10 Fifteen minutes before casserole is ready to serve, remove it from the oven. Skim sauce of fat if necessary. Add vegetable garnish and finely chopped parsley. Taste for seasoning, adding more salt or freshly ground black pepper, if necessary. Then cover casserole and return to the oven for a final 15 minutes. Serve immediately.

Note: If preferred, sauce may be strained and remains of sliced onions discarded before skimming and adding vegetable garnish.

Boeuf à la Bourguignonne

Serves 6

Indisputably one of the great dishes of France, worth every penny and every minute spent on it.

Start it the day before you intend to serve it to allow full marinating time – indeed, if you can plan it so that the casserole is *cooked* and left for 24 hours before serving, its flavour will be finer still.

Serve with plain boiled or steamed potatoes, or rice, or noodles.

1 The day before cooking the casserole, cut beef into neat, 1-inch cubes and put them in a large china or earthenware bowl.

2 To marinate beef: measure off about ¼ pint red wine and reserve it in a corked bottle for use the following day.

3 Pour the rest of the bottle of wine over beef. Add remaining ingredients listed for marinade and mix well. Cover bowl tightly with foil and leave overnight in a cool place.

4 The following day, start by blanching the pig's trotter (or calf's foot): wash it thoroughly; cover with cold water and bring to the boil over a moderate heat, adding a pinch of salt to bring the scum to the surface. Drain thoroughly and cool under the cold tap. Put aside.

5 Remove beef from marinade with a slotted spoon, letting as much liquid as possible drain back into the bowl. Put aside.

6 Pour marinade, including vegetables, into a saucepan. Bring to the boil and boil vigorously until reduced by about half.

7 In another pan, melt 2 level tablespoons butter. Blend in 2 level tablespoons flour with a wooden spoon and stir over a low heat to make a nutty brown *roux*.

8 Gradually add beef stock, stirring vigorously to prevent lumps forming, and bring to the boil, stirring. Add pig's trotter (or

3 lb topside of beef
1 pig's trotter or a piece of calf's foot
Salt
Butter
Flour
1 pint lightly seasoned beef stock (page 161)
2 tablespoons olive oil
2 level tablespoons finely diced fat salt pork
4 tablespoons brandy
Freshly ground black pepper

Marinade
1 bottle full-bodied red wine
2 Spanish onions, thinly sliced
2 large carrots, thinly sliced
2 stalks celery, thinly sliced
1 clove garlic, peeled
2 sprigs parsley
1 sprig thyme
1 bay leaf
2 tablespoons olive oil

Vegetable garnish
18 button onions, peeled
1/4 pint chicken stock (page 162)
1/2 level teaspoon sugar
2 level tablespoons butter
24 tight button mushrooms

calf's foot) and simmer, stirring frequently, until sauce has reduced by half, about 20 minutes.

9 Preheat oven to cool (225°F. Mark $\frac{1}{4}$).

10 Select a heavy, heatproof casserole large enough to hold beef comfortably, with room to spare for pig's trotter (or calf's foot) and the reduced marinade and stock sauce. Heat oil in it; add diced fat salt pork and sauté until transparent.

11 Dry beef cubes carefully with plenty of kitchen paper. Add beef to the casserole and brown on all sides over a steady, moderate heat.

12 Remove casserole from heat. Heat brandy in a metal ladle; ignite it and pour it over meat in casserole.

13 When flames die down, add the reduced marinade (with vegetables), stock sauce and pig's trotter (or calf's foot). Season to taste with salt and freshly ground black pepper and, with the casserole over a very low heat, bring to simmering point.

14 As soon as casserole simmers, remove from heat; cover tightly and transfer to the preheated oven.

15 Bake casserole for 3 hours, or until meat is meltingly tender but not disintegrating. During this time, the casserole should be taken out of the oven two or three times and the beef stirred; then brought back to simmering point over a low heat before replacing the lid and returning the casserole to the oven.

16 While beef is cooking, prepare the vegetable garnish: put button onions in a heavy pan with chicken stock, sugar and 1 level tablespoon butter. Bring to the boil; simmer until onions are tender and stock has evaporated; then continue to cook, shaking pan constantly, until onions are richly and evenly glazed. Put aside.

17 Wipe button mushrooms clean; trim stems and sauté mushrooms in remaining butter until tender and golden. Put aside.

18 Pour reserved $\frac{1}{4}$ pint wine into a small pan, enamelled if possible. Bring to the boil and boil hard until reduced to 2 tablespoons. Put aside.

19 When beef is tender, transfer it to a deep dish with a slotted spoon. Cover and keep hot.

20 Discard pig's trotter (or calf's foot).

21 Skim sauce; strain it through a fine sieve and return to the rinsed-out pan. Bring to the boil; simmer until slightly reduced and, if necessary, thicken with 2 to 3 level tablespoons *beurre*

manié (see page 370). Stir reduced wine into sauce and season carefully – sauce may already be adequately seasoned by the initial reduction of the stock.

22 Return beef to the sauce. Add button onions and mushrooms, and reheat gently, stirring and turning contents of casserole over to ensure that every morsel is thoroughly coated. Serve hot.

Boeuf à la Mode

To be started the day before serving.

1 Have your butcher lard the joint of beef with strips of larding pork fat, or do it yourself, using a special larding needle to draw the fat right through the length of the meat (see page 71). Season lightly with salt and freshly ground black pepper.

2 Combine marinade ingredients in a large porcelain or earthen-ware bowl. Turn beef in the marinade to coat it thoroughly; cover bowl and leave beef to marinate overnight, turning it over once or twice to ensure that it absorbs flavours evenly and remains well coated.

3 The following day, remove beef from marinade. Drain thoroughly and pat dry with kitchen paper. Reserve marinade.

4 Select a heavy, heatproof casserole large enough to hold beef comfortably (with room to spare for veal bones, etc., and the reduced marinade and stock sauce).

5 Melt dripping or lard in the casserole. When it is very hot, add the beef and brown well on all sides over a steady, moderate heat. Pour off excess fat. Cover casserole and put aside for the moment.

6 Pour marinade (including vegetables) into a saucepan and boil vigorously until reduced by half.

7 Meanwhile, in another pan melt 2 level tablespoons butter; blend in flour with a wooden spoon and stir over a low heat to make a nutty brown *roux*.

8 Gradually incorporate stock into *roux*, stirring constantly to prevent lumps forming. Bring to the boil, stirring; add veal knuckle and calf's foot or pig's trotter, both of which you have first blanched to prevent them throwing up scum into the sauce, and simmer, stirring frequently, for about 20 minutes, or until sauce has reduced by about half.

9 Preheat oven to cool (225°F. Mark ¼).

10 When marinade and sauce have reduced, pour them both

Serves 8

A 4- to 5-lb rolled joint of beef (topside or silverside), larded (see Step 1)

Salt and freshly ground black pepper

2 level tablespoons dripping or lard

4 level tablespoons butter

2 level tablespoons flour

1 pint well-flavoured beef stock (page 161)

1–1 1/2 lb veal knuckle bones, chopped and blanched

A piece of calf's foot or a pig's trotter, blanched

6 large carrots

24 button onions

2 level teaspoons sugar

Marinade

1 pint robust red wine

1 large Spanish onion, sliced

2 large carrots, sliced

2 cloves garlic

2 stalks celery, sliced

4 sprigs parsley

2 sprigs thyme

3–4 allspice berries

2 small bay leaves

4 tablespoons brandy

2 tablespoons olive oil

over the beef and surround with vegetables, knuckle bones and calf's foot or trotter. Bring to simmering point again; cover casserole tightly and transfer to the oven.

11 Bake for 2 hours. During this time, the casserole should be taken out of the oven two or three times for the beef to be turned and basted; then brought back to simmering point over a low heat before returning to the oven.

12 Meanwhile, peel carrots and cut them into sticks about 1 inch long and $\frac{1}{4}$ inch thick. Drop into boiling water; simmer for 5 minutes; drain and put aside.

13 At the same time, peel button onions and put them in a heavy pan with remaining butter. Sprinkle with sugar and cook over a high heat, stirring constantly, for 5 to 6 minutes until onions are well browned and caramelised. Put aside.

14 Remove beef from the casserole and strain sauce through a fine sieve. Return both to the casserole, together with prepared carrots and onions. Bring up to simmering point again; cover tightly and return to the oven for a further 2 hours, or until beef is meltingly tender. As before, it should be turned occasionally and the casserole brought back to simmering point before returning to the oven.

15 When beef is tender, lift it out on to a hot serving dish and discard trussing strings. Surround beef with button onions and carrot strips, and keep hot.

16 Skim sauce by drawing sheets of kitchen paper over the surface until no more fat is absorbed. Simmer, stirring, until reduced by about half, or less if you prefer a thinner but more abundant sauce.

17 Spoon some of the sauce over beef and vegetables, and serve remainder separately in a heated sauceboat. Serve meat thinly sliced across the grain to show off larding.

Pot-roasted Veal à la Suisse

Veal is an awkward meat to cook: it can be superbly flavoured or tasteless; moist or paper-dry, tender or rubbery, depending on its origin. If you are doubtful about it, this dish is the perfect answer: pot-roasting ensures that it remains moist and succulent, while the thin slices of Gruyère and raw ham with which you interleave it will transform the dullest joint without overwhelming its flavour, and turn a good joint into sheer magic.

For a really neat job, chill the meat thoroughly before carrying out Steps 1–3; then let it come to room temperature before going ahead with the rest of the recipe.

1 Choose a long thin joint of veal for roasting rather than a short one with a large diameter. Lay it on a board and, with a sharp knife, cut it into 7 even-sized slices (i.e. 6 cuts) without separating them completely – just as you would a French loaf for garlic bread. Open the slices out carefully and season generously with salt, freshly ground black pepper and a pinch of freshly grated nutmeg.

2 Lay a slice each of raw ham and Gruyère cheese neatly in each cut.

3 Pull the joint together again. Cover it with long, thin strips of fat salt pork or smoked bacon and tie up securely with string, first lengthwise and then horizontally in several places.

4 In a heavy, flameproof casserole which will hold the joint comfortably, melt half the butter and sauté veal until nicely browned all over. Remove from casserole and keep hot.

5 In the same fat, sauté finely chopped carrots and onions until golden brown.

6 Meanwhile, combine wine and crushed garlic clove in a small pan, and bring to the boil.

7 Lay veal on top of sautéed vegetables. Pour over brandy and flame.

8 As soon as flames have died down, moisten casserole with the boiling wine and garlic. Put a lid three-quarters on the pan and simmer over the lowest possible heat (diffused with an asbestos mat if you have one handy) for about 1 hour, or until veal is tender but not overcooked.

9 Meanwhile, fit button onions into the bottom of a heavy pan that will take them in one layer – this is important, otherwise onions will not glaze evenly. Add castor sugar, 1 level tablespoon butter, salt and freshly ground black pepper, to taste, and just enough water to cover.

A 2- to 2 1/2-lb joint of boned veal for roasting, rolled and tied

Salt and freshly ground black pepper

Freshly grated nutmeg

6 very thin slices (about 2 oz) raw ham: prosciutto, Westphalian or jambon de Bayonne

6 thin slices (about 4 oz) Gruyère

4–5 oz fat salt pork or fat smoked bacon, cut into long thin strips

4 oz butter

2 carrots, finely chopped

2 medium-sized onions, finely chopped

1/4 pint dry white wine

1 clove garlic, crushed

3 tablespoons brandy

30 button onions, peeled

1 level tablespoon castor sugar

24 tight white button mushrooms, thickly sliced

1/4 pint double cream

10 Bring to the boil and boil, uncovered, until liquid has completely evaporated, tossing occasionally towards the end to glaze the onions evenly.

11 In another pan, sauté thickly sliced mushrooms in 2 level tablespoons butter for 4 or 5 minutes until tender and golden. Sprinkle with salt and freshly ground black pepper, and put aside.

12 When veal is tender, remove it from the casserole; discard strings and keep meat hot on a heated serving dish while you finish sauce.

13 Strain sauce through a fine sieve, pressing some of the vegetables through as well. Return to the casserole; stir in cream and reheat gently without boiling. Correct seasoning.

14 Toss glazed onions and sautéed mushrooms in remaining butter for 2 to 3 minutes to heat them through.

15 To serve: garnish veal with onions and mushrooms. Spoon some of the sauce over the meat and vegetables, and serve remainder in a heated sauceboat.

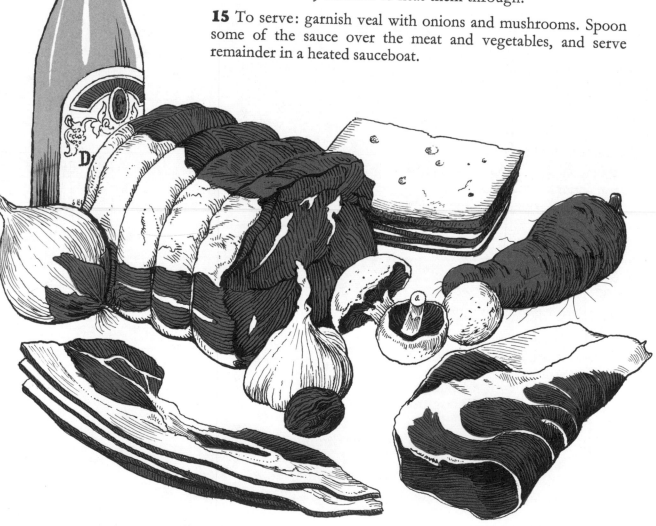

Blanquette de Veau

This recipe 'acidulates' the pieces of veal to ensure a pale creamy-coloured *blanquette*. Try this recipe, too, with lamb or chicken.

1 Cut shoulder or breast of veal, or a combination of the two, into 1½-inch cubes, discarding fat and gristle.

2 Place in a large bowl with the juice and rind of 1 lemon; cover with cold water and allow veal to 'blanch' for 12 hours, changing water two or three times.

3 Drain veal; place in a casserole; add stock; bring to simmering point and add coarsely chopped vegetables, the *bouquet garni* and the onion stuck with cloves. Cover and simmer over a low heat for 1¼ hours, or until veal is tender.

4 Wash button mushrooms, trim stalks and simmer mushrooms in a frying pan in 1 oz melted butter, sprinkling them with a few drops of lemon juice to preserve their colour. Cover and simmer gently until softened.

5 Melt another 1 oz butter in another pan and sauté button onions until golden, adding 2 tablespoons stock from the pan of veal. Season to taste with salt and freshly ground black pepper.

6 When veal is tender, remove pieces from pan with a slotted spoon and keep hot. Strain pan juices through a fine sieve into a bowl.

7 Rinse the pan and dry it thoroughly.

8 Melt 1 oz butter in the pan; add flour and stir over a low heat for 2 or 3 minutes to make a pale *roux*. Gradually add strained pan juices and bring to the boil, stirring constantly until sauce is smooth, then simmer for 2 or 3 minutes longer.

9 Add mushrooms and onions to the sauce; mix well and simmer for 10 minutes.

10 Beat egg yolks with cream and 1 tablespoon lemon juice. Beat in a few tablespoons of the hot sauce; then pour back into the pan and stir over a low heat until sauce thickens, taking care not to let it come to the boil, or it may curdle.

11 Add veal to the sauce and heat through for a few minutes longer, taking the same care not to let the pan come to boiling point. Serve *blanquette* immediately, garnished with finely chopped parsley, and accompanied by plain boiled or steamed rice.

Serves 4–6

- 2 1/2 lb boned shoulder or breast of veal
- 1 lemon
- 2 pints veal or chicken stock (page 162)
- 2 carrots, coarsely chopped
- 2 leeks, white part only, coarsely chopped
- *Bouquet garni* (2 sprigs parsley, 1 sprig thyme, 1 small bay leaf)
- 1 Spanish onion, stuck with 2 cloves
- 24 small button mushrooms
- Butter
- Lemon juice
- 24 button onions
- Salt and freshly ground black pepper
- 1 oz flour
- 2 egg yolks
- 4 level tablespoons double cream
- 2 level tablespoons finely chopped parsley

Serves 4–6

2 1/2 lb boned leg of veal
2 Spanish onions, finely
 chopped
2 cloves garlic, finely
 chopped
4 level tablespoons lard
2 level tablespoons paprika
1/4 level teaspoon caraway
 seeds
1/4 level teaspoon cayenne
 pepper
Generous pinch each of
 marjoram and thyme
Salt and freshly ground black
 pepper
2 bay leaves, crumbled
4 sweet red peppers
1 lb button mushrooms
1 14-oz can peeled tomatoes
Paprika
Finely chopped parsley
1/2 pint sour cream

Hungarian Veal Gulyas

Hungarian *gulyas* is not particularly remarkable – until you add the sour cream, and then it becomes one of the best casseroles I know.

1 Preheat oven to cool (250°F. Mark ½).

2 Cut veal into neat 1½-inch cubes, discarding any fat or gristle.

3 In a heavy, flameproof casserole, sauté finely chopped onions and garlic in lard for 3 to 4 minutes, or until soft and transparent.

4 Add veal and continue to sauté until meat is golden on all sides.

5 Sprinkle with paprika, caraway seeds, cayenne pepper, marjoram and thyme, and salt and freshly ground black pepper, to taste. Add crumbled bay leaves; mix well and cook gently for 10 minutes, stirring occasionally.

6 Core and seed peppers and slice thinly.

7 Wash mushrooms, trim stems and slice thinly.

8 Add peppers, mushrooms and canned tomatoes to casserole. Stir lightly and bring to simmering point over a very low heat.

9 Cover casserole tightly; transfer to the oven and cook for about 2 hours, or until veal is tender, stirring casserole occasionally.

10 Dust *gulyas* with paprika and finely chopped parsley, and serve with sour cream.

Normandy Pork with Apples

Serves 6

1 Preheat oven to cool (225°F. Mark ¼).

2 Divide pork into chops, allowing 1 large one or 2 small ones per person. Dust chops all over with well-seasoned flour.

3 In a heavy, flameproof casserole, heat olive oil with 1 level tablespoon butter and sauté finely chopped onion until a deep golden colour. Add blanched garlic cloves and allow them to colour lightly – be careful not to let them brown, though, or they will leave a bitter flavour. Discard garlic cloves and put sautéed onion aside on a small dish.

4 Sauté pork chops in remaining fat until well browned on both sides. Add button onions; sprinkle with crushed rosemary and sauté for 2 to 3 minutes longer.

5 Pour cider and chicken stock into the casserole, and scrape bottom and sides clean of crusty bits with a wooden spoon. Return sautéed onion to the pan, and add *bouquet garni*.

6 Cover casserole tightly; transfer to the oven and cook for 1½ hours. (Or, if more convenient, cook on top of the stove over the lowest possible heat, with an asbestos mat underneath for added protection.)

7 Peel, core and cut apples into eighths. Sauté in remaining butter until golden but not disintegrating; transfer apples to casserole with a slotted spoon and continue cooking for about ½ hour longer, or until meat is tender and apple slices soft but still in shape.

8 To serve: discard *bouquet garni*. Arrange chops in a deep, heated serving dish. Garnish with apples and button onions, and coat with pan juices.

2 lb loin of pork
Salt and freshly ground black pepper
2–3 level tablespoons flour
2 tablespoons olive oil
4 level tablespoons butter
1 Spanish onion, finely chopped
3–4 cloves garlic, peeled and blanched
18 button onions
1/4 level teaspoon crushed rosemary
1/2 pint cider
1/2 pint chicken stock (page 162)
Bouquet garni (parsley, thyme, 1 stalk celery, bay leaf)
2 lb Cox's orange pippins

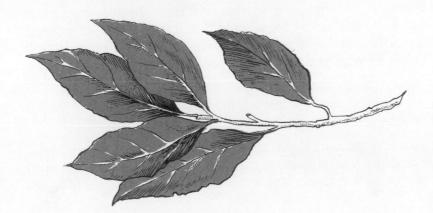

1 3/4 lb lean boned stewing
  lamb
Salt and freshly ground black
  pepper
Flour
2 tablespoons oil
1 level tablespoon butter
1/2 pint chicken stock, made
  with a cube
1 15-oz can Italian peeled
  tomatoes
1 clove garlic, very finely
  chopped
4 medium-sized carrots
8 button onions
4 small potatoes
8 oz frozen peas
2 level tablespoons finely
  chopped parsley

Basic Lamb Stew with Tomatoes

1 Cut lamb into 1- to 1½-inch cubes, discarding fat and gristle. Toss in seasoned flour until well coated.

2 Heat oil and butter in a heavy pan or flameproof casserole, and sauté lamb cubes over a steady heat until richly browned all over.

3 Stir in stock, Italian peeled tomatoes and garlic, and season to taste with salt and freshly ground black pepper.

4 Bring to the boil; lower heat; cover pan and simmer gently for 1½ hours, or until meat is almost tender.

5 Meanwhile, scrape carrots; halve them if they are thick and cut them into 2-inch lengths. Peel button onions. Peel and halve potatoes.

6 Add prepared vegetables to the stew and simmer, uncovered, for about 20 minutes, or until they, in their turn, are practically cooked.

7 Finally, stir in frozen peas and finely chopped parsley, and simmer until tender, about 5 minutes. Correct seasoning and serve.

Serves 4

1 3- to 3 1/2-lb roasting
  chicken
1 tablespoon olive oil
2 level tablespoons butter
3/4 pint chicken stock (page
  162)
2 leeks, white parts only,
  thinly sliced
1 carrot, thinly sliced
1 stalk celery, thinly sliced
8 button mushrooms
1 teaspoon lemon juice
4 level tablespoons finely
  chopped watercress leaves
1/4 pint double cream
2 egg yolks
Salt and freshly ground black
  pepper

Poulet au Cresson

1 Divide chicken into 8 joints, two from each leg and two from each breast. Skin them and wipe them dry.

2 In a shallow, heatproof casserole or sauté pan, large enough to take all the chicken pieces in one layer, heat olive oil with half the butter and sauté chicken joints, a few at a time, until golden on all sides.

3 Pour off fat remaining in the casserole and return chicken joints to it. Add chicken stock and thinly sliced leeks, carrot and celery. Bring to the boil over a moderate heat; then lower heat to a gentle simmer and cook, uncovered, for 15 minutes, turning chicken joints frequently.

4 Meanwhile, wipe button mushrooms clean. Trim stems and slice mushrooms thinly.

5 In a small pan, melt remaining butter. Add sliced mushrooms; sprinkle with lemon juice and sauté for 5 minutes, or until mushrooms are tender and most of their moisture has evaporated.

6 When chicken has been simmering for 15 minutes, add sautéed mushroom slices and continue to cook for a further 15 minutes, turning joints frequently as before.

7 Meanwhile, combine finely chopped watercress, cream and egg yolks in a bowl. Mix well and season to taste with salt and freshly ground black pepper.

8 When chicken joints are tender, transfer them to a deep, heated serving dish and keep hot in a cool oven while you finish sauce.

9 Mix a few tablespoons of the hot sauce with watercress cream. Remove casserole from heat and pour in watercress mixture, stirring vigorously. Return casserole to a low heat and stir sauce until it thickens just enough to coat chicken. This will take 10 to 15 minutes. Take great care not to let sauce boil, or egg yolks will curdle and ruin its appearance. Season sauce to taste with salt and freshly ground black pepper.

10 Spoon sauce and vegetables over chicken joints and serve immediately.

Quick Chicken Paprika

1 Preheat oven to moderate (375°F. Mark 5).

2 Skin chicken and cut it into 8 joints: 2 from each breast and 2 from each leg. Arrange joints in a casserole.

3 In a large, deep frying pan, heat butter and oil; add chopped onion and sauté gently for 10 to 15 minutes until very soft and golden but not brown.

4 Stir in paprika and continue to cook over a low heat for 2 to 3 minutes longer. Remove pan from heat.

5 Stir in contents of can of tomatoes; return to a low heat and slowly bring to the boil, stirring and mashing tomatoes with a spoon to reduce them to a purée. Simmer for 1 minute and remove from heat.

6 Stir in sour cream and chicken stock, and season to taste with salt, freshly ground black pepper and a generous pinch of sugar.

7 Rub sauce through a sieve over chicken joints in casserole. Cover casserole tightly and bake in the oven for 25 to 30 minutes until chicken is thoroughly hot and has absorbed some of the flavour of the sauce.

8 To serve: arrange chicken joints in the centre of a large, heated serving dish. Heap a ring of pilaff rice around them. Spoon

Serves 4

1 spit-roasted chicken, bought ready cooked, 3–3 1/2 lb
1 level tablespoon butter
1 tablespoon olive oil
1 large Spanish onion, very finely chopped
2 level teaspoons sweet paprika
1 8-oz can peeled tomatoes
1 1/4-pint carton sour cream
2 tablespoons chicken stock (page 162)
Salt and freshly ground black pepper
Generous pinch of sugar

To serve
Pilaff rice (page 417)
Sprigs of parsley
Thinly sliced cucumber

sauce over chicken. Garnish dish with tiny sprigs of parsley and an outer border of thin overlapping slices of cucumber.

Poulet en Cocotte Grand'mère

Serves 4

1 1/2 lb very small new potatoes
5 oz fat salt pork
3 level tablespoons butter
16–20 button onions
1 3- to 3 1/2-lb roasting chicken
Bouquet garni
Salt and freshly ground black pepper
2 level tablespoons finely chopped parsley

1 Preheat oven to moderate (350°F. Mark 4).

2 Scrape or peel new potatoes and pare them down if necessary so that they are all about the same size as the button onions. (You can, of course, use larger potatoes cut in half or quartered, and shaped with a knife into ovals to look like whole potatoes.)

3 Put potatoes in a pan; cover with cold water; bring to the boil over a moderate heat and drain thoroughly in a colander. Put aside.

4 Cut fat salt pork into 1/4-inch dice.

5 Melt 2 level tablespoons butter in a heavy, flameproof casserole just large enough to hold the chicken and vegetables comfortably. Add diced salt pork and button onions, and sauté over a moderately high heat until both are well browned.

6 Remove pork and onions with a slotted spoon; reserve.

7 In the resulting fat, brown chicken thoroughly on all sides over a steady heat. Remove from casserole and put aside.

8 Pour off fat from casserole into a bowl and leave for a few minutes to allow sediment to settle to the bottom. Meanwhile, wipe out casserole with kitchen paper.

9 Melt remaining butter in the casserole and carefully pour back in the fat, leaving sediment behind in the bowl.

10 Add potatoes and toss over a moderately high heat for 3 or 4 minutes until nicely browned all over.

11 Lay browned chicken in the centre of the casserole, and surround with potatoes, button onions and pork dice. Add *bouquet garni* and season well with salt and freshly ground black pepper. Cover casserole tightly.

12 Transfer casserole to the oven and pot-roast for 50 to 60 minutes, shaking casserole occasionally and only opening it when you wish to test the chicken: the juices should run clear when you pierce the thickest part of the leg closest to the body.

13 Transfer chicken to a very hot serving dish. Surround with vegetables and sprinkle with finely chopped parsley. Serve immediately. This dish is excellent when first made, but not particularly successful made in advance and reheated, as it tends to become heavy and greasy.

Poulet à l'Ail

(Chicken Casserole with Garlic I)

In this dish, garlic plays the role of a vegetable garnish as well as an aromatic. There is no need to feel apprehensive about 40 cloves of garlic – cooked in this way they are, if anything, less indigestible than a couple of finely chopped raw cloves of garlic would be. After all, we happily eat cooked stuffed onions as a dish in themselves, so why not garlic? It makes an unforgettable dish – rich and nutty and, strangely enough, not particularly strong in garlic flavour.

1 Preheat oven to cool (225°F. Mark ¼).

2 Wipe the chicken clean with a damp cloth and season both inside and out with salt and freshly ground black pepper.

3 Remove papery skins from garlic cloves, but leave them whole. Put garlic cloves in a small pan; cover with cold water; bring to boiling point and drain thoroughly. **Note:** garlic cloves must be plump and moist. Small dry cloves will be too strong in flavour.

4 Choose a heavy, flameproof casserole just large enough to hold the chicken comfortably, and equipped with a tight-fitting lid. In it sauté garlic cloves in 2 tablespoons each olive oil and butter for 3 to 4 minutes. Take the greatest care not to let the garlic cloves brown, or they will impart an unpleasantly bitter flavour to the whole dish. Remove garlic cloves from the casserole with a slotted spoon and reserve.

5 Add thinly sliced leeks to the casserole and sauté gently until slices are soft and a rich golden colour but not browned. Remove with a slotted spoon and put aside with the garlic cloves.

6 Add remaining oil and butter to the casserole. Raise heat and brown the chicken steadily and thoroughly on all sides.

7 Return sautéed garlic cloves and leeks to the casserole. Season to taste with salt and freshly ground black pepper; add the bay leaf and moisten casserole with wine and chicken stock.

8 Bring to the boil; cover casserole tightly and transfer to the oven. Bake for 1½ hours, or until chicken juices run clear when leg is pierced through the thickest part close to the body, and leeks have disintegrated to make a sauce.

9 Remove chicken from the casserole and place on a heated serving dish. Garnish with garlic cloves.

10 Skim pan juices; spoon some over chicken and serve remainder in a heated sauceboat.

Serves 4

1 3- to 3 1/2-lb chicken
Salt and freshly ground black pepper
40 plump whole cloves garlic (not dried ones)
3 tablespoons olive oil
3 level tablespoons butter
Whites of 4 fat leeks, thinly sliced
1 bay leaf
6–8 tablespoons dry white wine
6–8 tablespoons chicken stock

Serves 4

1 3- to 3 1/2-lb chicken, with
   giblets
Butter
Olive oil
2 oz fat salt pork, diced
20 plump whole cloves
   garlic, peeled
Bouquet garni (parsley,
   thyme, bay leaf)
Salt and freshly ground black
   pepper
Pinch of thyme
4–6 slices white bread

Poulet à l'Ail II
(Chicken Casserole with Garlic II)

1 With a damp cloth, wipe chicken clean both inside and out. Reserve the liver.

2 Select a heavy casserole large enough to hold chicken comfortably. Add 1 tablespoon each butter and olive oil, and fry chicken gently on all sides until skin is richly coloured, regulating heat so that the buttery cooking fat does not brown.

3 Add diced fat salt pork to the casserole; lower heat; add peeled whole garlic cloves and *bouquet garni*, and season contents of casserole generously with salt and freshly ground black pepper. Cover casserole tightly and simmer very, very gently until chicken is tender, $1\frac{3}{4}$ to 2 hours.

4 Towards the end of cooking time, sauté reserved liver in $\frac{1}{2}$ tablespoon each butter and oil just long enough to brown the exterior while remaining soft and pink inside. Dust with a pinch of thyme.

5 When chicken is tender, remove pork dice and garlic cloves from casserole with a slotted spoon. Rub them through a fine wire sieve (or purée in a vegetable mill) together with the sautéed liver. Blend purée thoroughly with a wooden spoon and taste for seasoning, adding more salt or freshly ground black pepper if necessary.

6 Discard *bouquet garni* from casserole and keep chicken and pan juices hot while you finish garnish.

7 Trim crusts from bread slices, cut slices into large triangles and toast lightly on both sides (or dry out slightly in the oven). Then sauté until crisp and golden in equal parts butter and olive oil.

8 Spread toast croûtons with garlic liver purée.

9 To serve: transfer chicken to a large, heated serving dish and garnish with croûtons. Skim pan juices if necessary and serve separately in a heated sauceboat. Straw potatoes (*pommes paille*) make a good accompaniment.

Poularde de Bresse à l'Estragon

Serves 4

Chickens from the region of Bresse are considered to be the finest in France. Their meat is particularly tender and succulent because of the corn on which they are fed.

Failing the genuine thing, try at least to use a free-range chicken or a chilled, as opposed to deep-frozen, bird, for in this exquisitely simple dish there is nothing behind which you can hope to camouflage an inferior flavour.

1 Wipe chicken clean both inside and out. Wash and dry giblets.

2 Lay half the tarragon sprigs in the cavity of the bird. Strip leaves from remaining sprigs and put stalks and leaves aside separately.

3 Season chicken all over with salt and freshly ground black pepper.

4 Select a heavy casserole just large enough to hold chicken comfortably. Melt butter in it and sauté chicken over a steady heat until a rich golden colour all over.

5 Pack giblets in around chicken, together with reserved tarragon stalks.

6 Cover casserole tightly and simmer over a low heat for $1\frac{1}{4}$ to $1\frac{1}{2}$ hours, or until chicken is tender and juices run clear and golden when you press a thin skewer into the thickest part of the leg closest to the body.

7 Remove chicken from casserole, allowing juices to drain back, and keep hot. Discard giblets and tarragon stalks.

8 Using a wooden spoon, stir chicken stock into juices remaining in casserole. Add reserved tarragon leaves and simmer for 2 to 3 minutes until juices have reduced by half, stirring and scraping bottom and sides of casserole clean with the spoon.

9 Beat cream with egg yolk until smoothly blended.

10 Lower heat under casserole even further; when juices have come off the boil, pour in cream mixture, stirring vigorously to blend them together smoothly. Continue to stir over a very low heat until sauce has thickened. Do not allow it to come to the boil, or egg yolk will curdle.

11 To serve: place chicken on a heated serving dish. Spoon sauce over the top and serve immediately. The simpler the accompaniment – potatoes, rice or a few noodles – the better, to avoid detracting from the delicate flavour.

1 3 1/2 lb roasting chicken, with giblets
4–6 sprigs fresh tarragon
Salt and freshly ground black pepper
4 level tablespoons butter
4–6 tablespoons chicken stock (page 162)
1/4 pint double cream
1 egg yolk

Serves 4–6

1 3 1/2 lb roasting chicken
4 oz unsmoked bacon, in one
 piece
3 level tablespoons butter
2 tablespoons olive oil
24 button onions, peeled
24 button mushrooms,
 trimmed
2 level tablespoons flour
Salt and freshly ground black
 pepper
2 cloves garlic, finely
 chopped
2 sprigs parsley
1 sprig thyme
2 small bay leaves
4 tablespoons brandy
1 pint full-bodied red wine
1/2 pint chicken stock (page
 162)
1 sugar lump
2 level tablespoons *beurre
 manié* (see step 15)
2 level tablespoons finely
 chopped parsley

Coq au Vin

1 Divide chicken into eight pieces, two from each breast and two from each leg. Wipe each piece dry.

2 Cut unsmoked bacon into $\frac{1}{4}$-inch dice.

3 In a large, heavy casserole, heat butter and olive oil, and sauté diced bacon until golden, 3 to 4 minutes.

4 Add button onions and mushrooms, and continue to sauté over a moderate heat until onions begin to turn transparent and mushrooms to brown. Remove from heat.

5 Remove onions, mushrooms and bacon bits from casserole with a slotted spoon. Keep warm.

6 Preheat oven to very slow (275°F. Mark 1).

7 Season flour with salt and freshly ground black pepper. Dust chicken pieces all over with seasoned flour.

8 Return casserole to the stove, and when fat is hot again, add chicken pieces. Sauté on one side for about 5 minutes, or until golden brown; then, using a blunt utensil to avoid piercing chicken, turn pieces over and sauté for 5 minutes on the other side. (You may find it more convenient to sauté chicken in two batches, in which case remove pieces as they begin to stiffen and keep them hot in a covered dish until they have all been prepared.)

9 Return sautéed onions, mushrooms and bacon bits to the casserole, together with finely chopped garlic, the parsley, thyme and bay leaves. Mix well with chicken pieces.

10 Cover casserole tightly and bake for 15 minutes.

11 Remove casserole from the oven. (Don't turn the oven off.) Lift out chicken pieces, vegetables etc. with a slotted spoon, and keep hot in a covered bowl.

12 Skim fat from juices left at the bottom of the casserole.

13 Place casserole over a high heat. Warm brandy in a soup ladle; pour it over juices and, standing well back, quickly set a match to it. Let the flames burn for a minute or two; then extinguish them by pouring in the wine and stock. Add sugar.

14 With casserole still over a high heat, bring sauce to the boil and reduce to half the original quantity.

15 Mash equal parts butter and flour smoothly to make a *beurre manié*. Stir tiny pieces of it into bubbling sauce, and simmer for a few minutes longer, stirring until they have 'dissolved' and sauce has thickened.

16 Strain sauce into a clean casserole. Add chicken pieces vegetables and bacon bits, and spoon sauce over them to coat' them thoroughly.

17 Bring casserole just to simmering point over a low heat; cover and return to the oven for 45 to 50 minutes, or until chicken pieces are tender and imbued with the flavour of the sauce.

18 Garnish with finely chopped parsley and serve hot, with plain boiled or steamed potatoes, which can be sprinkled with parsley as well.

Baked Egg and Potato Casserole

Serves 4

This is a first-class supper dish.

1 Preheat oven to moderate (375°F. Mark 5).

2 Peel and slice potatoes about $\frac{1}{16}$ inch thick. Put them in a pan with cold salted water to cover; bring to the boil over a moderate heat and drain in a colander.

3 Heat butter and oil in a large frying pan. Sauté finely chopped onion and bacon until onion is soft and golden; remove with a slotted spoon.

4 In the same fat, sauté parboiled potato slices over a moderate heat until golden brown on both sides and cooked through. Drain thoroughly and arrange in an even layer in a shallow, $2\frac{1}{2}$-pint gratin dish.

5 Scatter sautéed onion and bacon over the top and make 8 slight hollows in the surface. Break an egg carefully into each hollow.

6 Stir grated cheeses into cream and pour over the top. Season with a generous pinch of freshly ground black pepper.

7 Place gratin dish in a deep baking tin with hot water to come halfway up sides and bake for 10 to 12 minutes, or until eggs are just set, a minute or two longer if you prefer them slightly firmer. Serve immediately.

1 lb medium-sized potatoes
Salt
1 level tablespoon butter
1 tablespoon oil
1 medium-sized onion, finely chopped
4 level tablespoons finely chopped bacon
8 eggs
2 oz freshly grated Cheddar
2 oz freshly grated Parmesan
1/4 pint single cream
Freshly ground black pepper

Serves 4–5

Oxtail Stew

1 oxtail cut into sections
Seasoned flour
3 slices lean bacon
3 medium-sized carrots
2 medium-sized onions
2 small turnips
2 stalks celery
1 level tablespoon butter
1 tablespoon olive oil
1 pint beef (cube) stock
1/2 pint heavy red wine
1 clove garlic
A few parsley stalks
1/4 level teaspoon dried
  thyme
1 large bay leaf
6 black peppercorns
2 cloves
Beurre manié
1 level tablespoon tomato
  concentrate
Salt and freshly ground black
  pepper
2 level tablespoons finely
  chopped parsley

Vegetable garnish
12 small new potatoes
4 medium-sized carrots
12 button onions
12 button mushrooms

1 Trim excess fat from oxtail.

2 Put seasoned flour in a strong paper or plastic bag. Add oxtail, a few sections at a time, and, holding bag tightly closed, shake vigorously until meat is thoroughly coated with flour.

3 Chop bacon, carrots, onions, turnips and celery coarsely.

4 In a large, flameproof casserole, sauté chopped bacon until fat runs. Remove with a slotted spoon and put aside on a large plate.

5 Add butter and oil to casserole, and sauté oxtail sections over a moderate heat for 10 minutes, turning frequently, until well browned all over. The flour should darken considerably during this operation. Remove oxtail sections from casserole and put aside with bacon.

6 Cook chopped vegetables in fat remaining in casserole over a moderate heat for 10 to 15 minutes, or until soft and lightly coloured.

7 Return oxtail and bacon to casserole. Pour in stock (or $1\frac{1}{2}$ beef stock cubes, dissolved in 1 pint boiling water), $\frac{1}{2}$ pint red wine, garlic, parsley stalks, thyme, bay leaf, peppercorns and cloves.

8 Bring to the boil; skim froth from the top of the liquid; and then reduce heat to a bare simmer. Cover top of casserole with a double thickness of greaseproof paper and put on the lid. Cook for 3 hours over the lowest possible heat, checking occasionally that casserole maintains a gentle simmer.

9 Meanwhile, prepare vegetable garnish: peel potatoes, carrots and onions. Cut carrots into short lengths and round off edges with a potato peeler so that carrots, potatoes and button onions are all more or less the same size.

10 Wash or wipe mushrooms clean and trim stems.

11 Preheat oven to very slow (275°F. Mark 1).

12 When casserole has been simmering for 3 hours, lift the pieces of oxtail out with a slotted spoon.

13 Strain cooking liquid through a sieve into a 2-pint measuring jug, pressing vegetables against sides of sieve with a wooden spoon to extract all their juices without actually pushing them through.

14 Skim liquid of fat if necessary, using a spoon or by drawing squares of absorbent paper over the surface until no more fat is soaked up.

15 Note volume of stock; pour it back into casserole and reduce to about ¾ pint by fast boiling.

16 Make a *beurre manié* by mashing 1 level tablespoon each butter and flour to a smooth paste. Add to casserole in tiny pieces, stirring until they have quite dissolved. Then bring to the boil again and simmer for 2 minutes.

17 Blend tomato concentrate with 2 tablespoons hot sauce, stir into casserole.

18 Return oxtail pieces to casserole. Add prepared vegetable garnish, spooning sauce over them to make sure they are thoroughly coated. Bring to simmering point again; cover, transfer to the oven and bake for a further 2 hours, or until vegetables are soft and meat is practically falling off the bones.

19 Just before serving, taste and if necessary season with salt and freshly ground black pepper. Garnish with finely chopped parsley and serve from the casserole.

Tripe à la Provençale

Serves 4–6

1 Rinse tripe thoroughly. If you have bought it in a large sheet, cut it up into manageable chunks.

2 In a large pan, dissolve chicken stock cubes in 4 pints water. Add ½ level teaspoon salt and bring to the boil.

3 Meanwhile, tie components of *bouquet garni* up in a twist of muslin.

4 Add tripe to boiling stock, together with *bouquet garni* and the onion stuck with cloves. Boil gently, uncovered, for 1 hour.

5 Drain tripe thoroughly, reserving stock. Discard onion and *bouquet*. Cut tripe into strips ¼ inch wide and 2 to 2½ inches long.

6 In a large, deep frying-pan, heat olive oil and, when it is very hot, add tripe. Sauté over a high heat for about 15 minutes, keeping tripe constantly on the move with a large spatula to prevent it sticking fast to the pan. Remove from heat.

7 Melt butter in a heavy, medium-sized casserole, together with any remaining oil drained off from the frying-pan. Sauté sliced onions and crushed garlic until soft and golden.

8 Add tripe to casserole and mix well.

9 Strain ¾ pint tripe stock into the frying-pan. Bring to the boil, stirring and scraping pan clean with a wooden spoon. Pour over tripe and onions.

2 lb dressed tripe
2 chicken stock cubes
Salt
Bouquet garni (small bunch of parsley stalks, 1 stalk celery, chopped, 6 black peppercorns, 2 bay leaves, 1/2 level teaspoon dried thyme, small strips of lemon zest)
1 medium-sized onion stuck with 2 cloves
4 tablespoons olive oil
1 level tablespoon butter
2 large Spanish onions, sliced
2 cloves garlic, crushed
1/4 pint dry white wine
1 8-oz can peeled tomatoes
1/4 level teaspoon dried oregano
1/4 level teaspoon crushed rosemary
Freshly ground black pepper

10 Stir in dry white wine, contents of can of tomatoes and herbs, and season to taste with salt and freshly ground black pepper.

11 Bring to simmering point; cover and simmer gently for 2 hours.

12 Fifteen minutes before the end of cooking time, check consistency of casserole. If it is too liquid, finish cooking uncovered to allow some of the liquid to evaporate. Serve very hot with rice or French bread to mop up juices.

Philadelphia Pepperpot (A Casserole Soup)

Serves 6 hearty appetites

1 1/2 lb dressed tripe
3 chicken stock cubes
1 Spanish onion stuck with 3 cloves
1 medium-sized carrot, cut into thick slices
1 stalk celery, cut into thick slices
6 black peppercorns
1 bay leaf
4 slices lean bacon, chopped
2 level tablespoons butter
1 Spanish onion, finely chopped
3 stalks celery, finely chopped
2 sweet green peppers, seeded, cored and finely chopped
1 1 lb 12 oz can peeled tomatoes
1 2 1/4 oz can tomato concentrate
1/2 lb peeled potatoes, cut into 1/3-inch dice
1/4 level teaspoon dried thyme
Beurre manié (see Step 6)
Salt and freshly ground black pepper (optional)
2 level tablespoons finely chopped parsley

1 Rinse dressed tripe thoroughly under the cold tap. Then place it in a pan with cold water to cover; add 1 chicken stock cube, the onion stuck with cloves, sliced carrot and celery, pepper corns and bay leaf. Bring to the boil; reduce and simmer gently, uncovered, for 1 hour.

2 Drain tripe, reserving stock. Cut tripe into ½-inch squares.

3 In a large pan in which you intend to prepare the pepperpot, sauté chopped bacon over a moderate heat for 4 to 5 minutes until lightly golden.

4 Add butter to the pan and let it melt before adding finely chopped vegetables. Sauté over a moderately high heat for a further 5 minutes until excess moisture from vegetables has evaporated and they are beginning to colour.

5 Measure reserved tripe stock and make up to 2 pints with water. Add to pan, together with remaining stock cubes, contents of can of tomatoes, tomato concentrate diluted with a few tablespoons of the stock, diced potatoes and thyme. Bring back to the boil and simmer for about 12 to 15 minutes longer until potatoes are tender.

6 Prepare a *beurre manié* by working 2 level tablespoons each butter and flour to a smooth paste. Add to simmering soup in small pieces, stirring until they have dissolved. Simmer soup for 4 to 5 minutes longer.

7 Correct seasoning of soup, adding salt or freshly ground black pepper only if required. Garnish with finely chopped parsley and serve immediately, with fresh crusty bread.

L'Estouffat de Toulouse

Serves 6–8

1 Drain soaked beans and place them in a large pan with the next six ingredients. Season to taste with freshly ground black pepper but only a very little salt as bacon may already be salty enough. Cover with cold water.

2 Bring pan to the boil and lower heat to simmering point. Cover and simmer gently for about 45 minutes, or until bean skins blister and peel back when you blow on them.

3 Drain contents of saucepan in a colander, reserving liquor.

4 Remove the piece of bacon and cut it into 1-inch cubes.

5 Preheat oven to very slow (300°F. Mark 2).

6 In a frying-pan, simmer sausages in butter and oil for 10 minutes, turning them to colour them evenly. Add cubed bacon and continue to fry gently for a further 10 minutes.

7 Transfer contents of colander to a large, ovenproof casserole. Add contents of frying pan and mix them together, taking care not to crush beans.

8 Measure off 1 pint reserved bean liquor (make it up with water if there is not enough). Blend in tomato concentrate and pour over beans and pork. Taste for seasoning and add more salt or freshly ground black pepper if necessary. Finally, if you like it, you can sprinkle the surface with a ¼-inch layer of breadcrumbs before covering the casserole with a lid.

9 Bake casserole for 2 to 2½ hours, or until beans are very soft and have absorbed the flavours of the other ingredients. They should remain quite moist to the end, so check occasionally while they are cooking and add more bean liquor (or water) if they dry out too quickly.

10 Serve very hot from the casserole.

Note: Failing the traditional *saucisses de Toulouse*, use well-flavoured, meaty English (or Italian) pork sausages.

1 1/2 lb dried haricot beans, soaked overnight or parboiled and left to soak for 1 hour (see page 240)

1 lb unsmoked bacon, in one piece

2 Spanish onions, peeled and quartered

3 cloves garlic, peeled

1 bay leaf

1/2 level teaspoon thyme

2 level tablespoons lard

Salt

Freshly ground black pepper

6–8 *saucisses de Toulouse* (see Note)

1 level tablespoon butter

1 tablespoon olive oil

4 level tablespoons tomato concentrate

Soft white breadcrumbs (optional)

Lesson 15

Pasta, Rice and Polenta Dishes

Most of us are familiar with several varieties of pasta. Italians have more than a hundred different shapes and sizes to choose from, ranging from tiny golden specks called pastina, used mainly in light soups and broths to huge ribbed rigatoni, so large and hearty that they are often individually stuffed with meat, vegetables or cheese fillings.

It has always amazed me that no two pasta dishes taste alike, even when they are made with the same basic mixture and dressed with the same sauce. Pasta experts say that every variation of size and shape – long thin strands of spaghetti, fat thick tubes of macaroni, and flat ribbons of egg noodles, butterfly shapes, shell shapes and bow shapes – give a different proportion of pasta to sauce with every mouthful.

The very names of the different kinds of pasta and their sauces are music to the ear of any food-loving cook:

Pasta gialla The finest pasta dough, golden with fresh egg yolks.

Pasta asciutta Literally 'dry pasta' is the name given to noodles that are served as a dish in themselves, as opposed to . . .

Pasta in brodo, or 'pasta served in soup' – small shapes and broken lengths of macaroni used to garnish and add body to soups – from elegant clear consommés to hearty peasant *minestre* so thick that a spoon will stand up in them.

Al dente is a phrase you are probably familiar with already, for it has found its way into international cookery terminology. We use it when speaking about pasta and rice, but to the Italian cook other things, especially vegetables, can also be '*al dente*'. Literally meaning 'to the tooth', this phrase pinpoints a precise stage at which an ingredient is just cooked through and no more, no longer raw but still firm enough to offer a slight resistance when you bite through it.

A Pasta Collection

A detailed description of every size and shape of pasta with the history of their origin would fill a book in itself with enchanting pagan fairy stories, like that of the country cook who chanced to come upon Venus naked – she was spending the night at his *trattoria* – and was so impressed that he created the *tortellino* in memory of her beautiful navel.

Italian delicatessens, as well as ordinary stores in this country, now stock a fairly wide range of pasta, most of it imported, although very acceptable pastas are now also being produced here. They can roughly be divided into the following categories:

Ropes and strings These include spaghetti, spaghettini (a thinner version of spaghetti) and vermicelli, the finest of all.

Ribbons The most common names for ribbon noodles are *fettuccine*, *tagliatelle* and *tagliolini*.

Lasagne are large, flat strips of the same dough, much wider than the ribbons above. These are usually boiled until tender, then layered in a dish with a variety of sauces, and baked in the oven until golden and bubbling.

Tubular pastas The famous macaroni (*maccheroni*), *maccheroncini*, which are thinner, and *rigatoni*, ribbed noodles so large that just a couple make a good mouthful.

And finally, we are left with the whole range of *stricchetti* and *farfalletti* (bows and butterflies), *conchiglie* or 'little shells', little cupids' bows and kisses, stars and even letters of the alphabet.

Select them according to your need, using the larger ones to serve as a dish in themselves, and the smaller ones for garnishing soups.

The Pasta Dough (Pasta Gialla)

The two main ingredients of a pasta dough are flour and eggs. If you can get 'strong' flour, that is, a high-gluten flour, so much the better. If not, a perfectly acceptable pasta dough can be made with an ordinary plain flour.

Italian recipes for pasta usually call for eggs with dark yolks in order to give the noodles that appetising golden colour. Unless you can get free-range farm eggs, I am afraid you are going to have to cheat a little by adding a drop or two of yellow food colouring, for the yolks of battery farm eggs rarely have much colour of their own.

By the time you've made your dough, rolled it out, cut the noodles into the desired shapes and left them to dry, you will probably have had enough for one day. I prefer to break off at this stage anyway, leaving the noodles to dry overnight and setting about cooking them with renewed enthusiasm the following day.

Kneading the Dough

The first thing that will probably strike you when you start mixing the ingredients together is that there is far too little liquid to hold the dough together.

Keep at it a bit longer before you give up and decide to add more water. Of course, flours vary and some absorb more liquid than others, but you will probably find that with a little more effort you will be able to force all the flour into a hard ball.

Now start kneading in real earnest, pushing the ball of dough down and away from you with the heel of your hand, then pulling it towards you with your fingers as you draw your hand back. Each time you do this, turn the pad of dough round slightly so that every part of it is involved in the kneading. If you can develop a smooth, relaxed, regular kneading rhythm, you will find it much less tiring.

After about 15 minutes' steady kneading, the dough will have become supple and elastic, though still very firm. Little air blisters just under the surface are a sure sign that it has had enough.

'Resting' the Dough

If you were to try to roll the dough out at this stage, it would be very difficult indeed. The answer is to wrap the ball loosely in plastic (to prevent the surface drying out) and leave it to rest for a minimum of 1 hour – the longer the better. This gives the gluten in the flour a chance to relax and makes it yield more readily to the rolling pin. You can even leave it overnight at the bottom of the refrigerator if this is more convenient, but make sure the bag is not sealed, otherwise the dough will 'sweat'.

Rolling the Dough

When dealing with a large amount of dough, you will find it easier to roll it out a piece at a time. Cut off a portion of, say, 4 oz, and return the remainder to its plastic wrap to keep moist.

Flour your working surface lightly and flatten the piece of dough out with the palm of a lightly floured hand. *Don't* knead the dough at this stage: you will only revive its elasticity and make it more difficult to roll.

Dust your rolling pin with flour and start rolling the dough, using short light strokes in one direction only, and always working *outwards* from the centre to make a circle. Check occasionally that the sheet of dough has not stuck to the working surface, flouring a corner of the latter from time to time and swishing the sheet of dough over it to ensure that the underside keeps dry. The sheet of dough will resist all the way, but with perseverance you will finally get it paper-thin: if you press the surface firmly with a finger it should leave only the faintest indentation.

Cutting Noodles

When making stuffed, ravioli-type noodles, the dough should be used as soon as it is rolled, while it is still moist enough to stick to itself under the pressure of your fingers and seal in the filling.

For ribbon noodles, or large leaves of lasagne or cannelloni, it is safer to leave the sheet for 10 to 15 minutes to dry slightly before proceeding.

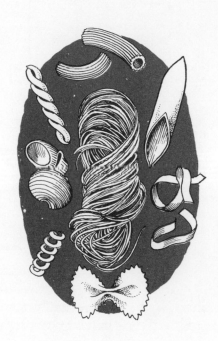

● Flour your hands lightly and sweep them over the surface of the dough.

● If making *cannelloni*, there is no need to fold the dough: just cut it neatly into 3- by 4-inch rectangles.

● Otherwise, fold the sheet up loosely into a long strip about 3 inches deep. Using a very sharp knife which will slice through the dough with minimum pressure, trim off uneven ends, then cut noodles as follows:

Tagliatelle (fettucine) Cut strips $\frac{1}{4}$ to $\frac{1}{2}$ inch wide.

Lasagne Cut strips 2 inches wide. Unravel each strip and divide into 4- or 6-inch lengths.

Drying the Noodles

Fresh, home-made noodles – whether stuffed or plain – must be left to dry for at least an hour before cooking, longer if possible, until they feel hard, if not exactly brittle like bought noodles. If they are not dry enough, they will absorb too much of the cooking water and turn slimy.

Dust a clean cloth with flour and, as you slice the noodles, shake the rolled ribbons loose and spread them out on the cloth. If you intend to leave them overnight, lay another cloth over the top to cover them completely.

Flat noodles should be laid out side by side, not overlapping.

Cooking Noodles

Specifying a cooking time for noodles is always a tricky business, whether you are dealing with home-made or bought ones. Roughly speaking, the former will take 6 to 8 minutes and the latter anything up to 11 minutes and beyond, depending on size, shape and how long they have been on the shelf. But the only reliable test is to lift out a strand or ribbon on a fork and bite it. As soon as it's *al dente* (see page 398), drain the noodles in a big colander, shaking out as much moisture as possible. Many recipes tell you to rinse the cooked noodles, some actually advising cold water. I find this has little effect other than to wash out all the flavour.

● Always boil pasta in plenty of salted water – 6 pints per pound of pasta is a reasonable amount – otherwise the noodles may stick together.

● Long noodles should never be broken: hold a sheaf upright in the water, pressing gently against the base of the pan and, as you feel it soften, gradually curl it around in the pan until it is completely submerged.

● Always add pasta gradually to the pan so that the water remains at a rolling boil.

● Once the strands or shapes are all in, give them a good stir with a fork to separate them and dislodge any that have stuck to the bottom of the pan.

● Never cover noodles while they are cooking: the pan is sure to boil over, and you will have the devil's own job cleaning up the sticky mess.

● Drain noodles as soon as they are cooked. Overcooking won't make them any more tender, and if they are left standing around in water they turn mushy and unpleasant.

● Always boil flat noodles like lasagne or cannelloni until *quite* tender before layering them with sauce or rolling them with stuffing for baking in the oven. For some reason, no amount of subsequent cooking will soften them further once they have been boiled and allowed to cool.

● Finally, never cook pasta too far in advance. But if you have to keep it hot for a little while before serving, set the colander over a saucepan containing an inch of boiling water and cover with a damp cloth until ready to serve.

Home-made Egg Pasta
(Pasta Gialla)

Serves 4–6

1 Sift flour and salt into a heap on a pastry board or in a large bowl. Make a well in the centre.

2 Break eggs into the well. Add oil and 3 tablespoons cold water.

3 With the fingers of one hand, gradually beat flour from sides of well into liquid ingredients. Then work dough until it holds together in a very stiff ball. Add a little more water only if necessary, but remember dough will soften quite a lot after kneading and resting.

4 Knead dough vigorously for about 15 minutes, or until smooth and elastic.

5 Roll dough into a ball; wrap loosely in plastic (or cover it with an upturned bowl) and leave to relax at room temperature for at least 1 hour.

6 When ready to roll dough, divide ball into four equal pieces and return three of them to the plastic bag.

7 Dust your working surface and rolling pin with flour and roll dough out as thinly as possible, working outwards from the centre and using more flour as necessary to prevent the sheet sticking to the board.

8 Cut noodles as described on page 401.

This portion of noodles (about 1 lb) tossed with a sauce or dressing will serve 4 as a main course or 6 as a first course.

1 lb plain strong or soft flour
1 level teaspoon salt
4 eggs
1 tablespoon oil
3 tablespoons cold water

Green Pasta
(Pasta Verde)

For making green ribbon noodles, cannelloni and lasagne.

1 Cook spinach according to directions on packet.

2 With a slotted spoon, remove spinach from pan, *not* draining it too thoroughly, and blend to a smooth purée in an electric blender. (There should be enough liquid left on the spinach to allow it to blend without clogging up blades.)

1 8-oz packet frozen leaf spinach
12 oz plain flour
3/4 level teaspoon salt
2 eggs
1 level tablespoon double cream

3 Sift flour and salt into a heap on a pastry board or in a large bowl. Make a well in the centre.

4 Add 5 level tablespoons puréed spinach, the eggs and cream.

5 Proceed as for Home-made Egg Pasta (page 403), adding a tablespoon or two of puréed spinach or cold water if you cannot get dough to hold together without it – this depends on the type of flour used and the amount of moisture left in the spinach.

Spaghetti with Garlic, Anchovy and Parsley Sauce

Serves 4 as a first course

1 lb spaghetti
Salt
4 level tablespoons butter
2 tablespoons olive oil
2 cloves garlic, finely chopped
8–10 large anchovy fillets
2–3 level tablespoons finely chopped parsley
Freshly ground black pepper
Freshly grated Parmesan cheese

1 Bring a large pan of salted water to the boil and cook spaghetti until tender but still firm.

2 Meanwhile, heat butter and olive oil in a small saucepan, and sauté finely chopped garlic cloves gently until they just begin to turn colour.

3 Strain butter and oil into a frying pan (reserving garlic); add anchovies and cook over the lowest possible heat, stirring, until they have dissolved into a paste.

4 Add finely chopped parsley and stir over a low heat for a few minutes longer. Stir in garlic and remove pan from heat.

5 Drain spaghetti thoroughly in a colander and pile it in a deep, heated serving dish.

6 Pour over sauce; toss well with a serving fork or spoon. Season to taste with freshly ground black pepper and a little salt if necessary. And add a little warm olive oil, if desired.

7 Serve very hot, accompanied by a large bowl of freshly grated parmesan.

Spaghetti with Prosciutto and Tomato Sauce

1 Prepare sauce: Chop *prosciutto* coarsely.

2 In a heavy saucepan, sauté chopped *prosciutto*, onion and garlic gently in butter and olive oil until vegetables are soft and golden, about 10 minutes.

3 Add canned tomatoes, sieved together with their juices, tomato concentrate, bay leaves, finely chopped parsley, oregano, lemon peel, and dry white wine.

Mix well and season to taste with salt and freshly ground black pepper.

4 Bring to the boil, stirring, cover pan and simmer very gently, stirring occasionally for 1 hour, or until ingredients are reduced to a thick sauce.

5 Meanwhile bring a large pan of salted water to the boil.

6 When sauce has been cooking for about 45 minutes, add spaghetti to boiling water (see page 402), and cook until tender, but not mushy.

7 As soon as spaghetti is ready, drain thoroughly in a colander.

8 To serve: heap spaghetti in a deep well-heated serving dish. Dot with butter. Pour sauce over the top and serve immediately, with plenty of freshly grated Parmesan to sprinkle over each portion.

Serves 4

1 lb spaghetti
Salt
2 level tablespoons butter
Freshly grated Parmesan cheese

Sauce

4 oz *prosciutto* (Parma ham)
1 Spanish onion, finely chopped
2 cloves garlic, finely chopped
2 level tablespoons butter
2 tablespoons olive oil
1 large can Italian peeled tomatoes
4 level tablespoons tomato concentrate
2 bay leaves
3 level tablespoons finely chopped parsley
1/4 level teaspoon oregano
1 small strip lemon peel
6 tablespoons dry white wine
Salt and freshly ground black pepper

Spaghetti alla Bolognese
(Spaghetti with a Rich Meat Sauce)

Serves 4

1 lb Spaghetti
Salt
Butter
Freshly grated Parmesan

Bolognese sauce
2 level tablespoons butter
4 tablespoons olive oil
1/4 lb *prosciutto* (Parma ham) or unsmoked bacon, coarsely chopped
1 Spanish onion, finely chopped
2 cloves garlic, finely chopped
2 carrots, finely chopped
1 stalk celery, finely chopped
1/2 lb lean beef, minced
1 strip lemon peel
1 bay leaf
4 level tablespoons tomato concentrate
1 large can Italian peeled tomatoes, sieved
1/4 pint dry white wine
Salt and freshly ground black pepper
Freshly grated nutmeg
4 level tablespoons freshly grated Parmesan

1 Prepare Bolognese sauce before cooking spaghetti: heat butter and olive oil in a large, heavy pan and sauté finely chopped *prosciutto* or bacon, onion, garlic, carrots and celery over a moderate heat until golden brown, stirring occasionally.

2 Add raw minced beef and continue to sauté until evenly browned, crumbling it with a fork.

3 Finally, stir in lemon peel, bay leaf, tomato concentrate, sieved Italian peeled tomatoes, white wine; season to taste with salt, freshly ground black pepper and a pinch of freshly grated nutmeg.

4 Cover pan and simmer very gently for 30 minutes, stirring occasionally.

5 Remove lemon peel and bay leaf, and continue to simmer sauce, uncovered, for 30 minutes longer, or until slightly thickened.

6 Stir in grated Parmesan and simmer gently for a final 2 to 3 minutes.

7 Twenty minutes before sauce is ready, bring a large pan of salted water to the boil. Add spaghetti, stir once or twice with a fork to prevent it sticking, and boil until tender but still *al dente* (page 398), 10 to 12 minutes depending on their quality. Drain thoroughly.

8 Heap spaghetti in a deep, heated serving bowl; add a good sized lump of butter and 4 level tablespoons grated Parmesan. Toss well and pour sauce over them. Serve with a large bowl of freshly grated Parmesan for each person to help himself.

Ribbon Noodles with Tomato and Basil Sauce

1 Prepare tomato and basil sauce. Finely chop onion, garlic, carrots and celery and place in a saucepan.

2 Chop fresh tomatoes coarsely and add to saucepan along with canned Italian peeled tomatoes, dry white wine and 12 fresh basil leaves. Bring to the boil, then lower heat and simmer, covered, for 1 hour.

3 Sieve the sauce, pressing vegetables through sieve with the back of a wooden spoon.

Note: If sauce is too thin, continue to simmer, uncovered, until it is the right consistency. Add butter, freshly grated Parmesan and salt and freshly ground black pepper, to taste.

4 Bring a large pan of salted water to the boil and cook ribbon noodles until tender, but still firm.

5 Drain noodles thoroughly and heap in a heated serving bowl. Add butter and freshly grated Parmesan and 12 basil leaves, shredded. Pour over heated tomato and basil sauce and mix well. Serve immediately.

Serves 4

1 lb ribbon noodles (tagliatelle or fettucine)
Salt
4 level tablespoons butter
4 level tablespoons freshly grated Parmesan, to serve
12 basil leaves, shredded

Tomato and basil sauce

1 Spanish onion
2 cloves garlic
2 carrots
1 stick celery
1 lb fresh tomatoes
1 lb canned Italian peeled tomatoes
1/4 pint dry white wine
12 fresh basil leaves
4 level tablespoons butter
4 level tablespoons freshly grated Parmesan
Salt and freshly ground black pepper

Macaroni alla Carbonara
(Macaroni with Bacon and Egg Dressing)

1 Bring a large pan of salted water to the boil and cook macaroni until tender but not mushy.

2 Meanwhile, heat butter and olive together in a heavy, medium-sized pan. Add finely chopped onion and simmer until soft and golden but not brown.

3 Add bacon strips and continue to sauté gently for about 5 minutes.

4 In a bowl, blend eggs with cream and 6 level tablespoons freshly grated Parmesan.

5 As soon as macaroni is cooked, drain thoroughly in a colander. Return macaroni to dry pan. Pour egg and cream mixture over hot macaroni and toss vigorously with a large fork and spoon so that heat of macaroni 'cooks' the sauce into a creamy dressing.

6 Add bacon and onion mixture and season to taste with salt and freshly ground black pepper.

Serves 6

1 lb macaroni
Salt
6 level tablespoons butter
2 tablespoons olive oil
3 level tablespoons finely chopped onion
6 oz streaky bacon, cut into thin strips
3 whole eggs
6 tablespoons single cream
Freshly grated Parmesan
Freshly ground black pepper

7 Serve immediately, piled in a well-heated serving dish, with more freshly grated Parmesan to sprinkle over each portion.

Serves 8

8 oz dried lasagne or 12 oz fresh lasagne
Salt
4 level tablespoons butter
Freshly grated Parmesan

Bolognese meat sauce
2 tablespoons olive oil
8 level tablespoons butter
1 Spanish onion, finely chopped
1 carrot, finely chopped
1 stalk celery, finely chopped
3 oz bacon, finely chopped
6 oz lean pork, minced
6 oz lean beef, minced
2 oz sausage meat
1/4 pint dry white wine
Salt and freshly ground black pepper
2 level tablespoons tomato concentrate
1/2 pint beef stock
3 tablespoons single cream
4 oz button mushrooms, sliced
1 clove garlic, crushed
1 level tablespoon finely chopped parsley

Cream sauce
3 oz butter
2 oz plain flour
1 3/4 pints milk
Salt
1 clove garlic, lightly crushed
2–3 large dried mushrooms, soaked in water
1 level tablespoon finely chopped parsley

Lasagne Bolognesi

1 Prepare Bolognese meat sauce: beat oil with 3 level tablespoons butter in a large, deep frying pan or wide saucepan, and sauté finely chopped onion, carrot and celery over a moderate heat until soft and golden brown.

2 Add bacon, minced pork and beef, and sausage meat, and continue to sauté gently until meats brown, crumbling them with a fork.

3 Moisten with wine and simmer until it evaporates. Then season to taste with salt and freshly ground black pepper.

4 Dilute tomato concentrate with a little of the stock and stir into meat mixture. Cover pan and simmer very gently for $1\frac{1}{2}$ hours, stirring occasionally and adding remaining stock gradually as sauce evaporates.

5 Meanwhile, prepare cream sauce: melt 2 oz butter in a heavy pan and stir in flour to form a *roux*. Continue to stir over a low heat for a minute or two, taking care not to let *roux* brown.

6 Gradually add $1\frac{1}{4}$ pints of the milk, stirring constantly, and bring to the boil slowly, stirring until sauce is smooth and thick.

7 Season to taste with a pinch of salt and put aside, with a piece of dampened greaseproof paper covering the surface to prevent a skin forming on top.

8 Melt remaining 1 oz butter and sauté crushed garlic clove for 2 or 3 minutes until golden brown. Remove garlic with a slotted spoon and discard it.

9 Pour soaked dried mushrooms into a small pan together with their soaking water. Bring to the boil and simmer gently for a few minutes until mushrooms have softened. Drain, reserving remaining water; chop finely and add to the pan with garlic-flavoured butter. Toss for 2 to 3 minutes over a low heat and add reserved mushroom water, finely chopped parsley, remaining $\frac{1}{2}$ pint milk and a pinch of salt, to taste. Simmer gently for 15 to 20 minutes.

10 Combine mushroom mixture with cream sauce and mix well.

11 Preheat oven to moderate (375°F. Mark 5).

12 Bring a large pan of salted water to the boil; drop in lasagne, bring to the boil again and simmer gently for 7 to 10 minutes (less if freshly made lasagne have been used), or until leaves are tender but still slightly resistant to the tooth. Drain, rinse with boiling water and drain again.

13 While lasagne are cooking, finish Bolognese meat sauce: stir in cream and continue to cook slowly for 5 to 10 minutes; then add 3 level tablespoons butter and stir over a low heat until melted.

14 Melt remaining butter (2 level tablespoons) in a deep frying-pan and sauté sliced mushrooms, crushed garlic and finely chopped parsley for 4 to 5 minutes, or until mushrooms are tender. Fold into Bolognese sauce.

15 To assemble lasagne: butter a deep, 7- by 12-inch, ovenproof dish. Cover base with a layer of cooked lasagne; spread thinly with cream sauce and Bolognese sauce, and sprinkle with 2 to 3 level tablespoons grated Parmesan. Continue in this manner until ingredients are used up, making as many layers as possible and ending with a layer of lasagne sprinkled with grated Parmesan. Dot with remaining butter.

16 Bake the dish of lasagne for 1 hour, or until golden brown and bubbling.

17 Serve straight from the baking dish, with a large bowl of additional grated Parmesan at hand so that each person can sprinkle more over his portion.

Serves 6–8

6 oz dry lasagne noodles
Salt
Butter
6 oz Fontina cheese (see
  note), thinly sliced
Freshly grated Parmesan

Meat sauce

1 Spanish onion, finely
  chopped
1 stalk celery, finely chopped
2 cloves garlic, finely
  chopped
2 tablespoons olive oil
8 oz lean beef, minced
1 14-oz can Italian peeled
  tomatoes
2 level tablespoons tomato
  concentrate
1/2 level teaspoon dried
  oregano
1/2 level teaspoon dried
  basil
Salt and freshly ground black
  pepper

Cream sauce

1 pint milk
1 chicken stock cube
3 level tablespoons butter
1 small onion, finely chopped
6 level tablespoons plain
  flour
1/4 pint single cream
6–8 white peppercorns
1 small bay leaf
Freshly grated nutmeg
3 level tablespoons freshly
  grated Parmesan
Salt

Lasagne al Forno

A simpler version, both as regards ingredients and method, of the classic recipe above. Fontina is a mild, soft, creamy Italian cheese with excellent melting qualities. If you can't find it, try to get Mozzarella or, failing that, any good creamy-melting cheese with not too sharp a flavour.

1 Start by preparing the meat sauce, which takes longest to cook: in a heavy, medium-sized saucepan, sauté finely chopped onion, celery and garlic in olive oil until soft and golden, about 5 minutes.

2 Add minced beef and cook for about 5 minutes longer, stirring and crumbling it with a fork to ensure that it browns evenly.

3 Stir in canned tomatoes, together with their juices, tomato concentrate and dried herbs, and season lightly with salt and freshly ground black pepper. Bring to the boil; cover tightly and simmer over a low heat for 1 hour, stirring occasionally.

4 Meanwhile, bring a large pan of salted water to the boil. Drop in lasagne (squares or rectangles) and simmer for 10 to 12 minutes, or until completely cooked but still *al dente*. Drain lasagne in a colander. Rinse them under the cold tap; then leave them to drain and cool, laid out in a single layer on sheets of absorbent paper.

5 Next, make cream sauce: pour milk into a pan; crumble in stock cube and bring to boiling point, stirring to make sure cube has dissolved. Remove from heat.

6 In a heavy pan, melt butter and sauté finely chopped onion over a low heat for 5 to 7 minutes until soft and transparent, making sure butter does not colour.

7 Blend in flour with a wooden spoon and stir over a low heat for 2 to 3 minutes longer to make a pale *roux*.

8 Gradually add flavoured milk, beating vigorously with the spoon to prevent flour lumping.

9 Stir in cream, whole peppercorns and bay leaf; season lightly with freshly grated nutmeg. Bring to the boil, stirring, and simmer very gently, uncovered, for 10 minutes, stirring frequently.

10 When sauce is thick, with no trace of raw flour in its flavour, remove pan from heat. Beat in freshly grated Parmesan; add a little salt if necessary and strain through a fine sieve. Keep hot.

11 Preheat oven to moderate (375°F. Mark 5).

12 Select an ovenproof baking dish, rectangular if possible, of about 3-pint capacity and not less than 2 inches deep. Grease it generously with butter.

13 To assemble dish: line base (not sides) with a single layer of lasagne, using about a third; spread evenly with half of the meat sauce, followed by a third of the cream sauce, and about half of the cheese slices. Repeat all these layers once more in the same order. Then finish with remaining lasagne and cover with remaining cream sauce. Sprinkle surface with 2 to 3 level tablespoons freshly grated Parmesan and dot with 1 to 2 level tablespoons butter.

14 Bake lasagne for 40 minutes, or until surface is golden brown and bubbling.

15 Remove from the oven and leave to settle for about 10 minutes before serving straight from the dish. A bowl of freshly grated Parmesan to sprinkle over each portion is a must.

Fettuccine al Burro e Formaggio
(Ribbon Noodles with Butter and Cheese)

Serves 4

1 lb fettuccine (ribbon) noodles
Salt
Freshly grated Parmesan

Dressing

4 oz softened butter
4–6 level tablespoons double cream
4 oz freshly grated Parmesan

1 Bring a large (6- to 8-pint) pan of salted water to the boil. Add noodles and cook until tender but still firm, stirring occasionally with a fork to keep strands separate. The cooking time will depend on whether the noodles are fresh or dry: say 6 to 8 minutes for the former, 11 minutes plus for the latter.

2 While noodles are cooking prepare dressing; place butter in the serving bowl and work with a wooden spoon until light and creamy.

3 Gradually beat in double cream, followed by freshly grated Parmesan.

4 As soon as noodles are cooked, drain them thoroughly in a colander; turn them into the serving bowl and toss vigorously with a serving fork and spoon until strands are thoroughly coated with the creamy dressing.

5 Sprinkle with more grated Parmesan and serve immediately.

Home-made Ravioli

Makes about 5 dozen

1/2 recipe Egg Pasta (page 403)
Meat filling (page 412)

1 Proceed according to basic egg pasta recipe as far as Step 8.

2 Roll dough out into a very thin sheet and cut it into long strips 1½ inches wide.

Melted butter, or
   tomato sauce
Freshly grated Parmesan

3 Take 2 strips at a time, leaving remainder covered with a damp cloth to prevent them drying out.

4 Arrange $\frac{1}{2}$ level teaspoon filling (see below) in neat mounds 1 inch apart down the length of one strip of pasta.

5 Cover very loosely with a second strip; then press down between each mound with your finger, or the side of a wooden spoon handle.

6 Now press strips together firmly all around each little mound so that it is tightly sealed.

7 Cut in between each mound to make little squares. Check again that each one is tightly sealed.

8 Fresh ravioli will need 20 to 25 minutes' cooking in boiling salted water. They can be served with melted butter or tomato sauce, depending on the filling, and accompanied by a large bowl of grated Parmesan.

**Makes enough for
5 dozen ravioli**

1 level tablespoon butter
1 1/2 teaspoons olive oil
4 oz cooked beef, minced
2 oz cooked veal, minced
1 level tablespoon stale white
   breadcrumbs
1 level tablespoon freshly
   grated Parmesan
2 level teaspoons finely
   chopped parsley
1 egg
1 tablespoon strong beef
   stock (page 161)
2 level teaspoons tomato
   concentrate
1/8 level teaspoon ground
   cinnamon
Salt and freshly ground black
   pepper

Meat Filling for Ravioli

1 Melt butter and oil in a heavy frying-pan or saucepan, and sauté minced meats for 5 minutes, stirring and tossing with a fork. Remove pan from heat.

2 Stir in breadcrumbs, grated Parmesan and chopped parsley.

3 Beat egg with beef stock and tomato concentrate. Stir into meat mixture.

4 Add cinnamon and season to taste with salt and freshly ground black pepper. Mixture should be quite moist and malleable. If not, work in a little more stock.

5 Allow to cool before using to make ravioli (see above).

Spinach and Chicken Filling for Ravioli

1 Melt butter and olive oil in a heavy frying pan or saucepan. Add spinach and minced chicken, and mix well. Remove from heat.

2 Add breadcrumbs and grated Parmesan, and mix well.

3 Stir in cream and chicken stock, and blend thoroughly. If mixture is not moist enough to shape into mounds, add a little more chicken stock.

4 Season to taste with salt, freshly ground black pepper and a little freshly grated nutmeg.

Makes enough for 5 dozen ravioli

1 level tablespoon butter
2 teaspoons olive oil
3 level tablespoons cooked chopped spinach, pressed dry
4 oz cooked chicken, minced
1 level tablespoon stale white breadcrumbs
1 level tablespoon freshly grated Parmesan
2 tablespoons single cream
2 tablespoons strong chicken stock (page 162)
Salt and freshly ground black pepper
Freshly grated nutmeg

Rice

It is said that Italians consume more beautiful, long-grained rice *per capita* than any other Western country. And they grow it, too. In fact, in Northern Italy, where it is grown extensively, rice vies with *polenta* for first place as the region's favourite dish. And the Italian method of cooking rice – first tossing it in butter and then simmering it in broth – leaves each grain separate and slightly resistant to the teeth – *al dente* – just like their *pasta*.

My favourite Italian rice dish, *risotto alla Milanese*, deliciously moist and saffron-flavoured, is one of the great specialities of Milano. Tossed with sweet, unsalted butter and sprinkled with freshly grated Parmesan cheese, it is a dish fit for the Gods.

My recipe on page 419 uses diced beef marrow and butter to give an authentic touch to this *Milanese* masterpiece.

Of course, there are many recipes for *risotto*; almost as many as there are cooks in Italy. But you'll find that most start off with a *risotto bianco* (the rice is tossed in butter, with or without onion, and is then simmered in chicken broth until tender) or a *risotto Milanese* (the rice is cooked exactly as above, but with the heady aroma and golden colour of saffron added) before the rice is combined with one or more of the following ingredients: cooked peas, artichoke hearts, thinly sliced mushrooms, clams, seafood of all sorts, thinly sliced white truffles, bits of cooked sausage and bacon or raw Parma ham, pine nuts, diced avocado and peeled, seeded and chopped raw tomatoes.

The Chinese, too, are famous for the way they use rice as the main component of a host of delicious dishes. Cooked rice, gently fried in the Chinese manner, can turn ordinary left-overs (cooked chicken, pork, shrimps or prawns, even vegetables) into superb party fare.

Chinese fried rice is not just one dish; it is a whole series of mouth-watering additions to your culinary repertoire; consisting first, of course, of rice, but with such delightful variations that the flavour combinations are infinite.

First of all you must have perfectly boiled or steamed rice: each grain dry, fluffy and distinct before you start. Then it is necessary only to pour a thin layer of corn or olive oil into your frying-pan; add the rice, and stir over a high heat until it is golden. The possible additives are limitless. I know of one Chinese recipe that combines diced duck, chicken, Chinese sausage, fried egg, soy sauce, ham, shrimp and lobster.

How to Cook Rice

The most common fault in the preparation of rice is over-cooking. A good general rule is to cook rice for sweets and puddings thoroughly so that it is quite soft, but for first courses, main dishes and vegetable accompaniments, to stop the cooking at the precise point where the rice just starts to get soft. Rice at its best should be magically tender – neither mushy soft nor unpleasantly hard.

When you cook rice in a tightly covered pan, you will find that it will absorb its own volume of liquid. Many recipes add twice the volume to make the rice more tender. But it also has the tendency to make the rice mushy. So you must, in the long run, be your own judge of how much liquid to use to produce rice to the exact consistency you prefer.

How to Keep Rice Hot Without Tears

Butter a bowl: spoon hot rice in carefully and lay a folded cloth over the top of the bowl. Cover tightly with a piece of foil (or a lid if you have one of the right size) and set bowl *over* a pan of simmering water. Rice can safely be kept hot in this manner for several hours.

Basic Boiled Rice

1 Bring a large pan of salted water (at least 4 pints) to the boil with lemon juice.

2 When water is bubbling vigorously, dribble in rice gradually through your fingers so that water does not come off the boil.

3 Stir once to dislodge any grains stuck to bottom of pan and boil rice for 15 to 18 minutes, or until tender but not mushy.

4 Drain rice in a colander and rinse thoroughly with hot water. Shake out all excess moisture. Toss rice gently with a little butter seasoned with salt and freshly ground black pepper; serve immediately.

Serves 4 to 6

12 oz long-grain rice
Salt
4 tablespoons lemon juice
Butter
Freshly ground black pepper

Basic Steamed Rice

1 Fill a large pan two-thirds full of water. Add lemon juice and a small handful of salt, and bring to the boil.

2 When water is bubbling briskly, shower in rice. Stir well to dislodge any grains that have attached themselves to the bottom and boil, uncovered, for 10 to 12 minutes. Rice should be cooked, but still very firm.

3 Drain rice thoroughly in a colander.

4 Cut a large square of double-thickness muslin. Heap rice in the centre and wrap up in a loose bundle.

5 Place bundle of rice in a steamer over boiling water. Cover steamer tightly and steam for 20 to 25 minutes, or until rice grains are fluffy, tender, and quite separate.

Note: You can wrap the rice in a clean tea towel instead of muslin, but make sure that any washing soap has been thoroughly rinsed out of it to avoid tainting the rice.

Serves 4–6

12 oz long-grain rice
4 tablespoons lemon juice
Salt

Serves 4, if
accompanied by 2 or
more other dishes

2 tablespoons corn oil
1 medium-sized onion,
  chopped
4 oz button mushrooms,
  coarsely chopped
About 1 lb cold, cooked
  long-grain rice (say 6 oz
  uncooked weight)
1 tablespoon soy sauce
Salt and freshly ground black
  pepper

Chinese Fried Rice with Mushrooms

1 Heat corn oil in a large, deep frying-pan and sauté chopped onion gently until golden, about 10 minutes. Add coarsely chopped mushrooms and continue to sauté, stirring, for 5 minutes longer.

2 Add cooked rice and continue to cook, stirring constantly, for 5 minutes until hot and thoroughly mixed with other ingredients.

3 Sprinkle with soy sauce; season to taste with salt and freshly ground black pepper, and stir over heat for a minute or two longer. Serve immediately.

Serves 3–4

6 tablespoons corn oil
2 eggs
Salt and freshly ground black
  pepper
1 medium-sized onion,
  chopped
1 medium-sized green
  pepper, cored, seeded and
  thinly sliced
1 4-oz slice cooked ham
1 4-oz slice cooked pork
1 4-oz packet frozen prawns
About 1 lb cold cooked
  long-grain rice (6 oz raw
  weight)
1–2 tablespoons soy sauce

Chinese Fried Rice with Prawns and Peppers

1 Heat 2 tablespoons corn oil in a 7- or 8-inch frying-pan. Beat eggs lightly with a fork and season with salt and freshly ground black pepper. Pour into pan and make a flat, thin omelette, flipping it over once it has set on one side to brown the other side. Slip out on to a plate and leave to cool.

2 Heat remaining oil in a large, heavy frying-pan. Sauté chopped onion and sliced green pepper, stirring occasionally, for 4 to 5 minutes, or until onion is soft but pepper strips are still rather crisp.

3 Meanwhile, cut ham and pork into $\frac{1}{4}$-inch dice.

4 Add frozen prawns to frying-pan and sauté over a moderate heat, gently prising the block apart with a fork to separate prawns without tearing them, 2 to 3 minutes.

5 Add cooked rice and diced meats to frying-pan, and continue to sauté over a moderate heat for about 5 minutes, stirring and turning contents of pan over with a spatula to mix them thoroughly and prevent rice sticking to bottom of pan.

6 Sprinkle with soy sauce; mix well and season to taste with salt and freshly ground black pepper. Fry for 1 to 2 minutes longer and transfer to a heated serving dish.

7 Roll omelette up tightly. Cut into strips about $\frac{1}{8}$ inch thick and use to garnish rice. Serve immediately.

Rice Pilaff

1 Preheat oven to moderate (375°F. Mark 5).

2 Melt 4 level tablespoons butter in a heavy, heatproof casserole, add olive oil and simmer finely chopped Spanish onion until golden brown.

3 Add rice and stir over a moderate heat for 2 or 3 minutes until grains are thoroughly coated with butter.

4 Dissolve stock cubes in 1¼ pints boiling water in a saucepan and bring to boiling point, ready to add to rice.

5 Pour 1 pint boiling stock into casserole (take care, as stock will sizzle up when it comes into contact with hot butter); season to taste with salt and freshly ground black pepper, and quickly cover casserole to prevent too much stock evaporating.

6 Bake casserole for 20 to 25 minutes, or until rice grains are fluffy and separate, and liquid has been absorbed, stirring once or twice and adding a little more boiling stock if it has all been absorbed before rice is tender.

7 To serve: transfer rice to a serving dish, add sliced sautéed mushrooms, (or plumped raisins, or pine nuts, or a combination of all three) and 2 level tablespoons butter, and toss with a fork to mix them in lightly; *or*, more simply, just stir in 4 level table-spoons butter with a fork; taste; and add more salt and freshly ground black pepper, if necessary.

Serves 6

Butter
2 tablespoons olive oil
1 Spanish onion, finely chopped
12 oz long-grain rice
1 1/2 chicken stock cubes
Salt and freshly ground black pepper
4 oz button mushrooms, sliced and sautéed in butter (optional)
2 oz seedless raisins, plumped in boiling water (optional)
1 oz pine nuts, sautéed in butter until golden (optional)

Simple Pilaff with Pine Nuts

1 Heat 1 tablespoon each butter and olive oil in a heavy, medium-sized saucepan with a tight-fitting lid. Add rice and stir over a moderate heat for 2 to 3 minutes, or until grains are transparent and thoroughly coated with hot fat.

2 Add ¾ pint boiling water. Season with salt and freshly ground black pepper; bring to the boil; reduce heat to a bare simmer and cover tightly with the lid.

3 Leave rice to simmer undisturbed for 15 to 20 minutes, or until stock has been absorbed, leaving rice tender but not mushy.

4 Melt 2 level tablespoons butter in a frying-pan; add pine nuts and sauté over a moderate heat until golden.

5 When rice is tender; transfer to a heated serving bowl; stir in pine nuts and butter and serve immediately.

Serves 4

Butter
1 tablespoon olive oil
8 oz long-grain rice
Salt and freshly ground black pepper
2 oz pine nuts

Serves 4–6

12 oz long-grain rice
Salt
4 level tablespoons butter
1/4 pound Mortadella
  sausage, cut in thin strips
2 level tablespoons finely
  chopped parsley
Freshly grated Parmesan
  cheese

Serves 4–6

4 level tablespoons butter
1/4 pound green bacon, or
  ham, diced
12 oz long-grain rice
Salt
2 egg yolks
6 level tablespoons double
  cream
Freshly grated Parmesan
Freshly ground black pepper

Serves 4–6

1 1/2 chicken stock cubes
5 level tablespoons butter
1 Spanish onion, finely
  chopped
1 clove garlic, finely chopped
12 oz long-grain rice
1 bay leaf
2 cloves
1-inch stick of cinnamon
1/2 level teaspoon turmeric
1/2 level teaspoon saffron
Salt and freshly ground black
  pepper
2 oz split blanched almonds

Italian Rice with Mortadella

1 Boil rice in boiling salted water until just tender. Drain and keep warm.

2 Melt butter in a thick-bottomed frying-pan; sauté the Mortadella in it for 3 minutes; add finely chopped parsley and keep warm.

3 Toss the hot rice with freshly grated Parmesan cheese, then with the Mortadella and parsley sauce.

4 Sprinkle with additional cheese and serve immediately.

Italian Rice with Bacon and Cream Sauce

1 Melt butter in a thick-bottomed frying-pan; add diced bacon (or ham), and sauté until crisp and golden.

2 Boil rice in boiling salted water until just tender. Drain; and transfer rice to a heated serving bowl.

3 Mix egg yolks and cream until smooth. Pour over hot rice and toss until heat of rice turns egg and cream mixture to a smooth sauce.

4 Add 6 level tablespoons freshly grated Parmesan cheese; bacon (or ham), pan juices, salt and freshly ground black pepper, to taste. Serve immediately with additional grated Parmesan.

Spicy Yellow Rice with Almonds

1 Preheat oven to moderate (375°F. Mark 5).

2 Dissolve stock cubes in $1\frac{1}{4}$ pints water in a saucepan and bring to boiling point, ready to add to rice.

3 In a heavy, flameproof casserole with a tight-fitting lid, melt 4 level tablespoons butter and gently sauté finely chopped onion and garlic for about 10 minutes until soft and transparent but not brown.

4 Add rice and stir over a low heat until grains are golden with butter.

5 Stir in bay leaf, cloves, cinnamon, turmeric and saffron. Season to taste with salt and freshly ground black pepper, and add 1 pint of the boiling stock. Stir once to dislodge any grains stuck to the bottom of the casserole. Cover casserole and transfer casserole to the oven. Bake for 20 to 25 minutes.

6 Meanwhile, melt remaining 1 tablespoon butter in a frying-pan and sauté blanched almonds over a moderate heat until golden brown all over, stirring constantly.

7 Remove casserole from the oven. All the moisture in the rice should have been absorbed, leaving the grains tender but firm and separate. If rice is not quite cooked, add a few tablespoons more boiling stock and return to the oven for a further 5 minutes or so, covered. Gently toss rice with a fork and fold in browned almonds. Taste – adding more salt or freshly ground black pepper if necessary – and serve immediately.

Risotto alla Milanese

1 In a large, heavy pan, melt 4 level tablespoons butter; add diced beef marrow and simmer finely chopped onion until soft and lightly golden but not brown, about 5 minutes.

2 Add rice and cook over a moderately low heat for 2 to 3 minutes longer, stirring constantly with a wooden spoon so that every grain is individually coated with butter.

3 Moisten rice with dry white wine and let it sizzle away.

4 Bring chicken stock or light beef stock to the boil. Pour about 1 pint into a saucepan and add saffron.

5 Pour saffron flavoured stock over rice.

6 Stir lightly to dislodge any grains stuck to bottom or sides of pan and simmer gently until most of the liquid has been absorbed.

7 When rice is moist but no longer wet, add a large ladleful (or 2 small ones) of simmering stock; stir again to dislodge grains stuck to pan and simmer over a low heat until stock has almost all been absorbed, leaving rice very moist.

8 Continue adding stock in this manner, stirring and scraping the bottom of the pan, with a fork, being careful not to crush the grains. Towards the end of cooking time, the *risotto* will need practically constant attention to prevent sticking. Stop adding stock when rice is cooked to creamy tenderness, without, however, the grains being mushy (see page 415). Total cooking time will be 20 to 25 minutes.

9 Remove pan from heat. With a large fork, gently fold in 2 level tablespoons butter and 3 to 4 level tablespoons freshly grated Parmesan, to taste.

10 To serve: mound *risotto* on a well-heated dish and serve immediately with more butter and a bowl of freshly grated Parmesan to sprinkle over each portion.

Serves 4–6

12 oz Italian *risotto* or long-grain rice

Butter

4 level tablespoons diced beef marrow

1/2 Spanish onion, finely chopped

6 tablespoons dry white wine

2 pints chicken (page 162) or light beef stock (page 161)

1/2 level teaspoon powdered saffron

Freshly grated Parmesan

Serves 4–6

1 recipe *Risotto alla Milanese*
(page 419)
1 oz dried wild mushrooms
(see note)
8 oz cooked ham, sliced
1/4 inch thick
Freshly grated Parmesan
Butter

Risotto con Funghi

(Risotto with Wild Mushrooms)

Dried wild mushrooms are comparatively easy to find in good stores and delicatessens. They are sold by the packet, or individually threaded on to fine string to make large garlands. *Boletus edulis* (the French *cèpe*) have the finest flavour, much richer than that of cultivated white mushrooms.

1 Place mushrooms in a bowl. Pour over $\frac{1}{2}$ pint boiling water and leave to soak for 1 hour.

2 When mushrooms have softened, pour contents of bowl into small pan. Bring to the boil and simmer for 7 to 10 minutes, or until mushrooms have swollen to about twice their original size and liquor is reduced to 6 or 7 tablespoons.

3 Drain mushrooms thoroughly, reserving liquor. Chop mushrooms coarsely and put aside until needed.

4 Trim cooked ham of fat if necessary. Cut ham into $\frac{1}{4}$-inch dice.

5 Preheat oven to moderate (350°F. Mark 4).

6 Make *Risotto alla Milanese* as directed on page 419, omitting the final butter and cheese. You can also leave out the saffron if you prefer, but the risotto will be less attractive.

7 When *risotto* is cooked, gently fold in coarsely chopped mushrooms, 6 tablespoons of their liquor, the diced ham and 4 to 6 level tablespoons freshly grated Parmesan, to taste. Use a large fork to avoid crushing the rice.

8 Grease a 3-pint casserole or deep baking dish liberally with butter.

9 Spoon *risotto* into casserole and cover tightly with a lid or a sheet of foil. Bake for 20 minutes.

10 Serve *risotto* immediately, with additional freshly grated Parmesan to sprinkle over each portion.

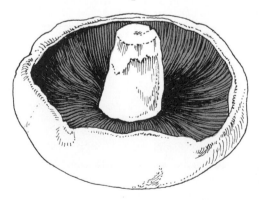

Risotto with Chicken Livers

Serves 4-6

1 recipe *Risotto alla Milanese*
  (page 419)
1 medium-sized onion
2 oz prosciutto or raw
  Westphalian ham
6 oz chicken livers
6 oz button mushrooms
3 level tablespoons butter
1/4 pint chicken stock
1–2 tablespoons Madeira
1 small bay leaf
Salt and freshly ground black
  pepper
1–2 level tablespoons finely
  chopped parsley
Freshly grated Parmesan

1 Peel and cut onion into paper-thin slices.

2 Shred *prosciutto* (or Westphalian ham) coarsely.

3 Wash chicken livers carefully. Cut each lobe into 2 or 3 slices and pat dry with absorbent paper.

4 Wash or wipe mushrooms clean with a damp cloth. Trim stems and slice mushrooms thinly.

5 Prepare *Risotto alla Milanese* as directed on page 419, up to but not including the final addition of butter and grated Parmesan.

6 When *risotto* is well under way, melt butter in a medium-sized, heavy pan. Add sliced onion and shredded *prosciutto*, and sauté gently for about 5 minutes.

7 Add sliced livers to the pan and cook over a moderate heat for a further 5 minutes, turning pieces carefully to brown them evenly without crushing them, and making sure onion slices don't colour too deeply.

8 Remove onion, *prosciutto* and chicken livers from pan. Keep hot.

9 To fat remaining in the pan add thinly sliced mushrooms. Sauté over a moderate heat for 5 minutes, or until soft and golden.

10 Return chicken liver mixture to the pan; add stock, Madeira and a small bay leaf, and season to taste with salt and freshly ground black pepper. Simmer over a very low heat for 5 minutes, stirring occasionally.

11 When *risotto* is ready, add chicken liver garnish, together with finely chopped parsley, and fold in gently but thoroughly with a large fork.

12 Mound *risotto* in a heated serving dish and serve immediately, with a bowl of freshly grated Parmesan to sprinkle over each portion.

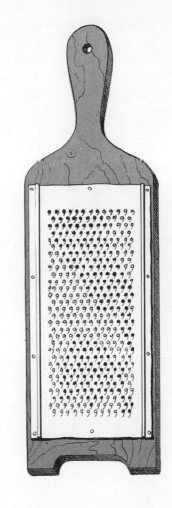

Serves 6

1 small sole, filleted, with bones and trimmings

1 small carrot, sliced

1 small piece (about 2 inches) celery stalk

4 sprigs parsley

4 white peppercorns

1 small bay leaf

Twist of thinly pared lemon zest

About 1/2-pint dry white wine

12 large, plump, live mussels

2 shallots, finely chopped

1 clove garlic, finely chopped

4 level tablespoons finely chopped parsley

4 oz peeled prawns

1/4 pint chicken stock (page 162)

1/2 level teaspoon saffron strands

2 tablespoons olive oil

Butter

1 Spanish onion, finely chopped

1 stalk celery, finely chopped

12 oz Italian *risotto* rice

Salt and freshly ground black pepper

4 level tablespoons freshly grated Parmesan

Seafood Risotto

1 Make a fish stock: place fish bones and trimmings in a pan; add carrot, a piece of celery stalk, parsley sprigs, white peppercorns, bay leaf and a twist of lemon zest. Cover with $\frac{1}{4}$ pint of the dry white wine and $\frac{3}{4}$ pint water. Bring to the boil; cover pan and simmer for 30 minutes.

2 Meanwhile, scrub mussels clean under cold running water, having made sure they are all alive. Place them in a heavy, medium-sized pan with 4 tablespoons of remaining white wine, the same of water, shallots, garlic and half the finely chopped parsley. Cover tightly and cook over a high heat, shaking pan frequently, for 5 to 7 minutes, or until all the mussels are wide open.

3 Remove mussels from their shells over the pan to avoid losing any liquor. Combine mussels with prawns in a bowl; cover and put aside until needed.

4 Filter mussel liquor through filter paper (or a sheet of absorbent kitchen paper, or fine, double-thick muslin) to trap any grains of sand that might have escaped from mussels. Strain fish stock through a fine sieve. Combine fish stock and mussel liquor in a deep frying pan.

5 Lay sole fillets in the frying-pan. Place over a moderately low heat and bring slowly to simmering point. As soon as you see the first bubbles breaking on the surface, remove pan from heat and lift out sole fillets. They should be barely cooked. Slice them crosswise into strips about $\frac{1}{3}$ inch thick and put aside with mussels and prawns.

6 Combine remaining fish stock and chicken stock in a large measuring jug, and if necessary make up to $1\frac{1}{4}$ pints with water. Pour into a pan; cover and bring to the boil. Remove from heat.

7 In a cup, soak saffron strands in 3 tablespoons of the boiling stock for 5 minutes; then mash strands against sides of cup with a spoon to make them release as much colour as possible.

8 In the pan in which you intend to cook *risotto* (a large, heavy one), heat the oil with 2 level tablespoons butter. Add finely chopped onion and celery, and simmer gently for about 10 minutes until soft and golden but not brown.

9 Add rice and cook over a moderately low heat for 2 to 3 minutes longer, stirring constantly with a wooden spoon so that every grain is individually coated with fat.

10 Moisten rice with 4 tablespoons dry white wine and let this sizzle away.

11 Add about a third of the hot chicken-fish stock, the saffron strands and the stock in which they were soaked; mix well; cover and cook slowly for 10 to 15 minutes, or until liquid is almost all absorbed but mixture can still find its own level when pan is tilted.

12 Stir in remaining stock and continue to simmer, covered, until this, too, has almost all been absorbed, leaving rice very moist indeed.

13 With a large fork, fold in 1 level tablespoon butter. Correct seasoning, adding salt and freshly ground black pepper, to taste (*risotto* may already be salty enough).

14 Carefully fold in mussels, prawns and strips of sole. Cover pan and return to a low heat for a final 3 minutes, by which time rice should be tender but in no way mushy and the whole mixture just thick enough to pile up in a dish.

15 Very gently fold in grated Parmesan and remaining chopped parsley. Turn into a heated serving dish and serve immediately.

Spanish Rice Salad

Serves 4–6

1 Combined cooked rice in a bowl with thinly sliced stuffed olives and red and green peppers, the diced *chorizo* sausage and finely chopped onion.

2 Make a vinaigrette dressing by combining in a small bowl the olive oil; lemon juice (or wine vinegar) and the finely chopped garlic. Add saffron and salt and freshly ground black pepper, to taste; mix well and pour over rice.

3 Drain tuna fish of oil; flake fish; add to the bowl and toss well.

4 Taste salad and correct seasoning, adding a little more olive oil, lemon juice or vinegar, and salt and freshly ground black pepper, if necessary.

1 pound cooked rice
8–12 stuffed olives, thinly sliced
1 red pepper, thinly sliced
1 green pepper, thinly sliced
1 cooked *chorizo* sausage, diced
1/2 Spanish onion, finely chopped
6 tablespoons olive oil
3 tablespoons lemon juice or wine vinegar
1 clove garlic, finely chopped
Generous pinch saffron
Salt and freshly ground black pepper
1 can tuna fish (about 7 oz)

Baked Barley and Mushroom Casserole

Serves 4

5 oz pearl barley
Butter
Salt
2 level tablespoons finely
  chopped onion
3/4 lb button mushrooms,
  thinly sliced
Freshly ground black pepper
1 egg, made up to 1/4 pint
  with single cream
2–4 level tablespoons grated
  cheese

Here's a dish which uses barley as we usually use rice. If you have never served barley as a dish in its own right, try this one. It is of Polish origin. Serve it as an accompaniment to meat or poultry, or as a supper dish instead of the usual macaroni-cheese.

1 Measure barley in a pint measuring jug or a cup and make a note of its volume. Put barley in a sieve and rinse under the cold tap until water runs clear. Drain well.

2 Measure double the volume of water as there is of barley into a heavy pan; add 1 level tablespoon butter and salt to taste. Bring to the boil.

3 Stir in barley; lower heat and simmer, covered, over the lowest possible heat until liquid has been absorbed and barley is cooked but not mushy, 20 to 30 minutes.

4 In a large frying-pan which has a lid, sauté finely chopped onion in 1 level tablespoon butter until soft and golden. Add sliced mushrooms and toss gently over a moderate heat for a few minutes. Season to taste with salt and freshly ground black pepper; moisten with 2 to 3 tablespoons water and simmer, tightly covered, until mushrooms are soft.

5 Preheat oven to moderate (375°F. Mark 5).

6 Butter a 2-pint baking dish and spread half of the barley evenly over the bottom. Cover with mushrooms and top with remaining barley.

7 Beat egg lightly with cream and a pinch of salt, to taste. Pour over the entire dish. Sprinkle surface with grated cheese.

8 Bake casserole for 20 minutes, or until golden and bubbling. Serve very hot.

Polenta

Serves 4–6

1 1/2 level teaspoons salt
12 oz fine cornmeal
Melted butter and freshly
  grated Parmesan, to serve

Polenta is nothing if not versatile. It goes magnificently well with richly sauced dishes of meat and game, even fish, especially salt cod. And you can serve it as it is; or grilled or fried; or allowed to cool, then stamped out or cut into shapes, and layered in a dish with other ingredients – butter, grated cheese or some rich meat sauce – before baking in the oven.

I am indebted to James Beard for this particularly fine manner of preparing polenta, which gives a much lighter texture than the more usual method of simmering over direct heat.

424

1 Measure $2\frac{1}{4}$ pints water into a heavy, large saucepan. Add salt and bring to the boil.

2 Slowly, to avoid water coming off the boil, pour in cornmeal, stirring vigorously with a wooden spoon to prevent lumps forming. Continue to cook, stirring vigorously, until mixture is quite thick and smooth, about 1 minute.

3 Line a metal sieve or colander with a double thickness of muslin.

4 Scrape polenta mixture into colander; fold ends of muslin neatly over top.

5 Fit sieve or colander over a pan of simmering water; cover with a lid and steam for $2\frac{3}{4}$ to 3 hours, until polenta has turned into a firm loaf.

6 Turn out on to a flat dish. Remove muslin and serve in slices with plenty of melted butter and freshly grated Parmesan.

Note: Left over polenta slices are delicious fried until crisp and golden in butter and oil.

Lesson 16

Making Perfect Pastry

The first pastries – created by the ancient Chinese – combined only flour and water to make delicious steamed or fried *won ton*, *shao m'ai* and pastes. The early Greeks and Romans produced pastries rich in oils and honey. The great houses of Britain and France were famous for their fabulous 'raised pies' – great set-pieces containing everything from game to pickled eggs, mushrooms and vinegar.

Today, our tastes are far simpler. We content ourselves with deep-set fruit pies or delicate glazed fruit flans; with meat, poultry, and game pies or French-inspired quiches.

But pastry is still king. For there is something wonderfully satisfying about the very making of pastry: the careful blending of the butter and the flour; the tender handling of the pastry itself; the choice of filling; and the baking.

Over the years, I have perfected a number of easy-to-make pastry recipes of the 'never fail' variety. Here I lay down a few 'musts' for making perfect pastry:

First, The Equipment

For measuring There's no guesswork when it comes to making perfect pastries, breads and cakes. Every good cook should have

Scales for measuring flour, sugar, fruit, etc.

Measuring spoons for all spoon measurements. It is too risky to use an ordinary spoon – they vary too much in size.

Measuring jug – marked in fluid ounces.

Other Equipment You Will Need

Nested mixing bowls of graduated sizes, from 1 pint to

3 quarts. Those with a flat 'grip-stand' side for easy handling when beating sauces are the best.

A wire pastry blender for shortcrust pastries. Blends flour and butter to crumbly stage quickly without danger of over-handling pastry. Particularly useful in warm weather.

An electric timer Reminds you when to take your pastry from the oven.

A metal sieve for sifting flour and other dry ingredients.

French pastry tins with loose bottoms Line with dough and bake according to instructions on page 429; then remove fluted ring and serve tart invisibly supported on loose metal bottom.

Wire whisks, small, medium and very large. These French whisks beat in more air than either a rotary whisk or an electric mixer.

The Flour

For most pastries I use a good-quality plain flour, sometimes 'weakened' with a little cornflour to reduce the gluten content and give an even finer texture.

All flour should be very dry and should be sieved with other dry ingredients for pastry-making. This not only ensures its being free from lumps, but makes the pastry lighter.

Don't use self-raising flour unless the recipe specially calls for it. Although a little baking powder can sometimes be added to plain flour to make a pastry shorter and lighter, especially if it is low in fat, but the proportion of raising agent is never as high as it would be if self-raising flour were used.

The Fats

Many cooks advocate the use of various combinations of butter, lard, margarine, clarified dripping, and the special whipped vegetable fats especially, to give a 'shorter' and 'lighter' texture to pastry. But for me there is only one fat: butter. For only butter can give that deliciously buttery texture and flavour to a crisp golden shell for a *quiche* or a fruit flan.

Use the butter firm, straight from the refrigerator. Cut it into tiny dice and toss the pieces in a bowl of sifted, flavoured flour immediately. Then, and only then, when they are thoroughly coated, you can start rubbing the butter into the flour. This

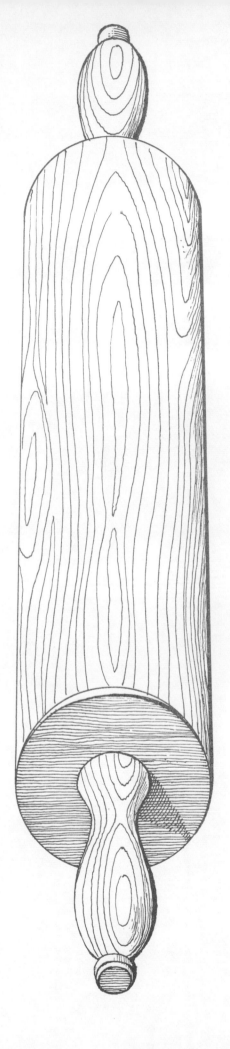

affords the butter some slight protection from the warmth of your fingers.

If, in spite of all precautions, you still can't prevent the butter turning oily, then your best bet is to use a pastry blender or two knives all through this process.

The Liquid

Water (and sometimes lemon juice or orange juice) is usually the only liquid required for mixing pastry. The liquid used should be as cold as possible, and in hot weather, a piece of ice should be added to it.

It is difficult to state exactly the amount of liquid to be used as so much depends on the consistency of the fat, and also upon the consistency of the flour. The finer the flour the more liquid it will require. For richer pastries, add a beaten egg or the yolk of an egg to the amount of water used.

Remember: using too much liquid is the most common cause of tough, badly shrunk pastry.

Remember, too, that a pastry that has been allowed to rest in the refrigerator is noticeably more moist when it comes out.

An egg yolk, which makes your pastry shorter and richer, also helps to keep the water content down, being largely composed of fat in a liquid form.

Dry Hands

Clean, dry hands are a must for pastry-making. In the summer, when hands are apt to be warm, mix the pastry as much as possible with a knife or a pastry-blender to keep it cool. Always make pastry in as cool a place as possible; the colder it is kept during the making the lighter your pastry will be.

Liquids should be added to the flour as quickly and lightly as possible. Some cooks do this on the board or slab by making a well in the centre of the flour and pouring the water into the centre as they mix. I find that mixing it in a large mixing bowl is much easier.

Chilling

Chilling is less important for simple pastries (i.e. half fat to flour) than for those rich in fat, but all pastries behave better after a thirty-minute rest in the refrigerator. This is particularly noticeable when you come to line tart tins, less important if the pastry is to be rolled quite thickly for covering a pie, etc.

To prevent the surface of the pastry drying out in the refrigerator, wrap it up in greaseproof paper, followed by a damp cloth, or in a piece of foil or plastic wrap. A plastic *bag* is not such a good idea as it tends to trap too much of the warm kitchen air inside it which then condenses and makes the ball of pastry 'sweat'.

To Roll Out Pastry

Remove dough from the refrigerator about ten minutes before you are ready to roll it out. This allows it to soften sufficiently for easy handling. Dust the pastry board or working surface lightly with flour. Then lay the ball of dough on it and work lightly with your hands until it is free from cracks.

Dust the rolling pin with flour; then press down the pastry and roll it out on one side only with sharp, quick strokes, trying to press equally with both hands on the rolling pin.

Never allow the pastry to stick to the board or working surface, but lift it occasionally on the rolling pin to dust some flour underneath. If any pastry has stuck to the board or working surface, carefully scrape it off with a knife before beginning to roll again.

Always sprinkle flour over board and pastry through a flour sifter, or a sieve, to make it finer and lighter, using as little flour as possible for this, as too much tends to make the pastry hard. If the rolling pin sticks to the pastry, dust with a little flour and then brush it off again lightly with a small brush kept for this purpose.

To 'Shape' Pastry

Roll out pastry as above ($\frac{1}{8}$ to $\frac{1}{16}$ inch thick). Then fold the rolled out sheet of pastry loosely over your rolling pin and transfer it to the tart tin. If you are using individual tart tins, cut rolled-out pastry into appropriately sized pieces to cover tins, leaving about 2 inches to spare. Then ease the pastry gently over the tart tin (or tins) and press it loosely down into the sides of tin (or tins) being careful not to pull or *stretch* it into place or it will just *shrink* out of shape again when it is baked.

It is better to press the pastry gently into position, using a little too much, and then pressing it against the sides of the tart tin

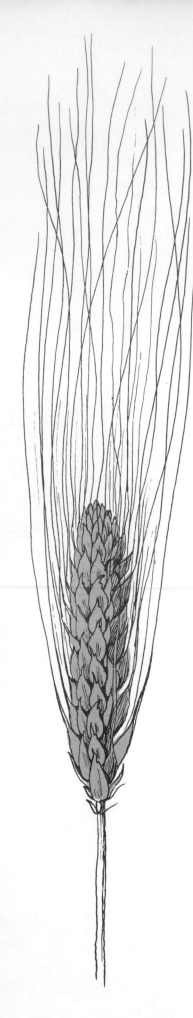

(or tins) and up, until it is of the thickness required. Then roll your rolling pin quickly across the top of the tin (or tins) to cut off the excess pastry neatly.

Prick the base and sides of your pastry shell (or shells) all over with the prongs of a dinner fork and chill pastry for 30 minutes in the refrigerator to minimise the danger of it 'running down' the sides of the tin (or tins) when it is first put into the oven.

Hot Oven

A relatively hot oven is required for pastry – for if it is not hot enough, the butter will 'melt' and run out of the pastry before the starch grains in the flour have time to burst and absorb it. But if the oven is too hot, the pastry will burn before it has risen properly. For flaky pastry the thermostat should register about 450°F (Mark 8) to begin with, and when the pastry is well risen the heat may be reduced to about 375°F (Mark 4). For meat pies, about 325°F (Mark 3) will be hot enough, and for the plainer kinds of pastry the temperature may be still a little lower.

Pastry should never be baked in an oven in which meat is being roasted, or with any other dish that generates steam, as moist heat is apt to destroy the pastry's crispness. Open and close the oven door as gently as possible, and not oftener than is necessary. If your pastry becomes too brown before it is sufficiently cooked, cover it over with a piece of aluminium foil or a double sheet of paper that has been slightly sprinkled with water. If the pastry is not to be used at once, allow it to cool slowly in the warm kitchen. Light pastry tends to become heavy when cooled too quickly.

Pastry Shells

To Bake an Unfilled Pastry Shell

To keep an unfilled pastry case from 'melting' down the sides of your tin – or bubbling up during baking, line the shell with greaseproof paper or foil and weight it down with raw dried beans or rice. I like to keep the beans or rice in a biscuit tin to use again and again. Push beans up against sides of shell to ensure that sides are properly supported.

Place the tin on a baking sheet and bake in a preheated, moderately hot oven (400°F. Mark 6) for 10 minutes. Remove from the oven and carefully lift out paper (or foil) and beans or rice. Allow to cool.

If tart shell is to be subjected to further baking after it has been filled, return the shell to the oven, minus beans and the lining paper without allowing it to cool (don't forget the baking sheet). Turn heat down to 350°F. (Mark 4) and bake for just 8 to 10 minutes longer to dry out the base without allowing it to brown. **Note:** If pastry starts to brown around the edges, cover edges lightly with foil.

If tart shell is to be cooked completely at this stage, leave it in the moderate oven for 10 to 15 minutes, or until it is set and a rich golden colour.

The base may bubble up slightly once it is no longer weighted down, but all you need to do is press it gently back into position again with a clean cloth folded into a wad.

Always leave the pastry shell to cool at room temperature. If it is cooled too quickly, it is liable to become tough.

Bottom Crust Pie

Using scissors, trim pastry ½ inch beyond edge of pan. Fold edge under, crimp with fingers. Bake 'blind' as above for 10 to 15 minutes to firm pastry. Then fill with uncooked mixture; bake as directed.

My Favourite Shortcrust Pastry (for Savoury Tarts, Flans and Quiches)

1 Sift flour, icing sugar and salt into a large bowl.

2 Cut cold (not chilled) butter into ¼-inch dice. Add to the bowl.

3 Using a pastry blender, or two knives held scissor-fashion one in each hand, cut diced butter into flour mixture until it resembles coarse breadcrumbs.

4 Discard pastry blender or knives. Scoop up some of the mixture in the palms of both hands and let it shower back lightly through your fingers, gently rubbing out the crumbs of fat between your fingertips. You should only need to do this six or seven times for the mixture be be reduced to fine breadcrumbs.

5 Beat egg yolk in a small bowl. Add lemon juice and 1 tablespoon iced water, and beat lightly until well mixed.

6 Sprinkle this over flour mixture, tossing and mixing with a fork. Rinse out bowl with another tablespoon of iced water and

8 oz plain flour
1 level teaspoon icing sugar
1/2 level teaspoon salt
5 oz cold butter
1 egg yolk
1 teaspoon lemon juice
Iced water

431

mix this into the pastry in the same way. Continue tossing and mixing with the fork until about three-quarters of the pastry is holding together. Then use your hand, cupped, to press the pastry lightly into one piece.

7 Shape pastry into a round. Wrap in a sheet of greaseproof paper, followed by a dampened tea towel, and chill for at least 1 hour before using.

To roll, shape and bake pastry: see pages 429 and 430.

Savoury Cornflour Shortcrust Pastry

4 oz plain flour
3 oz cornflour
1 level tablespoon castor sugar
Pinch of salt
1/2 level teaspoon baking powder
4 oz cold butter
1/4 teaspoon lemon juice
1 egg yolk
Milk

A well-behaved pastry with an exceptionally light, melting texture. It rolls out as thinly as you care to make it for delicate tart shells and hardly shrinks at all.

1 Sift first five ingredients into a bowl.

2 Dice butter coarsely and add it to the flour mixture, together with lemon juice. Toss until butter is well coated with flour; then rub it in lightly with your fingertips until mixture resembles fine breadcrumbs. Keep lifting your hands well above the bowl as you work so that the rubbed-in mixture is, as it were, aerated as it falls back into the bowl.

3 In a small bowl, beat egg yolk lightly with $1\frac{1}{2}$ tablespoons cold milk.

4 Sprinkle over flour mixture, stirring with a fork or a broad-bladed knife until pastry starts holding together in lumps. In the final stages, use a cupped hand to press pastry gently into a ball. (A little more milk may be added if pastry is too dry to shape into a ball, but as usual, keep the liquid down to a minimum, or pastry will be tough.)

5 Pastry may be used immediately, but if you have time to chill it for 30 minutes, wrapped in greaseproof paper or foil, so much the better.

To roll, shape and bake pastry: see pages 429 and 430.

Pissaladière

(Provençal Tomato and Onion Tart)

Serve as one large tart, cut in wedges, or in individual tart shells, as a first-rate appetiser or to hand around with drinks.

1 Preheat oven to moderately hot (400°F. Mark 6).

2 Brush interior of uncooked pastry shell with lightly beaten egg yolk and bake 'blind' for 10 to 15 minutes until crust is set but not brown. Remove from oven and allow to cool.

3 Reduce oven temperature to moderate (350°F. Mark 4).

4 Prepare filling: plunge tomatoes into boiling water for a minute to loosen skins; peel, seed and chop them.

5 Heat 4 tablespoons olive oil in a deep frying-pan; add chopped tomatoes, tomato concentrate, and freshly ground black pepper, to taste. Simmer over a low heat until excess moisture is cooked away, mashing occasionally with a wooden spoon to reduce tomatoes to a purée.

6 Slice onions and simmer them separately in butter, together with a pinch of freshly chopped rosemary, until soft and golden, but not brown.

7 Sprinkle bottom of pastry shell with freshly grated Parmesan. Add onions and cover with tomato purée. Arrange anchovies in a lattice pattern on top, and place a stoned black olive in the centre of each square. Brush olives and anchovies lightly with oil.

8 Bake tart for about 30 minutes. Serve hot, warm or cold.

Serves 6

An 8-inch shortcrust pastry shell (page 432)
1 egg yolk, lightly beaten

Filling
6 large ripe tomatoes
Olive oil
2 level tablespoons tomato concentrate
Freshly ground black pepper
3 Spanish onions
2 level tablespoons butter
Freshly chopped rosemary
2 level tablespoons freshly grated Parmesan
1 can anchovy fillets
Black olives, stoned

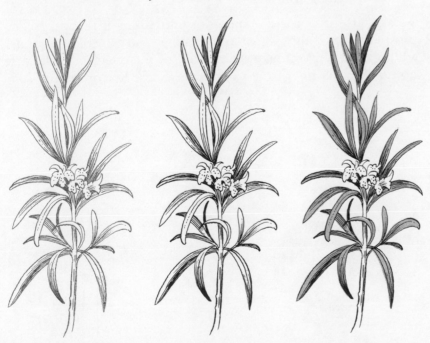

433

Serves 6

A 9-inch shortcrust pastry
case, prebaked (page 432)
4 level tablespoons butter
1 tablespoon olive oil
2 lb Spanish onions, very
finely shredded

Cream sauce

1/2 pint milk
1 bay leaf
1 clove
3 black peppercorns
1/2 chicken stock cube
1 level tablespoon butter
1 1/2 level tablespoons flour
3 egg yolks
2 level tablespoons freshly
grated Parmesan
Salt and freshly ground black
pepper
Freshly grated nutmeg

Onion Tart

1 Leave the pastry case in its tin. Lay it on a baking sheet and put aside until needed.

2 Melt butter with oil in a wide, heavy pan. Add finely shredded onions and sauté gently, stirring constantly with a wooden spoon, for 4 to 5 minutes, until onions have softened. Then cover pan, reduce heat even further and 'sweat' onions for 10 to 15 minutes longer, stirring occasionally. They should be meltingly soft but not coloured.

3 Preheat oven to moderate (350°F. Mark 4).

4 Prepare sauce: bring milk to the boil with the bay leaf, clove, peppercorns and stock cube. Remove pan from heat; cover and leave milk to infuse for 10 to 15 minutes. Strain into a jug.

5 In another, larger pan, melt butter; add flour and stir over a moderate heat for 2 to 3 minutes to make a smooth, pale *roux*. Stir in flavoured milk slowly and carefully to avoid making sauce lumpy, and when it is smooth again, simmer for a further 3 or 4 minutes until it thickens and loses its raw, floury taste.

6 Remove pan from heat. Beat in egg yolks, one at a time, followed by half the cheese, and season generously with salt, freshly ground black pepper and a pinch of freshly grated nutmeg.

7 Drain off any liquid which may have collected in the pan with the onions and fold onions gently into sauce.

8 Pour onion mixture into prebaked pastry case and sprinkle with remaining Parmesan.

9 Bake tart for 25 to 30 minutes, or until filling is set and golden brown on top. If top is slow in browning, you can colour it under a hot grill when you take the tart out of the oven, but take care not to char the rim of the pastry case. Serve hot or warm.

Creamed Button Onion Tart

Serves 6

1 To make filling: peel button onions. Put them in a pan with cold salted water to cover; bring to the boil over a moderate heat; boil for 2 minutes; then drain thoroughly in a colander.

2 In another pan, combine milk with bay leaf, peppercorns, cloves and half a chicken stock cube; bring to the boil, remove from heat and leave to infuse for ½ hour, covered with a lid.

3 Add onions to infused milk and return to the heat. Bring to the boil again and poach gently for 5 to 7 minutes, or until onions have softened but still hold their shape.

4 Preheat oven to moderate (350°F. Mark 4).

5 Place the prebaked tart case, still in its tin, on a baking sheet.

6 When onions are tender, remove them from the milk with a slotted spoon and arrange them side by side in the pastry case. Strain remaining milk through a fine sieve.

7 Melt butter in a heavy pan; add flour and stir over a low heat for a minute or two until well blended to make a pale *roux*. Then gradually blend in strained milk, stirring constantly to make a smooth sauce, and simmer for a few minutes longer until thickened.

8 In a large bowl, beat egg yolks lightly with cream until well mixed.

9 Gradually pour in a ladleful of hot sauce, beating all the while; then pour all the sauce into the top of a double saucepan and stir over hot water until it thickens, taking great care not to let it come to the boil, or the egg yolks will curdle.

10 Finally, stir in freshly grated Parmesan and season generously with salt, freshly ground black pepper and freshly grated nutmeg.

11 Spoon sauce over onions in tart shell.

12 Bake tart for 30 minutes, or until filling has set and top is a rich golden colour. If tart has not browned by the time filling is firm, brush top lightly with melted butter and slip under a hot grill for a minute or two to colour it. Serve hot.

An 8-inch shortcrust pastry case, prebaked (page 432)
Melted butter (optional)

Filling
2 lb tiny button onions
Salt
1/2 pint milk
1 bay leaf
3 black peppercorns
2 cloves
1/2 chicken stock cube
1/2 level teaspoon butter
1/2 level teaspoon flour
3 egg yolks
6 level tablespoons double cream
2 level teaspoons freshly grated Parmesan
Freshly ground black pepper
Freshly grated nutmeg

French Mushroom Tartlets

8 individual shortcrust
  pastry cases, prebaked
  (page 432) (see Step 1 of
  method)

1 lb small white button
  mushrooms

4 level tablespoons butter

2 tablespoons olive oil

Salt and freshly ground black
  pepper

Cayenne pepper

4 tablespoons Madeira

3 egg yolks

1/2 pint double cream

Finely chopped parsley, to
  decorate

1 The amount of mushroom mixture given will fill 8 fluted pastry cases 1¼ inches deep and 3 inches in diameter measured across the base, or 4 inches in diameter measured across the top. Bake them in loose-bottomed tins if possible, and don't unmould them until just before serving. While you are preparing the filling, arrange pastry cases on a baking sheet and pop them into a 350°F. (Mark 4) oven with the door open to reheat gently without cooking.

2 Wipe or wash mushrooms clean and trim rough stem ends.

3 In a large, heavy frying-pan, melt butter with olive oil and sauté mushrooms for 3 minutes (the mushrooms should stay 'crisp'). Season generously with salt, freshly ground black pepper and a dash of cayenne. Add Madeira and toss thoroughly. Remove pan from heat.

4 Whisk egg yolks lightly and blend with cream. Pour into top of double saucepan and stir over gently simmering water until mixture shows signs of thickening, 10 to 15 minutes.

5 Add mushrooms, together with all their juices, and continue to stir over simmering water until mushrooms are hot and sauce fully thickened, about 10 to 15 minutes longer. Take great care not to let sauce boil, or it will certainly curdle.

6 Taste sauce for seasoning. Then divide sauce and mushrooms between pastry cases.

7 To serve: carefully unmould tartlets on to a serving dish (or individual plates). Sprinkle with finely chopped parsley and serve immediately.

Note: Once you have mastered the art of thickening an egg sauce, you can dispense with the double saucepan. Simply pour the cream mixture into the frying pan with the mushrooms, and stir over a very low heat until sauce has thickened. It will take 20 to 25 minutes' patient stirring. Should the sauce seem to be heating too fast, whip the pan off the heat and, stirring constantly, let it cook from the heat of the pan itself for a minute or two before returning it to the stove.

French Leek Flan

1 Make the pastry case in a loose-bottomed tin if possible so that it need not be unmoulded until just before serving.

2 Slice leeks into rounds $\frac{1}{4}$ inch thick. Put them in a colander and rinse thoroughly under the cold tap. Drain well.

3 In a heavy saucepan, sauté leeks in 2 level tablespoons butter until they just start to colour, about 10 minutes. Add chicken stock; cover and simmer for 10 minutes, or until softened.

4 Preheat oven to moderate (375°F. Mark 5).

5 Drain leeks in a sieve over a bowl to catch the liquor, pressing them gently against sides of sieve with a spoon to extract as much moisture as possible without crushing them too much.

6 Pour liquor into a measuring jug and make it up to $\frac{1}{4}$ pint with milk if necessary. Alternatively, pour off excess to leave just $\frac{1}{4}$ pint.

7 Melt remaining butter in the top of a double saucepan. Blend in flour with a wooden spoon and cook over a direct, low heat, stirring constantly, to make a pale *roux*. Gradually add leek liquor, stirring briskly to avoid lumps forming. Bring to the boil and simmer for 2 to 3 minutes, stirring frequently. Remove from heat.

8 In a small bowl, beat cream and egg yolks together with a fork until well mixed. Pour into sauce gradually, stirring vigorously.

9 Fit pan over base containing simmering water. Cook sauce, stirring frequently, until slightly thickened, about 10 minutes, taking great care not to let it boil, or egg yolks will curdle. Remove from heat.

10 Beat in 1 oz grated cheese, and when melted, season to taste with salt and freshly ground black pepper.

11 To assemble flan: sprinkle base with another ounce of grated Gruyère. Fork over an even layer of cooked drained leeks. Spoon sauce over the top and sprinkle evenly with remaining cheese.

12 Place flan on a baking sheet and bake for 25 to 30 minutes, or until filling has set and surface is bubbling and golden. Serve hot or lukewarm.

A 9-inch shortcrust pastry case, prebaked
3/4 lb whites of leeks (about 6 medium-sized leeks)
3 level tablespoons butter
1/4 pint chicken stock (page 162)
Milk
1 level tablespoon flour
1/4 pint single cream
2 egg yolks
3 oz freshly grated Gruyère or Emmenthal
Salt and freshly ground black pepper

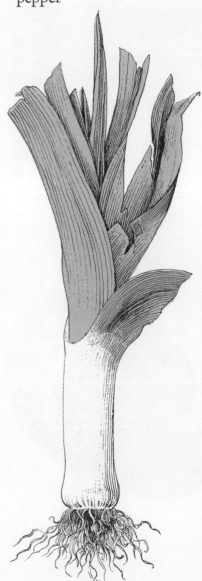

Serves 6

1/2 lb shortcrust pastry
  (page 432)
2 lb even-sized new potatoes
Salt and freshly ground black
  pepper
2 level tablespoons softened
  butter
3 level tablespoons freshly
  grated Parmesan
1/4 pint double cream
4 tablespoons milk
1 egg yolk

Gâteau de Pommes de Terre

(French Potato Tart)

1 Preheat oven to moderately hot (400°F. Mark 6).

2 Divide pastry in half. Roll one portion out $\frac{1}{8}$ inch thick and use it to line the bottom *only* of a loose-bottomed, 8-inch cake tin. Prick all over with a fork and bake blind for 10 minutes, or until pastry is set but not coloured. Remove from oven and leave to cool in the tin.

3 Reduce oven temperature to moderate (375°F. Mark 5).

4 Peel or scrape new potatoes and slice them into rounds about $\frac{1}{16}$ inch thick. Put potato slices in a pan; cover with cold salted water; bring to the boil over a moderate heat and boil for 1 minute. Drain thoroughly.

5 Take a small portion of the remaining pastry; roll out thinly and cut 4 bands each 6 inches long by 1 inch wide. These will be used to decorate the top of the tart.

6 Roll remaining pastry into a strip about $\frac{1}{8}$ inch thick, 4 inches wide and long enough to line the sides of the cake tin. Line the sides of the tin, sealing the strip carefully to the pastry base and allowing the excess to overhang the rim of the tin.

7 Layer potato slices in the pastry case, sprinkling each layer with freshly ground black pepper, a few flakes of softened butter and some of the grated Parmesan. Finish with a sprinkling of Parmesan.

8 Carefully fold the rim of loose pastry back over the top of the potatoes, pleating it at regular intervals to make a neat, even border.

9 In a bowl, beat double cream, milk and egg yolk lightly until well mixed. Put aside 3 level tablespoons for later use, and pour the remainder all over the potatoes.

10 Make a simple lattice on top with the 4 pastry bands, sealing them neatly to the border.

11 Bake potato tart for 35 to 40 minutes, or until potatoes feel soft when pierced with a thin skewer.

12 Spoon reserved cream mixture into potatoes, avoiding the pastry, and return to the oven for a further 10 minutes to brown the top.

13 Carefully unmould the tart and serve hot or warm.

My Favourite Shortcrust Pastry (For Sweet Tarts and Flans)

My favourite pastry of all for sweet tart shells. You can roll it out as usual, between $\frac{1}{8}$ and $\frac{1}{4}$ inch thick, but it also behaves beautifully when rolled even more thinly to make supremely light, crisp casings for delicate fillings of *crème pâtissière* and fresh fruits.

1 Sift flour, icing sugar and salt into a bowl.

2 Add softened butter in large pieces. Toss them about a little to coat them with flour mixture; then, very gently and lightly, rub butter into flour with your fingertips, lifting your hands well above the bowl as you work to aerate the mixture and help prevent butter becoming oily.

3 In a small bowl, beat egg yolk with 4 tablespoons iced water. Sprinkle over rubbed-in mixture and work in lightly with your fingertips until dough just holds together.

4 With a cupped hand, gently press moist dough into a flattened round. Wrap in greaseproof paper followed by a dampened cloth, or in a sheet of foil, and leave in the refrigerator for at least 1 hour to 'ripen'.

To roll, shape and bake pastry: see pages 429 and 430.

8 oz plain flour
2 level tablespoons icing sugar
1/4 level teaspoon salt
5 oz butter, softened
1 egg yolk
Iced water

Super-rich Shortcrust Pastry (For Sweet Tarts and Flans)

A fine, very short, sweet pastry, excellent for flan cases. It should be rolled between $\frac{1}{8}$ and $\frac{1}{4}$ inch thick.

1 Sift flour into a bowl.

2 Rub in butter with your fingertips until mixture resembles fine breadcrumbs.

3 Sift in icing sugar and stir until well mixed.

4 Make a well in the centre; drop in the egg yolk and quickly mix by hand to a soft dough. Knead lightly until smooth.

5 Roll dough into a ball. Wrap in a sheet of plastic or aluminium foil, or in greaseproof paper and a dampened cloth, and chill lightly for 30 minutes before using.

To roll, shape and bake pastry: see pages 429 and 430.

6 oz plain flour
4 oz butter
1 oz icing sugar
1 egg yolk

Cream Shortcrust Pastry (For Sweet Tarts and Flans)

8 oz plain flour
1 level tablespoon castor sugar
Pinch of salt
4 level tablespoons butter
1/4 pint double cream

Be prepared for a little more shrinkage than usual with this pastry, which has a fine, rich flavour.

1 Sift flour, sugar and salt into a bowl.

2 Rub in butter as usual – see preceding recipes – until mixture resembles fine breadcrumbs.

3 Add double cream gradually, stirring with a fork or a broad-bladed knife until about three-quarters of the pastry adheres together. Then discard the fork or knife and use a cupped hand to press the pastry gently into a ball.

4 Wrap pastry in a sheet of greaseproof paper, followed by a damp tea towel, or in a sheet of foil, chill for at least 30 minutes before proceeding.

To roll, shape and bake pastry: see pages 429 and 430.

Rich American Cookie Crust

5 oz butter
5 level tablespoons granulated sugar
1/4 level teaspoon salt
1 egg white
1/2 teaspoon vanilla essence or the juice of 1/2 lemon
8 oz plain flour

A buttery, vanilla-flavoured pastry with a firmer, crunchier texture than shortcrust – perfect for fruit tarts.

1 Cut butter into $\frac{1}{2}$-inch dice.

2 In a large bowl, combine diced butter with sugar and salt. Work these ingredients with a large fork until thoroughly mixed and mixture resembles coarse breadcrumbs.

3 In a small bowl or cup, beat egg white lightly with a fork. Add to butter mixture, together with vanilla or lemon juice, and continue to mix with the fork until thoroughly blended.

4 Gradually sift flour over butter mixture, mixing it in with the fork to begin with, then using your fingertips as it becomes stiffer, to make a smooth dough.

5 Roll dough into a ball. Wrap in a sheet of plastic, or in greaseproof paper and a dampened cloth, and chill lightly for 30 minutes before using.

This pastry is best rolled out just under $\frac{1}{4}$ inch thick. Otherwise, treat it as directed for shortcrust pastry (page 439). If you find that the outside rim browns more quickly during baking than an ordinary shortcrust, which it is liable to do, cover the top with a sheet of foil.

Crème Pâtissière I
(French Pastry Cream)

A light pastry cream for tarts, flans etc. It is not suitable for filling cream slices or choux puffs which require a stiffer consistency that stays put when cut with a knife – see Crème Pâtissière II, below.

1 Stir sugar with cornflour in the top of a double saucepan until cornflour is completely dispersed. Then add cold milk gradually, stirring with a wooden spoon to blend it in smoothly.

2 Cook over a moderate, direct heat, stirring constantly, until mixture comes to the boil; then simmer for 4 minutes, stirring, until sauce has thickened and no longer tastes of raw cornflour.

3 In a bowl, beat egg yolks lightly with a whisk. Pour on hot cornflour sauce in a thin stream, beating vigorously.

4 Return sauce to the pan and cook over lightly simmering water, stirring constantly, until thick and smooth, 10 to 15 minutes.

5 Strain sauce through a fine sieve into a bowl. Cool slightly; then beat in butter, followed by vanilla essence, to taste, and/ or any other flavouring called for in your recipe.

6 Allow pastry cream to cool, beating occasionally with a wooden spoon to prevent a skin forming on top. (If a skin *does* form, you will have to sieve the cream again before using it.) Cover surface with a piece of greaseproof paper.

Note: If you keep a supply of vanilla-flavoured castor sugar, this will give a far more subtle vanilla flavour than the essence.

Makes ¾ pint

4 oz castor sugar
2 level tablespoons cornflour
3/4 pint milk
4 egg yolks
4 level tablespoons butter
1/4–1/2 teaspoon vanilla essence and/or flavouring according to specific recipe

Crème Pâtissière II
(French Pastry Cream)

A pastry cream which is soft and delicate, yet firm enough to hold its shape when cut or bitten into.

1 Pour milk into a medium-sized pan and add vanilla pod, split to give out maximum flavour. Bring to boiling point over a low heat. Cover pan and put aside to infuse until needed.

2 In a bowl, whisk egg yolks with sugar until thick and light. Gradually whisk in flour and cornflour.

3 Fish out vanilla pod. Gradually pour milk into egg yolk mixture, beating with the whisk until well blended.

4 Pour mixture back into the pan. Bring to the boil over a

Makes about ¾ pint

3/4 pint milk
A 2-inch piece of vanilla pod, split
5 egg yolks
4 oz castor sugar
2 level tablespoons plain flour
1 level tablespoon cornflour
1 level tablespoon butter
A few drops of vanilla essence and/or flavouring according to specific recipe

moderate heat, stirring constantly. Then simmer for 3 minutes longer, beating vigorously with a wooden spoon to disperse lumps. (These lumps invariable form, but they are easy to beat out as the cream thickens.)

5 Remove pan from heat. Beat in butter and continue to beat for a minute or two longer to cool the pastry cream slightly before adding flavourings called for in your recipe.

6 Pass cream through a sieve if necessary. Put it in a bowl and cover with a sheet of lightly buttered greaseproof paper to prevent a skin forming on top.

7 Allow to become quite cold; then chill until required.

Fresh Fruit Tart Pâtissière

Summer travellers through the French countryside often return home full of praise for – among other things – French fruit flans: the golden shells of fresh baked pastry, with a hidden bonus of *crème pâtissière* (French pastry cream) which serves as a deliciously flavoured bed for fresh summer fruit – halved apricots, sliced bananas and oranges, apples arranged in concentric rings, alternate rows of strawberries, cherries and raspberries, or the caramelised gold of pineapple – all covered with a richly coloured apricot glaze flavoured with rum, brandy or kirsch.

The Pastry

Many cooks have their own recipes for pastry which do admirably for fruit tarts and flans of all kinds. My favourite is super rich in butter, the texture is sandy, not unlike that of an American 'cookie'. Sometimes I flavour it with cinnamon or finely ground almonds and lemon peel.

Pastry for Fresh Fruit Tart Pâtissière

8 oz plain flour
Pinch of salt
2 level tablespoons icing sugar
5 oz cold butter
1 egg yolk
2 teaspoons lemon juice
Iced water

1 Sieve the flour, salt and icing sugar into a large bowl.

2 Cut cold (not chilled butter) into ¼-inch dice. Add to bowl.

3 Using a pastry blender or two knives held scissor fashion, one in each hand, cut diced butter into flour mixture until it resembles coarse breadcrumbs.

4 Discard pastry blender or knives. Scoop up some of the mixture in the palms of both hands and let it shower back lightly through your fingers, gently rubbing out the crumbs of fat between your fingertips. You should only need to do this six or seven times for the mixture to be reduced to fine breadcrumbs.

5 Beat egg yolk in a small bowl. Add lemon juice and 1 tablespoon iced water, and beat lightly until well mixed.

6 Sprinkle this over flour mixture, tossing and mixing with a fork. Rinse out bowl with another tablespoon of iced water and mix this into the pastry in the same way. Continue tossing and mixing with the fork until about three-quarters of the pastry is holding together. Then use your hand, cupped, to press the pastry lightly into one piece.

7 Shape pastry into a round. Wrap in a sheet of greaseproof paper, followed by a dampened tea towel, and chill for at least 1 hour before using.

8 If chilled dough is too firm for handling, let it stand at room temperature until it softens slightly. Then turn onto a floured board, knead or pat lightly into a round, roll out and use as required.

9 Bake blind in a preheated fairly hot oven (425°F. Mark 7) for 15 minutes; lower heat to 350°F. (Mark 4) and bake for 30 minutes.

The Filling

The magic trick of the French fruit flan is the sweet, creamy filling hidden underneath the fruit. Crème pâtissière (page 441) holds its shape when cold yet is soft and never stiff in texture.

French Pastry Cream

The best French pastry cream to use for Fresh Fruit Tart Pâtissière is Crème Pâtissière II. Follow this recipe – steps 1 through 7 (see pages 441 and 442) for best results.

To Assemble Fresh Fruit Tart

Half fill baked pastry shell with French pastry cream; and arrange different fruits and berries – apricot halves, peach slices, strawberries, grapes, orange sections – in colourful rows on this bed. Coat with apricot glaze. (See recipe overleaf)

8 tablespoons apricot jam
4 tablespoons water
1–3 tablespoons rum, brandy
or Kirsch (optional)

Apricot Glaze

1 Heat apricot jam and water in a small saucepan, stirring constantly, until mixture melts. Strain.

2 If desired, stir in rum, brandy or Kirsch. Keep warm over hot water, until ready to use.

3 Brush surface of fruit to give a shiny glaze.

Tarte aux Abricots
(Apricot tart)

Line a pastry tin with tart or flan pastry (page 439 or 442); bake and cool. Half fill the tart shell with French Pastry Cream (page 441): place peeled, poached apricot halves, cut side down, on the cream and glaze with melted, sieved apricot jam. Let jelly set and sprinkle with chopped almonds.

Tartes aux Fraises
(Strawberry tarts)

Make individual tart shells of tart or flan pastry (page 439 or 442). Cool, spoon a little French Pastry Cream (page 441) into each shell and cover with ripe strawberries. Pour over each tart 1 tablespoon melted red currant jelly flavoured with $\frac{1}{2}$ teaspoon Kirsch. Cool and chill thoroughly.

Tarte aux Pommes à l'Alsacienne
(Alsatian Apple tart)

Line a pastry tin with tart or flan pastry (page 439 or 442); bake and cool. Half-fill with French Pastry Cream (page 441). Cover with overlapping rings of thinly sliced eating apples. Brush with melted butter and bake in a preheated hot oven (450°F. Mark 8) for 5 minutes. If apples do not brown sufficiently at edges to be attractive, put under grill for a minute or two. Cool tart and then glaze with sieved apricot jam flavoured with a little rum, brandy or Kirsch.

American Banana Pie

Line a pastry tin with tart or flan pastry (page 439 or 442); bake and cool. Half-fill with French Pastry Cream (page 441). Cover with thin slices of banana which you have dipped in lemon juice to preserve colour. Cover with thin layer of lemon jelly.

Ananas Bourdaloue
(Pineapple Bourdaloue)

Line a pastry tin with tart or flan pastry (page 439 or 442); bake and cool. Half-fill with French Pastry Cream (page 441). Arrange rings of fresh pineapple on this and brush with apricot jam. Serve chilled.

Tarte au Citron

1 Preheat oven to moderate (350°F. Mark 4).

2 Prepare Almond filling: whisk eggs with sugar until thick and creamy. Add remaining ingredients and beat vigorously with a wooden spoon until smoothly blended.

3 Fill pastry case with almond mixture and bake for 10 to 15 minutes until puffed and golden, and firm to the touch.

4 To make Lemon topping: slice lemons thinly, removing pips as you come across them. (If the pith on the lemons is very thick, first peel them with a sharp knife as you would an apple, otherwise they may be unpleasantly bitter.)

5 In a large, deep frying-pan, dissolve sugar cubes in $\frac{1}{4}$ pint water over a moderate heat. Bring to the boil; lay lemon slices in the syrup and simmer for 3 minutes.

6 Remove lemon slices with a slotted spoon.

7 Bubble remaining syrup over a moderate heat until reduced by half. Add apple jelly or sieved greengage conserve, and stir until melted to make a rich glaze.

8 Arrange lemon slices on top of tart in overlapping circles. Brush generously with glaze and slip under a hot grill for a few minutes until glaze is bubbling and caramelised, and edges of lemon slices are tinged with brown. Serve lukewarm or cold.

Serves 6–8

1 9-inch baked pastry shell
(page 439 or 442)

Almond filling

2 eggs
5 level tablespoons castor sugar
6 level tablespoons double cream
4 oz ground almonds
Juice and finely grated rind of 1 large lemon
1–2 drops almond essence

Lemon topping

4 thin-skinned lemons
3 oz sugar cubes
3 level tablespoons apple jelly or sieved greengage conserve

Tarte à l'Orange

Prepare as above, adding the finely grated rind of 1 bright-skinned orange to the filling.

For the topping, use 4 small oranges, thinly sliced and simmered in a light sugar syrup as above. **Note:** If pith is thick, first peel oranges with a sharp knife, as in recipe above.

Thicken the glaze with 3 level tablespoons orange jelly or sieved orange marmalade.

Serves 8

A 9-inch shortcrust pastry case, prebaked (page 439 or 442)

5 oz granulated sugar

1 3/4 pints water

4 large, ripe, round dessert pears

2 tablespoons brandy

1/4 pint plus 4 level tablespoons double cream

4 level tablespoons sour cream

1 level tablespoon cornflour

1 oz castor sugar

2 egg yolks, lightly beaten

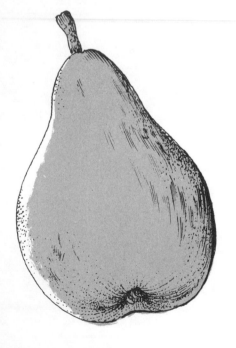

French Pear Tart

1 Make the pastry case in a loose-bottomed tin if possible, so that it can be left there until just before serving.

2 Make a light syrup by melting granulated sugar in $1\frac{3}{4}$ pints water, and let it simmer gently while you prepare pears.

3 Peel pears and cut them in half lengthwise. With a teaspoon, scoop out the central core and seeds; then take a small sharp knife and make a V-shaped incision to remove the fibres leading from the core to the stem.

4 As soon as pears are ready, lower them into the simmering syrup and poach them gently until very soft but not disintegrating. This will take about 15 minutes, depending on the variety of pears used and how ripe they are.

5 Lift pears out of syrup with a slotted spoon, draining them thoroughly, and put them in a bowl. Pour over brandy and leave them to macerate in it as they cool.

6 Preheat oven to very slow (300°F. Mark 2).

7 Blend double cream with sour cream in the top of a double saucepan. Mix cornflour and castor sugar together in a bowl (large enough to accommodate all the cream later). Add about 4 tablespoons of the cream mixture and mix until smoothly blended.

8 Bring remaining cream mixture to the boil over direct heat. Pour it over cornflour cream in a thin stream, stirring vigorously to blend them together smoothly.

9 Return mixture to top of double saucepan and stir over direct, moderate heat until it comes to the boil. Lower heat and simmer for 3 minutes, stirring constantly.

10 Remove pan from heat and blend in lightly beaten egg yolks. Fit top of pan over simmering water and cook, stirring frequently, until slightly thickened. Take great care not to let the mixture boil, or egg yolks may curdle. Remove from heat.

11 Pour off brandy syrup from pears and add it to the custard cream. Drain pears of any remaining syrup on absorbent paper.

12 Strain custard through a fine sieve. Spread a thin layer of it over base of pastry shell. Arrange pears in a circle in the pastry shell, cut sides down and stem ends pointing towards the centre. Spoon over remaining custard cream, making sure pears are completely coated.

13 Transfer tart, still in its tin, to a baking sheet. Bake for 30 minutes, or until custard cream has set.

14 If tops of pears have not coloured, slip the tart under a hot grill for 2 or 3 minutes to brown them lightly. Unmould just before serving and serve lukewarm or cold.

Black Bottom Pie

Serves 6

1 Sprinkle powdered gelatine over 2 tablespoons cold water in a cup and put aside to soften.

2 In the top of a double saucepan, stir cornflour into 3 oz castor sugar.

3 Beat egg yolks lightly; pour them over cornflour mixture, stirring vigorously with a wooden spoon until smoothly blended.

4 Bring milk to the boil; pour into egg mixture in a thin stream, stirring vigorously.

5 Cook over simmering water, stirring, for 15 to 20 minutes, or until custard coats back of spoon, taking great care not to let it boil, or egg yolks may curdle. Remove from heat.

6 Stand cup with gelatine in hot water (use the water in the bottom of the double saucepan) and stir until gelatine has dissolved and liquid is clear. Blend thoroughly with custard.

7 Melt chocolate on a plate over simmering water – yes, use the water left in the bottom of the double saucepan.

8 Pour two-thirds of custard mixture into one bowl, and remaining third into another.

9 Blend chocolate smoothly with larger portion of custard; flavour to taste with vanilla essence. Pour into pastry shell and chill until set on top.

10 When remaining portion of custard is on the point of setting, whisk egg whites with cream of tartar until soft peaks form; add remaining sugar gradually and continue to whisk to a stiff, glossy meringue.

11 Peel and cut 1 banana into very thin slices. Arrange on top of chocolate mixture.

12 Fold meringue into plain custard. Flavour to taste with vanilla essence and pile on top of chocolate mixture, covering it completely. Return to the refrigerator until quite set.

13 Just before serving, peel and slice remaining banana. Brush slices lightly with lemon juice to prevent them discolouring and arrange them on top of pie. Finish decoration with chocolate curls and a border of piped whipped cream.

1 deep, 8 1/2-inch shortcrust pastry case, prebaked (page 439)
1 level tablespoon powdered gelatine
1 level tablespoon cornflour
4 oz castor sugar
4 egg yolks
3/4 pint milk
3 oz bitter chocolate
Vanilla essence
3 egg whites
Pinch of cream of tartar
2 large bananas
Lemon juice
Chocolate curls and whipped cream, to decorate

Makes 12 tartlets

12 fluted tartlet shells,
3 inches in diameter, made
with about 4 oz shortcrust
pastry and prebaked (page
439)

12 very thin slivers
crystallised orange peel

Filling

4 level tablespoons cornflour
1/2 level teaspoon salt
6 oz castor sugar
1 level tablespoon butter
4 egg yolks, lightly beaten
8 tablespoons orange juice
2 tablespoons lemon juice
2 level teaspoons very finely
grated orange rind

Meringue

2 egg whites
Pinch of salt
4 oz castor sugar

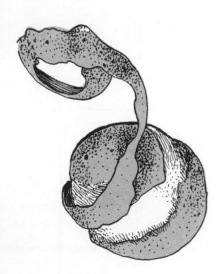

Orange Meringue Tartlets

1 Leave tartlet shells in the tins in which you baked them. Arrange them on one or two baking sheets.

2 Prepare filling: combine cornflour with salt and castor sugar in the top of a double saucepan. Mix to a smooth paste with $\frac{1}{4}$ pint cold water; then gradually pour on $\frac{1}{2}$ pint boiling water, stirring briskly. Cook over direct heat, stirring vigorously, until mixture comes to the boil.

3 Set top of pan over base containing boiling water, and simmer very gently for about 15 minutes, stirring occasionally, until sauce is thick and smooth, and no longer tastes of cornflour.

4 Beat in butter and lightly beaten egg yolks, and continue to stir over hot water until sauce thickens again. Take care not to let it boil at this stage, or egg yolks may curdle.

5 Pour sauce into a bowl and, while still hot, beat in orange juice, lemon juice and finely grated orange rind. Allow to cool, beating occasionally to prevent a skin forming on top.

6 Fill tartlets with orange filling, piling it up high in the shells.

7 Preheat oven to slow (325°F. Mark 3).

8 Prepare meringue: beat egg whites with a pinch of salt until soft peaks form. Add half of the castor sugar and continue to beat until stiff and glossy again; then carefully fold in remaining sugar with a metal spoon.

9 Divide meringue evenly between tarts, spreading it right down on to the rim of the pastry and covering filling completely. Decorate top of each tartlet with a strip of crystallised orange peel.

10 Bake tartlets for 15 to 20 minutes, or until meringue is crisp and lightly golden.

11 Carefully remove from tins. Serve lukewarm or cold.

Note: For lemon meringue tartlets, flavour custard with 6 tablespoons lemon juice and 2 level teaspoons very finely grated lemon rind. Decorate tops with slivers of crystallised lemon peel.

448

Orange and Lemon Chiffon Pie

Serves 6–8

An example of the famous American chiffon pie – you can flavour it as you like, with fresh limes, or any other sharp-flavoured fruit.

1 Preheat oven to moderate (375°F. Mark 5).

2 To make pastry: sift flour into a bowl. Make a well in the centre; add softened butter in small pieces, the icing sugar and egg yolk, and work together lightly to make a smooth paste. Roll into a ball, wrap loosely in foil and leave to rest in the refrigerator for ½ hour.

3 Press pastry into an 8-inch flan ring with a removeable base. Prick all over with a fork; line pastry shell with aluminium foil; fill with dried beans (to keep pastry from rising) and bake in preheated oven for about 20 minutes. Remove from oven and cool.

4 To make filling: sprinkle gelatine over 2 tablespoons cold water in a small bowl.

5 In the top of a double saucepan, beat egg yolks lightly with half the sugar, and all the grated orange rind, orange and lemon juice. Stir over simmering water until mixture thickens. Remove from heat.

6 Place cup containing gelatine in hot water remaining in the bottom of the double saucepan, and stir until gelatine has completely dissolved and liquid is clear. Beat into custard mixture and put aside until cold and on the point of setting.

7 Beat egg whites until stiff but not dry. Gradually beat in remaining castor sugar and continue to beat to a stiff, glossy meringue. Fold into cold custard mixture.

8 Whip double cream until soft peaks form. Fold into custard, together with chopped orange flesh. Chill mixture in the refrigerator until just on the point of setting and firm enough to hold its shape.

9 Pile filling into prebaked pastry case, swirling it up attractively, and decorate with orange and lemon segments.

10 Return to the refrigerator until firmly set.

Pastry
4 oz plain flour
3 oz softened butter
1 oz icing sugar
1 egg yolk

Filling
1 level tablespoon powdered gelatine
3 eggs, separated
4 oz castor sugar
Grated rind of 1/2 orange
Juice of 1 orange
Juice of 2 lemons
1/4 pint double cream
Flesh of 1 orange, chopped

To decorate
Orange and lemon segments

Making Perfect Puff Pastry

Rough puff, *flaky* (demi-feuilletée) *and puff* (feuilletée) are a formidable trio of pastries, to be treated with respect. If you have never experienced any difficulty in turning out a good puff pastry – each paper-thin layer separate, meltingly crisp and buttery – you are to be congratulated, for you are indeed a born pastrymaker.

For the rest of us, learning how to handle puff pastry, how to roll, fold and turn it so that the delicate layers build up, waiting for the moment when the intense heat of the oven will burst them apart again, is one of the great techniques of the kitchen.

The making of puff pastry is surrounded by something of a ritual – but unlike many culinary rituals, which can safely be relegated to obscurity, this is one to which you should pay careful attention, at least until you have found your feet.

The Ingredients

Flour

Good-quality, dry, plain flour should be used and *never* self-raising flour for the reasons already explained on page 427. And as when making shortcrust pastry, the flour should be sifted even if there are no obvious lumps in it, to incorporate air and, consequently, lightness.

Fat

Classic puff recipes do not recognise any fat apart from butter. It should be only lightly salted, if at all; otherwise you may find yourself with an oversalty pastry.

I have found, however, that other fats, used in small amounts, will improve the 'flake' of the pastry without interfering with its flavour which should, above all, be perfectly, deliciously buttery. Lard and whipped white vegetable fats are the ones I prefer.

Liquid

You will notice that our trio of recipes specially calls for *iced water*. This is all part of the general aim of keeping everything as cold as possible so that the butter is protected from softening too much. Simply drop a few ice cubes into a jug of water and leave for 10 minutes until water is thoroughly iced.

Lemon juice (some prefer vinegar) helps to develop the gluten in the flour which in simple language means that the structure of the pastry is strengthened.

Egg yolk, apart from contributing moisture, adds richness to texture and flavour.

The Technique

Rough puff, flaky and puff: this is the order in which you should tackle them.

Apart from being listed in ascending order of complexity (and fineness), the trio differ radically from each other in the manner in which flour and fat are brought together.

Rough puff Butter is all cut into small pieces and mixed with flour and liquid to make a rough paste. The knobbles of butter are gradually eliminated by a series of rollings and foldings.

Proportion of fat to flour can be as low as 1:2, rising to a maximum of 3:4.

Flaky Starts off by rubbing one-third of the fat into the flour; then binds this with water to make a sort of unleavened scone dough. This is then rolled into a rectangle and folded 4 times in all. Each time, a quarter of the remaining fat is dotted over two-thirds of the surface before the rectangle is folded in three.

Proportion of fat to flour is usually 3:4. Of the fat, no more than one-third should be lard and/or vegetable shortening.

Puff Here the basic flour-and-liquid dough or *détrempe* contains no fat at all. It is rolled into a circle and used to enclose a block of blended butter and fat. This 'parcel' is then rolled and folded 6 times in all.

The proportion of fat to flour is 1:1. We have found that 3 oz vegetable shortening to 13 oz butter gives excellent results.

For all these pastries, the same rules apply, with minor variations.

● Start Everything as Cold as Possible

If you can work on a marble slab, all to the good – it really does make a difference. And if you can actually get the marble inside the refrigerator to chill it between rollings as well, better still. The bowl of sifted flour can also be chilled for good measure if there is time and room left in the refrigerator.

● *Chill Between Rollings*

Unless you work with lightning speed – or in a refrigerated room – you are unlikely to be able to complete more than two rollings and foldings of the pastry at a time. The fat quickly starts to soften and becomes unmanageable.

Indeed, if you are a novice, or if the weather is hot (and, by the way, don't attempt puff pastry on a hot day until you are very, very experienced), be prepared to down tools *at any stage* if you feel the pastry start to soften under your rolling pin or notice a creaminess which indicates that the butter is going to start oozing through at any moment.

Finally, all these pastries improve if left to relax in the refrigerator for a few hours after the final folding. Be sure to wrap the pastry up closely in greaseproof paper, followed by a damp cloth, to prevent a crust forming on the surface.

This not only allows the alternating layers of butter and paste to firm up so that they remain even more well defined when baked, but also makes the pastry easier to roll.

Handling Puff Pastry

Here is where technique really comes into its own.

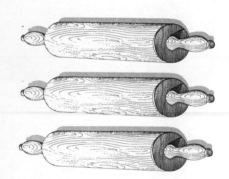

● First of all, get into the habit of rolling the rectangle of pastry always in the same direction, using long, smooth, light strokes. The easiest way is to work from the centre – rolling *up* away from you, then *down* towards you. Try not to roll *quite* over the ends, and don't be tempted to push hard or stretch the pastry with the rolling pin – all you will do is tear the layers you have gone to such lengths to build up.

● The pastry should be lifted occasionally to ensure it has not stuck to the marble, but do this carefully to avoid breaking any layering with your fingers.

● As the rectangle begins to take shape, use a ruler, or a knife with a long blade to knock sides straight and corners right-angled. This is important – a rounded edge falling short means a loss in that area of so many layers.

● Having folded the bottom third up towards the centre, brush off any loose flour adhering to the underside with a pastry brush before folding the top third down over it. You want to incorporate as little extra flour into the pastry as possible.

● Seal the folded rectangle by pressing gently but firmly against the seams with the rolling pin or the side of your hand.

● If in any doubt about the pastry's ability to take a further rolling and folding immediately, chill for 15 minutes.

● You may find it easier, when first starting to roll a thick, folded packet of pastry, if you press down on it several times with your rolling pin to flatten and spread it out slightly. The 'corrugated' look will soon disappear when you start rolling in earnest.

The 'Turns'

This term refers to the quarter-turn you give the slab of pastry each time you come to re-roll it. The best way to remember the initial position of the slab is to visualise a closed book lying in front of you with the front facing upwards. Thus the long, folded side will always be on your left-hand side when you start, and the long side last to be sealed on your right.

You should always make a note of the number of turns completed, either in the classic manner, by pressing light dents on the top of the folded pastry with the ball of a finger (not the tip – you might pierce the pastry with your fingernail), or simply by making a note of them on a sheet of paper. Otherwise, it's surprising how easy it is to lose your place after the second or third 'turn'.

Rough Puff Pastry

1 Sift flour and salt into a bowl.

2 Cut chilled butter into large dice (between $\frac{1}{4}$ and $\frac{1}{2}$ inch). Drop into bowl of flour and toss lightly until pieces of butter are thoroughly coated.

3 In a small bowl, beat egg yolk lightly with lemon juice and 4 tablespoons iced water.

4 Sprinkle egg mixture over flour and butter mixture, turning latter over and over from the bottom of the bowl with a spatula or a broad-bladed knife so that the two can be combined without breaking butter cubes.

5 Continue turning mixture over and sprinkling with more iced water until about three-quarters of the mixture holds together. Then, with cupped hands and the help of a little more iced water if necessary, gently push and press the mass into a moist but not sticky ball. You should be able to use it to wipe the bowl clean. This last stage will take another 3 and 4 tablespoons iced water, making a total of 7 or 8, not more.

7 Place the ball on a lightly floured marble or board. Dust your

8 oz plain flour
Pinch of salt
6 oz butter, chilled
1 egg yolk
1 teaspoon lemon juice
Iced water

rolling pin with flour as well, and gently roll the pastry into a rectangle about 12 inches long and 6 inches wide, pushing sides straight and corners as square as possible with the side of your ruler or a long-bladed knife.

8 With the back of your knife, mark a strip lightly across the width one-third from the bottom. Fold bottom third up over the centre; then fold remaining third down on top of it. Seal edges with your rolling pin or the side of your hand.

9 Wrap pastry in a sheet of greaseproof paper, followed by a damp cloth, and chill for 15 minutes. (Make a note that pastry has had 1 'turn'.)

10 Unwrap pastry and lay it in front of you on a lightly floured surface so that the fold is on your left-hand side and the longest sealed edge on your right (think of a closed book lying with its cover upwards).

11 Repeat rolling and folding *twice*. Wrap up and chill for 15 minutes. (Make a note that pastry has now had 3 'turns'.)

12 Repeat rolling and folding *twice*. Wrap up and chill for 15 minutes. (Pastry has now had 5 'turns'.)

13 Repeat rolling and folding *twice*. Wrap up and chill for 15 minutes. (Pastry has now had 7 'turns'.)

14 Finally, unwrap pastry and position bookwise once more. Roll and fold pastry for the last time. Pastry may now be used as it is, or wrapped up again and chilled in the refrigerator until needed.

Note 1: The ideal baking temperature for rough puff pastry is around 425°F. (Mark 7), but this will vary according to the use to which it is put.

Note 2: When time is limited, 6 'turns' of the pastry will give a perfectly satisfactory result. You will probably also find that as you gain expertise and speed, you will be able to complete three 'turns' at a time before the pastry becomes soft enough to require chilling.

Flaky Pastry
(Pâte Demi-feuilletée)

1 lb plain flour
1 level teaspoon salt
2 oz vegetable shortening
2 oz lard
8 oz butter
Iced water
1 tablespoon lemon juice

1 Sift flour and salt into a large bowl. If convenient, slip bowl into refrigerator until needed.

2 Place vegetable shortening and lard on a large soup plate. Using a spatula or a broad-bladed knife, work fats together until thoroughly blended. Shape into a brick; divide in half and refrigerate until firm again.

3 Remove bowl of flour from the refrigerator. Dice half the butter (i.e. 4 oz) into bowl and rub into flour with your fingertips until mixture resembles fine breadcrumbs. Make a well in the centre.

4 Carefully measure 10 tablespoons iced water into the well, together with lemon juice. Stir vigorously with a broad-bladed knife, gradually incorporating flour from sides of well; then start mixing in remaining flour, adding more iced water if necessary, a teaspoon at a time, until you have a ball of dough that is neither too sticky nor too dry, i.e. of such a consistency that you can use it to wipe the sides of the bowl clean. It will be easier to judge this if, in the final stages, you use your hands to push the dough gently together. In all, you will probably need another 3 to 4 tablespoons iced water, depending on the quality of your flour.

5 Turn dough out on to a lightly floured surface. Work it lightly with just a few turns (kneading would be too strong a word) to smooth out the texture without developing any elasticity.

6 Roll dough out into a rectangle 16 by 8 inches, pushing sides straight and corners as square as you can with the side of your ruler. If dough was kneaded too vigorously, it will probably start resisting before it has reached the right dimensions, but you will get it there if you keep on rolling with gentle perseverance.

7 With the back of a knife, make a light indentation across the width of the rectangle one-third from the bottom.

8 Use the tip of the knife to dot the upper two-thirds of the rectangle with half of the white fat mixture, covering the area down to the indentation with nut-sized flicks, and leaving a $\frac{1}{2}$-inch border clear on the three outer sides – if fat is put too near the edge, it may ooze out during rolling.

9 Fold rectangle in three as follows: fold the clear (i.e. free of fat) third of dough up towards the centre; then fold the remaining third down over the top of it. Seal all edges with your rolling pin or the side of your hand.

10 Wrap the pastry in greaseproof paper, then fold up in a damp cloth and chill for 15 minutes. (Make a note for yourself to indicate that pastry has had one rolling or 'turn'.)

11 Unwrap pastry and lay it on a lightly floured surface so that the fold is on your left-hand side and the longest sealed edge on your right (think of a closed book lying with its cover upwards).

Roll out again into a 16- by 8-inch rectangle, using firm, even strokes down towards you from the centre and upwards away from you – *never* roll pastry sideways or in different directions.

12 Repeat Steps 7–10, this time using half of remaining butter (i.e. 2 oz), and return packet to the refrigerator for 15 minutes. Make a note of the second 'turn'.

13 Give the pastry its third and fourth 'turns', using remaining white fat mixture for the third, and remaining butter for the fourth and final 'turn', and chilling pastry for 15 minutes in between.

14 After the final folding, seal edges of pastry; wrap the packet in greaseproof paper, followed by the damp cloth, and leave to rest in the refrigerator overnight, or for several hours at least.

Note: Once you have mastered the technique of making flaky pastry, you will probably find that you can work much more quickly and that, consequently, the fat stays firm enough to allow you to complete 2 turns at a time. Nevertheless, in very hot weather – or at the slightest suspicion of oozing – you would be well advised to follow the recipe step by step as described above.

Puff Pastry
(Pâte Feuilletée)

1 lb plain flour
1 level teaspoon salt
1 tablespoon lemon juice
Iced water
13 oz butter
3 oz vegetable shortening

1 Sift flour and salt into a tall mound on a pastry board or marble or, if you prefer, into a large bowl. Make a well in the centre, keeping the walls high, thick and even all around.

2 Measure lemon juice into the well, together with 6 tablespoons iced water.

3 Now, using the fingertips of one hand, gently mix the surrounding flour into the lemony water with a light beating motion until enough flour has been incorporated to produce the consistency of a smooth, thickish sauce.

4 Gradually add more water, all the while continuing to incorporate flour from the sides of the well. When you have added a further 7 tablespoons, making 13 in all, you should be able to make the whole mass on the pastry board adhere in a firmish ball of dough. Use the ball to 'mop up' remaining flour. Knead dough lightly a few times. At all costs avoid getting hard, dry flakes of flour in your dough. These are impossible to eliminate without hard kneading, which in turn develops the elasticity of the dough and makes it difficult to roll.

5 Shape dough into a pad. Wrap in greaseproof paper; fold up in a damp cloth and leave in the refrigerator for 30 minutes to relax.

6 Meanwhile, place butter and vegetable shortening on a plate or in a bowl, and work them together with a spatula or knife blade until smoothly blended. Scrape blended fats out on to a sheet of greaseproof paper and shape into a 4- by 6-inch rectangle. Cover with another sheet of greaseproof paper and leave in the refrigerator to firm up slightly. Ideally, the blended fat and the dough should be of the same consistency (softness) when they are brought together.

7 Flour your working surface and rolling pin lightly. Roll out prepared dough into a circle about 12 inches in diameter, using light, even strokes and always rolling *outwards* from the centre of the circle.

8 Place the rectangle of blended fat lengthwise in the centre of the circle. Bring dough on the two longer sides of the rectangle up to overlap over the fat. Seal with the rolling pin. Now bring dough on two shorter sides up again to meet and overlap in the centre.

9 Place the parcel of dough and fat before you with the two shorter sides on your left and right. Roll out into a 16- by 8-inch rectangle, pushing sides straight and corners as square as you can with the side of your ruler. Always roll in the same direction, using firm, even strokes down towards you from the centre and upwards away from you.

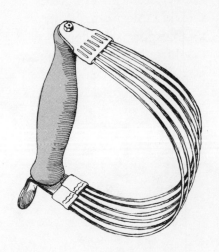

10 Fold pastry in three as follows: fold the bottom third up towards the centre and the upper third down on top of it. Seal edges with your rolling pin. Wrap tightly in greaseproof paper and fold up in a damp cloth. Chill for 15 minutes. (Make a note for yourself to indicate that pastry has had one rolling or 'turn'.)

11 Unwrap pastry and lay it on a lightly floured surface so that the fold is on your left-hand side and the longest sealed edge on your right, like a closed book with its cover upwards. Roll out again into a 16- by 8-inch rectangle and fold in three as before. Wrap up and return to the refrigerator. Make a note of the second 'turn'.

12 Repeat rolling and folding four times more, two 'turns' at a time (i.e. with only one rest period of 15 minutes in between).

13 After the final rolling and folding wrap pastry up in grease-proof paper, followed by a damp cloth and chill until firm, preferably overnight.

1 plump roasting chicken, weighing 3 1/2–4 lb

1–2 level tablespoons flour

2 tablespoons olive oil

4 level tablespoons butter

Salt and freshly ground black pepper

1/4 pint chicken stock (see note)

8 oz button mushrooms (half for chicken, half for sauce)

4 tablespoons Madeira

8 oz puff pastry

Lightly beaten egg yolk, to glaze

Sauce

1 level tablespoon butter

2 level tablespoons flour

2 tablespoons Madeira

Cooking juices from chicken

3 tablespoons cream

Pillows of Chicken

When preparing this dish for six, use half as much again of chicken, button mushrooms, Madeira and puff pastry for the chicken 'parcels'. The same amount of sauce will stretch to six quite comfortably.

The chicken carcass and trimmings make an excellent stock with coarsely chopped carrots, an onion stuck with a clove, a leek or two, a few stalks of celery, and a couple of over-ripe tomatoes if you have any lying around; add a *bouquet garni*, salt and freshly ground black pepper, to taste, cover with water and simmer until vegetables are tender. There will be more stock than needed for this recipe, but this can be strained and used as a base for soup at another meal.

1 Prepare chicken: with a sharp knife, cut legs off close to the body; then cut each leg into two pieces (drumsticks and thighs).

2 Bone both thighs and roll meat firmly into sausage shapes.

3 Take drumsticks and cut in around the top right down to bone to loosen flesh. Then, holding bone firmly between a finger and thumb, pull flesh down and over the end in one movement, turning flesh inside out; separate flesh from bone, and turn right side out again.

4 Slice down one side of breast as close to breast bone as possible; then take knife right across wingbone and through joint to sever breast from carcass. Repeat with the other breast.

5 Remove winglets and the other wing bone from each breast; cut breasts in half and roll each piece tightly into a sausage. You will now have 4 boned leg joints and 4 from breasts.

6 Make a rich stock with carcass and trimmings (see note above).

7 Dust chicken pieces with flour. In a heavy casserole, sauté chicken pieces in half the oil and butter until golden brown, seasoning generously with salt and freshly ground black pepper.

8 Strain $\frac{1}{4}$ pint chicken stock over chicken pieces; cover and simmer for 20 minutes, or until tender. Cool.

9 Slice mushrooms thinly. Sauté in remaining oil and butter until golden. Season with salt with freshly ground black pepper, and moisten with Madeira. Cool.

10 To make sauce: melt butter in a heavy pan; add flour and stir over a moderate heat to make a deep, golden *roux*. Remove from heat. Beat in Madeira and juices from cooked chicken; return pan to the heat and stir in cream. Bring to the boil, stirring constantly to make a smooth sauce.

11 Fold in half the sautéed mushrooms and simmer for 20 minutes longer, adding a little more stock if sauce becomes too thick.

12 Preheat oven to fairly hot (425°F. Mark 7).

13 Divide pastry into 4 and roll each piece out into a 6-inch square, trimming sides to give a neat shape. Make decorative leaves out of trimmings (2 or 3 per portion).

14 Place 1 piece chicken breast and 1 piece leg on each square of pastry; cover with a quarter of remaining mushrooms. Moisten with some of the mushroom juices; then fold pastry up over the filling like an envelope, and seal tightly, brushing seams with a little beaten egg yolk.

15 Arrange 'pillows' on a baking sheet, seam side down. Glaze with beaten egg yolk; decorate with pastry 'leaves', 'flowers' or 'tassels' and glaze these as well.

16 Bake pillows for 20 to 25 minutes, or until well risen, crisp and golden brown.

17 Reheat sauce and serve with pillows of chicken.

Pheasant and Mushroom Pie

Serves 6

1 Skin and bone pheasant.

2 Cut larger pieces of pheasant meat into neat strips; put them in a bowl; sprinkle with brandy or gin and leave to absorb flavours until needed.

3 Coarsely chop remaining pheasant meat, together with veal, pork and bacon.

4 Cut tongue into strips.

5 In a large, deep frying-pan, sauté finely chopped onion in butter over a low heat, stirring occasionally, until soft and golden but not brown, 5 to 7 minutes.

6 Add thinly sliced mushrooms; increase heat to moderate and continue to sauté until soft and golden.

7 Add chopped meats; mix well with mushrooms and onion, and sauté, stirring and turning contents of pan over with a spatula, until meats are lightly coloured, 3 to 4 minutes.

8 Remove pan from heat. Gently mix in strips of cooked tongue to avoid crushing them. Cool slightly.

9 Beat 1 egg lightly with cream. Stir into meat mixture and season

1 pheasant
3 tablespoons brandy or gin
4 oz lean veal
4 oz lean pork
2 oz unsmoked fat bacon
8 oz cooked tongue, in one piece
1 Spanish onion, finely chopped
4 level tablespoons butter
8 oz white button mushrooms, thinly sliced
2 eggs
2–3 level tablespoons double cream
Salt and freshly ground black pepper
3/4–1 lb shortcrust or flaky pastry (page 432 or 454)
4 juniper berries

to taste with salt and freshly ground black pepper. Leave to become quite cold.

10 Preheat oven to moderately hot (400°F. Mark 6).

11 Use two-thirds of the pastry to line a 2-pint ovenproof pie dish.

12 Cover base evenly with half of the sautéed meat mixture. Lay whole pieces of pheasant neatly on top, and cover with remaining meat mixture. Sprinkle with any brandy (or gin) left over at bottom of bowl and dot with juniper berries.

13 Roll remaining pastry out to make a lid for pie. Brush edges of bottom layer (lip of pie dish) with cold water; fit lid into position and seal to bottom layer by crimping the two together firmly.

14 Make a hole in centre of lid. Roll out leftover scraps of pastry; make pastry 'leaves', 'flowers' or 'tassels' and use them to decorate top of pie.

15 Beat remaining egg lightly. Brush over top of pie and decorations to glaze them.

16 Bake pie for 45 minutes, or until pastry is crisp and golden brown on top.

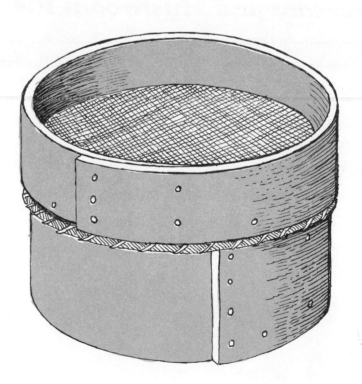

Old English Chicken Pie

1 Bone chicken.

2 Make a light stock by simmering wings, neck and bones in a little water with sliced onion and bay leaf for 20 minutes.

3 Re-form boned pieces of chicken; roll in flour and sauté in 2 tablespoons butter until golden. Add salt and freshly ground black pepper; cover and cook over a low heat for 20 minutes, turning occasionally.

4 Prepare white forcemeat mixture by grating bread and mixing it with finely chopped parsley and thyme, grated lemon rind, and grated nutmeg, salt and pepper, to taste. Add diced butter and egg yolk, and work to a smooth paste with fingers.

5 Make sausage forcemeat mixture by mincing liver and heart of chicken with sausage meat. Combine with chopped parsley and chives.

6 Form small balls out of two mixtures and brown lightly in butter in another pan.

7 Garnish a deep pie dish with chicken pieces, forcemeat balls and quartered hard-boiled eggs.

8 Stir 6 tablespoons stock into pan in which chicken was cooked, blending it well with butter and remaining juices. Pour this over the contents of pie dish and cover with layer of pastry.

9 Moisten edges of pie dish with water; press pastry to edge; crimping edge of crust with a fork. Cut one or two slits in the centre of crust to allow steam to escape. Decorate pastry crust as desired.

10 Bake in a moderate oven (375°F. Mark 5) for 30 minutes, or until done.

Serve with Chicken Velouté Sauce.

Serves 4–6

1 tender roasting chicken (about 3 lb)
1/2 Spanish onion, sliced
1 bay leaf
6 level tablespoons flour
2 level tablespoons butter
Salt and freshly ground black pepper
2 hard-boiled eggs, quartered
Flaky pastry for 1-crust pie (page 454)
Chicken velouté sauce (page 180)

White forcemeat

1/4 lb stale bread
1 level teaspoon finely chopped parsley
1/4 level teaspoon finely chopped thyme
Grated rind of ½ lemon
Pinch of freshly grated nutmeg
1/2 level teaspoon salt
Freshly ground black pepper
2 oz butter, diced
1 egg yolk

Sausage forcemeat

Liver and heart of the chicken
1/4 lb sausage meat
1 level teaspoon each finely chopped parsley and chives or onion greens

Making Choux Paste

Choux paste is something of a culinary phenomenon at first sight: a thick, close-textured paste – really a thick sauce – of flour, water and eggs, that puffs in the oven to become a crisp, delicate case of air.

Some people have difficulty in getting the puffs to stay crisp – or at least to prevent them turning chewy and tough – for more than an hour or two after they come out of the oven. The secret here lies in baking the puffs slowly, after an initial burst of high

461

heat, until as much moisture as possible has been dried out of them. In fact, you can carry on baking until the colour of the puffs forces you to take them out of the oven.

If you do this, it will not even be necessary to slit the puffs to allow the steam trapped inside to escape. However, to be on the safe side, this operation is advisable, especially when making larger puffs or éclairs. And if you find any uncooked (damp) paste lurking inside, simply scrape it out with your finger, or the back of a spoon.

● The paste itself is not difficult to make, provided that you follow the recipes below carefully. In Step 4, you must carry on beating until the mixture attaches itself around the spoon in a smooth, shiny ball, leaving the surface of the pan quite clean.

● Beaten eggs are then added to the *hot* mixture, a spoonful at a time, and when it has all been blended in, you must carry on beating vigorously until it develops a definite gloss or sheen.

● Choux paste should be used at once.

Filling Puffs and Eclairs

Creamy savoury or sweet fillings go equally well with choux puffs and éclairs, but they must never be filled too far in advance, or they may, after all, turn soggy.

The easiest filling is plain whipped cream, well chilled – served with a hot chocolate sauce, this makes a glamorous, easy sweet. But you can also use a thick *crème pâtissière* flavoured with vanilla, chocolate, coffee or liqueur.

Decorate with a sifting of icing sugar, glacé icing, caramel or, rather more tricky, spun sugar.

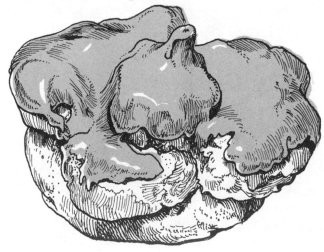

Basic Choux Paste

1 Sift flour on to a sheet of greaseproof or some other stiff paper.

2 In a heavy, medium-sized saucepan, combine diced butter and sugar (if used) with ¼ pint cold water. Bring to the boil slowly to give butter time to melt.

3 As soon as liquid is boiling briskly, remove pan from heat. Quickly pour in prepared flour all at once and immediately start beating vigorously with a wooden spoon.

4 Return pan to a low heat and continue to beat the paste until it attaches itself around the spoon in a smooth ball, leaving bottom and sides of pan clean, about 2 minutes. Remove pan from heat.

5 Add beaten eggs a little at a time, beating vigorously with the spoon. Then continue to beat until paste is glossy.

6 If paste is to be used in a savoury recipe, season generously with ¼ level teaspoon salt and a little white pepper, to taste. If sweet, beat in a few drops of vanilla essence, to taste. Use immediately.

Paste I (Savoury)

2 1/2 oz plain flour
1 1/2 oz butter, diced
1/4 pint cold water
2 eggs plus 1 egg yolk, beaten
1/4 level teaspoon salt
White pepper

Paste II (Sweet)

2 1/2 oz plain flour
2 oz butter, diced
1 level teaspoon sugar
1/4 pint cold water
2 eggs, beaten
Vanilla essence

To Make Profiteroles
(Choux Buns)

1 Place choux paste in a piping bag fitted with a plain, ½-inch tube.

2 Holding the piping bag vertically in your left hand, pipe out blobs about 1 inch in diameter on a lightly buttered baking sheet. Do not twist the bag; either pull it up sharply to disengage it from the piped blob, or cut the blob free with a knife dipped in cold water (held in the right hand). Any sharp points should be patted smooth with a damp knife blade, otherwise they will burn. Blobs should be spaced about 1 inch apart in case they spread.

3 Brush tops of blobs lightly with beaten egg, making sure egg does not run down sides on to baking sheet as this would anchor buns and prevent them rising to their full height.

4 Bake in a fairly hot oven (425°F. Mark 7) for 10 minutes; then reduce heat to slow (325°F. Mark 3) and continue to bake for 15 to 20 minutes, or until choux buns are crisp and light, and a rich golden colour.

5 As soon as choux buns come out of the oven, pierce or slit them with a sharp knife to allow steam to escape. Otherwise, the crisp buns will become damp and chewy as they cool. If necessary, any traces of uncooked paste may be scraped out of the hot buns.

6 Cool on a wire rack and either use immediately or store in an airtight container.

Makes about 40 small Choux buns

1 recipe Choux Paste II
Butter
1 egg, beaten

1 recipe Choux Paste II
  (page 463)
Butter
1 egg, beaten (optional)

To Make Eclairs

1 Proceed as on page 463, piping out 2½- to 3-inch lengths about 1 inch apart on to lightly buttered baking sheets. Hold the nose of your piping bag slightly above the surface of the baking sheet, so that the lengths remain rounded and are not deformed. Cut off with a knife dipped in water; or give the nose of the bag a slight sharp pull upwards to free it, then pat the point of the éclair smooth.

2 If you wish, éclairs may be glazed with beaten egg as above, but this is not necessary if you intend to cover them with chocolate.

3 Bake in a fairly hot oven (425°F. Mark 7) for 10 minutes; then reduce heat to slow (325°F. Mark 3) and continue to bake for about 20 minutes longer, or until éclairs are crisp, light and golden.

4 As soon as éclairs are ready, slit them to allow steam to escape. and if necessary remove any soft uncooked paste from the interior.

5 Cool on a wire rack and either use immediately or store in an airtight container.

Miniature Savoury Puffs and Eclairs – Hot and Cold

Hot, bite-sized choux puffs and éclairs make wonderful appetisers. Fill them full of creamed fish, curried chicken or creamed ham. Cold miniature choux puffs and éclairs can be filled with *pâté de foie gras* mixed with Madeira-flavoured whipped cream; cream cheese flavoured with garlic, lemon and finely chopped fresh tarragon, basil and chives; or chicken salad, duck salad, ham salad or egg mayonnaise. (Use Choux Paste I.)

Sweet Puffs and Eclairs

Sweet choux puffs and éclairs – when filled with (1) chilled whipped cream flavoured with a little cognac, rum or curaçao; (2) chocolate or vanilla ice cream; or (3) *crème pâtissière* – make a delicious sweet. Decorate sweet choux puffs and éclairs with a chocolate or caramel icing. (Use Choux Paste II.)

Anchovy Puffs

Serve a tray of these golden little choux pastry balls with drinks – the creamy anchovy filling makes a very good appetiser.

1 Preheat oven to fairly hot (425°F. Mark 7).

2 Prepare choux paste as directed on page 463.

3 Spoon paste into a piping bag fitted with a ½-inch nozzle, and pipe out 40 small balls on to greased baking sheets about ½ inch apart, cutting paste from nozzle with a knife dipped in water.

4 Dampen top of each ball with a little water and sprinkle with grated Parmesan.

5 Bake as directed in master recipe until puffed and crisp.

6 Remove puffs from oven and immediately make a small slit in the side of each one to allow steam to escape and keep pastry crisp. Leave to cool on a wire rack.

7 Meanwhile, prepare filling: melt butter in a small saucepan; add flour and cook over a low heat, stirring, for 1 minute to make a pale *roux*. Add milk gradually, stirring constantly to prevent flour forming lumps. Bring to the boil and simmer for 2 to 3 minutes.

8 Add tomatoes, tomato concentrate and anchovies; mix well and season generously with Tabasco, lemon juice and freshly ground black pepper. Allow to cool completely before filling puffs.

9 Fill puffs, allowing about 1 level teaspoon filling to each one. Do not fill them too long before serving to avoid pastry becoming soft.

1 recipe Savoury Choux
  Paste I (page 463)
1/2 oz freshly grated
  Parmesan
Butter for baking sheet

Filling

1 oz butter
1 oz plain flour
1/2 pint milk
2 tomatoes, peeled, seeded
  and chopped
2 level teaspoons tomato
  concentrate
1 can anchovies, drained and
  finely chopped
4 drops Tabasco
2 teaspoons lemon juice
Freshly ground black pepper

Gougère

This is a speciality of Burgundy. It is served very fresh, preferably straight from the oven, as an appetiser.

1 Preheat oven to moderate (375°F. Mark 5).

2 Prepare choux paste, following directions on page 463 and beating vigorously until paste is glossy.

3 Add grated Parmesan and Gruyère, and beat with a wooden spoon until thoroughly blended. Mix in strips of Gruyère and season with extra salt and freshly ground black pepper.

4 Grease a baking sheet with butter. Mark a circle on it about 6 inches in diameter.

Serves 6

1 recipe Choux Paste I
  (page 463)
1 oz freshly grated Parmesan
1 oz freshly grated Gruyère
2 oz Gruyère, cut into
  matchstick strips
Salt and freshly ground black
  pepper
Butter, for baking sheet

5 Dip a tablespoon in hot water and scoop out paste in 12 equal mounds, dipping the spoon each time and arranging mounds in a closed circle around the outside of the circle you marked on the baking sheet, i.e. *gougère* should be about 8 inches in diameter.

6 Bake *gougère* for 30 to 35 minutes, or until well puffed, crisp and golden brown. Serve hot or lukewarm.

Almond Fruits

Makes 20

1/2 recipe Choux Paste II (page 463)
Butter for baking sheet
12 oz almond paste (page 265)
Green and red food colouring
Sifted icing sugar

Crème pâtissière

2 oz castor sugar
1 1/2 level tablespoons cornflour
8 fluid oz milk
3 egg yolks, lightly beaten
1/2 level teaspoon vanilla essence
1 level teaspoon Kirsch (optional)

1 Preheat oven to fairly hot (425°F. Mark 7).

2 Prepare choux paste (see page 463).

3 Butter a baking sheet lightly. Spoon choux paste into a piping bag fitted with a plain, ½-inch nozzle and pipe out 20 balls of uniform size, leaving an inch clear between them in case they spread a little.

4 Bake for 10 minutes, or until balls are puffed up; then reduce oven temperature to slow (325°F. Mark 3), and continue to bake for a further 15 to 20 minutes, or until puffs are crisp and a rich golden colour.

5 As soon as puffs come out of the oven, make a tiny slit in the *base* of each one to allow steam to escape. Then leave them to cool completely on a wire rack.

6 Prepare *crème pâtissière*: combine sugar and cornflour in the top of a double saucepan. Stir in milk and cook over direct heat, stirring constantly, until mixture comes to the boil. Boil for 1 minute.

7 Beat egg yolks and add a little of the hot cornflour mixture to them. Mix well, then pour back into top of double saucepan. Cook over hot water for 5 to 10 minutes, or until custard is thick, taking care not to let it boil, or egg yolks may curdle. Strain and cool. Stir in vanilla and Kirsch, if desired, and chill thoroughly.

8 Fill choux puffs with *crème pâtissière* through the slits made earlier, using a piping bag fitted with a small (about ⅛-inch), plain nozzle.

9 Colour almond paste very faintly with a drop or two of green food colouring, kneading thoroughly to distribute colour evenly. Divide paste into 20 pieces and roll or pat each piece out into a circle ⅛ inch thick, large enough to enclose a puff. Dust board and rolling pin with a little sifted icing sugar if paste tends to stick.

10 Place a choux puff in the centre of a circle of almond paste, slit side upwards. Draw sides of circle up to seal puff; then shape paste into fruit: apple, pear, fig, or what have you. Brush with red or red and green food colouring as appropriate.

Les Réligieuses

So called because the little choux puffs, one coated with dark chocolate, the other with a paler coffee icing, resemble the habits of fat little nuns.

1 Make up Almond Praline recipe. When quite cold and hard, crush it finely either with a pestle and mortar, or by feeding no more than 2 oz praline at a time through the hole in the lid of an electric blender on to turning blades; run blender until praline is reduced to a fine powder. Sieve crushed praline; re-pound any small pieces that refuse to go through. Store in an airtight container in the refrigerator until required.

2 Make up Butter Cream Mousseline, adding 2 to 3 oz crushed praline immediately after beating in the butter. Taste and add more praline if desired. Store in the refrigerator in an airtight container until required.

3 Make up *Crème Pâtissière* II, up to but not including the final addition of butter.

4 Have ready chocolate, melted over hot water or softened in the oven; and $\frac{1}{2}$ level teaspoon coffee granules dissolved in $\frac{1}{2}$ teaspoon boiling water.

5 Divide *crème pâtissière* between two bowls, two-thirds on one and one-third on the other.

6 Into the larger portion, beat in melted chocolate, dissolved coffee granules and 2 level teaspoons butter.

7 Dissolve 2 level teaspoons coffee granules in 2 teaspoons boiling water. Beat into the smaller portion of *crème pâtissière*, together with 1 level teaspoon butter and a few drops of vanilla essence, to taste.

8 Store the two portions of custard in separate, airtight containers in a cool place until required.

9 Preheat oven to slow (325°F. Mark 3).

10 Make up Scotch Shortbread according to recipe, up to and including Step 3.

11 Roll out dough $\frac{1}{8}$ inch thick on a lightly floured surface and stamp out rounds with a plain, $1\frac{1}{2}$-inch cutter.

1 recipe Almond Praline (page 564)
1 recipe Butter Cream Mousseline (page 266)
1 recipe Crème Pâtissière II (page 441)
2 oz bitter dessert chocolate
Coffee granules
Butter
Vanilla essence
1 1/2 recipes Scotch Shortbread (page 261)
1 recipe Basic Choux Paste II (page 463)

Coffee glacé icing
4 oz icing sugar, sifted
2 level teaspoons coffee granules

Chocolate icing
1 1/2 oz bitter dessert chocolate
3 tablespoons single cream

12 Transfer rounds to a lightly buttered baking sheet, or sheets, and bake for 20 to 25 minutes until a pale golden colour. Allow to cool and harden slightly before leaving to cool completely on wire racks. Store in an airtight container until required.

13 Butter 3 baking sheets.

14 Make up Choux Paste II, omitting sugar and essence. Place in a piping bag fitted with a plain, $\frac{1}{2}$-inch nozzle.

15 Preheat oven to fairly hot (425°F. Mark 7).

16 Have 2 baking sheets in front of you. Pipe out a round no larger than a 2- (new) penny piece in diameter on one sheet, followed by a round about the diameter of a $\frac{1}{2}$- (new) penny piece on the other. Continue piping the two sizes alternately, moving across to the third baking sheet when the first two are full. In this way, you ensure an even number of balls in the two sizes.

17 Smooth down any sharp points with a wetted knife as described in the master recipe. Leave unglazed.

18 Bake choux balls for 10 minutes; then reduce heat to 325°F. (Mark 3) as directed in the master recipe. Bake smaller balls for a further 10 to 15 minutes, and larger ones for 15 to 20 minutes longer. With the mixed sheet, sweep off the smaller balls with a spatula on to a cooling rack when they are ready, and return sheet to the oven as quickly as you can. The aim is to dry the balls out as much as possible. They should be a rich, deep golden colour.

19 To assemble *réligieuses*: place *crème pâtissière* mixtures in separate piping bags with plain, $\frac{1}{8}$-inch nozzles. Fill larger balls with chocolate mixture and smaller ones with coffee mixture.

20 Prepare coffee glacé icing by beating sifted icing sugar with coffee granules dissolved in 2 teaspoons boiling water until smooth.

21 Prepare chocolate icing by melting chocolate over hot water or in the oven, and beating in cream until smoothly blended.

22 Dip chocolate-filled balls in chocolate icing until they are three-quarters covered. Let excess drip back into bowl before leaving on a wire rack to harden.

23 Dip coffee-filled balls in coffee glacé icing in the same way, and leave to harden.

24 Put praline-flavoured mousseline in a small piping bag fitted with a small, star-shaped nozzle. Pipe a little blob in the centre of each round of shortbread and stick a chocolate ball firmly on top.

Then pipe another small blob in the centre of each chocolate ball and sit a small coffee ball firmly on top of that.

25 Decorate base of each *réligieuse* with small rosettes of praline cream. Chill until ready to serve.

FOURTH COURSE

Lesson 17

First Course Salads and Vegetable Appetisers

If you have been following our cookery school methodically, you will sail through the recipes below without turning a hair. If not, turn to Lesson 1 (page 24) and read the introductions to Simple Appetisers and Basic Green Salad. When making first-course salads and vegetable appetisers, bear the following important points in mind:

● An appetiser salad or vegetable dish is designed to stimulate the appetite without satisfying it.

● It must be attractive to the eye as well as the palate – this is the first impression your guests will get of the meal you have prepared for them, and we all know how first impressions linger the longest.

● Make a point of using the finest, fruitiest olive oil, a mellow wine vinegar, freshly ground black peppercorns and a good, coarse salt when you come to dress a salad, prepare a mayonnaise or simmer vegetables for a cold antipasto or a dish à la Grecque.

● Finally, remember that just as a salad ought to be crisp, so cooked vegetables must never be taken beyond the stage where textures break down to a uniform, lifeless mush. They should be neither raw, nor overcooked, but *al dente* – the stage at which texture and, as a result, flavour are at their peak.

472

Belgian Appetiser Salad

1 Trim and wash beans. Wash potatoes without peeling them. Boil beans and potatoes until tender in separate pans of salted water, 12 to 15 minutes for the beans, and about 25 minutes for the potatoes.

2 In the meantime, melt butter in a deep frying-pan or sauté dish and sauté bacon strips until crisp and golden, about 5 minutes.

3 Add finely chopped onion and sauté until soft but not coloured.

4 Sprinkle with wine vinegar and heat gently for a further 3 minutes. Keep hot.

5 When beans are tender, drain them thoroughly and place them in a salad bowl.

6 Drain potatoes; peel them and cut into $\frac{1}{4}$-inch-thick slices. Add them to the beans and season lightly with salt and freshly ground black pepper.

7 Pour bacon mixture over hot beans and potatoes, and toss gently until well mixed. Serve lukewarm, sprinkled with finely chopped parsley.

Serves 4

3/4 lb green beans
3/4 lb new potatoes
Salt
2 level tablespoons butter
8–10 oz streaky bacon, cut in strips
1 Spanish onion, finely chopped
4 tablespoons wine vinegar
Freshly ground black pepper
2 level tablespoons finely chopped parsley

Provençal Cauliflower Salad

1 Trim cauliflowers and cut out any bruised spots. Break into flowerets; rinse well and poach gently in lightly salted water for about 5 minutes. They should remain crisp and if anything slightly undercooked.

2 Drain flowerets carefully and leave them in a bowl of cold water until ready to use.

3 In a small bowl, combine finely chopped anchovies, black olives, parsley, garlic and capers with olive oil and wine vinegar. Season to taste with salt and freshly ground black pepper.

4 When ready to serve: drain flowerets and dry them carefully in a cloth. Arrange them in a serving dish; spoon anchovy dressing over the top and serve immediately, tossing salad lightly at the table.

Serves 6

2 medium-sized cauliflowers
Salt
6 anchovy fillets, finely chopped
12 black olives, pitted and chopped
3 level tablespoons finely chopped parsley
1 clove garlic, finely chopped
1 level tablespoon finely chopped capers
6 tablespoons olive oil
2 tablespoons wine vinegar
Freshly ground black pepper

Serves 6

2 cloves garlic

1/4 pint olive oil

2 heads Cos lettuce

1/2 level teaspoon salt

1/4 level teaspoon each dry mustard and freshly ground black pepper

4 tablespoons lemon juice

2 eggs

3–4 slices bread, 1/4 inch thick

4 anchovy fillets, finely chopped (optional)

8 level tablespoons freshly grated Parmesan

Caesar Salad

1 Peel garlic cloves and crush them lightly in a small bowl. Add the olive oil and leave them to steep for about 2 hours, so that the oil becomes heavily impregnated with their flavour. Strain oil through a fine sieve, discarding garlic.

2 Wash and drain Cos lettuce, and pat each leaf dry with a clean cloth. (This is important, as any water remaining on the leaves would dilute the dressing.) Break leaves into a salad bowl in fairly large pieces.

3 Combine salt, dry mustard and freshly ground black pepper with lemon juice. Beat in 6 tablespoons of the garlic-flavoured oil to make a vinaigrette dressing.

4 Drop eggs into boiling water; simmer for just 90 seconds and drain immediately. (This is known as 'coddling'.)

5 Cut bread slices into ¼-inch cubes. Heat remaining garlic oil in a frying pan and sauté bread cubes until crisp and golden brown all over, adding a little more oil if necessary. Drain well on absorbent paper.

6 To assemble salad: toss lettuce with vinaigrette dressing and chopped anchovies, if used. When the leaves are well coated with dressing, break coddled eggs into the centre and toss again. Finally, add garlic croûtons and finely grated Parmesan, and toss lightly but thoroughly until there is no more dressing left at the bottom of the bowl. Serve immediately.

Herbed Salad Niçoise

1 Boil potatoes in their jackets in salted water until just tender, 15 to 20 minutes.

2 Meanwhile, prepare dressing: whisk or beat olive oil, wine, wine vinegar and mustard together until they emulsify. Stir in grated shallot and season to taste with salt and freshly ground black pepper.

3 As soon as potatoes are tender, cool the pan under cold running water until they can just be handled. Peel and slice them into a salad bowl.

4 Pour 4 or 5 tablespoons dressing over hot potato slices. Mix gently and leave to cool.

5 Add herbs to remaining dressing.

6 Boil eggs for 10 minutes. Drain, cover with cold water and leave to cool.

7 Soak onion rings in cold water for 10 minutes. Drain, pat dry and add to bowl.

8 Halve, core and seed pepper, and slice into thin strips. Add to salad bowl.

9 Slice celery stalks ¼ inch thick. Add to the bowl together with coarsely flaked tuna, and mix thoroughly, taking care not to break potato slices.

10 Halve tomatoes and cut each half into three wedges.

11 Shell and quarter hard-boiled eggs.

12 Arrange tomato wedges, quartered hard-boiled eggs and halved anchovy fillets decoratively on top of salad. Dot with pitted black olives, halved if they are very large. Spoon over some of the dressing and serve remainder separately.

Serves 4

1 lb small waxy potatoes
Salt
2–3 eggs
1/4 Spanish onion, thinly sliced and separated into rings
1 medium-sized green pepper
4 stalks celery
1 7-oz can tuna, drained and coarsely flaked
4 large firm tomatoes, peeled
1 2-oz can anchovy fillets, drained and sliced in half lengthwise
12 black olives, pitted

Dressing

1/4 pint olive oil
2 tablespoons dry white wine
2 tablespoons wine vinegar
1/2 level teaspoon French mustard
1 shallot, grated
Salt and freshly ground black pepper
1 level tablespoon finely chopped parsley
1/4 level teaspoon each dried marjoram, chervil and tarragon

Russian Chicken and Potato Salad

Serves 4

1/2 cooked chicken
1/2 lb potatoes, boiled in
  their jackets
2 large dill pickles
1 7½-oz can button
  mushrooms, drained
2 teaspoons Worcestershire
  sauce
8 level tablespoons lemon-
  flavoured mayonnaise
  (page 43)
Salt and freshly ground black
  pepper
6 black olives, pitted and
  halved
2 hard-boiled eggs, sliced

1 Skin and bone chicken, and cut meat into short, thin strips.

2 Peel boiled potatoes and cut them into strips of the same size.

3 Cut dill pickles into matching strips.

4 In a bowl, combine chicken, potatoes and pickles with button mushrooms. Mix lightly, taking care not to break potatoes.

5 Beat Worcestershire sauce into 6 level tablespoons of the mayonnaise and carefully fold into salad with a large spoon, adding salt and freshly ground black pepper, to taste.

6 Mound salad in a shallow serving dish. Mask with remaining mayonnaise and decorate with pieces of olive and slices of hard-boiled egg.

7 Chill until ready to serve.

German Potato Salad with Bacon

Serves 4, or 6–8 as part of a selection of hors-d'œuvres

1 1/2 lb small new potatoes
Chicken stock (made with a
  cube)
3–4 slices bacon
1 medium-sized onion, finely
  chopped
6 tablespoons olive oil
3 tablespoons cider vinegar
1 level tablespoon sugar
1 teaspoon Worcestershire
  sauce
2–3 drops Tabasco
Salt and freshly ground black
  pepper

1 Scrub potatoes clean. Boil them in their jackets in water flavoured with a chicken stock cube until just tender. (If potatoes are large, cut them in half to allow flavour of stock to penetrate.)

2 Meanwhile, dice bacon finely and fry until crisp in a small pan. Put aside.

3 When potatoes are tender, drain and cool them slightly; then peel and dice them (or slice them if they are small enough) and put them in a bowl.

4 To the crisp-fried bacon add finely chopped onion, olive oil, cider vinegar, sugar, Worcestershire sauce and Tabasco. Heat gently, stirring, without allowing mixture to come to the boil.

5 Pour hot dressing over hot potatoes; mix lightly and leave to cool.

6 Season salad to taste with salt and freshly ground black pepper, and chill lightly before serving.

Chick Peas Rémoulade

1 Drain soaked chick peas and cover with fresh water in a saucepan. (Do not salt the water, or chick peas will not soften.) Bring to the boil and simmer until chick peas are tender, about 45 minutes, depending on their quality and age. Drain and leave until cold.

2 Combine next five ingredients in a bowl.

3 Flavour thick mayonnaise with French mustard. Blend with chopped anchovy mixture.

4 Fold enough of the anchovy-flavoured mayonnaise into chick peas to dress them richly. Any left over mayonnaise may be served separately in a bowl so that people may help themselves to more if they wish.

5 Season chick peas with salt and freshly ground black pepper, to taste, and a little lemon juice if you like.

6 Garnish with parsley sprigs and chill until ready to serve.

Serves 6–8 as part of a selection of *hors-d'œuvres* dishes

1/2 lb chick peas, soaked overnight
1 can anchovy fillets, drained and chopped
1 clove garlic, crushed
2 level tablespoons capers, chopped
1 level tablespoon finely chopped shallots or spring onions
2 level tablespoons finely chopped parsley
1/4 pint thick mayonnaise (page 43)
1 level teaspoon French mustard
Salt and freshly ground black pepper
1 tablespoon lemon juice (optional)
Parsley sprigs, to garnish

Pois Chiches en Salade

1 Drain soaked chick peas and cook them in a fresh portion of unsalted water until tender, as above.

2 Drain chick peas thoroughly, and while still hot, toss in a salad bowl with finely chopped spring onions, parsley and garlic.

3 To make dressing: beat ingredients together with a fork until they form an emulsion, adding salt and freshly ground black pepper, to taste.

4 Pour dressing over chick peas. Add flaked tuna fish and toss together lightly until well mixed.

If you want to serve the salad on its own, use a $7\frac{1}{2}$-oz can of tuna instead of the smaller size.

Serves 4–6 as part of a selection of *hors-d'œuvres* dishes

6 oz chick peas, soaked overnight
6 spring onions, finely chopped
2 level tablespoons finely chopped parsley
1 clove garlic, finely chopped
1 3 1/2-oz can tuna fish, drained and flaked

Dressing
8 tablespoons olive oil
2 tablespoons wine vinegar
1 tablespoon lemon juice
Salt and freshly ground black pepper

Brussels Sprout Appetiser

Serves 4, or 6-8 as part of a selection of *hors-d'œuvres* dishes

1 lb baby sprouts
Salt
1/4 pint olive oil
2–3 tablespoons wine vinegar
Generous pinch of dry mustard
Generous pinch of sugar
Freshly ground black pepper
A few lettuce leaves
2 level tablespoons finely chopped onion
4 level tablespoons finely chopped parsley

1 Trim Brussels sprouts, removing overblown or yellowed leaves, and nicking a small cross in the base of each stem so that heat will penetrate and cook them evenly.

2 Bring a pan of salted water to a brisk boil. Drop in Brussels sprouts; bring to the boil again and simmer until just tender, 5 to 7 minutes.

3 Meanwhile, beat olive oil and wine vinegar with a fork, adding mustard, sugar, salt and freshly ground black pepper, to taste.

4 Drain Brussels sprouts thoroughly. Shake them gently in the pan for a few seconds over moderate heat to evaporate any remaining moisture. Put them in a bowl.

5 Pour dressing over hot sprouts. Toss lightly and leave to marinate for an hour or two.

6 To serve: line a salad bowl with lettuce leaves. Pile Brussels sprouts and juices in the centre, and garnish with finely chopped onion and parsley.

French Cabbage Salad

Serves 4

1/2 head firm white or green cabbage (8–10 oz)
4 tablespoons olive oil
1 tablespoon lemon juice
2 level tablespoons sour cream
1 clove garlic, crushed
2 level tablespoons castor sugar
Salt and freshly ground black pepper
1 crisp dessert apple, peeled, cored and chopped

1 Shred cabbage very thinly. Soak in cold water for 5 minutes. Drain thoroughly, pressing out as much moisture as possible.

2 Make a dressing by beating oil and lemon juice with a fork until they form an emulsion. Add sour cream gradually, beating constantly. Flavour dressing with crushed garlic and sugar, and season to taste with salt and freshly ground black pepper.

3 In a serving bowl, toss drained cabbage with freshly chopped apple. Pour over dressing; mix well and chill until ready to serve.

Stuffed Cucumber Appetiser

Serves 4–6

1 Trim both ends of cucumber. Peel off skin very thinly and cut cucumber across into three thick chunks. Drop pieces into boiling salted water and simmer for 10 minutes. Drain thoroughly; then soak in iced water for 10 minutes to firm them.

2 Carefully scoop out seeds from each piece of cucumber to leave a ring $\frac{3}{8}$ inch thick. Leave to drain while you prepare filling.

3 Pound well-drained tuna fish to a paste with butter. Add herbs; mix well and season to taste with salt and freshly ground black pepper.

4 Fill cucumber rings tightly with tuna fish paste and chill in refrigerator until firm.

5 Serve chilled cucumber cut in thin slices and arranged on a bed of lettuce leaves.

1 cucumber
Salt
Iced water
1 7-oz can tuna fish in oil
3 level tablespoons softened butter
1/4 level teaspoon each thyme, oregano, tarragon and chives
2 level teaspoons finely chopped parsley
Freshly ground black pepper
Lettuce leaves, to garnish

Italian Pepper Appetiser

Serves 6

1 Place peppers side by side in a grill-pan and grill steadily under a moderate heat until their skins blister and blacken all over, and peppers become rather limp. Keep turning them so that every part is exposed to the heat.

2 Plunge grilled peppers into a large bowl of cold water. Leave them for 2 minutes; then drain and peel. Skins will slip off quite easily if peppers have been correctly and evenly grilled. Slice peppers in half; cut out pith and rinse out seeds under cold running water. Pat each piece of pepper dry and cut it in four across the width.

3 Cut anchovy fillets into $\frac{1}{4}$-inch lengths and combine them in a deep serving dish with peppers and finely chopped garlic and parsley. Toss lightly until well mixed.

4 Heat olive oil with lemon juice in a small pan. When it is very hot, pour it all over the peppers and mix lightly. Leave to become quite cold – the dressing helps to develop and blend flavours together as it cools in a way that a simple cold dressing could never do. Serve chilled.

Note: This dish is so strongly flavoured that you are unlikely to need either salt or pepper, but taste and judge for yourself.

8 sweet peppers
6–8 anchovy fillets
3 cloves garlic, finely chopped
3 level tablespoons finely chopped parsley
4 tablespoons olive oil
2 teaspoons lemon juice
Salt and freshly ground black pepper (optional)

2 lb firm salad potatoes

Salt

3–4 tablespoons dry white
 wine

2 tablespoons tarragon
 vinegar

Freshly ground black pepper

8–12 oz cooked tongue,
 sliced 3/8-inch thick

1/2 pint thick lemon
 mayonnaise (page 43)

2 level tablespoons finely
 chopped parsley

1–2 level teaspoons tarragon
 (see note)

2–3 crisp dessert apples

Lettuce leaves and chopped
 parsley, to garnish

Potato and Tongue Salad

1 Scrub potatoes thoroughly and boil them in salted water until just soft. Cover with cold water until cool enough to handle; then peel carefully and cut into small, chip-like strips. Place in a large bowl.

2 While potatoes are still warm, sprinkle with a mixture of white wine and tarragon vinegar; toss lightly and season to taste with salt and freshly ground black pepper.

3 Cut sliced tongue into strips of the same size. Mix carefully with warm potatoes and leave until quite cold.

4 Meanwhile, prepare a well-seasoned lemon mayonnaise. Add finely chopped parsley and tarragon, to taste.

5 Peel, core and dice apples, folding pieces into the bowl of mayonnaise as soon as you have cut them to prevent discoloration.

6 Combine potato-tongue mixture with apple mayonnaise. Taste and add more salt or freshly ground black pepper if necessary.

7 Serve cold but not chilled in a lettuce-lined bowl, dusted with more chopped parsley.

Note: When fresh tarragon is not available, use $\frac{1}{2}$–1 level teaspoon 'infused' for 10 minutes in boiling water and drained on a sheet of absorbent paper.

Serves 4

1/2 lb cooked chicken, diced

4 stalks celery, thinly sliced

2 oz flaked almonds, toasted

2 level tablespoons very
 finely chopped onion

1 tablespoon lemon juice

1/4 pint thick home-made
 mayonnaise (page 43)

4 level tablespoons double
 cream, lightly whipped

Tabasco

Salt and freshly ground black
 pepper

Lettuce leaves, to garnish

Almond Chicken Salad

1 Combine chicken with celery and half the almonds in a large bowl.

2 In another bowl, mix very finely chopped onion with lemon juice, mayonnaise, lightly whipped cream and a dash of Tabasco. Add to chicken and celery, and toss until well coated with dressing.

3 Season salad to taste with salt and freshly ground black pepper, and chill until ready to serve.

4 To serve: line 4 individual serving dishes with lettuce leaves. Divide salad between them and decorate with remaining toasted almonds.

Curried Rice Salad

A creamy mayonnaise aspic with a faint flavour of curry, served with a light rice salad spiked with crisp pieces of sweet pepper. Use curry paste if you can get it, as uncooked curry powder tends to leave a crude aftertaste.

1 Prepare Mayonnaise Aspic Mould: In a large bowl, blend mayonnaise thoroughly with curry paste and flavour with lemon juice.

2 Turn contents of can of tuna fish into a small bowl and work to a paste with a fork – alternatively, purée at moderate speed for 30 seconds in an electric blender. Add to the curried mayonnaise and mix well.

3 Cut both green and red peppers in half; remove cores, seeds and stems, then slice green peppers into thin strips and the red ones into small dice. Add half of each pepper to the mayonnaise, and reserve remainder for the salad.

4 When aspic is on the point of setting, stir into mayonnaise gently, to avoid creating air bubbles. Season generously with salt and freshly ground black pepper.

5 Lightly oil a plain, 2-pint ring mould (choose one with a wide hole in the centre, into which you can later pile the rice salad). Pour in mayonnaise aspic and chill in the refrigerator for $1\frac{1}{2}$ to 2 hours, until firmly set.

6 Meanwhile, prepare Rice Salad: turn cooked rice into a large bowl. Add flaked tuna fish and remaining green and red peppers, and mix lightly.

7 Slice button mushrooms thinly and toss with lemon juice to prevent discolouration. Add them to the rice mixture, together with finely chopped parsley, and toss again.

8 Make a dressing for the salad with olive oil, wine vinegar, curry paste, and salt and freshly ground black pepper, to taste. Pour over salad; give it a final good toss and taste for seasoning, adding more salt or freshly ground black pepper if necessary. Chill until ready to serve.

9 Just before serving: turn ring mould out in the centre of a large flat dish. (Do this by turning the mould upside down on the dish, wrapping a cloth wrung out of hot water round the top and sides for a few seconds, then shaking the mould gently until it comes loose. You may have to use the hot cloth several times, but do not leave it for more than a few seconds each time, or the surface of the mayonnaise aspic will start to melt.)

Mayonnaise aspic mould

1/2 pint thick home-made mayonnaise (page 43)

2 level teaspoons curry paste

2 teaspoons lemon juice

1 3 1/2-oz can tuna fish

1 large green pepper

1 large red pepper

1/2 pint liquid aspic

Salt and freshly ground black pepper

Rice salad

8 oz long-grain rice, cooked and drained

1 7-oz can tuna fish, coarsely flaked

8 oz white button mushrooms

Juice of 1/2 large lemon

2 level tablespoons finely chopped parsley

6 tablespoons olive oil

3 tablespoons wine vinegar

1/2 level teaspoon curry paste

Salt and freshly ground black pepper

Garnish

1 small pepper, multi-coloured if possible

10 Heap the rice salad in the centre of the mould. Core and seed remaining pepper; cut it into thin strips, and use it to decorate top of ring mould and salad. Serve any left over rice salad in a separate bowl.

Cauliflower à la Grecque

Serves 4–6

1 cauliflower, about 2 lb
8–10 tablespoons olive oil
2 carrots, finely diced
1 Spanish onion, finely chopped
1/4 pint dry white wine
12 black peppercorns, lightly crushed
Bouquet garni
1 fat clove garlic
18 coriander seeds
1/2 lb tomatoes, peeled and seeded
Salt
Lemon juice
2 level tablespoons finely chopped parsley
8–12 black olives, pitted

1 Wash cauliflower and break into flowerets of roughly the same size. Put aside.

2 Heat 4 tablespoons olive oil in a heavy saucepan or flameproof casserole and sauté carrots and onion over a moderate heat for 5 minutes until golden.

3 Remove pan from heat. Add white wine, lightly crushed peppercorns, *bouquet garni*, garlic clove, coriander seeds and peeled, seeded tomatoes. Mix well; then add pieces of cauliflower, turning them over carefully to coat them thoroughly with the sauce.

4 Season to taste with salt and cook over a moderate heat for 15 to 20 minutes, or until cauliflower is tender but still on the crisp side, stirring occasionally and adding a little more wine (or water) if sauce evaporates too quickly. Sauce should be rather scarce by the time the cauliflower is cooked. Remove from heat and allow to cool.

5 When mixture is cold, remove *bouquet garni* and garlic clove. Stir in remaining olive oil. Correct seasoning if necessary and add a little lemon juice to bring out flavours.

6 Arrange cauliflower in a serving dish. Garnish with finely chopped parsley; dot with black olives and chill lightly until ready to serve.

Courgettes à la Grecque

1 Heat 4 tablespoons olive oil in a heavy pan or casserole; add finely chopped onion and garlic, and sauté until transparent. Add wine, ¼ pint water, *bouquet garni*, coriander seeds, black peppercorns, the juice of 1 lemon, and salt, to taste. Bring to the boil and simmer gently for 5 minutes.

2 Wipe courgettes with a damp cloth. Trim ends; quarter courgettes and cut them into 2-inch segments (they should not be peeled). Add courgettes to simmering sauce and cook over a low heat for 20 to 25 minutes, or until tender but still firm.

3 Transfer courgettes to a deep serving dish, discarding *bouquet garni*. Pour over cooking juices and allow to cool. Then chill until ready to serve.

4 Just before serving, moisten with remaining olive oil. Sprinkle with the finely chopped parsley and a little lemon juice, to taste, and serve immediately.

Serves 4–6

6 tablespoons olive oil
1 large Spanish onion, finely chopped
1 large clove garlic, finely chopped
1/4 pint dry white wine
Bouquet garni
12 coriander seeds
12 black peppercorns
Lemon juice
Salt
1 1/2 lb small sweet courgettes
2–4 level tablespoons finely chopped parsley

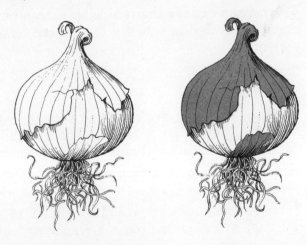

Onions à la Grecque

1 Peel onions.

2 Combine in a saucepan with 1 pint water, the dry white wine, sugar, plumped-up raisins, tomato concentrate and olive oil. Add wine vinegar, salt, freshly ground black pepper and cayenne pepper, to taste, and simmer for about 45 minutes, or until onions are tender, but still quite firm.

3 Serve cold, garnished with coarsely chopped parsley.

Serves 4

2 lb button onions
1/4–1/2 pint dry white wine
5 oz sugar
5 oz plumped-up raisins
4 level tablespoons tomato concentrate
4 tablespoons olive oil
2–4 tablespoons wine vinegar
Salt and freshly ground black pepper
Cayenne pepper
Coarsely chopped parsley

Serve 6

6 tender artichokes
Juice of 1–2 lemons
6 oz onions, minced or
    grated
12 button onions
Salt
6–8 tablespoons olive oil
Freshly ground black pepper

Artichoke Hearts à la Grecque

Only the hearts of the artichokes are used in this dish. Boil the leaves separately in salted, acidulated water until tender, and serve them with a bowl of melted butter or vinaigrette to dip into. They are far too good to waste.

1 To prepare artichokes: lay each artichoke on its side and slice off the leaves level with the choke. Then, holding the artichoke firmly, peel round with a sharp knife from the base to remove remaining leaves right down to the heart. Have ready a bowl of cold water heavily acidulated with lemon juice and immerse the artichoke in it as soon as you have cut down to the heart. Otherwise it quickly goes black when exposed to the air.

2 Now scrape out all the fibres or 'choke' growing on the heart, dipping it into the bowl of lemon water occasionally to keep it white.

3 Prepare remaining artichoke hearts in the same way.

4 Arrange artichoke hearts side by side in one layer in a wide, shallow pan. Spoon some of the minced or grated onion over each one.

5 Slip button onions in between hearts and barely cover with salted water.

6 Bring to the boil; cover pan and simmer gently until artichoke hearts and onions are tender, about 20 minutes. Then remove lid; pour in olive oil and raise heat under the pan. Boil hard for about 10 minutes, or until water has evaporated, leaving the oil behind.

7 Transfer artichoke hearts and button onions to a shallow serving dish, spooning pan juices over them. Season to taste with freshly ground black pepper and more salt if necessary. Sprinkle with a little lemon juice and chill until ready to serve.

Note: If you feel the dish is too dry, you can spoon over a little more raw olive oil just before serving.

Lesson 18
Pancakes

The Pancake

Take the cooking of any country and you are practically certain to come across a pancake in one guise or another. Indeed, pancakes may well have been the earliest form of bread – finely ground grain mixed with water, formed into flat cakes and baked on hot stones – before the discovery of leavening agents, and they still are in some parts of the world.

Large or small, fat or thin, stuffed or plain, and made with every conceivable type of flour, from robust maize and buckwheat to the silkiest white wheat, pancakes come under a variety of names: German pfannkuchen and palatschinken, Russian bliny, Jewish blintzes and latkes (potato pancakes), Spanish-Mexican tortillas, Swedish plättar, Norwegian lefser, even, at a pinch, the Indian paratha, but the most famous of them all is the Great French Crêpe.

Once you have learned how to produce a good crêpe, thin and delicate in texture, well worth eating in its own right with sugar and lemon or simmered in an aromatic syrup, yet substantial enough to wrap around a sweet or savoury filling without coming apart – the variations are child's play.

The pancake pan Choose a frying-pan (5 to 6 inches in diameter is the usual size) heavy enough to disperse the heat evenly, yet not too heavy, so that you can do the tossing trick with it when so inclined. Rounded sides are an advantage as they make it possible to slip a flexible spatula or knife blade around the edge of the pancake to ease it away from the bottom of the pan.

If you intend to devote a pan exclusively to crêpes, cast-iron or lined copper are both good choices, or heavy aluminium. Before using the pan for the first time, 'season' it with oil just like an omelette pan – see page 285.

The Pancake Batter

A crêpe-type batter is a simple mixture of flour smoothly blended with milk (or milk and water, or cream), with eggs to make the batter rise slightly, a dash of salt, perhaps a pinch of sugar (not too much, though, for sweet batters scorch more easily), a little oil or melted butter to help prevent pancakes sticking – and the merest drop of cognac, rum, wine or beer.

There is practically no difference between a savoury pancake batter and a sweet one.

● The batter must not be overbeaten, as this seems to result in tough pancakes.

● It should be absolutely smooth. If necessary, strain through a fine sieve before use.

● The lighter the batter, the thinner the coating you can spread over the pan and, consequently, the more delicate your pancake will be. Flours vary so much in quality, and eggs in size, that you should always be ready to adjust the liquid specified in the recipe, so that your batter ends up with the consistency of single cream.

● Conversely, if your pancakes tear easily when you handle them, either the batter is too thin, or you have not used enough eggs.

'Resting' the Batter

According to time-honoured rules, pancake batters should be left to rest for a couple of hours before they are used. Some people claim that they cannot discern any difference between a batter used straight away and one left to rest. However, one's own experience can be the only guide in such matters, and mine tells me that a batter which is used immediately just will not behave as it should. Resting develops its elasticity so that it runs effortlessly and evenly over the surface of the pan, instead of making ragged streaks that refuse to join up.

Greasing the Pan

There are two ways of doing this. In both cases the pan must first be made very hot. Shake a little cold water on to the surface: when the pan is hot enough, it will roll about in little drops and sizzle away almost immediately.

● Then either melt a small knob of butter in the pan, swirling it around quickly to glaze the bottom and sides evenly . . .

● Or simply rub the hot pan all over with a thick wad of kitchen paper dipped in oil or smeared over with lard. (Watch your fingertips!)

The aim is just to grease the pan, *not* to provide fat for the pancake to fry in.

Repeat after every pancake.

Frying the Pancake

You now have a very hot, greased pan. Lift it away from the heat with your left hand (or your right hand if you're left-handed) and, holding the pan ready to tilt, with your other hand pour a tablespoon of batter into the centre, followed by another tablespoon round the outer perimeter. Immediately start tilting the pan about until the two 'rings' of batter close up to make a thin, even pancake.

● Another method that guarantees paper-thin pancakes, although it is slightly wasteful, pours a good splash of batter into the hot pan from a ladle or jug. As soon as the batter is in the pan, tilt it round and round as before until a thin, even coating has set over the entire surface. Then, if you find you have used too much batter, simply pour the excess back into the bowl as soon as enough has set on the surface, and next time use less.

The 'trail' left behind on the side of the pan can be scraped off with a spatula.

Return the pan to a moderately high heat to cook the pancake until it becomes opaque and dry on top, and little bubbles of air start forming underneath. Then draw a knife blade or flexible spatula round the edges of the pancake to loosen them and either flip it over on the spatula, or give the pan a quick, firm flick to toss it on to the other side. Carry on cooking the pancake for a few seconds longer, but take care not to burn it – the second side always scorches more easily.

● You may find that the first pancake of the batch refuses to form itself properly and sticks badly in spite of careful greasing. Before you start blaming the batter, try making a second pancake. The first one is often a failure, especially when the pan is not kept exclusively for pancakes. In fact, this is a good way of 'seasoning' a pan for the pancakes to come. Just scrape away the offender; rub the pan clean of any burnt scraps with a wad of kitchen paper, and start again.

● It is impossible to colour a pancake evenly on both sides. The second side usually ends up with unattractive dark spots. Make

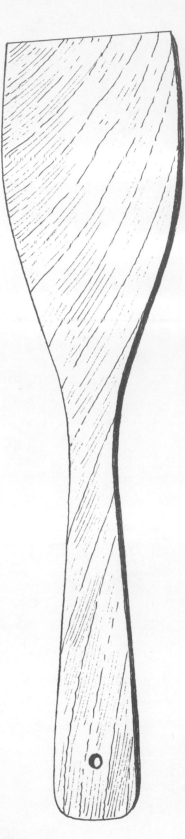

sure when folding or rolling your pancake that this is discreetly turned inwards.

● Finally, the best way to regulate the cooking heat when making pancakes is to draw the *pan* away from the flame or ring when you feel that it's getting too hot and continue cooking the pancake from the heat of the pan itself as it cools down again. This is far more effective than fiddling with the gas or electric controls. I have often found that in a heavy, hot pan I can finish cooking a pancake on one side before I need to return it to the stove for a heat boost.

Stacking Pancakes (to be served immediately)

The way you stack your pancakes depends on whether you want them to be tender or slightly crisp. The former are better for rolling or folding as they don't crumble at the edges.

● For soft pancakes, place an upturned soup plate over a pan of hot water and cover it with a clean tea towel folded in four. As soon as the first pancake is ready, slip it out of the pan on to the soup plate and cover it with the cloth. Then repeat with remaining pancakes, stacking them on top of one another.

In this way, the hot steam generated by pancakes is trapped around them, keeping them warm and softening overcrisp edges.

● For drier pancakes, either stack them as above and keep them hot, uncovered, in a low oven; or cool individually on a wire rack so that all the excess moisture evaporates.

To Reheat Pancakes

The inverted soup plate over hot water method is equally good for reheating pancakes: cover the plate of pancakes with a bowl and gently reheat the water underneath. In this way the pancakes will warm up gradually without becoming rubbery.

● Stuffed pancakes are usually rolled or folded and then either slipped into a moderate oven or under the grill (not too hot, otherwise the pancakes may burn before the heat has penetrated the filling), or gently fried in butter.

Storing Pancakes

Pancakes store well in a refrigerator – which makes them a good standby for the busy host or hostess – and they can also be deep-frozen.

● See that they are quite cold before you put them away, otherwise they may become rubbery when reheated.

● To refrigerate pancakes: wrap the stack of pancakes in an airtight plastic bag or foil. They will keep for several days under mild refrigeration.

● To deep-freeze pancakes: stack the pancakes as above, but this time put a sheet of lightly oiled greaseproof paper between each layer to prevent them sticking together. Wrap securely in foil or a plastic bag and make sure all the air is expelled before sealing tightly. Deep-frozen pancakes should not be kept longer than about 8 weeks.

Savoury Pancakes
Basic Crêpe Batter

Makes 12–15 thin crêpes

4 1/2 oz plain flour
Pinch of salt
1 egg
1/2 pint milk
Olive oil

1 Sift flour and salt into a bowl, and make a well in the centre; break in egg and gradually add milk, stirring from the centre with a wooden spoon to incorporate flour smoothly. When batter is quite free of lumps, stir in 2 teaspoons olive oil. Leave to rest for at least 1 hour before making *crêpes*.

2 When ready to fry *crêpes*: have ready an upturned soup plate covered with a folded cloth.

3 Heat a small, heavy *crêpe* pan about 6 inches in diameter. When it is very hot, rub entire surface very lightly with a wad of kitchen paper moistened with oil.

4 Pour about 2 tablespoons batter into centre of hot pan, tilting it quickly so that it coats bottom of pan very thinly and evenly all over before it has had a chance to set. If you find you have used too much batter, pour excess back into the bowl once a thin layer has set on the bottom of the pan, and scrape away the 'trail' it leaves on the side of the pan. Then use a little less batter for the next *crêpe*.

5 Cook steadily for about 1 minute, drawing a spatula or the point of a knife round edges of *crêpe* to loosen it. As soon as small bubbles begin to form under the *crêpe*, flip it over and cook for 60 to 90 seconds longer.

6 Slip out on to the prepared plate and cover with the cloth.

7 Continue in this manner until you have made 12 *crêpes* in all, with an extra one or two as a reserve, stacking them on top of each other under the cloth. The pan should be oiled again *very* lightly between each *crêpe*.

8 Allow *crêpes* to become quite cold; then store in the refrigerator, covered, until needed.

3 oz plain flour
1/4 level teaspoon salt
1 egg
7 fluid oz lager
1 tablespoon melted butter

Crêpe Batter with Beer

The taste of lager is not as pronounced as you might suppose in pancakes made with this batter. It comes through just enough to complement and give a boost to savoury fillings of ham, shellfish or cheese.

1 Sift flour and salt into a bowl, and make a well in the centre.

2 Separate egg.

3 Beat egg yolk lightly with lager. Pour into the well slowly, stirring from the centre and gradually incorporating flour from sides of well with a wooden spoon. Then beat vigorously until smooth.

4 Stir melted butter into batter. Strain through a fine sieve if you have not succeeded in eliminating every pocket of flour, and leave to rest for at least 30 minutes before frying *crêpes*.

5 Just before using batter, whisk egg white until stiff but not dry and fold in carefully but thoroughly with a metal spoon.

6 Cook *crêpes* as directed under Basic Crêpe Batter, Steps 3–8, above.

Curried Crab Pancakes

1 Make up pancake batter 2 hours in advance to allow it time to rest: sift flour, castor sugar and salt into a bowl, and make a well in the centre.

2 Add the whole egg plus an egg yolk, and with a wooden spoon start working them into the flour, gradually incorporating the latter from the sides of the well and adding milk in a thin stream. Beat the batter vigorously until quite smooth.

3 Stir in melted butter and brandy, and if any pockets of flour remain, strain batter through a fine sieve.

4 While batter is resting, prepare Filling: melt butter in a heavy pan and sauté apple slices and finely chopped shallots over a moderate heat until golden brown.

5 Remove pan from heat; stir in curry paste, crushed coriander, Béchamel sauce and lemon juice, and season well with salt and freshly ground black pepper.

6 Fold in flaked crabmeat. Allow to cool.

7 Cook pancakes as usual, using 2 to 3 tablespoons batter to make thin ones 6 inches in diameter. You should have 10 to 12 pancakes.

8 When ready to serve, preheat oven to moderate (350°F. Mark 4). Butter an 11- by 7-inch gratin dish.

9 Reheat crabmeat mixture over a gentle heat, and divide it between the pancakes, rolling each one up as you fill it, and tucking the ends under to prevent filling oozing out.

10 Arrange pancakes side by side in the gratin dish. Dot with about 2 level tablespoons butter and sprinkle with freshly grated Parmesan.

11 Bake pancakes for 15 to 20 minutes until thoroughly hot. Then, if top has not coloured, slip the dish under a hot grill for a few minutes to glaze it. Serve immediately.

Pancake batter
2 oz plain flour
1 level teaspoon castor sugar
Pinch of salt
1 egg
1 egg yolk
8 fluid oz milk
1 tablespoon melted butter
1 tablespoon brandy

Curried crab filling
2 level tablespoons butter
1/2 tart apple, peeled, cored and sliced
2 shallots, finely chopped
1–1 1/2 level teaspoons curry paste
1/2 level teaspoon crushed coriander seeds
1/2 pint Béchamel sauce (page 178)
1 tablespoon lemon juice
Salt and freshly ground black pepper
1 7 3/4-oz can crabmeat, drained and flaked

Olive oil to fry pancakes
Butter
2 level tablespoons freshly grated Parmesan

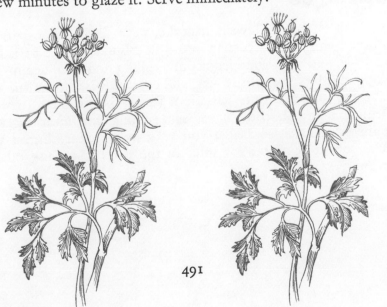

12 thin *crêpes*, 5 inches in
  diameter (page 489)
1 oz butter
1 oz plain flour
6 fluid oz hot milk
2 oz freshly grated Gruyère
Salt and freshly ground black
  pepper
2 eggs, separated
4 level tablespoons freshly
  grated Parmesan

Crêpes Souflées au Fromage

This dish is not as awkward as it sounds to prepare as a first
course for guests. The *crêpes* can be fried and stacked well in
advance, and the filling prepared right up to the point of beating
in the egg yolks. Don't go any further, though – the final stages
must wait until your guests are just about to sit down to the
table.

1 Preheat oven to moderately hot (400°F. Mark 6). Butter 2
large baking sheets.

2 Make the *crêpes*, following the recipe on page 489, and stack
them on an upturned soup plate covered with a folded tea towel
to keep them moist while you prepare filling.

3 To make filling: melt butter in a thick-bottomed saucepan. Add
flour and cook for 2 to 3 minutes over a low heat, stirring constantly with a wooden spoon, to make a smooth, pale *roux*.
Add milk gradually, beating all the time until sauce is smooth
and thick.

4 Beat freshly grated Gruyère into sauce. When sauce is smooth
again, season generously with salt and freshly ground black
pepper, and allow to cool slightly.

5 When sauce is lukewarm, beat in egg yolks.

6 Whisk egg whites until stiff but not dry, and fold lightly but
thoroughly into sauce with a metal spoon or spatula.

7 Put a generous tablespoon of cheese mixture on half of each
crêpe and fold in two, pressing filling lightly towards the open
edge.

8 Transfer *crêpes* to prepared baking sheet with a wide spatula
and sprinkle each one with a level teaspoon of grated Parmesan.

9 Bake *crêpes* for 12 to 15 minutes, or until they are puffed up and
crisp golden brown on top. Serve immediately.

5 oz plain flour, sifted
1 level teaspoon salt
4 eggs, well beaten
1/2 pint milk or water (see
  note)
Butter or oil, to fry

Blintzes

A blintz is a thin Jewish pancake, very like a French *crêpe*,
although in fact it is Russian in origin. Blintzes are first fried on
one side, and then wrapped round a filling and fried again. The
filling may be sweet or savoury, and every Jewish housewife will
have her own favourite variation. Remember, though, that an
Orthodox Jewish cook never serves milk and meat together
at the same meal, so that if you are making meat blintzes you
must substitute water for milk in the batter, and use oil for
frying.

1 Sift flour and salt into a bowl, and make a well in the centre. Combine well beaten eggs with milk or water and pour into the well. Incorporate liquid into flour gradually with a wooden spoon to make a smooth batter.

2 Heat a small knob of butter or oil in a heavy frying-pan 6 inches in diameter. Pour in enough batter to make a very thin layer, tilting the pan to coat the base evenly. Cook over a steady, low heat on one side only until top of blintz is dry and lightly blistered. Transfer to a clean cloth or a piece of greaseproof paper, fried side up.

3 Repeat until batter is used up, stacking blintzes on top of each other with a sheet of greaseproof paper between each one to prevent them sticking together.

4 To fill blintzes: lay each blintz fried side down and spread a tablespoon of chosen filling (see below) in centre. Fold vertical sides inwards to enclose filling; then fold up neatly to make an envelope. Blintzes may be prepared in advance and stored in the refrigerator until needed.

5 When ready to serve: fry blintzes in butter or oil over a low, steady heat until they are crisp and golden brown on both sides, and the filling is hot and well cooked.

Meat Blintzes

1 For authentic Jewish meat blintzes, prepare the batter with water and fry in oil.

2 Mix filling ingredients lightly but thoroughly with a fork.

3 Fill blintzes and fry slowly in oil over a low heat so that meat inside is well cooked. Serve hot.

Bliny

A classic Russian dish: small, thick pancakes made with a mixture of buckwheat and plain flour, raised with yeast. Serve them straight from the pan. Each guest helps himself to a pancake and assembles it as follows: first a brushing of melted butter, then some smoked fish, e.g. salmon, trout or even skinned and boned buckling (or substitute a generous layer of salt herring butter – overleaf – anchovy butter – see page 218 – or both), and finally a dollop of soured cream.

On extra-special occasions, serve bliny with black caviar.

Makes 16 blintzes

1 recipe Blintzes (page 492)
Oil, for frying

Filling
3/4–1 lb minced raw beef
1 egg
Salt and freshly ground black pepper
2–3 tablespoons meat stock

8 oz plain flour
8 oz buckwheat flour
2 level teaspoons dried yeast
1 pint lukewarm milk
Generous pinch of sugar
2 eggs, separated
1 oz butter, melted
Salt
3 oz fat, for frying

Bliny

1 Sift plain flour into a large bowl and buckwheat flour into a smaller one.

2 Dissolve yeast according to instructions on the can or packet, using a little of the lukewarm milk sweetened with a pinch of sugar.

3 Make a hollow in the centre of the plain flour; pour in dissolved yeast and work into flour gradually, beating with a wooden spoon, and adding enough of the remaining milk to make a thick, smooth batter. Cover bowl and leave batter to rise in a warm place until light and bubbly, and doubled in bulk.

4 Beat in buckwheat flour and enough of the remaining milk to make a batter with the consistency of double cream. When batter is absolutely smooth again, beat in egg yolks, melted butter and salt, to taste.

5 Whisk egg whites until stiff but not dry. Fold them lightly but thoroughly into batter with a spatula or a metal spoon, and leave to rise until almost doubled in bulk again.

6 Heat a heavy frying-pan 4 or 5 inches in diameter and brush lightly with a little fat. Ladle $\frac{1}{4}$ inch batter into pan, swirling to distribute it evenly, and cook over a steady, moderate heat until underside is golden and little bubbles have formed all over the top; then flip over with a spatula and brown the other side.

7 Continue in this manner until batter is used up, greasing pan every time and either serving bliny straight from the frying-pan, or stacking them on a large dish over a pan of simmering water, covered with a clean napkin, until they are all prepared. Serve very hot (see above).

Makes about $\frac{1}{2}$ lb

1/2 lb salted herrings
2 hard-boiled egg yolks
4 oz unsalted butter, softened

Salted Herring Butter

To serve with hot bliny (see page 493), as a canapé spread, or with baked potatoes or potato pancakes (see page 495).

Herrings pickled in vinegar or other acid are of no use for this recipe. You must get real salted herrings from a barrel and you will probably find them at a delicatessen specialising in Eastern European food.

1 Desalt herrings thoroughly by soaking them in a bowl of cold water for at least 24 hours, changing water frequently. It is advisable to leave them under running water for the first half-hour.

2 Drain herrings thoroughly and pat dry with kitchen paper. Then fillet them, removing every scrap of skin and bone.

3 Chop herrings finely and pound smoothly to a paste in a mortar, together with hard-boiled egg yolks.

4 Turn paste into a bowl. Add softened butter and beat until very smooth and fluffy. Shape into a neat brick and chill until firm.

Polish Potato Pancakes

These hearty pancakes are not only economical, but very versatile, too: you can serve them savoury, on their own, spread with a herring or anchovy butter, or mushroom sauce, or as an accompaniment to casseroled beef; or sweet – traditionally sprinkled with sugar and topped with a dollop of sour cream.

1 Line a sieve with a double thickness of muslin and set it over a bowl.

2 Peel, wash and dry potatoes, and grate them very finely into the muslin-lined sieve.

3 Draw up sides of muslin and gently press excess moisture out into the bowl.

4 Allow liquid in the bowl to stand for a few minutes; then pour it off carefully, leaving behind the starch, which will have settled on the bottom.

5 Combine grated potatoes with potato starch. Add the egg, flour, and salt to taste, and blend thoroughly with a wooden spoon. Potato mixture should be quite thick.

6 Fry pancakes two or three at a time. In a large frying-pan, melt 2 or 3 tablespoons lard (or a combination of butter and oil). When sizzling, drop in a tablespoon of potato mixture for each pancake and, with a spatula or the back of a spoon, spread out into a thin oval (the thinner the layer, the crisper will be the pancake). Fry on one side until pancake is crisp and golden underneath; then flip over and continue to fry until other side is golden.

7 Drain pancakes thoroughly on absorbent paper. They are at their best served straight from the pan, but you can keep them hot in a slow oven until you have finished frying them. Do not lay them on top of each other, though, or they will turn limp and rubbery.

**Serves 3–4
(12 Pancakes)**

1 lb floury potatoes
1 egg
1 level tablespoon plain
  flour
Salt
Lard or butter and oil, for
  frying

Serves 4

Wholewheat flour
1/2 level teaspoon salt
Butter (optional)

Chappatis

1 Sift 8 oz wholewheat flour and salt into a bowl.

2 Gradually sprinkle on about $\frac{1}{3}$ pint cold water, working flour with your fingertips to make a stiff dough which you can just knead. Knead until smooth; roll into a ball and leave to rest for 30 minutes, covered with a damp cloth.

3 Dust your hands lightly with extra wholewheat flour and knead dough vigorously for 2 to 3 minutes until it loses its stickiness.

4 Divide dough into 8 equal pieces. Flour your rolling pin and surface generously, and roll each piece into a thin circle 5 inches in diameter.

5 Heat an ungreased griddle or heavy frying-pan until very hot and cook chappatis for 2 to 3 minutes on each side until brown spots appear on the floury surface.

6 Serve chappatis very hot just as they are or lightly spread with butter on one side only.

Serves 4

Wholewheat flour
1/2 level teaspoon salt
5 oz softened butter
Freshly ground black pepper
Ground cumin

Parathas

A traditional accompaniment for curry.

1 Sift 10 oz wholewheat flour and salt into a bowl.

2 Rub in 1 oz softened butter until thoroughly incorporated. Then gradually sprinkle on about $\frac{1}{4}$ pint cold water, working and kneading mixture to a smooth, stiff dough. Roll into a ball. Cover bowl with a damp cloth and put dough aside to rest for 30 minutes.

3 Divide dough into 4 equal pieces. Reserve 1 oz of the remaining butter for frying the *parathas*, and put the rest on a plate.

4 Dust your rolling pin and surface with a little extra wholewheat flour, and roll each piece of dough into a thin circle about 7 inches in diameter. Spread with a little butter; fold circle in half and seal edges by pinching them firmly between your fingers. Then spread with more butter, fold in half again to make a triangle, and seal edges once more. Finally, roll each triangle into a circle, this time making it about 6 inches in diameter.

5 To fry *parathas*: heat a heavy frying-pan thoroughly and grease with some of the reserved butter. Fry each *paratha* for 2 to 3 minutes on each side until golden and rather flaky.

6 Dust hot *parathas* with freshly ground black pepper and a pinch of ground cumin, and serve immediately.

Bacon Pancakes

1 Sift flour into a bowl with a pinch of salt and make a well in the centre.

2 Pour in lightly beaten egg and the milk, and stir with a wooden spoon, working from the centre of the well and incorporating flour very gradually from sides until blended to a perfectly smooth batter. Stir in oil. The batter should have the consistency of thick cream. If too thick, beat in a little more milk. (**Note**: If batter is lumpy in spite of all precautions, strain it through a fine sieve.) Put aside to rest for at least 1 hour.

3 Preheat oven to fairly hot (425°F. Mark 7).

4 The pancakes can be baked in 4 individual round heatproof dishes 6 inches in diameter, or in a 9- by 11-inch roasting tin. Melt butter in the chosen dish(es) and fry bacon slices slowly until crisp, allowing 3 or 4 per person according to size.

5 Pour over batter.

6 Bake pancakes for 20 to 25 minutes until puffy and golden brown. Serve very hot.

Serves 4

4 oz plain flour
Salt
1 egg, lightly beaten
1/4 pint milk
1 tablespoon oil
4 level teaspoons butter
12–16 slices streaky bacon

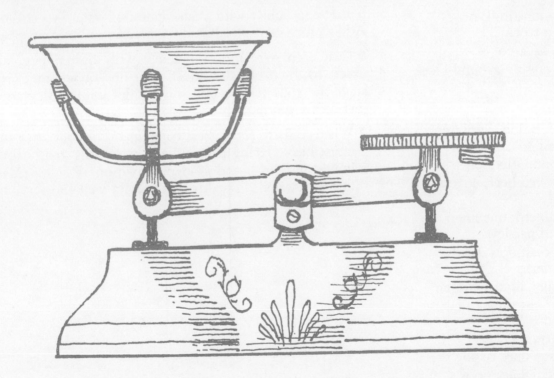

497

12 *crêpes*, 6 inches in
diameter (page 489)

1 egg

Salt and freshly ground black
pepper

2–3 oz fine stale breadcrumbs

Butter and olive oil, for frying

Chicken filling

1 Spanish onion, very finely
chopped

1 tablespoon olive oil

8 oz cooked chicken meat,
coarsely minced

4 level tablespoons finely
chopped parsley

1/2 level teaspoon dried
mixed herbs

2 egg yolks, lightly beaten

4 level tablespoons double
cream

4 tablespoons milk or
chicken stock

4 drops Tabasco

Salt and freshly ground black
pepper

Beef filling

1 Spanish onion, very finely
chopped

1 tablespoon olive oil

12 oz cooked beef, coarsely
minced

6 level tablespoons finely
chopped parsley

3/4 level teaspoon dried
mixed herbs

2 egg yolks, lightly beaten

3 tablespoons milk or beef
stock

1/2–1 teaspoon
Worcestershire or soy sauce

1 1/2 level tablespoons
concentrated tomato purée

Salt and freshly ground black
pepper

Crisp-fried Pancake Rolls with Chicken or Beef

Serve these crisp-fried pancake rolls with bowls of steaming hot, clear consommé, or as a supper dish, accompanied by a tomato or mushroom sauce.

They are a very useful way of using up left over cooked meats.

1 Prepare *crêpes* in advance. They should be quite thin, but sound and free of holes.

2 The method for both fillings is exactly the same: sauté finely chopped onion in olive oil for 3 or 4 minutes until transparent and lightly coloured. Turn into a mixing bowl.

3 Combine with remaining ingredients and blend thoroughly, adding salt and freshly ground black pepper, to taste.

4 Lay a *crêpe* flat. Put 2 level tablespoons meat filling in the centre, moulding it into a small, thick sausage with your fingers (filling will be stiff enough to hold its shape). Fold two sides of *crêpe* in over filling and roll up into a neat, secure parcel. Repeat with remaining *crêpes* and filling.

5 Beat egg lightly with a tablespoon of water in a shallow dish. Add a pinch each of salt and freshly ground black pepper.

6 Coat each *crêpe* roll completely with beaten egg, allowing excess to drain off, and cover with fine breadcrumbs. (At this stage the rolls can be put aside under mild refrigeration until just before serving.)

7 When ready to serve: heat equal quantities of butter and oil in a large, heavy frying-pan and fry *crêpe* rolls gently for 7 or 8 minutes until crisp and golden brown on all sides. (Make sure filling has heated right through.) Drain well and serve immediately.

Sweet Pancakes

Basic Batter for Dessert Crêpes

1 Sift flour, salt and castor sugar into a bowl, and make a well in the centre.

2 Beat egg lightly and pour into the well. Slowly add milk, stirring from the centre with a wooden spoon and gradually incorporating flour from sides of well. Then beat batter until smooth.

3 Stir in oil and brandy. Strain batter through a fine sieve if necessary and leave to rest for at least 1 hour before making *crêpes*.

4 Cook *crêpes* as directed under Basic Crêpe Batter, Steps 3–8, page 489.

Makes twelve 6-inch crêpes

4 oz plain flour
Pinch of salt
1 level teaspoon castor sugar
1 egg
8 fluid oz milk
1 tablespoon corn or peanut oil
1 tablespoon brandy

Kirsch Butter Crêpes

1 Prepare Kirsch butter: soften butter in a bowl. Add castor sugar and beat until very light and fluffy. When mixture is almost white, add Kirsch a little at a time, beating vigorously with a wire whisk. Scrape butter into a mound and chill until firm.

2 To assemble *crêpes*: put an eighth of the butter at one end of each *crêpe*. Roll up and fold ends under to close the parcel.

3 Pack *crêpes* tightly side by side in a fireproof dish with folded ends underneath. *Crêpes* may be left like this in a cool place for several hours.

4 Just before serving, sift icing sugar over the top of the *crêpes* and place under a hot, preheated grill until glazed and golden. Serve immediately.

Serve 2 per person. The filling is very rich

8 *crêpes*, 6 inches in diameter (see recipe above)
2 level tablespoons icing sugar

Kirsch butter

4 level tablespoons unsalted butter
4 level tablespoons castor sugar
3 tablespoons Kirsch

12 *crêpes*, 5 to 6 inches in diameter (page 499)

Orange butter

4 oz unsalted butter, softened

2 oz castor sugar

Finely grated rind of 1 large orange

2 tablespoons orange liqueur

5 tablespoons orange juice

To flame

1 level tablespoon castor sugar

2 tablespoons orange liqueur

2 tablespoons brandy

Crêpes Suzette

1 Prepare *crêpes* in advance. They should be thin, but not paper-thin.

2 Prepare orange butter: in a bowl, cream softened butter with sugar and grated orange rind, and when fluffy, beat in orange liqueur and juice a little at a time. The butter will probably curdle, but this does not matter.

3 Melt the orange butter in a chafing dish, a large electric frying pan, or a heavy frying-pan (the pancakes might scorch in a thin one). Let it bubble over a low heat for 3 or 4 minutes until slightly reduced.

4 Keeping the heat low, immerse a *crêpe* in the bubbling butter and, with the aid of a fork and spoon, fold it in half and then in half again, and push it to the side of the pan. Repeat with remaining *crêpes*.

5 To flame: when all the *crêpes* are in the pan, sprinkle surface with castor sugar and pour over orange liqueur mixed with brandy.

Light a match and, standing well clear, set the alcohol alight. Remove pan from heat. Keep spooning the flaming syrup over the *crêpes* until the alcohol burns itself out. Serve immediately.

Serves 6

12 *crêpes*, 6 inches in diameter (page 499)

Sifted icing sugar

1 tablespoon each cognac and Grand Marnier (optional)

Soufflé mixture

1 oz plain flour

2 oz granulated sugar

4 egg yolks

1/4 pint milk

2 lemons

3 egg whites

Crêpes Soufflées au Citron

Souffléed *crêpes* make a spectacular dish for a dinner party. The pancakes can be cooked and stacked, and Steps 1 and 2 of the soufflé mixture completed in the morning. Steps 3, 4, 5 and 6 should be seen to before you sit down to the table, leaving Steps 7 to 11 until just before serving.

1 Prepare soufflé mixture: combine flour with sugar, 2 egg yolks and 4 tablespoons of the milk in a bowl. Bring remaining milk to the boil and pour over flour mixture, beating vigorously. Return to the pan and cook over a low heat, stirring constantly, for 2 or 3 minutes longer. Remove from heat.

2 Grate the rind of the 2 lemons very finely and beat into the mixture, together with 1 tablespoon lemon juice.

3 Clear a surface and lay out pancakes side by side. If necessary, trim ragged edges with a pair of scissors. Select a shallow baking dish large enough to hold all the pancakes folded in half, and suitable for serving at table.

4 Put egg whites in the bowl of your electric mixer (or have them ready in a bowl with a hand beater beside it). Have icing sugar and a small sieve ready to use. Assemble cognac and Grand Marnier, a metal ladle and a box of matches if you intend to flame the *crêpes*.

5 Beat remaining 2 egg yolks into soufflé mixture.

6 Preheat oven to fairly hot (425°F. Mark 7).

7 Just before serving: whisk egg whites until stiff but not dry, and fold them into soufflé mixture with a large metal spoon or spatula.

8 Lay a trimmed pancake in the baking dish; put 3 level tablespoons soufflé mixture in centre and fold pancake in two so that top half overlaps bottom half by about ½ inch.

9 Fill all 12 pancakes in this manner. Dust all over with icing sugar and bake for 10 minutes, or until puffed and golden.

10 Meanwhile, if you intend to flame the *crêpes*, heat the ladle in hot water. Dry it thoroughly. Pour in cognac and Grand Marnier, and swirl around for a few seconds to warm them gently.

11 As soon as *crêpes* come out of the oven, set a match to the alcohol and, when flames are burning brightly, dribble them up one row of *crêpes* and down the other. Serve at once.

Coffee–Chocolate Crêpes

Serves 6

1 Sift flour into a bowl with 1 level tablespoon castor sugar, the salt, powdered chocolate and instant coffee. Make a well in the centre.

2 Beat eggs lightly. Pour into well and start stirring from the centre with a wooden spoon, adding milk in a thin stream as you gradually incorporate flour from sides of well with your spoon.

3 When batter is smoothly blended, beat in melted butter and strain through a fine sieve to ensure there are no pockets of unblended flour left. The batter should have the consistency of thin cream. Allow it to stand for at least 2 hours before frying *crêpes*.

4 Heat a 6-inch *crêpe* pan until a drop of water shaken on to it sizzles and rolls about on contact. Rub base and sides of hot pan with a wad of kitchen paper dipped in oil.

4 oz plain flour
Castor sugar
Pinch of salt
1 level tablespoon powdered chocolate
1 level tablespoon instant coffee powder
2 eggs
3/4 pint milk
2 tablespoons melted butter
Oil
1/2 pint double cream, chilled
1 tablespoon rum

5 Pour about 2 tablespoons batter into the pan, and quickly swirl it around so that base is entirely covered before batter has had a chance to set.

6 Cook over a fairly high heat for a minute or two until *crêpe* is coloured and slightly crisp underneath; then flip it over with a palette knife and cook for a further 1 or 2 minutes.

7 Continue to make pancakes in this manner until batter is all used up, stacking them on top of each other on an upturned soup plate over a pan of hot water, and oiling the pan lightly for every pancake.

8 Just before serving, whip chilled cream until very thick and flavour with rum and a little castor sugar, to taste.

9 Spread each *crêpe* with rum-flavoured cream and roll up. Serve immediately before cream starts melting from warmth of *crêpes*.

Note: Poached pear slices make a delicious garnish for these *crêpes*. For the above portion of *crêpes*, allow 3 ripe pears, peeled, cored and thinly sliced, and poached in a vanilla-flavoured syrup until tender but not mushy.

Souffléed Apple Pancakes

Serves 4–6 (2 pancakes per person)

Pancake batter
2 1/2 oz plain flour
2 level tablespoons castor sugar
Salt
3 eggs
1/2 pint milk
1/4 teaspoon finely grated lemon rind
Few drops of vanilla essence
3 crisp dessert apples
Lemon juice
Oil or butter
Sifted icing sugar
Ground cinnamon

1 To make pancake batter: sift flour, castor sugar and $\frac{1}{4}$ level teaspoon salt into a large bowl, and make a well in the centre.

2 Break 1 egg into a bowl. Separate 2 remaining eggs, adding yolks to the bowl with the whole egg, and putting whites aside for the moment.

3 Beat whole egg lightly with yolks. Pour into the flour mixture.

4 Gradually pour in milk, stirring from the centre with a wooden spoon and incorporating flour from sides of well a little at a time to prevent lumps forming. When batter is smooth and well blended, add finely grated lemon rind and a few drops of vanilla, to taste, and continue to beat vigorously for a minute or two longer. Leave batter to rest while you prepare apples.

5 Peel, core and slice apples thinly into a bowl with a little water acidulated with lemon juice to prevent them discolouring.

6 When ready to make pancakes, add a small pinch of salt to the egg whites and whisk them until stiff but not dry. Fold gently into batter with a metal spoon or spatula.

7 Heat a 6-inch *crêpe* pan over a moderate heat and either brush bottom and sides with a wad of kitchen paper dipped in oil, or melt a small knob of butter in it, swirling it around so that the entire surface is coated.

8 Pour 2 to 3 tablespoons batter into the pan, tilting it quickly back and forth to coat entire surface before batter has had a chance to set. Cook steadily over a moderate heat for about 1 minute until pancake is set and golden underneath.

9 Cover each pancake with some drained apple slices and pour another 2 or 3 tablespoons batter over it. Then, with a wide spatula, turn pancake over and continue to fry until other side is golden brown. Pancake should remain slightly creamy in the centre.

10 Fold pancake over in two or three and transfer to a heated serving dish. Dust with icing sugar and sprinkle with a good pinch of cinnamon. Keep hot.

11 Continue in this manner until batter and apples are used up, greasing pan with oil or butter before every pancake. Serve immediately.

Polish Cottage Cheese Pancakes

1 To make filling: cover sultanas or raisins with boiling water and put them aside to plump up and soften for a few minutes.

2 Drain off any excess liquid from cottage cheese. Rub cheese through a fine sieve into a bowl.

3 Add softened butter and beat vigorously with a wooden spoon until smoothly blended.

4 Beat in remaining ingredients, together with the soaked sultanas, drained and pressed dry against the sides of a sieve.

5 Divide cheese mixture between prepared *crêpes*. Roll them up and tuck ends under to seal in filling.

6 Butter a heatproof rectangular dish and arrange *crêpe* rolls in it side by side. They may be left like this for several hours, covered with foil, in the refrigerator.

7 When ready to serve: dust *crêpes* with sifted icing sugar and dot with flakes of butter.

Serves 4–6

12 thin *crêpes*, 6 inches in
  diameter (page 499)
Butter

Filling

2 level tablespoons sultanas
  or raisins
8 oz cottage cheese
2 oz unsalted butter, softened
2 egg yolks
2 level tablespoons castor
  sugar
1/4 teaspoon vanilla essence
Finely grated rind of 1 small
  lemon
2 teaspoons lemon juice
1/4 level teaspoon ground
  cinnamon

Topping

2 level tablespoons icing
  sugar
2 level tablespoons unsalted
  butter

8 Slip dish under a hot, preheated grill for 5 to 7 minutes, or until *crêpes* are golden and bubbling on top, and hot through. Serve immediately.

Note: Instead of grilling the *crêpes*, you can fry them gently in butter until crisp and golden on the outside, and thoroughly hot in the centre.

Kaiserschmarrn

Serves 4-6

2–3 oz raisins or sultanas
12 pancakes (not too thin)
2–3 oz blanched almonds, slivered
3 level tablespoons butter
1–2 level tablespoons icing sugar

1 Cover raisins or sultanas with boiling water and leave to plump up and soften for 15 minutes.

2 Meanwhile, cut the pancakes into $\frac{1}{2}$-inch squares or diamonds.

3 Drain soaked raisins or sultanas thoroughly and toss with pancake pieces and almond slivers in a bowl.

4 Melt butter in a frying-pan. When it is foaming, add pancake mixture and sauté over a moderate heat for 3 to 4 minutes, tossing with a fork, until hot and golden brown.

5 Pile mixture into a heatproof serving dish. Sift icing sugar over the top.

6 Slip dish under a very hot, preheated grill for about 30 seconds so that sugar caramelises without burning. Serve immediately.

Apple Blintzes

Serves 3-4

1/2 recipe (8) Blintzes (page 492)
2–3 tart eating apples
1 1/2 level tablespoons ground almonds
1 egg white
1 level tablespoon icing sugar
1/4 level teaspoon ground cinnamon
Lemon juice (optional)
Cinnamon sugar, to serve

1 Prepare and fry blintzes, following directions on pages 492 and 493.

2 Peel, core and chop apples finely.

3 Add ground almonds, the egg white, icing sugar and cinnamon, and toss until well mixed. Add a little lemon juice if apples are too sweet, more icing sugar if they seem tart.

4 Fill blintzes and fry as described in the master recipe.

5 Serve hot with cinnamon sugar.

Cherry Blintzes

1 Prepare and fry blintzes, following direction on pages 492 and 493.

2 Toss cherries with flour, cinnamon, sugar and grated lemon rind until well mixed.

3 Fill blintzes and fry as described in the master recipe.

4 Serve hot with thick sour cream or cinnamon sugar.

Serves 3–4

1/2 recipe (8) Blintzes (page 492)

8 oz fresh or canned pitted cherries

1 level tablespoon plain flour

1/4 level teaspoon ground cinnamon

1/4 level teaspoon castor sugar

Finely grated rind of 1/2 lemon

Sour cream or cinnamon sugar, to serve

Lesson 19
Great Boiled Dishes

The title of this lesson is something of a misnomer, for 'boiling' as such plays little or no part in the dishes that follow. In some cases one does boil, but only for a carefully limited time, in order to force out scum.

The crucial lesson to be learned here, as in so many branches of cooking, is control of heat. Once you have done with any initial fast boiling, the liquid in your pot should *never* again be allowed to progress beyond a light shudder, with tiny bubbles breaking here and there on the surface at irregular intervals. If you can't get the heat of your stove low enough to achieve this (and if you're cooking on gas, do make sure there are no draughts to puff out the tiny flame), try using an asbestos mat or, if that doesn't help, raise the pot slightly above the cooking top by standing it on a trivet or metal rack.

Meat subjected to this almost imperceptible cooking remains tender and juicy instead of being reduced to a bundle of tough, dry rag – as inevitably happens if it is allowed to boil fast.

Skimming

See directions for skimming stock on page 160. The important points to remember are:

(1) To use salt – with discretion – to force out scum without oversalting the stock itself. (Bear in mind that the stock will probably reduce quite considerably during cooking so that what tastes adequately salted at the beginning will be oversalty by the end.)

(2) To refrain from skimming until foam on the surface becomes a definite scum that won't slip through the holes in your slotted spoon.

Preparing the Meats

If you are using different meats in pieces of vastly varying size, it is a good idea to divide the larger ones so that all the lumps are roughly the same size, say 2 lb in weight. This gives you a better chance of having everything in the pot ready at the same time.

To make it easier to test the various meats for doneness, tie a string around each piece, leaving one end long enough to hang over the side of the pot so that you can draw out any piece you wish to test without trouble.

● The 'boiled' dishes we have given below may at first glance appear quite a to-do. But don't forget that in many of them, you are getting a *whole* main course, vegetables and all, from one pot, plus a bonus of rich stock to serve as a soup on its own, or to use for cooking and flavouring a pot of rice, or to turn into a sauce, or to keep for later use as the foundation of some other delicious soup.

Boiled Collar of Bacon with Horseradish Cream Sauce

Serves 4–6

1 Soak collar of bacon overnight in a large bowl of water, changing it as often as possible.

2 The following day, drain bacon thoroughly and place it in a pan with cold water to cover. Bring slowly to the boil; drain again and cover with fresh water. Add quartered onion, bay leaf, cloves and mace; bring gently to the boil again and simmer very slowly, allowing 20 minutes per lb, plus 20 minutes over – i.e. 1 hour for a 2-lb joint.

3 About ½ hour before the end of cooking time, prepare sauce: combine milk and stock cube in a pan, and bring to the boil, stirring until cube has dissolved.

4 In another, medium-sized pan, simmer finely chopped onion in butter over a very low heat for 10 minutes, or until soft and transparent but not coloured.

5 Blend in flour and continue to stir over a low heat for 2 to 3 minutes to make a pale *roux*.

6 Gradually add hot, flavoured milk, stirring vigorously to prevent flour forming lumps, and when sauce is smooth, blend in cream.

One 2-lb piece collar of
   bacon
1 onion, quartered
1 bay leaf
2 cloves
2 blades mace

Horseradish Cream Sauce
1 pint milk
1 chicken stock cube
1 small onion, finely chopped
3 level tablespoons butter
4 level tablespoons flour
1/4 pint single cream
Grated horseradish
Wine vinegar or lemon juice
Salt and freshly ground black
   pepper

7 Add horseradish to taste. The amount will depend on the type of horseradish you have been able to get – freshly grated, packed in vinegar, or dehydrated. Simmer gently for 10 minutes, stirring occasionally.

8 Flavour sauce with white wine vinegar or lemon juice, again depending on how your horseradish was prepared. Season lightly with salt and freshly ground black pepper.

9 When bacon joint is tender, remove strings; pull off rind – it will come away easily if joint is sufficiently cooked.

10 Place bacon joint on a heated serving dish and serve hot, with the sauce handed around separately.

Boiled Forehock of Bacon with Fruit Sauce

For this dish, you can use a 'boil-in-the-bag' joint.

1 Pierce bag containing bacon joint; place it in a pan with water to cover; add quartered onion, peppercorns, cloves and bay leaf. Bring to the boil slowly; turn down heat and simmer gently for about 30 minutes per lb, or until cooked through but not stringy.

2 To make fruit sauce: drain can of pineapple cubes, reserving syrup in a measuring jug. Cut each pineapple cube in four.

3 Finely grate rind from orange on to a plate. Peel orange and divide into segments, holding it over the measuring jug as you do so to catch any juices that may escape. Cut each orange segment in half.

4 Make syrup and orange juice up to $\frac{1}{4}$ pint with water if necessary.

5 In a small pan, blend remaining sauce ingredients together smoothly. Gradually add pineapple syrup mixture and bring to the boil, stirring constantly. Simmer, stirring, for 2 to 3 minutes.

6 Gently stir in pineapple and orange segments. If necessary, thin sauce with a tablespoon or two of the bacon stock. Flavour to taste with a pinch of grated orange rind and season with salt and freshly ground black pepper.

7 When bacon is tender, drain bag and remove it. Pull skin off joint – it will strip away easily if bacon is sufficiently cooked.

8 Place joint on a heated serving dish and serve immediately, accompanied by sauce in a separate heated sauceboat or bowl.

Serves 4

1 smoked bacon forehock, about 1 3/4 lb (see note)

1 medium-sized onion, quartered

4 black peppercorns

2 cloves

1 bay leaf

Fruit sauce

One 12-oz can pineapple cubes

1 orange

1 level tablespoon cornflour

1 level tablespoon Demerara sugar

1 tablespoon soy sauce

2 tablespoons olive oil

1–2 tablespoons white wine vinegar

Salt and freshly ground black pepper

Boiled Knuckle of Bacon with Parsley Sauce

1 Boil the bacon knuckle in its bag (pierced) as directed in the recipe for Boiled Forehock of Bacon (see opposite), allowing 30 minutes per lb.

2 About 15 minutes before bacon is due to finish cooking, prepare parsley sauce: in a heavy pan, melt butter, blend in flour and cook over a low heat, stirring constantly, for 2 to 3 minutes to make a pale *roux*.

3 Gradually add milk, stirring vigorously to prevent lumps forming. Bring to the boil, stirring; add finely chopped parsley and continue to simmer, stirring frequently, for 3 to 4 minutes until sauce is thick and smooth, and no longer tastes floury. Season lightly with salt and freshly ground black pepper.

4 Serve bacon as above, accompanied by sauce in a separate, heated sauceboat.

Serves 3–4

1 smoked 'boil-in-the-bag' bacon knuckle, 2–2 1/4 lb
1 medium-sized onion, quartered
4 black peppercorns
2 cloves
1 bay leaf

Parsley sauce

3 level tablespoons butter
2 level tablespoons flour
1/2 pint milk
3–4 level tablespoons finely chopped parsley
Salt and freshly ground black pepper

Boiled Fresh Ox Tongue

1 Scrub tongue with a stiff brush under cold running water to clean it thoroughly, and trim away any gristle or excess fat from root or underside. Then leave tongue to soak in a bowl of cold water for 1 hour.

2 Meanwhile, prepare vegetables and tie the components of your *bouquet garni* up in a piece of muslin.

3 Drain tongue and fit it into a large cooking pot with 8 pints cold water. Add coarse sea salt and bring to the boil over a low heat, skimming frequently as liquid approaches boiling point until surface is clear of froth.

4 As soon as liquid starts simmering, add vegetables and *bouquet garni*. Keep liquid at a gentle simmer for the next $3\frac{1}{2}$ to 4 hours.

5 To test if tongue is cooked, pull at the little bones embedded at the root. They should come out easily and cleanly.

6 When tongue is cooked, lift it out of the pot, allowing all the stock to drain back – this can be used to make an accompanying sauce, or kept for soup. Rinse tongue briefly under the cold tap so that surface is cool enough to handle. Peel skin off in strips. It should come away very easily, but it may be necessary here and there to pare it off with a knife. Tongue is now ready to serve.

Serves 6–8

1 fresh ox tongue, 4–4 1/2 lb
1 Spanish onion, quartered
2 leeks, trimmed
2 carrots, cut into chunks
2 stalks celery, cut into chunks
3 level tablespoons coarse sea salt (gros sel)

Bouquet garni

About 8 sprigs parsley
1 level teaspoon dried thyme
2 bay leaves
1 (unpeeled) clove garlic
6 allspice berries
6 black peppercorns

Serves 6–8

1 fresh ox tongue, 4–4 1/2 lb
Coarse sea salt (gros sel)

Pickling brine

6 oz coarse sea salt
3 oz Demerara sugar
1/2 oz saltpetre (potassium
   nitrate)
1 bay leaf
6 black peppercorns
3 juniper berries

Pickled Ox Tongue

1 The day before immersing the tongue in brine, scrub it thoroughly under cold running water. Trim root and underside. Pat tongue dry. Prick all over with a skewer and rub liberally with coarse salt. Place tongue in a bowl; cover and leave overnight in a cool place.

2 The following day, prepare Pickling brine: combine ingredients in a pan with 4 pints cold water. Bring to the boil over a low heat; boil for 2 to 3 minutes; remove from heat and leave until quite cold.

3 Rinse tongue thoroughly. Place it in a large glazed bowl. Strain cold brine over it, and if necessary, weight tongue so that it is completely submerged. Cover bowl tightly with plastic wrap or foil. Leave in a cool place for 7 days.

4 Before proceeding to cook pickled tongue, rinse it thoroughly under the cold tap and leave to soak for 1 hour in a bowl of cold water.

Note: You can obtain saltpetre from any well-stocked chemist.

Boiled Pickled Tongue

A pickled tongue is boiled in exactly the same way as a fresh one (see page 509), except that for obvious reasons the salt is omitted from the stock.

Boiled Ox Tongue and Carrots with Horseradish Chantilly

Boil a fresh or pickled tongue as directed in the master recipe (page 509).

About 30 minutes before tongue is cooked, scrape 2–2½ pounds carrots; cut them in halves or quarters, according to size; place them in a pan and strain over enough of the tongue stock to cover. Boil carrots until tender. Drain.

Serve tongue on a large, heated platter surrounded by carrots, and accompanied by a bowl of Horseradish Chantilly.

To make horseradish chantilly: Whisk ¼ pint double cream until soft peaks form. Add 2 tablespoons iced water and continue to whisk until thick and fluffy again. Fold in freshly grated horseradish or bottled horseradish sauce to taste, and season lightly with salt.

Pressed Tongue

Serves 6

1 pickled ox tongue, 4–4 1/2 lb, boiled (page 510)

1 packet aspic jelly powder, or enough to set 1/2 pint

2 tablespoons port or Madeira (optional)

1 As soon as tongue is cooked, lift it out of the stock; skin it and remove any bones at the root. Trim root end neatly.

2 Select a deepish, round dish into which the tongue will just fit when curled up tightly. (For the size of tongue specified above use a soufflé dish 5½ inches in diameter.)

3 Curl hot tongue tightly into dish.

4 Bring cooking stock to the boil and cook rapidly, uncovered, to reduce it until either saltiness prevents you going further, or the stock juices taste rich and meaty.

5 Strain ½ pint reduced stock into a measuring jug. Add 1 packet aspic jelly powder, or enough to set ½ pint, and stir until dissolved. If liked, jelly may be flavoured with a little port or Madeira: remember when adding it – and any further seasonings – that the aspic will lose a lot of flavour once it sets.

6 Pour enough liquid aspic over tongue almost to cover it. Place a flat plate on top and weight down with cans until tongue is completely submerged. (Left over aspic may be set on a plate; then chopped and used to decorate tongue.)

7 Cool tongue and chill until set.

8 To serve: dip mould for a few seconds in hot water and turn out on to a flat plate. Serve cut in thin slices, accompanied by pickles and salad.

Tongue with Italian Green Sauce

Serves 6–8

1 pickled tongue, 4–4 1/2 lb, boiled (page 510)

Italian green sauce

2 large bunches watercress

6 level tablespoons finely chopped parsley

1 level tablespoon grated onion

1/2 clove garlic, crushed

1 tablespoon lemon juice

12 tablespoons olive oil

8 anchovy fillets

1 level tablespoon roughly chopped capers

Salt and freshly ground black pepper

1 Prepare tongue as directed on page 510.

2 Prepare Italian green sauce: Rinse watercress in a colander under cold running water until you are sure it is quite free of grit. Shake dry and strip leaves from stalks.

3 Bring a pan of water to the boil. Throw in watercress leaves; blanch for 1 minute; drain thoroughly in the colander and 'refresh' with cold water.

4 Combine blanched watercress, chopped parsley, onion, garlic and lemon juice in the container of an electric blender. Set blender in motion and, when contents are reduced to a purée pour in olive oil slowly, a tablespoon at a time. Finally, add anchovy fillets and blend until smooth.

5 Scrape sauce into a bowl. Stir in roughly chopped capers and season with salt if necessary (anchovies may already have made sauce salty enough) and freshly ground black pepper. You may also prefer a little more lemon juice.

6 To serve: slice cold boiled or pickled tongue and arrange in an overlapping row on a serving dish. Spoon some of the sauce down centre and serve remainder in a separate bowl or sauce boat.

Note: If you have no blender, sauce may either be pounded in a mortar, or you can chop blanched watercress leaves as finely as possible with the chopped parsley; then put them in a bowl and whisk in remaining ingredients with a hand-held electric mixer, or a rotary whisk.

Serves 6

1 leg of lamb, 3 1/2–4 lb

Salt and freshly ground black pepper

Bouquet garni (2 sprigs parsley, 2 stalks celery, 2 bay leaves, coarsely chopped, 1 sprig thyme or 1/4 level teaspoon dried thyme)

2 Spanish onions, each stuck with a clove

Butter

1 lb small carrots, scraped

1 lb small onions, peeled

Finely chopped parsley, to garnish

Dill sauce

About 1 pint reduced lamb stock (see Step 10)

3 level tablespoons butter

3 level tablespoons flour

1–1 1/2 teaspoons dried dill weed

2 egg yolks

1/4 pint single cream

Salt and freshly ground black pepper

Squeeze of lemon juice

Boiled Lamb with Dill Sauce

Mutton is, of course, *the* meat traditionally used for this great Scandinavian dish, but as it is so difficult to get, we have used lamb, which is even more succulent and no more expensive than mutton nowadays.

1 Ask your butcher to remove shank bone from leg of lamb.

2 Trim most of fat from leg and shave away any official 'stamps'. Rub leg with salt and freshly ground black pepper. Wrap it up tightly in muslin and tie ends securely with string.

3 Tie components of *bouquet garni* in a twist of muslin.

4 Select a deep pan that will hold leg comfortably. Fill with water (allowing for displacement by the joint); salt it and bring to the boil.

5 Lower in the leg of lamb; bring back to the boil and boil vigorously for 10 minutes, skimming off any scum that rises to the surface.

6 Reduce heat under pan to a bare simmer. Add *bouquet garni* and the onions stuck with cloves, and simmer very, very gently until lamb is tender. There should be a suspicion of pink about the juices that run when you pierce it through to the centre with a skewer. Allow 25 to 30 minutes per lb.

7 About 30 minutes before lamb is due to finish cooking, pour 6 tablespoons of its stock into each of 2 medium-sized saucepans. Add 1 level tablespoon butter to each pan and melt over a high heat.

8 Place carrots in one pan and onions in the other. Lower heat to a gentle simmer. Push a sheet of buttered greaseproof paper down over contents of each pan; half-cover with a lid and cook gently, shaking pans frequently, for about 20 minutes until vegetables are just tender and all the stock has either evaporated or been absorbed. Vegetables should be *very* lightly glazed, if at all.

9 When leg of lamb is cooked, unwrap it and place it on a large, heated serving dish. Surround with cooked carrots and onions. Cover dish tightly with foil to prevent meat drying out and keep hot in a cool oven while you prepare the dill sauce.

10 Skim lamb stock of fat if necessary. Ladle $1\frac{1}{2}$ pints of it through a sieve into a pan. Boil briskly until reduced by about one-third. Remove from heat.

11 To make dill sauce: in the top of a double saucepan, melt butter over direct heat. Blend in flour with a wooden spoon and stir over a low heat for 2 to 3 minutes to make a pale *roux*.

12 Gradually add reduced stock, stirring vigorously to prevent lumps forming, and bring to the boil, stirring until sauce is smooth and thickened.

13 Stir in dill – if you have not cooked with dill before, start with the smaller amount, then add more to taste if you wish – and simmer gently for 2 to 3 minutes.

14 Meanwhile, beat egg yolks and cream together until well mixed.

15 Remove pan from heat. Blend in egg and cream mixture; fit pan over simmering water and continue to cook gently for a further 4 to 5 minutes until sauce has thickened again. Do not allow sauce to boil, or egg yolks may curdle. It should have a pleasant, thickish-coating consistency. If it is too thick, add a little more strained lamb stock.

16 Season sauce to taste with salt and freshly ground black pepper, and sharpen flavour with a squeeze of lemon juice. Pour into a heated sauce boat.

17 To serve: garnish lamb and vegetables with finely chopped parsley and serve accompanied by dill sauce.

Serves 4–6

1 5- to 5 1/2-lb boiling fowl,
dressed weight
1 Spanish onion, stuck with
2 cloves
2 large carrots, scraped or
peeled
1 stalk celery, cut into
2-inch lengths
2 cloves garlic, peeled
2 pints chicken (cube) stock
1/4 pint dry white wine
4–6 black peppercorns
Butter

Lemon cream sauce

3 level tablespoons butter
3 level tablespoons flour
3/4 pint stock (from
casserole), strained
1 tablespoon lemon juice
Salt and freshly ground black
pepper
2 egg yolks

Boiled Chicken with Lemon Cream Sauce

Serve the chicken on a bed of saffron rice or, more adventurously, with rice flavoured with pine nuts and a handful of currants. Recipes below.

1 Clean and truss boiling fowl if necessary.

2 In a casserole just large enough to hold the fowl comfortably, combine onion, carrots, celery, garlic, chicken stock, dry white wine and peppercorns, and bring to the boil.

3 Place fowl on its side in the liquor. Bring back to the boil and immediately turn down heat so that fowl barely simmers.

4 Cover exposed side of bird with a sheet of buttered greaseproof paper. Put on the lid and simmer for $2\frac{1}{2}$ hours, turning chicken over on to its other side at the half-way stage.

5 About 10 minutes before cooking time of fowl is up, start the rice (see page 515), pouring off $\frac{3}{4}$ pint simmering stock from the casserole as you need it, and leaving fowl to carry on barely simmering over a low heat.

6 While rice is cooking, prepare lemon cream sauce: in a heavy-based pan, melt butter; blend in flour with a wooden spoon and stir over a low heat for 2 to 3 minutes to make a pale *roux*. Remove from heat.

7 Pour off a further $\frac{3}{4}$ pint stock from casserole. (Again, let the fowl continue to cook – or rather keep hot – in the remains of the simmering stock.)

8 Return *roux* to a low heat. Gradually strain in stock, stirring vigorously to prevent lumps forming. Bring to the boil and simmer gently, stirring, for 3 to 4 minutes. Add lemon juice; season to taste with salt and freshly ground black pepper, and remove from heat.

9 Whisk egg yolks in a small bowl. Whisk in a little of the hot sauce; then blend with remaining sauce in the pan (still *off* the heat). Keep hot over hot water while you dish up bird and rice.

10 To serve: drain fowl thoroughly of remaining stock and arrange it on a large, heated serving dish. Mix 1 to 2 level tablespoons butter into rice with a fork, and spoon around bird.

11 Mask bird with some of the sauce and serve immediately, accompanied by remaining sauce in a heated sauce boat.

Saffron Rice

1 Pour a little of the hot, strained stock over saffron strands in a cup and leave to 'infuse' until required.

2 Melt butter in a heavy, medium-sized pan with a tight-fitting lid, and simmer finely chopped onion until transparent but not coloured, 2 to 3 minutes.

3 Add rice and stir over a low heat until grains are coated with buttery juice. Remove from heat.

4 Mash saffron strands against sides of cup with a spoon to extract as much colour as possible.

5 Add saffron mixture to rice, together with remaining hot stock. Season to taste with salt, freshly ground black pepper and a pinch of freshly grated nutmeg. Bring to the boil and reduce heat to a slow simmer.

6 Cover pan tightly and leave rice to simmer undisturbed for 15 to 20 minutes, or until liquid has been absorbed, leaving rice tender but not mushy.

3/4 pint stock (from casserole), strained
Generous pinch of saffron strands
1 level tablespoon butter
1 Spanish onion, finely chopped
8 oz long-grain rice
Salt and freshly ground black pepper
Freshly grated nutmeg

Pilaff with Pine Nuts and Currants

1 Heat butter and oil together in a heavy, medium-sized pan with a tight-fitting lid. Add pine nuts and sauté gently until golden but not brown.

2 Add rice and currants, and stir over a moderate heat for 2 to 3 minutes longer until grains are transparent and thoroughly coated with hot fat.

3 Add boiling stock. Season to taste with salt and freshly ground black pepper; bring back to the boil; reduce heat to a bare simmer and cover tightly with the lid.

4 Leave rice to simmer undisturbed for 15 to 20 minutes, or until stock has been absorbed, leaving rice tender but not mushy.

1 level tablespoon butter
1 tablespoon olive oil
2 oz pine nuts
8 oz long-grain rice
1 oz currants
3/4 pint boiling stock (from casserole), strained
Salt and freshly ground black pepper

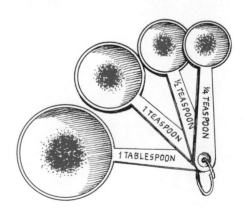

Serves 4–6

2 lb beef for pot-au-feu (see note)
1 lb shin of beef on the bone
1 lb shin of veal on the bone
2 oz ox liver
1 chicken liver
3 large carrots
1 large or 2 small turnips
2 large leeks
2 stalks celery
Coarse salt
2–3 sprigs parsley
1 sprig thyme or a pinch of dried thyme
1 small bay leaf
1 Spanish onion, stuck with 1 clove
1 fat clove garlic

To serve
Coarse salt and freshly ground black pepper
Various mustards and pickles
Horseradish Chantilly (page 510).

Pot-au-feu

A pot-au-feu may seem quite a performance at first sight, but remember that you are getting two dishes for the price of one: a rich bouillon to start with, followed by a steaming platter of beef and vegetables.

The English cuts of beef most closely resembling the *tranche grasse*, *gîte à la noix* and *paleron* or *macreuse* traditionally used by French cooks for a *pot-au-feu* are, respectively, thick flank, silverside and blade bone or chuck, but you can also use brisket, top rib, top round or shoulder, or a combination of two of these when preparing a double portion of the recipe, plus shin of beef and shin of veal with their bones for the gelatinous content.

1 Ask your butcher to roll and tie each piece of meat so that it holds its shape during cooking. The pieces of shin should first be boned and the bones chopped into large chunks. When making *pot-au-feu* for a larger number of people, the beef should be divided up so that no piece weighs more than about 2 lb; otherwise it will be difficult to calculate the cooking time. It is also a good idea to leave a length of string attached to each piece of beef to allow you to fish it out of the pot when you want to test it.

2 Put the bones in a large pot (for the ingredients listed, I used a 2-gallon pot), and lay the meat and livers on top. Add 5 pints cold water, or a combination of water and light stock if you have some handy. Bring to a simmer over a *very* low heat.

3 Meanwhile, peel carrots and turnip(s), and quarter them lengthwise. Split leeks down the centre and wash them thoroughly under cold running water. Trim and wash celery stalks.

4 Reassemble leeks, sandwiching a celery stalk inside each one, and tie them together firmly with string. If the bundle won't fit your pot whole, cut it in half.

5 When the water begins to shudder, add a little salt to help the scum disengage itself from the meat and bones – not too much, though, for the liquid will reduce during cooking and may end up too salty. At first, a white foam will rise to the surface. Curb your impatience until this forms itself into a distinct scum, otherwise it will slip through your slotted spoon when you try to skim it off. On the other hand, don't wait too long before skimming, or the scum will disperse throughout the liquid again and make your stock cloudy. Skim several times, each time adding $\frac{1}{4}$ pint cold water to settle the surface for a few moments and bring a new rise of scum to the surface, until only a little white froth remains. Don't worry about this; it will of its own accord be consumed in the cooking. Finally, wipe the sides of the pot clean.

6 Add carrots and turnips, parsley, thyme and a small bay leaf; bring back to the boil very slowly and skim again if necessary. Then put the lid on at a tilt to allow steam to escape and leave for 1 hour, occasionally checking that the pot has not started boiling

7 After the first hour, add leek bundles, the onion stuck with a clove and garlic. Leave the pot to tremble gently as before for a further 2 hours, or until meat and vegetables are tender.

8 When ready to serve: lift meat and vegetables out of the pot, letting them drain back into it. Discard strings; cut each piece of meat into serving pieces and arrange in the centre of a large, hot platter. Surround meat with the vegetables, grouping them by colour. Moisten with a little of the stock; cover the platter with foil and keep hot.

9 Remove grease from stock (see page 160); strain stock through a muslin-lined sieve and reheat it.

10 Serve the stock first, followed by the platter of beef and vegetables, accompanied by coarse salt, a large peppermill, various mustards and pickles, and my own favourite accompaniment for *pot-au-feu*, Horseradish Chantilly.

Note: Cabbage, not usually a part of a classic *pot-au-feu* but excellent with it nevertheless, should be cooked separately, as its flavour would overpower the stock. Cook wedges in water first; then finish them in a little of the stock poured off into another pan, and serve with meat and vegetables. The platter can also be garnished with some boiled or steamed potatoes.

517

2 lb beef, topside, flank or
brisket

Bouquet garni (parsley,
thyme, bay leaf)

1 onion, stuck with 2 cloves

1 stalk celery, halved

3 large carrots, halved

2 large turnips, halved or
quartered

4 leeks, trimmed and cut in
three

1/2 lb shin of beef

Salt and freshly ground black
pepper

2 large marrow bones

6 small slices bread, trimmed
of crusts

Boeuf Bouilli
(Boiled Beef)

1 Put the topside, flank or brisket of beef, the *bouquet garni* and
the onion stuck with cloves in a large pan or stock pot. Add 4
pints water and bring to the boil over a very low heat, allowing
the scum to accumulate on the surface. When a thick skin has
formed, pour in about $\frac{1}{4}$ pint cold water to stop the stock from
boiling any further, and skim scum off carefully with a slotted
spoon.

2 Bring to the boil again, still keeping heat under pan very low,
and add the prepared vegetables and the shin of beef. Simmer
very slowly for 3 hours – the more gentle the heat, the clearer
your stock will be.

3 After 2 hours' simmering, add salt and freshly ground black
pepper to taste.

4 Twenty minutes before the end of cooking time, tie the marrow bones in a piece of muslin to prevent marrow seeping out
into the stock. Add them to the pot and simmer for 20 minutes.

5 Meanwhile, toast bread slices. Heat a shallow serving dish.

6 Remove marrow bones from the pan, unwrap muslin and
scoop out marrow. Spread it on toast and cut in half to make
triangles. Sprinkle lightly with salt.

7 Arrange meat and vegetables on the serving dish, and garnish
with toast triangles. Serve very hot, preceded by cups of hot
stock, which you have first skimmed of excess fat.

Serves 4

1 lb carrots

1 lb small, sweet turnips

2 pints well-flavoured beef
stock (page 161)

8 oz small white button
mushrooms

4 tournedos steaks, about
6 oz each

4 thin strips pork fat

Freshly ground black pepper

4 teaspoons brandy

Boeuf à la Ficelle

Boeuf à la ficelle or 'beef on a string' takes its name from the
length of string on which the steak is suspended as it poaches
gently in a well-flavoured beef stock.

1 Peel carrots. Cut them into $\frac{1}{4}$-inch-thick slices, then into strips
$\frac{1}{4}$ inch wide and $1\frac{1}{2}$ inches long. Peel turnips and cut them into
strips of the same size.

2 Select a wide pan which will take all the tournedos steaks comfortably side by side. Pour in well-flavoured beef stock and carrot
strips, bring to the boil and simmer for 10 minutes. Then add
turnips and simmer for 5 minutes longer.

3 Meanwhile, wipe or wash mushrooms clean; trim stems. Add
them to the simmering pan and continue to cook gently for
another 5 minutes, or until all the vegetables are tender. Drain

vegetables and put them aside with a little stock. Return remaining stock to the pan.

4 Wrap a thin strip of pork fat round the middle of each tournedos. Cut 4 pieces of string long enough to go round each tournedos and hang over the side of the pan when submerged in stock. Tie one end of each string quite firmly round each tournedos to keep the pork fat in place.

5 Just before serving: bring stock to the boil and lower in tournedos side by side. Simmer for 5 minutes if you like them rare, 8 minutes for medium, and 12 minutes for well done.

6 When tournedos are ready, fish them out by their strings. Drop vegetables into simmering stock to reheat them.

7 Remove strings and strips of pork fat from tournedos and arrange on a shallow, heated serving dish.

8 Season each steak liberally with freshly ground black pepper and sprinkle with a teaspoon of brandy. Garnish the dish with reheated vegetables; moisten them with some of the cooking stock and serve immediately.

519

Serves 6

A plump boiling fowl, about
   5 lb, with giblets
Bouquet garni (parsley,
   celery, bay leaves)
1 onion, stuck with 2 cloves
1 clove garlic, crushed
3 large carrots
3 turnips, halved
4 leeks, white parts only
1 stalk celery
Salt and freshly ground black
   pepper
1 large, firm cabbage
3 large potatoes, halved

Stuffing
The chicken giblets
2 (extra) chicken livers
6 oz lean veal or chicken
   meat
6 oz unsmoked streaky
   bacon
4 oz cooked ham
6 oz stale white breadcrumbs
Milk
2 Spanish onions, finely
   chopped
3 level tablespoons butter
2 level tablespoons finely
   chopped parsley
2 tablespoons brandy or
   armagnac
1/4 level teaspoon ground
   allspice
Salt and freshly ground black
   pepper
1 egg
3 level tablespoons double
   cream

Poule au Pot à la Béarnaise

1 To make stuffing: mince chicken giblets together with 2 extra chicken livers, the veal or chicken meat, bacon and ham. Put into a large bowl and blend together.

2 Soak breadcrumbs in milk for 10 minutes; then squeeze out as much moisture as possible.

3 Sauté finely chopped onions in butter over a moderate heat for 5 to 6 minutes, or until soft but not coloured.

4 Combine sautéed onions and soaked breadcrumbs with minced meat mixture, and mix again, adding finely chopped parsley, brandy or armagnac, allspice, and salt and freshly ground black pepper, to taste.

5 Beat egg with cream; add to the bowl and blend until stuffing is smooth and homogeneous.

6 Stuff cavity of boiling fowl with half the mixture and sew up all the openings with a needle and strong thread.

7 Pour 4 pints water into a large pan; add *bouquet garni*, the onion stuck with cloves, crushed garlic, the stuffed chicken, and all the vegetables except cabbage and potatoes. Season to taste with salt and freshly ground black pepper; bring to the boil over a gentle heat, skimming off scum. If chicken is not totally submerged in liquid, cover protruding part with buttered greaseproof paper. Cover pan tightly and simmer as gently as possible for 2 hours.

8 In the meantime, bring another large pan of water to the boil and plunge in the cabbage, head downwards. Cover and simmer for 7 to 10 minutes; then drain and remove six of the best outer leaves. Rinse them in cold water and lay them out flat to drain on a clean cloth or paper towels.

9 Divide remaining stuffing between the leaves. Fold over sides of each leaf and roll up tightly. Wind a thin string round each cabbage roll to prevent it coming apart.

10 When chicken has been simmering for about 1¾ hours, add cabbage rolls to the pan.

11 Quarter the cabbage heart and add it to the pan at the end of the 2 hours' cooking time, together with potatoes, and continue to cook gently for 25 to 30 minutes longer, or until potatoes and cabbage are tender but not disintegrating, and chicken is cooked through but still juicy.

12 To serve: remove cabbage rolls from pan with a slotted spoon, taking great care not to crush them, and arrange them to one side on a large, heated serving platter. Lay the chicken in the centre of the dish, and surround with carrots, turnips, potatoes and cabbage wedges. The deliciously rich stock will probably require skimming of excess fat, and can be served before the chicken.

Stuffed Whole Cabbage

Serves 4-6

A whole cabbage scooped out and stuffed with a mixture of ham and mushrooms flavoured with onion, oregano and grated Cheddar. Serve with a simple, fresh-tasting tomato sauce and floury boiled potatoes.

1 Remove outer leaves of cabbage and, with a sharp knife, cut out a hole in the top of the cabbage about 4 inches in diameter. Scoop out centre to about three-quarters of its depth.

2 Bring a large pan of salted water to the boil. Plunge cabbage in it and simmer, covered, for 5 to 10 minutes, making sure that the hole in the centre is filled with water. Drain thoroughly.

3 Heat oil with half the butter in a heavy pan; add finely chopped onion and sauté over a moderate heat for 8 to 10 minutes until soft and golden brown. Stir in chopped ham and mushrooms, cooked rice and finely chopped red pepper; sprinkle with oregano, mix well and cook over a moderate heat, stirring occasionally, for 7 to 10 minutes longer, to allow flavours to blend.

4 Add grated Cheddar and lemon juice to the mixture; mix well and season to taste with salt and freshly ground black pepper.

5 Pile mixture into the hollowed-out cabbage. Dot top with remaining butter and cover with a piece of foil.

6 Fit a colander (or a large sieve) over a pan of water. Bring to a fast boil; place cabbage in the colander; cover pan and steam for 20 to 25 minutes, or until cabbage is cooked through but still very firm. Serve immediately.

1 large Savoy cabbage
Salt
1 tablespoon oil
4 level tablespoons butter
1 Spanish onion, finely chopped
1 lb cooked ham, chopped
1/2 lb button mushrooms, chopped
3 level tablespoons long-grain rice, boiled and drained
2 level tablespoons finely chopped red pepper
1 level teaspoon dried oregano
1-2 level tablespoons finely grated Cheddar cheese
Juice of 1/2 lemon
Freshly ground black pepper

Serves 8–10

5 lb corned brisket of beef
1 lb salt pork
3 bay leaves
6 black peppercorns
1 small boiling fowl, about
   4 lb
12 large carrots, scraped
6 medium-sized onions,
   peeled
6 large potatoes, peeled
3 medium-sized turnips,
   peeled and quartered
1 medium-sized cabbage,
   quartered
Horseradish chantilly

New England Boiled Dinner

1 Wipe corned beef with a damp cloth; tie into shape and put into a large stockpot or heavy saucepan. Cover with cold water and bring to the boil; drain and rinse beef. Repeat this operation.

2 Cover brisket with fresh boiling water; add salt pork, bay leaves and peppercorns; cover and simmer over the lowest heat possible for 3 to 4 hours, or until meat is tender, adding chicken after the first hour.

3 Cool pot slightly; skim excess fat and add carrots, onions, potatoes and turnips. Cook for about 20 minutes, then add cabbage wedges; cook until all the vegetables are tender but not disintegrating – cabbage should remain on the crisp side.

4 Serve meats on a platter, garnished with pot vegetables. Accompany with horseradish chantilly.

6–8 tablespoons double
   cream
1–2 level tablespoons
   freshly grated raw
   horseradish
Pinch of salt

Horseradish Chantilly

1 Whip double cream until it holds shape in soft peaks. Add 1 to 2 tablespoons iced water and whisk until thick and light again.

2 Fold in freshly grated horseradish to taste, and season with a pinch of salt.

Olla Podrida
(Spanish Boiled Dinner with Chick Peas)

1 Trim beef, lamb and gammon of excess fat, and cut them into 1-inch cubes.

2 In a large frying pan, brown beef and lamb cubes thoroughly on all sides in olive oil, a portion at a time so that pan is not over-crowded. Remove meat cubes to a plate with a slotted spoon.

3 Chop 2 onions coarsely. Add them to the fat remaining in the frying-pan, together with finely chopped garlic and diced green pepper.

4 Sprinkle with turmeric and sauté over a moderate heat until vegetables are soft and lightly coloured, 10 to 15 minutes. Remove from heat.

5 Rinse chicken joints and place them in a large pot or deep casserole. Cover with $2\frac{1}{4}$ pints water. Add remaining onion, quartered, chopped celery, *bouquet garni*, stock cube, and salt and freshly ground black pepper, to taste.

6 Place pot over a low heat and slowly bring to simmering point, skimming off scum as it rises to the surface. As soon as liquid simmers, remove pan from heat.

7 Add browned beef and lamb, gammon, sliced *chorizo*, the contents of the frying-pan, tomatoes and the well-drained chick peas. Mix well.

8 Return pot to a low heat and very slowly bring it to simmering point again. Regulate heat so that liquid in pot barely bubbles; cover and continue to cook very gently for 1 hour, or until meats are just tender. If pot is allowed to come to a rolling boil at any time, meats will turn tough and stringy.

9 Add quartered potatoes and whole carrots, and continue to simmer very gently for a further 15 minutes.

10 Finally, add French beans and cabbage wedges, and continue to simmer for 20 minutes, or until all the vegetables are cooked and meats are very tender indeed.

11 To serve: drain off stock into another pan. Correct seasoning; bring to the boil and serve about three-quarters of it as a soup in deep bowls.

12 Pile meats, chick peas and vegetables on a large, heated serving dish, grouping them attractively. Moisten with remaining stock and serve as the main course.

Serves 5–6

1/2 lb stewing beef
1/2 lb lean leg of lamb
1/2 lb gammon
3 tablespoons olive oil
3 medium-sized Spanish onions
2 cloves garlic, finely chopped
1 small green pepper, seeded, cored and diced
1/2 level teaspoon turmeric
1 1/2 lb boiling chicken joints
1 large stalk celery, coarsely chopped
Bouquet garni (3 sprigs parsley, 1 sprig thyme, 1 bay leaf)
1 chicken stock cube
Salt and freshly ground black pepper
1/2 lb Spanish chorizo sausages, skinned and sliced 1/2 inch thick
2–3 large ripe tomatoes, peeled and seeded
1 lb chick peas, soaked overnight
3 potatoes, peeled and quartered
6 baby carrots, scraped, topped and tailed
1/2 lb French beans, trimmed and cut into 2-inch lengths
1/2 small head firm cabbage, cut into 6 wedges

Serves 6

1 3- to 3 1/2-lb roasting
  chicken
Salt and freshly ground black
  pepper
3 tablespoons olive oil
2 level teaspoons paprika
1 level teaspoon ground
  ginger
1/2 level teaspoon ground
  cinnamon
1/4 level teaspoon saffron
  strands
2 chicken stock cubes
2 level tablespoons tomato
  concentrate
1 lb packaged couscous
  (see note)
4 level tablespoons chopped
  parsley
2 level tablespoons butter
Ground ginger, cayenne and
  tomato concentrate, to
  finish sauce.

Bouquet garni

1 stalk celery, cut into 1-inch
  lengths
6 black peppercorns
3 cloves
1 bay leaf
1 clove garlic, peeled
1/2–1 level teaspoon cumin
  seed

Vegetables

1 Spanish onion, diced
4 small turnips, diced
1/2 lb carrots, diced
2 medium-sized green
  peppers, seeded, cored and
  cut into large dice
4 oz chick peas, soaked
  overnight
1 8-oz packet frozen broad
  beans

Couscous

The famous dish that goes under the name of *couscous* is composed of two distinct parts: the *couscous* or grain itself, and the stew of fish, meat or poultry over which it steams, and whose flavours it is intended to absorb.

A special pot, known in French-speaking North Africa as a *couscousière*, is used to make it, but you can substitute a saucepan with a steamer and a bowl, both of which fit snugly over the top.

Until the last few years, *couscous* would have been quite impractical for the European kitchen as the grain demands a great deal of tedious and highly expert pre-preparation before it will separate to light fluffiness when cooked. Nowadays, though, the grain is exported ready for its final steaming, which is child's play.

Here is a version of *couscous* with chicken. You can also add shoulder of lamb, cut into serving portions, if you wish.

1 Cut chicken in half and season with salt and freshly ground black pepper.

2 Collect ingredients for *bouquet garni* and tie them up in a square of muslin.

3 Select a large saucepan, and a steamer which will fit over it tightly, (see introductory note). Heat 2 tablespoons olive oil in it and sauté chicken halves steadily until golden brown all over 10 to 15 minutes. Transfer chicken halves to a plate.

4 In the same oil, sauté diced onion, turnips, carrots and green peppers for 15 minutes, or until golden. Sprinkle with paprika, ginger, cinnamon and saffron, and mix well.

5 Pour over 2 pints boiling water; add stock cubes, tomato concentrate, *bouquet garni* and soaked chick peas. Bring to the boil; reduce heat to a gentle simmer; cover and cook gently for 10 minutes.

6 Meanwhile, prepare *couscous*: place the grain in a bowl and moisten with 6 tablespoons cold water, one at a time, working it in evenly with your fingertips, rather as though you were rubbing fat into flour to make a pastry. The grain will absorb this water without any trouble, and look and feel almost as it did when it came out of the packet.

7 Line steamer with a clean tea cloth (wrung out of boiling water just in case any trace of detergent remains). Place *couscous* in this.

8 Remove lid from pan in which chicken is simmering. Fit steamer over the top and continue to simmer gently, uncovered. Steam *couscous* in this way for 30 minutes, occasionally drawing a fork through the grains to aerate them and ensure that they do not stick together in lumps.

9 After 30 minutes, remove *couscous* from steamer. Spoon grain into a heatproof bowl that will fit snugly over the pan. Sprinkle with remaining tablespoon of olive oil and gradually add a further 6 tablespoons cold water, working it in evenly as before. Season to taste with salt.

10 Add frozen broad beans to stew. Stir in chopped parsley. Fit bowl over the pan; cover bowl with lid and continue to simmer for a further 30 minutes.

11 Add butter to *couscous* and leave to melt while you finish sauce.

12 Strain off ½ pint liquid from stew. Pour into a small pan. Flavour with a further ¼ level teaspoon ground ginger, a pinch of cayenne and a teaspoon of tomato concentrate. Taste and adjust flavourings/seasonings – sauce should be quite strong. Reheat to boiling point.

13 Toss *couscous* with a fork to mix in melted butter. Heap it around the sides of a large, oval, heated serving platter.

14 Place chicken pieces in the centre. Spoon over as much of the vegetables and juices that your dish will take and serve immediately, handing sauce around separately. Any remaining vegetables and juices can be kept hot in reserve to reinforce the dish if necessary.

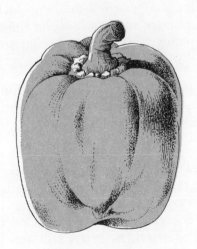

Lesson 20
Minced Meat/Loaves

Minced meat dishes started off as a clever way of dealing with tough meat in the days when practically all meat was tough. And it is significant to note that meat balls and patties, sauces, and stuffings made with minced meat are still a staple part of the diet in the poorer countries of the world: think of the Mediterranean, for example, and the countries of North Africa.

On the other hand, the steak-loving Americans have developed the hamburger and the baked meat loaf to a fine art. Is this, I wonder, something they have learnt from their immigrants – hamburgers from Hamburg, sauced meat balls from the Mediterranean, and so on?

So much for the past. What *has* changed is the ease with which meat loaves and meat balls can be prepared. With an electric mincer or blender, the actual preparation time is literally reduced to minutes. And they *still* make about the most economical meat dish you could hope to have.

● **The texture** of a meat loaf is a matter of taste. Some prefer a rougher mixture which still has a little bite. And a hamburger should always be coarsely ground. In this case use the coarse blade of your mincer. Others like a super-smooth texture, which can be achieved by dropping cubes of meat, a few at a time, on to turning blades, and blending away until the right consistency is reached.

● **Mixing** of the meats and aromatics can be done right in the blender, or in an electric mixer, but I prefer to work it with my hands, which gives me the best idea of whether the mixture is wet enough.

● **Moistening** the mixture. The most common mistake people make is not using enough liquid in a meat loaf mixture, with the result that the baked loaf is dry. In the majority of cases, the mixture should tend towards the sloppy when raw. Don't be afraid to add a cupped handful of water, or better still, stock, if towards the end of mixing the mixture still feels a little on the dry side.

● **Shaping patties and meat balls** This again is best done by hand. If you have been mixing by hand as well, wash your hands carefully, but leave them thoroughly wet. Scoop up a portion of the mixture and lightly roll or pat into the required shape. Drop straight on to the flour or breadcrumbs with which the patty is to be coated. If, after shaping several patties, the mixture starts to stick to your hands again, simply rinse well and moisten with more water.

● **Flavouring** the raw mixture. Unless it contains pork, go ahead and *taste* it. But if that makes you feel squeamish, a more laborious way is to sauté off a small ball of the mixture in a little butter and oil. Sometimes, the taste of a meat mixture doesn't quite seem to 'jell'. Reach for a bottle of ketchup or tomato purée or Worcestershire sauce, or Tabasco, or try a little French mustard or garlic salt, and see if that makes a difference. It will, but if by chance it doesn't, sauté your onions to a deeper colour next time.

● **A combination of meats** can give a very successful flavour: You can use two kinds, or even three together, chosen from beef, lamb, veal and pork, the last two tending to 'lighten' taste and texture, but remember that *one* of them should always predominate in a (maximum) ratio of 2:1.

Blender Meat Loaf

A trouble-free dish for a Sunday supper. You can serve the meat loaf *au naturel*, with its cooking juices, or make a simple tomato sauce to go with it. If the container of your blender is not very large, blend the mixture in two stages, then mix thoroughly in a bowl.

1 Preheat oven to slow (325°F. Mark 3).

2 Put eggs in the container of an electric blender. Start blending at low speed, dropping beef, pork and bacon gradually on to turning blades. Then turn up speed to high and continue to blend until smooth.

3 Add remaining ingredients, seasoning generously with salt and freshly ground black pepper, and continue to blend until flavourings are thoroughly incorporated.

4 Press mixture into a 2-lb loaf tin and bake for 45 minutes to 1 hour, or until loaf is cooked through and firm to the touch.

5 When ready to serve, drain off juices into a small pan; skim off as necessary, and keep hot while you slice loaf thickly. Arrange in overlapping slices on a heated serving dish; pour over hot juices and serve immediately.

Serves 6–8

2 eggs
1 lb lean beef, minced
1/2 lb lean pork, minced
1/2 lb streaky bacon, chopped
2 level tablespoons tomato concentrate
1 teaspoon Worcestershire sauce
1/2 level teaspoon oregano or marjoram
Generous pinch of thyme
3 drops Tabasco
1 Spanish onion, finely chopped
1–2 level tablespoons finely chopped parsley
2 slices bread, soaked in chicken stock (not squeezed)
Salt and freshly ground black pepper

Meat loaf
Butter
1 Spanish onion, finely
  chopped
3 slices stale white bread
  cut from a large loaf
1/4 pint beef stock (page
  161)
3/4 lb lean minced beef
1/4 lb lean minced pork
2 level tablespoons finely
  chopped parsley
1/2 level teaspoon mixed
  herbs
1 egg, beaten
1 teaspoon Worcestershire
  sauce
Dash of Tabasco
1/2 level teaspoon salt
Freshly ground black pepper

To wrap in shirtsleeves
8 oz frozen puff pastry,
  defrosted
3 level tablespoons French
  mustard
Beaten egg, to glaze

Meat Loaf in Shirtsleeves

For best results, make the meat loaf first thing in the morning of the day you intend to serve it, or even the night before, so that it will be quite cold and firm before you attempt to wrap it in pastry.

1 Preheat oven to fairly hot (425°F. Mark 7).

2 Grease a 1-lb loaf tin generously with butter.

3 To make Meat Loaf: simmer finely chopped onion in 2 level tablespoons butter over a low heat until very soft and golden but not brown, 10 to 15 minutes.

4 Trim crusts from bread slices. In a large bowl, soak bread slices in beef stock for 10 minutes; then shred to a pulp with a fork.

5 Add remaining ingredients to bowl, including sautéed onion and the butter in which it was cooked; beat with a wooden spoon or knead by hand until thoroughly blended.

6 Pack meat mixture into prepared loaf tin and level off with a spatula or the back of a spoon. Cover tin tightly with foil.

7 Bake meat loaf for 45 minutes. Remove from oven and leave to become quite cold, covered, before wrapping 'in shirtsleeves'.

8 When ready to proceed, preheat oven to moderately hot (400°F. Mark 6).

9 Roll puff pastry into a 12-inch square.

10 Turn meat loaf out of its tin. Scrape off any excess fat and spread exposed surfaces with 2 level tablespoons mustard.

11 Set meat loaf in the centre of the pastry square with the remaining, unspread surface upwards (use two forks to lift the loaf). Spread with remaining mustard.

12 Wrap meat loaf up in pastry like a parcel, sealing edges with a little beaten egg and trimming off excess pastry. Cut out small vents in the centre top to allow steam to escape. Decorate with leaves and tassels made from trimmings. Brush pastry all over with beaten egg.

13 Transfer pastry-wrapped meat loaf to an ungreased baking sheet and bake for 30 minutes, or until pastry is crisply puffed and a rich golden colour all over.

14 Serve hot, cut into thick slices, and if you wish, accompanied by a simple tomato sauce.

Cumberland Pork Loaf

1 Preheat oven to moderate (350°F. Mark 4).

2 Leave breadcrumbs to soak in milk until needed.

3 Blend Cumberland topping ingredients together. Spread over the base of a 2-lb loaf tin.

4 In a large bowl, combine minced pork, sausage meat, soaked breadcrumbs, together with any milk left unabsorbed, and lightly beaten egg. Blend thoroughly by hand or with a wooden spoon. Season with at least 1 level teaspoon salt and freshly ground black pepper, to taste.

5 Spoon meat mixture carefully over topping, which is very wet, tapping tin firmly several times to settle mixture and eliminate air pockets. Level off top with the back of the spoon. Lay bay leaves on surface.

6 Cover tin tightly with foil.

7 Bake loaf for 1 hour.

8 To serve: allow meat loaf to 'settle' for a few minutes. Then remove bay leaves and invert loaf carefully on to a heated serving dish, which should be curved to contain the sauce created by the topping mixture. Garnish with finely chopped parsley and serve immediately.

Serves 6

2 oz fresh white breadcrumbs
1/4 pint milk
1 1/2 lb lean minced pork
1/2 lb pork sausage meat
1 egg, lightly beaten
Salt and freshly ground black pepper
2 bay leaves
Finely chopped parsley, to garnish

Cumberland topping

4 level tablespoons redcurrant jelly
4 level tablespoons Demerara sugar
Finely grated rind of 1 orange
2 tablespoons orange juice or 1 tablespoon each orange juice and port
2 level teaspoons French mustard

Liver and Sausage Luncheon Loaf

1 Grease a 2-lb loaf tin generously with butter and line base with buttered greaseproof paper.

2 Preheat oven to moderate (350°F. Mark 4).

3 Put liver, onion and garlic through the standard blade of a mincer. 'Chase' them through with the bread.

4 Add sausage meat, the egg, parsley, ketchup, Worcestershire and Tabasco, and beat with a wooden spoon until smoothly blended. Mixture should be rather loose.

5 Season with about 1 level teaspoon salt and freshly ground black pepper to taste. (Bought sausage meat is usually seasoned already.)

6 Pack mixture in loaf tin. Level off top with the back of a spoon. Sprinkle surface evenly with breadcrumbs.

7 Bake loaf for 1¼ hours.

Serves 6

Butter
1 1/2 lb beef liver
1 small onion, peeled and quartered
1 clove garlic, crushed
3 oz trimmed white bread
12 oz pork sausage meat
1 egg, lightly beaten
2 level tablespoons finely chopped parsley
1 level tablespoon tomato ketchup
1 teaspoon Worcestershire sauce
Dash of Tabasco
Salt and freshly ground black pepper
4 level tablespoons stale white breadcrumbs

8 Remove from oven and allow to 'rest' for 10 minutes before turning out on to a heated serving dish. Serve immediately.

Note: A light mushroom, mustard or onion sauce makes a pleasant accompaniment.

Hamburgers

Try these hamburgers, then let your imagination run riot with different flavourings and seasonings. Do not mince the meat too finely or the hamburgers will lose their succulent, crumbly texture.

1 Preheat grill to very hot.

2 With a fork, mix minced meat with seasonings, adding salt and freshly ground black pepper to taste. Shape lightly into a round, about $\frac{3}{4}$ inch thick.

3 Sprinkle grill-pan with salt (or place a piece of foil on rack of grill pan and sprinkle that with salt). Place hamburger on top and grill for about 3 minutes on each side. Serve immediately, with cooking juices spooned over the hamburgers.

Makes 1 hamburger

Recipe I

4 oz lean steak, coarsely minced

1 level teaspoon finely chopped parsley

1 level teaspoon finely chopped onion

Salt and freshly ground black pepper

Recipe II

4 oz lean steak, coarsely minced

1 teaspoon tomato ketchup

1/4 teaspoon Worcestershire sauce

Salt and freshly ground black pepper

Recipe III

4 oz lean steak, coarsely minced

1/4 teaspoon soy sauce

2 drops Tabasco

Salt and freshly ground black pepper

Albóndigas
(Spanish Meat Balls)

These meat balls are a popular dish in Spain, Portugal and many of the South American countries Here is one version.

1 Put minced meats in a large mixing bowl.

2 Soak breadcrumbs in milk.

3 Sauté finely chopped onion in 2 tablespoons olive oil until soft and golden. Add to minced meats and mix well.

4 Add soaked breadcrumbs, salt, thyme, cayenne pepper, lemon rind and beaten eggs. Knead thoroughly by hand or mix with a wooden spoon until mixture is smooth and ingredients are well blended. Refrigerate for 30 minutes.

5 When meat mixture is firm, shape it into walnut-sized balls. Sauté gently in a little olive oil until meat balls are cooked through and a rich golden brown, about 15 minutes.

6 Serve hot with a rich tomato sauce.

Serves 4–6

1/2 lb minced beef
1/2 lb minced veal
1 lb minced pork
1/2 lb streaky bacon, minced
4 level tablespoons fresh white breadcrumbs
4 tablespoons milk
1 Spanish onion, finely chopped
Olive oil
1 level teaspoon salt
1/2 level teaspoon dried thyme
1/4 level teaspoon cayenne pepper
Grated rind of 1/2 lemon
2 eggs, beaten
Tomato sauce, to serve

Côtelettes de Volaille à la Crème

Although this classic French recipe usually calls for white chicken (or turkey) meat alone, we have found that it works very well indeed with a mixture of white and dark, used in the proportions you would get naturally from a whole chicken.

If you do not have an electric blender to purée the raw meat, put it through the fine blade of a meat mincer, then pound it to a paste with a mortar and pestle before rubbing it through a sieve.

1 Skin and bone the chicken, picking out sinews and tendons as you go. (The trimmings will come in useful for flavouring your Velouté sauce.)

2 Put the meat, white and dark together, in an electric blender and blend to a smooth purée.

3 Rub purée through a fine sieve into a bowl.

4 Season to taste with salt, freshly ground black pepper and a small pinch of freshly grated nutmeg. Then incorporate chilled cream, a tablespoon at a time, beating vigorously with a wooden spoon between each addition. Correct seasoning.

5 Cover bowl and chill purée for 2 hours, or until firm enough to shape by hand.

Serves 4–6

1 2 1/2- to 3-lb chicken
Salt and freshly ground black pepper
Freshly grated nutmeg
1/2 pint double cream, chilled
About 2 oz plain flour
1 egg
About 4 oz stale white breadcrumbs
2–3 level tablespoons butter

To serve
Buttered green peas
3/4 pint Velouté sauce (page 180)

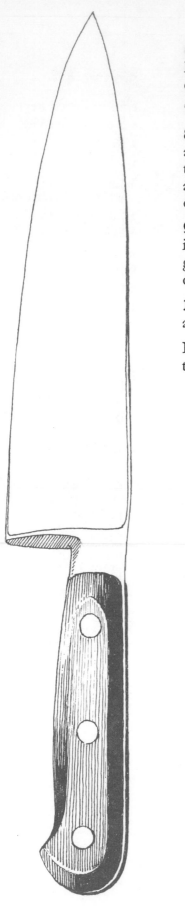

6 Sprinkle flour over a large plate. In a shallow bowl, beat egg lightly with a fork until well mixed. Sprinkle a layer of bread-crumbs over another large plate.

7 Divide chicken mixture into 12 even-sized pieces.

8 Shape each *côtelette* as follows: roll in flour until coated all over and pat into a cutlet shape, tapering at one end and about $\frac{1}{2}$ inch thick; dip in beaten egg, making sure surface is entirely covered, and allowing excess to drain back into the bowl; roll in bread-crumbs, again making sure no bare patches remain.

9 Melt butter in a large frying-pan (or divide it between two pans if your largest one won't take the cutlets all at once). Fry cutlets gently over a low heat for 7 to 8 minutes on each side, or until cooked through and golden but not brown.

10 Serve on a heated dish garnished with buttered green peas and accompanied by a Velouté sauce.

Note: For a nice final touch, push a small chicken bone into the tapering end of each cutlet after coating it with breadcrumbs.

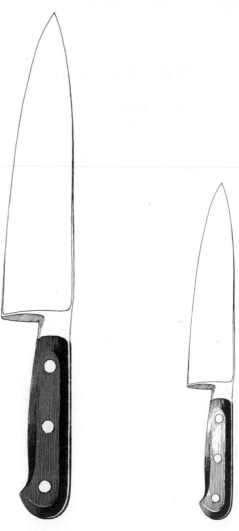

Lesson 21

American and Continental Cheesecakes

There are two basic types of cheesecake: the continental, or cooked cheesecake, usually baked in a pastry case of some kind, and the American-inspired 'uncooked' cheesecake, which relies on gelatine instead of flour and/or eggs to set it. Another reliable guide to origin is the preference that Americans have for using crushed biscuits fused together with butter to make the base.

Which Cheese to Use

American cheesecakes use a lot of *cream cheese*, 'Philadelphia' in particular. This is excellent when you want the cheese to give texture and rely on other ingredients to provide flavour.

My favourite is ordinary *curd cheese*, similar to the French *fromage blanc*. Unfortunately, English curd cheese is often badly drained, and in its bought state contains enough moisture to upset the balance of the remaining ingredients. To counteract this, wrap the cheese tightly in a double thickness of muslin; shape it into a ball and leave it to drain overnight in a colander, heavily weighted with a panful of water or a board topped with as many cans of food as you can muster. You will be surprised by the amount of moisture this will force out of it. The following day, finish the operation by twisting the ends of the muslin and squeezing the ball of cheese until no more beads of moisture spring to the surface.

Unfortunately, curd cheese is still not universally available in this country. A good alternative is *cottage cheese*. This will probably also need draining like curd cheese, though the moisture seems to be easier to extract and may not require the initial overnight draining under weights; then, unless the recipe calls for thorough beating with an electric mixer, rub cottage cheese through a sieve to smooth out the lumps.

Baking a Cheesecake

You will notice that most of our cheesecakes, especially those high in egg content, bake slowly. This preserves their smooth, uncurdled texture, stops them cracking on the surface, and also avoids too excessive a rise, which usually results in the cake sinking in the middle as it cools. A tiny amount of flour in the cheese mixture helps to prevent this by strengthening the structure of the cake, but basically, controlled heat is the answer.

If, in spite of these precautions, the cheesecake persists in sinking, then I suspect the cheese has not been drained well enough and the raw mixture has been too liquid for the eggs and flour to be able to set it firmly enough.

American Cheesecake with Black Cherry Topping

Makes 8 portions

Biscuit crust

4 oz wholemeal biscuits
1 level tablespoon castor sugar
1 oz unsalted butter, softened

Cheese filling

1 lb curd or cottage cheese
6 oz castor sugar
Finely grated rind of 2 lemons
Finely grated rind of 1 orange
3 eggs
1 1/2 level tablespoons self-raising flour
4 level tablespoons double cream

Cherry topping

2 14-oz cans pitted black cherries
1–2 tablespoons lemon juice
1 level teaspoon arrowroot

1 To make biscuit crust: crush biscuits finely or put them through a mincer. Stir in sugar and work in butter until thoroughly dispersed throughout mixture.

2 Press biscuit mixture evenly over the base of a loose-bottomed, 7½-inch cake tin.

3 Preheat oven to moderately hot (400°F. Mark 6).

4 To make cheese filling: if using curd cheese, squeeze it out in a double thickness of muslin to extract as much moisture as possible. If using cottage cheese, rub it through a fine-meshed sieve.

5 Put cheese in a bowl. Add sugar and beat until soft and creamy.

6 Beat in finely grated lemon and orange rinds; then add eggs, one at a time, beating well between each addition.

7 Sift flour into the bowl; add double cream and mix gently just enough to blend in ingredients.

8 Spoon cheese mixture over prepared crust.

9 Bake cheesecake for 10 minutes; then reduce heat to very slow (275°F. Mark 1) and bake for about 2 hours, or a little longer, until cake is an even golden colour and feels firm when pressed in the centre.

10 Allow cheesecake to cool in its tin. Chill for 3 hours, or overnight.

11 To make cherry topping: drain canned cherries, reserving syrup. Pit them if necessary and arrange them tightly side by side on top of the cheesecake.

12 Measure 3 fluid oz cherry syrup into a small pan. Add lemon juice, to taste.

13 Cream arrowroot smoothly with a little of the prepared syrup. Heat remaining syrup and when it is hot, stir in creamed arrowroot. Bring to the boil, and simmer until glaze is thick and translucent. Cool.

14 Spoon glaze over cherries and return cake to the refrigerator to set before taking it out of its tin.

Apricot Cheesecake

Serves 6–8

Canned apricots may be used to make this cheesecake when fresh ones are out of season, but if you do so, you may have to use less sugar (or more lemon) in the cheese filling, and sharpen the flavour of the glaze with a little lemon juice as well.

1 Preheat oven to slow (325°F. Mark 3).

2 To make crust: crush biscuits finely and blend with softened butter. Press mixture evenly into an 8-inch, loose-bottomed cake tin. Bake for 10 minutes; remove from oven and allow to cool.

3 To make filling: put halved, stoned apricots in a pan with ¼ pint water; simmer, mashing occasionally with a wooden spoon, until apricots are reduced to a pulp. Cool and drain off excess moisture.

4 Combine cheeses, sugar and vanilla essence in a large bowl. Add lemon juice, grated lemon rind and beaten egg yolks, and whisk until smooth.

5 Soften gelatine in 2 tablespoons cold water in a small cup; then place cup in a bowl of hot water and stir until gelatine has completely dissolved. Add to cheese mixture and blend thoroughly.

6 Whip cream lightly and fold into mixture, together with apricot pulp.

7 Whisk egg whites until stiff but not dry and fold gently into cheese mixture.

8 Spoon cheese mixture over crumb base, and chill in the refrigerator until set.

9 To make topping: dissolve sugar in ½ pint water over a low heat. Poach apricots in this syrup until just cooked, 10 to 15

Crust
6 oz digestive biscuits
2 oz softened butter

Filling
3/4 lb ripe fresh apricots, halved and stoned
2 3-oz packets Philadelphia cream cheese
8 oz cottage cheese
4 level tablespoons castor sugar
1 teaspoon vanilla essence
Juice and finely grated rind of 1 lemon
2 egg yolks, beaten
1 level tablespoon powdered gelatine
1/2 pint double cream
2 egg whites

Topping
2 oz sugar
1 lb fresh apricots, halved and stoned
2 level tablespoons apricot jam, sieved
1 level tablespoon toasted flaked almonds

minutes, depending on ripeness. Drain fruit, reserving syrup; remove skins carefully; pat apricot halves dry and arrange them on top of chilled cheesecake, close together.

10 Add sieved apricot jam to syrup and spoon over top of cheesecake. Sprinkle with toasted flaked almonds. Serve very cold.

Bilberry Cheesecake

Serves 6-8

1 9-inch tart shell, prebaked (page 431)

Filling

10 oz cottage cheese, sieved

2 eggs

1/2 pint sour cream

4-6 level tablespoons castor sugar

3-4 teaspoons lemon juice

1 teaspoon vanilla essence

3 drops almond essence

Pinch of salt

Topping

1 16-oz jar bilberries in light syrup (see note above)

1 1/2 level tablespoons cornflour

2 teaspoons lemon juice

Pinch of salt

Pinch of ground cinnamon

Fresh bilberries appear all too briefly in English shops in late summer. However, you can also buy excellent bilberries bottled in light syrup, with a full, fresh flavour (if possible, don't buy a can, where you can't see whether the bilberries are whole as they should be, or all mushed up). Or you can equally well substitute blackcurrants in syrup, which may be easier to track down.

Prepare this cheesecake in your favourite crust – I like a crisp, thin shortcrust shell to act as a foil to the delicate filling, but you may prefer to use a crushed biscuit crust made with 1 lb crushed digestive biscuits, 6 oz melted butter, $\frac{1}{4}$ level teaspoon cinnamon and a pinch of salt. It should be at least 2 inches deep to hold the filling comfortably, and baked in a loose-bottomed tin to facilitate removal.

1 Preheat oven to moderate (375°F. Mark 5). Leave the baked tart shell in its tin.

2 To make filling: combine sieved cheese with remaining ingredients and beat vigorously with a wooden spoon until smooth and creamy. (If you have an electric blender, it is not necessary to sieve cheese; simply blend ingredients at speed 4 for about 2 minutes, or until smooth.)

3 Pour filling into prepared shell and bake for 45 minutes, or until set. Remove from oven and allow to cool completely.

4 To make topping: drain bilberries. Blend cornflour smoothly with a few tablespoons of the bilberry syrup and combine with remaining syrup in a small, heavy pan.

5 Cook over a moderate heat, stirring until smooth and thick, about 4 minutes from the time mixture comes to the boil. Allow to cool. Stir in bilberries and flavour to taste with lemon juice, a tiny pinch of salt and a larger one of cinnamon.

6 Spoon bilberry topping over cheesecake and chill until firm.

7 Serve cheesecake very cold, but not chilled, unmoulded on to a flat dish.

Little French Cheesecakes

Serve with tea or coffee, or as a sweet after an informal meal.

1 Leave prepared pastry cases in their tins and lay them on a baking sheet.

2 Preheat oven to slow (325°F. Mark 3).

3 Wrap curd cheese in a double thickness of muslin and twist firmly to extract moisture. If using cottage cheese, press through a fine sieve.

4 In a bowl, beat cheese with castor sugar until smooth and creamy. Blend in lightly beaten egg yolks, followed by melted butter.

5 When mixture is smooth again, flavour with lemon juice, cinnamon and a few drops of vanilla essence, and stir in raisins.

6 Spoon cheese mixture into pastry cases and bake for about 40 minutes, or until filling is set and a rich golden colour.

7 Serve the little cheesecakes warm or cold.

Makes 6

6 individual pastry cases 4 inches in diameter, baked blind

Cheese filling

8 oz curd or cottage cheese

2 oz castor sugar

2 egg yolks, lightly beaten

3 oz butter, melted

2 teaspoons lemon juice

1/8 level teaspoon ground cinnamon

A few drops of vanilla essence

3 level tablespoons raisins

German Cheesecake

1 Preheat oven to slow (325°F. Mark 3).

2 To make pastry case: sift flour into a large bowl and make a well in the centre.

3 In another bowl, cream butter and sugar together.

4 When mixture is light and fluffy, blend in the egg yolk and finely grated lemon rind.

5 Finally, work in flour to make a smooth, softish dough.

6 Press dough evenly over the base of a deep, loose-bottomed cake tin 7 inches in diameter.

7 Bake for 20 minutes until firm but not coloured.

8 Remove pastry base from oven and allow to cool in the tin. At the same time, reduce oven temperature to very slow (275°F. Mark 1).

9 To make cheese filling: toss sultanas with rum in a small bowl or cup and leave to macerate until required.

10 Rub cottage cheese through a fine sieve into a large bowl.

11 Beat in egg yolks and finely grated lemon rind until smoothly blended.

Serves 6–8

Pastry base

6 oz plain flour

4 oz softened butter

2 oz castor sugar

1 egg yolk

1/4 level teaspoon finely grated lemon rind

Cheese filling

2 oz sultanas

1–2 tablespoons dark rum

12 oz cottage cheese

4 eggs, separated

1 level teaspoon finely grated lemon rind

4 oz castor sugar

1 level tablespoon plain flour, sifted

12 In another bowl that is perfectly clean and dry, whisk egg whites until stiff but not dry. Then gradually whisk in castor sugar and sifted flour, and continue to whisk to a stiff, glossy meringue.

13 With a large metal spoon or spatula, carefully fold meringue into cheese mixture.

14 Spoon mixture over prebaked pastry case. Sprinkle surface with rum-soaked sultanas.

15 Bake cheesecake for 40 to 50 minutes until firm to the touch.

16 Cool; remove from tin and chill lightly before serving.

Makes 8–10 portions

Pastry base

6 oz plain flour

2 oz icing sugar

3 oz butter, softened

1 egg yolk

2 tablespoons iced water

Cheese filling

1 1/4 lb curd cheese

5 oz butter, softened

5 eggs, separated

7 oz icing sugar, sifted

Juice and finely grated rind of 2 lemons

1/2 teaspoon vanilla essence

1 1/2 oz plain flour

2 oz raisins or coarsely chopped sultanas

1 oz chopped candied peel

Sifted icing sugar or a light lemon water icing, to decorate

Viennese Cheesecake

The Viennese are possibly the most ardent, as well as the most discriminating cake- and pastry-lovers in Europe. The names of their great pastry-shops or *Konditorei* such as Sacher's and Gerstner's are famous throughout the world. Sharing pride of place with their *Torten*, *Krapfen*, *Stollen*, and other *Kuchen* with equally rich-sounding names, is this cheesecake, lighter than most, yet at the same time as rich in flavour as you could wish.

1 Prepare pastry base: sift flour and icing sugar into a bowl and rub in softened butter with your fingertips until mixture resembles fine breadcrumbs.

2 Make a well in the centre; drop in the egg yolk; sprinkle with iced water and mix together with a fork. Then knead lightly and quickly by hand to make a smooth dough.

3 Roll dough into a ball. Wrap in greaseproof paper and refrigerate for 1 hour.

4 Preheat oven to moderately hot (400°F. Mark 6).

5 Flour a board and rolling pin lightly, and roll dough out $\frac{1}{8}$ inch thick.

6 Line base and sides of a deep, loose-bottomed cake tin 9 inches in diameter with dough. Prick all over with a fork. Cover dough with a sheet of greaseproof paper and weight down with baking beans. Return to refrigerator for 10 minutes.

7 Bake pastry shell 'blind' for 10 minutes. Then remove beans and paper, and continue to bake for 10 to 15 minutes longer, or until pastry is cooked through and lightly coloured.

8 Remove pastry from oven and leave to cool. Reduce oven temperature to moderate (375°F. Mark 5).

9 Prepare cheese filling – an electric mixer will come in very useful if you have one. Squeeze out as much moisture from the cheese as possible: wrap it in a double thickness of muslin; twist the ends of the cloth as hard as you can, and squeeze the ball of cheese between your hands until the milky liquid stops oozing out of it.

10 Beat softened butter in electric mixer until light and fluffy. (Or use a wooden spoon.)

11 Have egg yolks, sifted icing sugar and curd cheese ready in three separate dishes. With the mixer turned to medium speed, add them alternately to the butter, a little at a time. Then continue to beat until smoothly blended, scraping sides of bowl towards the centre with a spatula to ensure that all of the mixture comes under the beaters.

12 Flavour cheese mixture sharply with lemon juice and grated rind, and add vanilla to taste, bearing in mind that flavours are weakened by cooking, and that this cheesecake should be rather lemony.

13 Sift flour over raisins or sultanas and candied peel. Toss fruit to coat them thoroughly and fold into cheese mixture.

14 Beat egg whites until stiff but not dry. Fold into cheese mixture with a large metal spoon or spatula.

15 Fill pastry case with cheese mixture, piling it up in the centre, as the cake tends to sink slightly in the middle when it cooks.

16 Bake cheesecake for 50 to 55 minutes until firm in the centre and well risen. If top of cake browns too quickly, cover it with greaseproof paper or crumpled foil.

17 When cake is cooked, remove from the oven and allow to cool in the tin before carefully unmoulding on to a serving dish.

18 To decorate: sift icing sugar over the top, or ice with a lemon water icing.

Makes 12 generous portions

2–2 1/4 lb curd cheese

6 egg yolks

10 oz vanilla-flavoured castor sugar

1/2 pint double cream

1/2 lb unsalted butter, softened

3–4 oz blanched almonds, slivered

3 level tablespoons finely chopped candied peel

1 level tablespoon raisins

1 level tablespoon sultanas

1 level tablespoon finely chopped glacé cherries

1 level tablespoon finely chopped angelica

2–3 tablespoons lemon juice

Finely grated rind of 1 large lemon

Finely grated rind of 1 orange

1/4–1/2 teaspoon vanilla essence

To decorate

Candied fruit, raisins, glacé cherries and angelica

Paskha

(Russian Easter Cheesecake)

A king among cheesecakes. *Paskha* is traditionally made just once a year, at Easter time, when Russians of the Orthodox faith break their strict Lenten fast with an incredibly rich bout of feasting.

The beautifully decorated dome of cheese shares pride of place with a feathery, brioche-like yeast cake called *kulich* which is also baked in a tall mould. The two are sliced and served together as a climax to the Easter feast.

As you will see, you have to start preparing a *paskha* at least 2 days before you wish to serve it. The cheese must first be squeezed dry of as much moisture as possible; then the *paskha* is left to drain and firm up under a heavy weight for at least 24 hours before unmoulding.

1 Use the larger amount of cheese if it seems very moist. Wrap it up tightly in a double thickness of muslin. Place in a colander with a heavy weight on top and leave to drain overnight.

2 The following day, take the muslin-wrapped ball of cheese and twist the ends of the cloth firmly to squeeze out remaining liquid.

3 When cheese seems dry, unwrap it and put it in a large mixing bowl, or preferably in the bowl of an electric mixer.

4 Next, take a clean 6-inch flowerpot, an earthenware one if possible, as it absorbs moisture, and line it with a double thickness of muslin wrung out of cold water, cutting enough to fold over the top of the pot when it is full.

5 In the top of a double saucepan, whisk egg yolks with vanilla-flavoured castor sugar until thick and lemon-coloured. Gradually whisk in double cream until smoothly blended.

6 Set top of pan over simmering water and cook, stirring constantly, for 10 to 15 minutes, or until custard coats back of spoon thickly. Do not allow it to boil, or egg yolks will curdle. As soon as custard has thickened sufficiently, plunge base of pan into cold water to halt the cooking process.

7 Beat cheese vigorously with a large wooden spoon, or at medium speed in an electric mixer. When cheese is smooth, add softened butter a piece at a time, and continue to beat until smoothly blended. (If using an electric mixer, keep scraping sides of bowl with a spatula to make sure all of the mixture comes under the beaters.)

8 Add hot custard, beating vigorously until mixture is well blended again.

9 If you have been using an electric mixer, switch it off at this stage and remove the bowl from the stand. Stir in remaining ingredients; then give the mixture a final beating to disperse them evenly throughout it.

10 Taste mixture and add more lemon juice or vanilla if necessary. It should be fragrant and rather sharply flavoured.

11 Pour cheese mixture into muslin lined flowerpot and fold overlapping sides of muslin over the top to cover it completely.

12 If mixture is still rather liquid, as it will be if the custard was very hot when you blended it in, allow to cool. Then cover with a flat plate or saucer which just fits inside the rim of the flowerpot; weigh down heavily and leave in the refrigerator for at least 24 hours, standing on a dish to catch the syrupy liquid which will drain out of it.

13 To unmould *paskha*: fold back muslin and turn out on to a flat dish. Carefully peel off the muslin, which will have left an attractive pattern on the surface of the cheese.

14 To decorate *paskha*: stud the surface with small pieces of candied fruit, raisins, glacé cherries and angelica. Traditionally, the letters 'XB', which stand for the Easter salutation 'Christ is risen!' in the cyrillic alphabet, are incorporated into the decoration.

Any left over will keep for several days, covered, in the bottom of the refrigerator.

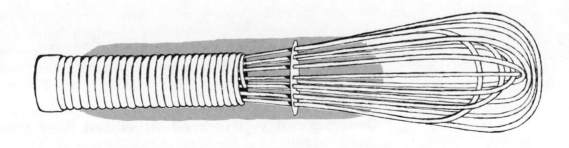

Lesson 22

Steamed and Boiled and Moulded Desserts

British Steamed Puddings

The steamed pudding is a peculiarly British institution. A Continental cook might raise an eyebrow and wonder at the menu that would tolerate such a hearty finale. And indeed, solid English puddings have acquired something of a reputation abroad. But, as with so many aspects of traditional British cooking, when a steamed pudding is good, it is very good indeed. And the traditional Christmas pudding, made to some treasured family recipe and carefully matured over many months, can be a positive triumph.

Steamed puddings suit the British winter – that uncomfortable blend of mildness and chilling damp, which penetrates clothing that would be adequate in a dry climate well below zero. They are substantial, but they need not be intolerably heavy. Even a Christmas pudding should have a light crumbly texture. And a steamed sponge pudding can be positively feathery.

The Pudding Batter

Basically, there are two types of batter suitable for steaming. One is a sponge-cake-type mixture in which butter is either creamed with the sugar, or rubbed into the flour. The other uses suet instead of fat. It's quite easy to see the difference: a steamed suet pudding has a much more crumbly, and in some ways lighter texture.

Commercially prepared shredded beef suet is a great convenience. If you want to prepare your own, make sure it is fresh, hard and dry. Remove any papery membrane or fibres before chopping it up into fine shreds with a long-bladed knife. (Use some of the flour from your recipe to prevent the suet clogging up your knife blade.)

Fine *white breadcrumbs* may be substituted for part (usually half) of the flour to lighten the texture even more.

If you want a well-risen, airy pudding, aim for a rather soft batter. A Christmas-pudding-type affair, on the other hand, is quite stiff from the start, and hardly rises at all: it may swell up slightly in the centre, though, so to counteract this, hollow out a slight indentation in the middle with the back of your spoon.

Preparing the Pudding Basin

The pudding basin must be carefully buttered to make sure that the pudding comes out cleanly at the end. If butter refuses to adhere to the glazed surface, which it will do if there is the slightest suspicion of moisture there, or if the bowl is very cold, you will save a lot of time by using melted butter and applying it generously with a brush. When this sets, you can, if you wish, dust the surface with fine browned breadcrumbs, biscuit or macaroon crumbs, brown sugar or even chopped fruit and/or toasted nuts, shaking out the excess as you would from a cake tin.

Frequently the bottom of the basin is spread with jam, syrup or treacle which melts in the heat and, apart from its main aim of decorating the top of the pudding, makes it easier to turn it out. When no provision of this kind is made, you'd be safer to line the base with a circle of buttered greaseproof paper.

Having filled the basin, cover the surface of the pudding with another circle of buttered greaseproof paper.

Traditionally, the basin is sealed by tying on a cloth, but aluminium foil makes a far more effective and more convenient seal, tied tightly under the rim with a loop knot to make it easier to unravel.

If you still prefer to use a cloth, first rinse and wring it out of boiling water to make sure no trace of soap or detergent remains, then dust it lightly with flour. Tie on the cloth; bring the ends up over the top and pin them together neatly with a safety pin.

If the basin fits into the pan without much room to spare, fashion a string handle on top, or put the whole basin in one of those old-fashioned string shopping bags – not plastic or nylon, though – to enable you to lift it out again without scalding your fingers.

To Steam a Pudding

First find a saucepan large enough to take the pudding basin and cover tightly with a lid once it's in. A piece of wood or wad of newspaper in the bottom of the pan will prevent the pudding basin coming in too-direct contact with the heat.

Place the basin in the pan; pour in very hot water to come half or three-quarters of the way up the sides and bring to the boil.

Cover pan tightly; adjust heat so that water boils steadily and strongly without actually making the pudding basin rattle, and allow to boil for the required time. If you have to top up the pan, use boiling water; otherwise, you may crack the basin.

Alternatively, you can use a steamer. Again, it must be large enough to take the basin when the lid is firmly on, and care must be taken not to allow the pan underneath to boil dry.

To Boil a Pudding

A heavy suet pudding can also be boiled, literally, in a cloth.

First prepare the cloth as above, scalding it with boiling water and wringing it dry. Sprinkle lightly with flour and arrange in a round-bottomed bowl or colander, floured side up. Put in the pudding mixture; draw the sides of the cloth up over the top and tie together, leaving room for pudding to swell.

Immerse pudding completely in a pan of boiling water; bring to the boil again and boil steadily for the required time, topping up with more boiling water as necessary.

To Turn Out a Pudding

Lift the basin out of the pan, steamer or whatever, and let it stand for a minute or two. Otherwise, the sudden outburst of steam might crack the surface of the pudding.

Remove cloth, foil and greaseproof paper, lay a heated serving dish on top of the basin and invert the two together. Shake gently once or twice until you feel the pudding come loose.

Carefully lift off basin, and peel off any greaseproof paper lining the bottom of the pudding.

If the pudding has been boiled in a cloth, let it drain thoroughly in a colander. Untie the string and gently pull the cloth away from the sides. Then invert pudding on to a serving dish and peel the cloth away completely.

To Serve a Pudding

The traditional English steamed or boiled pudding is rather dry, and fairly cries out for a sauce of some kind, a light custard or jam sauce, or hot syrup sharpened with lemon juice.

Nègre en chemise goes beautifully with chilled whipped cream, but this is rather lost on the more usual type of steamed pudding.

Always serve steamed puddings as hot as possible.

Basic Steamed or Boiled Sponge Pudding

1 Butter a 2-pint pudding basin and spread jam or syrup etc., over the bottom and about a quarter of the way up sides.

2 Sift flour and baking powder into a bowl.

3 Rub in butter with your fingertips until mixture resembles fine breadcrumbs. Stir in sugar and make a well in the centre.

4 Beat eggs lightly. Pour them into the well, together with enough milk to make a batter with a good dropping consistency. Beat vigorously with a wooden spoon until batter is smoothly blended.

5 Beat in chosen flavouring.

6 Pour batter into prepared basin. Cover surface with a disc of buttered greaseproof paper; then cover basin tightly with a double thickness of foil, or tie on a pudding cloth.

7 Steam or boil pudding for 1½ to 2 hours until well risen and firm to the touch.

8 To serve: turn pudding out on to a hot serving dish and serve immediately with a custard or fruit sauce.

Serves 6

8 oz plain flour
2 level teaspoons baking powder
4 oz butter
4 oz castor sugar
2 eggs
About 1/4 pint milk

Flavourings
Vanilla essence
Grated lemon rind
Mixed spice, cinnamon or ginger
2 oz sultanas or raisins

To decorate basin
Butter
4–6 level tablespoons tart jam or warm syrup, honey or treacle

To serve
Fruit or custard sauce (Crème Anglaise – page 145)

Steamed Apricot Pudding

1 Grease a 3-pint pudding basin generously with butter.

2 Cream 3 oz butter with the castor sugar until light and fluffy.

3 Sift flour; beat half of it into creamed mixture, together with 1 egg.

4 Beat vigorously until batter is well blended; then add remaining egg and flour, and beat again until smooth.

Serves 6

Butter
3 oz castor sugar
4 oz plain flour
2 eggs
12 canned apricot halves
Generous pinch of ground cinnamon

545

Finely grated rind of 1 orange
Juice of 1 lemon
2 level teaspoons baking
powder
3/4 pint apricot or custard
sauce (Crème Anglaise –
see page 145), to serve

5 Pat apricot halves dry. Chop them up into ½-inch squares and fold them gently into the mixture, together with a generous pinch of cinnamon, the finely grated orange rind and lemon juice.

6 Finally, add baking powder and stir until well mixed.

7 Spoon batter into prepared basin. Cover surface with a disc of buttered greaseproof paper; then seal bowl with a double thickness of foil or by tying on a pudding cloth.

8 Boil or steam pudding for 1½ hours, or until well risen and firm to the touch.

9 To serve: turn pudding out on to a heated serving dish and serve hot with an apricot or custard sauce.

Brown Bread and Apple Pudding

1 Trim bread of crusts and butter each slice generously.

2 Butter a 2-pint pudding basin generously and line base and sides completely with some of the bread slices, buttered sides inwards.

Serves 4–6

About 14 slices brown bread
cut medium thick from a
small loaf
About 4 oz butter
1 1/2 lb cooking apples
Juice and finely grated rind
of 1 large lemon
3 oz Demerara sugar
2 level tablespoons raisins
Generous pinch of ground
cloves
1/4 level teaspoon ground
cinnamon
3/4 pint rich custard sauce
(Crème Anglaise – see
page 145), to serve

3 Peel, core and cut apples into small chunks. Toss them thoroughly with lemon juice and finely grated lemon rind, the sugar, raisins and spices. (If using dessert apples, cut sugar by 1 oz.)

4 Pack half the apple mixture into the bread-lined basin and dot with a level tablespoon of butter in flakes.

5 Cover surface with more bread slices, buttered side up, and fill to the top with remaining apple mixture. Press down lightly; dot with another tablespoon of butter and cover surface entirely with remaining bread slices, buttered side down this time.

6 Cover basin tightly with a sheet of buttered greaseproof paper and then with a piece of foil.

7 Steam pudding for 1½ hours.

8 Remove foil and greaseproof paper. Turn pudding out carefully and serve hot with a custard sauce (or cream).

Canary Pudding

1 Butter a 2-pint pudding basin generously.

2 Sift flour with a pinch of salt.

3 In a bowl, beat softened butter with a wooden spoon until creamy.

4 Add sugar and grated lemon rind, and beat until light and fluffy.

5 Beat in 1 egg; then add half the sifted flour and blend thoroughly.

6 Add remaining eggs one at a time alternately with remaining flour, beating vigorously to make a smooth batter.

7 Finally, sift in baking powder and blend thoroughly.

8 Turn mixture into prepared pudding basin, making a slight hollow in the centre with the back of your spoon so that pudding will rise evenly. Cover with a buttered paper.

9 Tie on a cloth with string or seal top of bowl tightly with a double thickness of foil to ensure that no water can seep in.

10 Steam or boil pudding for 1½ hours.

11 To serve: turn pudding out on to a serving dish. Mask with some of the Crème Anglaise and serve remainder in a sauceboat.

Serves 6

Butter
3 standard eggs plus their weight in softened butter castor sugar and plain flour (about 6 oz of each)
Pinch of salt
Finely grated rind of 1 lemon
1/2 level teaspoon baking powder
3/4 pint Crème Anglaise (see page 145) flavoured with a little lemon rind and juice

Castle Puddings

1 Butter six ¼-pint dariole or turret moulds and decorate with a few small pieces of glacé cherry.

2 Prepare mixture as for Canary Pudding, Steps 2–7 (above).

3 Half-fill moulds with pudding mixture. Cover surface of each pudding with a disc of lightly buttered greaseproof paper and seal moulds with foil.

4 Arrange moulds in a pan with boiling water to come a third of the way up sides and simmer, covered, for 40 minutes.

5 Turn out and serve with Crème Anglaise (page 145) or melted jam sauce sharpened with lemon juice.

Serves 6

Butter
3 standard eggs plus their weight in softened butter, castor sugar and plain flour (about 6 oz of each)
Pinch of salt
Finely grated rind of 1 lemon
1/2 level teaspoon baking powder
3/4 pint Crème Anglaise flavoured with a little lemon rind and juice (or a little jam) sauce sharpened with lemon juice, to serve

To decorate moulds
Butter
Pieces of glacé cherry

Serves 6

1–2 level tablespoons butter
4 oz shredded beef suet
4 oz fresh white breadcrumbs
4 oz plain flour
1 level teaspoon baking
  powder
Pinch of salt
4 oz currants
4 oz raisins
1/4 pint treacle
1/2 pint milk
Custard sauce (Crème
  Anglaise – see page 145),
  to serve

Chelsea Treacle Pudding

1 Grease a 2-pint pudding basin with butter.

2 In a large bowl, combine beef suet with breadcrumbs. Sift in flour together with baking powder and a pinch of salt, and mix well.

3 Wash dried fruit if necessary and squeeze out as much moisture as possible in a clean cloth. Add to the bowl; stir until well mixed and make a hollow in the centre.

4 Warm treacle gently in a heavy pan. Stir in milk. Then pour liquid into the hollow of the mixture, beating vigorously with a wooden spoon to make a smooth batter.

5 Pour batter into prepared basin. Cover surface with a disc of buttered greaseproof paper; then cover bowl tightly with a double thickness of foil, or tie on a pudding cloth.

6 Boil or steam pudding for 3 hours, topping up with more water as necessary to prevent it boiling dry.

7 To serve pudding: turn out on to a heated serving dish and mask with a rich custard sauce. Serve more sauce separately in a sauceboat.

Serves 6

4 oz trimmed white bread
1/2 pint double cream
Softened butter
4 eggs
2 egg yolks
1 oz ground almonds
Castor sugar
4 oz bitter chocolate, melted

Nègre en Chemise

1 Soak bread in ¼ pint cream for 5 minutes.

2 In a large bowl beat 2 oz softened butter until fluffy. Work in soaked bread until completely blended. Add eggs, egg yolks, ground almonds and 1 oz sugar, beating vigorously between each addition. (Mixture may curdle when eggs are added, but this does not matter as chocolate will bind it again.)

3 Add half of egg mixture to melted chocolate and beat well; then combine with remaining egg mixture and continue to beat vigorously until thoroughly blended.

4 Butter a tall, tapering, 1½-pint mould – a metal measuring jug will do – and line base with a circle of buttered greaseproof paper. Pour in chocolate mixture and make a slight hollow in the centre with the back of your spoon. Cover top of mould tightly with foil or a pudding cloth.

5 Place mould in a pan with water to come halfway up sides. Bring to the boil; cover pan and steam for 1½ hours, topping up water in the pan as necessary.

6 To serve: whip remaining cream and sweeten lightly with castor sugar.

7 Turn mould out; pipe generous swirls of cream around base and serve immediately before cream melts from heat of pudding.

Old English Christmas Pudding

Makes 2 puddings

As you will see, a home-made Christmas pudding is no last-minute whim. First the raw mixture has to stand overnight before cooking, and then the pudding must be left to mature in a cool, dry place for a minimum of 4 months, preferably longer. Those who insist that a Christmas pudding should be allowed to mature for a year manage to do this by preparing during one Christmas season the pudding they intend to serve at the next, thus keeping one step ahead of themselves all the time, a degree of dedication I have never quite achieved.

1 Pick over dried fruit; wash and dry thoroughly on a cloth only if necessary.

2 In a large porcelain or earthenware bowl, assemble first twelve ingredients and toss together until thoroughly mixed. Make a large well in the centre.

3 In another, smaller bowl, blend treacle or syrup thoroughly with grated orange and lemon rinds. Blend in orange and lemon juice gradually, and when mixture is smooth again, beat in lightly beaten eggs, barley wine and brandy.

4 Pour this mixture into dried ingredients and stir vigorously with a large wooden spoon until well blended. (Don't forget to make a wish with the last three stirs!)

5 Cover bowl with a damp cloth and leave overnight in a cool place to allow flavours to develop.

6 The following day, start by preparing your pudding basins. Grease two 2½-pint basins with butter and line bottoms with circles of buttered greaseproof paper.

7 Divide pudding mixture evenly between prepared basins, levelling off tops.

8 Cover top of each pudding with another circle of buttered greaseproof paper; then cover basins with pudding cloths and tie down with string.

9 Steam puddings for 3 hours, taking care not to let water underneath dry out. Allow to cool before storing in a cool, dry cupboard.

10 On the day you wish to serve a pudding, steam it slowly for 2 hours until thoroughly reheated.

12 oz sultanas
12 oz raisins
12 oz currants
12 oz shredded suet
8 oz fresh white breadcrumbs
8 oz soft dark brown sugar
4 oz self-raising flour, sifted
4 oz chopped mixed peel
2 oz grated raw carrot
1 level teaspoon mixed spice
1/2 level teaspoon freshly grated nutmeg
1/4 level teaspoon salt
2 level tablespoons treacle or golden syrup
1/2 level teaspoon finely grated orange rind
1/2 level teaspoon finely grated lemon rind
4 tablespoons fresh orange juice
2 tablespoons lemon juice
4 large eggs, lightly beaten
1/4 pint barley wine (or stout)
6–8 tablespoons brandy

For pudding basins
Butter
Greaseproof paper
Pudding cloths and string

To serve
A sprig of holly
Sifted icing sugar
Brandy
Brandy sauce (page 550) or Brandy butter (page 550)

11 To serve: turn pudding out on to a heated serving dish. Decorate with holly (if it's Christmas time) and a sifting of icing sugar, and flame with brandy at the table. (To avoid an anti-climax it is best to heat the brandy in a large metal ladle or spoon and set it alight *before* pouring it over the pudding.) Serve with brandy sauce, brandy butter or whatever accompaniment is traditional in your family.

This recipe makes 2 puddings, each serving 8. In some families the second pudding is saved up for Easter, by which time its flavour has reached a peak of perfection.

Brandy Sauce (for Christmas Pudding)

Makes ½ pint

4 egg yolks
4 level tablespoons double cream
4 tablespoons brandy
2 level tablespoons castor sugar

1 Combine ingredients in the top of a double saucepan. Add 4 tablespoons water.

2 Set pan over lightly simmering water and whisk for 6 to 8 minutes to make a thick, frothy sauce. Do not allow sauce to boil, it will curdle.

3 Serve warm or cold.

Brandy Butter (for Christmas Pudding)

Makes ½ lb

4 oz butter
4 oz castor sugar
2 tablespoons brandy

1 Soften butter with a wooden spoon; then beat until smooth and fluffy.

2 Put aside 1 level tablespoon castor sugar. Add remainder to creamed butter gradually, beating vigorously until mixture is very fluffy and almost white.

3 Soak remaining sugar in brandy. Incorporate into butter cream a little at a time, and beat until smooth again. Chill until firm.

Moulded Desserts

Although we no longer go in for great towering edifices of moulded desserts like those that grace the colour plates of Victorian cookery books – the tension when turning these out must have been quite unbearable – a pretty moulded cream, set just firmly enough to hold its shape without rubberising the texture, is a satisfying thing to make.

The simplest example of a moulded dessert is a jelly. Then come the Bavarian creams and cold soufflés, which are two variations on the same theme of whisked egg yolks, cream and stiffly beaten egg whites, helped to set with gelatine.

Indeed, with the exception of the clear jellies, you should never regard gelatine as the major setting agent in moulded sweets, but rather as an aid to the cooked eggs and whipped cream which should do most of the work themselves.

How to Use Gelatine

Handling gelatine no longer presents the problems that it once did, what with clumsy, thick brown sheets that often burned before they would melt, had a nasty flavour reminiscent of carpenter's glue, and varied considerably and quite unpredictably in strength from brand to brand. Nowadays, powdered gelatine of high quality is packed in clearly labelled sachets which state the weight, or, in some cases, the setting power. You should always look out for this, especially when using a brand that is new to you. If, for example, your recipe calls for $\frac{1}{2}$ oz and the contents of the sachet are said to be *the equivalent of* $\frac{1}{2}$ oz, be guided by the manufacturer, even though the contents may not actually *weigh* $\frac{1}{2}$ oz exactly. (Our recipes all give gelatine in fractions of an ounce, except for very small quantities of less than a tablespoon, to allow for any adjustment you may need to make.)

Leaf gelatine, which used to be the usual form in which it was sold, has now largely been superseded by the powdered variety. If you prefer to use leaf gelatine, weigh out the exact equivalent of $\frac{1}{2}$ oz and make a note of the number of leaves for future reference – usually it works out to about 6 fine leaves to the ounce.

Gelatine should never be added to a mixture in its dry state. The usual procedure, which applies to both leaf and powder, is first to soak it thoroughly, then to heat the soaked mixture gently until completely dissolved.

To dissolve powdered gelatine Sprinkle granules over cold liquid in a small bowl or cup (water, or a little of the recipe liquid, according to the recipe method), and leave to soak for several minutes. The gelatine will absorb the liquid and, if only a little liquid has been used, be quite solid again. Now place the cup in hot water, and when gelatine starts to melt around the sides, stir gently until liquid is quite, quite clear.

For some dishes, especially those in which the gelatine is combined with a hot mixture, the second stage can be omitted. The gelatine is simply softened in a larger amount of liquid, and beaten into hot liquid. Remember, though, that gelatine should not be boiled, so all the cooking must be finished and the pan removed from the heat *before* it is added.

Working with gelatine Dissolved gelatine is usually added to a mixture when it is *just* lukewarm. For best results, the liquid gelatine and the mixture should be at the same temperature. If the mixture is too cold, you run the risk of the gelatine setting into nasty little lumps or 'ropes' before you have had time to blend it in.

Having thoroughly incorporated the gelatine, the mixture is usually left to cool until it is *just on the point* of setting, i.e. it must not be stiff enough to hold a clean edge, otherwise you will not be able to fold anything else in smoothly. On the other hand, if it is too liquid, anything airy that you attempt to incorporate, such as beaten egg white, will have all its volume and lightness crushed out of it.

When time is short and you want to speed up the cooling process of a gelatine mixture, stand the bowl in a few inches of cold water and leave to cool, occasionally drawing a large metal spoon around the sides and through the centre to prevent the mixture setting firmly around the sides and on the base, where it is in contact with the cold bowl.

On the other hand, should you find that the mixture has set suddenly when your back was turned, just replace the bowl over a pan of hot water for $\frac{1}{2}$ minute or so and let it soften again, folding and drawing it away from the sides of the bowl with your spoon to keep the texture even.

Folding Ingredients into a Gelatine Mixture

Cream Many dishes have whipped cream folded into the gelatine mixture towards the end. The important thing to remember here is that the consistency of the cream should be more or less the same as that of the mixture into which it is being incorporated. This means that the cream must be whisked with great care, preferably by hand, since it is only too easy to overbeat it, and if it is too stiff, you are likely to end up with pockets of unblended cream in your mixture. Some recipes advise adding a tablespoon or two of very cold milk to the cream before beating it. This makes it easier to control by slowing down the rate at which it thickens.

Egg whites Stop whisking as soon as they stand up in firm, soft peaks when the beaters are lifted. Do not let them go 'dry'.

In either case, if you have overbeaten by mistake and feel that the cream or egg whites will not fold in easily, reverse the process and start by folding some of the cool gelatine mixture into the cream (or egg whites). Then, having loosened the latter, carefully fold it all back into the gelatine mixture.

To Turn Out a Jelly or Moulded Sweet

The moment of truth that causes so much unnecessary heart-break. I have found no justification for rinsing the mould out with cold water as so many cookbooks advise. Provided the mould is clean and the contents quite set, you should have no trouble in turning it out.

● Fill a basin with very hot water.

● Select the dish on which you intend to serve the jelly or mould. It should be large and flat for the mould to stand steady. Wet the plate lightly so that if the mould does not land on it dead centre you will be able to coax it into position.

● Draw the tip of a knife around the outer rim of the mould. Then immerse the mould in hot water for *1 or 2 seconds only* – no longer. Far better to repeat the dipping if the mould refuses to come out than to risk melting the surface away.

● Lay the plate in position on top of the mould and, holding the plate and mould together with both hands, quickly reverse them. Halfway over, give them a quick jerk to loosen the side so that if the mould is being held fast by an airlock, this will be released. Turn the mould right over on to the dish. Give one or two firm shakes – you will feel the weight of the jelly or pudding transfer itself to the plate.

● When you are sure it has come loose, lay the plate down and slowly, with both hands, slip the mould off.

● Wipe the sides of the dish clean.

● If the outer surface of the pudding has melted slightly, slip it into the refrigerator to firm up again.

● Metal moulds need a very short immersion in water as they conduct heat so efficiently. In fact, it is often enough to wrap a cloth wrung out of very hot water around them for a second or two to loosen the contents. Porcelain and earthenware moulds are trickier, and may require more than one dipping before the pudding comes loose.

To Serve Moulded Desserts

There is one golden rule – never serve a moulded dessert that has been set with gelatine straight from the refrigerator, especially if it has been left there to chill overnight. Aim to allow it about an hour at room temperature to take the chill off and restore softness to the texture.

And if the mould has been damaged on its way out, remember that a piping-bagful of whipped cream, judiciously used, will camouflage all but the most disastrous mishap.

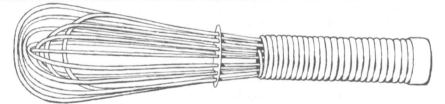

Cold Soufflés

The cold soufflé (*soufflé froid*) is not really a soufflé at all, but a concoction of whipped eggs, sugar and cream, flavoured with fruit, chocolate, or whatever, and made light and delicate with stiffly beaten egg whites.

The texture of the soufflé is all important, and for this reason great care must be taken when adding gelatine. Too little, and it will not hold its shape – too much and it will be just like trying to eat your way through foam rubber.

The illusion of a soufflé is created by extending the height of the soufflé dish with a firm collar, enabling you to take the mixture about a third again above the rim. The soufflé is then left to set and, just before serving, the paper collar is peeled off to reveal what to all appearances is a genuine soufflé with a beautifully risen 'head'.

To Shape a 'Collar' for a Cold Soufflé

The best way of shaping a collar is to cut a band of greaseproof paper about 10 inches wide, and long enough to go around the soufflé dish with an overlap of about $1\frac{1}{2}$ inches. Fold it in half lengthwise, i.e. to make a long band 5 inches wide.

Wrap the band around the dish and, with a pencil, mark the spot where the two ends meet. Then remove dish and pin the two ends of the band together at the base corner, making the collar slightly tighter than indicated by your pencil mark.

Now comes the test: carefully drop the dish down into the collar and pull the latter up around it to come about 3 inches above the rim of the dish. *The fit should be tight enough to allow you to lift the dish by its collar without any fear of it slipping off.*

Pin the top of the collar in position. Finally, stand the prepared soufflé dish on a plate, so that you will be able to transport it back and forth without damaging the collar.

I realise that many people simply tie the collar on as tightly as possible with string. If this method works for you, well and good. However, I think you will find the procedure outlined above worth the little extra time it takes in that it guarantees a neat, safe result.

To Remove Collar

Just before serving, and having made sure the soufflé is quite set, unpin the collar. Take a knife with a long blade and hold it upright, handle upwards, against the side of the soufflé, close to the end where you intend to start pulling the paper away. Then, with your other hand, take hold of the paper collar and carefully peel it away against the back of the knife. In this way you will avoid pulling large chunks of soufflé off with the paper.

The exposed sides of the soufflé can either be left bare to show off its texture, or decorated by pressing on chopped nuts or coarsely grated chocolate. Finish with piped whipped cream and fruit or chocolate curls on top.

Serves 6–8

1 medium-sized orange
1 level tablespoon instant
    coffee
5 oz bitter chocolate
1/2 oz powdered gelatine
6 eggs
4 oz castor sugar
1/2 pint double cream
1–2 tablespoons brandy, rum
    or liqueur (optional)
Coarsely grated bitter
    chocolate and whipped
    cream, to decorate

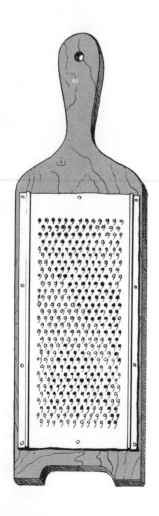

Cold Chocolate Soufflé

1 Fit a standing collar of greaseproof paper around a 7-inch soufflé dish (measured across the top), to come 3 inches above the rim (see page 555).

2 Select two bowls, a large one for beating the eggs and a smaller one for melting chocolate. Find a saucepan over which both bowls will fit securely. Pour in water. Fit each bowl in position over the pan and check that base does not touch water. Put water on to heat gently.

3 Scrub the orange clean and dry it thoroughly with a cloth. Finely grate rind into the smaller bowl. Squeeze juice and strain it into the same bowl. Add instant coffee, dissolved in 3 tablespoons boiling water, and chocolate, broken into small pieces. Put aside.

4 In a small bowl or cup, sprinkle gelatine over 4 tablespoons cold water and put aside to soften until needed.

5 Break eggs into the large bowl. Add sugar.

6 When water in saucepan comes to the boil, reduce heat to a bare simmer. Fit bowl containing eggs and sugar over pan, and whisk vigorously until mixture is light and bulky, and leaves a trail on the surface when beaters are lifted.

7 Remove bowl and in its place put the smaller bowl containing chocolate mixture. Heat gently until chocolate has completely melted.

8 Meanwhile, continue to whisk egg mixture until barely luke-warm.

9 When chocolate has melted, remove from heat. Remove saucepan of water from heat as well. Stand bowl (or cup) containing softened gelatine in the hot water and stir until completely dissolved. Remove.

10 Whisk chocolate mixture lightly to ensure it is quite free of lumps.

11 When chocolate mixture and dissolved gelatine are both just warm, blend them together thoroughly.

12 Pour cream into a bowl and whisk carefully until it is just thick enough to leave a barely perceptible trail on the surface. (If you have been using an electric mixer so far, this operation may be safer done with a hand whisk to avoid overbeating cream.)

13 Quickly and lightly fold chocolate gelatine mixture into cream. Then, before mixture has had a chance to start setting, fold it into the cooled whisked egg mixture, together with brandy, rum or liqueur, if used. Stop folding as soon as you have got rid of chocolate 'streaks' in mixture.

14 Stand prepared soufflé dish on a plate. Pour in soufflé mixture, taking care not to dislodge or crumple paper collar. Leave it to firm slightly for 15 to 20 minutes before transferring dish to the refrigerator.

15 Chill soufflé for 2 to 3 hours until firmly set.

16 Just before serving: peel off paper collar (see page 555). Press coarsely grated bitter chocolate around exposed sides of soufflé and decorate top with grated chocolate and piped whipped cream.

Cold Lemon Soufflé

Serves 4–5

1 Fit a standing collar of greaseproof paper around a $5\frac{3}{4}$-inch soufflé dish (measured across the top) to come at least 3 inches above the rim (see page 555).

2 Select two bowls, one larger than the other, and a saucepan over which the larger bowl will fit securely. Pour 2 or 3 inches water into pan and put it on to heat. Make quite sure that smaller bowl is perfectly clean and dry.

3 Separate eggs, dropping yolks into larger bowl and whites into smaller one.

4 Sprinkle gelatine over 4 tablespoons cold water in a cup and leave to soften.

5 Add sugar to egg yolks. Fit bowl over pan of water, which should be barely simmering, and whisk vigorously until mixture is thick and light, and leaves a trail on the surface when beaters are lifted.

4 eggs
1/2 oz powdered gelatine
7 oz castor sugar
Finely grated rind and strained juice of 4 large lemons
1/2 pint double cream
Whipped cream and chopped toasted nuts, to decorate (optional)

6 Gradually whisk in lemon juice and continue to whisk until mixture thickens again. This time it will just manage to hold a trail on the surface. Remove pan from heat and lift off bowl.

7 Place cup containing softened gelatine in the hot water to dissolve, stirring occasionally.

8 Meanwhile, continue to whisk egg yolk mixture until just lukewarm.

9 When gelatine has completely dissolved, remove cup from water. Allow to cool slightly. Whisk into egg yolk mixture. Fold in finely grated lemon rind.

10 Whisk cream until a trail just holds its shape on the surface, being careful not to let it go too far, or it will be difficult to fold in. The texture should be about the same as that of the egg mixture.

11 Make sure your whisk is perfectly clean and dry. Whisk egg whites until they hold their shape in floppy peaks.

12 With a large metal spoon or spatula, fold cream into egg mixture, followed by beaten egg whites, working as lightly and quickly as possible.

13 Stand prepared soufflé dish on a plate. Pour in soufflé mixture, taking care not to dislodge or crumple paper collar. Leave it to firm slightly for 15 to 20 minutes before transferring dish to the refrigerator.

14 Chill soufflé for 2 to 3 hours until firmly set.

15 Just before serving: peel off paper collar (see page 555). If liked, decorate top of soufflé with swirls of piped whipped cream and press chopped toasted nuts around exposed sides.

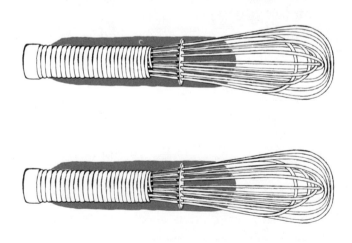

Cold Orange Soufflé

Serves 6–8

1 Fit a standing collar of greaseproof paper around a 7-inch soufflé dish (measured across the top), to come 3 inches above the rim (see page 555).

2 Select a large bowl and a saucepan over which it will fit comfortably. Fill saucepan with water to a depth of about 2 inches; bring water to simmering point.

3 Scrub oranges and lemon. Finely grate rinds of 2 oranges and 1 lemon into bowl. Squeeze juice of all the oranges and the lemon, and strain into bowl.

4 Pour off 3 tablespoons strained juice into a small bowl or cup. Sprinkle gelatine over it and leave to soften.

5 Separate eggs, dropping yolks into bowl with fruit juice, and whites into another bowl that is quite clean and dry.

6 Add sugar to bowl containing egg yolks and juice. Fit bowl over pan of simmering water and beat with a whisk until mixture is very fluffy and pale, and leaves a trail on the surface when beaters are lifted.

7 Remove bowl and pan from heat. Place bowl on the table. Stand cup or bowl containing softened gelatine in the remaining hot water and let it dissolve completely, stirring occasionally.

8 Meanwhile, continue to whisk orange egg mixture until cool.

9 Add dissolved gelatine and continue to whisk until thoroughly blended. Leave until completely cold and on the point of setting.

10 Whisk egg whites until stiff but not dry.

11 Whisk cream until floppy and of the same consistency as the cold orange mixture.

12 With a large metal spoon or spatula, fold cream into orange mixture, followed by stiffly beaten egg whites and liqueur, if used.

13 Stand prepared soufflé dish on a plate. Pour in soufflé mixture, taking care not to dislodge or crumple paper collar. Leave it to firm up slightly for 15 to 20 minutes before transferring dish to the refrigerator.

14 Chill soufflé for at least 2 hours until firmly set.

15 Just before serving: peel off paper collar (see page 555) and decorate soufflé with piped whipped cream and sections of fresh orange.

5 medium-sized oranges
1 lemon
3/4 oz powdered gelatine
6 eggs
8 oz castor sugar
1/2 pint double cream
2–3 tablespoons Grand Marnier (optional)
Whipped cream and fresh orange segments, to decorate

Serves 6–8

4 level teaspoons powdered
  gelatine
8 oz bitter chocolate
2 egg yolks
4 1/2 oz icing sugar
17 fluid oz milk
1 level tablespoon powdered
  coffee
1 pint double cream
Vanilla essence
Coarsely grated chocolate,
  to decorate

Mousse Glacée au Chocolat

1 Sprinkle gelatine over 2 tablespoons cold water in a cup and put aside to soften.

2 Break chocolate into the top of a double saucepan and allow to melt over simmering water, stirring occasionally with a wooden spoon.

3 Put egg yolks in a large bowl; sift in icing sugar and beat until smooth and fluffy.

4 Dissolve gelatine by standing cup in a bowl of hot water and stirring until liquid is quite clear.

5 When chocolate has melted, bring milk to the boil. Add to chocolate gradually, beating well with a wooden spoon to avoid small lumps forming. Beat in powdered coffee, followed by dissolved gelatine.

6 Pour hot chocolate milk over egg yolk mixture in a thin stream, beating vigorously with a wire whisk. Allow to cool.

7 When mixture is on the point of setting, beat cream with a whisk until it stands in soft peaks. Fold gently but thoroughly into chocolate mixture, using a metal spoon. Flavour with a few drops of vanilla essence.

8 Pour chocolate mixture into a 2-pint mould and leave to set in the refrigerator, preferably overnight.

9 To serve: turn out mould on to a flat serving dish (see page 554). Decorate with coarsely grated chocolate and serve.

Apple Apricot Mousse

Serves 6

If you have an electric blender, you can make a smoother purée of the fruit than obtainable with a sieve but, of course, the apples must then be cored and peeled before they are cooked.

The type of dried apricots used makes a difference to the final result: try to find the soft, plump variety which are paler in colour and less tart than the small, hard, bright orange kind.

The mousse can also be made with dried peaches.

1 Drain soaked apricots and measure off ¼ pint soaking liquid into a medium-sized pan. Add apricots.

2 If intending to use an electric blender to purée fruit (see note above), peel and core apples. Otherwise simply wipe them with a damp cloth. Chop apples coarsely and combine with apricots. Add finely grated rind and juice of ½ lemon.

3 Place pan over a moderate heat. Bring to the boil; cover and simmer gently for about 20 minutes, or until apricots are very soft and apples disintegrating.

4 Meanwhile, sprinkle gelatine over 5 tablespoons cold water in a small bowl or cup and leave to soften for about 5 minutes. Then stand bowl (or cup) in hot water and stir until gelatine has dissolved and liquid is quite clear. Cool slightly.

5 Beat egg yolks lightly with a fork.

6 When fruits are cooked, rub them through a fine sieve or purée in an electric blender, together with all their juices.

7 Blend egg yolks into hot fruit purée and sweeten to taste with sugar.

8 Pour fruit purée into a 2-pint measuring jug. When purée is just lukewarm, beat in dissolved gelatine.

9 Measure purée and if necessary, stir in a little cold water to make it up to 1½ pints. Pour into a large bowl and allow to cool until just on the point of setting.

10 Whisk cream until just stiff enough to leave a faint trail on the surface when beaters are lifted. It should be of about the same consistency as the fruit purée.

11 Make sure your whisk is perfectly clean and dry. Whisk egg whites until they hold their shape in floppy peaks.

12 With a large metal spoon or spatula, fold cream into fruit purée, followed by beaten egg whites.

13 Flavour mousse to taste with vanilla and just a drop or two

1/2 lb dried apricots (see note at head of recipe), soaked overnight
1 lb cooking apples
Finely grated rind and juice of 1/2 lemon
1 1/2 oz powdered gelatine
2 eggs, separated
3 oz sugar, or to taste
1/4 pint double cream
1 teaspoon vanilla essence
1–2 drops almond essence
1–2 drops orange food colouring (optional)
Whipped cream and toasted almond slivers, to decorate

of almond essence. If the apricots have not coloured mousse sufficiently, you can liven it up with a drop or two of orange (or mixed red and yellow) food colouring.

14 Pour mousse into a 2½-pint mould. Chill until set.

15 To serve: turn mould out on to a dish (see page 554). Decorate with blobs of whipped cream and spike with toasted almond slivers.

Coffee Cream Bavarois

Serves 6–8

1 1/2 oz bitter chocolate
3/4 pint milk
6 egg yolks
6 oz castor sugar
2 level tablespoons instant coffee
2 tablespoons orange liqueur
1/2 oz powdered gelatine
4 tablespoons very cold milk
1/2 pint double cream
Flavourless cooking oil, for mould

To decorate

2 level tablespoons freshly roasted coffee beans
1 tablespoon orange liqueur
Whipped cream

Use a good-quality dark chocolate for a really rich, smooth flavour.

1 Break chocolate into small pieces. In the top of a double saucepan, scald milk over direct heat. Add chocolate and stir until dissolved.

2 Beat egg yolks with sugar until fluffy and lemon-coloured. Add scalded milk mixture gradually, beating constantly.

3 Dissolve instant coffee in 3 tablespoons boiling water. Stir into milk mixture. Pour back into top of double saucepan and cook over lightly simmering water, stirring constantly, until mixture coats back of spoon, about 20 minutes. Take care not to let it boil, or egg yolks will curdle.

4 As soon as custard has thickened, plunge pan into cold water to arrest cooking process and cool custard slightly. Stir in liqueur.

5 Soften gelatine in 3 tablespoons cold water. Then put basin in a pan of hot water (the bottom half of the double saucepan is the most convenient), and stir until gelatine has completely dissolved and liquid is clear. Stir into cooling custard. Leave until cold and just on the point of setting.

6 Add cold milk to double cream and whisk until floppy. Ideally, it should have the same consistency as the cold custard, so that the two can be combined with the minimum of folding. Fold cream into cold custard.

7 Brush a 2-pint mould with flavourless oil. Pour in *bavarois* mixture and chill until set, 2 hours at least.

8 To unmould *bavarois*: dip mould in hot water *for 2 to 3 seconds only* to loosen cream – not too long, or cream will begin to melt. Turn out carefully on to a serving dish, and return to the bottom of the refrigerator until an hour before serving.

9 To decorate *bavarois*: macerate coffee beans in orange liqueur for at least 30 minutes, longer if possible. Drain them and chop them coarsely with a knife.

10 Just before serving: decorate *bavarois* with whipped cream and sprinkle with chopped coffee beans.

Hazelnut Bavarois

Serves 6–8

A *bavarois* need not necessarily be made with chocolate, coffee or fruit. Here is a deliciously rich one flavoured with hazelnuts and praline.

Failing home-made praline, use bought almond (or even peanut) brittle, crushed with a rolling pin or pounded in a mortar.

1 Grill hazelnuts under a hot grill, shaking the pan frequently to prevent them burning, until skins become dry and brittle. Rub skins off by rolling hazelnuts between the palms of your hands (or between two sheets of greaseproof paper). Grind 6 oz hazelnuts in a *mouli*. Chop remainder coarsely or leave them whole.

2 In the top of a double saucepan, stir milk with sugar and salt over direct heat until sugar has melted.

3 Beat egg yolks in a bowl. Blend in a little of the hot milk mixture, then pour back into the pan and continue to cook over hot water until custard thickens, stirring frequently. Do not allow custard to boil, or egg yolks will curdle.

4 Remove pan from heat and plunge base into cold water to halt cooking process. Cool slightly; add lemon juice and vanilla essence, to taste, and leave to become quite cold, stirring occasionally to prevent a skin forming on the surface.

5 Brush a 2-pint, straight-sided mould with flavourless oil.

6 Sprinkle gelatine over 2 tablespoons cold water in a cup, and leave for 5 minutes until softened. Then stand cup in a bowl of hot water and stir until gelatine has dissolved and liquid is quite clear. Blend dissolved gelatine with cooling custard, and leave until on the point of setting.

7 Whip cream until floppy. Fold into custard, together with all the hazelnuts and praline.

8 Pour into prepared mould and chill in the refrigerator until firmly set.

7 oz hazelnuts
1/4 pint milk
4 oz castor sugar
Pinch of salt
4 egg yolks
1 tablespoon lemon juice
1 teaspoon vanilla essence
Flavourless cooking oil, for mould
1/2 oz powdered gelatine
1 pint double cream
2–3 level tablespoons crushed praline (see note)

9 To unmould: dip mould in hot water for just 10 seconds to loosen it, and turn out carefully on to a flat serving dish (see page 554). The *bavarois* may be decorated with hazelnuts dipped in caramel or a sprinkling of more finely pounded praline.

To make praline In a small, heavy pan, melt 4 oz granulated sugar with 4 tablespoons water and 1 teaspoon lemon juice. Bring to the boil and boil until syrup turns into a rich, golden caramel (340°F. on a sugar thermometer). Add 4 oz almonds, blanched and toasted to a deep golden colour. Mix well. Pour on to a marble slab, or some other cold surface which you have brushed with oil, and leave until cold and hard. Use as required.

Raspberry Bavarois

Serves 6

1 lb frozen raspberries
3 oz castor sugar
3 egg yolks
1/2 pint milk
1/2 oz powdered gelatine
Juice of 1 lemon
1/2 pint double cream
Butter, for mould

1 Place frozen raspberries in a sieve over a bowl and sprinkle with 1 oz of the castor sugar. Leave until completely defrosted.

2 Whisk remaining sugar with egg yolks until light and fluffy.

3 Scald milk. Pour over egg and sugar mixture gradually, beating constantly.

4 Transfer mixture to the top of a double saucepan and stir over simmering water until sauce thickens enough to coat the back of a wooden spoon. Take care not to let it boil, or egg yolks will curdle. Remove from heat and cool slightly.

5 Meanwhile, soften gelatine for 5 minutes in 4 tablespoons of the syrup drained from the raspberries; then stir over hot water until liquid is clear and gelatine completely dissolved.

6 Cool gelatine mixture slightly. Blend with cooling custard.

7 Crush two-thirds of the raspberries, reserving the best ones, and press them through a sieve to make a purée. Blend purée with custard; then fold in whole fruit, taking care not to crush them. Add lemon juice, to taste.

8 Whip half the cream lightly. Fold into raspberry custard.

9 Brush a 2-pint decorative mould with about 1 tablespoon melted butter. Pour in the raspberry cream and chill in the refrigerator until firm.

10 When ready to serve: whip remaining cream stiffly.

11 Dip mould for 1 or 2 seconds only into very hot water. Turn *bavarois* out on to a serving dish and pipe whipped cream in a decorative pattern over top and sides. Serve very cold.

Semolina Cream Mould with Blackcurrant Sauce

Serves 4–6

Do not be dismayed at the thought of a semolina pudding. Nothing could be less like the hated memories of your childhood than this elegant French sweet.

1 Remove stalks from fresh blackcurrants. Rinse them quickly in a sieve or colander under the cold tap; drain well, shaking off as much moisture as possible. If using frozen currants, defrost them according to instructions on packet.

2 Rub blackcurrants through a fine sieve; or blend them in an electric liquidiser, then rub purée through the sieve. Beat in sifted icing sugar.

3 Bring milk to the boil in a heavy pan. Stir in semolina and simmer, stirring frequently, for 15 to 20 minutes, or until mixture is thick and semolina well cooked. Remove from heat and allow to cool slightly.

4 Whisk egg yolks with castor sugar until thick and light; beat into semolina mixture, together with cream, vanilla and lemon juice.

5 Butter a decorative 2½-pint mould.

6 Whisk egg whites until stiff but not dry. Fold into semolina mixture gently but thoroughly. Pour into mould and chill until set.

7 To serve: turn mould out on to a large, flat serving dish (see page 554). Pour blackcurrant sauce over the top and serve immediately.

1 lb fresh or frozen blackcurrants
4 oz icing sugar, sifted
1 pint milk
3 oz semolina
2 eggs, separated
3 oz castor sugar
4 level tablespoons double cream
1 teaspoon vanilla essence
1 tablespoon lemon juice
1 level tablespoon softened butter

Serves 6

1/2 oz powdered gelatine
1/4 pint pineapple juice, fresh
  or canned
6 egg yolks
6 oz granulated sugar
1 level tablespoon cornflour
3/4 pint milk
5 egg whites
Generous pinch of salt
1 level tablespoon castor
  sugar
3 tablespoons lemon juice
1/4 pint double cream, chilled
3–4 slices pineapple, fresh
  or canned, shredded
Pineapple rings, maraschino
  cherries and angelica
  'leaves', to decorate

Pineapple Cream

The addition of stiffly beaten egg whites turns this delicate sweet into a cross between a Bavarian cream and a cold soufflé. To make an orange cream, substitute orange juice for pineapple juice and intensify the flavour with the freshly grated zest of 2 large oranges.

1 Sprinkle powdered gelatine over pineapple juice and leave to soften.

2 In a large bowl, whisk egg yolks with sugar until fluffy and lemon-coloured; add cornflour and continue to whisk until smoothly blended.

3 Scald milk; add to egg yolk mixture in a thin stream, beating vigorously with the whisk. Then pour into top of double saucepan and cook over simmering water, stirring frequently. As soon as custard coats back of spoon, plunge base of pan into cold water to arrest cooking process. Do not under any circumstances allow custard to boil, or egg yolks will curdle.

4 Add gelatine and pineapple juice mixture to hot custard, stirring until completely melted. Pour custard into a large bowl.

5 Beat egg whites with salt until soft peaks form. Add castor sugar and continue to beat to a stiff meringue. Fold gently but thoroughly into hot custard mixture and flavour to taste with lemon juice. Flavour should be rather sharp. Allow mixture to become quite cold, drawing a large metal spoon through it occasionally to prevent it separating.

6 When custard mixture is on the point of setting, whip chilled cream (by hand for maximum volume) until floppy and with the same consistency as the pineapple custard mixture. Fold into custard, together with shredded pineapple.

7 Rinse a 3-pint mould with cold water, shaking out all excess. Fill to the brim with pineapple cream; cover with greaseproof paper and chill until firmly set, preferably overnight.

8 To serve: dip mould into very hot water for 1 second only and turn out on to a flat serving dish. Decorate with halved pineapple rings, maraschino cherries and angelica 'leaves', and return to refrigerator until ready to serve.

Rice à la Royale

1 Put (unwashed) rice in a heavy, medium-sized pan. Cover with cold water to come 2 inches above rice. Bring to the boil; stir to dislodge any grains stuck to the pan and simmer for 5 minutes.

2 Drain rice thoroughly in a colander. Return to the pan. Add granulated sugar and half the milk. Bring to simmering point, stirring frequently, and simmer gently, uncovered, until rice is soft and most of the milk has been absorbed, about 20 minutes. Remove pan from heat; cover and allow to cool.

3 Blend cornflour to a smooth, thin paste with a little of the remaining milk. Then combine cornflour mixture with all the remaining milk in the top of a double saucepan. Bring to the boil over direct heat and simmer gently for 5 minutes, stirring constantly. Remove from heat.

4 Combine egg yolks and castor sugar in a bowl, and whisk until light and fluffy. Add cornflour sauce in a thin stream, whisking. Return mixture to top of double saucepan.

5 Fit top part of pan over base containing simmering water and cook, stirring frequently, for about 20 minutes, or until custard is thick enough to coat back of spoon. Remove from heat and allow to cool, beating occasionally to prevent a skin forming on top.

6 Sprinkle gelatine over 4 or 5 tablespoons cold water in a cup and leave to soften.

7 When custard is cold, place cup containing gelatine in a bowl of hot water and stir until gelatine has completely dissolved. Beat gelatine into custard and flavour to taste with vanilla essence.

8 Combine custard with cooked rice mixture, cream and Kirsch, to taste.

9 Pour mixture into a deep, round, 3-pint mould. Chill until firmly set, preferably overnight.

10 To unmould rice: dip mould for just 1 or 2 seconds into very hot water. Place a large serving dish on top; invert and gently shake rice mould out on to dish. Decorate with halved and cored pears which you have poached in a light syrup or, if they are really ripe and soft, simply brushed all over with lemon juice to prevent discolouration. Finish decoration with swirls of piped whipped cream, halved glacé cherries and 'leaves' cut out of angelica. Serve very cold.

Serves 8

6 oz short-grain rice

6 level tablespoons granulated sugar

2 1/4 pints milk

3 level tablespoons cornflour

6 egg yolks

7 level tablespoons castor sugar

3/4 oz powdered gelatine

1–1 1/2 teaspoons vanilla essence

6 level tablespoons double cream

3–4 tablespoons Kirsch

To decorate

3–4 small, ripe dessert pears, halved, cored and poached in light syrup or brushed with lemon juice

Whipped cream

Glacé cherries, halved

Angelica 'leaves'

Serves 6

Sponge finger biscuits, or strips of sponge cake
1/2 oz powdered gelatine
8–9 juicy oranges (see Step 4)
3 sugar lumps
4 tablespoons lemon juice
6 oz granulated sugar
3 eggs, separated
3 level tablespoons castor sugar
1/2 pint double cream
Vanilla essence (optional)
Lightly sweetened whipped cream and orange segments, to decorate

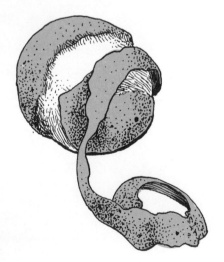

Charlotte Russe à l'Orange

A classic French mould for a Charlotte Russe is made of metal, with plain, slightly sloping sides, and two little heart-shaped handles. You can also use a soufflé dish or any other mould with tall, plain sides and a flat bottom.

When it comes to lining the mould, you can choose between sponge finger biscuits and strips of sponge cake. If you use sponge fingers, they will fit better (and the finished result is more attractive) if you alternate brown and white sides on the outside. If you have difficulty making them stand up around the sides, try brushing them with a little egg white to hold them in place.

1 Line base of a 2½- to 3-pint charlotte mould with a circle of dampened greaseproof paper. Line sides of mould with a tight layer of sponge fingers (see note above).

2 Sprinkle gelatine over 3 tablespoons cold water in a cup and put aside to soften.

3 Scrub 2 oranges and dry them. Rub sugar lumps all over their zest until thoroughly impregnated with orange oil.

4 Squeeze oranges to make ¾ pint strained juice. Combine with lemon juice in the top of a double saucepan.

5 Add sugar lumps and granulated sugar, and stir over direct heat until sugar has dissolved. Do not boil juices as this tends to make them bitter.

6 In a bowl, whisk egg yolks until frothy. Gradually pour in hot juices, whisking vigorously.

7 Return mixture to top of double saucepan and cook over simmering water, stirring, until slightly thickened, 10 to 15 minutes. Remove from heat and allow to cool.

8 Meanwhile, stand bowl containing gelatine in the hot water remaining in the bottom of the double saucepan and stir until thoroughly dissolved. Mix with cooling orange 'custard'. Leave until quite cold but not set.

9 In a medium-sized bowl, whisk egg whites until stiff but not dry. Gradually whisk in castor sugar, and continue to whisk to a stiff, glossy meringue.

10 Slowly add cold orange mixture, whisking vigorously.

11 In another bowl, whisk cream lightly until barely thick enough to hold a trail. Fold in orange mixture and flavour, if liked, with a few drops of vanilla essence. Leave until on the point of setting.

12 When orange cream is very thick, pour into sponge-lined mould and leave in a cool place until set.

13 To turn out: with a pair of scissors, snip off tips of sponge fingers level with top of filling. If charlotte has stuck to mould, dip briefly in and out of very hot water. Turn out on to a flat serving dish. Remove paper.

14 Decorate charlotte with lightly sweetened whipped cream and, if liked, orange segments.

Crown of Apples

1 Brush a plain, 2-pint ring mould with melted butter.

2 In a large, heavy pan, combine sugar, lemon zest and vanilla pod, if used (but not vanilla essence), with ¾ pint water. Bring to the boil over a low heat, stirring until sugar has melted; then lower heat to a simmer. If using vanilla essence, do not add it until syrup is simmering to minimise evaporation.

3 Prepare two apples at a time by cutting them into quarters, coring and peeling them, and slicing them about ⅛ inch thick. As soon as they are ready, drop slices into simmering syrup and poach for 5 minutes, or until translucent and soft but not disintegrating. Remove slices from syrup with a slotted spoon and spread out on a plate to cool.

4 Prepare remaining apples in the same way.

5 Arrange poached apple slices in regular, overlapping circles, close together and with the peeled side of the slices towards the outside edge of the mould. Press each layer lightly with the back of a spoon to 'settle' it.

6 When mould is full, cover tightly with foil and chill overnight.

7 The following day, prepare a glaze by melting apricot jam with a tablespoon of the apple poaching syrup in a small, heavy pan over a low heat. Sieve into a bowl. Cool slightly and flavour with brandy, Kirsch, or a few drops of lemon juice, to taste.

8 Dip ring mould into hot water for just a second to loosen apples, and turn it out on to a large, flat serving dish.

9 Brush apple ring with warm apricot glaze, taking care not to dislodge slices. Chill until ready to serve.

10 Use a sharp knife to slice crown of apples into portions, and serve with a light Crème Anglaise.

Serves 6–8

Melted butter
3/4 lb sugar
Spiral of thinly pared lemon zest
A piece of vanilla pod, split, or vanilla essence
3/4 pint water
4 lb firm, tart dessert apples, e.g. Coxes or Golden Delicious
Crème Anglaise (page 145), to serve

Glaze
6 level tablespoons apricot jam
1 tablespoon apple syrup
1 tablespoon brandy, Kirsch etc., or lemon juice

FIFTH COURSE

Lesson 23
Aspics and Pâtés

How to Make a Perfect Aspic

One of the most agreeable first courses I know is a simple poached egg set in tarragon-flavoured aspic. The amber tinted aspic, shimmering and cool, just firm enough to hold the egg; the egg itself, cooked to the point of perfection with its yolk still soft and runny; a design of tender tarragon leaves glinting greenly against the soft whiteness of the egg.

And yet, this dish in its perfect simplicity is rarely encountered in this country, where far too often the egg is a hard tasteless spheroid encased in a dark molasses tinted rubber-like jelly, marred by the unmistakably unpleasant sharpness of tarragon vinegar.

The use of aspic jelly in *pâtés* and *terrines* is very important. Indeed there are many pâtés whose bodies are made up entirely of aspic – the famous *pâté d'anguilles*, for instance, served by Madame Point at Vienne; a savoury concoction of tender slices of river eel, mushrooms and thin lemon slices, set in a deliciously fragrant aspic of blended white wines of the region spiked with fresh herbs. Restaurant 'La Bourgogne' in Paris, famous for its Burgundian specialities, features a most unusual pâté of ham in aspic called *jambon persillé à la mode de Bourgogne*, tender pink morsels of ham simmered lovingly in a stock made rich with veal and wine; and then set in aspic with freshly chopped parsley; a pink and green pâté which is a joy to behold.

Aspic plays a major part in most terrine and pâté recipes. When I make a terrine or pâté, I always place a board or flat plate on top of it to weight it down as it cools. The pâté mixture shrinks in cooling and this weight (use an iron, tinned foods or a brick) compresses it just enough to eliminate the tiny air holes that make the pâté difficult to slice when chilled.

Your pâté should be firm and moist, and must not fall apart as you cut it. The aspic serves to hold it together as well as to add to the general flavour and appearance of the finished dish. Of course, when you bake a *pâté en croûte* you will not be able to weight it down. The aspic jelly, which you pour in through a hole in the top of your crust, will fill the tiny holes formed during baking and will serve to fill the space created by shrinkage during the baking process.

Any well-flavoured *consommé* will serve as a base for your aspic. The clarity of the consommé, its delicate flavour, and above all its correct consistency are the important points to watch for. A really successful aspic should be just firm enough to hold its shape, shivering gently when moved, ready to fall away at the touch of a fork. It is far better to err on the side of too fragile a mixture than to make one which is tough and rubbery and resistant to the touch.

Aspics

Moulding in aspic jelly is a favourite way of preparing appetisers because the jelly adds a delicious flavour and gives them a delightful shimmering appearance. Cold dishes in aspic fit particularly well in Christmas entertaining because they can be made ready in advance and chilled, thus eliminating much last-minute cooking.

Though you would never believe it from deb dances, aspics can be made in several ways. The simplest, the most common and, I am afraid, the most unsatisfactory is to add unflavoured gelatine to tinned consommé or bouillon. One tablespoon of granulated gelatine will jell one pint of liquid. First soften gelatine for 5 minutes in cold liquid, then dissolve it in boiled liquid.

More particular cooks, of course, make their own aspic from a rich soup stock, clarified with chopped lean beef and egg white. If enough bones are used in making the stock (especially calf's feet or chicken feet which are high in gelatine content) the mixture will stiffen or 'jell' when cold. When bones are unobtainable, or when making a fruit or vegetable juice aspic, commercial gelatine can be used in the proportion of 1 tablespoon gelatine to each pint of liquid.

Clarification

For each pint of bouillon made, chop $\frac{1}{4}$ lb lean raw beef, mix it with the green part of a leek finely chopped and a little tarragon, beat the whole mixture with the whites of two eggs. Add this to the bouillon; bring it very slowly to the boil, stirring constantly. Lower the flame and simmer gently for about 25 minutes. If the liquid boils too hard, the whites will come to the surface and the impurities will remain at the bottom of the saucepan. Pass the liquid through a wet flannel or muslin placed over a sieve. And before the aspic is cold, add a little Port wine, Sherry or Madeira and a drop of Cognac for good measure.

Test your Aspic

Before you make use of your aspic, test it for density and flavour. Pour a tablespoon or two in a soup plate resting on ice and let the liquid form a jelly. If the consistency is right, use it; if not, correct it in one of the following ways:

If aspic is too stiff Add a little more Port or Sherry.

If aspic is too thin You can make the gelatine more dense if you add a little granulated gelatine to the liquid.

If aspic is flavourless Add a greater amount of ground lean beef when you clarify it.

To coat with aspic Always wait until the food to be coated with aspic is completely cold. Decorate it beforehand with leaves of tarragon, thin rounds of cooked carrot, truffles, lemon peel or hard-cooked egg white. Heat the aspic; cool it until it is syrupy; then pour it, spoon by spoon, over the food to be coated. Place food on a wire rack over a shallow plate before coating with aspic so that aspic overflow is not wasted.

To line mould with aspic Fill the mould with liquid aspic and place in a bowl of crushed ice until the aspic starts to set at the sides. Then pour off the liquid and your mould will be evenly lined.

For chopped aspic Pour a thin layer of liquid aspic into a cake tin; allow it to cool and then remove to a chopping board and chop finely.

574

Basic Meat Aspic

1 Put beef bones, the carcass or chicken joint, and the calf's foot or chicken feet in a large stock-pot or saucepan, and cover with 4 pints cold water. Bring to the boil very slowly; then, as bubbles begin to break on the surface, add a little salt to draw out scum. Skim it off with a slotted spoon and repeat skimming until bones cease to throw up scum. The clarity of your aspic will largely depend on doing this thoroughly and conscientiously.

2 Add roughly chopped vegetables, herbs and a little freshly ground black pepper; bring back to the boil; skim again if necessary and leave stock to simmer for about 3 hours, skimming occasionally.

3 Strain off stock and measure it: if it is more than 1 pint, pour into a clean pan and simmer until reduced to a pint. Leave to cool before skimming fat from the surface.

4 The stock must now be clarified: in a heavy pan, beat egg white lightly. Add raw beef and herbs; mix well, then stir in cooled stock.

5 Bring to the boil over a low heat, stirring constantly. As soon as a pad of scum begins to form on the surface, stop stirring. Leave stock to simmer gently for 15 minutes.

6 Pass hot stock through a sieve lined with a double thickness of muslin. Skim any remaining fat from the surface by drawing sheet after sheet of absorbent paper over it. Allow to cool.

7 Aspic may now be flavoured in any of the following ways:

Sherry aspic Stir in 1 tablespoon dry sherry.

Madeira aspic Stir in 1 tablespoon Madeira.

Port aspic Stir in 1 tablespoon port.

Allow aspic to cool until very syrupy and on the point of setting before using it.

8 oz veal or beef bones, chopped chicken or duck carcass, or an 8-oz chicken joint
1 calf's foot, split, or 4 chicken feet, well scrubbed
Salt
1 Spanish onion, roughly chopped
1 leek, roughly chopped
2 carrots, roughly chopped
2 stalks celery, roughly chopped
2 sprigs parsley
1 sprig thyme or 1/4 level teaspoon dried thyme
1 bay leaf
Freshly ground black pepper
1 egg white
1/4 lb raw lean beef, minced or chopped
1 level teaspoon each finely chopped fresh tarragon and chervil (or 1/2 amount dried herbs)

Eggs in Aspic

The success of an egg in aspic depends entirely on the flavour of your aspic (remember that flavours tend to weaken after cooling) and the care that you put into its decoration. Be sure to allow enough time for jelly to set between stages.

1 Flavour a well-seasoned aspic with Madeira, to taste. Pour a thin layer over the base of four ½-pint moulds. Leave to set in the refrigerator.

1 pint liquid aspic (page 573)
2 tablespoons Madeira
4 thin slices cooked carrot
1 sprig tarragon, blanched
4 eggs, poached and trimmed (page 57)
4 slices ham

2 Cut carrot slices into flower shapes and arrange them on top of the aspic, surrounding them with little pieces of tarragon to make 'leaves'. Spoon a $\frac{1}{4}$-inch layer of liquid aspic over them and chill again until set.

3 Place a neatly trimmed poached egg in each mould. Fill almost to the brim with aspic and chill until firmly set.

4 Cut ham slices to diameter of moulds and fit them in over the top. Set them in place with a little more aspic. Chill.

5 To unmould aspics: dip each mould in hot water to within $\frac{1}{4}$ inch of the top for no more than 10 seconds and turn out carefully on to an individual serving dish.

Fruits de Mer in Aspic, Sauce Verte

1 To make fish aspic: ask your fishmonger for a selection of fish heads, bones and trimmings. Put them in a large pan with the stock cube, dry white wine, onion, carrots, tomato, parsley stalks, and salt and freshly ground black pepper, to taste. Cover with 1 pint water; bring to the boil and simmer for 20 minutes.

2 Meanwhile, sprinkle gelatine over 2 tablespoons cold water in a cup and leave to soften.

3 To clarify aspic: strain stock through a fine sieve. Rinse pan and return stock to it. Add sliced leek, minced beef, crushed egg shells and softened gelatine.

4 Whisk egg whites until foamy and add to the pan. Heat gently until stock foams up to the top of the pan. Quickly draw pan off heat and allow foam to subside. Repeat this process three times in all, then strain stock through a sieve lined with muslin. It should be crystal clear.

5 To assemble moulds: decorate the bases of 6 individual moulds or soufflé dishes with a few tarragon leaves and a piece of lobster or king crab. Arrange halibut or sole, pieces of salmon and a few shrimps in each dish. Spoon over liquid aspic to cover and chill in the refrigerator until firm. Pour remaining aspic into a wide, shallow dish and allow this to set as well

6 To serve: wrap a cloth wrung out of hot water around each mould (one at a time) for 2 to 3 seconds only to loosen it without melting aspic too much, and turn out on to individual dishes garnished with lettuce leaves and quartered tomatoes. Chop remaining aspic and arrange a little around each mould. Serve with Sauce Verte.

Serves 6

1 cooked lobster or king crab, shelled and sliced (page 363 or 355)
1/2 lb halibut or sole, poached
1 salmon steak, poached
1/4 lb frozen shrimps, defrosted

Fish aspic
Fish bones and trimmings
1 chicken stock cube
4 tablespoons dry white wine
1 Spanish onion, sliced
2 carrots, sliced
1 large tomato, chopped
2 stalks parsley
Salt and freshly ground black pepper
1/2 oz powdered gelatine
1/2 leek, thinly sliced
2 oz minced lean beef
2 egg shells, crushed
2 egg whites

To decorate and garnish
Fresh tarragon leaves
1/2 small head lettuce
Quartered tomatoes

Sauce Verte

Makes ½ pint

Use egg yolks left over from clarifying fish stock to make mayonnaise.

1 Wash sprigs of watercress, parsley and chervil carefully, and plunge them into a small pan of boiling salted water. Bring back to the boil and simmer for 5 to 6 minutes. Drain well and press dry between the folds of a cloth or absorbent paper.

2 Pound blanched herbs to a paste in a mortar (or purée in an electric blender). Add to mayonnaise and mix well.

3 Stir in finely chopped herbs and lemon juice, and season to taste with salt and freshly ground black pepper.

1 oz each watercress, parsley and chervil
Salt
1/2 pint well-flavoured mayonnaise (page 43)
1 level tablespoon each finely chopped watercress, parsley, chervil and fresh tarragon
1 tablespoon lemon juice
Freshly ground black pepper

Foies de Volaille en Gelée

Serves 6

1 Choose nice, whole livers, not badly crushed or torn ones. Clean them thoroughly; snip off any sinews, membrane or green parts, and pat them dry with kitchen paper.

2 Put livers in a bowl. Sprinkle with salt and freshly ground black pepper, the very finely chopped onion and sage, and moisten with 1 tablespoon port. Mix lightly until livers are well coated with dressing, and leave to absorb flavours for at least 30 minutes, turning them occasionally.

3 Stir remaining port into aspic.

4 Pick out 18 of the best tarragon leaves. Put them in a small sieve and pour some boiling water over them to 'set' their colour.

5 Coat bottoms of six ¼-pint ramekins with a couple of teaspoons of the aspic and carefully decorate each one with 3 tarragon leaves in an attractive pattern (a pair of tweezers would come in useful here). Leave to set in the refrigerator.

6 Melt butter in a heavy frying-pan. When it is very hot, add chicken livers and their juices, and sauté over a high heat until juices have evaporated and livers are just cooked but still rather pink inside, 3 to 5 minutes.

7 Turn livers out on to absorbent paper and leave to cool.

8 When livers are cold, slice them into small, thin escalopes and divide them between the ramekins.

9 Fill each ramekin to the brim with port-flavoured aspic and chill until firmly set, at least 2 hours. Any leftover aspic should be poured into a soup plate and allowed to set as well.

6–8 oz chicken livers
Salt and freshly ground black pepper
2 level tablespoons very finely chopped onion
Generous pinch of dried sage
3 tablespoons port
3/4 pint liquid aspic
2–3 sprigs fresh tarragon (18 leaves)
1 level tablespoon butter

10 To turn ramekins out: loosen sides of aspic with your fingers or by drawing a sharp knife blade around the edge of the dish. Dip bottom of mould into very hot water for just 1 or 2 seconds and shake out on to a serving dish. Chop leftover aspic roughly and use it to decorate dish.

Pâté de Foie Gras in Aspic

Serves 2

1/4 pint liquid aspic
1–2 tablespoons Madeira
2 2-oz slices *pâté de foie gras*

To decorate
2 black olives, pitted and
  finely slivered
1 small firm tomato, seeded
  and slivered
A few fresh tarragon leaves

Like the eggs in aspic (page 575), so these little turrets of *pâté de foie gras* in aspic can be made or marred by the quality of your basic ingredients; use the best *pâté* available and a well-seasoned, flavoursome aspic, and for very special occasions, decorate the base of each ramekin with a thin sliver of black truffle.

1 Flavour aspic – which should be on the point of setting – with Madeira, stirring it in gently to avoid creating air bubbles.

2 Cover base of 2 ramekins 2 inches in diameter with a table-spoon each of Madeira-flavoured aspic. Chill until set.

3 Remove ramekins from refrigerator. Decorate base of each one with small slivers of olive and tomato, and a few leaves of fresh tarragon, dipping each morsel in aspic so that it will stick firmly in place. Return to the refrigerator to set again.

4 Trim each slice of pâté with a plain, 2-inch pastry cutter and fit one into each ramekin. Pour in enough aspic to fill ramekins to the brim. Chill until very firmly set.

5 When ready to serve: turn each ramekin over on to an individual, flat serving dish and wrap a very hot wet cloth wrung out of very hot water round the base and sides of the ramekin *for a few seconds only*. Remove cloth and, holding the ramekin and dish together firmly, shake gently until you feel the aspic coming loose – you may have to use the hot cloth again, but do not leave it wrapped round the ramekin for more than a few seconds at a time, or the aspic will start to melt and spoil the appearance of the dish.

Beef in Aspic

A pleasant luncheon or buffet dish. Serve cut in thick slices and accompanied by a salad and a dish of pickled cucumbers.

1 Cut meat into strips, carefully discarding any sinew or gristle.

2 Combine marinade ingredients in a large bowl. Add meat and leave to marinate for about $1\frac{1}{2}$ hours.

3 Transfer meat to a pan, together with marinade. Bring to simmering point over a low heat; cover tightly and simmer very gently for 1 hour. Uncover pan; stir in liquid aspic and continue to simmer for about 30 minutes longer, or until meat is tender.

4 Drain meat, reserving pan juices, and discard marinade vegetables. Strain pan juices through a fine sieve.

5 Brush a 2-pint mould with oil and dust all over with 2 level tablespoons finely chopped parsley. Arrange meat in the mould.

6 Add brandy and dry sherry to strained juices. Correct seasoning, adding more salt or freshly ground black pepper if necessary, and stir in remaining parsley.

7 Pour sauce over meat and chill until firmly set, preferably overnight.

8 To unmould aspic: dip mould in boiling water for a few seconds and shake out gently on to a flat serving dish.

Serves 8

3 lb rump steak or fillet ends
1 pint liquid aspic (page 573)
Olive oil
4 level tablespoons finely chopped parsley
1 teaspoon brandy
1 teaspoon dry sherry

Marinade

3/4 pint red wine
1 tablespoon wine vinegar
2 Spanish onions, finely chopped
2 carrots, diced
1 clove garlic
1 shallot
1 level tablespoon finely chopped parsley
1/4 level teaspoon dried thyme
6 juniper berries
2 cloves
Salt and freshly ground black pepper

Jellied Chicken Loaf

1 Select a heavy casserole or saucepan just large enough to hold chicken comfortably, with a tight-fitting lid. Lay chicken in it; add finely chopped shallots, parsley sprigs and $\frac{3}{4}$ pint cold water; season lightly with salt and freshly ground black pepper, and bring just to simmering point over a low heat. Cover tightly and continue to simmer very gently until chicken is tender, about 45 minutes.

2 Lift chicken out of the casserole, allowing all the stock to drain back, and put it aside to cool.

3 Strain stock through a fine sieve into a bowl and leave it to cool as well.

4 Transfer 2 tablespoons of the stock to a small bowl or cup. Sprinkle powdered gelatine over the surface and leave to soak until required.

5 Meanwhile, skin and bone chicken carefully, and cut meat into $\frac{1}{2}$-inch dice. Put it in a bowl.

Serves 6

1 3-lb chicken
2 shallots, finely chopped
2 sprigs parsley
Salt and freshly ground black pepper
2 level teaspoons powdered gelatine
2 1/4-inch-thick slices ham, about 2 oz each
4 stalks celery
Lemon juice
Lettuce leaves, to garnish
Sauce Verte (page 577) or plain mayonnaise (page 186), to serve

6 Cut ham slices into ¼-inch dice. Combine with chicken.

7 Chop celery stalks finely. Add them to the chicken and ham.

8 Toss chicken, ham and celery together with a fork until well mixed. Arrange in a 2-lb loaf tin.

9 Stand bowl with softened gelatine in hot water; stir until gelatine has dissolved and liquid is completely clear.

10 Stir gelatine into remaining stock. Correct seasoning with more salt or freshly ground black pepper, and sharpen flavour with a few drops of lemon juice.

11 Pour stock into loaf tin. Chill for at least 3 hours, or until set.

12 To unmould: run a knife round the edge of the jelly; then dip base of tin into hot water for 2 or 3 seconds *only* and turn loaf out on to a serving dish lined with lettuce leaves. Serve with Sauce Verte or a well-flavoured mayonnaise.

Poularde en Gelée

Inevitably served as part of a large cold buffet, this dish can be magnificent provided the aspic is richly flavoured and the chicken itself highly perfumed with herbs and carefully seasoned.

1 Preheat oven to moderate (350°F. Mark 4).

2 Wipe chickens both inside and out with a damp cloth, and dry them carefully with paper towels.

3 Set aside a few sprigs of tarragon. Chop remainder very coarsely; combine with softened butter and season generously with salt and freshly ground black pepper. Push this mixture under the skin of the breast of each bird and into the body cavity. Sprinkle chickens all over with salt and freshly ground black pepper.

4 Roast chickens for 1 to 1¼ hours, or cooked through, basting several times with the butter that runs out of them.

5 Heat chicken stock in a large saucepan. Add minced beef, frothy egg whites and crushed egg shells. Whisk mixture with a balloon whisk for about 30 seconds; then bring to the boil, allowing froth to rise to the top of the pan. Remove pan from heat and leave to stand for about 10 minutes.

6 Sprinkle powdered gelatine over 3 to 4 tablespoons cold water in a cup. Allow to soften for a few minutes; then place cup in a bowl of hot water and stir until liquid is quite clear. Pour dissolved gelatine into stock mixture. Bring to the boil again,

Serves 8

2 small roasting chickens
Bunch of fresh tarragon
4 oz softened butter
Salt and freshly ground black pepper
2 pints well-flavoured chicken stock (page 162)
4 oz raw minced beef
2 egg whites, whisked until frothy
1–2 egg shells, crushed
1 oz powdered gelatine
1/2 pint dry white wine
4 tablespoons Madeira or Port
4 large firm tomatoes
24–30 black olives, stoned and halved
1 lettuce

letting mixture froth up to the top of the pan. Then leave to stand for a further 5 minutes.

7 Finally, stir in white wine and Madeira or port. Bring to the boil, remove from heat and leave until egg whites and shells have gathered in a thick scum on top of the liquid aspic.

8 Strain aspic into a bowl through a sieve lined with a double thickness of fine muslin. Chill in the refrigerator until aspic is syrupy and on the point of setting.

9 When chickens are cold, skin them carefully and divide into serving pieces.

10 Dip remaining sprigs of tarragon into boiling water for a second or two to rid them of their surface oil so that they can be coated with aspic. Dry leaves carefully; dip them in aspic and arrange them decoratively on chicken joints.

11 Coat each piece of chicken with aspic, allowing two or three coats in all, and returning pieces to the refrigerator each time to allow the jelly to set.

12 Skin tomatoes or leave them unskinned, as you prefer. Cut them in half in a decorative fretwork pattern, and carefully scoop out seeds and pulp with a sharp spoon. Sprinkle inside of each tomato with salt and leave upside down to drain for 10 to 15 minutes.

13 Fill tomato shells with black olives; mask with aspic and chill in refrigerator until set.

14 Wash lettuce leaves carefully and dry them one by one. Arrange them on a large serving dish and lay chicken pieces on top. Garnish with prepared tomatoes. Serve cold.

Pâtés and Terrines

If there is one everyday institution that I cherish above all others in France, it is the *charcuterie* – the shop that makes a living selling pâtés, terrines, sausages and cold meats of all kinds, as well as cheeses and ready-to-serve salads.

The *charcutier* plays a major role in the life of every town and village in France, side by side with the butcher and baker. Many of them have now branched out for their livelihood to include frozen and other convenience foods, but the best of them still boast a selection and variety of freshly cooked pâtés, terrines, home-cured hams and sausages, both fresh and preserved, that would put the delicatessen counters of some of our most sophisticated food stores to shame.

One day, we too may come to know the pleasures of having a *charcuterie* around the corner, a source of a delicious variety of pâtés – to replace the ubiquitous grilled chops and omelettes when we are pressed for a quick meal; to serve as a noble first course for unexpected guests; or, with wine and fresh bread picked up from the neighbouring shops in some village high street, to replace the horrors of self-service cafeteria food with a roadside picnic fit for a king.

Meanwhile, let us explore the delights of home-made pâtés and terrines, for they are not at all difficult to make. And if the preparation often seems a long drawn-out affair, this is counterbalanced by the fact that you are free to make it well in advance at your own convenience, for a pâté positively needs to mature over 2 or 3 days, during which time its flavour undergoes a quite dramatic improvement.

Making Pâtés and Terrines

There is no real difference between a pâté and a terrine mixture – the latter simply takes its name from the dish in which the mixture is baked. One could possibly say that the texture of a terrine is likely to be coarser than that of a pâté, but even this cannot be treated as a general rule.

Texture What most pâté and terrine mixtures have in common is a high proportion of fat – usually fresh pork fat, occasionally fat unsmoked bacon, and even smoked bacon if, for example, the basic meat is highly flavoured game. The fat content can also be supplemented by adding plenty of double cream.

If you have never made a pâté (or terrine) before, you would be forgiven for querying the amounts of fat used, but don't; for without it your pâté would be dry, crumbly and quite uninteresting.

Texture is also improved by beating in *breadcrumbs* which have been soaked either in some of the cream or in stock.

Eggs play a dual role in both binding the pâté, thus making it easier to slice, and enriching the texture.

Finally, as a general rule, bear in mind that for the texture of a pâté to come through several hours' slow cooking unscathed, the uncooked mixture should be very moist – even sloppy – to start with. If it appears to be on the stiff and dry side, counteract this with more cream or a little stock.

Flavouring the Mixture

By far the trickiest part of making terrines and pâtés is getting the right balance of seasoning. Not many people relish the idea of tasting a pâté mixture raw, and as a result they tend to season too cautiously. However, there is a simple way around this: when the mixture is ready to be packed into its baking dish, take a spoonful of it; shape it into a patty and sauté until cooked through in a little butter. When you taste it, make allowance for the fact that the 'tone' of the seasoning will be appreciably weaker after cooking and maturing.

The other point worthy of mention in this context is the term *quatre épices* which you will come across in French pâté recipes. The French are able to buy a commercial spice mixture specially blended for seasoning pâtés. Sometimes it comes in the form of *sel épicé* – or salt seasoned with this special spice blend.

Don't despair if you can't persuade anyone to bring some over for you (for as far as I know, the blend is not as yet imported into England). At the end of this introduction you will find instructions for making your own spice blend. First try it as it is and then, if you wish, adjust the formula to make it even more personally yours.

The Terrine or Baking Dish

Pâtés and terrines are traditionally baked in deep, glazed earthenware dishes, rectangular, round or oval, covered with a lid which has a hole in it to allow steam to escape. However, as such dishes are not easily available in this country, you will probably have to make do with a loaf tin covered with foil.

Lining the Baking Dish

To protect the sides and base of the pâté, your baking dish must first be lined completely with paper-thin slices of fat salt pork or bacon.

Fat salt pork Should you have difficulty in slicing this thinly enough (I use a rotary cutter), try chilling – even freezing – the block of fat first. Pounding thicker slices between sheets of greaseproof paper, a measure often recommended, tends to make them disintegrate as there are no fibres in fat, as there are for example in a slice of meat, to hold them together.

Fat bacon Thinly sliced bacon should be stretched to paper-thinness with the back of a knife.

Baking Pâtés and Terrines

Most pâtés are baked *au bain marie*, i.e. with the baking dish standing half or one-third submerged in a larger container of hot water. Like the lining of fat, this aims primarily to protect the parts of the pâté in closest contact with the heat, and to prevent them turning hard and crumbly.

The temperature of the oven is kept quite low throughout baking for the same reason.

To tell whether the pâté is cooked, pierce it through the thickest part with a skewer: the juices should run perfectly clear, without a trace of blood. At the same time, the liquid fat surrounding the pâté should be quite transparent, and free of pink or red juices. The pâté itself will have shrunk quite considerably and be bathed in melted fat and juices.

To Finish a Pâté

Having cooked the pâté, you can either weight it or encase it in aspic, or even adopt a combination of both, first weighting the pâté; then draining off the juices and reinforcing them with a little dissolved gelatine before pouring them back. The object of all these operations is to make the pâté cut in neat, firm slices. *Weighting* it eliminates air bubbles and closes up the texture. While *liquid aspic* seeps into all the little crevices and sets there to hold the meat together and prevent the slices crumbling as you cut them.

To Weight a Pâté

Have ready a board or flat dish that fits the top of the pâté as closely as possible. When you remove the pâté from the oven, pour off the water in the larger container and leave the dish standing in it (in case the juices overflow when you weight it). Lay the board or dish on top of the hot pâté and weight it down – with balance scale weights, tins of food etc., until the surface of the pâté is submerged in liquid fat and juices. Leave until cold and set.

The coarser the texture of the original mixture, the heavier the weights must be – from 2 lb up to 8 lb as, for example, in our chunky terrine of veal (see page 590).

To Aspic a Pâté

Remove pâté from oven. Leave uncovered for a few minutes to allow cooking to subside, *or* leave for 15 minutes lightly weighted as above. Pour off fat and juices into a measuring jug. Skim off fat.

Supplement juices with a little concentrated stock if you don't think there are enough to cover the pâté completely. For a firm set that will cut well, use ½ oz gelatine per ½ pint of juices.

When pâté is cool, pour over juices. Leave until quite cold before chilling.

● The only exception to this is the *pâté en croute*, or pâté baked in a pastry crust (see page 600). Here, because the juices are inaccessible under the crust, you must use a liquid aspic, prepared separately, to fill in all the empty spaces left as the pâté mixture inside the crust shrank.

To Store Pâtés and Terrines

If you intend to store a pâté for longer than the maturing period specified, make perfectly sure that the top of the dish is completely sealed with fat – fresh lard is best.

A weighted pâté will have a good surface layer of fat anyway, but under this fat you will probably find quite a lot of lightly jellied juices. These are best scraped away if you mean to keep the pâté for any length of time, as they tend to be the first to go off.

A well-sealed pâté will be safe under mild refrigeration for about 10 days. The only exception is a pâté with a high bread content, which might go sour if kept for more than a week.

To Serve Pâtés and Terrines

Pâtés can be turned out, sliced and served in individual portions, garnished with a leaf of lettuce and a slice of tomato, or cut into chunky slices and served straight from the dish, depending on the occasion.

If you are not going to use it all at once, scrape the fat off the surface of as much as you need, and keep it to spread over the surface of the last cut side.

Pâtés are not light, so keep portions quite modest. And always have plenty of fresh toast or French bread with them to act as a foil for their rich, concentrated flavours.

Spice Blend for Pâtés and Terrines

2 level tablespoons paprika

1 level tablespoon each:
ground bay leaves, dried
sage, marjoram and
rosemary, and ground
mace

1/2 level tablespoon each:
cayenne pepper, ground
cinnamon, ground cloves,
and freshly grated nutmeg

5 level tablespoons white
peppercorns

1 Take all the ready ground spices and measure them out on to a large sheet of greaseproof paper.

2 Measure peppercorns into an electric blender and blend to a powder (or grind in a mortar). Sift mixture through a fine sieve on to the sheet of greaseproof paper. If some of the peppercorns do not go through the sieve the first time, return them to blender or mortar; blend or pound and sift again.

3 Sift the spices all together once more on to another sheet of greaseproof paper to mix them together thoroughly.

4 Store in a tightly stoppered jar.

You are now in business for making pâtés and terrines.

Chicken Liver Terrine

Makes 10–12 portions

1 1/4 lb fresh chicken livers,
cleaned

6 tablespoons port

Pinch of dried thyme

4 bay leaves

4 slices white bread,
trimmed of crusts

1/4 pint milk

2 level tablespoons butter

4 slices cooked ham

6 oz sausage meat

6 oz lean pork, minced

1/2 clove garlic, finely
chopped

Freshly ground black pepper

Thin slices of streaky
bacon or fat salt pork

Melted lard

As this terrine is rather rich, you will probably find that one good slice per person makes an ample *hors-d'œuvre*, leaving about half to serve on another occasion.

1 Place chicken livers in a large bowl. Add port, a pinch of thyme and 2 bay leaves, crumbled. Toss lightly and leave to marinate for at least 2 hours.

2 Soak bread in milk and squeeze dry.

3 Remove chicken livers from marinade with a slotted spoon. Reserve marinade.

4 Sauté livers in butter until they begin to stiffen.

5 Reserve a quarter of the best livers and put remainder through a mincer together with ham, sausage meat, minced pork and soaked bread. Work lightly with a spoon, adding enough of the reserved marinade to produce a rather wet mixture. Then stir in finely chopped garlic and season to taste with freshly ground black pepper.

6 Preheat oven to moderate (375°F. Mark 5).

7 Line a 2-pint terrine or a 2-lb loaf tin with slices of fat bacon which you have stretched out thinly with the back of a broad-bladed knife. (Or, for a more subtle flavour, use paper-thin strips of fat salt pork – see page 583 – alternately with bacon to line the dish.)

8 Spread half of the liver and sausage meat mixture evenly over base of dish. Arrange whole livers down centre. Then cover with remaining liver and sausage meat mixture, smoothing it out evenly, and top with thin slices of bacon and 2 bay leaves. Cover dish tightly with a lid or a sheet of foil.

9 Place dish in a deep baking tin; add boiling water to come half-way up sides, and bake for $1\frac{1}{4}$ to $1\frac{1}{2}$ hours, topping up with more *boiling* water if it evaporates too quickly.

8 Remove dish from oven; uncover and place a weight on the terrine to press out all excess juices. Leave terrine to cool under the weight.

9 When quite cold, seal top of terrine with a little melted lard. Its flavour will 'mature' and improve considerably if it is left in the refrigerator for 2 or 3 days before serving.

Pâté Liégeoise

Serves 6

1 Cover livers with salted water; bring to the boil and simmer, covered, for 20 minutes. Drain livers, pat them dry with paper towels, and put twice through the finest blade of your mincer – or purée in an electric blender.

2 Return paste to the pan and beat over a moderate heat for 1 minute to evaporate excess moisture. Cool.

3 Work butter with a wooden spoon until soft and creamy. Flavour with onion, mustard, nutmeg and cloves; then beat in minced livers. Season to taste with salt and freshly ground black pepper. If you prefer an absolutely smooth texture, rub pâté through a fine sieve.

4 Pack pâté firmly into one or two small earthenware pots or terrines, and chill until ready to serve. Serve with hot toast. Any left over will keep well in the refrigerator.

1 lb chicken livers
Salt
8 oz unsalted butter
4 level tablespoons finely grated Spanish onion
2 level teaspoons dry mustard
1/2 level teaspoon freshly grated nutmeg
1/4 level teaspoon ground cloves
Freshly ground black pepper
Hot toast, to serve

Serves 4–6

8 oz pork liver

8 oz fat belly of pork, rind removed

1 shallot, finely chopped

1 clove garlic, finely chopped

3–4 tablespoons brandy

3–4 tablespoons Madeira

1/2 level teaspoon salt

Generous pinch of allspice

Freshly ground black pepper

About 8 oz thinly sliced fat salt pork or unsmoked streaky bacon

4 oz chicken livers, cleaned and trimmed

1 bay leaf

1 level teaspoon powdered gelatine

Pork and Liver Terrine

1 Preheat oven to slow (325°F. Mark 3).

2 Coarsely mince pork liver and fat pork belly into a bowl.

3 Add finely chopped shallot and garlic, brandy, Madeira, salt, a generous pinch of ground allspice and freshly ground black pepper, to taste. Blend thoroughly with a wooden spoon. Mixture will seem rather sloppy, but this is as it should be.

4 Line base and sides of a $1\frac{1}{2}$-pint terrine with paper-thin slices of fat salt pork or unsmoked streaky bacon (see page 583).

5 Spread half of minced mixture evenly over base of terrine. Arrange chicken livers on top in a neat, evenly spaced layer, and cover with remaining minced mixture, levelling it off with the back of a spoon. Cover top of mixture with more thin slices of fat salt pork or bacon. Lay a bay leaf in the centre.

6 Cover terrine with a lid. Stand it in a roasting tin and transfer to the oven. Pour in water to come a third of the way up sides of terrine.

7 Bake terrine for $1\frac{3}{4}$ hours, or until juices run clear when a skewer is pushed through the centre and melted fat surrounding terrine is also clear. Top up roasting tin with more hot water if it evaporates too quickly.

8 Remove terrine from roasting tin. Pour off water; replace terrine; take off lid; cover surface of terrine with a board or plate and place a 2-lb weight on top. Leave for 15 minutes.

9 Remove weight and carefully pour off the fat and juices surrounding terrine into a bowl. Cover terrine with a lid and put aside.

10 Allow juices to cool. Skim off fat. Sprinkle gelatine over skimmed juices and leave for a few minutes to soften. Then stand bowl in a pan of hot water and stir gently until gelatine has completely dissolved.

11 Pour gelatine mixture over terrine. Weight it down as before and leave in a cool place to set.

12 Store terrine under refrigeration for at least 48 hours before serving to allow flavours to develop and mature.

Pâté de Canard

Serves 6–8

1 Remove meat from duck, discarding all skin, fat and sinews. You should be left with about 1 lb duck meat.

2 Combine duck meat with pie veal and raw gammon, and put 3 times through the coarse blade of a mincer.

3 Place minced meats in a bowl. Add brandy and port; mix well; cover bowl tightly and leave to develop flavours for 24 hours.

4 The following day, preheat oven to moderate (350°F. Mark 4).

5 In another bowl, whisk eggs until well mixed. Whisk in cream; stir in breadcrumbs and leave them to absorb moisture for 10 to 15 minutes.

6 Beat egg mixture into minced meats. Add grated onion, ground bay leaves, paprika, and salt and freshly ground black pepper, to taste.

7 Beat vigorously, preferably using a sturdy electric stand mixer, until mixture is reduced to an almost smooth, paste-like consistency.

8 Gently fold in cubes of tongue and skinned, halved pistachio nuts so that they are evenly distributed throughout the mixture.

9 Line base and sides of a 2-lb loaf tin (measuring $9\frac{1}{4}$ by $2\frac{1}{4}$ by $2\frac{3}{4}$ inches) with thin strips of fat salt pork.

10 Add duck mixture. Tap tin firmly against table to settle mixture and eliminate air bubbles, and level off top with the back of a spoon.

11 Cover top of tin tightly with foil. Place in a larger pan with simmering water to come half-way up sides.

12 Bake pâté for $1\frac{3}{4}$ to 2 hours, or until juices run clear when centre of pâté is pierced with a skewer.

13 Cool pâté. Then leave at the bottom of the refrigerator for at least 24 hours to allow flavours to develop.

1 3 1/2- to 4-lb duck, dressed weight
4 oz pie veal, coarsely cubed
4 oz raw gammon, coarsely cubed
4 tablespoons brandy
4 tablespoons port
3 eggs
1/4 pint single cream
2 oz stale white breadcrumbs
1/2 small onion, grated
1/4 level teaspoon ground bay leaves
1/4 level teaspoon paprika
Salt and freshly ground black pepper
6 oz ox tongue, cut into 1/2-inch cubes
2 oz pistachio nuts, blanched, skinned and halved
6–8 oz paper-thin strips fat salt pork

1 1/2 lb lean veal, leg or
  shoulder
1/2 level teaspoon salt
Freshly ground black pepper
1/2 level teaspoon ground
  ginger
1/4 level teaspoon cayenne
  pepper
Grated rind of 1 orange
Juice of 3 oranges
4 tablespoons white wine
1 tablespoon Cointreau
1 8-oz piece pork rind
8 oz fat unsmoked bacon
  slices
3 oranges, to garnish
Parsley sprigs and lettuce
  leaves to garnish

Terrine of Veal à l'Orange

Prepare and bake this terrine the day before you intend to serve it.

1 Cut meat into neat, $\frac{3}{4}$-inch cubes and put them in a large bowl. Add the salt, a sprinkling of freshly ground black pepper, the ground ginger, cayenne, grated orange rind and juice, white wine and Cointreau. Toss until cubes of veal are well coated; cover and leave to absorb flavours for $2\frac{1}{2}$ to 3 hours. Mixture should taste very highly seasoned, as flavours weaken considerably after the terrine has been cooked.

2 Meanwhile, put pork rind in a pan of cold water. Bring to the boil and boil for 8 minutes; drain and rinse well under the cold tap. Remove fat from rind.

3 Preheat oven to fairly hot (425°F. Mark 7).

4 Select a 2-pint earthenware terrine with a lid, and a piece of wood which just fits the top of the terrine (for weighting it down after it has been cooked).

5 Lay prepared pork rind at the bottom of the terrine, skin side down. Cover with a layer of veal cubes, then a layer of bacon slices, and continue in this manner until veal and bacon are used up, ending with a layer of veal. Pour any remaining juices left over from veal over the top.

6 Cover terrine with a lid. Place it in a larger pan with hot water to come halfway up sides and bake for $1\frac{3}{4}$ hours, or until meat feels tender when pierced with a thin skewer.

7 Remove terrine from oven; uncover and place the plank on top. Weight the plank down (you will need at least 8 lb weight) and leave to cool under pressure. Then chill in the refrigerator, still under pressure, until the following day.

8 Just before serving: peel and divide two of the oranges reserved for garnish into segments. Cut the remaining one, unpeeled, into thin slices.

9 To serve: turn terrine out on to a board and cut into slices. Arrange them on a serving dish with a segment of orange on each slice. Decorate dish with orange slices and any remaining orange segments, and a few parsley sprigs or crisp lettuce leaves.

Terrine de Lapin

1 Bone rabbit as follows: chop off hind legs. Carefully slice fillets away from either side of the backbone, from the neck right down to where legs were removed. Put aside. Take as much meat from ribs as possible. Slice off front legs. Turn rabbit over, so eviscerated side is uppermost. Remove the small fillets of meat to be found on either side of the backbone in what was the stomach area. Trim off any remaining meat from carcass. Remove meat from legs, keeping flesh from top half of legs as whole as possible. You should be left with a total weight of between 2 and $2\frac{1}{2}$ lb meat.

2 Separate large pieces of rabbit meat (from backbone and legs) from the scraps.

3 Coarsely chop 2 oz of the pork fat. Sauté in a frying-pan until fat runs and coats base of pan. Sauté large pieces of rabbit in hot fat, a few at a time, until lightly coloured all over, and remove with a slotted spoon so that fat drains back into pan.

4 Chop rabbit liver coarsely. Sauté in fat remaining in pan just long enough to set the blood and turn the liver beige, 3 to 4 minutes.

5 Cut sautéed pieces of rabbit into strips, a finger thick and $1\frac{1}{2}$ to 2 inches long.

6 Cut gammon and a further 2 oz pork fat into $\frac{1}{4}$-inch cubes.

7 Combine rabbit strips with cubed gammon and pork fat in a bowl. Add brandy, Madeira, pâté spice, $\frac{1}{4}$ level teaspoon salt and freshly ground black pepper, to taste. Toss lightly to coat meats thoroughly; cover bowl and leave to absorb flavours for 1 hour.

8 Meanwhile, put pork fillet, remaining pork fat, rabbit scraps, and the rabbit liver, together with all the fat and juices left in the frying pan, through the coarse blade of a mincer. Blend thoroughly with chopped parsley, thyme, about $\frac{1}{2}$ level teaspoon salt and freshly ground black pepper; to taste.

9 Preheat oven to moderate (375°F. Mark 5).

10 Line base and sides of a $1\frac{1}{2}$-pint terrine with paper-thin strips of fat salt pork or unsmoked bacon (see page 583).

11 Divide minced mixture in three. Spread one-third evenly over base of terrine, pressing it down firmly.

12 Divide marinated mixture in half, making sure different types of meat are equally distributed between the two portions. Arrange one portion neatly on top of minced layer, laying the

Makes 12 thick slices

1 $4\frac{1}{2}$-lb rabbit, dressed weight, with liver

8 oz fresh pork fat

5 oz raw gammon, not too salty (see note below)

4 tablespoons brandy

4 tablespoons Madeira

1/2–3/4 level teaspoon pâté spice (see page 586)

Salt and freshly ground black pepper

10 oz pork fillet

3 level tablespoons chopped parsley

1/2 level teaspoon dried thyme

Thin slices of fat salt pork or unsmoked bacon

591

strips of rabbit in neat, parallel rows running lengthwise. Sprinkle with some of the marinating juices.

13 Repeat layer of minced mixture; cover with remaining strips and cubes of meat, arranging them in the same fashion, and sprinkle with remaining marinade juices. Cover with a final layer of minced mixture.

14 Cover top of terrine with more thin strips of fat salt pork or bacon. Put on the lid.

15 Stand terrine in a roasting tin. Place it at the door of the oven and pour in boiling water to come one-third of the way up sides of dish.

16 Bake terrine for about 1 hour, or until melted fat surrounding meat is quite clear, and juices flow golden without a trace of pink when terrine is pierced through the centre with a thin skewer.

17 Remove terrine from roasting tin. Pour off water; return terrine to tin and let it stand for 15 minutes before weighting it down with a board and a 3- to 4-lb weight (scale weights or cans). Leave until quite cold.

18 Replace lid and leave terrine at the bottom of the refrigerator for at least 48 hours before serving to allow flavours to develop and mature.

19 Serve from the dish, cut in thick slices.

Note: Make certain the gammon is mild, otherwise it could overpower the flavour of the whole terrine. If in any doubt, leave it to soak overnight in a large bowl of cold water.

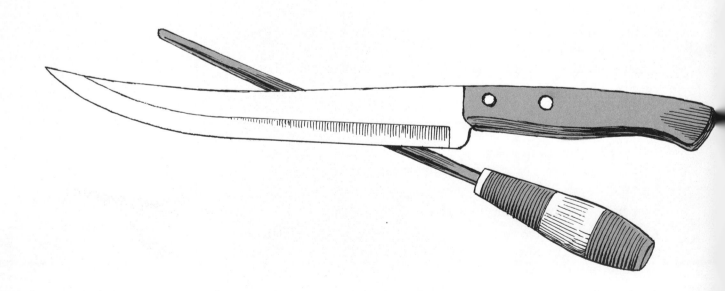

Terrine de Lièvre

Makes 24 thick slices

A long-term project, calling for 48 hours' marination and a 'maturing' period of at least 3 days, preferably up to a week.

1 Prepare hare meat cut off legs. With a sharp knife, remove 'fillets' of meat that run down either side of the backbone from just behind the head to where the hind legs were removed. Turn the carcass over. You will find two small fillets on either side of the spine in the area that contained the stomach. Remove these as well. Cut off all the flesh from the legs.

2 Reserve one of the back fillets. Cut remainder of hare meat into chunks and place them in a bowl.

3 Take reserved hare fillet. Cut it lengthwise into strips about 2 inches long and slightly thinner than your little finger. Place strips in a second bowl.

4 Take chicken breast meat, 4 oz gammon and 4 oz fresh pork fat, and cut them into ¼-inch dice. Add to second bowl. Season to taste with salt and freshly ground black pepper.

5 Cut remaining gammon and fresh pork fat into chunks. Add to first bowl.

6 Cut pork spareribs into chunks. Add to first bowl. Sprinkle with crumbled bay leaves; season to taste with salt and freshly ground black pepper, and toss well.

7 Divide brandy, Madeira and port evenly between the two bowls. Toss well. Cover bowls tightly with plastic wrap or foil and leave for 48 hours in a cool place to develop flavours.

8 When ready to make terrine, sauté finely chopped onion in butter and oil until soft and golden but not brown. Cool.

9 Take contents of the first bowl. Put it twice through the fine blade of a mincer, together with cold sautéed onion and its pan juices.

10 If you have a sturdy electric mixer on a stand, put the minced mixture in the bowl and allow mixer to beat at moderate speed for 3 to 4 minutes while you gradually add the double cream and beaten eggs. If this is not possible, beat vigorously with a wooden spoon while you incorporate these ingredients; then continue to beat until mixture is almost a smooth paste.

1 small hare, to give 2 lb boned meat
8 oz chicken breast meat
6 oz gammon
12 oz fresh pork fat
Salt and freshly ground black pepper
8 oz pork spareribs (meat only)
2 bay leaves, crumbled
4 tablespoons brandy
2 tablespoons Madeira
2 tablespoons port
1 Spanish onion, chopped
1 level tablespoon butter
1 tablespoon olive oil
1/4 pint double cream
2 eggs, beaten
1/2 level teaspoon pâté spice (see page 586)
About 1 1/4 lb fat salt pork
About 6 level tablespoons finely chopped parsley

11 Season paste with salt, freshly ground black pepper and pâté spice. Check seasonings by sautéeing a small nut of the mixture in butter. This will give you a fair idea of whether more seasoning is needed.

12 Now take the contents of the second bowl. Lift out all the strips of hare meat. Fold remainder of contents into the minced mixture, together with any juices left at the bottom of the bowl.

13 Preheat oven to moderate (350°F. Mark 4).

14 Line two 3-pint terrines with paper-thin slices of fat salt pork (see page 583).

15 Divide pâté mixture into 4 equal portions. Spread a quarter (i.e. one portion) evenly over base of each terrine.

16 Roll reserved strips of hare in parsley. Lay them in neat rows over the surface of the mixture in each terrine.

17 Spread remaining portions of pâté mixture evenly on top.

18 Cover surfaces with more paper-thin slices of fat salt pork. Cover terrines with lids.

19 Stand terrines in a large, deep roasting tin with hot water to come a third of the way up sides. Bake for about $1\frac{1}{2}$ hours, or until juices run quite clear when surface is pierced deeply with a skewer.

20 Remove terrines from the oven. Uncover and place a small board (or small, flat, rectangular dish) on the surface of each terrine. Weight down so that surface is submerged in juices. Leave until quite cold.

21 Remove weights and allow terrines to mature for a minimum of 3 days under mild refrigeration before serving.

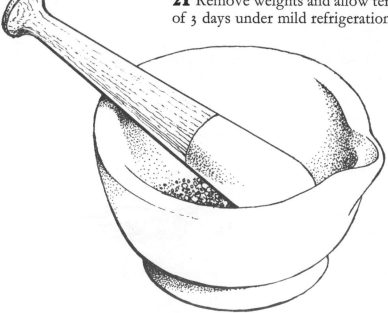

Galantine of Chicken with Pistachio Nuts

This dish is undeniably difficult and time-consuming, and must be started the day before you intend to serve it. Nevertheless, it deserves its fine reputation and will provide the highlight to a memorable cold luncheon or buffet table.

1 Ask your poulterer to bone the chicken, leaving the wings and drumsticks intact. If this is not possible, proceed as follows: with a very sharp knife, cut off the head, if still intact, then slit along the back from the neck to the parson's nose. Remove the latter, together with the neck, leaving as much of the skin behind as possible. Then, with the tip of your knife, start detaching the skin and flesh from the carcass, taking great care not to pierce skin. When you come to the wings and legs, disjoint them at the wing tips and drumsticks; draw the bones out, and continue boning bird until carcass can be lifted out completely.

2 Place boned bird on a board, skin side down. Sprinkle it with a tablespoon of cognac. Place chopped raw chicken meat and strips of raw chicken breast in a bowl and moisten with 1 tablespoon cognac. Leave both to absorb flavours for 2 to 3 hours.

3 Melt butter in a small pan; add very finely chopped onion, cover and simmer over a very low heat until soft but not coloured. Remove from heat and allow to cool.

4 Drain marinated chopped chicken meat, reserving juices. Mince it to the same consistency as veal and pork. Then blend veal, pork and chicken together thoroughly in a bowl.

5 In another bowl, beat egg with 2 level tablespoons double cream, adding remaining cognac and the drained-off marinade. Add sautéed onion and soaked, squeezed breadcrumbs; mix well. Then blend this mixture thoroughly with minced chicken and meat mixture. Season liberally with salt, freshly ground black pepper and a pinch of allspice, and work in halved or coarsely chopped pistachio nuts.

Serves 6–8

A 3- to 3 1/2-lb roasting chicken

4 tablespoons cognac

8 oz raw chicken meat, finely chopped

1 raw chicken breast, cut lengthwise into thin strips

2 level tablespoons butter

1 Spanish onion, very finely chopped

4 oz minced veal

4 oz minced lean pork

1 egg

2 level tablespoons double cream

2 oz fresh white breadcrumbs, soaked in cream and squeezed dry

Salt and freshly ground black pepper

Pinch of allspice

2 oz shelled pistachio nuts, halved or very coarsely chopped

4 slices lean unsmoked bacon, sautéed and coarsely chopped

5 pints white stock

3/4 pint liquid aspic

2 tablespoons Madeira

1 teaspoon lemon juice

To decorate

Thin strips of cucumber peel, sliced stuffed green olives, thin slices of cooked carrot, hard-boiled eggs, sliced, sprigs of flat-leaf parsley, capers etc.

6 Arrange half of the meat mixture down the centre of the boned chicken, pushing it inside the pockets left by the wings and legs. Cover with half the strips of chicken breast, and all the sautéed and coarsely chopped bacon. Spread remaining stuffing on top, again filling every crevice. Lay remaining strips of chicken breast down centre.

7 Bring two sides of chicken skin up to enclose stuffing completely, and sew up neatly, 'darning' ends of wings and legs as well to prevent stuffing seeping out, and reshaping bird as much as possible into its original form as you sew it.

8 Wrap stuffed chicken fairly tightly in muslin and tie securely at both ends with string, taking care not to distort the shape of the chicken as you do so.

9 Bring stock to the boil in a large pan or casserole. Reduce heat to simmering point and carefully lower in bird. Bring to the boil again slowly and simmer, with the water barely bubbling, for $1\frac{1}{2}$ hours.

10 When the bird is cooked, drain it and leave to 'set' for 30 minutes in its muslin before unwrapping it. Cool and chill overnight.

11 The following day, carefully remove threads from chicken. Flavour liquid aspic with Madeira, lemon juice and salt, to taste, and chill until syrupy and just on the point of setting. Coat bird with a thin layer of aspic and chill until firmly set.

12 Decorate chicken as desired, dipping each piece of decoration in liquid aspic before laying it in position. Spoon another coating of aspic over bird and pour remainder into a soup plate. Chill both chicken and remaining aspic until firm.

13 When ready to serve: lay chicken in the centre of a large, oval serving dish. Chop remaining aspic roughly and heap it decoratively around the sides of the dish.

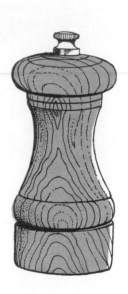

Galantine of Game

1 Bone pheasant, following directions for Chicken Galantine, above, but removing wing tips and boning legs completely. Reserve carcass.

2 Lay pheasant out flat on a large, shallow dish and add chicken meat, diced bacon and pheasant liver (or use a chicken liver). Season with salt and freshly ground black pepper, and sprinkle with thyme. Moisten with Madeira and half the brandy and *marc de Bourgogne*, mixed. Leave to marinate for 2 to 3 hours.

3 Preheat oven to moderately hot (400°F. Mark 6).

4 To make stock: split calf's foot or pig's trotters and break up veal bone (or have this done by your butcher). Put them in a roasting tin together with the pheasant carcass, and roast in the oven until well browned, about 45 minutes.

5 Transfer roasted bones to a large pan. Rinse out roasting tin with $\frac{1}{2}$ pint water and add to pan. Add chopped vegetables and the shin of veal. Cover with about $3\frac{1}{2}$ pints water and add salt and freshly ground black pepper, to taste. Bring to the boil, lower heat and simmer very gently for about 3 hours, skimming off scum as it rises to the surface.

6 In the meantime, take diced bacon, chicken meat and pheasant liver, shaking marinating juices back into the dish. Put them through the finest blade of your mincer twice, together with tongue, to make a smooth paste.

7 Add remaining brandy and *marc*, the juices in which meats were marinated, egg yolks, cream, softened butter and finely chopped onion, and mix well. Finally, beat in *foie gras* and grated lemon rind. Taste for seasoning, adding a little more salt and freshly ground black pepper if necessary.

8 Cut a piece of muslin large enough to enclose pheasant completely and lay the boned pheasant on it, skin side down.

9 Pat stuffing into an oval ball and place it on the pheasant. Bring skin up round the stuffing and stitch it together with a large needle and strong thread, moulding the bird back into its original shape as much as possible, and 'darning' holes left by wings and legs. Then wrap it in muslin and tie ends securely.

10 Strain stock and return to pan. Lower galantine into stock; bring back to simmering point over a low heat and cook gently, with the water barely bubbling, for $1\frac{1}{2}$ to 2 hours.

11 Drain galantine, reserving stock. Allow to cool for about 30 minutes before unwrapping muslin. Place a heavy, flat weight on top of galantine, and leave in refrigerator overnight.

1 large pheasant, with liver
8 oz chicken meat
6 oz unsmoked fat bacon, diced
Salt and freshly ground black pepper
Pinch of thyme
4 tablespoons Madeira
4 tablespoons brandy
4 tablespoons *marc de Bourgogne*
4 oz cooked tongue
2 egg yolks
4 tablespoons cream
1 level tablespoon softened butter
1/2 Spanish onion, finely chopped
2 oz *foie gras*
1 level teaspoon grated lemon rind

Stock
1 calf's foot or 2 pig's trotters
1 veal bone
Pheasant carcass
3–4 carrots, chopped
2 stalks celery, chopped
2 ripe tomatoes, chopped
1 Spanish onion, chopped
3/4 lb shin of veal on the bone
Salt and freshly ground black pepper

To clear aspic

3 oz lean minced beef

2 egg shells

2 egg whites

To decorate

Thin strips of cucumber
peel, thin slices of cooked
carrot, sliced stuffed green
olives, hard-boiled eggs,
sliced, capers, sprigs of
flat-leaf parsley etc.

12 Simmer remaining stock until reduced by half to make an
aspic. Pour it into a bowl and when cool, skim off fat. Correct
seasoning if necessary.

13 If aspic is cloudy, clear it as follows: return it to the pan; add
minced beef and crushed egg shells. Beat egg whites until frothy
and add to the pan. Bring to the boil, drawing pan off the heat
just as foam rises to the top, and allow to settle. Repeat this
process twice more. Finally, pour aspic through a muslin-lined
sieve and allow to cool to the point of setting.

14 When aspic is syrupy, coat galantine with it. Return galantine
to the refrigerator to set the coating.

15 Decorate galantine as described in the preceding recipe,
coating it with further layers of aspic until it is glossy and
completely covered. Set any remaining aspic in a shallow dish and
use it, roughly chopped, to decorate the base of the galantine on
its serving dish.

Makes 12–15 portions

A 4- to 5-lb duck

1 lb lean pork

1 lb pie veal

4 oz brown chicken meat
   (1 leg)

2 eggs

1 black truffle, finely
   chopped (optional)

2 level tablespoons chopped
   pistachio nuts

4 tablespoons cognac

4 oz *mousse de foie gras*

2 oz cooked tongue, diced

2 oz cooked ham, diced

Generous pinch each of
   cayenne, ground ginger,
   cloves, cinnamon,
   coriander and cumin

Salt and freshly ground black
   pepper

2 tablespoons olive oil

Ballottine of Duck

The only difficult part about making this ballottine is boning the
duck, but if you follow the instructions carefully and patiently,
and above all make sure that your boning knife is razor-sharp
before you start, you should be able to make a success of it.

This ballottine is roasted, rather than poached in stock. I find that
this gives a richer flavour. See which method you prefer.

The ballottine looks incredibly inviting, arranged in thin slices on
a serving dish, and decorated with orange slices and seeded
white grapes. Serve it as part of a cold buffet, or as an *hors-
d'œuvre* with each portion arranged on a lettuce leaf, accompanied
by crisp slices of hot toast.

For special occasions, garnish the stuffing with small sticks of *foie
gras* individually wrapped in paper-thin slices of pork fat.

1 Pull skin back from neck of duck and cut off neck, leaving skin
intact. Lay duck on board, breast down, and slit skin open down
the back with a very sharp knife; then carefully bone back of
duck, working your way to the wing and leg joints. Break joints
and leave legs and wings intact for the moment. Turn duck over
and ease skin and meat away from breast bone, taking particular
care as meat is very thin over the top of the breast, and you are
most likely to tear the skin at this point. Lift out the carcass and,
finally, bone wings and legs, keeping skin intact.

2 Preheat oven to moderate (375°F. Mark 5).

3 Remove any skin, fat and nerves from pork, veal and chicken leg. Dice and pass through the finest blade of your mincer three times, or until meats are reduced to a paste.

4 Put minced meats in a bowl; add next seven ingredients and blend thoroughly. Season to taste with spices, salt and freshly ground black pepper. Mixture should be highly seasoned at this stage as flavours tend to weaken when ballottine has been cooked.

5 Lay boned duck out flat on a board, skin side down, and arrange meat stuffing down centre. Bring sides of skin up to enclose stuffing completely and shape into a large sausage. Sew up neatly with coarse thread, taking care not to leave any openings, and tie the ballottine with string at 2-inch intervals, not too tightly, to hold it in shape.

6 Place ballottine in a roasting tin; pour over oil and roast for $1\frac{1}{2}$ hours, basting frequently with pan juices. Test duck by pushing a skewer through the thickest part; leave it there for a few seconds, then remove – the part of the skewer that came in contact with the centre of the stuffing should be hot. (If duck browns too quickly before it is cooked through, cover it with a piece of crumpled foil.)

7 Allow ballottine to become quite cold before removing string and threads. (To serve: see note above.)

Françoise's Pâté of Grouse

Serves 8–10

The ideal fate for a grouse of doubtful age. This pâté should be allowed to 'mature' for several days in the refrigerator before serving. However, if you are planning to make it more than 3 or 4 days in advance, it will be safer to seal the terrine by pouring a layer of melted pork or bacon fat over the top.

1 Bone grouse and cut flesh into chunks. Put them in a dish; add olive oil, red wine and herbs, and leave to marinate for 24 hours in a cool place.

2 The following day, drain pieces of grouse, reserving marinade juices, and place them in a bowl.

3 Mince the pork and veal coarsely, and add to the grouse, together with finely chopped onion, the chicken livers, crushed garlic and parsley. Mix well and season generously with salt and freshly ground black pepper.

4 Preheat oven to slow (325°F. Mark 3).

1 oven-ready grouse
4 tablespoons olive oil
6–8 tablespoons red wine
1/4 level teaspoon each dried thyme and oregano
2 lb lean pork belly
1 lb stewing veal
1 medium-sized onion, finely chopped
1/2 lb chicken livers
1 clove garlic, crushed
3–4 level tablespoons finely chopped parsley
Salt and freshly ground black pepper
1/2 lb fat bacon, thinly sliced
2 teaspoons powdered gelatine

5 Line bottom and sides of an ovenproof earthenware terrine with thin slices of bacon. Pack grouse mixture into terrine; pour over marinade juices and cover with a lid. If you are using a loaf tin, instead of a terrine, cover with foil.

6 Bake terrine for $2\frac{1}{2}$ to 3 hours, topping up with any remaining marinade or a little extra red wine if pâté dries out while it cooks.

7 Remove terrine from the oven. Pour off juices and put terrine aside to cool.

8 Soften gelatine in 1 tablespoon cold water. Skim terrine juices of fat; add to gelatine and stir over warm water until gelatine has completely dissolved. Taste and correct seasoning if necessary. (A small piece of chicken stock cube may be dissolved in the juices as well, if you feel the flavour is too thin.)

9 Pour juices back into terrine and allow to cool; then cover and chill in the refrigerator for several days before serving.

Serves 6–8

1 lb boned leg of venison
1 lb boned lean leg of pork
1 tablespoon olive oil
3 level tablespoons butter
1 tablespoon Madeira
1 tablespoon port
1/4 cooking apple, peeled, cored and chopped
2 oz button mushrooms, chopped
1/2 small onion, chopped
3 tablespoons brandy
6 oz chicken livers, separated into lobes and cleaned
1/4 pint single cream
1 egg
1/4 level teaspoon dried rosemary

Venison Pâté en Croûte

A *pâté en croûte* is traditionally shaped in a special tin with spring-form sides, which makes unmoulding it a comparatively simple matter. These tins are not, however, universally available, even in specialised kitchen-ware shops, so we have adapted the recipe to a standard 2-lb loaf tin (i.e. one measuring $9\frac{1}{4}$ by $5\frac{1}{4}$ by $2\frac{3}{4}$ inches). Should you wish to use some other mould, check first that the capacity matches.

You can, if you like, prepare this pâté in two stages, breaking off on completion of Step 10 and leaving all the 'components' tightly covered under mild refrigeration until the following day.

1 Remove about 4 oz neat strips from boned venison, 3 inches long and finger-thick. Put remaining venison once through a meat mincer and leave in a large bowl, covered, until needed.

2 Cut boned pork into 1-inch cubes and place in another bowl.

3 In a large frying-pan, heat oil with 1 level tablespoon butter. Sear venison strips in hot fat for about 3 minutes, or until well browned on all sides.

4 With a slotted spoon, transfer venison strips to a small bowl. Add Madeira and port; toss lightly; cover and leave to marinate in a cool place until required.

5 Add chopped apple, mushrooms and onion to cubed pork, and toss together until well mixed. Turn contents of bowl into the (same) frying-pan and sauté over a moderately high heat for about 5 minutes until lightly coloured.

6 Heat brandy in a melted ladle or small pan. Carefully set it alight and, when flames are burning briskly, pour over contents of frying-pan. Allow flames to burn out of their own accord; then scrape contents of pan back into bowl and leave to cool, covered.

7 Meanwhile, heat remaining 2 level tablespoons butter in the frying-pan and sear chicken livers over a high heat, tossing and turning constantly with a spatula, for about 3 minutes until well browned on the outside but still very pink inside. Remove from pan with a slotted spoon; place on a plate; cover and put aside until needed.

8 When pork mixture is cold, put it through the mincer. Then combine with minced venison and mince the mixture once more. Place in the bowl of a large, sturdy electric stand-mixer if you have one.

9 Beat cream and egg together until well blended. Add to minced meats, together with herbs, pâté spice, crushed garlic and crumbled bay leaf.

10 If using an electric mixer, beat the mixture at high speed until it is reduced to a smooth paste. If you do not have a large mixer on a stand (a hand-held electric mixer is unlikely to be sturdy enough for this purpose), keep beating and pounding the mixture with a wooden spoon until soft and pasty.

11 Drain venison strips thoroughly, and beat their marinating juices into pâté mixture. Season pâté to taste with salt and freshly ground black pepper. Add halved pistachio nuts, diced fat salt pork and ox tongue, mixing thoroughly but gently to avoid breaking down the cubes.

1/4 level teaspoon dried marjoram

1/4 level teaspoon dried thyme

1/4 level teaspoon pâté spice (see page 586)

1/2 clove garlic, crushed

1 bay leaf, crumbled

Salt and freshly ground black pepper

2 oz pistachio nuts, skinned and halved

4 oz fat salt pork, cut into 1/4-inch dice

4 oz cooked ox tongue, cut into 3/4-inch dice

About 4 oz fat salt pork, sliced paper-thin (see page 583)

Pastry for croûte

10 oz plain flour

1/4 level teaspoon salt

2 oz butter

2 oz lard

2 egg yolks

3 tablespoons water

Butter

Beaten egg yolk, to glaze

About 1/2 pint liquid aspic, flavoured with 2 tablespoons Madeira

12 Wrap strips of venison in paper-thin fat salt pork, using just enough to wrap once around each strip and no more. Put aside.

13 Preheat oven to very slow (300°F. Mark 2).

14 To make pastry for *croûte*: sift flour and salt into a bowl. Rub in butter and lard with your fingertips until mixture resembles fine breadcrumbs. Make a well in the centre.

15 Beat egg yolks lightly with 3 tablespoons warm water. Pour into well and knead to a firm, pliable dough, adding a tablespoon more of lukewarm water if necessary.

16 When dough is smooth, divide into two portions, one of them two-thirds of the total amount and the other one-third.

17 Place larger piece of dough on a floured board and shape into a rectangle. Roll out into a 16- by 11-inch rectangle approximately $\frac{1}{8}$ inch thick. (Do not trim pastry at this stage unless your rolling was wildly inaccurate.)

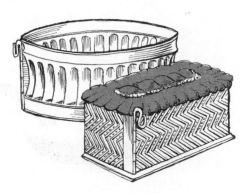

18 Grease a pâté mould or a 2-lb loaf tin (see note above) liberally with butter. If you are using a loaf tin, cut two strips of foil 6 inches wide, one long enough to run the length of the tin and up the sides with a 3-inch overlap at each end, and the other long enough to do the same across the breadth. Fold each strip in three lengthwise to make long strips 2 inches wide. Fit them in position to make a cross on the base of the tin. You will thus have strong little 'handles' which will help you to lift the pâté out when it is cooked. Butter strips of foil as well.

19 Lift sheet of pastry on a rolling pin and gently ease it into the tin, pressing it lightly on to base and into corners with the side of your hand. Avoid stretching pastry if at all possible. Trim off excess pastry, leaving a $\frac{1}{2}$-inch overlap around edge of tin.

20 Line base and sides of pastry-lined tin with paper-thin strips of fat salt pork, again allowing a good overlap around the top edge.

21 Cover base of lined tin evenly with half the minced meat mixture. Arrange wrapped venison strips on top in rows, running down the length of the tin. Cover with remaining meat mixture and level off top smoothly.

22 Fold overhanging strips of fat salt pork in over the surface of the pâté. Cover bare pâté with more strips of fat salt pork.

23 Roll remaining piece of pastry into a 'lid' which will cover top of tin with a $\frac{1}{2}$-inch overlap. Brush edges of pastry lining with beaten egg yolk. Lift pastry 'lid' on the rolling pin and carefully place it in position on top of pâté.

24 Gently but firmly bring edges of pastry lining and 'lid' together to seal them. Brush underside of pastry lining with water and roll the edges of the pastry under – like the hem of a silk scarf. Decorate the raised edge thus created by pressing all around it with the tines of a fork.

25 Using a $\frac{1}{2}$-inch, plain piping tube (or some other sharp, round cutting tool of $\frac{1}{2}$ inch diameter), carefully stamp out two holes at either end of the pastry lid.

26 Roll out pastry trimmings. With another, slightly larger cutter, stamp out two more circles. Then take the smaller cutter again and stamp out their centres to make little round 'collars'.

27 Brush edges of holes in lid with a little beaten egg yolk and fit pastry 'collars' in position around them.

28 Decorate top of pâté with 'leaves' cut from remaining pastry. Stick them in position with beaten egg yolk. Finally, glaze top and rim of pâté completely with more beaten egg yolk.

29 If you have 2 plain metal piping tubes, stick these firmly into the holes in the pastry lid to make funnels, taking care not to pierce the lining of fat salt pork underneath. Otherwise, improvise funnels from cornets of greaseproof paper.

30 Place pâté on a baking sheet and bake for $1\frac{3}{4}$ to 2 hours. Juices will bubble up into the funnels and be quite clear by the time pâté is cooked, and pastry will be a rich golden colour.

31 Remove pâté from oven. Leave to cool until just lukewarm. If using a loaf tin, pâté should be unmoulded at this stage before topping up with liquid aspic. Have ready a little malleable, *cold* butter to plug any holes and seal cracks that may appear during this operation.

32 Remove funnels (the juices will have subsided into the pâté by this time) and pour liquid Madeira-flavoured aspic into the holes. Do this a little at a time, through both holes alternately, to avoid an overflow. Leave pâté to become quite cold; then chill until firmly set. Pastry will cut more easily if left for 24 hours, and pâté continues to improve in flavour for up to a week under mild refrigeration.

Lesson 24

Pan Frying and Sautéeing

Most young cooks begin their culinary experiments with the minimum of equipment: a small saucepan, a heatproof casserole and that old stand-by, a frying-pan. To professional chefs, too, a really good frying-pan is one of the first requisites.

Choosing Your Frying-pan

An all-purpose frying-pan should be heavy, with a handle that doesn't conduct heat and won't melt if inadvertently left over a gas flame. The pan should have a flat bottom so that it stands steady and conducts heat evenly. If it's really meant to be an *all-purpose* pan, choose one with sloping sides (especially for omelettes and pancakes). Given a choice between a well-seasoned (see page 285), old-fashioned iron pan and a modern coated one, I'd go for the former every time. Black iron is the professionals' choice, though you do need to look after it carefully, wiping it with a film of oil to prevent rust getting a grip on it and storing in a dry place, especially if it's not to be used again for several days.

(For directions on how to season a frying-pan, see page 285).

General Rules for Pan-frying

At the risk of repeating advice and admonition from earlier lessons, do bear in mind the following:

● It is always safer to use butter in conjunction with oil or rendered fat salt pork (or both) when frying: butter, with its low burning point, needs this protection if the heat is high and/or prolonged. Or you can clarify the butter to rid it of the foam-like substance – which is what causes the trouble.

● Don't use fat skimmed from stock or jellied roasting juices and suchlike for dry-frying: it's impossible to get rid of *all* the moisture, and if left, this is liable to spit like mad once it heats up.

Keep them for the steady browning of meat intended for a pot-roast or casserole.

● It's easier to calculate the cooking time if all the morsels in the pan are of the same *thickness* – size is less important.

● If you want an ingredient to brown, don't overcrowd the pan. This makes it difficult for the steam to escape and lowers the heat in the pan so that, instead of being sealed, the ingredients end up simmering in their own juice.

● Coated foods (egg-and-breadcrumbed, for example) are more likely to remain coated if you chill them for an hour or so before frying. They are best fried in a plentiful supply of butter and oil, as they tend to absorb quite a lot and burn easily, if the pan 'dries out'.

● Use tongs or two wooden spoons to turn steaks, chops, etc., and avoid the juices pouring out of the pinpricks made by a fork.

General Rules for Dry-frying

Dry-frying is the answer for anyone who is cursed with an inferior grill that refuses to heat up to the necessary intensity. *You can fry successfully any cut of meat that can be grilled.*

The principle is as follows: a heavy, well-seasoned pan is heated up to the stage where a drop of water shaken on to the surface sizzles away almost instantaneously. The pan is then wiped quickly all over with a piece of fat (from the steak or chop) impaled on a long fork or a thick wad of absorbent paper dipped in oil. This should start smoking lightly almost immediately. Slap on your steak or chop, and when seared brown on both sides, reduce heat to moderate and continue to cook according to the individual tables on pages 608, 614 and 616.

● This method, which practically reproduces the charred surface of a grilled or barbecued steak, is *not* suitable for coated foods.

● The precious mixture of fat and juices left over at the end must *never* be discarded. Either pour them over as they are, or deglaze the pan with a splash of water, lemon juice, well-flavoured stock or wine and pour them over the meat. A small knob of butter stirred in at the last moment will make the juices rich and glossy.

Dry-frying Beef Steaks

● Only individual beef steaks can be dry-fried, i.e., you couldn't do a super steak in a frying-pan.

● Use the same quality of beef as for grilling.

● Similarly, steaks should be at room temperature before you start.

● Season with freshly ground black pepper as soon as you take them from the refrigerator to allow its flavour to permeate the meat, but leave salting until the last moment.

To Dry-fry a Steak

1 Leave a little border of fat around the steak (keep any you trim off for greasing the pan). Slash fat around steak to prevent it curling up. Sprinkle steak with salt – you will have peppered it in advance, see note above.

2 Heat a heavy frying-pan over a moderately high heat until drops of water shaken on to the surface bounce and sizzle away on contact.

3 Grease pan thoroughly with some of trimmed-off fat (*don't* forget the sides) impaled on a fork, or with a thick wad of absorbent paper soaked in oil.

4 When pan is practically smoking, slap on the steak and sear for just 2 minutes on each side, turning once.

5 Reduce heat to very moderate and time carefully according to the chart on page 608 to achieve the chosen degree of doneness.

6 Half a minute before steak is due to come out of the pan, add a good lump of butter. Let it froth and turn golden.

7 Transfer steak to a heated serving dish.

8 Pour butter pan juices over steak as they are. *Or* add a good splash of water, lemon juice, well-flavoured stock or wine, and stir briskly over a moderate heat to 'fuse' the fat and liquid into a flavoursome emulsion. Remove the pan from the heat before all added liquid has evaporated again (or you'll be back to square one.) Pour over steak and serve immediately.

607

TIMETABLE FOR INDIVIDUAL BEEF STEAKS

Cut	Weight	Thickness	Cooking time each side*	Degree of doneness
Fillet	4–6 oz	$1\frac{1}{4}$ inches	3 minutes 4 minutes 7–8 minutes $9\frac{1}{2}$–10 minutes	blue rare medium well-done
Tournedos	4–6 oz	2 inches	$3\frac{1}{2}$–4 minutes $5\frac{1}{2}$–6 minutes 7 minutes $8\frac{1}{2}$ minutes	blue rare medium well-done
Chateaubriand (serves 2–3)	16 oz	$1\frac{3}{4}$ inches	$2\frac{1}{2}$ minutes $3\frac{1}{2}$ minutes 4–$4\frac{1}{2}$ minutes 6–$6\frac{1}{2}$ minutes	blue rare medium well-done
Thick sirloin (serves 2)	11–12 oz	$1\frac{1}{2}$ inches	$2\frac{1}{2}$ minutes $3\frac{1}{2}$ minutes 4–$4\frac{1}{2}$ minutes 6–$6\frac{1}{2}$ minutes	blue rare medium well-done
Thick rump (serves 2)	14–16 oz	$1\frac{1}{4}$–$1\frac{1}{2}$ inches	3 minutes 4 minutes 7–8 minutes $9\frac{1}{2}$–10 minutes	blue rare medium well-done
T-bone	16 oz (weight including bone)	$1\frac{1}{4}$ inches	$2\frac{1}{2}$–3 minutes $3\frac{1}{2}$–4 minutes 7–8 minutes $9\frac{1}{2}$–10 minutes	blue rare medium well-done

* Including initial 2 minutes at high heat on each side (see note p. 607).

Tournedos with Red Wine Sauce

Per tournedos

Salt and freshly ground black
  pepper
Butter
3–4 tablespoons red
  Burgundy
Pinch of sugar
1 level tablespoon finely
  chopped chives or parsley

1 Dry-pan-fry tournedos to the desired degree (see table above). During this, it will probably be necessary to pour off excess juices – retain these in a small cup or bowl.

2 Transfer steak to a heated serving dish and keep hot while you prepare sauce.

3 Pour wine into frying-pan and return any juices that have been drained off. Stir in 1 level teaspoon butter.

4 Add sugar, salt and freshly ground black pepper, to taste; bring to a brisk boil, stirring; pour over steak; sprinkle with finely chopped chives or parsley and serve immediately.

Tournedos Chasseur

Make a point of having all the ingredients for the sauce measured, chopped etc., before you start, so that fried steaks do not have to wait longer than necessary.

1 Dry-pan-fry tournedos steaks to the desired degree (see table on page 608). During frying, it will be necessary to pour off pan juices (after about 3 minutes). Reserve these in a cup for later use.

2 Remove steaks from pan and keep hot.

3 Melt 1 level tablespoon butter in the same frying-pan and sauté finely chopped mushrooms and shallot for 2 to 3 minutes.

4 Add wine, chervil, tarragon and a tiny piece of stock cube, together with reserved pan juices, and continue to cook at a moderate pace so that mushrooms and shallot have softened by the time mixture has reduced by about half.

5 Stir in a further teaspoon of butter and the parsley; season to taste with salt and freshly ground black pepper; add any juices that may have collected around steaks while they were waiting.

6 Pour sauce over tournedos and serve at once.

2 tournedos steaks
Salt and freshly ground black pepper
Butter
3 oz button mushrooms, finely chopped
1 small shallot, finely chopped
1/4 pint dry white wine
1/2 level teaspoon dried chervil
Pinch of dried tarragon
Tiny piece of beef stock cube
1 level teaspoon finely chopped parsley

James Beard's Steak au Poivre

An example of dry-frying. This recipe by James Beard has an added refinement in that the crushed peppercorns are first marinated in cognac.

1 Take steak out of the refrigerator well in advance of cooking it. Nick fat in several places to prevent steak curling up as it cooks.

2 Crush peppercorns coarsely in a mortar; or place them between 2 sheets of greaseproof paper and crush with a rolling pin.

3 Put peppercorns in a small, screwtop jar. Sprinkle with a teaspoon of cognac; screw on lid and shake vigorously. Then leave to marinate for 3 hours.

4 Press generous amounts of marinated peppercorns on to both sides of steak.

5 Heat a small, heavy frying-pan until a sprinkling of water sizzles and evaporates on contact. Spear a piece of beef suet on to a fork (a trimming of fat from the steak itself is ideal) and rub all over base and sides of hot pan.

6 Return pan to heat, and when it is very hot again, slap on the steak. Time cooking according to the chart on page 608.

1 8-oz rump steak
12 black peppercorns
Cognac
Beef suet
Salt
Watercress sprigs, to garnish

7 Remove steak to a hot plate. Sprinkle with salt and keep hot.

8 Pour 2 tablespoons cognac into the frying-pan. Stir briefly and scrape bottom and sides with a wooden spoon. Then quickly pour over steak and serve immediately, garnished with sprigs of watercress.

Pan-fried Beef Patties with Tomato Sauce

Serves 6

3 oz fresh white breadcrumbs

1/4 pint milk

2 oz butter

3 tablespoons olive oil

2 medium-sized onions, finely chopped

4 oz good-quality sausage meat

1 lb leftover cooked beef, minced

1–2 cloves garlic, finely chopped

2 level tablespoons finely chopped parsley

Salt and freshly ground black pepper

1 egg, lightly beaten

1 oz flour

Tomato sauce

3 shallots, finely chopped

2 tablespoons olive oil

1 14-oz can peeled tomatoes

Generous pinch of thyme

1 small bay leaf

2 sprigs parsley

1/4 pint beef stock

Salt and freshly ground black pepper

1 level teaspoon sugar

A good dish for a family supper. Serve with tomato sauce on a bed of freshly cooked spaghetti.

1 Soak breadcrumbs in milk for 10 minutes. Squeeze out excess moisture.

2 Heat half the butter with 2 tablespoons olive oil in a frying-pan, and sauté finely chopped onions until soft and golden but not brown.

3 Add sausage meat and sauté until lightly coloured, crumbling it with a fork and mixing it thoroughly with the onions.

4 Add minced beef and, with the pan still over the heat, mix well. Stir in soaked breadcrumbs, together with the garlic and half the parsley, and season to taste with salt and freshly ground black pepper.

5 Remove pan from heat and blend in lightly beaten egg. Cool.

6 Prepare a simple tomato sauce: sauté finely chopped shallots in 2 tablespoons olive oil until soft and golden.

7 Add canned tomatoes, thyme, bay leaf and parsley sprigs, and simmer for a minute or two longer.

8 Moisten with stock; season to taste with salt, freshly ground black pepper and a little sugar, and simmer, covered, for 20 minutes, or until tomatoes are reduced to a purée.

9 While sauce is simmering, shape meat mixture into 12 balls the size of an egg. Dust with flour and flatten slightly to make round patties.

10 Fry patties in remaining butter and oil until golden brown on all sides.

11 Strain sauce over meat patties through a fine sieve and simmer gently for a final 3 or 4 minutes. Garnish with remaining parsley and serve immediately.

Pan-frying Veal Chops

Buy loin, rib or shoulder chops 1 to 1¼ inches thick. Ask your butcher to trim off the corner of the backbone of each chop so that the meat will lie as flat as possible on each side.

Trim veal chops if necessary, but leave a border of fat to moisturise and protect the meat.

Wipe dry with kitchen paper; season with freshly ground black pepper. If meat has spent some time in the refrigerator, allow it to come to room temperature. Season chops with salt just before cooking it.

Veal chops are best fried for 3 or 4 minutes on each side in a mixture of oil and butter, until they are well browned, and then cooked slowly in a covered frying-pan or casserole for 15 or 20 minutes or until their juices have turned from rose to clear.

Season veal chops with rosemary, tarragon, marjoram, and a little lemon juice or dry white wine.

Veal must always be well cooked. But be careful not to over cook it for veal, at its best, is moist and juicy, not dry.

Sautéed Veal Scallopini with Rosemary

1 Season veal on both sides with salt and freshly ground black pepper and cut veal into squares about 2 inches wide.

2 Heat oil with 2 level teaspoons butter in a frying-pan. When fat froths, add rosemary and leave over a moderate heat for a minute longer.

3 Add squares of veal in one layer. Cook for 1 minute on each side, or until cooked through but still juicy.

4 Transfer veal to a heated dish with a slotted spoon. Keep hot.

5 Add remaining butter to the pan, together with a teaspoon or two of dry white wine or water. Heat gently, scraping surface of pan clean with a wooden spoon.

6 Pour pan juices over hot veal and serve immediately.

Per portion

4 oz boneless veal, loin or
  fillet, sliced 1/4 inch thick
Salt and freshly ground black
  pepper
1 teaspoon olive oil
3 level teaspoons butter
1/4 level teaspoon dried
  rosemary
Dry white wine (optional)

Sautéed Veal Scallopini with Madeira

Per portion

4 oz boneless veal, loin or
  fillet, sliced 1/4 inch thick
Salt and freshly ground black
  pepper
1 teaspoon olive oil
3 level teaspoons butter
2–3 teaspoons Madeira

1 Season veal and cut into squares as above.

2 Heat oil with 2 level teaspoons butter in a frying-pan.

3 When fat froths, lay veal squares in it in one layer and cook for 1 minute on each side, or until cooked through but still juicy.

4 Transfer veal to a heated dish with a slotted spoon. Keep hot.

5 Add remaining butter to the pan together with Madeira and 1 or 2 teaspoons water. Heat gently, scraping surface of pan clean with a wooden spoon.

6 Pour pan juices over hot veal and serve immediately.

Sauté of Veal with Asparagus

Serves 4–6

1 lb asparagus tips
1 lb tender asparagus stems
Salt
2 lb veal
3 oz butter
Freshly ground black pepper
4 spring onions or shallots,
  finely chopped
1 1/2 oz flour
1/4 pint double cream
1 teaspoon lemon juice

An incredibly subtle yet simple dish. The asparagus stems should of course, be very tender, but for the sauce you can use tips that are past their prime.

1 Wash asparagus tips and stems carefully. Cook them in separate pans of simmering salted water: the tips will take about 8 minutes, the stems 3 to 5 minutes longer. Drain well, reserving cooking liquor, and keep hot.

2 Cut veal into 2-inch cubes, discarding any fat or gristle.

3 Melt butter in a deep frying-pan or heavy casserole without letting it colour. Add pieces of veal and sauté gently on all sides until golden.

4 Season veal to taste with salt and freshly ground black pepper. Add finely chopped spring onions or shallots, and sauté for a few minutes longer.

5 Sprinkle veal and onions with flour, and simmer gently until flour is cooked, taking great care as before not to let ingredients brown.

6 Moisten with $\frac{3}{4}$ to 1 pint of the reserved asparagus liquor; stir well, cover and simmer for 15 to 20 minutes, or until veal is tender.

7 Purée asparagus tips in a blender or by rubbing them through a fine sieve.

8 Stir purée into the veal, together with cream and lemon juice. Taste for seasoning, adding more salt, freshly ground black pepper or lemon juice, if necessary. (Remember that the asparagus liquor will already have contributed some salt.) Simmer for 7 to 8 minutes longer.

9 Transfer veal to a heated, large, deep serving dish. Pour over sauce. Arrange asparagus stems attractively in small bunches around sides of dish and serve immediately.

German Veal with Almonds

Serves 6

1 Sauté mushrooms in 1 tablespoon each butter and olive oil until soft and golden. Add salt and freshly ground black pepper, to taste; sprinkle with Madeira and allow to cool.

2 Beat escalopes out as thinly as possible.

3 Cut tongue into thin strips; divide into 6 bundles and pile each bundle in the centre of an escalope. Spoon mushrooms over the top and fold each escalope into an envelope.

4 Beat egg(s) lightly with a little water. Toss breadcrumbs with flaked almonds.

5 Dust veal 'envelopes' with flour; dip into beaten egg and coat with almond-breadcrumb mixture, patting it on firmly. Chill.

6 To cook veal: melt remaining butter and oil, and fry veal 'envelopes' slowly on both sides until golden brown, about 10 minutes. Serve immediately with a Quick Hollandaise Sauce.

6 oz button mushrooms, thinly sliced
4 tablespoons butter
4 tablespoons olive oil
Salt and freshly ground black pepper
2 tablespoons Madeira
6 veal escalopes, about 4–5 oz each
6 oz cooked tongue
1–2 eggs
3 oz fine dry breadcrumbs
2 oz flaked almonds
Plain flour

Quick Hollandaise Sauce

Serves 6

1 Melt butter in a small pan, taking care that it does not bubble or sizzle.

2 Warm goblet of an electric blender and in it combine egg yolks with 1½ teaspoons lemon juice, 1½ tablespoons water, and a pinch each of salt and freshly ground white pepper.

3 Switch blender to moderate speed and when yolks are well mixed, remove lid and pour in butter in a thin stream. If butter is poured in slowly enough, sauce will thicken into a genuine Hollandaise. However, if it remains too liquid, transfer to the top of a double saucepan and stir over hot water for a few seconds to thicken it; conversely, an over-stiff sauce may be thinned by beating in a tablespoon or two of very hot water.

4 Add more salt, pepper or lemon juice, if necessary, and keep sauce warm over warm water. Do not let it boil or sauce will curdle.

6 oz butter
6 egg yolks
Lemon juice
Salt and white pepper

Pan-frying Lamb Chops

● Trim lamb chops if necessary, but leave a border of fat to moisturise and protect the meat. Wipe dry with kitchen paper; season with freshly ground black pepper, and if meat has spent some time in the refrigerator, allow it to come to room temperature (most important when so much of our lamb is frozen). Season chop with salt just before cooking it.

● Lamb chops are best fried in a mixture of oil and butter, or you can wipe the hot pan around with a piece of discarded lamb fat.

● When pan is thoroughly hot but *not* smoking, sear chop over a moderately high heat for 2 minutes on each side. Then reduce heat to moderate and continue to fry according to the chart below.

● A minute or so before chop is ready, add a knob of butter to the pan and when it has melted, turn chop over in it briefly to glaze it.

● Deglaze pan with a drop or two of water if liked; stir in a little more butter and pour over chop. Serve at once.

TIMETABLE FOR INDIVIDUAL LAMB CHOPS

Cut	Weight	Thickness	Cooking time each side*	Degree of doneness
Chump chop	about 6 oz	1 inch	3–3½ minutes 4 minutes	rosé well-done
Loin chop	about 5 oz	1 inch	3 minutes 4 minutes	rosé well-done
Best end of neck chop	about 3 oz	1 inch	3 minutes 4 minutes	rosé well-done

* Including initial 2 minutes at high heat on each side.

Important:
Marinated chops will take about 1 minute longer on each side.

Pan-fried Lamb Chops with Oregano or Marjoram

Serves 4

1 Heat olive oil and butter in 2 large frying-pans, then brown the chops, 4 at a time in each pan, for 3 to 4 minutes on each side (see chart), sprinkling chops generously with salt, freshly ground black pepper and dried oregano or marjoram, as you turn them.

2 Transfer cooked chops to a heated serving dish and keep warm.

3 Add lemon juice and parsley to pan and cook, scraping all crusty bits from sides of pan into sauce. Pour over chops and serve immediately.

8 thick loin lamb chops
2 tablespoons olive oil
2 level tablespoons butter
Salt and freshly ground black pepper
Dried oregano or marjoram
Juice of 1 lemon
2 level tablespoons finely chopped parsley

Pan-fried Lamb Chops with Herb Sauce

Serves 4

1 Preheat oven to 325°F. (Mark 3).

2 Heat olive oil and butter in a large frying-pan, then brown the chops, 4 at a time, for 3 minutes on each side. As they are done, season with salt and freshly ground black pepper and arrange them in a heatproof casserole, overlapping chops slightly.

3 To make herb sauce: pour off fat in the pan and add 4 level tablespoons of softened butter. When it has melted, add finely chopped onion and cook gently for 1 minute. Add dry white wine and finely chopped herbs and allow to simmer for a few minutes, scraping brown crusty bits from sides of pan into sauce.

4 Spoon herb and onion mixture over chops in casserole and heat casserole on the top of the stove until the liquid is simmering. Cover and cook in preheated oven for 15 minutes, turning the chops and basting them with their liquid in the casserole 2 or 3 times.

5 Transfer chops to a heated serving dish. Add chicken stock to the casserole and boil rapidly on top of the stove until the liquid has reduced and thickened slightly. Pour sauce over chops and serve immediately.

8 thick loin lamb chops
2 tablespoons olive oil
2 level tablespoons butter
Salt and freshly ground black pepper
Softened butter
4 level tablespoons finely chopped onion
8 tablespoons dry white wine
1 level tablespoon finely chopped fresh tarragon or chives, or a combination of the two
1 level tablespoon finely chopped parsley
4 tablespoons chicken stock (page 162)

615

Pan-frying Pork Chops

● Trim pork chops if necessary, but leave a border of fat to moisturise and protect the meat – it can always be cut off later if someone doesn't like it. Wipe dry with kitchen paper; season with freshly ground black pepper, and if meat has spent some time in the refrigerator, allow it to come to room temperature. Season chop with salt just before cooking it.

● Pork chops may be fried in lard, or a mixture of oil and butter; or the pan may be whisked round with a piece of the trimmed-off fat so that there is just enough to prevent it sticking to the pan.

● Heat frying-pan thoroughly over a moderately high heat; grease it, and when hot but *not*, this time, smoking, add the chop and brown quickly for 2 minutes on each side. Then lower heat to moderate and continue to cook for the time specified below.

● There is only one degree of 'doneness' for pork: moist and juicy, but without a trace of pink in the flesh. Test it by slipping a knife blade down between meat and bone, where it always takes longest to cook, and if necessary, continue to cook for a few minutes longer.

● Transfer chop to a heated serving dish.

● Deglaze pan with a teaspoon or two of water (or stock, or cider, or wine); stir in a small knob of butter to make it glossy; pour over chop and serve at once.

TIMETABLE FOR INDIVIDUAL PORK CHOPS				
Cut	Weight (including bone)	Thickness	Cooking time each side*	Degree of doneness
Chump chop	12–14 oz	1¼–1½ inches	6 minutes	well-done but juicy
Loin chop	9–10 oz 12 oz	¾ inch 1 inch	7 minutes 8 minutes	well-done but juicy
* Including initial 2 minutes at high heat on each side.				

Pork Chops with Almonds

Serves 4

1 Trim pork chops of excess fat if necessary. Sprinkle them with curry powder and salt and freshly ground black pepper, to taste.

2 In a heavy frying-pan, fry chops in butter over a moderate heat for 7 to 8 minutes on each side, or until cooked through but still juicy. Transfer chops to a heated serving dish and keep hot.

3 Pour off excess fat from frying-pan. Add flaked almonds and toss over a moderate heat for 2 to 3 minutes until golden. Take great care, as they burn easily.

4 Sprinkle chops with sautéed almonds and serve immediately, accompanied by whipped potatoes and a tossed green salad.

- 4 thick pork chops
- 1 level teaspoon curry powder
- Salt and freshly ground black pepper
- 1 level tablespoon butter
- 2 oz flaked almonds

Pork Chops à la Normande

Serves 4

1 Preheat oven to 325°F. (Mark 3).

2 Trim excess fat from pork chops. Chop up fat and place in a frying-pan over a moderate heat until fat has melted and pieces are shrivelled and crisp.

3 Dry chops with absorbent paper. Season generously with salt and freshly ground black pepper.

4 Remove fat bits from pan with a slotted spoon. Add thinly sliced onions and fry until onions are soft and are just beginning to turn gold. Remove onions with a slotted spoon. Reserve.

5 Add chops and fry over a moderately high heat for 5 minutes on each side.

6 When chops are well browned on both sides and practically cooked through, transfer them to a heatproof casserole, add fried onions; cover casserole and place in pre-heated oven.

7 Core and slice apples thickly into strips. Brush with lemon juice; dust with sugar.

8 Pour off most of the pork fat from frying-pan; add butter and, when it has melted, sauté apples for 2 to 3 minutes in the fat until apples are coloured on both sides and beginning to soften.

9 Cover chops and onions with apple rings and continue to cook in oven for a further 5 to 10 minutes, or until chops are cooked through.

10 Meanwhile, add apple juice or apple cider (or apple cider and water) to the pan. Return to a moderate heat and bring to the boil, scraping surface of pan clean with a wooden spoon. Taste and add salt or freshly ground black pepper if necessary.

11 Remove casserole from oven. Arrange chops on a heated serving dish and garnish with sautéed apple rings and onions. Pour over pan juices and serve immediately.

- 4 pork chops, 3/4 inch thick
- Salt and freshly ground black pepper
- 1 Spanish onion, thinly sliced
- 3 crisp tart dessert apples
- Juice of 1 lemon
- 2 level tablespoons castor sugar
- 2 level tablespoons butter
- 4 tablespoons apple juice or apple cider (or 2 tablespoons each apple cider and water)

Pork Chops Stuffed with Apple

Serves 4

4 thick pork chops
2 tart eating apples
1 level teaspoon soft brown
  sugar
2 level tablespoons flour
1/2 level teaspoon ground
  ginger
2 level tablespoons butter
Salt and freshly ground
  black pepper

1 Trim pork chops of fat if necessary. With a sharp knife, cut a horizontal slit in each chop, starting at the fat end and going right through to the bone, to make a 'pocket'.

2 Peel and core apples; slice them $\frac{1}{2}$ inch thick, then cut each slice in half. Sprinkle 4 half-slices with brown sugar and push one deep into each pocket. Reserve remaining apple slices.

3 Mix flour and ginger together on a flat plate. Coat chops with some of flour mixture, patting them firmly with the palm of your hand to close up pockets.

4 In a large, heavy frying-pan, fry chops in half the butter over a moderate heat for 7 to 8 minutes on each side, or until cooked through but still juicy. Transfer to a heated serving dish; sprinkle with salt and freshly ground black pepper, and keep hot.

5 Dust reserved apple slices with remaining flour mixture.

6 Add remaining butter to the pan in which chops were fried and, when melted, sauté apple slices until golden brown on both sides. Take care not to overcook them, or they will become mushy.

7 Serve chops garnished with sautéed apple slices. A few potatoes and a tossed green salad are all you need to accompany this informal dish.

Variation: Omit apples; in their place, stuff pork chops with 8 whole cocktail onions and 8 gherkins, finely chopped, which you have tossed together in a teaspoon of Worcestershire sauce.

Breaded Pork Chops with Rosemary

Serves 4

4 thick pork chops
1 level teaspoon grated
  onion
1 level teaspoon finely
  chopped parsley
1/2 level teaspoon dried
  rosemary
1 egg
Salt and freshly ground black
  pepper
Fresh white breadcrumbs
Lard or oil, for frying

1 Combine onion, parsley, rosemary and egg in a wide, shallow dish. Beat well with a fork and season generously with salt and freshly ground black pepper.

2 Have breadcrumbs ready on another wide plate.

3 Trim excess fat from chops if necessary – trimmings may be chopped, rendered down and used for frying the chops instead of the lard or oil. Wipe chops dry with absorbent paper.

4 Coat each chop first with seasoned egg mixture, allowing excess to drain back into dish, and then with breadcrumbs, pressing them on firmly. Put them on a plate and chill lightly for at least 30 minutes to set coating and at the same time allow flavours to penetrate meat.

5 When ready to fry chops, sauté any trimmings with a little lard or oil in a large frying-pan until they shrivel up and turn crisp. Lift them out with a slotted spoon. There should be a generous layer of melted fat in the pan, say $\frac{1}{8}$ inch deep.

6 Lay chops in hot fat – two at a time if necessary. Fat should be hot enough to foam when chops come in contact with it. Fry them over a moderate heat for 4 to 5 minutes on each side, or until coating is crisp and golden brown, and chops are cooked through. Meat in contact with bone should be quite beige, without a trace of pink. Drain on absorbent paper and serve immediately.

Pan-fried Liver with Apples

1 Have liver cut into slices $\frac{1}{4}$ inch thick. Dust with seasoned flour just before frying.

2 Heat 1 level tablespoon each butter and lard or bacon drippings in a large frying-pan over a moderate heat, and when hot, fry liver slices in batches (so that there is only a single layer in the pan at a time) for 30 seconds on each side. Remove liver slices to a plate.

3 Add remaining butter to pan and simmer onions over a moderate heat until a rich golden brown colour, about 10 minutes.

4 Add sliced apples to pan and continue to fry for a further 3 minutes, turning contents of pan over and over with a spatula to colour apples evenly.

5 Pour in stock and cider vinegar; bring to simmering point.

6 Return liver slices to pan, together with any juices that may have accumulated around them on the plate. Stir in parsley and heat through over a moderately low heat. Season to taste with salt and freshly ground black pepper, and serve immediately.

Serves 4

1 lb calves' or lambs' liver
Seasoned flour
3 level tablespoons butter
1 level tablespoon lard or bacon dripping
2 medium-sized onions, thinly sliced
2 crisp tart dessert apples, peeled, cored and sliced
1/4 pint beef stock
2 teaspoons cider vinegar
2 level tablespoons finely chopped parsley
Salt and freshly ground black pepper

Serves 4

1 lb calves' liver, thinly
   sliced (see note)
3 level tablespoons flour
Salt and freshly ground black
   pepper
1/2 lb button mushrooms
2 level tablespoons butter
2 tablespoons olive oil
Lemon juice

Garnish
Thin slices of lemon
Sprigs of parsley

Calves' Liver with Mushrooms

For this dish, the liver should be sliced about $\frac{1}{8}$ inch thick, providing roughly 16 *small* slices to the lb.

1 Mix flour, $\frac{1}{2}$ level teaspoon salt and a good sprinkling of freshly ground black pepper together on a plate.

2 Wash or wipe button mushrooms clean. Trim stalks and slice mushrooms thinly.

3 In a heavy pan, melt 1 level tablespoon butter with 1 tablespoon oil and a tablespoon of lemon juice. Add sliced mushrooms; toss well to coat them with lemony butter, and sauté over a moderate heat until soft and golden, 5 to 7 minutes. Season to taste with salt and freshly ground black pepper, and keep hot.

4 Dry liver slices on absorbent paper; then coat them with seasoned flour.

5 Melt remaining oil and butter in a large frying-pan. When fat is sizzling, arrange liver slices in it in one layer (unless you use two pans, you will have to fry the liver in two batches). Fry quickly on one side for about a minute, or until droplets of blood appear on the uncooked surface. Then flip slices over and fry quickly for 1 minute on the other side. Liver should be nicely browned on the surface but still faintly pink inside. Transfer slices to a well-heated serving dish, and fry remaining liver in the same way, using more butter and oil if necessary.

6 Garnish liver with sautéed mushrooms and their juices. Decorate with lemon slices and parsley sprigs, and serve immediately.

Serves 2–3

6 lamb's kidneys, about 1 lb
Butter
1 medium-sized onion,
   finely chopped
2 level teaspoons Dijon
   mustard
2 level teaspoons yellow
   French mustard
1/2 pint single cream
Croûtons of fried bread
1 tablespoon brandy
Salt and freshly ground black
   pepper
Finely chopped parsley, to
   garnish

Kidneys in Mustard Sauce

1 Skin kidneys. Cut out cores with scissors. Slice each kidney in two or three. Pat dry with absorbent paper.

2 Melt 2 level tablespoons butter in a frying-pan and simmer finely chopped onion gently until golden, about 10 minutes.

3 Stir in mustards and gradually blend in cream. Boil gently, stirring frequently, until sauce is reduced by about one-third.

4 Have *croûtons* ready on a large serving dish in a low oven.

5 While sauce is reducing, melt 2 oz butter in another frying-pan until hot and sizzling. Add sliced kidneys and sauté for 5 to 8 minutes, or until well seared on the surface but still a little pink inside.

6 With a slotted spoon, transfer kidneys to the *croûtons* in the oven.

7 Heat brandy in a large metal spoon or ladle; set it alight and pour over pan juices left behind by kidneys.

8 When flames have died down, combine pan juices with reduced cream sauce. Season to taste with salt and freshly ground black pepper. Sauce should have a good, coating consistency. If too thin, reduce a little further; if too thick, stir in a tablespoon or two of hot water.

9 Spoon sauce over kidneys, sprinkle with finely chopped parsley and serve immediately.

French Pan-fried Chicken

Serves 4

1 Cut chicken into serving pieces, reserving backbone.

2 Season chicken pieces well with salt and freshly ground black pepper, and put pieces, flesh side down, in a sauté pan or thick bottomed frying-pan just large enough to hold them comfortably. Add butter and olive oil and sauté chicken pieces until they are browned on all sides – about 10 minutes.

3 Add backbone and *bouquet garni*; cover pan and simmer gently for 20 minutes, removing wings and breasts after 15 minutes. They are the most delicate, and cook more quickly. Keep warm.

4 Remove remaining pieces and sauté finely chopped onion in pan juices until transparent. Then add garlic and dry white wine, and continue cooking until wine is reduced to half the original quantity.

5 Add tomatoes and simmer gently for 5 minutes more.

6 Return sautéed chicken to the pan and allow it to simmer gently, covered, over the lowest of heats for 5 minutes. (Note: Do not allow liquid to boil or your chicken will be tough.)

7 Wash mushrooms and trim stems. Combine butter and lemon juice in a small frying-pan; add mushrooms and simmer until mushrooms are tender. Season with salt and freshly ground black pepper.

8 Transfer chicken and sauce to a heated serving dish; garnish with mushroom caps and serve immediately.

1 tender chicken (2 1/2 to 3 lb)
Salt and freshly ground black pepper
2 level tablespoons butter
2 tablespoons olive oil
Bouquet garni (2 sprigs parsley, 1 sprig thyme, 1 bay leaf)
2 level tablespoons finely chopped onion
1 small clove garlic
4 fluid ounces dry white wine
1 pound ripe, red tomatoes, peeled, seeded and chopped

Garnish:
4 button mushrooms
2 level tablespoons butter
Juice of 1/4 lemon
Salt and freshly ground black pepper

Pan-fried Chicken with Mustard

Serves 4

1 3 1/2-lb frying chicken
2 level tablespoons German
  mustard
1 level tablespoon Dijon
  mustard
2 egg yolks
2 level tablespoons double
  cream
About 5 oz stale white
  breadcrumbs
Flour
Salt and freshly ground black
  pepper
Corn oil, for frying

1 Divide chicken into 8 joints, two from each breast and two from each leg. Pull off skin, using a piece of absorbent paper to give you a better grip, and pat each joint dry.

2 In a medium-sized bowl or deep soup plate, blend mustards smoothly with egg yolks and cream.

3 Have breadcrumbs spread out on one sheet of greaseproof paper, and a little flour on another.

4 Season each chicken joint with salt and freshly ground black pepper. Dust it with flour. Dip it in mustard mixture, turning it over to make sure it is entirely coated, and roll in bread-crumbs, patting them on firmly.

5 Place joints on a plate and chill for 3 to 4 hours to firm up the coating and allow the mustard flavour to penetrate the chicken.

6 When ready to fry chicken, select one large, deep, frying-pan (or two smaller ones) that will take all the joints comfortably in one layer. Pour in corn oil to a depth of about 1 inch and place pan(s) over a moderate heat.

7 When oil is hot enough to make a bread cube froth on contact, add the chicken joints – oil should not quite cover them. Fry over a moderate heat for 15 to 20 minutes, or until chicken is cooked through, crusty and golden brown, turning occasionally. (Use a pair of tongs or two spoons to avoid piercing the chicken.)

8 Drain chicken joints on kitchen paper and serve immediately.

Note: If you have to fry the chicken in two batches – or if it is not to be served immediately – you can keep it hot in an oven at the lowest setting for 15 to 20 minutes.

Lesson 25
Deep-frying

In many homes, deep-frying is a thing of the past. Cooks are reluctant to attempt it on their home ground, knowing full well that without adequate ventilation the whole house is liable to reek of fat. Unless your kitchen is equipped with a powerful extractor or you can keep the kitchen door shut and the window wide open while you work, you may be forgiven if you don't care to deep-fry when you're all dressed up for a formal dinner party. But please don't let this deter you from treating your family to crisp fritters and *beignets*, and nutty, home-made potato chips on less formal occasions.

Deep-frying Equipment

For easy, foolproof deep-frying, you should equip yourself with a large deep-frying pan and frying basket, and a thermometer for measuring the temperature of the fat or oil. However, you can start out without either of these if necessary.

Deep-frying pan Provided you have a large, wide, heavy saucepan with a flat base that sits securely on the hob, a long handle and a well-fitting lid to clamp on in case the fat catches fire, you are ready to go. Instead of the frying-basket, have a large slotted spoon to fish out the food when it's ready. Then, if deep-frying appeals to you, get a proper deep-fryer. It is much more convenient to use (a) because of the frying-basket, and (b) because the fat can be left in it between reasonably frequent frying sessions.

Fat thermometer A thermometer for measuring the temperature of fat, sugar syrups etc. is an invaluable piece of equipment to have around in the kitchen. In deep-frying, the temperature of the fat is probably the one most important factor: too hot, and the food will set and burn on the surface before it has had a chance to puff up and cook (or reheat) all the way through; not hot enough, and the surface will not be sealed quickly with the result that the fritter will be sodden with fat.

623

Until you get a proper thermometer, use the bread test to determine the temperature of the fat: cut a 1-inch cube of day-old bread. When you think the fat is hot enough, drop it in. The table below gives, roughly, the time it will take for the bread cube to turn crisp and golden brown:

> 350°F. – 90 seconds
> 375°F. – 60 seconds
> 425°F. – 30 seconds

Fat for Deep-frying

You can choose between lard, olive oil and one of the anonymous vegetable oils now on the market. *Lard* contributes more richness of flavour than any of the others, and I prefer it above all for doughnuts, sweet fritters and deep-fried pastries. *Olive oil* imparts a characteristic nutty flavour – some people love it, others dislike it intensely. If you enjoy the food of the Mediterranean, you will like to try potato chips, vegetables and fish deep-fried in olive oil. *Vegetable oils* are for dishes where you want no interference in the flavour of the food itself.

Butter and margarine are useless for deep-frying. Their burning point is way below the 375°F. usually required for deep-frying.

Regulating the temperature One of the trickiest parts about deep-frying is keeping the temperature of the fat or oil steady once you have heated it to the required level. If you're not careful, the temperature will continue to rise. In extreme cases, you can lower it quickly and efficiently by adding a lump of cold lard to the pan, or pouring in more cold oil. If you realise it in time, though, you can draw the pan to one side and carry on frying *off* the heat until the temperature settles down again.

A drastic drop in temperature may be caused if you attempt to deep-fry too many chips or fritters at one time. Avoid this either by frying them in small batches, or by turning up the heat briefly as soon as they go in.

Storing fat or oil There is no need to discard the fat (or oil) used after each session provided you filter out all the impurities before putting it away. If you keep adding more fresh fat (or oil) to the current batch, you will find this makes it last much longer. The fat should be discarded once it discolours badly, smells less than fresh and develops a tendency to smoke at a moderate temperature (375°F.).

Rules for Deep-frying

1 Never leave a pan of fat or oil to heat unattended. If it overheats, it will at best acquire a nasty, burnt flavour and have to be discarded, at worst catch fire.

2 Make sure that the level of the fat leaves at least $2\frac{1}{2}$ inches clear at the top of the pan. There is always a certain amount of frothing when the food is added, and if the fat spills over, it may cause a nasty fire. On the other hand, the *minimum* depth of oil or fat you can deep-fry in is between 2 and 3 inches.

3 Because of points 1 and 2 above, always have a metal lid near at hand so that if the fat does catch fire, you can quickly contain it by depriving the flames of oxygen. *Never* try to extinguish a burning pan of fat with water.

4 Make sure that the thermometer and any spoons etc. that come in contact with the hot oil are perfectly dry. Water causes the oil to spit viciously and you could give yourself a nasty burn.

5 For the same reason, carefully dry off uncoated (i.e. unbattered) food, chips for example, before adding them to the pan.

6 Don't fry too many fritters, or whatever, at a time. As we have already pointed out, this is likely to cause a sharp fall in temperature, and it may also result in fritters sticking together as they puff up. There should be enough room for the whole batch to bob about freely on the surface without getting in each others' way.

7 Recheck the temperature of the fat frequently.

8 Drain deep-fried morsels thoroughly on a bed of crumpled absorbent paper and *serve them immediately* as they rapidly lose their crispness.

Chips with Everything

Follow the simple rules below and limp, sodden chips will be a thing of the past.

● Use plenty of fat for frying chips – 3 pints should be enough for up to 2 lb potatoes – so that they don't crowd and stick together.

● Dripping, lard or vegetable oil can all be used. Olive oil gives a distinct and delicious flavour all of its own. Make sure your fat is fresh and sweet, and don't hesitate to throw it out if you suspect that it's going rancid.

● Use a proper deep-frying pan with a basket, and make sure it is large enough for your needs: the level of the fat should be at least $2\frac{1}{2}$ inches below the top of the pan, otherwise it may froth up over the top, and then you're in real trouble. (If the pan does catch fire, clap on a lid as quickly as you can, or failing that, cover the top completely with a heavy baking sheet to cut out the oxygen.)

● Chipped potatoes should always be rinsed thoroughly to remove excess starch from the surface, then dried carefully with a cloth. This is crucial not only for the sake of safety, but also because excess moisture would lower the heat of the fat as it evaporates and cause the chips to become saturated.

● Be very careful when you lower the basket of potatoes into the pan. There will inevitably be a certain amount of spitting and foaming, so stand well back.

● Finely cut potatoes such as game chips, *pommes allumettes* and *pommes pailles* should be cooked a handful at a time to give them plenty of room, and also because they tend to froth more vigorously.

● English chips and French fries are cooked in two stages. The first of these, which leaves the chips soft but still very pale, can be done well in advance (the same day, of course); the second stage takes place just before serving so that the chips come hot and crisp to the table. Always make sure that the second frying temperature is appreciably higher than the first. If it is not, your chips will be drunk with fat.

● Have by you plenty of crumpled absorbent paper. As soon as the chips are cooked, tip them out on to the paper to drain thoroughly. Serve immediately with a light sprinkling of salt.

Chips – English Style

Serves 4–6

2 lb medium-sized potatoes
3 pints fat or oil for deep-frying (see above)
Salt

1 Peel potatoes. Wash them and cut them lengthwise into slices $\frac{1}{2}$ inch thick. Then cut each slice lengthwise into sticks $\frac{1}{2}$ inch wide. Rinse potato sticks thoroughly under the cold tap to rid them of their surface starch and dry carefully with a clean cloth.

2 In a deep-frying pan, heat fat or oil to 350°F., or until a cube of bread dropped into it browns within 90 seconds. Lower heat to keep temperature steady.

3 Place potato sticks in the frying-basket. Lower them gently into the fat, at the same time raising the heat under the pan for a minute or two to compensate for the temperature loss that this will have caused.

626

4 Deep-fry potatoes for 5 minutes, or until soft but still pale.

5 Lift out the basket. Shake it lightly over the pan to get rid of the worst of the excess oil; then tip the chips out on to absorbent paper and drain thoroughly. (If chips are not to be given their second frying for some time, wrap them loosely in greaseproof paper and put aside.)

6 When chips are required, reheat pan of fat or oil to 425°F., or until a fresh bread cube browns in 30 seconds.

7 Return chips to frying basket; lower them into the hot fat, raising the heat as before to maintain the temperature. Fry chips for 2 minutes, or until crisp and golden.

8 Tip chips out on to fresh absorbent paper. Drain thoroughly and serve at once, sprinkled with salt.

Chips – French Style

Cut peeled potatoes lengthwise into slices $\frac{1}{3}$ inch thick, then into sticks $\frac{1}{3}$ inch wide. Proceed as above but give potato sticks 3 minutes' frying instead of 5 the first time around.

Pommes Allumettes

Cut peeled potatoes into slices $\frac{1}{8}$ inch thick, then into sticks $\frac{1}{8}$ inch wide. Wash and dry as above. Deep-fry once only, at 425°F., for 2 to 3 minutes, or until crisp and golden.

Pommes Pailles

Cut peeled potatoes into slices $\frac{1}{16}$ inch thick (paper-thin), then into fine strips, or use a special cutter. Wash and dry as above. Deep-fry once only, at 425°F., for about 2 minutes, or until crisp and golden.

Crisps (Game Chips)

Cut peeled potatoes into slices $\frac{1}{16}$ inch thick (paper-thin), or use a mandolin cutter if you have one. Wash and dry as above. Deep-fry once only, at 425°F., for 1 to 2 minutes, or until crisp and golden.

Pommes Soufflées

It would be dishonest of me to pretend that these crisp, puffed little pillows are easy to make. Luck plays a part in it, as well as the type of potato used, and even professional chefs admit to a high failure rate – i.e. of 'pillows' that have declined to puff.

The best potatoes to use are old, red-skinned ones. New potatoes don't work.

The theory is simple enough: potatoes are cut into slices $\frac{1}{8}$ inch thick, then trimmed into little oval pillows about 2 inches long and $\frac{3}{4}$ inch wide. Don't rinse them.

Deep-fry a small portion at a time at 275°F. for 2 minutes only until soft but not at all coloured. Drain and cool.

For the second frying, preheat fat or oil to 475°F. It is the sudden shock of this high temperature that turns the moisture left inside the pillows to steam and – in theory – puffs them up. Lower in the basket and turn the little pillows about gently with a slotted spoon so that they cook evenly.

Drain on absorbent paper and serve immediately – and console yourself with the fact that any pillows which have not puffed up will make excellent crisps.

Deep-fried Vegetables

Deep-fried Aubergines

Serves 4–6

4 large ripe aubergines
Salt and freshly ground black
  pepper
Plain flour
Olive oil for deep-frying

Serve deep-fried aubergines piping-hot as a summer appetiser, sprinkled with cinnamon and accompanied by a bowl of plain, cool yoghourt. Or, as an accompaniment to grilled meats or poultry. You'll find they are compulsive eating.

1 Wipe aubergines clean and trim off stems.

2 Cut aubergines in thin slices horizontally or vertically, depending on whether they are the long or round variety. Sprinkle with salt and leave in a colander for at least 30 minutes to allow bitter juices to drain away.

3 Rinse aubergine slices thoroughly. Pat them dry with paper towels and dust lightly with seasoned flour.

4 Preheat a pan of olive oil to 375°F.

5 Deep-fry aubergine slices in hot oil for 5 minutes, or until crisp and golden brown. Drain thoroughly on absorbent paper and serve immediately, otherwise they quickly become limp again.

Deep-fried Courgettes

Deep-fried courgettes make an excellent accompaniment to grilled meats or poultry.

1 Wipe courgettes clean and trim off stems.

2 Cut courgettes in thin rounds and dust lightly with seasoned flour.

3 Preheat a pan of olive oil to 375°F.

4 Deep-fry courgette slices in hot oil for 5 minutes, or until crisp and golden brown. Drain thoroughly on absorbent paper and serve immediately.

Serves 4–6

8 courgettes
Plain flour
Salt and freshly ground black pepper
Olive oil for deep-frying

Batters

Fritter Batter

A light, all-purpose fritter batter.

1 Sift flour and salt into a bowl, and make a well in the centre.

2 Pour in olive oil and 8 tablespoons tepid water, and stir with a wooden spoon, gradually incorporating flour from sides of well until blended to a smooth batter. Leave to rest for 30 minutes.

3 When ready to use batter: whisk egg whites until stiff but not dry, and fold in gently but thoroughly. Use immediately.

Makes $\frac{3}{4}$ pint

4 oz plain flour
Pinch of salt
2 tablespoons olive oil
8 tablespoons tepid water
2 egg whites

Beer Batter I

A light batter for meat, poultry, vegetables, fish and shellfish.

1 Sift flour and salt into a bowl, and make a well in the centre.

2 Pour in olive oil and gradually add beer, stirring with a wooden spoon to incorporate flour from sides of well. Batter should be completely smooth and slightly thicker than a *crêpe* batter. Leave to rest for 2 hours.

3 When ready to use batter: whisk egg white until stiff but not dry, and fold in gently but thoroughly. Use immediately.

Makes $\frac{3}{4}$ pint

5 oz plain flour
Pinch of salt
2 tablespoons olive oil
1/4 pint beer, preferably lager
1 egg white

Beer Batter II

Makes ¾ pint

6 oz plain flour
1/2 level teaspoon salt
2 eggs, separated
4 fluid oz lager
2 tablespoons melted butter

This rather strongly flavoured version of beer batter is excellent for deep-frying savoury morsels such as shrimps or prawns, or thin onion rings which you have first sprinkled with salt or blanched to mellow their flavour.

1 Sift flour and salt into a bowl, and make a well in the centre.

2 Beat egg yolks lightly with lager and pour into well. With a wooden spoon, gradually stir in the flour from the sides of the well to make a smooth batter.

3 When batter is free of lumps, stir in melted butter. Allow batter to rest for about ½ hour.

4 When ready to use batter: whisk egg whites until stiff but not dry, and fold in gently but thoroughly.

Japanese Tempura Batter

Makes ¾ pint

1 egg
8 fluid ounces water
1 tablespoon soy sauce
4 ounces plain flour

Whisk egg, water and soy sauce together until smooth; gradually sift flour into mixture, whisking lightly. For best results batter should remain a little lumpy, so don't over mix.

To Deep-fry Fish

Fish, when properly fried, should be light golden brown in colour and dry and crisp in texture, and as free from fat as if it had never touched it.

Small fish are better fried whole. Large ones should be filleted or cut into even-sized steaks, cutlets or fingers before frying. If whole fish, or fish segments, are very thick, make small slits in the sides to allow the fish to cook more evenly.

Always make sure that your fish is perfectly dry before frying. I usually pat any fish for frying dry with a clean cloth or paper towel before coating it with well seasoned flour, fine oatmeal or cornmeal, beaten egg and dry breadcrumbs, or a frying batter. Any of the above coatings will keep fat from entering the fish while it is immersed in the hot cooking fat or oil. And it will add a flavoursome crunchy coating to the fried fish, which adds immeasurably to the flavour.

If seasoned flour or flour and milk are used as a coating, apply it just before the fish is to be cooked, or the flour will become moist and the fish will not fry well.

Batter, too, should be applied only at the last moment. But the fish may be coated with egg and dry breadcrumbs sometime before it is to be fried – even the night before, if you intend to serve the fish for breakfast.

For best results, place a single layer of fish in a frying basket so that fish is not overcrowded and the hot oil can be in contact with all sides of the fish when frying.

Preheat your oil to 375°F. and fry the fish at 375° for about 3 to 4 minutes, or until golden brown. Transfer fish to absorbent paper to drain off excess fat and keep warm while you cook remaining fish in the same manner.

Always make sure your oil is reheated to 375°F. before adding the next batch of fish to be fried.

Deep-fried 'Fish-n-Chips'

Serves 4–6

1 Cut fish into serving pieces, 2 or 3 pieces per serving.

2 Place fish in a flat porcelain bowl and sprinkle with lemon juice, finely chopped onion and salt and freshly ground black pepper, to taste. Allow fish to marinate in this mixture for 1 hour.

3 To make 'chips': wash and peel the potatoes, cutting them into strips about $\frac{1}{8}$ inch square and about 3 inches long. Rinse in cold water and drain thoroughly.

4 Heat oil to 375°F. Fill frying-basket one-half to two-thirds full of potatoes and immerse it gently into the hot oil. Shake the basket from time to time while frying to keep potatoes from sticking together. Continue to fry until potatoes are nearly tender. Drain well and spread on a pan lined with paper towels to absorb excess oil while you fry remaining potatoes.

5 Make batter.

6 Sift flour, paprika, 1 level teaspoon salt, and freshly ground black pepper and cayenne pepper to taste, on to a flat dish. Dust the fish thoroughly in the seasoned flour.

7 Dip fish, piece-by-piece into the batter and deep-fry in the same oil (make sure heat is 375°F.) until golden brown and crisp. Place fish in a pan lined with paper towels and keep warm.

8 Bring oil to 375°F. again and refry potatoes in small quantities in frying-basket until golden brown. Drain.

9 Serve fish and chips together in a heated serving dish. Garnish with lemon wedges.

1 1/2 pounds cod or halibut
6 tablespoons lemon juice
1/2 Spanish onion, finely chopped
Salt and freshly ground black pepper
6 medium sized potatoes
Oil for deep frying
1 recipe batter
4 ounces sifted flour
1 level teaspoon paprika
Cayenne pepper
2 lemons, cut into wedges

8 scallops
2 eggs
4 tablespoons milk
2 tablespoons water
Salt and freshly ground black
    pepper
Flour
Fine breadcrumbs
Oil or melted fat for
    deep-frying
Tartare sauce, to serve

Deep-fried Scallops

1 Prepare scallops: Rinse scallops if necessary. Trim off any ragged edges, but leave red 'corals' attached. They are a delicacy. Slice each scallop into 3 pieces.

2 Beat eggs, milk and water together. Season with salt and freshly ground black pepper, to taste.

3 Combine 4 level tablespoons flour and 8 level tablespoons fine breadcrumbs in a flat bowl.

4 Dust scallops with flour and then roll them in flour and breadcrumb mixture.

5 Drop scallops, a few at a time, into deep hot fat or oil (375°F.). Fry for 4 minutes, or until golden brown. Skim oil or fat and reheat to 375°F. before frying remaining scallops.

6 Drain in a pan lined with absorbent paper. Serve very hot with tartare sauce.

Serves 4

1 recipe Tempura Batter
    (page 630)
24 large raw prawns
4 scallops
8 thin slices aubergine
8 thin slices courgette
8 sprigs parsley
Oil for deep-frying

Japanese Tempura

Batter dipped seafood and vegetables, deep-fried in hot vegetable oil until they are delicately golden, are a famous Japanese speciality which makes a deliciously different 'fry-up' for Western kitchens.

1 Make Tempura Batter (page 630).

2 Shell prawns, leaving tail fins attached. Remove black veins. Wash and drain dry.

3 Wash and trim scallops and cut into thin slices. Drain dry.

4 Make sure that all vegetables and seafood are thoroughly dry.

5 Fill a deep casserole or deep-fryer three-quarters full of oil for frying. Heat to between 355° and 370°F.

6 Dip prawns, sliced scallops and then vegetables, one by one, into the batter; holding each for a moment against the sides of the bowl so that all excess batter drips off. Then lower ingredients, one piece at a time, into the hot oil. When batter is golden brown (about 2 to 3 minutes) the *tempura* is done. Drain pieces as you cook them on absorbent paper.

How to Deep-fry Chicken

I love fried chicken – whether it is simply shaken in a bag with well-seasoned flour and then fried in oil or lard, or whether it is first immersed in a delicious beer batter and then deep-fried in oil to a rich, crunchy gold. It is delicious served cold with a spicy dipping sauce, or hot 'in the basket'.

Cut chicken – tender young birds are best for frying – into serving portions. Pat dry and cover with the coating of your choice. One of my favourites is the following which dips the chicken pieces first into a lemon- and herb-scented flour, then in beaten eggs and finally into fine dry breadcrumbs before deep-frying them in fat or oil.

1 To make lemon- and herb-scented flour: combine in a mixing bowl 5 oz plain flour, 2 level teaspoons dried rosemary, 3 level tablespoons finely chopped parsley and 1 level teaspoon finely grated lemon rind and season generously with salt and freshly ground black pepper.

2 Beat 3 eggs in another bowl with 3 tablespoons water.

3 Place 4 oz fine dry breadcrumbs in a shallow bowl. This is enough for 2, 3-lb frying chickens.

4 Coat each chicken joint with seasoned flour; dip in beaten egg (allowing excess egg to drain off) and repeat this process once more. Then coat with breadcrumbs. Chill for at least 1 hour before frying.

5 When ready to fry: heat fat to 350°F. or until a cube of bread fries golden brown within 60 seconds. Place 3 or 4 chicken pieces in frying-basket and fry for 20 to 25 minutes, or until juices run clear when chicken is pricked deeply with a skewer, and the breadcrumb coating is crisp and brown.

6 Drain deep-fried chicken pieces on absorbent paper while you fry the remainder of the chicken in the same way.

Note: Always remember that the white meat of chicken cooks faster than dark meat. So it is best to add the white-fleshed pieces after the dark meat has begun to brown.

Serves 4

1 frying chicken, about 2 1/2
  lbs
4 level tablespoons flour
1 level teaspoon salt
Freshly ground black pepper
Cayenne pepper
Oil or fat for frying

Serves 2–4

1 tender young chicken,
  2 1/2 to 3 lbs
Juice of 1/2 lemon
Salt and freshly ground black
  pepper
1/2 level teaspoon paprika
2 eggs
2 tablespoons water
Flour
Fine breadcrumbs
Lard for deep-frying
1 lemon, cut into wedges

Easy Fried Chicken

1 Cut chicken into serving pieces.

2 Shake chicken pieces in a paper bag with flour seasoned generously with salt and freshly ground black pepper and cayenne, to taste.

3 Place oil to a depth of 1 inch in a heavy frying-pan and heat to a temperature of 370°F. Drop the seasoned chicken pieces into the hot oil and fry 6 to 8 minutes. Turn chicken and continue to cook for 6 more minutes, turn once more and continue to cook until chicken is golden brown and tender.

Transfer the pieces to absorbent paper to drain off excess fat.

Serve immediately.

Wiener Backhendl (Viennese Fried Chicken)

1 Cut young chicken into 4 pieces.

2 Rub chicken pieces with lemon juice, salt, freshly ground black pepper and paprika.

3 Beat eggs with water until well beaten.

4 Dust chicken pieces with flour; dip in beaten egg and water mixture and then in fine breadcrumbs.

5 Melt lard in a large frying pan to a depth of at least 1 inch. Carefully place chicken pieces into the boiling fat and fry them to a golden brown on all sides.

6 Lower heat and continue to cook chicken until tender, without letting it take on any more colour. About 10 to 15 minutes.

7 Remove chicken pieces from fat with a slotted spoon and allow them to drain in a pan lined with kitchen paper to absorb excess fat.

8 Serve fried chicken on a heated serving dish with lemon wedges.

Oven-finished Fried Chicken

Serves 6

1 Cut chickens into serving pieces.

2 Beat eggs well with milk and water. Pour into a shallow bowl.

3 Spread fine breadcrumbs on a piece of aluminium foil. Sprinkle another piece of foil with sifted flour which you have seasoned with salt and freshly ground black pepper.

4 Preheat oven to moderate (350°F. Mark 4).

5 Heat equal quantities of butter (or lard) and olive oil in a large frying pan to give you a depth of at least 1 inch.

6 Dip chicken pieces into seasoned flour; into the egg and milk mixture and then roll well in fine breadcrumbs.

7 Place chicken pieces carefully into hot fat, turning them with a spoon and fork as they cook until they are golden brown.

8 Transfer chicken pieces to casserole; season with salt and freshly ground black pepper and place casserole in preheated oven.

9 Continue frying remaining chicken pieces until they are golden brown, as above, and then transfer to casserole. Allow chicken to cook 20–25 minutes in the oven.

2 tender young chickens, 2 1/2–3 lbs
3 eggs
3 tablespoons milk
3 tablespoons water
Fine breadcrumbs
8 level tablespoons flour, sifted
Salt and freshly ground black pepper
Butter or lard
Olive oil

Mushroom Beignets

Serves 4–6

Serve these crisp, golden mushroom fritters accompanied by a bowl of sharply flavoured tomato sauce. They make an excellent appetiser.

1 First prepare beer batter, which has to rest for 2 hours before using.

2 Wash mushrooms carefully, and trim stems and place them in a saucepan with dry white wine, lemon juice and salt and freshly ground black pepper to taste. Simmer until tender but still very firm, about 10 minutes. Cool.

3 Drain thoroughly and leave to become quite cold; then season generously with salt and freshly ground black pepper.

4 Heat a pan of oil for deep-frying to 375°F.

5 Whisk egg white (in Beer Batter I recipe) until stiff but not dry and fold lightly but thoroughly into batter.

6 Dip mushrooms (halve them if too large) into batter, a few at a time; shake off excess batter and deep-fry for 4 to 5 minutes, or until a rich golden colour. Drain thoroughly on absorbent paper and serve immediately.

1 recipe Beer Batter I (page 629)
8 oz firm white button mushrooms
3 tablespoons dry white wine
2 tablespoons lemon juice
Salt and freshly ground black pepper
Oil for deep-frying

Makes about 24

5 egg whites
6 oz freshly grated Gruyère
2 oz freshly grated Parmesan
1 egg yolk
Pinch of cayenne pepper
Freshly ground black pepper
6 level tablespoons very fine
  dry breadcrumbs
Oil for deep-frying

Souffléed Cheese Boulettes

Useful for serving with drinks. Prepare *boulettes* just before serving as they tend to become rubbery if left lying around too long.

1 Beat egg whites until stiff but not dry. Gently but thoroughly, fold in grated Gruyère and Parmesan.

2 Beat egg yolk lightly with a fork, adding a pinch of cayenne and freshly ground black pepper, to taste. Fold lightly into beaten egg white and cheese mixture.

3 Spread breadcrumbs in a shallow dish. Form balls of the cheese mixture and roll in breadcrumbs until thoroughly coated.

4 Heat a large pan of oil for deep-frying to 350°F.

5 Drop in *boulettes* a few at a time and deep-fry until puffed and golden.

6 Remove with a slotted spoon; drain on absorbent paper and serve immediately.

Serves 4–6

1 12-oz can whole-kernel
  corn, drained
2 eggs, lightly beaten
1/2 level teaspoon salt
Freshly ground black pepper
1 level teaspoon sugar
3 level tablespoons plain
  flour
About 2 oz butter

Corn Fritters

Corn fritters – crisp and golden – are the traditional accompaniment for Southern Fried Chicken. Try them next time you serve fried chicken or oven-fried chicken.

1 To make batter: mix first six ingredients together in a bowl, and stir lightly until well blended.

2 Melt butter in a frying-pan. Drop in batter using 2 level tablespoons for each small flat fritter, and spacing them well apart to allow them to spread. Fry over a moderate heat, turning fritters once only with a spatula, for about 3 minutes, or until golden brown on both sides.

3 Drain fritters on paper towels and serve hot.

Belgian Cheese Fritters

An excellent appetiser which should be served fresh and piping hot, before the fritters lose their crispness.

1 Prepare beer batter and leave to rest for 2 hours.

2 Prepare a thick white sauce: Melt butter in the top of a double saucepan. Stir in flour and cook over a medium heat, stirring constantly, until well blended. Add milk and cook, over hot water, until sauce is thick and smooth.

3 Add grated cheese(s), mustard, egg yolk, cayenne and cream, and beat vigorously with a wooden spoon until sauce is smooth and well blended. Season to taste with salt and freshly ground black pepper, and allow to cool.

4 When cheese sauce is lukewarm, whisk egg white until stiff but not dry, and gently but thoroughly fold it into the sauce.

5 Shape cheese mixture into walnut-sized balls, and chill in the refrigerator for ½ hour to firm them up slightly.

6 Heat a pan of oil for deep-frying. When it reaches 350°F., lower the heat so that the temperature remains steady.

7 Meanwhile, whisk egg white belonging to Beer Batter and fold it in as directed in the basic recipe.

8 Coat fritters with batter, making sure no bare patches remain, and deep-fry a few at a time for about 5 minutes, flipping them over as soon as one side is golden. Drain well on absorbent paper and serve very hot.

Serves 6

1 recipe Beer Batter I (page 629)
2 oz butter
2 oz flour
1/2 pint milk
4 oz freshly grated Gruyère or Parmesan (or half and half)
1 level teaspoon French mustard
1 egg, separated
Pinch of cayenne
4 level tablespoons double cream
Salt and freshly ground black pepper
Oil for deep-frying

Makes about 24

Filling

1/2 pint milk
1 small onion stuck with 2–3 cloves
1 bay leaf
2 oz butter
2 oz plain flour
1 medium-sized potato, cooked and mashed
1 level tablespoon finely chopped parsley
1 clove garlic, crushed
24 anchovy fillets, crushed
1 tablespoon lemon juice
Salt and freshly ground black pepper

Batter

4 oz plain flour
Pinch of salt
1 egg yolk
1/4 pint milk

Plain flour for coating
Oil for deep-frying

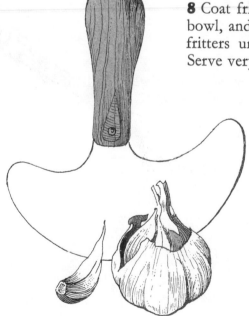

Anchovy Fritters

For these fritters the batter should not be too thin; otherwise there is a danger that the filling will seep out before the batter has had a chance to set.

1 To make filling: pour milk into a heavy pan. Add the onion stuck with cloves and the bay leaf; bring to boiling point, then remove from heat, cover and leave to infuse for about ½ hour.

2 In another saucepan, melt butter; blend in flour and cook over a low heat for 1 minute, stirring constantly, to make a pale *roux*.

3 Strain milk into *roux* gradually, beating vigorously to prevent lumps forming. Bring to the boil and simmer until thick, 4 to 5 minutes, stirring constantly.

4 Add mashed potato, finely chopped parsley, crushed garlic, anchovy fillets and lemon juice, and mix well. Season to taste with salt and freshly ground black pepper, and allow to become quite cold.

5 When mixture is cold and very stiff, take a teaspoonful at a time and shape into a ball. Roll in flour and chill in the refrigerator for at least 1 hour.

6 Meanwhile, prepare batter: sift flour and salt into a bowl; make a well in the centre; add egg yolk and milk, and work in flour gradually from sides of well, beating with a wooden spoon until batter is smooth.

7 Heat a pan of oil for deep-frying to 375°F.

8 Coat fritters with batter, allowing excess to drain back into bowl, and drop from a spoon into hot oil, a few at a time. Fry fritters until golden brown; drain well on absorbent paper. Serve very hot.

Chicken Croquettes

Serves 3–4

1 In a bowl, toss cooked chicken with finely chopped mushrooms, parsley, lemon juice and grated lemon rind.

2 Melt butter in a heavy pan. Blend in flour with a wooden spoon and stir over a low heat for 1 minute to make a pale *roux*.

3 Gradually add hot milk, stirring vigorously to prevent lumps forming; bring to the boil and simmer, stirring, for a further 3 or 4 minutes until sauce is smooth and thick. Then beat in a small piece of chicken stock cube and season to taste with salt and freshly ground black pepper.

4 Add lightly beaten egg in a thin stream, beating vigorously to prevent sauce curdling.

5 Fold sauce into chicken mixture. Cool and chill for 1 hour. Mixture should be very stiff.

6 Flour your hands and divide mixture into 8 equal portions. Shape into croquettes and chill in the refrigerator for 15 minutes to firm them up.

7 To coat croquettes: beat egg thoroughly with milk in a shallow dish. Have 2 other dishes ready, one with more flour, the other with fine dry breadcrumbs.

8 Dust each croquette with flour; dip in egg mixture, allowing excess to drain back into dish, and coat with breadcrumbs.

9 Heat a pan of oil for deep-frying to 375°F., and deep-fry croquettes for about 3 minutes, or until crisp and golden. Drain on absorbent paper and serve immediately.

12 oz cooked chicken, finely chopped
2 oz white mushrooms, blanched and finely chopped
4 level tablespoons finely chopped parsley
1 tablespoon lemon juice
1/4 level teaspoon finely grated lemon rind
4 level tablespoons butter
6 level tablespoons flour
12 fluid oz hot milk
1/4 chicken stock cube
Salt and freshly ground black pepper
1 egg, lightly beaten

To coat croquettes
1 egg
2 tablespoons milk
Flour
4 oz fine stale breadcrumbs

Oil for deep-frying

Almond Croquettes

Serves 4–6

1 Sift 2 oz flour into a heavy saucepan. Make a well in the centre and pour in milk. Beat with a wooden spoon, gradually incorporating flour from sides of well to make a smooth batter.

2 Place pan over a low heat and cook, stirring, until mixture becomes very thick. Continue to beat over a low heat for 1 minute.

3 Remove pan from heat. Beat in butter, ground almonds, sugar, a pinch of salt, and finally the egg yolks. When ingredients are smoothly blended, return pan to a low heat and stir gently for 1 or 2 minutes longer, or until mixture thickens again.

4 Spread mixture out on a shallow plate. Leave until quite cold and firm.

Plain flour
1/2 pint milk
1 oz butter
2 oz ground almonds
2 level tablespoons sugar
Pinch of salt
2 egg yolks
1 whole egg
3 oz stale white breadcrumbs
Oil for deep-frying
4 level tablespoons icing sugar, sifted
2 level tablespoons grated dark chocolate (optional)

5 When mixture has set, cut into 30 or 32 even-sized pieces. Dust your hands with a little additional flour and roll pieces into small croquette shapes.

6 In a shallow dish, beat whole egg until smoothly mixed. Put breadcrumbs on another dish.

7 Dip each croquette in beaten egg, allowing excess to drain back into dish, and coat with breadcrumbs. If croquettes are not to be fried immediately, return them to the refrigerator.

8 Heat a pan of oil for deep-frying to 375°F.

9 Deep-fry a batch of croquettes at a time for 1 minute, or until golden brown. Drain thoroughly on absorbent paper.

10 Pile up on a dish. Dust with sifted icing sugar (or sugar mixed with grated chocolate) and serve warm.

Serves 4–6

1 recipe Fritter Batter
 (page 629)
4 crisp eating apples, about
 1 lb
Lemon juice
Oil for deep-frying

Apple Fritters

There can be few people who will not succumb to the temptation of a crisp apple fritter. Serve them sprinkled with sugar (granulated, castor, or cinnamon-flavoured) or doused in hot syrup, and serve them quickly – no fritter will remain crisp if made to wait.

1 Prepare batter and put aside to rest for 30 minutes.

2 Meanwhile, peel apples and cut them into thin slices. Carefully remove core from each slice. Drop apple slices into a bowl of water acidulated with lemon juice as you prepare them to prevent discolouration.

3 When ready to fry fritters: whisk egg whites (in Fritter Batter recipe) until stiff but not dry, and fold into batter lightly but thoroughly.

4 Heat a pan of oil for deep-frying to 375°F.

5 Drain apple slices and dry each one carefully with a clean cloth or kitchen paper.

6 Coat slices in batter, holding them over the bowl for a few seconds to drain off excess, and deep-fry in hot oil, a few at a time, until crisp and golden, turning once.

7 Drain thoroughly on absorbent paper and serve immediately (see note above).

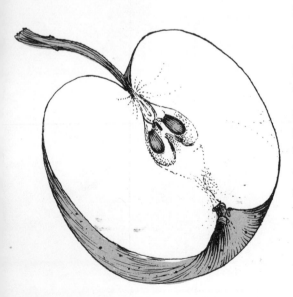

Banana Fritters

You can vary the flavour of these banana fritters by macerating them in rum instead of lemon juice.

1 Prepare fritter batter and put aside to rest for 30 minutes.

2 Peel bananas and cut each one into four chunks. Toss with lemon juice to prevent discolouration and sprinkle with castor sugar.

3 When ready to fry fritters: whisk egg whites (in Fritter Batter recipe) until stiff but not dry and fold into batter gently but thoroughly.

4 Heat a pan of oil for deep-frying to 375°F.

5 Coat each banana chunk with batter and deep-fry, a few at a time, until crisp and golden.

6 Drain fritters thoroughly on absorbent paper. Dust with cinnamon sugar or sifted icing sugar, and serve very hot.

Makes 24 fritters

1 recipe Fritter Batter (page 629)
6 bananas
3 tablespoons lemon juice
2 level tablespoons castor sugar
Oil for deep-frying
1 level tablespoon cinnamon-flavoured castor sugar or 1–2 level tablespoons sifted icing sugar

Bilberry Fritters

When fresh bilberries are out of season, you can use well-drained canned ones instead, restoring their sharpness if necessary with 1 or 2 teaspoons lemon juice.

1 Sift flour, baking powder, sugar and salt into a bowl, and make a well in the centre.

2 Beat egg yolks with 8 tablespoons water; pour into the well gradually, stirring in flour mixture with a wooden spoon to make a smooth, thick batter.

3 Fold in bilberries.

4 Heat a pan of oil for deep-frying to 375°F.

5 Whisk egg whites until stiff but not dry. Fold into batter with a large metal spoon.

6 Drop teaspoons of the batter into hot oil, a few at a time; deep-fry for 2 minutes, flip over and continue to fry for 2 minutes longer, or until fritters are puffed and golden.

7 Remove fritters from fat with a slotted spoon; drain on absorbent paper and serve immediately with a liberal dusting of sifted icing sugar.

Serves 4–6

6 oz plain flour
1 level teaspoon baking powder
1 level tablespoon castor sugar
1/2 level teaspoon salt
2 eggs separated
4 oz bilberries
Oil for deep frying
Icing sugar, sifted

Serves 4

1 1/2 lb young rhubarb stalks
Oil for deep-frying
Castor sugar, to serve

Fritter batter
4 oz plain flour
2 level tablespoons castor
  sugar
2 eggs, separated
1 tablespoon olive oil
1/4 pint milk
Pinch of salt

Rhubarb Fritters

1 Wash and trim rhubarb, and cut each stalk into 2-inch lengths.

2 To make fritter batter: sift flour and sugar into a bowl, and make a well in the centre. Add egg yolks and olive oil, and with a wooden spoon work them smoothly into the flour mixture, gradually adding milk. Then beat batter vigorously and if any lumps remain, strain it through a fine sieve.

3 Whisk egg whites and a pinch of salt until stiff but not dry. Fold into batter.

4 Heat a pan of oil for deep-frying to 375°F.

5 Coat each piece of rhubarb with batter, allowing excess to drip back into bowl, and deep-fry, a batch at a time, until crisply puffed and golden brown. Rhubarb inside should be soft but not disintegrating.

6 Drain fritters on absorbent paper and dust generously with castor sugar. Serve immediately.

Makes about 12

4 oz plain flour
1 level tablespoon castor
  sugar
1 egg
1 tablespoon brandy
5 tablespoons cold water
Oil for frying

Moulded Fritters

To make these pretty little fritters you will need special metal moulds. These look rather like branding irons and come in a variety of shapes – flowers, stars, butterflies. Children love them with golden or maple syrup, honey, vanilla or cinnamon sugar, and whipped cream.

1 Sift flour and castor sugar into a bowl, and make a well in the centre.

2 Break in the egg; add brandy and 3 tablespoons cold water. Using a wooden spoon or a wire whisk, beat them together, gradually incorporating flour from sides of well and adding more water to give a stiffish mixture, rather thicker than a pancake batter. You will probably need another 2 tablespoons water to achieve this.

3 In a deep, wide frying-pan, pour oil to the depth of the fritter mould, usually $\frac{1}{2}$ inch, plus $\frac{1}{4}$ inch or so. Heat to 400°F.

4 Rest mould(s) in hot oil for 3 minutes initially to heat them through.

5 To make a fritter, dip hot mould in batter, making sure it does not flow over top of mould; count slowly to 5; then, holding mould level, quickly transfer it to hot oil. Count to 5 again, by which time the fritter should have detached itself from the mould of its own accord, or with a little help from a spatula. When fritter is golden on the underside, flip it over and continue to fry until crisp and golden all over. Remove with a slotted spoon and drain on absorbent paper.

6 Continue making fritters 2 or 3 at a time as above, dipping the bare mould into hot oil for a count of 5 each time to reheat it.

7 Cool fritters slightly before serving.

Sweet Cheese Fritters

Before cooking with curd cheese, it is vital to extract as much moisture from it as possible. Even if the cheese seems dry when you buy it, do not ignore the draining process outlined below. You will be amazed by the amount of liquid that will be pressed out, and that would otherwise ruin the balance of the recipe.

1 Wrap cheese in a double thickness of fine muslin; place it in a colander with a heavy weight, such as a large pan of water, on top and leave it to drain for several hours. The cheese will become quite crumbly and very dry.

2 Prepare a batter by beating flour with oil, salt and 2 tablespoons water until free of lumps. Beat egg white until firm but not dry, and fold into batter gently but thoroughly. Leave to rest while you prepare cheese mixture.

3 Beat cheese thoroughly with egg yolks, sugar, salt, flour and rum or lemon juice, to taste.

4 Blend cheese mixture smoothly with prepared batter. Flavour with finely grated lemon rind and cinnamon.

5 Heat a pan of oil for deep-frying.

6 Whisk egg whites until stiff but not dry. (If they are beaten too stiffly they will be difficult to incorporate into the batter and the extra folding will cause loss of air.) Fold them carefully but thoroughly into cheese mixture.

7 When temperature of oil reaches 375°F., drop teaspoonfuls of cheese mixture into it, a few at a time to prevent them either sticking together or lowering the temperature of the oil too sharply. Hold the spoon still as the mixture runs off it, otherwise the fritters will ribbon out and not have a full, round shape. Flip them over almost immediately and deep-fry for 4 minutes in all. Lift fritters out with a slotted spoon and drain thoroughly on absorbent paper. Continue until all the mixture is used up.

8 Pile fritters up on a serving dish. Dust with sifted icing sugar and serve very hot and crisp.

Makes about 24

Cheese mixture
7 oz curd cheese
3 eggs, separated
4 level tablespoons castor sugar
Pinch of salt
5 level tablespoons plain flour
2 tablespoons rum or lemon juice
Finely grated rind of 1–1 1/2 lemons
1/4 level teaspoon ground cinnamon

Batter
5 oz plain flour
2 tablespoons oil
Pinch of salt
1 egg white

Oil for deep-frying
Sifted icing sugar

Lesson 26
Game

In years gone by, one could have filled a book with recipes for game birds and animals alone. Today, such books – and surprisingly enough, they are still being written – largely make escapist reading. When did you last see, or come to that, have you *ever* seen widgeon, teal or some of the other exotica that apparently still breed in these islands? As for wild duck, snipe, woodcock and capercailzie, we cooks rarely get a chance at them, and then only if we make friends with an enthusiastic hunter or go out there and shoot them ourselves.

The town-dweller must content himself with the few species that have survived the disappearance of hedgerows, and the havoc wreaked by chemical pesticides. And of those, it may not be long before the exquisite little partridge has become no more than a nostalgic memory. Remember what happened to the rabbit?

On the other hand, the British can still point with pride to their grouse, plentiful supplies of pheasant and superb venison, while more and more farmers are realising the profit to be made from rearing guinea fowl and quail. So the picture may still not be as black as it first appears.

General Rules for Cooking Game

Choosing a method The first thing to do is to determine the age of the beast. This is not too difficult, provided it's still feathered or, so to speak, on the hoof. But once it's plucked, or skinned and cut up into joints, as the case may be, the matter becomes more complicated.

A good poulterer on whose advice you can rely is worth his weight in gold. And it's also true that with experience one begins to develop an instinct for game and meat of all kinds, so that one can tell from its appearance if its a tender piece or likely to cause trouble.

All this is very important indeed for the cooking of game.

General rule number one in my book says: *Only the finest, most tender young game should be roasted.* If in doubt, forget about roasting and instead think in terms of a pot-roast, casserole, pie or terrine. The point is that unlike roasting, all those methods provide a built-in safeguard against drying out the precious juices – which are rare enough in game at the best of times – even if it takes longer to cook than you expected.

'Moisturising' game

All game, including artificially bred species like guinea fowl and quail, has one important characteristic in common: the meat is by its very nature dry, even in young birds, and it grows drier with age. There are several steps we can take to counteract this:

Barding This is advisable for all game, from a tiny quail to a haunch of venison. You simply take thin sheets of fat salt pork, fresh pork fat or fat unsmoked bacon, and wrap them all around the bird or joint, tying them in position with string. When the sheets melt, the fat runs down the sides of the meat, providing it with a continuous basting. Then, as the sheets of fat shrivel up, you take over, basting with the juices that have collected in the roasting tin – supplemented with wine, stock or water – and turning the bird or joint over at regular intervals.

Larding A slightly more tricky operation in that to do it professionally you require both a special tool (a larding needle or *lardoire*) and the knack of using it.

Larding is recommended for joints which are too thick to benefit from a barding strip. In fact, it's a sort of barding from within, whereby strips of fat (pork, salt pork or bacon) are pulled throughout the length of the joint (i.e. with the grain), or if the structure of the joint doesn't allow this, pushed down into the meat as deeply as possible from either end, so that the meat is subjected to constant moisturising as the fat melts from the heat of the oven or casserole.

Sturdy, professional *lardoires* are very difficult to come by. There are small ones to be found in kitchen-ware shops, which work on the principle of a sewing needle, i.e. you attach the strip of fat to one end and pull it through, but these are useless for a large joint, as the fragile fat invariably breaks after the first inch or two.

A *lardoire*, on the other hand, *pushes* the strip of fat through. It looks like a long, narrow metal trough ending in a point like an old-fashioned pen-nib. The other end of the trough is attached to a strong wooden handle.

Take a long strip of fat and press it into the trough. Push the trough through the length of the meat, turning gently in one direction so that the strip doesn't come loose, until the tip of the 'pen nib' emerges at the other end. Then dig the strip of fat out of the trough at either end and carefully draw the *lardoire* out again, wriggling it gently from side to side so that the fat stays embedded in the meat.

Failing a *lardoire*, the next best thing is your finger: simply make deep slits in the meat with the point of a narrow-bladed knife and push the strips of fat down as far as you can. In this case, though, you'll have to lard the meat *against* the grain unless the joint's quite short.

Marinating Another first-class way of moisturising, tenderising *and* improving the flavour of strong game is to soak it for a day or two in a highly flavoured marinade of wine, vinegar and vegetables. The marinade can be raw or cooked. If it is a cooked one, make sure it's *quite* cold before you add the meat.

If you're larding the meat as well, do so *before* putting it into the marinade – the latter will penetrate more easily and consequently work faster.

At the other end of the scale, tiny game birds like quail can also be marinated for a couple of hours to add interest to their otherwise delicate flavour.

Roasting Game

Here again, the rules are simple: *game birds* should be roasted as quickly as possible at a high temperature so that they get the minimum opportunity to dry out. Conversely, *larger game* which requires a longer time in the oven anyway, should be taken more slowly, otherwise the joint will be dry and fibrous on the surface by the time it has cooked through to the centre.

Casseroling Game

The technique of casseroling game is the same as that for all other meat and poultry – see Lesson 14. Briefly, keep the casserole down to a bare simmer throughout its cooking time, and if you find this difficult to regulate on top of the stove, try using the oven instead. As we have seen, an oven temperature of 250°F. or 275°F. (Mark $\frac{1}{2}$ to 1) is sufficient to keep a tightly covered casserole simmering gently once you've brought it up to bubbling point on top of the stove.

Grouse

The king of the moors, grouse has a subtle yet distinct flavour of the heather on which it feeds. Gourmets eagerly await the start of the season, when the first birds are rushed by rail, sea and air to the tables of grand restaurants all over the world.

A great deal of the aura that surrounds grouse stems from its rarity. Although many different birds around the world are described as 'grouse', the red or Scotch grouse has so far defied all attempts to transplant it from the British Isles.

The finest grouse for the table is the bird shot in the season of the same year in which it was hatched. Small at first, and no more than a portion for one, the birds grow and fatten as autumn passes until they are large enough to split in two.

Look for soft down under the wings and distinctly pointed flight feathers. Slim, pliable feet indicate a young bird, but don't look for spurs on the cock bird as a grouse does not have them.

Only young grouse should be roasted. The others fare best in casseroles, pies and terrines.

Season 12 August–10 December; best in mid-September to October.

Hanging About 7 days, longer in very cold weather.

Roast Grouse

1 Preheat oven to fairly hot (425°F. Mark 7).

2 Wipe bird carefully both inside and out with a damp cloth or absorbent paper. Reserve liver.

3 In a small bowl or cup, blend 1 level tablespoon softened butter with lemon juice and a generous seasoning of salt and freshly ground black pepper. Stuff seasoned butter into body cavity of grouse.

4 Bard breast of grouse with thin slices of fat salt pork or bacon and tie in place with fine string. Rub bird all over with salt and freshly ground black pepper.

5 Butter a small roasting tin or baking dish. Lay grouse in it.

6 Roast grouse for 35 to 45 minutes, depending on its size and whether you prefer it slightly pink or well done. Test by piercing flesh between leg and breast with a fine skewer or toothpick. You will be able to judge the state of the bird from the colour of the juices. For well-done meat they should run quite clear.

Serves 1

1 young grouse, 3/4–1 lb dressed weight, trussed, with liver

Butter

1 teaspoon lemon juice

Salt and freshly ground black pepper

2 thin slices fat salt pork or unsmoked bacon

1 slice bread, 1/4–1/2 inch thick, trimmed, to serve as base for grouse

1 tablespoon clarified butter

1 tablespoon olive oil

Cayenne pepper (optional)

Sprigs of watercress, to garnish

647

7 10 to 15 minutes before grouse is ready, fry bread in a mixture of clarified butter and olive oil until crisp and golden brown on both sides. Drain well on absorbent paper. Place on a heated serving dish and keep hot.

8 In a small pan, sauté grouse liver for 2 to 3 minutes in 1 level teaspoon hot butter, mashing with a fork. Scrape contents of pan into a small bowl. Add 1 level tablespoon butter and mash to a smooth paste. Season to taste with salt and freshly ground black pepper or a pinch of cayenne.

9 When ready to serve: spread fried bread *croûte* with liver mixture. Remove grouse from the oven; discard trussing thread and barding strips, and place bird on *croûte*. Skim pan juices of fat if necessary and spoon over bird. Garnish with sprigs of watercress and serve immediately. Bread sauce or browned breadcrumbs, game chips and redcurrant jelly are the usual accompaniments.

Gilbert Harding's Roast Grouse

Serves 2

2 young grouse, each 3/4–1 lb dressed weight, trussed, with livers
Butter
2 teaspoons lemon juice
Salt and freshly ground black pepper
1 apple, sliced
1/2 Spanish onion, sliced
2 small pieces of raw beef steak
2 thin slices fat salt pork or unsmoked bacon
2 slices bread, 1/4–1/2 inch thick, trimmed, to serve as base for grouse
1 tablespoon clarified butter
1 tablespoon olive oil
Cayenne pepper (optional)
Sprigs of watercress, to garnish

1 Preheat oven to fairly hot (425°F. Mark 7).

2 Wipe birds carefully both inside and out with a damp cloth or absorbent paper. Reserve livers.

3 In a small bowl or cup, blend 2 level tablespoons softened butter with lemon juice and a generous seasoning of salt and freshly ground black pepper. Rub body cavities of grouse with this flavoured butter.

4 Place sliced apple and onion in cavity of each bird with a piece of raw beef steak. You'll find that this will moisturise and flavour birds.

5 Continue to prepare grouse as in Steps 4–8 of Roast Grouse recipe above.

6 When ready to serve: spread fried bread *croûtes* with liver mixture. Remove grouse from the oven; discard trussing thread and barding strips; remove sliced apple and onion and beef pieces and place birds on *croûtes*. Skim pan juices of fat if necessary and spoon over birds. Garnish with sprigs of watercress and serve immediately.

648

Casseroled Grouse

1 Preheat oven to cool (250°F. Mark ½).

2 Wipe grouse clean and dry both inside and out, using a damp cloth or absorbent paper. Season inside and out with salt and freshly ground black pepper.

3 In a heavy, heatproof casserole large enough to hold grouse comfortably, sauté diced fat salt pork over a moderate heat until fat runs.

3 Add whole button onions, thickly sliced carrots and mushroom stalks to the casserole, and sauté until golden brown, 7 to 10 minutes.

4 With a slotted spoon, remove vegetables and pork bits to a plate, leaving behind fat. Add olive oil and butter to the casserole, and when hot, brown grouse thoroughly on all sides in the resulting mixture of fats for about 10 minutes.

5 Lower heat. Return sautéed vegetables and pork bits to casserole. Add *bouquet garni*, red wine and stock, and season to taste with salt and freshly ground black pepper and heat gently. At the first sign of a simmer, remove casserole from heat; cover tightly and transfer to the oven.

6 Bake casserole for about 2 hours, or until grouse are meltingly tender, regulating heat if necessary so that sauce never advances beyond a bare simmer, and turning grouse over occasionally to keep them moist.

7 About 30 minutes before the end of cooking time, prepare sautéed mushroom caps: heat butter and lemon juice in a small pan, and sauté mushroom caps gently for 5 to 8 minutes until golden. Add them to the casserole for the final 15 minutes of cooking.

8 To finish sauce: when grouse are tender, transfer them to a heated serving dish; remove any trussing strings or skewers. Pour sauce through a sieve into a saucepan. Garnish grouse with vegetables from sauce and return to the oven to keep hot.

9 Mash 2 level teaspoons each butter and flour to a smooth paste to make a *beurre manié*. Place saucepan over a moderate heat; add *beurre manié* in tiny pieces, stirring until they have dissolved into the sauce; bring to the boil and simmer, stirring, for 2 to 3 minutes until slightly thickened.

10 Flavour sauce with a little redcurrant jelly (to counteract bitterness of old grouse); correct seasoning, adding more salt or freshly ground black pepper if necessary, and spoon over grouse and vegetables. Serve immediately.

2 old grouse, dressed
Salt and freshly ground black pepper
2–3 level tablespoons finely diced fat salt pork
8 button onions, peeled
2 small carrots, thickly sliced
8 mushroom stalks (from caps, see below)
1 tablespoon olive oil
1 level tablespoon butter
Bouquet garni (3 sprigs parsley, 1/4 level teaspoon or 1 sprig of thyme, 1 bay leaf)
1/4 pint red wine, preferably Burgundy
1/4 pint chicken stock (page 162)

Sautéed mushroom caps
1 level tablespoon butter
1/2 teaspoon lemon juice
8 button mushroom caps

To finish sauce
2 level teaspoons butter
2 level teaspoons flour
1/2 level teaspoon redcurrant jelly

Serves 1

1 tender young grouse, trussed

1/4 cooking apple, cored

1/4 small Spanish onion

1/4 level teaspoon dried thyme

Salt and freshly ground black pepper

2 barding strips fat salt pork or unsmoked bacon

1 level tablespoon butter

1 tablespoon olive oil

Corn oil

To finish gravy

2 tablespoons stock, red wine or water

1 level teaspoon butter

Grouse en Papillote

1 Preheat oven to fairly hot (425°F. Mark 7).

2 Wipe grouse clean both inside and out with a damp cloth or absorbent paper.

3 Coarsely chop apple and onion. Mix them together in a small bowl, adding thyme and a generous seasoning of salt and freshly ground black pepper. Stuff body cavity of grouse with this mixture.

4 Rub grouse all over with salt and freshly ground black pepper. Bard breast with strips of fat salt pork or bacon, tying them in place with fine string.

5 In a small, heavy pan, thoroughly brown grouse all over in butter and olive oil over a steady heat, 10 to 15 minutes.

6 Take a strong white or glazed brown paper bag large enough to hold grouse comfortably. Brush bag well with corn oil, both inside and out.

7 Place browned grouse in paper bag, taking care not to tear or pierce the latter in any way. Use a paper tie tag (or string) to seal bag tightly. Lay bag on a wire rack.

8 Roast grouse *en papillote* for 20 minutes. Remove from the oven. Grouse may now be left to cool, still tightly sealed in its bag.

9 About 30 minutes before you intend to serve grouse, return the bag to the oven on its rack. Roast for 10 minutes.

10 Remove grouse from oven. Slit open paper bag and transfer bird to a heatproof baking dish just large enough to hold it comfortably. Discard barding strips. Pour over all the juices left behind in the bag.

11 Return grouse to the oven for a further 10 to 15 minutes to brown and finish cooking, basting with a tablespoon of stock, wine or water halfway through. To test bird: pierce the thickest part between leg and body with a small skewer or wooden toothpick. Juices should run clear or, if you prefer grouse slightly underdone, with the faintest trace of pink.

12 When grouse is cooked to your liking, transfer to a heated serving dish. Discard trussing threads or skewers. Keep hot.

13 Add remaining tablespoon of stock, wine or water to juices remaining in baking dish. Place over a moderate heat and bring to simmering point, stirring and scraping up all the crusty bits stuck to dish. Add 1 level teaspoon butter and stir until melted. Remove from heat. Taste for seasoning, adding a little more salt or freshly ground black pepper if necessary.

14 Spoon juices over grouse and serve immediately.

Guinea Fowl

The guinea fowl, like the partridge, is a cross between turkey and pheasant in flavour. Indeed, it can claim to be *the* original turkey. The guinea fowl as we know it is a farm-raised bird; though once dead, it must be hung like a game bird.

A young guinea fowl weighing up to 3½ or 3¾ lb is quite exquisite in flavour. But take care when buying an unplucked bird: the abundant purple-grey plumage flecked with white belies the size of the body inside.

Season As a domesticated bird, the guinea fowl has no season as such, but generally it is available from the beginning of the year to early summer, thus taking over neatly and conveniently when the true game birds are out of season.

Hanging Allow 4 to 7 days at most, depending on the age of the bird.

Serves 2

1 guinea fowl, about 1 1/2 lb
 dressed weight
Salt and freshly ground black
 pepper
Thin strips of fat salt pork
 or fat unsmoked bacon
2 level tablespoons softened
 butter
1/4 chicken stock cube
Sprigs of watercress, to
 garnish

Stuffing

2 oz unsmoked bacon
2 oz lean pork
1 oz fresh white breadcrumbs
Generous pinch of dried
 tarragon
Generous pinch of mixed
 spice
1 egg yolk beaten with 4–5
 tablespoons milk
1–2 level tablespoons finely
 chopped parsley
Salt and freshly ground black
 pepper

Roast Stuffed Guinea Fowl

1 Preheat oven to fairly hot (425°F. Mark 7).

2 Wipe guinea fowl both inside and out with absorbent paper. Pick off any remaining quills or feathers. Season cavity with a little salt and freshly ground black pepper.

3 To make stuffing: put bacon and pork through the finest blade of a meat mincer (or twice through the coarse blade).

4 Blend minced meats thoroughly with remaining stuffing ingredients, adding salt and freshly ground black pepper to taste. Stuffing should be fairly soft.

5 With a dessertspoon, pack stuffing into body cavity of bird. Skewer vent shut with a couple of small wooden toothpicks.

6 Season bird generously with salt and freshly ground black pepper. Truss it and wrap it completely in thin strips of fat salt pork or unsmoked bacon, tying them in place with string. Spread breast of bird with butter.

7 Place bird in a small roasting tin (or a larger tin in which you have put a smaller lining shaped of double-thickness foil to prevent roasting juices spreading out too thinly). Roast for 40 to 50 minutes, basting every 10 minutes with pan juices. Guinea fowl is ready when juices flow clear from a skewer prick through the thickest part of the inside leg.

8 When guinea fowl tests cooked, remove trussing threads, strings, skewers and remains of barding strips. Place bird on a heated serving dish; cover with foil and return to the oven. Switch off oven and leave for 10 minutes while you make a gravy with roasting juices.

9 Add just enough water to the roasting tin to deglaze it (about ¼ pint). Flavour with ¼ chicken stock cube and bring to the boil, scraping all the crusty bits from bottom and sides of tin into gravy with a wooden spoon. Simmer, stirring, until gravy has reduced slightly and has a good flavour. More salt or freshly ground black pepper should not be necessary. Pour gravy into a heated sauceboat.

10 Remove guinea fowl from the oven; garnish vent of bird with a few sprigs of watercress and serve immediately, accompanied by gravy.

Roast Pintadeau à la Flamande

(Roast Guinea Fowl with Apple Raspberry Garnish)

Steps **1–7** as in Roast Stuffed Guinea Fowl opposite.

8 As soon as the guinea fowl has gone into the oven, start preparing garnish. Peel and core apples. Place them in a small ovenproof casserole and brush with melted butter. Cover tightly with a lid or foil.

9 When bird has been roasting for 15 minutes, place the casserole of apples in the oven with it, near the bottom.

10 Toss partially thawed raspberries lightly with castor sugar.

11 When guinea fowl tests cooked, remove from oven and take away trussing threads and strings, skewers and remains of barding strips. Place bird on a heated serving dish; cover with foil and return to oven.

12 Remove apples from oven. Stuff cavities with sweetened raspberries. Cover and return to the oven. Switch off oven and leave for 10 minutes while you make a gravy with roasting juices (Step 9 in recipe opposite).

13 Remove guinea fowl and apples from the oven. Arrange apples around guinea fowl.

14 Stir any juices that have escaped from apples into the gravy. Pour gravy into a heated sauceboat.

15 Garnish vent of bird with a few sprigs of watercress and serve immediately, accompanied by gravy.

Serves 2

1 guinea fowl (about 1 1/2 lbs dressed weight), stuffed and roasted as in Steps 1–7 of the recipe opposite
1/4 chicken stock cube
Salt and freshly ground black pepper
Sprigs of watercress, to garnish

Apple raspberry garnish

4 crisp tart dessert apples
1 tablespoon melted butter
4 oz frozen raspberries, partially thawed
1 level tablespoon castor sugar

Guinea Fowl au Calvados

1 Wipe guinea fowl both inside and out with absorbent paper. Pick off any remaining quills or feathers.

2 Season bird both inside and out with salt and freshly ground black pepper. Cover breast completely with strips of fat salt pork or unsmoked bacon, and secure in place with fine string. Truss legs together to give bird a neat shape.

3 In a heavy, heatproof casserole just large enough to hold bird comfortably, heat half the butter and olive oil together. Brown bird thoroughly on all sides in hot fat, about 10 minutes.

4 Moisten with chicken stock. Immediately cover casserole; lower heat and cook very, very gently for 40 to 50 minutes, turning bird from time to time. When juices run clear from the thickest part of the inside leg, bird is cooked.

Serves 2

1 guinea fowl, about 1 1/2 lb dressed weight
Salt and freshly ground black pepper
Thin strips of fat salt pork or fat unsmoked bacon
2 level tablespoons butter
2 tablespoons olive oil
4 tablespoons chicken stock (page 162)
2 slices white bread, 1/4 inch thick, from a small loaf
2 crisp tart dessert apples
4 tablespoons Calvados

653

5 Meanwhile, prepare *croûtons* for garnish. Trim bread slices into squares and cut each slice diagonally from corner to corner twice to make 4 triangles (8 in all).

6 Fry bread triangles in remaining butter and oil until crisp and golden on both sides. Drain on absorbent paper.

7 Peel, quarter and core apples.

8 When guinea fowl is cooked, remove trussing strings and remains of barding strips.

9 Heat 2 tablespoons Calvados in a small metal ladle or pan. Carefully set it alight, and when flames are burning briskly, pour over guinea fowl in casserole. Allow flames to burn out of their own accord.

10 Transfer guinea fowl to a heated serving dish. Surround with *croûtons*. Keep hot in a cool oven while you finish garnish.

11 Add quartered apples to juices remaining in casserole. Cook over a moderate heat, tossing gently, for 5 to 7 minutes, or until soft, but still firm.

12 Flame as before with remaining Calvados.

13 Remove apples from casserole with a slotted spoon. Arrange on *croûtons*.

14 Skim casserole juices if necessary. Spoon over guinea fowl and serve immediately.

Note: Failing a guinea fowl, this recipe works beautifully with a baby (2-lb) chicken.

Partridge

For those who are not over enthusiastic about the strong flavours of game, partridge is the answer. The flavour of a young, plump partridge is quite exquisite, delicate like chicken, yet with a fullness and richness no farmyard bird would have.

A young partridge will have pale, yellow-brown feet and when plucked, the flesh will be a shade paler than that of an older bird. The latter is betrayed by its first flight feather which is rounded, rather than pointed at the tip, and darker, brownish feet.

The French draw a distinction between the younger partridge, which is known as a *perdreau*, and birds over six months old, which are called *perdrix*. Whence the saying:

> *A la Saint-Rémi*
> *Tous perdreaux sont perdrix.*

(After 1 October, all '*perdreaux*' turn into '*perdrix*'.)

Season 1 September to 31 January; best halfway through the season in October/November.

Hanging Prolonged hanging damages the delicate flavour of the partridge. Do not leave it for longer than 3 or 4 days.

Roast Partridge

Serves 1–2 according to its size

1 young partridge
Butter
1/4 level teaspoon dried thyme
Lemon juice
Salt and freshly ground black pepper
Barding strip of fat pork (or 2 unsmoked bacon slices)
Flour
Stock and wine, to finish gravy
Sprigs of watercress, to garnish

1 Preheat oven to fairly hot (425°F. Mark 7).

2 Wipe bird carefully both inside and out with a damp cloth or absorbent paper. Reserve liver.

3 Blend 2 level tablespoons of softened butter with dried thyme, lemon juice and salt and freshly ground black pepper, to taste. Stuff seasoned butter into the cavity of the bird, together with its liver.

4 Truss partridge. Cover breast with a paper-thin slice of barding pork fat or 2 slices of fat unsmoked bacon, and tie in place with string. Brush bird with a tablespoon of softened butter.

5 Lay partridge in a roasting tin or casserole just large enough to hold it so that cooking juices do not spread over too large an area – and roast until tender but still very juicy. The time will depend very much on the age and size of birds: a young and tender one will be ready in 25 to 30 minutes, while an older one will need closer to 45. Baste frequently with pan juices through-out cooking time, otherwise there is a danger of the flesh being on the dry side.

6 Ten minutes before the end of cooking time, untie the barding fat and discard it. Dredge breasts of partridge with flour and return to the oven to finish cooking and brown breast.

7 Transfer partridge to a hot serving dish and remove trussing threads or skewers. Keep hot while you make a gravy with the pan juices, a little stock and a splash of wine.

8 Garnish partridge with sprigs of watercress and serve with its own gravy. Bread sauce or browned breadcrumbs are the traditional accompaniments.

Serves 1

1/2 tender partridge
Corn oil
1 level tablespoon butter
1 tablespoon olive oil
Salt and freshly ground black
  pepper
Pinch of thyme or marjoram
1 slice cooking apple, cored
1 thin slice Spanish onion

Partridge en Papillote

1 Preheat oven to fairly hot (425°F. Mark 7).

2 Wipe partridge with a damp cloth or absorbent paper.

3 Take a strong white or glazed brown paper bag large enough to hold the piece of bird comfortably. Brush bag, both inside and out with corn oil.

4 Heat butter and olive oil in a frying-pan, and sauté bird until well browned on all sides. Remove to a plate with a slotted spoon. Sprinkle with salt, freshly ground black pepper and a generous pinch of thyme or marjoram.

5 In the same fat, sauté apple and onion slices for 1 to 2 minutes on each side until golden. Remove from pan with a slotted spoon and lay on top of bird.

6 Carefully slide bird into the oiled paper bag, taking care not to tear or pierce the latter in any way. Use a paper tie tag (or string) to seal bag tightly. Lay bag on a wire rack.

7 Roast bird for 20 minutes. Remove from the oven. Bird may now be left to cool, still tightly sealed in its bag.

8 About 25 minutes before serving, return bag to the oven on its rack. Roast for 10 minutes.

9 Transfer paper bag to a small roasting tin (or a large one into which you have fitted a smaller inner lining shaped from foil). Slit the bag open and fold paper back.

10 Return to the oven for a final 10 minutes to finish cooking and brown the top. Bird should be juicy, but juices should run clear when it is pierced through the thickest part with a tooth-pick or skewer. Serve each *papillote* opened, on a heated plate. Or if you prefer, remove half partridge and its garnish from bag and serve with juices and garnish on a heated plate.

Partridge with Lentils

1 Wipe partridges clean with a damp cloth, but do not wash them. Season both inside and out with salt and freshly ground black pepper.

2 Select a heavy pan with a tight-fitting lid. It should be large enough to hold partridges comfortably side by side. Heat butter and oil in it, and sauté finely diced fat salt pork until transparent.

3 Brown partridges in the resulting mixture of fats for 6 to 8 minutes, or until well coloured on all sides. Transfer partridges to a plate and keep warm.

4 In the same fat, sauté sliced onion and carrots until lightly browned.

5 Return partridges to the pan. Pour over dry white wine; bring to simmering point and simmer until reduced by half. Then add chicken stock. Season with a little more salt and freshly ground black pepper if necessary, and gently bring to simmering point again.

6 Cover pan tightly and continue to simmer over a low heat for 40 to 45 minutes, or until partridges are tender and juicy. (Older birds may take a little longer.)

7 When partridges have been simmering for about 15 minutes, start cooking lentils, which have already been soaked overnight. Drain them thoroughly and place them in a medium-sized pan with enough cold water to cover them by about 1 inch. Add remaining ingredients. Bring to the boil; lower heat; cover and simmer for about 20 minutes. Lentils should be tender without any suspicion of mushiness.

8 When lentils are cooked, drain them thoroughly and discard onion, garlic cloves and parsley stalks.

9 To serve: arrange partridges in the centre of a large, deep, heated serving dish. Heap lentils around them. Skim partridge juices if necessary and pour them over partridges and lentils, preferably through a sieve. Serve immediately.

2 dressed partridges, trussed
Salt and freshly ground black pepper
2 level tablespoons butter
2 tablespoons olive oil
4 oz fat salt pork, finely diced
1 Spanish onion, sliced
2 medium-sized carrots, sliced
1/4 pint dry white wine
1/4 pint chicken stock (page 162)

Lentils

12 oz large brown lentils, soaked overnight
1 medium-sized onion, stuck with 2 cloves
2 cloves garlic, peeled
3–4 parsley stalks
1/2 level teaspoon dried thyme

657

Serves 4

1 large green crinkly
   cabbage about 2 1/2 lb
Salt
1 old partridge
4 level tablespoons goose fat
   or lard
1 Spanish onion, sliced
2 carrots, thinly sliced
8 oz thick Continental ham
   sausage
12 oz smoked bacon (e.g.
   collar)
3/4–1 pint beef stock (page
   161)
Freshly ground black pepper
1 plump young partridge,
   part-roasted
   (see page 656 and the Note
   page 659)

Chartreuse of Partridge

A rather elegant, modern version of a very old French country dish. Once the old partridge has done its job of flavouring the cabbage, it is discarded, to be turned into a delicious clear game soup (see recipe opposite), and a freshly roasted bird is put in its place.

1 Preheat oven to very slow (300°F. Mark 2).

2 Rinse cabbage thoroughly under the cold tap. Hollow out the thick core from the base with a potato peeler, otherwise it will still be hard by the time remainder of cabbage is cooked.

3 Select a large, deep, short-handled pot or ovenproof casserole that will hold the whole head of cabbage with room to spare. Fill about two-thirds full with salted water and bring to the boil. As soon as water boils, place the cabbage in, head first. Make sure it is completely immersed; cover and cook for 5 minutes.

4 Drain cabbage and quickly immerse it in a bowl of cold water. Leave under the cold tap to cool.

5 Cut the old partridge into 4 joints, two from the breast and two legs.

6 Rinse and dry pot. Melt goose fat or lard in it and brown partridge pieces all over. Transfer to a plate.

7 In the same fat, sauté sliced onion and carrots for about 5 minutes until golden.

8 Cut sausage into 4 equal chunks and prick skin with a fork to prevent it bursting. Add to pot and continue to sauté for a further 5 minutes until coloured all over. Remove sausage chunks to plate with partridge.

9 Strip 3 or 4 of the large outer leaves from the cabbage. Lay them over the vegetables at the bottom of the pot.

10 Drain cabbage thoroughly and carefully ease apart its leaves. Tuck pieces of partridge deep down among the leaves. Fit the cabbage into the pot.

11 Cut bacon into 4 equal slices and lay them around the cabbage, together with sausage chunks. Pour over half the stock and sprinkle with salt and freshly ground black pepper.

12 Cover pot tightly and bake for 40 minutes. Then moisten with remaining stock and continue to bake for a further 40 minutes.

13 Cut the partially roasted partridge into 4 joints.

14 Remove pot from the oven. Replace joints of old partridge with fresh joints of roast partridge. Pour over juices from roasting tin. Cover and return to the oven for a final 10 to 15 minutes to reheat partridge and finish cooking.

15 To serve: lift out whole cabbage on to a large, deep serving dish. Lift the pieces of roast partridge out; lay them on top and surround with bacon slices and sausage chunks. Moisten dish generously with about three-quarters of the strained cooking juices (or as much as it will take), and serve immediately.

Note: Ideally, two ovens would be employed in making this dish, one for the pot of cabbage, the other to roast the partridge, but few people will be able to do this. Instead, roast the partridge *before* tackling the cabbage. *Remove it from the oven 10 minutes* before it is quite ready (so that it can finish cooking with the cabbage), and put aside until needed, covering the roasting tin tightly with foil to prevent the partridge drying out as it cools.

Clear Game Soup

Serves 3–4

1 Remove breast meat of partridge, keeping pieces as large as possible. Chop up remaining carcass and meat into small pieces.

2 Slice shin of beef thinly across the grain.

3 In a medium-sized pan, sauté chopped bacon in butter until fat runs. Add onion, carrot and celery, and continue to sauté over a steady heat for 10 to 15 minutes until well browned. Lower heat.

4 Add stock and sliced beef. Bring to the boil very slowly; add *bouquet garni* and season lightly with salt and freshly ground black pepper – seasoning will become more concentrated as stock reduces, so do not use too much. Simmer very gently, uncovered, for 1½ hours.

5 Strain stock through a sieve lined with absorbent paper or double-thick muslin. Leave until quite cold, preferably overnight in the refrigerator.

6 Prepare vegetable garnish shortly before serving. Peel or scrape carrot(s); peel baby turnip; wash leek thoroughly. Cut vegetables into short, matchstick-thick strips.

7 Skin reserved breast of partridge and cut it into slivers to match vegetables.

8 Remove every scrap of fat from surface of partridge stock. Pour into a pan and reheat gently.

1 old partridge, cooked (see recipe for Chartreuse of Partridge, page 658).
4 oz shin of beef (meat only)
1 slice unsmoked fat bacon, chopped
1 level tablespoon butter
1 onion, quartered
1 carrot, thickly sliced
1 stalk celery, chopped
1 1/2 pints beef (cube) stock
Bouquet garni (3 sprigs parsley, 1/4 level teaspoon or 1 sprig thyme, 1 bay leaf)
Salt and freshly ground black pepper
1–2 tablespoons medium dry sherry

Vegetable garnish
1–2 small carrots
1 baby turnip
1/2 leek, white part only

9 Poach carrot and turnip strips in a very little of the stock for 10 minutes, or until just tender. After the first 5 minutes, add leek and partridge strips.

10 Drain vegetable garnish and transfer to a heated soup tureen. Pour over partridge stock and stir in sherry to taste. Serve immediately.

Pheasant

Pheasants are the most beautiful wild birds still to be found in this country. The brilliant plumage of the cock and the soft, muted browns of the hen make a handsome sight when paired together in a brace.

A young cock bird will have short, rounded spurs which lengthen and sharpen with age. The hen is an altogether rounder, plumper creature. A young one will have soft, pliable feet and her plumage will be a shade lighter than that of an old bird. The feathers under the wing should be soft and downy, and the flight feathers rounded rather than pointed.

Young pheasants make superb roasts, but if in any doubt, play safe with a pot-roast or casserole to ensure that the flesh cooks to tenderness without becoming dry and stringy.

Season 1 October to 1 February; best halfway through the season in November/December.

Hanging In cold weather, a pheasant should be hung (by the neck) for 10 to 14 days, but it will only need half that time, even less in warm weather. Test it by pulling at the longest tail feather: it should pluck out quite easily.

Roast Pheasant

1 Preheat oven to fairly hot (425°F. Mark 7).

2 To make stuffing: in a small pan, sauté finely chopped onion in olive oil until soft and lightly coloured. Drain onion with a slotted spoon and transfer to a bowl.

3 Peel apple and grate it coarsely into the bowl. Quickly add lemon juice and toss with apple and onion to prevent apple turning brown.

4 Add softened butter. Blend ingredients together with a fork and season to taste with salt and freshly ground black pepper.

5 Wipe pheasant clean and pick off any stray feathers. Pack stuffing into body cavity, pushing it right in – the handle of a wooden spoon makes a good 'rammer'.

6 Cover breast of bird completely with strips of thinly pounded pork fat or slices of unsmoked bacon. Tie in place with fine string or strong thread.

7 Spread pheasant with butter and sprinkle lightly with salt and freshly ground black pepper. Place it in a small roasting tin.

8 Mix red wine and chicken stock together in a small jug, ready for basting pheasant.

9 Roast bird for 50 to 60 minutes, basting every 10 minutes, the first time with some of the wine and stock mixture, then alternately with pan juices and more wine and stock. Bird is ready once juices run clear when you pierce the thickest part of the inside leg with a skewer. Do not overcook it, or flesh will be dry.

10 Lift pheasant out of roasting tin, letting juices from body cavity drain back into tin. Place it on a heated serving dish. Remove trussing strings, skewers and remains of barding fat. Cover dish with foil and keep hot in a cool oven while you finish gravy.

11 Skim roasting juices of fat. Place tin over a moderate heat; add remainder of wine and stock mixture, and bring to simmering point, stirring and scraping the tin clean with a wooden spoon.

12 Stir in redcurrant jelly and breadcrumbs, and continue to simmer, stirring constantly, until sauce has thickened slightly. Taste and add salt or freshly ground black pepper, if necessary. Pour into a heated sauceboat.

13 Place a bunch of watercress sprigs in vent of pheasant for garnish, and serve with gravy. Bread sauce or browned breadcrumbs are the traditional accompaniments.

1 2- to 2 1/2-lb plump young pheasant, dressed weight, trussed
Strips of barding pork fat or unsmoked fat bacon
1 level tablespoon softened butter
Salt and freshly ground black pepper
6 tablespoons red wine
6 tablespoons chicken stock (page 162)
1 level tablespoon redcurrant jelly
2 level tablespoons fresh white breadcrumbs
Sprigs of watercress, to garnish

Stuffing
2 level tablespoons finely chopped onion
1 tablespoon olive oil
1 medium-sized cooking apple
1 teaspoon lemon juice
4 level tablespoons softened butter
Salt and freshly ground black pepper

1 tender young pheasant,
2–2 1/2 lb dressed weight,
with liver

Salt and freshly ground black
pepper

Barding strips of fat salt
pork or unsmoked bacon

Butter

1 tablespoon olive oil

2 medium-sized onions,
thickly sliced

1 small carrot, thickly sliced

Flour

1/2 pint chicken stock (page
162)

6–8 tablespoons dry white
wine

1 clove garlic, crushed

Bouquet garni (2 sprigs
parsley, 1 sprig thyme,
1 bay leaf)

2 tablespoons brandy

4 oz white button
mushrooms, trimmed

1 shallot, finely chopped

2 level tablespoons *foie gras*

1 level tablespoon double
cream

Croûtons of fried bread, to
serve

Salmis de Faisan à l'Ancienne

1 Preheat oven to fairly hot (425°F. Mark 7).

2 Wipe pheasant clean both inside and out with a damp cloth or absorbent paper, and season with salt and freshly ground black pepper. Bard breast with strips of fat salt pork or unsmoked bacon, tying them on with fine string. Lay pheasant in a small roasting tin.

3 Roast pheasant for 30 minutes, or until you judge it to be about two-thirds cooked.

4 Divide pheasant into 4 joints, taking the breast meat away from the carcass with each leg and wing, so that the main part of the carcass itself, including the breastbone, is left behind. Put aside in a covered dish.

5 Chop carcass up with a cleaver or heavy knife.

6 In a medium-sized pan, heat 1 level tablespoon butter with the oil. Add chopped carcass, thickly sliced onions and carrot, and brown them thoroughly over a moderate heat, 10 to 15 minutes. Sprinkle with $\frac{1}{2}$ level tablespoon flour and continue to sauté until lightly coloured, 2 to 3 minutes longer.

7 Add chicken stock, dry white wine, crushed garlic clove, *bouquet garni*, and a sprinkling of salt and freshly ground black pepper. Bring to the boil; reduce heat to simmering point; cover and simmer gently for 1 hour. Put aside until required.

8 If the pheasant is intended to serve 4, and you wish to give each person both dark and white meat, divide each joint in two. Arrange pieces of pheasant side by side in a large, shallow, heat-proof casserole or deep sauté dish.

9 Heat brandy in a large metal ladle over an open flame, or in a small pan. Carefully set brandy alight with a match and, when flames are burning strongly, pour all over pheasant. Allow flames to burn themselves out.

10 Add whole button mushrooms. Strain pheasant stock over contents of casserole, discarding carcass and vegetables.

11 Set casserole over a low heat and slowly bring to simmering point. Reduce heat to the barest simmer; cover casserole and cook very gently until pheasant is tender. This will take 15 to 20 minutes for a young bird; longer for an older one.

12 Meanwhile, in a small pan, sauté finely chopped shallot in 1 level tablespoon butter for 5 minutes until soft and golden.

13 Cut pheasant liver into chunks. Add it to the pan and continue to sauté gently for about 3 minutes, just long enough for liver to turn beige. Remove from heat.

14 Rub contents of pan, buttery juices as well, through a fine sieve into a small bowl. Blend in *foie gras* and cream with a fork. Taste and season with salt or freshly ground black pepper.

15 Prepare a *beurre manié* by mashing 1 level teaspoon each butter and flour to a smooth paste.

16 When pheasant is tender, transfer pieces to a heated serving dish with a slotted spoon. Keep hot while you finish sauce.

17 Add *beurre manié* to pan juices in tiny pieces, stirring until they have completely melted; bring to the boil and simmer until sauce has thickened slightly, stirring.

18 Reduce heat to very low. Blend liver mixture into sauce and reheat gently without letting it come to the boil again.

19 Pour sauce over pheasant. Garnish with fried croûtons and serve immediately.

Pheasant à la Crème

Serves 3–4

1 Wipe pheasant both inside and out with a damp cloth or absorbent paper, and sprinkle with salt and freshly ground black pepper. Reserve liver for later use.

2 Select a heavy, heatproof casserole large enough to hold pheasant comfortably. Heat 2 level tablespoons butter and the oil in it, and brown pheasant on all sides over a steady, moderate heat for 10 to 15 minutes.

3 Turn down heat. Add finely chopped onion and carrot, thyme and crumbled bay leaf. Cover casserole tightly and simmer gently for 20 minutes. Remove from heat.

4 Heat 2–3 tablespoons brandy gently in a large metal ladle over an open flame, or in a small pan. Carefully set brandy alight with a match and, when flames are burning strongly, pour all over pheasant and vegetables.

5 When flames have died down, pour in double cream. Bring to simmering point over a low heat; cover and simmer very gently until pheasant is tender and sauce slightly reduced. Turn pheasant occasionally and baste with creamy sauce to prevent it drying out. A young bird will take 30 to 40 minutes; an older one will need considerably longer.

6 While pheasant is cooking, trim slice of bread into a rectangle large enough to serve as a base for pheasant. Place it on a wire

1 tender pheasant, trussed, with liver
Salt and freshly ground black pepper
Butter
2 tablespoons olive oil
4 level tablespoons finely chopped onion
4 level tablespoons finely chopped carrot
1/4 level teaspoon dried thyme
1 bay leaf, crumbled
Brandy
1/2 pint double cream
1 large slice bread, 1/2 inch thick
Lemon juice
1 level teaspoon flour

663

rack and bake in a moderate oven (375°F. Mark 5) until lightly golden, crisp and dry. (This is known as a *croûte*.)

7 Shortly before pheasant is ready, melt 1 level tablespoon butter in a small pan and sauté pheasant liver over a high heat just long enough for it to change colour, turning and crushing lightly with a fork.

8 Transfer contents of pan to a small bowl. Add another tablespoon of butter and mash to a paste with your fork, flavouring the mixture with 1 or 2 drops of brandy and a squeeze of lemon juice. Season to taste with salt and freshly ground black pepper.

9 Spread liver mixture over *croûte*. Place it on a warmed serving dish and keep hot.

10 When pheasant is tender, lift it out of the casserole and discard trussing threads and skewers. Place pheasant on the *croûte* of bread and keep hot in a slow oven while you finish sauce.

11 Make a *beurre manié* by mashing flour to a smooth paste with 1 level teaspoon butter. Add to sauce in small pieces; place over a moderate heat and stir until dissolved. Bring to the boil and simmer, stirring, for 2 to 3 minutes until sauce has thickened slightly. Taste for seasoning, adding more salt or freshly ground black pepper if necessary.

12 Spoon sauce over pheasant and serve immediately.

Pheasant in Red Wine

Serves 4

1 pheasant, trussed, with liver
Salt and freshly ground black pepper
2 shallots, finely chopped
Butter
1 tablespoon olive oil
8 button mushrooms, with stalks
1/2 pint good red wine, preferably Burgundy
1/2 level tablespoon flour
8 button onions
1 level tablespoon sugar
1/2 teaspoon lemon juice
Chicken or game stock (made with a cube and/or trimmings of pheasant)

1 Wipe pheasant clean both inside and out with a damp cloth or absorbent paper. Season inside and out with salt and freshly ground black pepper. Stuff body cavity of bird with finely chopped shallots and its own liver.

2 In a sauté pan or deep frying-pan, melt 1 level tablespoon butter with olive oil. Over a steady, moderate heat, brown pheasant thoroughly all over for 15 to 20 minutes. Transfer pheasant to a medium-sized, ovenproof casserole with a tight-fitting lid. Cover and keep warm.

3 Trim stalks from button mushrooms. Put mushroom caps aside, and add stalks to sauté pan, together with wine. Bring to the boil over a high heat, stirring and scraping bottom and sides of pan clean with a wooden spoon. Boil until reduced by half. Remove from heat.

4 Make a *beurre manié* by mashing flour to a smooth paste with ½ level tablespoon butter. Add to hot wine sauce in small pieces, stirring until they have completely dissolved. Return pan to heat;

bring to the boil again and simmer, stirring, for 2 to 3 minutes longer until sauce has thickened.

5 Strain sauce over pheasant. Replace lid and put aside.

6 Preheat oven to very slow (275°F. Mark 1).

7 Simmer button onions in salted water to cover for 10 minutes; drain thoroughly.

8 Add 1 level tablespoon butter to pan and swirl over a low heat until melted. Then sprinkle with sugar; turn heat up to moderate and sauté for about 10 minutes, or until button onions are coated with a rich caramel glaze. Add glazed onions to casserole.

9 Melt 1 level tablespoon butter in another small pan. Add mushroom caps; sprinkle with lemon juice (to preserve their whiteness), salt and freshly ground black pepper to taste, and toss over a low heat for 8 to 10 minutes until lightly coloured. Add to casserole.

10 Set casserole over a low heat and slowly bring to simmering point. Cover tightly and transfer to the oven.

11 Bake casserole until pheasant is meltingly tender. If it is a young bird, it will be done in 40 to 50 minutes. An older one will take considerably longer. Turn pheasant and baste occasionally with wine sauce as it cooks to keep it moist, adding a little game or chicken stock if sauce cooks away too quickly.

12 To serve: transfer pheasants to a heated serving dish and remove trussing threads and skewers. Surround with onions and mushroom caps. Taste sauce for seasoning; skim off fat if necessary and spoon over pheasant. Serve immediately.

1 young pheasant, about 2 lb
dressed weight, with liver
(see note)
2 slices bread, 1/4 inch
thick, cut from a large
white loaf
Salt and freshly ground black
pepper
2 barding strips of fat salt
pork or slices
of unsmoked bacon
1 tablespoon olive oil
Butter
2 shallots, finely chopped
2 level tablespoons *foie gras*
1/4 chicken stock cube
4 oz button mushrooms,
thinly sliced
4–6 oz large green grapes,
halved and seeded
4–6 oz large red or black
grapes, halved and seeded
1–2 tablespoons brandy or
marc de Bourgogne
6–8 level tablespoons double
cream

Faisan à la Vigneronne

1 Preheat oven to fairly hot (425°F. Mark 7).

2 Trim slices of bread sparingly so that you are left with approximately 4-inch squares. Cut each square in half horizontally and then vertically, making 8 smaller squares; then divide each of these in two crosswise so that finally you are left with 16 triangles. Arrange in a single layer on a cake rack and put aside until required.

3 Wipe pheasant clean both inside and out with a damp cloth or absorbent paper, and season inside and out with salt and freshly ground black pepper. Bard breast with thin strips of fat salt pork (or fat unsmoked bacon), tying them on securely with string. Secure legs close to the body with string.

4 Select a shallow, heavy casserole large enough to hold pheasant comfortably. Brown pheasant in it on all sides in a mixture of olive oil and 1 level tablespoon butter for 10 to 15 minutes over a steady heat.

5 Transfer casserole to the oven and roast pheasant, uncovered, for 25 to 30 minutes, or until juices run clear when you pierce the thickest part of the flesh between leg and breast with a small skewer or toothpick. At the same time, place the rack of bread triangles lower down in the oven to dry out to a crisp golden brown.

6 Meanwhile, prepare a liver garnish for *croûtons* as follows: in a small pan, simmer finely chopped shallots in 1 level teaspoon butter until soft and golden but not brown, 10 to 12 minutes.

7 Chop pheasant liver coarsely; add to the pan and sauté for 2 to 3 minutes longer, mashing with a fork to reduce liver to a pulp. Remove from heat as soon as liver turns beige.

8 Scrape contents of pan into a small bowl. Beat in *foie gras*. Taste and season with a little salt or freshly ground black pepper if necessary. Put aside.

9 When pheasant is tender, lift it out of the casserole, allowing juices to drain back, and place it on a large chopping board. With a cleaver or heavy knife, cut it into 4 joints, 2 breasts and 2 legs; then cut these neatly in half again so that each person can have a portion of both white and dark meat. Arrange pheasant pieces on a heated serving dish; cover with foil and keep hot in the oven, which you have turned down to very slow (275°F. Mark 1).

10 Scrape all the juices and scraps left behind on the chopping board into a small pan. Add a piece of stock cube and $\frac{1}{4}$ pint water; bring to the boil and cook briskly until reduced to about 3 tablespoons of gamey stock.

11 Place casserole in which you roasted pheasant over a moderate heat. Add sliced button mushrooms and sauté gently for 10 minutes. After 7 minutes, add grapes and continue to sauté, turning carefully to avoid crushing grapes.

12 Heat brandy or *marc* in a metal soup ladle or small pan. Carefully set it alight with a match, and when flames are burning briskly, pour over mushrooms and grapes.

13 As soon as flames have burnt themselves out, strain in game stock; add cream and continue to heat gently, uncovered, for 5 minutes until sauce has reduced and thickened slightly. Taste and add salt or freshly ground black pepper if necessary.

14 Spread *croûtons* with *foie gras* mixture.

15 Spoon sauce, grapes and mushrooms over pheasant pieces. Arrange *croûtons* around sides of dish.

16 Return dish to the oven for a minute or two longer to heat *croûtons* through. Serve immediately.

Note: If you have not been given the pheasant's liver, substitute a chicken liver instead.

Quail

It is unlikely that you will be able to buy wild quail in England, since quail-farming has grown into quite a flourishing little industry. So now you can *order* quail from good poulterers.

These tiny little birds have a very delicate flavour at the best of times, and I have a feeling that reared quail have even less. However, they make such a pretty and elegant dish for a special occasion that it is worth spending time and trouble flavouring them up.

Keep the cooking of quail short and sharp. They need plenty of butter to prevent them drying out, and will be done in a matter of minutes.

It is quite correct to use your fingers when eating quail; a knife and fork look gigantic beside the lilliputian bird, and will be of little use when you come to the legs – so have fingerbowls of warm, lemony water on the table.

Serves 2-4

4 dressed quails
Salt and freshly ground black
pepper

Mustard butter
6 oz butter
1 1/2 shallots, very finely
chopped
1 1/2 level teaspoons Dijon
mustard
3/4 level teaspoon dried
thyme
Salt and freshly ground black
pepper

Spit-roasted Quails with Mustard Butter

1 To make mustard butter: beat butter until creamy. Blend in remaining ingredients, adding salt and freshly ground black pepper to taste.

2 Take one-third of the prepared butter; place it on a small square of greaseproof paper and roll up into a roll 3 to 4 inches long and of approximately 1-inch diameter. Wrap up and refrigerate until required.

3 Mix a little salt and freshly ground black pepper on a saucer. Dip your finger in it and rub the quails all over, both inside and out.

4 Using remainder of flavoured butter, put a small knob of butter in the body cavity of each quail. Spread quails with the remainder. Arrange them on a plate and leave at the bottom of the refrigerator for 2 hours to absorb flavours.

5 If using an oven rôtisserie – preheat it to fairly hot (425°F. Mark 7). Fashion a long, narrow trough from double-thick aluminium foil to catch juices from quails as they revolve, and lay it beneath the spit. (If juices are left to drip into a large pan, they are likely to burn).

6 Thread quails lengthwise on to a spit, and spit-roast for 15 to 20 minutes, or until juices run clear when they are pierced with a thin skewer around the inside leg area where the meat is thickest.

7 When quails test done, transfer them to a heated serving dish.

8 Cut chilled butter into 4 parts. Top each quail with a pat of butter and serve immediately.

Serves 2-4

4 dressed quails
Salt and freshly ground black
pepper

Orange wine butter
3/4 pint red wine
6 oz butter
12 anchovy fillets, finely
chopped
Finely grated rind of 1 1/2
oranges
1 1/2 teaspoons orange juice
Freshly ground black pepper

Spit-roasted Quails with Orange Wine Butter

1 To make orange wine butter: boil wine briskly until reduced to about 3 tablespoons. Cool.

2 In a small bowl, beat butter until creamy. Add finely chopped anchovy fillets and grated orange rind, and continue to beat until well blended.

3 Gradually beat in reduced wine and orange juice, and season to taste with freshly ground black pepper – you will probably not need salt because of the anchovy fillets.

4 Proceed as in Steps 2–6 of the preceding recipe.

Old English Quail Pudding

Serves 4

1 Start by making up a half-portion of Quick Espagnole Sauce (page 182). When it is lukewarm, flavour to taste with port.

2 Prepare sausage forcemeat balls: sprinkle breadcrumbs with milk. Mince pork coarsely. Combine soaked breadcrumbs with pork, sausage meat and herbs; season to taste with salt and freshly ground black pepper, and mix well. Shape mixture into 16 small balls.

3 Sauté forcemeat balls in equal parts butter and oil until well browned on all sides. Remove from frying pan with a slotted spoon; drain on absorbent paper and put aside until needed.

4 To make butter crust: sift flour, salt and a good pinch of freshly ground black pepper into a bowl. Rub in butter until mixture resembles fine breadcrumbs. Stir in herbs and finely grated lemon rind.

5 Beat egg yolks lightly with 2 tablespoons cold water. Sprinkle over rubbed-in mixture and toss with a fork until dough begins to hold together. Then gather it into a ball with your hands and knead lightly once or twice to eliminate cracks.

6 Roll pastry into a circle which will cover an upturned $2\frac{1}{2}$-pint pudding basin. Cut out a wedge, roughly a quarter of the total amount, and put it aside to use as a lid.

7 Butter the pudding basin and line it with the larger piece of pastry, joining the edges of the removed section together neatly. Trim off edges of pastry that come above the rim of the basin.

8 Re-roll remaining pastry to make a lid that fits the top of the basin exactly.

9 In the same fat in which forcemeat balls were browned, sauté quail halves for 2 to 3 minutes until golden brown all over. Drain on absorbent paper.

10 Spread base of pastry-lined basin with about 3 level tablespoons port-flavoured Espagnole sauce. Scatter with a few forcemeat balls and lay 2 quail halves on top. Repeat until these ingredients are used up, packing them in quite tightly and ending with a good coating of sauce.

11 Place pastry lid in position. Brush outside rim with a little cold water and fold top of outer lining over the lid to seal the pudding.

4 dressed quails, halved
1/2 recipe Quick Espagnole Sauce (page 182)
3–4 tablespoons port
Butter and oil for frying

Sausage forcemeat balls
1 oz white breadcrumbs
2 tablespoons milk
2 oz lean pork
2 oz pork sausage meat
1 level teaspoon finely chopped parsley
Pinch of dried sage
Salt and freshly ground black pepper

Butter crust
8 oz self-raising flour
1/4 level teaspoon salt
Freshly ground black pepper
3 oz butter
1 level teaspoon finely chopped parsley
1/4 level teaspoon dried thyme
Finely grated rind of 1/2 lemon
2 egg yolks
2 tablespoons cold water

12 Cover top of basin with a sheet of buttered greaseproof paper which you have pleated down the middle so that pastry can rise. Then cover with a sheet of foil, similarly pleated, and tie securely with string.

13 Stand basin on a wad of paper in a large pan. Add hot water to come a third of the way up sides. Bring to the boil; reduce heat to simmering point; cover pan and simmer for 2 hours, topping up with more boiling water as it evaporates.

14 Serve pudding very hot, straight from the basin.

Wild Rabbit or Young Hare

Wild rabbit or young hare used to be extremely popular in this country. But with the coming of progress, the spread of townships and cities, the recent bout of myxamatosis which decimated the rabbit population of our hedgerows, young rabbit is as rare on our tables today as it is in America. Is it because we regard fluffy young tame bunnies as household pets? Or is it just that we tend to limit ourselves more and more to quail, guinea fowl, grouse, partridge and pheasant when we think of cooking with game?

Grilled Young Rabbit

Surely the simplest way of cooking rabbit, if it is young and tender, is to grill it – over charcoal or under the grill. Skin the animal, draw it, and then split it down the backbone. Rub the flesh well with salt, freshly ground black pepper and a touch of dried thyme or rosemary. Dribble a little melted butter over it, squeeze half a lemon over it, and place the rabbit on the grid of your grill about 4 inches from the heat.

Grill the rabbit for about 12 to 15 minutes per side, brushing with melted butter several times during the cooking process. Then place in a well-buttered gratin dish in a preheated moderately hot oven (400°F. Mark 6), brush with melted butter, sprinkle with lemon juice and cook the rabbit for 10 minutes more to finish the cooking.

Le Cul de Lapin à l'Estragon

Serves 4–6

1 If fresh tarragon is not available, use dried tarragon, pretreated as follows: put it in a small bowl; pour over 1 tablespoon boiling water and leave to infuse for a few minutes (as you would tea leaves).

2 If the rabbit's head has not been removed, chop it off with a sharp knife. Then joint the rabbit as follows. Cut off the front of the rabbit at the ribs and divide it in two. Cut off legs at the thigh. Chop the saddle in two crosswise.

3 Slice fat salt pork thinly. Arrange slices on a sheet of grease-proof paper, well spaced apart, and roll with a rolling pin until virtually paper-thin.

4 Preheat oven to hot (450°F. Mark 8).

5 If tarragon has been 'infused', drain it. Mix tarragon with mustard.

6 Season each piece of rabbit with salt and freshly ground black pepper, and spread lightly with tarragon mustard.

7 Wrap each piece of rabbit in fat salt pork, securing it in place with string.

8 Select an ovenproof casserole or lidded baking dish that will take the rabbit pieces in 1 layer. Grease it with butter and cover base with a layer of sliced onions and tomatoes. Sprinkle with chopped garlic, thyme, crumbled bay leaf and a little salt and freshly ground black pepper. Lay rabbit pieces on bed of vegetables.

9 Bake, uncovered, for 20 minutes, or until rabbit pieces are lightly coloured.

10 Remove casserole from the oven and turn heat down to slow (325°F. Mark 3).

11 Moisten casserole with dry white wine. Cover tightly and return to the oven for a further 1 to $1\frac{1}{4}$ hours, on until rabbit is tender.

12 Untie rabbit joints and discard pork fat. Arrange joints in a shallow, ovenproof serving dish and return them to the oven to keep hot while you finish sauce.

13 Strain contents of casserole through a fine sieve into a saucepan, pressing the vegetables against the sides of the sieve with the back of a spoon to extract their juices without rubbing them through.

1 4 1/2-lb rabbit (skinned and cleaned weight)

1 level tablespoon finely chopped tarragon

About 2 oz fat salt pork, in one piece

1 level tablespoon yellow French mustard

Salt and freshly ground black pepper

Butter

2 medium-sized onions, sliced

4 medium-sized tomatoes, sliced

2 cloves garlic, chopped

1/4 level teaspoon dried thyme

1 bay leaf, crumbled

1/4 pint dry white wine

2 level teaspoons cornflour

671

14 Mix cornflour smoothly with 2 to 3 tablespoons of the sauce. Stir into remaining sauce; bring to the boil and simmer, stirring, for 2 to 3 minutes, or until sauce has thickened and no longer tastes of raw cornflour.

15 Spoon sauce over rabbit joints and serve immediately. Hot buttered noodles make an excellent accompaniment.

Lapin en Gelée

1 Wipe rabbit clean with a damp cloth. Cut it up into 7 joints (2 hind legs, 2 forelegs, 2 pieces of saddle and the rib cage).

2 Arrange pieces of rabbit in a wide, heavy pan or casserole. Add the next seven ingredients and bring to simmering point over a moderate heat.

3 Lower heat. Cover pan and simmer gently for about 30 minutes, or until rabbit is tender.

4 Remove pan from heat and put it aside, covered, to cool until rabbit can be handled.

5 Lift rabbit out of pan. Strain stock through a muslin-lined sieve and discard all the flavourings except carrots and bay leaf.

6 Pour 2 or 3 tablespoons stock into a small bowl. Sprinkle gelatine over the top and leave to soften.

7 Peel and slice shallot (or onion) paper-thin. Poach slices gently in a few tablespoons of the remaining stock until slightly 'wilted', 3 to 4 minutes. Lift out with a slotted spoon and return any leftover stock to the main quantity.

8 Slice half of the cooked carrot thinly; then cut slices into $\frac{1}{2}$-inch rounds, using a plain, $\frac{1}{2}$-inch piping nozzle if you have one.

9 With a small cleaver or heavy knife, chop rabbit joints into largish pieces. Check that the bones have not splintered anywhere. If they do, pick the splinters out.

10 Measure all remaining stock. If necessary, reduce to 1 pint by fast boiling. Cool slightly.

11 Place bowl with softened gelatine in a pan of hot water. Stir until gelatine has completely melted. Combine with stock and taste for seasoning. Stock should be highly flavoured as it weakens considerably when set.

Serves 4-6

1 3- to 4-lb rabbit, dressed weight
2 carrots, cut into 2-inch lengths
1 onion, quartered
Small twist of thinly pared lemon zest
4 black peppercorns
1 bay leaf
1 pint chicken stock (page 162)
1/4 pint dry white wine
1 level teaspoon powdered gelatine
1 shallot or small onion
Salt and freshly ground black pepper
2–3 level tablespoons finely chopped parsley
4 paper-thin slices lemon
Lemon wedges, to serve

12 Toss rabbit pieces with chopped parsley.

13 Arrange parsleyed rabbit in a long, wide 2½- to 3-pint dish. Scatter rounds of carrot and poached shallot slices over them, and lay paper-thin lemon slices in a row down centre. Place bay leaf in the middle. Pour over jelly stock.

14 Allow to cool; then chill lightly, overnight if possible, until softly set.

15 To serve: scoop up portions of rabbit and jelly with a large spoon – this dish is not intended to be turned out. Some people may like to squeeze a little lemon juice over their portions, so serve lemon wedges on a separate little plate.

Hare

Hare is a much stronger meat than rabbit, considered by many to be on a par with venison. Like venison, it tends to be dry unless precautions are taken, such as barding, larding and steeping in a marinade.

The tenderness of a hare is greatly improved if you first pare off as much as you can of the tough, opaque, outer membrane that holds the carcass together. (It does not matter if you can't strip it completely.) This allows the meat to absorb the flavours of the marinade and to cook through in a shorter time. Unlike other game, hare should *never* be served rare.

Season There is no close season, but hare is in best condition in the autumn, when it has got itself in shape to face the rigours of winter.

Hanging Hang a hare by its hind legs for a week to 10 days in cold weather (less in hot weather). It is best gutted after the first 3 or 4 days, but you can leave this operation until the end if more convenient: the result will be an even gamier flavour.

Serves 6

1 young hare, about 3 lb
dressed weight
4 level tablespoons French
mustard
1 level teaspoon powdered
rosemary
1/2 level teaspoon dried
thyme
Olive oil
Salt and freshly ground black
pepper
Butter (optional)
2 shallots, finely chopped
1 level teaspoon flour
1–2 tablespoons wine
vinegar
1/2 pint sour cream
3 juniper berries, crushed
and chopped

Spit-roasted Hare with Sour Cream Sauce

1 If using an oven rôtisserie spit, preheat oven to moderate (375°F. Mark 5).

2 Prepare hare: chop off head. With a small, sharp knife, carefully remove as much as possible of the tough outer membrane on the hare. This will come off the saddle quite easily but the limbs are more difficult to deal with. However, provided you take off as much as you can, any remaining scraps will have disappeared by the time the hare is cooked.

3 Dry hare thoroughly with absorbent paper. Thread it on to a spit, running the latter through the whole length of the body. Fasten legs tightly to the body with metal skewers. Finally, make sure that laden spit rotates freely when attached to rôtisserie mechanism, and disconnect it again.

4 In a small bowl, blend mustard with rosemary, thyme, 2 tablespoons olive oil, 1 level teaspoon salt and a generous pinch of freshly ground black pepper.

5 Spread hare all over with mustard mixture.

6 Re-attach spit to rôtisserie mechanism and place a large, shallow drip pan underneath to catch all the juices.

7 Spit-roast hare for 50 to 60 minutes, basting with a tablespoon of olive oil every 15 minutes. Test by piercing the thickest part of the meat with a skewer: hare is ready when juices run clear.

8 Remove hare from spit. Place it on a board and divide into joints, chopping the saddle in two. The rib cage, which has little meat on it, can go towards making a soup.

9 Arrange hare joints in a deep, hot serving dish. Cover with foil and keep hot in a 250°F. (Mark ½) oven while you finish sauce.

10 Place drip pan over a low heat. If juices look rather dry, add 1 level teaspoon butter. Then add finely chopped shallots and sauté until soft and golden.

11 Blend in flour and stir over a low heat for 1 or 2 minutes longer to make a golden *roux*. Add wine vinegar and mix well.

12 Gradually blend in sour cream, stirring and scraping bottom and sides of pan clean of all the flavoursome morsels. Stir in chopped juniper berries. Continue to stir until creamy sauce comes to the boil and thickens slightly. (If it is too thick, thin down with a tablespoon or two of water.)

13 Correct seasoning and pour sauce over hare. (If you prefer, sauce may be strained through a fine sieve.) Serve immediately.

Jugged Hare with Forcemeat Balls and Glazed Onions

1 You will need to make special arrangements with your butcher or poulterer to have the blood of the hare saved for you. Ask him to skin the animal carefully and remove the intestines without disturbing the liver, heart and kidneys. If the hare has been hanging head downwards, all the blood will have collected around the rib cage, so that little should escape during this operation. Take the skinned hare home in a water-tight plastic bag.

2 Suspend hare, head downwards, over a large bowl, and leave it until most of the blood has dripped off. Pour blood into an air-tight container and store in the refrigerator until required.

3 Combine marinade ingredients in a large porcelain or earthenware bowl.

4 Remove liver, heart and kidneys from hare – they will be needed for the forcemeat balls which traditionally accompany this dish.

5 Chop the head off and discard it. Chop off hind legs at the top joint. Cut saddle in two between hind legs and rib cage. Remove forelegs. Split rib cage in two lengthwise along the spine. (This gives 8 joints in all.)

6 Place joints in marinade. Cover and leave in a cool place to marinate for 24 hours, turning joints occasionally to ensure that they remain well coated with marinade.

7 When ready to cook hare, preheat oven to very slow (300°F. Mark 2).

8 Remove joints from marinade (reserve marinade and vegetables) and pat them dry with absorbent paper.

9 Select a large, heavy casserole with a tight-fitting lid. In it, sauté fat salt pork in olive oil until fat runs.

10 Add 4 pieces of hare at a time and brown them thoroughly on all sides. Transfer browned joints to a plate.

11 Remove casserole from heat. With a slotted spoon, lift carrot and onion slices and the strip of lemon rind out of marinade, and lay them at the bottom of the casserole. Add chopped

1 4-lb hare, dressed weight, complete with blood, liver, heart and kidneys
2 level tablespoons diced fat salt pork
1 tablespoon olive oil
1 stalk celery, roughly chopped
1 pint beef stock
Bouquet garni (parsley, thyme, bay leaf)
4 allspice berries, crushed
Juice of ½ lemon
Salt and freshly ground black pepper
Glazed onions (page 676)
Forcemeat balls (page 677)
2–3 tablespoons port
1–2 level tablespoons redcurrant jelly
Beurre manié (see Step 16)

Marinade
1/2 pint red wine
1 tablespoon olive oil
1 small onion, sliced
1 carrot, sliced
Strip of lemon rind
1/2 level teaspoon mixed spice
1 clove
1/4 level teaspoon mixed herbs
1 bay leaf
Freshly ground black pepper

celery. Arrange browned hare joints on top. Pour over beef stock; add *bouquet garni*, crushed allspice berries and lemon juice, and season to taste with salt and freshly ground black pepper.

12 Return casserole to a moderate heat. Bring to simmering point. Cover tightly with a lid; then cover top of casserole with foil to ensure that it is completely sealed.

13 Bake casserole for 2 hours. During this time, prepare glazed onions and forcemeat balls (see recipes below).

14 Test hare after 2 hours. If not quite cooked, return to the oven for a little longer. When hare is tender, remove joints from casserole with a slotted spoon. Keep hot.

15 Strain sauce through a sieve into a saucepan. Correct seasoning and flavour to taste with port and redcurrant jelly.

16 Prepare a *beurre manié* (1 level tablespoon each butter and flour mashed to a smooth paste) and add to the sauce in tiny pieces over a low heat. Bring to the boil, stirring, and simmer for 2 to 3 minutes until sauce has thickened. Remove from heat.

17 Return hare to casserole. Add glazed onions.

18 Stir marinade into sauce, together with 1 tablespoon hare's blood. Return to a low heat until sauce is hot again, *but on no account allow it to boil*. A sauce thickened with blood behaves just like an egg custard, and will certainly curdle if overheated.

19 Pour sauce over hare and onions. Make sure casserole is thoroughly hot. Garnish with forcemeat balls and serve immediately.

Glazed Onions

12 button onions
Salt
1 level tablespoon butter
1 level tablespoon castor
   sugar

1 Peel onions. Place them in a small pan.

2 Cover with cold salted water. Bring to the boil and simmer, covered, for 10 minutes. Drain thoroughly.

3 Dry the pan and melt butter in it without letting it colour. Stir in sugar.

4 Return onions to pan. Toss lightly to coat them with sugary butter and sauté gently over a low heat until richly glazed.

5 Remove from heat. Cover pan and leave on one side until needed.

Hare Forcemeat Balls

Makes 12 balls

1 Rinse liver, heart and kidneys of hare. Place them in a small pan. Cover with cold salted water and slowly bring to the boil. As soon as water boils, drain thoroughly. Rinse and dry pan.

2 Coarsely mince hare offal into a bowl.

3 In the same pan, simmer finely chopped onion gently in 2 oz butter for 10 to 15 minutes until very soft but not coloured.

4 Add sautéed onion and its butter to minced offal, together with fresh breadcrumbs, herbs and grated lemon rind. Mix well and season to taste with salt and freshly ground black pepper.

5 Beat egg lightly and gradually work into mixture to bind it to a firm paste.

6 Dust your hands lightly with flour and shape mixture into 12 balls. Roll them in flour and leave on a plate until needed.

7 Just before hare is ready to serve, brown forcemeat balls thoroughly in a mixture of oil and 1 level tablespoon butter. Use them to garnish jugged hare as directed above.

Liver, heart and kidneys of hare
Salt
1 small onion, finely chopped
Butter
4 oz fresh white breadcrumbs
2 level tablespoons finely chopped parsley
1/4 level teaspoon dried thyme
Finely grated rind of 1/2 lemon
Freshly ground black pepper
1 egg
Plain flour
2 tablespoons olive oil

Venison

The term venison can be applied to the flesh of any deer – roe, fallow and red. It makes excellent eating, but care must be taken when cooking it, as it tends to be dry by nature.

All venison improves with marinating and generous larding or barding with fat salt pork or fat bacon. Leg and loin, used separately, or in the form of a haunch or saddle, make superb roasts. The remainder of the carcass should be casseroled, put in a pie or turned into a game stock.

Season Legally, there is no close season for venison. Fresh venison is most commonly found in the shops in the autumn and early winter, but you are also likely to come across it at other times of the year when herds are culled. Frozen venison is also becoming more popular.

Hanging Ideally, the animal should be skinned and cleaned as soon as it is shot. How long you then leave it hanging in a cold, airy place depends on how 'ripe' you like it. Strange as it may sound, venison that has been left until virtually maggoty acquires superb texture. You then shave away the surface of the meat (the maggots do not penetrate very deeply) before marinating and cooking the meat.

Serves 6

1 leg of well-hung venison,
   4 1/2–5 lb
Salt
Long strips of fat salt pork
   for larding
Thin slices of fat salt pork
   for barding
2 level tablespoons butter
2 tablespoons olive oil
6 level tablespoons double
   cream
3–4 tablespoons tawny
   port
1/2 level teaspoon crushed
   black peppercorns
2 level tablespoons *beurre
   manié* (see Step 11)

Marinade

1 level tablespoon finely
   diced fat salt pork
1/2 lb carrots, finely chopped
1/2 lb onions, finely chopped
1/4 lb celery (tops included),
   finely chopped
1 bottle red wine
1/4 pint red wine vinegar
1 level tablespoon chopped
   parsley
1 level teaspoon dried thyme
1 level teaspoon crumbled
   bay leaves
2 level teaspoons allspice
   berries
1/2 level teaspoon crushed
   black peppercorns
1/2 level teaspoon salt

Roast Leg of Venison with Crushed Pepper Sauce

A leg of venison marinated for 48 hours in a separately cooked marinade to tenderise and flavour it before roasting.

1 Start by preparing marinade, which must be quite cold when used: in a medium-sized, heavy saucepan with a lid, sauté diced fat salt pork until fat runs and little bits are crisp and browned. Press browned bits against sides of pan with a spoon to extract as much fat from them as possible and discard them.

2 Add chopped vegetables to pan; mix well and cook gently, tightly covered, for 15 minutes until soft but not coloured – shake covered pan vigorously from time to time in case vegetables stick to the bottom.

3 Add remaining ingredients; top up with $1\frac{1}{4}$ pints water and bring to the boil. Boil gently, uncovered, for 30 minutes. Remove from heat and allow to become quite cold.

4 Trim leg of venison and remove the tough outer membrane. Lard it lengthwise with two or three strips of $\frac{1}{4}$-inch-thick fat salt pork.

5 Pour cold marinade into a large porcelain or earthenware bowl. Add the leg of venison and turn it over several times to coat it thoroughly. Cover and leave for 2 days, turning occasionally.

6 When ready to cook venison, preheat oven to moderately hot (400°F. Mark 6).

7 Remove venison from marinade; drain and dry it thoroughly. Season with salt and cover with thin sheets of fat salt pork, tying them in place with fine string.

8 Place venison in a roasting tin with butter and olive oil. Roast for $1\frac{1}{2}$ hours if you like venison medium-rare, 15 minutes longer if you prefer it more thoroughly cooked. Baste and turn joint occasionally to keep it moist.

9 Transfer venison to a heated serving dish and remove remains of barding pork. Keep hot.

10 Skim fat from pan juices. Place roasting tin over a moderate heat; add 2 to 3 tablespoons water and scrape surface of tin clean with a wooden spoon.

11 Blend in double cream, port and crushed black peppercorns, and, when hot, stir in a *beurre manié* (equal parts butter and flour mashed to a smooth paste) in tiny pieces. Simmer for 2 to 3 minutes until they have completely dissolved and sauce has thickened.

12 Correct seasoning of sauce with more salt if necessary and serve in a heated sauce boat with venison.

Roast Saddle of Venison in Sour Cream Sauce

Serves 4–6

For this dish, the venison requires to be marinated overnight.

1 Carefully remove tough outer membrane from saddle of venison and cut away sinews etc. Keep trimmings and any bones for making game stock.

2 Beat olive oil and lemon juice together with a fork. Pour over saddle of venison in a bowl, turning it until thoroughly coated, and leave, covered, to marinate overnight.

3 The following day, preheat oven to moderate (350°F. Mark 4).

4 Drain venison thoroughly and pat dry with absorbent paper. Lard along the length of the saddle with strips of fat salt pork, allowing 2 rows of larding on each side.

5 In a mortar, crush juniper berries with salt. Rub into saddle.

6 Place the saddle, meaty side upwards, in a roasting tin. Scatter onion rings around it and add the strip of lemon zest. Pour vinegar and 4 tablespoons hot melted butter over the saddle.

7 Place roasting tin in the oven.

8 Meanwhile, turn 2 cartons sour cream into a small pan and warm it gently, stirring.

9 When venison has been roasting for 15 minutes, baste with half of the warmed sour cream. Return to the oven for a further 20 minutes, basting once or twice during this time.

1/2 saddle well-hung venison, 2 1/2–3 lb dressed weight

1/4 pint olive oil

Juice of 1 lemon

4 larding strips of fat salt pork, the length of the saddle and about 1/4 inch square

1 level teaspoon juniper berries

1 level teaspoon salt

1 medium-sized onion, sliced

1 3-inch strip of lemon zest

2 tablespoons wine vinegar

6 level tablespoons melted butter

2 5-fluid-oz cartons plus 3–4 level tablespoons sour cream

1 level tablespoon sifted flour

1/4 pint game stock (made by simmering trimmings of game in a little water or stock, with chopped onion, carrot and a *bouquet garni*).

10 Turn saddle so that rib bones face upwards. Pour over remainder of warmed sour cream and continue to roast for a further 15 minutes.

11 Remove roasting tin from the oven. Increase temperature to fairly hot (425°F. Mark 7).

12 Turn saddle meaty side up again. Dust roasting tin and venison with sifted flour; sprinkle with remaining butter and return to the oven for 10 minutes longer.

13 Check venison: if it is too rare for your taste, add water (no more than 3 tablespoons) to the roasting tin and return to the oven for 10 minutes, or until venison is cooked to your liking.

14 Transfer saddle to a heated serving dish and return to the turned-off oven to keep hot while you make a sauce with the pan juices.

15 Place roasting tin over a moderate heat. Add game stock, stirring and scraping bottom and sides of pan clean with a wooden spoon. Bring to the boil; simmer for 2 minutes and remove from heat. Allow bubbling to subside, then finish sauce by stirring in remaining sour cream. Correct seasoning if necessary.

16 Strain some of the sauce over meat and serve remainder in a separate sauce boat.

Casseroled Saddle of Venison with Pears

Serves 4–6

1/2 saddle of well-hung venison, 2 1/2–3 lb dressed weight
Flour
2 level tablespoons butter
2 tablespoons olive oil
1/2 pint beef or game stock (page 161 or see *Roast saddle of Venison*)
2 level teaspoons tomato concentrate
1/2 chicken stock cube
2 level tablespoons *beurre manié* (see Step 16)
4 level tablespoons double cream
2 level tablespoons jelly from cranberry preserve or redcurrant jelly
Salt and freshly ground black pepper

This dish must be started 2 days in advance to allow for marinating.

1 Prepare saddle of venison by trimming away the tough membrane covering the meat and removing any sinews etc.

2 In a large porcelain or earthenware bowl, assemble marinade ingredients. Mix well; add saddle of venison and turn it over until thoroughly coated. Cover bowl tightly and leave in a cool place for 2 days, turning meat from time to time.

3 When ready to cook venison, preheat oven to cool (250°F. Mark ½).

4 Remove saddle from marinade, allowing the latter to drain back into the bowl. Dry meat thoroughly with absorbent paper and dust with flour.

5 Strain marinade into a saucepan, reserving vegetables, and boil briskly until reduced to half the original volume.

6 In a flameproof casserole large enough to hold saddle comfortably, heat 1 tablespoon each butter and oil; add marinade vegetables and sauté over a moderately high heat for 10 to 12 minutes, or until lightly browned. Transfer vegetables to a plate with a slotted spoon.

7 Add remaining butter and oil to casserole, and when hot, sear venison on all sides for 10 to 15 minutes until thoroughly browned.

8 Return browned vegetables to casserole, together with reduced marinade, game (or beef) stock and tomato concentrate. Bring just to boiling point over a gentle heat; cover and quickly transfer to the oven.

9 Bake venison for $1\frac{1}{2}$ to $1\frac{3}{4}$ hours, or until very tender. For maximum tenderness, casserole should be kept down to a barely perceptible simmer.

10 Meanwhile, prepare pears: combine sugar, wine vinegar, cinnamon stick, clove and lemon zest in a pan with $\frac{1}{4}$ pint water. Bring to the boil, swirling pan gently until sugar has dissolved; then boil vigorously until syrup is reduced by half.

11 Peel, halve and core pears, and arrange them in a shallow baking dish in a single layer.

12 Pour over hot syrup; cover with a sheet of buttered grease-proof paper, and place in the oven on a shelf below the casserole after the latter has had its first half-hour.

13 After 1 hour, increase the temperature of the oven to very slow (275°F. Mark 1).

14 When venison is tender, remove casserole from the oven and increase temperature to 350°F. (Mark 4) to complete cooking of pears. They will take a further 15 minutes or so, giving you time to finish the sauce.

15 Remove saddle from casserole and place it on a large, thoroughly heated serving dish. Keep hot.

16 Stir $\frac{1}{2}$ stock cube into casserole juices until dissolved. Then add *beurre manié* (equal parts butter and flour mashed to a smooth paste) in small pieces; bring to the boil, stirring, and simmer for 3 to 4 minutes until thickened.

17 Remove casserole from heat. Stir in cream and cranberry or redcurrant jelly, and season to taste with salt and freshly ground black pepper. Strain sauce through a fine sieve.

18 Drain pears and arrange them around the venison, cored side up. Fill each hollow with a teaspoon of tart-flavoured whole cranberry preserve. Glaze venison with a few tablespoons of the sauce and serve remainder separately in a heated sauce boat.

Marinade

2 medium-sized onions, sliced

2 medium-sized carrots, thinly sliced

2 stalks celery, sliced

1 clove garlic, peeled and left whole

12 black peppercorns

6 juniper berries

1 bay leaf

1/2 level teaspoon dried thyme

1 pint red wine

4 tablespoons wine vinegar

Poached pears

4 oz sugar

1/4 pint wine vinegar

1 1-inch piece of cinnamon stick

1 clove

Small strip of lemon zest

4 small (Comice) pears

Butter

Tart-flavoured whole cranberry preserve

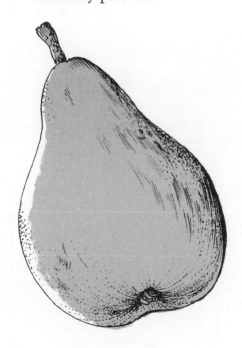

Lesson 27
Baking with Yeast

Bread

There is something supremely basic about the ancient ritual of kneading, proving and shaping a yeast dough, far removed from the clinical chemistry of baking powders and quick-mix cakes. Baking with yeast is a very personal activity. Yeast is a living organism and you will soon realise that, just like people, each dough has a character of its own: some bounce back irrepressibly, others are soft and gentle, and a little slower to react.

People are said to have a light hand with pastry and cakes. With yeast doughs, 'feel' would be a better word. Recipes can describe the consistency of a particular yeast dough, but only you, as you gain experience, will be able to judge whether it is soft or firm enough, whether it is pliable and elastic, or should be kneaded some more. Your eye will learn to recognise the smug sheen on a ball of dough that has had its full share of pummelling and kneading – I can only give you a rough guide of how long it takes me, but you may work more quickly, or less vigorously, than I do. And only you can tell how long it will take for your dough to double in bulk, because I don't know how cool or warm your kitchen will be on any particular day.

The Basic Ingredients

If you can get *fresh yeast*, so much the better. There is something eminently pleasing about its soft, creamy-crumbly texture and strong aroma. I instinctively prefer it, although I can find little justification for this attitude, except for the fact that you can tell by its appearance when fresh yeast has gone stale and won't work (throw it away once it's turned brown or gone hard), whereas there is no way of checking how long a can or packet of dried yeast has been lying around on the grocer's shelf.

Assuming that it really is fresh when you buy it, a lump of fresh yeast in a polythene bag can be stored for 4 to 5 days in a cool place, up to a month in the refrigerator in an air-tight container, and, tightly wrapped, up to a year in a deep freeze.

Dried yeast, provided the can is kept tightly closed, will stay fully active for 6 months. After that, it is cheaper to discard any left over rather than risk spoiling a whole batch of dough. Or at least, before embarking on a baking session, test suspect yeast by sprinkling a teaspoon over a little lukewarm water. If there is no sign of activity after the usual 10 minutes, or if activity is very weak, go out and get some more.

When substituting dried yeast in a recipe that calls for fresh, use half the quantity specified:

1 oz fresh yeast = $\frac{1}{2}$ oz or 1 level tablespoon dried yeast
$\frac{1}{2}$ oz fresh yeast = $\frac{1}{4}$ oz or $1\frac{1}{2}$ level teaspoons dried yeast
$\frac{1}{4}$ oz fresh yeast = $\frac{1}{8}$ oz or $\frac{3}{4}$ level teaspoon dried yeast

To dissolve or 'cream' fresh yeast Use some of the liquid specified in the recipe. Unless a reliable, tested recipe instructs you to cream the yeast with sugar, this method should be avoided.

To dissolve dried yeast In a small bowl, dissolve a little sugar in some of the measured recipe liquid (individual recipe will specify the amount of each required). Sprinkle dried yeast over the top and beat it up thoroughly with a fork. Then leave it for at least 10 minutes. The liquid should be very frothy and not a trace of the hard little granules should remain. If they are not thoroughly dissolved at this stage, they will still be in evidence when the bread/cake comes out of the oven.

● In plain bread-type mixtures, $\frac{1}{2}$ oz fresh yeast ($\frac{1}{4}$ oz dried) will leaven 1 lb flour, but note that this proportion changes with larger quantities, so that 3 lb flour requires only 1 oz fresh yeast.

Doughs which are rich in sugar and butter need more yeast, and also rise much more slowly.

Flour

Strong flour is ideal for plain breads because of the high proportion of gluten it contains, but don't worry if you can't get it. Good-quality plain flour will also give good results. Self-raising flours should *never* be used.

When you buy a fresh bag of flour, transfer it to a glass jar or some similar airtight container (earthenware, tin, etc.) with a tight-fitting lid, and store in a cool, dry place.

The recipes that follow have been tested with perfectly dry, plain flour. If your flour is slightly damp, or you are using strong flour, be prepared to adjust the amount of liquid.

Working with Yeast

Providing your yeast is fresh and your recipe accurate, there is very little that can go wrong when you're working with yeast.

Yeast doughs fall more or less into two categories, those that can be kneaded into a pliable, compact mass that leaves the bowl or working surface and your fingers clean (bread and bun doughs etc.) – and those that are so soft and rich that they have to be slapped rather than kneaded, and even refrigerated before they can be handled (brioches and savarins, for example).

● Make it a rule *never* to let your dough get too hard. Far better to start off with a too-soft mixture and add flour – within reason of course – than to decide halfway through kneading that you are going to have to work in more liquid. Somehow, the dough never seems to recover fully from this.

● Remember that while cold will only retard the growth of a yeast dough, excessive heat will kill it. For this reason, check the temperature of any ingredient that has been heated (water, milk or melted butter, for example) and make sure that it is at blood heat before incorporating it into your dough.

● Again, while it is a good idea to have your flour gently warmed before mixing it with the yeast liquid, this is not, strictly speaking, necessary. The same applies to the place where you leave your dough to rise: if it is cold, you will simply have to wait longer. Yeast doughs rise quite happily in a refrigerator – see Croissants (page 691) for example – and the slower the rise, the stronger will be the gluten framework of the flour. But if it is too warm, the dough will rise too fast and have a coarse, open texture. For a steady, even rise which doesn't take too long, aim for an average to warm room temperature.

● At all stages of its preparation, a yeast dough should be protected to prevent the surface drying out. *A dry crust on the surface means dead yeast cells*.

If the dough is a firm one, shape it into a ball, lift it out of the bowl and brush the bowl with a few drops of flavourless, odourless oil. Put the ball of dough back in it and roll it around so that the entire surface is coated with an almost imperceptible film of oil.

Then – and this applies to firm and loose dough alike – either slip the bowl into a large, oiled plastic bag and tie the ends, or cover the top of the bowl tightly with self-clinging plastic wrap (which allows you to see what's going on underneath) or foil, and seal tightly. (The bowl must be big enough so that the fully risen dough isn't held back by the covering.)

Apart from keeping the dough moist, the wrapping also helps to contain the heat that the yeast has generated of its own accord. This is quite noticeable when you lift the wrapping off.

When the dough has been shaped and put into tins ready for its second rising, cover it again, loosely this time, with oiled plastic wrap or a just-damp cloth.

● Baking with yeast is inevitably a slow process and, as we have seen, there is little you can do to speed it up. Don't ever, for example, be tempted to add more than the amount of yeast specified in the recipe – the baked dough will reek of yeast and have a bad texture.

Having kneaded the basic dough, however, you can break off whenever you like, even leave it until the following day. Just slip the bowl into a large plastic bag or cover with foil; seal tightly and chill in the refrigerator until you are ready to continue. Once the dough has come back to room temperature, it will carry on rising as if nothing had happened.

Plain White Bread I

Makes a 1 lb loaf

1 If using fresh yeast, dissolve it in a small bowl with castor sugar and a little of the lukewarm milk. If using dried yeast, first dissolve sugar in 4 tablespoons milk; sprinkle dried yeast over the top; beat well with a fork and leave for about 10 minutes, or until liquid is frothy and yeast granules have completely dissolved.

2 Sift flour and salt into a warmed bowl. Rub in butter with your fingertips and make a well in the centre.

3 Pour in creamed yeast, the lightly beaten egg and enough of the remaining milk to make a moderately firm dough. Knead vigorously until dough comes away from sides of bowl and is smooth, shiny and elastic.

4 Roll dough into a ball; mark a deep cross in the centre with the side of your hand. Cover the bowl with a cloth or plastic wrap and leave dough to rise until doubled in bulk, about 1 hour.

5 When dough is well risen, turn it out on a floured board and punch it down again. Knead vigorously for 10 to 15 minutes until dough has regained its elasticity and has a deep sheen.

6 Shape dough into an oblong, making sure that top is smooth. Place it in an oiled 1-lb loaf tin. Cover tin with a cloth and leave to rise until doubled in bulk again.

7 Preheat oven to moderate (375°F. Mark 5).

1/2 oz fresh yeast or 1/4 oz (1 1/2 level teaspoons) dried yeast
1/2 level teaspoon castor sugar
1/2 pint lukewarm milk
1 lb plain flour
1/2 level teaspoon salt
1 oz butter
1 egg, lightly beaten
Flavourless oil, for loaf tin

8 When loaf has risen to the required height, bake in the oven for about 35 minutes. It should be a rich golden colour on top and sound hollow when rapped on the base with your knuckles. Cool on a wire rack before serving.

Plain White Bread II

1 If using fresh yeast, dissolve it in a small bowl with 4 tablespoons lukewarm water. If using dried yeast, sprinkle it over 4 tablespoons lukewarm water in a small bowl. Beat well with a fork and leave for about 10 minutes until granules have dissolved and mixture is frothy.

2 Combine milk, sugar, salt and butter in a large, heavy saucepan, and stir over a low heat until butter has melted. Do not let mixture become hot.

3 Sift a third of the flour into the warm milk mixture and beat until smooth. Pour in dissolved yeast and beat again. Add remaining flour, gradually, beating vigorously. By the time all the flour has been incorporated you will have a very tacky, soft dough.

4 Scoop dough out on to a floured surface and knead vigorously. After about 5 minutes, you will begin to notice the difference as gradually dough becomes less sticky, and when you have kneaded for 5 minutes longer, it will be soft, springy and smooth, leaving your fingers and working surface clean.

5 Shape dough into a ball and place in a bowl which you have brushed lightly with flavourless oil. Roll dough around in it until entire surface is greased. Cover bowl with a cloth or plastic wrap and leave dough to rise in a warm place for about $1\frac{1}{2}$ hours, or until doubled in bulk.

6 Grease two 1-lb loaf tins.

7 Turn dough out again on to a lightly floured surface and cut it in half. Shape each piece into a smooth ball. Cover and leave to rest for 10 minutes. Then flatten each piece into a rectangle about 15 by 7 inches; roll up each rectangle like a Swiss roll, sealing it down at each turn with your fingertips, and using a little more flour if necessary. Press the ends of each roll with the sides of your hands to make flat flaps, and turn them underneath.

8 Place loaves in prepared loaf tins; cover with a cloth and leave to rise again in a warm place for about 1 hour, until doubled in bulk.

9 Preheat oven to moderate (375°F. Mark 5).

Makes 2 1 lb loaves

1 oz fresh yeast or 1/2 oz
   (1 level tablespoon)
   dried yeast
3/4 pint milk
2 level tablespoons sugar
2 level teaspoons salt
1 level tablespoon butter
1 1/2 lb plain flour
Flavourless oil

10 When loaves are well risen, bake them for 35 minutes or until they make a hollow sound when you rap them on the bottom with your knuckles. They sould be a rich golden colour on top; cover them with a little crumpled foil if they brown too quickly. Cool on a wire rack before serving.

Wholemeal Bread

Makes a 1 lb loaf

1 oz fresh yeast or 1/2 oz (1 level tablespoon) dried yeast
1/2 pint lukewarm milk
12 oz wholemeal flour
4 oz plain flour
1 level teaspoon salt
1 1/2 oz cracked wheat
Butter, for loaf tin

A little plain white flour must be added to wholemeal bread to prevent it being too heavy. As with white bread, a gradual, even rise is crucial to the final texture.

1 Dissolve fresh yeast in a few tablespoons of lukewarm milk. If using dried yeast, sprinkle it over 4 tablespoons luke warm milk in a small bowl. Beat well with a fork and leave until granules have completely dissolved and mixture is bubbly, about 10 minutes.

2 Sift wholemeal and plain flours and salt into a large, heated bowl; stir in 1 oz cracked wheat.

3 Make a well in the centre and pour in yeast mixture. Start working the mixture by hand, gradually adding enough of the remaining milk to make a dough which is soft but still on the firm side. Knead until smooth, shiny and elastic.

4 Roll dough into a ball; cover bowl with a cloth or plastic wrap and leave in a warm place to rise until doubled in bulk.

5 Butter a 1-lb loaf tin and coat it with remaining cracked wheat.

6 When dough has risen, punch it down again and knead lightly until smooth. Shape it into a loaf and place in the prepared tin. Cover with a cloth and leave to rise again until it has doubled in bulk.

7 Preheat oven to moderate (375°F. Mark 5).

8 Bake loaf for 35 minutes, or until top is golden brown and loaf sounds hollow when you rap it with your knuckles. Cool on a wire rack before serving.

Makes 1 loaf

1/2 pint dark beer
Melted butter
1 oz fresh yeast or 1/2 oz
   (1 level tablespoon) dried
   yeast
2 level tablespoons brown
   sugar
1/2 level teaspoon salt
1 egg, lightly beaten
1/2 lb plain flour
1/2 lb wholewheat flour

Beer Bread

In spite of the comparatively large amount of beer used, the flavour of this bread remains very subtle, if rich. It keeps extremely well.

1 Bring beer to boiling point in a large saucepan. Stir in 2 tablespoons melted butter and cool to lukewarm.

2 If fresh yeast is used, cream it with a little of the lukewarm beer before stirring it into the pan. If using dried yeast, sprinkle it over the lukewarm beer, beat well with a fork and leave for about 10 minutes, or until granules have completely dissolved and liquid is frothy.

3 Combine beer mixture with brown sugar, salt and the lightly beaten egg.

4 Sift plain and wholewheat flours into a large, warmed bowl. Make a well in the centre and gradually add beer mixture, working it with your fingertips to make a dough which is fairly soft but on the firm side.

5 Knead dough vigorously until smooth, shiny and elastic. Roll it into a ball; cover bowl with a cloth or plastic wrap and leave in a warm place to rise until doubled in bulk, about 2 hours, depending on the surrounding temperature.

6 Brush a 2-lb loaf tin with melted butter.

7 Punch risen dough down again and knead very lightly until smooth; shape it into an oblong and fit it into the loaf tin. Brush top with melted butter and cover tin with a cloth. Leave to rise until doubled in bulk again.

8 Preheat oven to moderate (375°F. Mark 5).

9 When fully risen, place loaf in the oven and bake for 30 to 40 minutes, or until it is crisp and brown on top, and sounds hollow when you tap it on the bottom with your knuckles.

10 Turn out and cool on a wire rack before serving.

French Bread

When it comes to baking fine white bread, the French are the world's acknowledged experts. But unless you have had the good fortune to taste a crusty French loaf warm from the ovens of a bakery somewhere in France, you would be forgiven for having some reservations on this point – the wooden sticks stuffed, or so it seems, with damp feathers, which so often pass for 'French bread' in England, hardly afford an inducement to crossing the Channel.

Part of the secret of French bread, it is said, stems from the fact that the French are prepared to buy a fresh supply every day, and sometimes even twice a day, and admittedly this is a habit that few people would have the time or inclination to acquire in these days when more and more housewives have to combine shopping and cooking for the family with a full-time career outside their homes.

However, next time you are spending a leisurely Sunday at home, why not make a batch of these light, crusty loaves? If you put the dough to rise after clearing away lunch, by suppertime the house will be fragrant with the aroma of baking bread and you will be able to find out for yourself just how indescribably delicious fresh French bread can be.

1 Combine 1 level tablespoon butter with salt and sugar in a large bowl. Pour in ¾ pint boiling water, stirring until all is dissolved, and allow to cool to lukewarm.

2 Meanwhile, sprinkle dried yeast over ¼ pint lukewarm water; beat with a fork and leave for about 10 minutes, or until granules have completely dissolved. (If using fresh yeast, simply cream it with a few tablespoons of the lukewarm water just before using it, and add the remainder of the water to the mixture separately.)

3 Pour dissolved yeast into butter mixture and mix well. Gradually sift in flour, stirring at first, then beating vigorously with a wooden spoon to make a smooth mixture which is a cross between a dough and a batter.

4 Now discard the spoon and use your hand to work the dough, slapping and kneading it vigorously, and sifting a little more flour over the surface until it *begins* to lose its tendency to stick to the fingers. (This can be done in the bowl, if it is large enough, or on a pastry board.) Unlike other bread doughs, this one will remain rather sticky and very soft until it is shaped.

5 Gather the dough into a ball; butter the bowl and return dough to it. Cover with a sheet of lightly buttered greaseproof paper; then cover bowl with two or three thicknesses of tea towel.

Makes 3-6 french loaves

Butter
1 level tablespoon salt
1 level tablespoon sugar
1 oz fresh yeast or 1/2 oz (1 level tablespoon) dried yeast
1 1/2 lb plain flour plus 1–3 oz for kneading
2–3 level tablespoons yellow cornmeal

Leave to rise in a warm, draught-free place, away from direct heat, for about 1½ hours, or until dough has doubled its bulk.

6 When dough has risen, slap it down to deflate it; cover as before and let it rise until doubled in bulk again – this time it should be ready in an hour.

7 Grease two large baking sheets with butter and dust with cornmeal, shaking off excess.

8 Punch dough down and turn out on to a well-floured surface. Flour your hand and knead dough lightly until smooth and homogenous; then divide into 3 or 6 equal portions.

9 Dust a rolling pin lightly with flour and roll each portion into a rectangle, larger balls into 8- by 12- or 14-inch rectangles, depending on the length of your baking sheets, smaller ones the same lengths but somewhat narrower. The dough will be so elastic at this point that it resists rolling, but with a little effort it can be done.

10 Roll each rectangle up tightly like a swiss roll, starting at one of the longer sides. Pull each roll into shape if necessary.

11 Place loaves, seam side down, on prepared baking sheets; cover with a clean cloth and leave to rise again until doubled in bulk, about 1 hour.

12 Transfer baking sheets to the refrigerator for 20 minutes to firm the dough. At the same time, preheat oven to moderately hot (400°F. Mark 6).

13 Remove loaves from the refrigerator; pinch them into shape if necessary and brush top of each loaf with cold water. Using a razor-sharp knife to avoid crushing dough, cut three or four shallow, diagonal slashes across the top of each loaf.

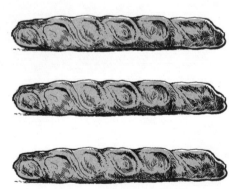

14 Pour an inch of boiling water into a wide, shallow pan (a roasting tin, for example) and place it in the bottom of the oven. Place baking sheets in the oven and bake loaves for 45 minutes if thin, about 1 hour if fatter, brushing tops with more cold water every 15 minutes. If loaves brown too quickly, cover them with a piece of crumpled foil. (The combination of a steamy oven and regular brushing of the loaves with cold water gives the characteristic crisp crust of real French bread.)

15 When loaves are ready – they should sound hollow when rapped with the knuckles – remove from the oven and cool on wire racks.

Croissants

1 The day before you wish to *serve* croissants, put 3 tablespoons of the lukewarm milk and water mixture in a cup. Add 1 level teaspoon castor sugar and stir until dissolved. Sprinkle dried yeast over the surface; beat lightly with a fork and leave for about 10 minutes, or until liquid is frothy and yeast granules have completely dissolved.

2 Meanwhile, sift flour, salt and remaining castor sugar into a warmed bowl, and leave to warm gently.

3 Make a well in the centre of the flour and pour in dissolved yeast. Rinse cup out with remaining milk and water, and add to the flour, kneading to make a smooth dough which is quite soft, but firm enough to roll into a ball.

4 When dough is smooth and homogenous, gradually add melted butter, kneading vigorously until dough is smooth and springy again.

5 Roll dough into a ball. Lay a sheet of buttered greaseproof paper, plastic wrap or foil on top; then cover bowl with a cloth and leave in a warm place to rise to *three* times its original bulk. This will take approximately $3\frac{1}{2}$ hours.

6 When dough has risen, scoop it out on to a very lightly floured surface. Press it gently with the palm of your hand to deflate it; then fold it over on to itself to make a ball again; return to the bowl, cover as before and leave to rise again. This time it should take about 2 hours to double its bulk.

7 Deflate dough once again. Pat it into a rectangle 8 by 4 inches and seal in a tight, neat parcel of foil. Chill for 30 minutes.

8 Towards the end of this time, take chilled butter and work it with your fingertips to make it malleable, *but not oily*. If your hands are warm, hold your wrists under the cold tap for a minute or two to cool them.

9 Unwrap dough. Place it on a lightly floured surface and roll out into a 12- by 8-inch rectangle with a floured rolling pin. Take small knobs of chilled butter; pinch them out into paper-thin flakes between your fingertips and dot upper two-thirds of rectangle with them so that the entire surface is evenly covered, leaving a $\frac{1}{4}$-inch border round the three outer sides unbuttered.

10 Fold unbuttered third of rectangle up over the centre; then fold the top (buttered) third down, making a neat packet composed of three layers of dough sandwiched with two layers of butter.

Makes 12 croissants

6 tablespoons lukewarm milk mixed with 3 tablespoons lukewarm water

3 level teaspoons (1 level tablespoon) castor sugar

1 1/2 level teaspoons dried yeast

1/2 lb plain flour

1 level teaspoon salt

3 tablespoons melted butter

3 oz unsalted butter, chilled

Egg yolk beaten with a little water, to glaze

691

11 Dust board and rolling pin lightly with more flour if necessary, and roll packet out into a 12- by 8-inch rectangle again. Use your rolling pin with short, light strokes to avoid stretching the dough beyond its capacity, or it will tear and allow butter to seep through. Fold in three as before; wrap in foil and chill for 15 minutes.

12 Remove foil and give packet a quarter-turn to the right, i.e. so that top now faces right. Repeat rolling and folding twice more, giving dough a quarter-turn to the right, and chilling it for 15 minutes in between. After the second rolling and folding, seal packet tightly in foil and chill overnight, or for at least 2 hours.

13 *To shape croissants:* on a lightly floured board, roll dough into a 15- by 5-inch rectangle. Cut it in three to make three 5-inch squares and return two of them to the refrigerator.

14 Roll the remaining square into a rectangle 10 by 5 inches. Cut it in half to make two 5-inch squares again, and cut each square into two triangles.

15 Roll each triangle up quite tightly from the broadest end to the tip. Pull into a horseshoe shape, twisting ends round themselves slightly, and lay on an ungreased baking sheet, with the tip underneath.

16 Repeat with the two remaining squares of pastry, taking them from the refrigerator one at a time.

17 Cover croissants with a cloth and leave to rise again until doubled in bulk, about 30 minutes.

18 Preheat oven to fairly hot (425°F. Mark 7).

19 When croissants are well risen, brush them all over with beaten egg yolk and bake for 8 to 10 minutes, or until light and crisp, with a rich golden glaze.

20 Serve croissants lukewarm, or gently reheated just before serving.

Pizza

Basic Pizza Dough

This recipe makes enough dough for a substantial round pizza base 10 to 11 inches in diameter, or a rectangular one measuring 12 by 8 inches. However, rolled out to half the thickness, the same portion of dough will stretch to two pizzas of either size. It's all a matter of taste. I prefer the thicker base for a pizza to be served as an informal main course and the thinner one when serving it with drinks or, Italian style, as a first course before a (light) main dish of meat or fish.

1 Sift flour and salt into a bowl. Make a well in the centre.

2 Dissolve sugar in 2 tablespoons warm water. If using fresh yeast, 'melt' it with sweetened water. If using dried yeast, sprinkle over the water; mix well with a fork and leave until granules have completely dissolved and mixture is bubbly, about 10 minutes.

3 Combine milk with 2 fluid oz hot (not boiling) water to give a lukewarm mixture.

4 Pour dissolved yeast into well in flour, together with enough of the milky liquid to give a firm, soft dough.

5 Turn dough out on to a board and knead for 10 minutes, or until it loses its stickiness and becomes pliable and elastic. You should need very little extra flour for this operation.

6 Flatten dough out and make deep indentations all over it with your fingertips. Sprinkle with 1 tablespoon olive oil; fold dough up to enclose oil and knead again until the latter has been completely absorbed. Roll dough into a ball.

7 Sprinkle bowl with a few drops of oil and roll the ball of dough about in it to coat it entirely with a thin film.

8 Cover bowl tightly and leave dough to rise until doubled in bulk. It will take about 1 hour or even less, depending on surrounding temperature, as it is such a plain dough.

9 When dough has risen, deflate it again and knead lightly before rolling it out to the required shape and thickness.

Makes 1 pizza base

8 oz plain flour
1/2 level teaspoon salt
1/4 level teaspoon sugar
1/2 oz fresh yeast or 1 1/2
   level teaspoons dried yeast
2 fluid oz milk
Olive oil

Basic Pizza Dough for 1
round or rectangular base
(see introductory note to
recipe, page 693)
Olive oil

Topping

1 8-oz can Italian peeled
tomatoes

2 level tablespoons tomato
concentrate

Salt and freshly ground black
pepper

About 3 oz cooked ham,
thinly sliced

About 3 oz Mozzarella or
Emmenthal cheese, thinly
sliced

1 canned red pimento, cut
into thin strips

1 2-oz can anchovy fillets in
oil, drained and halved

6–8 black olives, pitted

1 level teaspoon dried
marjoram or oregano

1 teaspoon olive oil

Pizza alla Casalinga

1 Prepare Basic Pizza Dough and prove it as directed in the preceding basic recipe.

2 Preheat oven to fairly hot (425°F. Mark 7).

3 Use dough to line a round or rectangular baking sheet, pushing it into the required shape with the palm of your hand, or by rolling it lightly with a rolling pin. With the thumb of one hand and forefinger of the other, build up outside edge of dough slightly to prevent filling spilling over. Brush entire surface with olive oil.

4 To make topping: drain tomatoes and rub them through a sieve. Add tomato concentrate, season to taste with salt and freshly ground black pepper, and mix well. Spread over prepared base to within $\frac{1}{2}$ inch of the edges.

5 Cut thinly sliced ham and cheese into strips about 2 inches wide. Arrange ham and cheese strips alternately and overlapping slightly on top of tomato purée.

6 Criss-cross surface attractively with strips of pimento and halved anchovy fillets.

7 Dot with olives and, finally, sprinkle with herbs and olive oil.

8 Bake pizza near the top of the oven for 15 to 20 minutes. Then check that the underside is cooked through and coloured by lifting one side of the pizza up carefully with a fish slice or broad spatula. If it is still very white and doughy, return pizza to the oven for a further 5 to 10 minutes. Top may be covered loosely with foil if it browns too quickly.

9 Serve immediately, in wedges if it is a round pizza, rectangles or squares if you have made a rectangular one.

Onion Pizza

1 Prepare Basic Pizza Dough as directed in the recipe on page 693.

2 While dough is proving, prepare topping: heat olive oil in a large frying pan; add thinly sliced onions and sauté gently for 10 to 15 minutes until soft and a pale golden colour.

3 Add contents of can of tomatoes, tomato concentrate and herbs; mix well. Season to taste with salt and freshly ground black pepper.

4 Cook over a moderate heat, stirring occasionally, until excess moisture has evaporated, leaving onion mixture with a thick, jam-like consistency, 20 to 25 minutes. Cool slightly.

5 Preheat oven to fairly hot (425°F. Mark 7).

6 When dough has doubled its bulk, deflate it; knead lightly and use it to line a round or rectangular baking sheet. Build up outside edges and brush entire surface with olive oil (see Step 3 of preceding recipe).

7 Spread warm onion mixture over pizza base to within ½ inch of edges.

8 Garnish by snipping anchovy fillets over surface, then sprinkling with slivered olives, followed by freshly grated Parmesan.

9 To bake and serve pizza: see Steps 8 and 9 of preceding recipe.

Making Brioches

I find it puzzling that the English, who have taken to croissants in such a big way, should at the same time practically have ignored the finest of all French breads – the brioche. Light and feathery, and delicately rich in butter and eggs, brioches will be a revelation to you. The two basic types of brioche are the *brioche commune* or standard brioche, and the *brioche mousseline*, which is even lighter and finer.

For traditional *brioches à tête*, the dough is baked in fluted tins with gently sloping sides (large or individual). The tins are brushed with melted butter or flavourless oil to make the brioche crusty and golden brown on the outside. Then the dough is placed in the tins in two balls, a large one underneath and a small one (the little head or *tête*) on top. The brioches are left to rise again and glazed with beaten egg yolk just before going into the oven.

If you can't get hold of the right sort of tin – they are becoming

Serves 4–6

Basic Pizza Dough for 1 round or rectangular base (see introductory note to recipe, page 693)
Olive oil

Topping

3 tablespoons olive oil

1 lb Spanish onions, thinly sliced

1 14-oz can Italian peeled tomatoes

1 level tablespoon tomato concentrate

1 bay leaf

1/4 level teaspoon dried marjoram

1/4 level teaspoon dried oregano

Salt and freshly ground black pepper

Garnish

1 2-oz can anchovy fillets in oil, drained

6–8 black olives, pitted and slivered

2 level tablespoons freshly grated Parmesan

easier to find – don't despair: brioches will bake quite happily in any small, individual tins, preferably with sloping sides, in a large ring mould, or in tall, narrow pans.

The same dough is also used (as an alternative to puff pastry) for koulibiac; for wrapping around a fillet of beef *en croûte* – much easier to cut than puff pastry, which has a habit of crumbling off – and similar savoury pies; for wrapping around savoury foods such as a length of continental sausage; or for little pastry fingers wrapped around batons of dark chocolate, which are a great favourite with French children.

Fresh brioches with plenty of butter and home-made jam, served for breakfast, or with tea or coffee, are irresistible. But have you ever used brioches as cases for delicate fillings of pâté, meat, fish or shellfish in a rich, creamy sauce, or fruits poached in syrup? For this you will need brioches at least one day old: carefully remove the 'head' and set aside; scoop out the soft pith of the brioche with a small, sharp spoon, leaving a firm case. Then brush the inside of the brioche with a little melted butter or dust with castor sugar, and slip back into a slow oven to crisp through. Fill; set the little 'heads' back on top and serve.

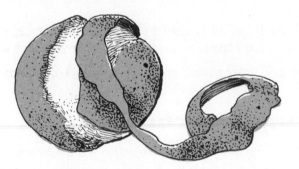

Brioche dough should present no problems, but bear in mind the following points:

● Unlike bread dough, brioche dough cannot be kneaded to a point where it leaves the fingers quite clean when first made. In fact, it will appear impossibly soft and sticky before it is put away to rise the first time, and for this reason . . .

● It is essential to chill the dough overnight to allow the gluten in the flour to 'relax'. The following day the dough, though still very soft, will be much less sticky, and capable of being kneaded and shaped without too much trouble.

● Keep the surrounding temperature steady but not too high while dough is proving so that the brioches will have an even, fine texture, neither heavy nor coarse.

Brioches I

Start dough the day before you wish to serve brioches.

1 If using fresh yeast, cream it with 8 tablespoons lukewarm water. Sprinkle dried yeast over 8 tablespoons lukewarm water in a small bowl; beat well with a fork and leave for about 10 minutes until liquid is frothy and yeast granules have completely dissolved.

2 Sift flour, sugar and salt into a large, warmed bowl and make a well in the centre.

3 Beat eggs with lukewarm milk; stir in vanilla essence and add to the flour, together with dissolved yeast. Mix well.

4 Add half the softened butter, diced, and beat with a wooden spoon until dough is smooth. The dough will be very soft at this stage. Dot surface with remaining butter; cover bowl with a clean cloth and leave in a warm place to rise until doubled in bulk, about 1½ hours.

5 Punch dough down again and beat vigorously by hand for 5 minutes, or until it no longer sticks to the sides of the bowl (flour your hands from time to time while beating).

6 Cover bowl tightly with a sheet of plastic wrap or foil and refrigerate overnight. Brioche dough is very rich and sticky, and chilling it overnight helps to make it easier to handle.

7 The following day, brush 12 individual brioche moulds with melted butter.

8 Turn dough out on a lightly floured surface and knead a few times until smooth again. Weigh dough and cut off a quarter, making two balls. Divide each ball into 12 pieces of equal size. Roll the 12 larger pieces into balls and place them in prepared moulds. Roll each of the smaller pieces into a ball; snip top of each larger ball twice with scissors to form a cross, and set one of the smaller balls on top. Place moulds on a baking sheet and leave brioches to rise again until doubled in bulk, about 30 minutes.

9 Preheat oven to moderately hot (400°F. Mark 6).

10 When brioches have risen, brush tops with egg yolk beaten with a little water. Bake for 15 to 20 minutes, or until firm and well risen, and a rich golden colour.

11 Turn out and cool on a wire rack.

Makes 12 brioches

1 oz fresh yeast or 1/2 oz (1 level tablespoon) dried yeast

1 1/4 lb plain flour

4 level tablespoons castor sugar

1/2 level teaspoon salt

4 eggs

8 tablespoons lukewarm milk

1 teaspoon vanilla essence

4 oz softened butter

Melted butter, for moulds

1 egg yolk beaten with a little water, to glaze

Makes 12

1/2 oz fresh yeast or 1/4 oz
(1 1/2 level teaspoons) dried
yeast
12 oz plain flour
4 level teaspoons castor
sugar
1/2 level teaspoon salt
3 eggs, lightly beaten
4 oz softened butter
Flavourless oil or melted
butter, for mould
1 egg yolk beaten with a
little water, to glaze

Brioches II

1 If fresh yeast is used, cream it with 4 tablespoons lukewarm water. Sprinkle dried yeast over 4 tablespoons lukewarm water in a medium-sized bowl; beat well with a fork and leave for 10 minutes, or until liquid is frothy and granules have completely dissolved.

2 Gradually beat in $2\frac{1}{2}$ oz sifted flour. Cover bowl and leave to rise until very frothy and doubled in bulk, about 20 minutes.

3 Sift remaining flour, sugar and salt into a large bowl. Make a well in the centre; add yeast mixture and lightly beaten eggs, and incorporate into flour gradually, beating vigorously by hand or with a wooden spoon.

4 When dough is smooth, beat in butter, which should be soft to the point of melting. Beat or work by hand until thoroughly incorporated. The dough should be soft and shiny.

5 Cover bowl with a cloth or plastic wrap and leave dough in a warm place to rise until doubled in bulk, about $1\frac{1}{2}$ hours. Then replace cloth with a tight covering of foil (leave it if it is plastic); place dough in refrigerator and chill overnight.

6 When ready to shape brioches: brush 12 brioche tins lightly with oil or melted butter.

7 Scoop dough out of bowl on to a floured surface; with floured hands knead lightly until smooth. Cut dough into 12 equal pieces.

8 Shape brioches as usual and place them in prepared tins (see page 695).

9 Place brioche tins on a baking sheet. Cover loosely with a cloth and leave to rise for $1\frac{1}{2}$ to 2 hours, or until doubled in bulk.

10 Preheat oven to moderately hot (400°F. Mark 6).

11 Brush each brioche lightly with beaten egg. Bake for 12 minutes, or until well risen and a rich golden colour.

12 Remove baking sheets from oven. Turn brioches out of tins and leave them to cool on a wire rack. Store in an air-tight tin.

Chocolate Brioches

Makes 24–26

These little pastries are sold by French bakers, still warm from the oven, in time for breakfast. They are delicious dunked in a cup of milky coffee.

1 Prepare chocolate as follows: divide bar into double squares. Heat a sharp-bladed knife by dipping it in boiling water for a few minutes; then slice each double square of chocolate in three lengthwise to make long, thin fingers, using as little pressure as possible to avoid splintering the chocolate, and reheating the knife blade as it cools.

2 Roll dough out ⅛ inch thick; cut into 2-inch squares.

3 In the centre of each square place a rectangular piece of chocolate. Roll square of dough round it to enclose it completely.

4 Place rolls on buttered baking sheet and leave to rise in a warm place until doubled in bulk, about 1 hour.

5 Preheat oven to moderately hot (400°F. Mark 6).

6 Brush brioche rolls lightly with beaten egg and bake for 12 minutes, or until golden. Cool on wire racks and serve very fresh.

About 2 oz plain, thin chocolate squares
1/2 recipe Brioche Dough II
Butter, for baking sheet
Beaten egg, to glaze

Brioche Mousseline

Makes 12–14

As its name suggests, this brioche is even lighter and more delicate than the two doughs given above – it is so fine and rich that it hardly needs spreading with butter at all.

1 If using fresh yeast, dissolve it in 4 tablespoons lukewarm water in a bowl. If using dried yeast, sprinkle granules over 4 tablespoons lukewarm water in a bowl; beat well with a fork and leave for 10 minutes, or until liquid is frothy and granules have completely dissolved.

2 Gradually sift 2½ oz of the flour into dissolved yeast, mixing with a spoon to make a stiff batter. Cover bowl and leave to rise until frothy and doubled in bulk, about 20 minutes.

3 Sift remaining flour with sugar and salt into a large bowl. Make a well in the centre; add yeast mixture and lightly beaten eggs, and incorporate into flour gradually, beating vigorously by hand or with a wooden spoon.

4 When dough is smooth, beat in softened butter. Continue to beat or work the dough by hand until butter is thoroughly incorporated. The dough should be soft and shiny.

1 oz fresh yeast or 1/4 oz (1 1/2 level teaspoons) dried yeast
9 oz plain flour
2 level tablespoons castor sugar
1/2 level teaspoon salt
3 eggs, lightly beaten
7 oz softened butter
Flavourless oil or melted butter, for moulds
1 egg yolk beaten with a little water, to glaze

5 Cover bowl with a cloth or plastic wrap and leave dough in a warm place to rise until doubled in bulk, about $1\frac{1}{2}$ hours. Then replace cloth with a tight covering of foil (leave it if it is plastic); place dough in refrigerator and chill overnight.

6 When ready to shape brioches: grease 12 brioche moulds with oil or melted butter.

7 Remove dough from refrigerator. Gather it up out of bowl and place on a floured surface; with floured hands knead lightly until smooth. Cut dough into 12 equal pieces. (Do this as quickly as you can so that butter does not have a chance to soften again.)

8 Shape brioches as usual and place them in prepared tins (see page 695).

9 Arrange tins on a baking sheet. Cover loosely with a cloth and leave to rise for $1\frac{1}{2}$ to 2 hours, or until doubled in bulk.

10 Preheat oven to moderately hot (400°F. Mark 6).

11 Brush each brioche lightly with beaten egg and bake for 12 minutes, or until well risen and a rich golden colour.

12 Remove baking sheet from oven. Turn brioches out of moulds and leave them to cool on a wire rack. Store in an airtight tin.

Gugelhupf

The Viennese are renowned for their famous sweet yeast breads, and the *Gugelhupf* is probably the most famous of them all. However, as with so many Central European delicacies, you will find the Poles claiming the same cake as their very own *Babka*, while Russians call it *Kulich* and serve it at Easter-time, traditionally accompanied by a delectable cheese confection called *Paskha* (see page 540). Even the Italian *Panettone* bears a suspicious resemblance to it. The only way to steer clear of these gastronomic jealousies is to bake your *Gugelhupf* in a fluted, tubular tin, *Babka* in either a tube tin or a fluted one without a hole in the middle, and *Kulich* in a tall, round pan of slightly smaller capacity, so that the dough rises above the rim to make a lovely, mushroom top.

The rather off-beat method of making the dough gives the cake a moist texture which retains its freshness particularly well. However, if you are ever left with stale *Gugelhupf*, slice and toast it – delicious served with butter and good jam.

Gugelhupf

1 Sift 5 oz of the flour into a medium-sized bowl. Bring $\frac{1}{2}$ pint milk to the boil. Pour it into the sifted flour all at once, beating vigorously with a wooden spoon to make a stiffish dough free of lumps. Beat dough for a minute or two longer; then put it aside to cool to blood heat.

2 Meanwhile, if using dried yeast, sprinkle it over 3 tablespoons lukewarm water in a small bowl; beat well with a fork and leave for about 10 minutes, or until liquid is frothy and yeast granules have completely dissolved. Fresh yeast should be creamed with the water just before it is needed.

3 Test temperature of flour and milk dough by pushing a finger right into the centre, where it will be warmest. When it feels neither hot, nor cold (i.e. blood heat), blend in creamed yeast. Cover bowl closely with plastic wrap, foil or a damp cloth, and leave to rise in a warm place until doubled in bulk, 30 to 40 minutes.

4 Meanwhile, warm a further $\frac{1}{4}$ pint milk in a small pan, adding saffron strands if available to enrich the colour of the dough. Remove from heat and allow to cool to lukewarm, pressing strands against sides of pan with a spoon to extract as much colour as possible.

5 Sift 11 oz flour and a pinch of salt into a large, warmed bowl. Sift a further 2 oz flour on to a plate and put it on one side, ready to dip into while working the dough if needed.

6 Whisk egg yolks with castor sugar until thick and light.

7 Melt butter over a low heat, taking care not to let it sizzle, and put aside to cool to lukewarm.

8 When yeast mixture has risen, make a well in the centre of flour. Add yeast mixture and whisked egg and sugar mixture. Mix together by hand, gradually adding enough saffron milk to make a soft dough.

9 Now work the dough vigorously, pulling it up in handfuls and twisting it as you do so, then slapping it down again. Gradually, the dough will develop elasticity and lose most of its stickiness, so that when you lift up a handful and let it drop back again, it will leave your palm comparatively clean. This stage takes about 20 minutes. If you find you have used too much milk, and dough remains unmanageable, work in as much as you need of the flour held in reserve for this purpose.

About 1 lb 2 oz plain flour

Milk

1 oz fresh yeast or 1/2 oz (1 level tablespoon) dried yeast

A few saffron strands (optional)

Salt

6 egg yolks

5 oz castor sugar

4 oz good butter

2 oz sultanas

2 oz raisins

1 oz mixed candied peel, finely chopped

4 glacé cherries, chopped

2 oz blanched almonds, slivered

Freshly grated rind of 1 large orange and 1 lemon

Vanilla essence

1–2 drops almond essence (optional)

Melted butter, for baking tin

Sifted icing sugar or water icing, to decorate

10 Next, cup your kneading hands and pour in some of the lukewarm melted butter, taking care not to disturb the sediment, which should have fallen to the bottom. Work this into the dough until it has completely disappeared. Add remaining butter in the same way, leaving behind the sediment. By the end, dough will have lost its remaining stickiness, although it will still be very soft.

11 Knead in fruits, slivered almonds and enough of the flavourings to make the dough positively fragrant – if this causes dough to become slightly sticky again, don't worry.

12 When fruits are well distributed throughout dough, cover dough closely with plastic wrap, foil or a damp cloth, and leave to rise until doubled in bulk. A rich dough like this is a slow riser and will take between 3 and 4 hours at average room temperature.

13 Brush a 6-pint, tubular, fluted *Gugelhupf* tin liberally with melted butter.

14 When dough has risen, knead it very lightly once or twice until smooth again, and gently shape it into an even coil that fits into the base of the tin. Make sure the two ends of the coil are 'fused' together, then carefully fit the coil into the tin. Cover closely as before, and leave to rise until doubled in bulk again.

15 Preheat oven to moderate (350°F. Mark 4).

16 Bake *Gugelhupf* until well risen (it should fill the tin), cooked through and golden brown on top, 45 to 50 minutes. A thin metal skewer pushed through the thickest part should come out feeling dry and quite clean.

17 Remove *Gugelhupf* from the oven and allow to cool in the tin for 5 minutes before turning out on to a wire rack. Leave to become quite cold before either (1) dredging with sifted icing sugar or (2) brushing with a thin water icing.

Note: You can, of course, divide the dough between two tins, tubed or otherwise. The important thing to remember is the total capacity, which should not be less than 6 pints, unless you want a mushroom top.

Baba au Rhum

If you succeed in getting the consistency of your raw dough right, this recipe will provide you with the most feathery *baba* in the world! Remember that with all yeast doughs it is far better to thicken the consistency with extra flour than to have to thin down an excessively stiff dough with extra liquid.

1 Sift flour into a large bowl and allow to warm gently while you sponge yeast as follows: in a small bowl, mix fresh yeast with 1 level teaspoon of the sugar; add 2 level teaspoons of the flour and enough of the milk to give a batter-like consistency. Leave in a warm place until bubbly. If using dried yeast, sprinkle it over 4 tablespoons lukewarm milk; beat well with a fork and leave for 10 minutes until liquid is frothy and yeast granules have completely dissolved. Then make batter as above with flour and sugar.

2 Beat egg yolks with remaining sugar and grated lemon rind until fluffy.

3 In a small, thick-bottomed pan, melt butter over a very low heat, taking care not to let it sizzle. Remove from heat and allow sediment to fall to the bottom. Then carefully strain butter through fine muslin, discarding sediment.

4 When yeast mixture is spongy, make a well in the flour. Pour in yeast mixture and beaten eggs, and mix thoroughly by hand, adding milk gradually to make a very soft dough (precise amount of milk will depend on the quality of your flour).

5 Continue to work dough until very smooth; then gradually add clarified butter, kneading and slapping dough, which will be very soft indeed by this stage – a very thick batter, in fact – until it no longer sticks to the palm of your hand.

6 Cover bowl with a cloth or plastic wrap and leave dough to rise in a warm place until doubled in bulk.

7 Preheat oven to moderate (375°F. Mark 5).

8 Brush a 3-pint ring mould generously with melted butter.

9 When dough is well risen, slap it down again. Half-fill mould; cover and allow to rise again until dough comes almost to top of mould.

10 Bake *baba* for 30 to 40 minutes, or until firm and golden. A thin metal skewer pushed through the thickest part should feel quite dry to the touch. Allow *baba* to cool slightly before turning it out.

1/2 lb plain flour
1/2 oz fresh yeast or 1/4 oz (1 1/2 level teaspoons) dried yeast
1 oz castor sugar
About 1/4 pint lukewarm milk
4 egg yolks
Grated rind of 1/2 lemon
4 oz butter
Melted butter, for mould
1 pint warm rum-flavoured sugar syrup
4–6 tablespoons apricot glaze
Fresh or crystallised fruit
Whipped cream, to decorate

11 Cool *baba* on a wire rack. While it is still slightly warm, place it on a deep, wide dish. Prick lightly all over with a toothpick and pour over warm syrup, spooning it back over *baba* as it runs out, until cake is heavily saturated.

12 Allow *baba* to become quite cold. Then brush it lightly with apricot glaze and decorate sides with pieces of fruit, brushing them with a little glaze as well. Fill centre with whipped cream just before serving.

Note: Ideally, the *baba* should still be warm from the oven when the syrup is poured over it. If you have made it a day or two in advance, slip it into a slow oven (325°F. Mark 3) for a few minutes until just lukewarm again.

Petits Babas aux Fraises

1/2 lb plain flour
1/2 oz fresh yeast or 1/4 oz (1 1/2 level teaspoons) dried yeast
1 oz castor sugar
About 1/4 pint lukewarm milk
4 egg yolks
Grated rind of 1/2 lemon
4 oz butter
Melted butter for moulds
1 pint warm sugar syrup
6 tablespoons Kirsch
4–6 tablespoons apricot glaze
2 punnets small fresh strawberries
Whipped cream, flavoured with Kirsch, to serve

1 Make individual *babas*, following the directions in Steps **1–7** of the *Baba au Rhum* recipe above, but using cylindrical individual *baba* moulds, 2 inches deep and 2 inches in diameter.

2 Brush insides of *baba* moulds generously with melted butter. Lightly cut off about 1 tablespoon of dough, enough to fill about ⅓ of each mould. Press dough lightly into the bottom of each mould.

3 Place the moulds, uncovered, again in a warm place and allow to rise 1 to 2 hours more, or until the dough is about ¼ inch over the rim of the moulds.

4 As soon as the dough has risen this second time, bake *babas* for 15 minutes – or until nicely browned and slightly shrunk from the sides of moulds.

5 Allow *babas* to cool slightly before turning out.

6 Cool *babas* on a wire rack. While they are still warm, place in a wide serving dish. Prick lightly all over with a toothpick and pour over warm syrup which you have flavoured with Kirsch, spooning it back over *babas* as it runs out.

7 Allow *babas* to become quite cold. Then brush lightly with apricot glaze. Surround *babas* with strawberries and pour over remaining Kirsch-flavoured syrup. Serve Kirsch-flavoured whipped cream separately.

Lesson 28

Ice Creams and Bombes

A childhood passion for ice cream lies dormant in most adults, however sophisticated they may subsequently grow. But having once tasted real, home-made ice cream, I doubt if even the most enthusiastic ice addict will ever again look kindly on the stop-me-buy-one or supermarket deep-freeze variety.

Many people are discouraged from trying their hand at ice cream because they believe that it can't be done without special and rather expensive equipment. Before we go into this, let me reassure you that you can make perfectly delicious, velvety ice creams and bombes so long as your refrigerator has a freezer large enough to accommodate the container or mould in which the mixture is to be frozen. The texture of the ice creams in the chapter that follows would undoubtedly be even smoother if made in one of the gadgets described below. However, having made a point of testing them in the freezer of a normal household refrigerator, we found that they still beat any commercial variety we had tasted hands down, *provided they were transferred to the ordinary chilling compartment of the refrigerator for at least an hour to soften slightly before they were served.*

As for the special equipment you can buy, this ranges from a hand-operated ice-cream bucket to a power-driven automatic model. Both of these work independently of the refrigerator or freezer. We are not enthusiastic about the electric ice cream churns that are designed to be used in conjunction with the fridge or freezer – the lead invariably gets in the way and makes it impossible to shut the door or lid of the freezer completely. If you don't want to go to the effort of about 20 minutes' churning by hand, and can't or won't invest in an expensive, fully automatic ice cream maker (and it really isn't worth it unless you are crazy about ices), then ordinary freezing is the answer.

Hand-operated churn This consists of a wooden bucket with a tube-like, tightly covered metal container which fits in the middle. Long paddles reach down into the inner container, with a handle attached to the other end, over the lid.

Chipped ice and freezing (rock) salt are packed tightly into the bucket around the container. The liquid ice cream or sorbet mixture is poured into the container and covered tightly with the lid, to which the handle is then attached. You turn the handle steadily, churning the mixture until an increasing resistance to the paddles tells you that the ice cream is ready. Remove the paddles, scraping them clean of ice cream, and the handle, and plug the hole in the lid left by the handle. Pour off melted ice from the bucket, pack to the top again with more ice and salt if necessary. Cover the contraption with a blanket and leave for at least 1 hour before serving.

Take great care each time you open or close the container not to let in any of the surrounding salt.

Electric ice cream maker Using one of these is child's play. You simply pack with ice and salt as above, set it in operation and wait until the hum of the motor changes to a laboured whine, indicating that the ice cream is frozen thick.

Remove paddles, scraping them down, replace lid, and either top up the outer bucket with fresh ice and salt, or transfer the inner container to the refrigerator until required.

● Both of these pieces of equipment call for large quantities of ice, and rock salt to slow down the rate at which it melts. If your refrigerator cannot provide you with enough ice, try your local fishmonger, who will also be able to supply you with the salt.

If he delivers it in a large, unwieldy block, you will have to break it down into large chips with a small chisel or strong skewer and a mallet or hammer. Don't make the chips too small, though, or they will melt too quickly.

The refrigerator-freezer method The easiest of all. Just remember to turn the refrigerator down to its lowest temperature (i.e. highest setting) before you start, if possible at least an hour in advance.

Water Ices (Sorbets, Granitas) and Ice Creams
Frozen ices fall into two categories, water ices and ice creams.

Water ices Basically a simple sugar syrup flavoured with fruit juice, or a purée of fruit, or simply an essence such as strong coffee, with whipped egg white folded in when the ice is partly frozen.

Water ices need more attention than ice creams when freezing by the refrigerator-freezer method. The absence of any fat in the syrup permits large ice crystals to form, and in order to break these down, the mixture must be beaten up vigorously with a fork at regular intervals before being allowed to freeze hard.

Ice creams These are based on a rich egg custard. Whipped cream is folded in for an even more velvety texture. Indeed, it is this high fat content that gives an excellent texture even with uninterrupted freezing. Gelatine is sometimes added as well if the cream is to be moulded and turned out.

When using the simple refrigerator method, you will save a lot of time if you freeze ice creams in individual serving dishes – a short cut which would be impractical for water ices, for obvious reasons.

Flavouring Ices and Ice Creams

There is only one thing to remember here: prior to freezing, the mixture should, if anything, taste *over*-flavoured and *over*-sweetened. You will be surprised how much flavour is lost with freezing.

To Serve Ices and Ice Creams
A water ice or ice cream served rock-hard, straight from the freezer, is practically impossible to savour with anaesthetised tastebuds, and can be positively painful to eat.

Ices (sorbets) are best served scooped into glass coupes, one stage harder than slushy, i.e. just firm enough to hold a shape in the scoop.

Ice cream should be transferred to the main compartment of the refrigerator, turned to a moderate setting, for at least 1 hour before serving, or long enough to soften slightly without melting.

A purée of soft fruits or a hot (or warm) sauce (chocolate, or butterscotch – see pages 276 or 255), or just softly whipped double cream can be served as an accompaniment.

Vanilla Ice Cream

Serves 4

4 egg yolks
4 level tablespoons castor sugar
Salt
3/4 pint single cream
1 vanilla bean

1 Turn refrigerator to its lowest temperature (i.e. highest setting).

2 Combine egg yolks and castor sugar and a pinch of salt in a bowl, and whisk until light, fluffy and lemon-coloured.

3 Scald cream with a vanilla bean. Remove vanilla bean and pour vanilla-flavoured cream over egg yolk mixture in a thin stream, whisking vigorously. Add a pinch of salt, whisk again.

4 Pour mixture into the top of a double saucepan and stir over lightly simmering water until it thickens into a custard which coats back of spoon. Take great care not to let it boil, or egg yolks will curdle.

5 Strain custard through a fine sieve and leave to cool.

6 Pour cooled custard into a freezing tray and freeze, stirring the mixture up vigorously with a fork every half-hour, until half-frozen, then leaving it for a further 2 or 3 hours until frozen hard.

7 Transfer ice cream to main cabinet of refrigerator about 1 hour before serving.

Coffee Ice Cream

Serves 4

4 egg yolks
2 oz castor sugar
Pinch of salt
3/4 pint single cream
4–6 level teaspoons instant coffee
Vanilla essence

1 Turn refrigerator to its lowest temperature (i.e. highest setting).

2 Combine egg yolks, sugar and salt in a bowl, and whisk until light and lemon-coloured.

3 In the top of a double saucepan, scald single cream with instant coffee over direct heat.

4 Add scalded cream to whisked egg mixture in a thin stream, whisking vigorously all the time.

5 Pour mixture back into top of double saucepan and cook over simmering water, stirring constantly, until it thickens to a custard which coats back of spoon.

6 Remove pan from heat; strain custard through a fine sieve and leave to cool.

7 Flavour custard with a few drops of vanilla essence, to taste.

8 Pour into a freezing tray and freeze until firm, about 3 hours, giving the ice cream a good stir with a fork after the first hour.

9 Transfer ice cream to the main cabinet of the refrigerator about 1 hour before serving.

Chocolate Ice Cream

Serves 6

4 egg yolks
2 oz castor sugar
Pinch of salt
3/4 pint single cream
2 oz dark chocolate
2 level teaspoons instant coffee
Vanilla essence
1/2 pint double cream, chilled

1 Turn refrigerator to its lowest temperature (i.e. highest setting).

2 Combine egg yolks, sugar and salt in a bowl, and whisk until light and lemon-coloured.

3 In the top of a double saucepan, scald single cream over direct heat.

4 Pour scalded cream over whisked egg yolks in a thin stream, whisking vigorously.

5 Break chocolate into a bowl and leave to melt over hot water.

6 Pour egg mixture back into top of double saucepan and cook over simmering water, stirring constantly, until it thickens to a custard which coats the back of the spoon. Take great care not to let the custard boil, or egg yolks will curdle.

7 Blend in melted chocolate and instant coffee; strain through a fine sieve and leave to cool.

8 When custard is lukewarm, flavour to taste with a few drops of vanilla essence.

9 Whisk chilled double cream until it holds its shape in soft peaks.

10 Fold in chocolate custard mixture.

11 Pour mixture into a freezing tray and freeze until firm, at least 3 hours.

12 Transfer ice cream to the main cabinet of the refrigerator about 1 hour before serving.

Champagne Ice Cream

A note of high luxury on which to end an extra-special dinner party. Serve with brandied strawberries (a pound of small ripe strawberries, hulled, tossed with 2 or 3 tablespoons brandy and *a little* sugar, to taste, and left to macerate for about 2 hours) or other fruit treated in the same manner.

12 oz sugar
1/4 pint dry champagne
4 tablespoons brandy
3 tablespoons lemon juice
1/4 pint double cream, chilled
Brandied strawberries or other fruit, to serve (see note)

1 Turn refrigerator to its lowest temperature (i.e. highest setting).

2 In a heavy pan, stir sugar with $\frac{1}{2}$ pint water over a low heat until melted. Raise heat to bring syrup to the boil; then reduce it again to simmer slowly for 15 minutes.

3 Remove pan from heat and allow syrup to cool.

4 Stir in champagne, brandy and lemon juice.

5 Pour syrup into a large freezing tray and freeze for about 2 hours, or until mixture has the consistency of wet snow.

6 Whisk chilled double cream until it holds its shape in soft peaks.

7 Turn half-frozen champagne syrup into a bowl. Fold in whipped cream.

8 Pour mixture back into the freezing tray and freeze until firm. It will take about 3 hours longer.

9 Transfer ice cream to the main cabinet of the refrigerator about 1 hour before serving.

10 To serve: scoop ice cream into champagne glasses; top with brandied strawberries (or other fruit) and serve.

Mango Ice Cream

Serves 3–4

2 large fresh mangoes (see Note)
2 teaspoons lemon juice
4 oz sugar
8 fluid oz double cream
1/8 teaspoon salt

My favourite ice cream, The mangoes must be very juicy and perfectly ripe, if anything bordering on over-ripe, so that their delicate flavour is at its most concentrated.

1 Turn refrigerator down to its lowest temperature (i.e. highest setting).

2 Cut mangoes in half; remove stones and scoop out pulp.

3 Purée mango pulp in an electric blender and rub through a fine sieve – or simply rub through the sieve. Stir in lemon juice.

4 In a heavy saucepan, dissolve sugar in 7 tablespoons water. Bring to the boil and simmer very gently for 15 minutes. Cool syrup.

5 Combine mango purée with sugar syrup and stir until well blended.

6 Pour into freezing tray and freeze until mixture has the consistency of wet snow, about 1 hour.

7 Whisk double cream with salt until soft peaks form. Fold thoroughly into half-frozen mango mixture.

8 Return ice cream to the freezer. When it starts hardening around the sides (after about 1 hour), beat it up again with a fork. Then leave until firmly frozen, 2 to 3 hours.

9 Transfer ice cream to the main cabinet of the refrigerator about 1 hour before serving.

Note: I have also made quite a good mango ice cream with canned mangoes, although unfortunately it can never quite match up to one made with fresh fruit.

Take a 1 lb 3 oz can of mangoes in syrup. Drain, reserving syrup; remove stones and purée mangoes through a sieve.

Proceed as above, substituting syrup from can for the made-up sugar syrup in the original recipe.

250 Gr.

Tea Ice

A very elegant ice cream, provided you use a tea with an interesting flavour: tea bags are out, of course, but you must also beware of using a brand that is excessively perfumed. Try a combination of half Earl Grey and half good Ceylon, then make your own experiments with the teas available from your grocer.

5 eggs
4 oz castor sugar
1/4 pint very strong tea (see note)
1/2 pint milk
1/4 pint single cream
Flavourless oil, for freezing tray
Sweet wafers, to serve

1 Turn refrigerator to its lowest temperature, i.e. highest setting.

2 In a bowl, whisk eggs and castor sugar together until thick enough for beaters to leave a trail on the surface.

3 Combine tea, milk and cream in the top of a double saucepan, and bring to the boil over direct heat.

4 Pour boiling tea cream on to egg mixture in a thin stream, beating vigorously to prevent eggs curdling.

5 Pour mixture back into double saucepan and stir over lightly simmering water for 5 to 7 minutes, or until custard coats back of spoon. Take care not to let it boil, or eggs will curdle.

6 As soon as custard coats back of spoon, plunge base of pan into cold water to arrest the cooking process. Leave to cool, stirring occasionally to prevent a skin forming on top.

7 Brush a 1½-pint freezer tray (or a loaf tin) lightly with flavourless oil. Pour in cold custard mixture.

8 Freeze ice cream for a minimum of 4 hours. After the first and second hours, remove tray (or loaf tin) from the freezer and beat contents up vigorously with a fork to ensure that any ice crystals are eliminated.

9 The ice cream should be transferred to the main cabinet of the refrigerator for 1 hour before serving to allow it to soften again slightly. Serve with sweet wafers.

Iced Soufflés au Grand Marnier

Serves 6

1 Turn refrigerator down to lowest temperature, i.e. highest setting.

2 Select 6 individual soufflé dishes about 2½ inches wide across the base and tie double-thickness collars of greaseproof paper around them to come 1 inch above the top.

3 In a small cup, sprinkle gelatine over 1 tablespoon cold water and leave to soften.

4 In a bowl, beat egg yolks with sugar until thick and light.

1/2 level teaspoon powdered gelatine
4 egg yolks
4 oz granulated sugar
1/2 pint milk
3 tablespoons Grand Marnier
Few drops of vanilla essence
1/2 pint double cream
6 small Italian macaroons (*amaretti*), crushed

711

5 Pour milk into the top of a double saucepan and bring to the boil over direct heat. Then whisk into egg mixture in a thin stream.

6 Return mixture to double saucepan and stir over gently simmering water until it coats back of spoon, taking care not to let custard boil, or egg yolks will curdle. Cool slightly.

7 Dissolve softened gelatine by standing cup in hot water and stirring until liquid is clear. Blend into cooling custard, together with Grand Marnier and a few drops of vanilla essence, to taste.

8 Beat double cream until soft peaks form. Fold into custard.

9 Divide mixture between prepared soufflé dishes. It should come well above the rim of each dish.

10 Freeze for about 5 hours, or until very firm. Then transfer to the main compartment of the refrigerator for about 1 hour before serving.

11 To serve: sprinkle top of each iced soufflé with finely crushed macaroons, patting the crumbs in lightly to make them stick; then carefully peel off paper collars. Serve immediately.

Frozen Almond Creams

Serves 6–8

1/2 pint double cream
2 egg whites
Pinch of salt
4 level tablespoons castor sugar
1/4 lb almonds, blanched, coarsely chopped and toasted
4 tablespoons brandy, Marsala or medium sherry

1 Turn refrigerator down to its lowest temperature (i.e. highest setting).

2 Whip cream until it holds its shape.

3 In another bowl, whisk egg whites with a pinch of salt until you can make soft, floppy peaks with the beaters.

4 Whisk in castor sugar, a tablespoon at a time; then continue to whisk to a stiff, glossy meringue.

5 Fold whipped cream into meringue, together with all but 2 level tablespoons of the toasted almonds.

6 Flavour cream with brandy, Marsala or a medium sherry, and spoon into individual custard cups or soufflé dishes each holding 4 or 5 fluid oz.

7 Decorate centre of each cream with a generous pinch of chopped almonds, and freeze in the freezing compartment of the refrigerator for 3 to 4 hours until very firm.

Bombes

Having mastered the simple technique of making ice creams, you are now well on the way to one of the most delightful dinner party sweets imaginable – the ice cream bombe.

The bombe is a frozen mould consisting of an outer shell of ice cream filled with either a mousse-like mixture – the Basic Bombe Mixture on page 714 – or an ice cream of a contrasting or complementing flavour, and refrozen. The combination of flavours is endless. You can also enhance the filling with chopped fruits macerated in liqueur, crushed chocolate or praline, chopped toasted nuts and crushed macaroons. In fact, the only limitations are the bounds of your own imagination.

Bombes are governed by all the same rules that apply to ice creams.

Here, too, the question of special equipment can be postponed until you decide if you are going to use it often enough to justify the expense. So start off by using an ordinary bowl. And only then, if the idea really appeals to you, treat yourself to a real bombe mould. Copper ones are particularly attractive. The simplest kind are dome-shaped. A flat little disc attached to the rounded end allows it to stand steady while the filling is poured into the centre. Bombe moulds come with a lid.

To Line a Bombe Mould

1 Before you start, chill the empty mould thoroughly in the freezer.

2 Turn the ice cream with which the mould is to be lined into a bowl and work it with a spatula until just soft enough to spread.

3 Line bottom and sides of mould evenly with ice cream, smoothing the surface with a spatula or the back of a large spoon. If the ice cream has accidentally softened too much, line half of the mould only and return it to the freezer until frozen hard before proceeding with the remaining half. Then return to the freezer until entire lining is quite firm before filling it up.

To Unmould Bombe

A bombe is best unmoulded while it is still frozen hard, i.e. before its 'softening up' period in the main cabinet of the refrigerator.

1 Remove lid (or foil covering) and invert mould on to a serving dish.

2 Wrap a cloth wrung out in hot water around it for about 30 seconds, longer if an earthenware bowl has been used, redipping cloth in hot water and wringing it out again as it cools.

3 Carefully lift off mould. If you find you have overdone it slightly and melted the surface of the bombe, smooth it over with a knife blade and return to the freezer. (If quite a lot of the surface has melted away you will have to repeat this 'reshaping' process several times at 15-minute intervals.) Finally, for a perfect surface, heat the knife blade thoroughly in a jug of hot water, dry it and draw it over the surface of the bombe with a few rapid strokes.

● If you have a deep-freeze, you can lay in a variety of bombes for special occasions, using the same mould. As each bombe is prepared, unmould it as above, return to the freezer until rock-hard again, then store in a sealed polythene bag, until, say, a couple of hours before serving. Then unwrap, place on a serving dish and leave in the main compartment of the refrigerator until ready to serve. What could be more convenient?

Makes 1 pint basic bombe mixture

5 oz granulated sugar
5 egg yolks

Basic Bombe Mixture

This mixture forms the foundation for a pint of bombe filling and, with flavourings and garnish added, will be sufficient to fill the centres of four 1-pint bombes. If not used at once, it may be stored in a sealed container in the refrigerator for up to 1 week.

1 Dissolve sugar in $\frac{1}{4}$ pint water and bring to the boil, stirring. Simmer over a moderate heat until thermometer reads 217°F. Remove from heat and allow to cool.

2 In the top of a double saucepan, beat egg yolks until light and creamy. Add syrup gradually, beating constantly with a wire whisk.

3 Cook egg mixture over hot water, beating constantly with the whisk, until mixture is thick and has doubled its bulk, about 15 minutes. Then remove from heat; plunge pan into a bowl of iced water and whisk until mixture is smooth and cold.

Bombe Filling (for 1-pint bombe mould lined with ice cream)

1 Pour Basic Bombe Mixture into a bowl. Fold in whipped cream, together with chosen flavouring and garnish.

2 Whisk egg white until stiff but not dry, and fold in lightly but thoroughly. Use as required

Variations on the flavoured Bombe theme

1 First line interior of your chilled bombe mould (see page 714) with slightly chilled ice cream of your choice (chocolate, coffee, raspberry, mango, etc.), smoothing it out with the back of a spoon to make an even layer about ½ inch thick. Freeze until firm.

2 In the meanwhile pour Basic Bombe Mixture into a bowl. Fold in whipped cream, together with ½–1 teaspoon chosen flavouring (or 2 teaspoons Cognac or liqueur) and 2–3 level tablespoons of the garnish of your choice. (See suggested flavour combinations opposite.)

3 Whisk egg white until stiff but dry, and fold it into the mixture lightly but thoroughly.

4 Pour filling into lined mould and freeze until firm, preferably overnight.

5 Transfer bombe to main compartment of refrigerator about 1 hour before you intend to serve it.

6 To unmould: remove lid and invert mould on to a serving dish. Wrap a cloth wrung out in hot water around it for about 30 seconds, redipping cloth in hot water and wringing it out again when it cools. If the surface of the ice cream melts slightly as you unmould it, smooth over with a knife and return to the freezer for 15 to 30 minutes.

7 Serve bombe decorated with piped whipped cream and a little of the chosen garnish.

Makes enough to fill one 1-pint Bombe mould lined with ice cream

Slightly softened Ice Cream of your choice: chocolate, coffee, raspberry, mango, etc. (about 3/4 pint)
1/4 pint Basic Bombe Mixture (see page 714)
2 level tablespoons whipped double cream
1 egg white
Piped Whipped cream

Flavourings, choice of:
Vanilla essence
Grated Orange rind
Rum
Cognac or liqueur (about 2 teaspoons)

Garnish, choice of:
(Use 2–3 level tablespoons, to taste)
Coarsely grated chocolate
Crumbled macaroons
Finely chopped glacé cherries
Toasted flaked almonds
Chopped nuts
Halved small strawberries
Crushed raspberries (use about 4 oz)
Diced peaches, bananas or pears

Raspberry ice cream

1 lb raspberries
8 fluid oz double cream
1/2 teaspoon lemon juice
2 teaspoons Kirsch
2 level tablespoons castor
   sugar

Filling

1/4 pint Basic Bombe
   Mixture (see page 714)
2 level tablespoons whipped
   cream
1 level teaspoon grated
   orange rind
2 teaspoons Grand Marnier
2 level tablespoons thinly
   flaked almonds
1 egg white
Fresh raspberries and
   whipped cream, to
   decorate

Raspberry Bombe

Either fresh or frozen raspberries may be used for this exciting bombe. If using frozen berries, sprinkle them with castor sugar while they are defrosting, then purée and reduce them as directed below. This prevents the development of the characteristic metallic taste which frozen fruit can sometimes have.

1 Turn refrigerator down to its lowest temperature, i.e. highest setting.

2 Purée raspberries through a sieve and simmer until reduced to 8 fluid oz. Cool.

3 Whip cream and fold into raspberry purée together with lemon juice, Kirsch and sugar. Pour into an ice tray and freeze until almost set, stirring occasionally.

4 Put empty bombe mould into freezer.

5 When ice cream is almost set, line interior of mould with it, smoothing it out with the back of a spoon to make an even layer about $\frac{1}{2}$ inch thick. Freeze again until firm.

6 Meanwhile, prepare filling: to Basic Bombe Mixture add cream, grated orange rind and Grand Marnier, and whisk until well blended. Fold in flaked almonds.

7 Whisk egg white until stiff but not dry, and fold into mixture.

8 Pour filling into lined mould and freeze until firm, preferably overnight.

9 Transfer bombe to main compartment of refrigerator about 1 hour before you intend to serve it.

10 To unmould: remove lid and invert mould on to a serving dish. Wrap a cloth wrung out in hot water around it for about 30 seconds, re-dipping cloth in hot water and wringing it out again when it cools. If the surface of the ice cream melts slightly as you unmould it, smooth over with a knife and return to the freezer for 15 to 30 minutes.

11 Serve bombe decorated with whole raspberries and piped whipped cream.

Cherry Praline Bombe

Serves 6

Serve this pretty bombe decorated with piped whipped cream and a few Maraschino cherries, either whole or halved.

1 Turn refrigerator down to its lowest temperature, i.e. highest setting.

2 Combine vanilla ice cream with crushed praline or peanut brittle stirring as little as possible to avoid ice cream becoming too soft. Line a 1-pint bombe mould with an even layer about ¾ inch thick. Return mould to freezer to set firmly.

3 To the Basic Bombe Mixture add lightly whipped cream, Maraschino liqueur and quartered Maraschino cherries.

4 Whisk egg white until stiff but not dry and fold into mixture.

5 Pour filling into lined mould; cover and freeze until firm, preferably overnight.

6 To unmould bombe: see Steps 9 and 10 on page 716.

3/4 pint vanilla ice cream (page 707)

3 oz almond praline (page 564) or peanut brittle, crushed

1/4 pint Basic Bombe Mixture (see page 714)

2 level tablespoons lightly whipped cream

2 teaspoons Maraschino liqueur

2 level tablespoons quartered Maraschino cherries

1 egg white

Bombe au Chocolat

Serves 6

A delicious combination of rich chocolate ice cream with a creamy coffee- and brandy-flavoured centre.

1 Turn refrigerator down to its lowest temperature, i.e. highest setting.

2 Prepare chocolate ice cream: beat egg yolks with sugar and salt until light and lemon-coloured.

3 Scald single cream and add to egg mixture, beating vigorously until well blended.

4 Pour into the top of a double saucepan and cook over hot water for about 10 minutes, stirring, until mixture coats back of spoon.

5 Melt chocolate in milk and add to custard. Mix well; strain and cool.

6 When chocolate custard is cool, fold in whipped double cream. Pour into a freezing-tray and freeze until quite firm, 2 to 3 hours.

7 Place a 1-pint bombe mould in freezer as well if there is room for it.

8 Line chilled bombe mould with the chocolate ice cream, coating half of the mould at a time and chilling it until firm if ice cream is still rather soft at this stage.

Chocolate ice cream

2 egg yolks

2 oz castor sugar

Pinch of salt

7 fluid oz single cream

3 oz plain chocolate

3 tablespoons milk

1/4 pint double cream, whipped

Filling

2 level teaspoons instant coffee

1 tablespoon brandy

1/4 pint Basic Bombe Mixture (see page 714)

2 level tablespoons lightly whipped cream

1 egg white

9 To make filling: dissolve instant coffee in brandy and whisk into Basic Bombe Mixture. Fold in whipped cream.

10 Whisk egg white until stiff but not dry and fold into filling.

11 Pour filling into lined mould; cover with a lid and freeze until very firm, preferably overnight.

12 To unmould bombe: see Steps 9 and 10 in Rasberry Bombe recipe.

Serves 8

2 pints chocolate ice cream
(see note)
1 can (about 1 lb) sweetened
chestnut purée (*crème de marrons*)
1 egg white
1/2 pint double cream

To decorate

1 egg white
1/4 pint double cream
Icing sugar
Vanilla essence
Marrons glacés, candied
violets and angelica
'leaves'

Chocolate Chestnut Bombe

If you wish to use home-made chocolate ice cream, which is infinitely superior to most of the bought varieties available, make up $1\frac{1}{2}$ times the recipe on page 717.

1 Chill a $2\frac{1}{2}$-pint bombe mould thoroughly in the freezer, which you have turned down to its lowest temperature, i.e. highest setting.

2 Soften chocolate ice cream slightly and, with a spatula, spread it smoothly over base and sides of mould to make an even layer about 1 inch thick. Return to freezer until ice cream is firm again.

3 Meanwhile, turn sweetened chestnut purée into a bowl. If necessary, beat with a spoon or spatula to eliminate lumpiness.

4 Whisk egg white until stiff but not dry.

5 Whisk double cream until it just leaves a trail on the surface when beaters are lifted.

6 Fold chestnut purée gently into whipped cream until mixture is no longer streaky. Fold in beaten egg white.

7 Pour chestnut mixture into mould. Cover mould with a lid or a sheet of foil. Freeze until firm, preferably overnight.

8 To unmould bombe: see Steps 9 and 10 in Raspberry Bombe.

9 Just before serving, make a Crème Chantilly as follows: whisk egg white until stiff but not dry. Whisk cream until it holds its shape in stiff peaks, adding a little icing sugar and a few drops of vanilla essence to taste – cream should be only faintly sweet. Fold enough beaten egg white into cream to lighten its texture without making it flow.

10 Pipe Crème Chantilly decoratively over and around bombe, and finish decoration with a few marrons glacés (glacéed chestnuts), candied violets and angelica 'leaves'.

Index

This index lists each recipe alphabetically under the heading of its principal ingredient, as well as its actual name, *i.e.* No-Roast Beef Roast appears under Beef, roast, and No-Roast Beef Roast. Recipe names given in French appear under their French title and under the heading of the principal ingredient. In addition, recipes are listed under menu categories, as *Hors-d'œuvres*, Salads, Soups, Sauces, and under the names of specific preparations, as Aspic Dishes, Fritters, Mousses, Soufflés and so on. The reader should look for a salmon dish under Salmon rather than under Fish, for a potato recipe under Potato rather than Vegetable; under general terms such as Fish or Vegetable are listed only those recipes in which these words are part of the recipe name, plus general information. Where entries and/or page numbers appear in brown, this indicates basic information on preparation and cooking rather than a specific recipe.

724

733

737